D0801847

AREA HANDBOOK
for
VENEZUELA

Co-Authors

Thomas E. Weil

Jan Knippers Black
Howard I. Blutstein
Kenneth W. Martindale
David S. McMorris
Sally Engle Merry
Frederick P. Munson
Charles Townsend

Research and writing were completed
December 1970

Published 1971
(This pamphlet supersedes DA Pam 550-71,
February 1964)

DA Pam 550-71

Library of Congress Catalog Card Number: 74-611208

For sale by the Superintendent of Documents, U.S. Government Printing Office
Washington, D.C. 20402–Price $4.00

FOREWORD

This volume is one of a series of handbooks prepared by Foreign Area Studies (FAS) of The American University, designed to be useful to military and other personnel who need a convenient compilation of basic facts about the social, economic, political, and military institutions and practices of various countries. The emphasis is on objective description of the nation's present society and the kinds of possible or probable changes that might be expected in the future. The handbook seeks to present as full and as balanced an integrated exposition as limitations on space and research time permit. It was compiled from information available in openly published material. An extensive bibliography is provided to permit recourse to other published sources for more detailed information. There has been no attempt to express any specific point of view or to make policy recommendations. The contents of the handbook represent the work of the authors and FAS and do not represent the official view of the United States government.

An effort has been made to make the handbook as comprehensive as possible. It can be expected, however, that the material, interpretations, and conclusions are subject to modification in the light of new information and developments. Such corrections, additions, and suggestions for factual, interpretive, or other change as readers may have will be welcomed for use in future revisions. Comments may be addressed to:

The Director
Foreign Area Studies
The American University
5010 Wisconsin Avenue, N.W.
Washington, D.C. 20016

PREFACE

At the end of 1970 Venezuela was enjoying the benefits of increasing national wealth and the strengthening of democratic institutions. These and other significant developments during the late 1960s underlined the need for a revison of the *Area Handbook for Venezuela* published in February 1964. It was researched and written under Chairman Wendell Blanchard, by a team made up of Frederic H. Chaffee, Edwin E. Erickson, Susan G. Fortenbaugh, Skaidrite Maliks, and John Hughes Stodter.

The book represents an effort to provide a compact and objective exposition and analysis of the dominant social, political, and economic characteristics of Venezuelan society. It is designed to give readers both within and outside the government an understanding of the dynamics of the component elements of Venezuelan society and an insight into the needs, goals, and achievements of the people. A large number of consultants, many of them with first-hand knowledge of the country, have provided data not available in printed sources. The authors alone are responsible for the final draft.

English usage follows *Webster's Third New International Dictionary* (unabridged). Spanish words and phrases, used only when adequate English equivalents are lacking, are defined at first appearance. If they are employed frequently, they are listed in the Glossary. Spanish is based on *Appleton's New Cuyás Dictionary* (Fifth Edition). Unless otherwise stated, the tons used in production and commodity figures are metric tons.

Government actions reported after completion of research and writing substantially altered conditions affecting foreign investment in Venezuela. In mid-December 1970 the National Congress passed unanimously a banking law that called for all foreign banks to be at least 80 percent Venezuelan owned. Foreign banks would not be permitted to accept savings accounts or deal in foreign exchange except as agents of the Central Bank of Venezuela (Banco Central de Venezuela); restrictions on loans by foreign banks to other foreign corporations were to be imposed.

In mid-December 1970 the National Congress also approved legislation increasing the tax on profits of the largely foreign owned petroleum companies from 50 to 60 percent. Adding royalties and other taxes paid by the petroleum companies, this measure increased the effective government share of petroleum profits from about 70 to 80 percent. In February 1971 this proportion was the highest paid by private industry anywhere in the world. The legislation provided that the government would unilaterally establish the reference prices on which petroleum taxes are based and also increased the taxes established for mining concerns owned by foreign interests. In January 1971 the minister of mines and hydrocarbons announced that the country's reserves of natural gas would be placed under state control; foreign participation in this industry was to be limited to minority positions.

COUNTRY SUMMARY

1. COUNTRY: Republic of Venezuela (República de Venezuela).
2. GOVERNMENT: Federal Republic. Independent legislative, executive, and judicial branches. Strong executive powers. Constitution of 1961 in effect in 1970. Capital: Caracas.
3. POPULATION: Nearly 11 million in 1970. Heaviest concentration in northern mountain region; 75 percent of total is urban. Between 10 and 25 percent of population white, with Spanish and Italian origins predominating; most of remainder a mixture. Small numbers of Negroes and Indians.
4. SIZE: About 352,000 square miles. Sixth country in size in Latin America. Greatest north-south extent, about 790 miles; east-west, 928 miles.
5. TOPOGRAPHY: In north, ranges of mountains with peaks up to 16,000 feet extend in an arc from Colombian border in west to Atlantic Ocean in east. In south, sparsely populated Guiana Highlands make up nearly half of national territory. Extensive lowlands of Orinoco River lie between the two upland regions. Another lowland region surrounds Lake Maracaibo in northwest. More than 1,000 rivers. Most important river, the Orinoco, provides drainage for four-fifths of country.
6. LANGUAGES: Spanish, the official language, spoken almost universally. Some Indian dialects still in use in more remote areas, but slowly dying out as Indians are absorbed into the Venezuelan culture. English used increasingly in business and professional circles.
7. RELIGION: Roman Catholicism the professed religion of some 91 percent of the population. No state religion, but Catholic church has strong ties with government. Religious freedom guaranteed by constitution since 1836. Small but growing number of Protestants; a very small number of Indians continue to practice their traditional religions.
8. EDUCATION: More than 2.2 million students enrolled in school system in 1970; about 85 percent in public schools. Education free to all levels and compulsory to the age of fourteen. Six-year course in primary schools, where three-fourths of all students are enrolled; five-year intermediate academic and vocational schools; and up to six years in universities. In 1968 some 81 percent of population over age ten considered literate.
9. HEALTH: Generally excellent. Low death rate and high and

increasing rate of longevity reflect rapid improvement in health conditions since World War II. Medical facilities and personnel concentrated in Caracas and other major cities. Most hospitals and other facilities operated by government with charges for services based on ability to pay. Free hospitalization and outpatient care provided for the 20 percent of total population covered by social security program. Improvement in health conditions attributed principally to control of malaria, yellow fever, and other endemic diseases through successful environmental health programs.

10. CLIMATE: Almost no seasonal change. Dry season commonly referred to as summer; the remainder of year, as winter. Average temperatures vary with altitude, ranging from torrid at sea level to cold in high mountains. Corresponding variety in rainfall. High humidity in most localities.

11. JUSTICE: Supreme Court of Justice composed of nine members elected by National Congress for nine-year terms. All other judiciary appointed by the Council of the Judiciary. Maximum sentence for any crime, thirty years.

12. ADMINISTRATIVE DIVISIONS: Federal District, twenty states, two territories, and about seventy-two Caribbean islands administered as federal dependencies.

13. ECONOMY: Estimated gross national product (GNP) in 1970, Bs50 billion (US$11 billion), or over Bs4,762 (US$1,058) per person. Estimated growth rate in 1970 was 5 percent.

14. INDUSTRY: Major industries: petroleum and refining; mining of iron ore; foodstuffs and beverages; chemicals; textiles and clothing; primary metals and metal products; and transport equipment.

15. LABOR: Labor force estimated at 3 million in 1970; about one-fifth, female. Nearly half of total belonged to unions. Collective contracts negotiated often between groups of employers and federations of unions. Generally harmonious relations between unions and employers and fairly low incidence of strikes. Close association between unions and political parties.

16. EXPORTS: Bs11.5 billion (US$2.55 billion) in 1969. Principally petroleum and petroleum products (about 90 percent); iron ore (5 percent); cocoa, coffee, sugar, fruits, and rice (2 percent).

17. IMPORTS: Bs7.3 billion (US$1.62 billion) in 1969. Principally machinery and equipment, certain industrial raw materials, manufactured consumer goods, and some agricultural products (wheat, powdered milk, and cotton).

18. FINANCE: Budget deficit frequently occurs; 1969 deficit, Bs1.2 billion (US$267 million). Central government budget only part of total public sector expenditures. Autonomous institutions, states, and local governments combined spend more than central government.

19. COMMUNICATIONS: National Telephone Company of Venezuela, 95 percent government owned and responsible for telephone system throughout country; 340,000 telephones in 1968. Submarine cable provides voice communication with United States. More than 100 radio broadcasting stations; 5 television stations.
20. RAILROADS: 300 miles of railroad track. State owned except for 126 miles. Plans to increase trackage suspended because railroads have not successfully competed with efficient highway system.
21. ROADS: In 1970, 10,000 miles of paved roads and 12,000 miles of gravel and dirt roads. Highways most popular means of transport. In 1967 vehicle registration was 642,000.
22. RIVER TRANSPORTATION: Orinoco-Apure river system and Lake Maracaibo most important waterways. Both can accommodate oceangoing vessels.
23. PORTS AND PORT FACILITIES: La Guaira, Puerto Cabello, Maracaibo, and Cumaná most important coastal ports. Ciudad Bolívar important Orinoco River port. Orinoco and Lake Maracaibo require constant dredging.
24. AIRFIELDS: 64 major airfields. Maiquetía International Airport on coast north of Caracas most important and being expanded to handle Boeing—747 aircraft. Thirty-two cities connected by air taxi service.
25. PRINCIPAL AIRLINES: Two national airlines, one government owned and one privately owned. Together they formed a third line for international service. International service to North, Central, and South America and to Europe.
26. MERCHANT MARINE: 35 oceangoing vessels totaling 315,000 tons. In 1967, 10,000 shipping arrivals discharged 3 million tons of cargo.
27. INTERNATIONAL AGREEMENTS AND TREATIES: Organization of Petroleum Exporting Countries; International Coffee Agreement; Andean Development Corporation; Inter-American Treaty of Reciprocal Assistance; Latin American Nuclear Free Zone Treaty; and Alliance for Progress.
28. AID PROGRAMS: Through 1969, loans from Export-Import Bank of United States, US$203 million; and Inter-American Development Bank, US$109 million. Through mid-1970, International Bank for Reconstruction and Development, US$298 million. Technical assistance from United Nations Development Program.
29. OVERSEAS TERRITORIES: None.
30. INTERNATIONAL OBLIGATIONS AND MEMBERSHIPS: Organization of American States; Inter-American Development Bank; and Latin American Free Trade Association. The United Nations and specialized agencies: World Bank and affiliates; International Monetary Fund; Food and Agriculture Organization; Inter-

national Labor Organization; International Telecommunications Union; United Nations Development Program; Economic and Social Council; Universal Postal Union; World Health Organization; World Meteorological Organization; International Atomic Energy Agency; United Nations Conference on Trade and Development; and Economic Commission for Latin America.

31. ARMED FORCES STRENGTH: Two-year conscription required. Armed forces total about 30,000. Police forces, including national guard, also about 30,000. Most items of armed forces equipment procured from foreign sources.

VENEZUELA

TABLE OF CONTENTS

			Page
Foreword			iii
Preface			v
Country Summary			vii
Section	I.	SOCIAL	
Chapter	1.	General Character of the Society	1
	2.	Physical Environment Natural Features—Boundaries and Political Subdivisions—Settlement Patterns	7
	3.	Historical Setting Discovery and Exploration—Conquest and Colonization—The Struggle for Independence—Authoritarian Government—The Liberal Experiment—Resurgence and Rejection of Authoritarian Rule	31
	4.	Population and Ethnic Groups Population—Development of the Ethnic Structure—The Contemporary Ethnic Structure	53
	5.	Social Structure Development of the Modern Social Structure—Urban Society—Rural Society—The Family	81
	6.	Living Conditions Diet and Nutrition—Housing—Dress—Patterns of Living and Leisure—Health and Sanitation—Welfare	97
	7.	Education Historical Background—Education and Society—Administration and Finance—The School System—Teachers—Literacy and Adult Education	125
	8.	Artistic and Intellectual Expression The Colonial Period—The Quest for a National Culture—Twentieth-Century Innovations—Contemporary Trends	149
	9.	Religion Historical Background—The Contemporary Roman Catholic Church—Protestantism	171
	10.	Social Values The Individual—Human Relations and the Social Order	193
Section	II.	POLITICAL	
Chapter	11.	The Governmental System The Course of Constitutional Government—The Constitution of 1961—The Functional Aspects of Government—Electoral Machinery—Civil Service	205
	12.	Political Dynamics Sociopolitical Development—The Emergence of Parties—Institutionalization of the Democratic Process—Political Forces and Interest Groups—The Party System	231
	13.	Foreign Relations Historical Background—Relations with the United	253

States—Relations with Latin America—International Organizations and Commitments—Foreign Policy Decision-making—Policies of the Caldera Government
14. Public Information 269
Freedom of Expression—Newspapers—Radio—Television—Motion Pictures—Periodicals and Books
15. Political Values and Attitudes 291
Determinants of Political Values—Attitudes Toward the Nation—Attitudes Toward the State and the Political System—Attitudes Toward the Caldera Government—Symbols of the Nation
Section III. ECONOMIC
Chapter 16. Character and Structure of the Economy 303
Petroleum—Growth and Employment—Agriculture
17. Agriculture 315
Land Tenure—Agricultural Production—Role of the Government
18. Industry 335
Manufacturing—Petroleum—Natural Gas—Construction—Power Resources—Mining—Role of the Government
19. Labor 365
Structure and Dynamics of the Labor Force—The Labor Movement—Conditions of Employment—Labor Relations—Labor Organizations
20. Trade 387
Foreign Trade—Tourism—Domestic Trade—Transportation—Communications
21. Finance 405
National Budget—State and Municipal Finances— Public Debt—Balance of Payments—Banking and Currency
Section IV. NATIONAL SECURITY
Chapter 22. Public Order and Internal Security 429
The Police System—The Administration of Justice—Incidence of Crime—Threats to Public Order—Governmental Measures
23. The Armed Forces 441
The Place of the Military in National Life—Position in the Government—The Military Establishment and the National Economy—Foreign Influence—Mission and Top Control—The Army, Navy, and Air Force—Manpower—Training—Logistics—Military Justice—Uniforms and Insignia—Awards and Decorations—Civic Action—Conditions of Service
Bibliography for February 1964 Edition 457
Bibliography for Revised Edition 487
Glossary 507
Index 509

LIST OF ILLUSTRATIONS

Figure | Page
1 Venezuela xiv
2 Geographic Regions of Venezuela 11
3 Population Densities of Venezuela, 1961 25

LIST OF TABLES

Table		Page
1	Major Venezuelan Dailies	273
2	Major Venezuelan Radio Stations	280
3	Venezuelan Television Television Stations	287
4	Employment in Venezuela, 1961 and 1968	365
5	Economically Active Population of Venezuela by Occupational Group, November 1968	366

64
60
CARIBBEAN SEA
GRENADA (U.K.)
12
9
23
TRINIDAD AND TOBAGO
8
10
Port of Spain
ATLANTIC
OCEAN
18
17
16
21
8
20
GUYANA
22
BRAZIL
International boundary
State boundary
National capital
State capital
0 50 100 150
Miles
BRAZIL
64
60

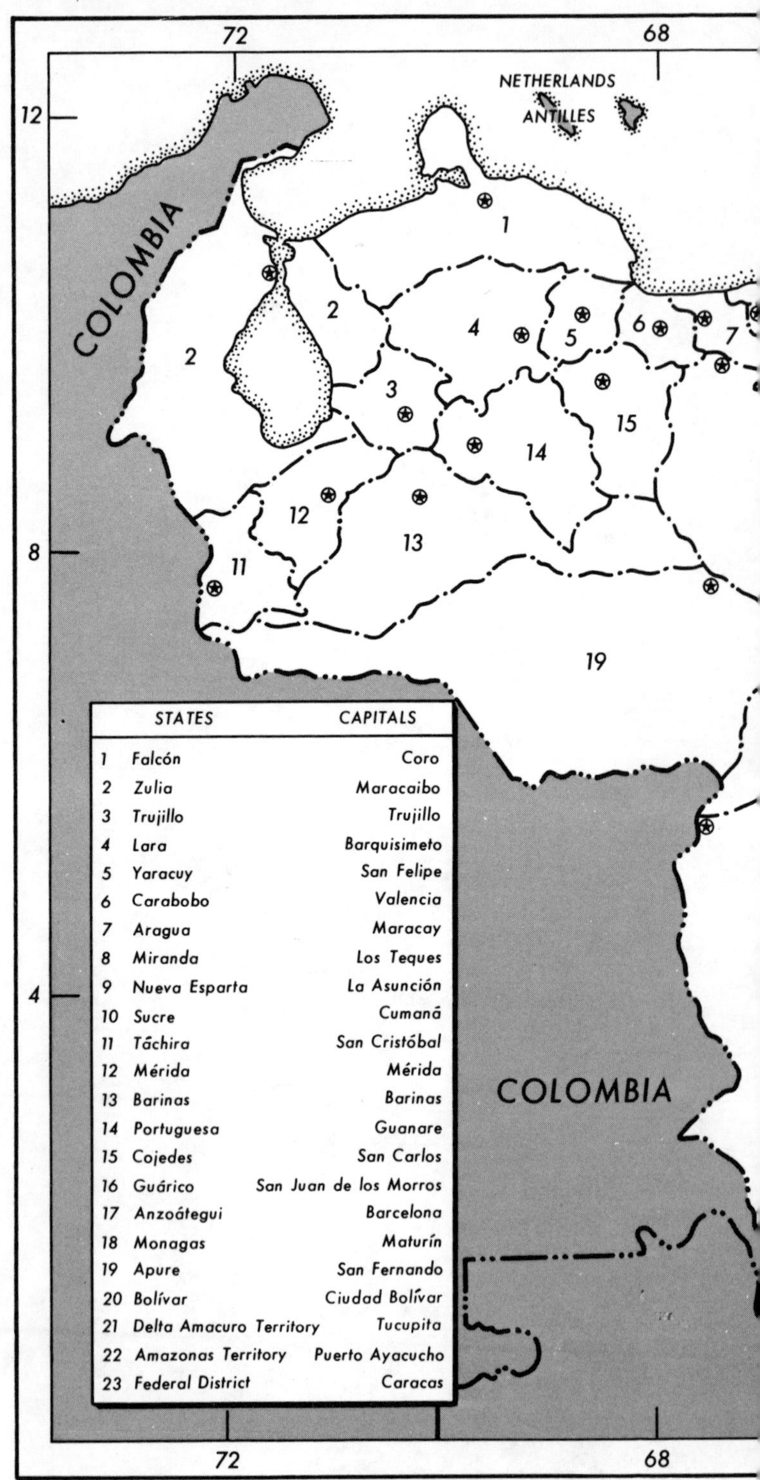

Figure 1. Venezuela

SECTION I. SOCIAL

CHAPTER 1

GENERAL CHARACTER OF THE SOCIETY

In 1971 the Republic of Venezuela, the world's leading exporter of petroleum and the third largest producer, was a federal republic with a popularly elected government engaged in strengthening democratic institutions; promoting increased agricultural and industrial production; enlarging education, housing, and public health programs; and continuing the development of hydroelectric power and communication and transportation facilities. A rapid increase in national wealth had been generated by the exploitation of petroleum resources after 1900. Public administration, formerly characterized by the personal rule of dictators, had, after the middle of the twentieth century, taken the form of popular self-government.

Located entirely in the tropics on the northern coast of South America, astride the major sea and air routes linking the northern and southern portions of the Western Hemisphere, the country, with some 11 million people, has an area of more than 350,000 square miles and a coastline of 1,750 miles on the Caribbean Sea and the Atlantic Ocean.

The country comprises four distinct geographical regions: the Northern Mountains and adjacent hill country in the northwest; the Maracaibo Lowlands, bordering on Lake Maracaibo and the Gulf of Venezuela; the Orinoco Lowlands, extending eastward from the Colombian frontier into the Orinoco Delta; and the Guiana Highlands, south of the Orinoco River, a mixture of tropical savanna grasslands and tropical forest.

The highlands are generally warm in the daytime and cool at night. The lowland coastal region is humid and hot, as are the inland river valleys. There are more than 1,000 rivers, but the Orinoco drains some four-fifths of the country.

The effects of the physical environment on the people are indicated by the fact that early agricultural development and urban settlements were in the valleys of the Northern Mountains, whereas the Orinoco Lowlands, best suited to cattle raising, attracted a scanty population. After World War I, however, development of the petroleum industry and manufacturing triggered a rapid increase in the population of the Maracaibo basin and other coastal areas. After

World War II cities were established in the richly endowed Guiana Highlands.

Discovered by Columbus on his third voyage in 1498, Venezuela was one of the first colonies in the New World to revolt against Spain, and it achieved independence in 1821 under the leadership of Simón Bolívar, the native son who became the country's national hero. During the nineteenth century the country's history was marked by frequent outbreaks of revolutionary turbulence, periods of political instability, and dictatorships.

Not until the discovery of oil in the twentieth century did Venezuela attain prosperity. The result was a flourishing of the cosmopolitanism to which upper class Venezuelans assign positive values without, however, abandoning their basic Hispanic culture pattern. In the twentieth century, after long periods of authoritarianism, three consecutive democratic elections were held—in 1958, 1963, and 1968.

The population, estimated at nearly 11 million in 1970, was growing rapidly. Rising birth rates after World War I reflected improving living conditions and a moderate amount of immigration, but after the mid-1950s the net gain of immigration over emigration declined. In 1970 the country was becoming rapidly urbanized as a result of crowding of agricultural lands, the demand for urban workers generated by the development of the petroleum industry, and the establishment by the government of new industrial centers. The population was concentrated in the coastal and Andean regions, but the development of industry in the Guiana Highlands was drawing people to new urban centers, such as Ciudad Guayana, during the 1960s.

The ethnic makeup of the population is largely the result of a mingling of Indians, Europeans, and Africans; most Venezuelans share a sense of ethnic identity and a common culture based on Hispanic traditions, colored by Indian and African influences. The number of tribal Indians was decreasing in 1970, and many of these were adjusting to the national culture. In 1970 a substantial number of foreigners lived in the country. Thus the process of ethnic amalgamation is remarkably advanced, and ethnic labels for groups are little used. There remains a correlation between racial descent and class, with notable white dominance at the upper levels, but persons of all degrees of mixed ancestry are found at all levels.

The national language is Spanish, spoken by almost all Venezuelans. It is flavored with an admixture of foreign loan words.

Changes in the structure of the society have been spurred by economic factors—notably the oil boom. In the colonial period society was stratified. After independence rivalry developed between European-born Spaniards and American-born descendants of Spanish settlers. In the twentieth century a middle class evolved and exercised an increasing influence on national affairs. Entrance into this class was facilitated by expanded educational opportunities, especially the increase in the number of secondary schools.

The society has been profoundly influenced by the rapid development of the educational system. A campaign during the 1960s reduced illiteracy from 37 percent in 1961 to an estimated 14 percent in 1970. In the 1960s there was emphasis on the growing role of technical education.

In 1970 Roman Catholicism was the religion of the great majority of the people. Religious freedom was guaranteed by the Constitution, and a small number of Protestants and Jews practiced their religions freely.

During the War of Independence there was a diversity of opinion among the clergy and hierarchy of the Roman Catholic Church in Venezuela, and during the nineteenth century political leaders limited the church's influence and power. In the twentieth century there was an improvement in church-state relations and increasing interest among the clergy and the hierarchy in social reform.

In 1970, after more than a decade of democratic government, habits of voter participation and peaceful transfer of office had been established. Within a multiparty system all major contenders sought mass bases of support and advocated social reform. Important elements in the society competing for influence in the political system were the landed aristocracy, the armed forces, organized labor, the business community, the Roman Catholic Church, and student organizations.

Power that had been concentrated for generations in the hands of the landed aristocracy and the military had been diffused through universal suffrage, direct elections, and large-scale political organization embracing such groups as peasants and urban labor. The first party to develop a base of broad popular support was the Democratic Action (Acción Democrática—AD) party, which in 1958 elected Rómulo Betancourt to the presidency.

In 1970 the military continued as an important political force; universities were centers of leftist political activism; the traditional conservatism of the Catholic hierarchy was significantly affected by reformist trends; and the influence of the private sector on government policies was offset by organized labor and peasant groups.

Political attitudes in 1970 were characterized by general acceptance of the authority of the Constitution and the ballot, and the great majority of the adult population had demonstrated its fundamental belief in the democratic process by going to the polls. Political education, formerly carried out almost entirely by the family and the church, was also influenced significantly by schools, labor unions, local political organizations, and the communications media.

Traditional sources of national pride—the achievements of Venezuelan patriots in the independence movement—have been supplemented by a sense of national purpose stimulated by the materialization of democratic processes and the undertaking of large-scale social reform. Ethnic homogeneity and the erosion of regionalist sentiment have strengthened national unity, and expansion of the educational system and extensive urbanization have given formerly isolated peasants a greater sense of participation in the national community.

Important foreign policy objectives of the government in 1970 were expansion of export trade and increased diplomatic and commercial ties, especially with the developing countries of Africa and Asia and with Eastern Europe. Simón Bolívar, a national hero, was the initiator of the first Pan American Conference, held in 1826. Venezuela participated in the League of Nations and was a charter member of the United Nations. After World War II the country became a party to the Río Treaty and the Latin American Nuclear Free Zone Treaty and participated in the activities of the Inter-American Development Bank (IDB), the Organization of American States (OAS), the Latin American Free Trade Association (LAFTA), and other hemispheric organizations.

Significant structural changes in the economy occurring in 1970 included an increase in the manufacturing sector's proportion of the gross national product (GNP), resulting from efforts to diversify the economy, and forward strides after 1963 in strengthening the economy with the assistance of loans from international financial agencies and other sources. The country continued to depend on petroleum for the great bulk of its foreign exchange and a large portion of its government revenue.

Although large portions of the rural population had migrated to the cities, agricultural workers in 1970 constituted the largest single segment of the labor force. The government's policy of attaining self-sufficiency in agriculture had greatly reduced food imports, and an agrarian reform program put into operation in 1960 had resulted in the distribution of unsettled land and provided credit to farmers.

In 1970 the country was rapidly increasing its manufacturing output and undertaking to reduce the need for imports. The government played an important role in setting prices, providing industrial development incentives, and serving as an entrepreneur through its national and regional agencies. The labor force was growing in significance and, with the sharp rise in population, was becoming younger. Labor unions tended to function more as extensions of political parties than directly as collective bargaining agents.

In 1970 literate Venezuelans took a lively interest in public affairs. Mass media included more than 100 radio stations, 5 television stations, and some 35 daily newspapers. Government censorship of the media was virtually nonexistent, and freedom of expression was guaranteed by the Constitution of 1961.

In colonial times cultural development was limited. Most early chronicles and scholarly works were written by Spanish priests. During the eighteenth century doctrines of the Enlightenment influenced leaders of the revolutionary movement, and patriotic verse and political polemics became popular forms of expression. In the twentieth century scholars showed new interest in the colonial period and in the Spanish influence on the country's social system. In novels and poetry modernism and realism predominated, and in painting the neoclassic tradition yielded to impressionism.

In 1970 there was a preoccupation with national characteristics—not only in philosophy and science but also in a variety of art forms. Cultural expression tended to reflect the beliefs and aspirations of a new generation of Venezuelans, imbued with a sense of national responsibility and a feeling of pride in their country.

CHAPTER 2

PHYSICAL ENVIRONMENT

Sixth in size among the countries of Latin America, Venezuela has an area of 352,000 square miles, a 1,750-mile coastline extending along the Caribbean Sea and the Atlantic Ocean, and some 3,000 miles of continental border with Colombia, Brazil, and Guyana (see fig. 1). Dominant among the natural features influencing the course of its evolution have been the mountains that rise in the north. The site of most of the first colonial estates, agricultural estates, and urban settlements, they remained the administrative, economic, and social heartland of the country in 1970.

The principal northern mountain ranges extend eastward in a great arc from the Colombian frontier to the Atlantic, descending northward to narrow coastal terraces or directly to the Caribbean, except in the west, where two spur systems reach northward to enclose an extensive lowlands around Lake Maracaibo and the Gulf of Venezuela. The southern flank of the mountains slopes more gradually to a nearly featureless lowland of grasses that extends east and west the full length of the country. The Orinoco River, flowing along the lowland's southern rim, provides drainage for most of the country. South of the Orinoco, the land rises into highlands made up of geologically ancient plateaus, deeply dissected by swiftly running streams and blanketed by dense tropical forests interspersed with grassy savannas. This region takes up nearly half of the national territory, but it is remote from population and transportation centers, and in 1970 much of its tangled forest land had yet to be explored.

Where rainfall is plentiful, the country's natural vegetation varies with altitude—from the luxuriantly tropical through the temperate to sparse alpine growths at higher levels. In semiarid areas dry forest and desertlike growth predominate, and in seasonally watered lowlands, where quality and depth of the soil are insufficient to support more sophisticated growth, prairie grasses provide most of the natural cover.

The tropical heat of the lowlands gives way to progressively cooler and more invigorating environments at higher altitudes, and seasonal variations of a few degrees at sea level are replaced by year-round constant averages in the higher parts of the mountains. Although there are no real deserts and the amount of rainfall is adequate in most localities, seasonal variations are considerable, and in some places, the land is alternately inundated and parched. In the greater part of the country, land is better suited to forest or pasture than to agriculture, and much otherwise arable land has been relatively neglected because of adverse weather conditions or lack of access to markets. At the same time, heavily worked soils of limited fertility in coastal terraces and in parts of the densely populated mountains have continued to be intensively cultivated.

With the exception of sugar estates in the lowlands around Lake Maracaibo, coffee plantations on the northern approaches to the Cordillera de Mérida, great cattle ranches on the lowlands of the Orinoco, and occasional subsistence farms in forests where shifting agriculture was practiced, there was little settlement outside the prosperous intermont valleys and basins of the mountains until well after the beginning of the twentieth century.

Before that time, population growth had been slow, but improving health and sanitary conditions after World War I and heavy immigration in the years immediately after World War II combined to cause a sharp rise in the growth rate and accelerate a previously sluggish trickle of migration from rural to urban areas (see ch. 4, Population and Ethnic Groups).

This movement was hastened by development of the petroleum industry that followed the discovery of petroleum near Lake Maracaibo. There are important iron mines and a variety of other mineral deposits, particularly in the highlands south of the Orinoco, but it is primarily petroleum wealth that has urbanized the country and made possible the growth of population centers beyond the limits of the mountain region. Satellite industries were established in the petroleum centers, and new urban job opportunities were available in construction work and in the services sector. By 1970 some 75 percent of the population was urban.

In the late 1950s the government commenced reshaping the pattern of settlement. Under already existing agrarian reform legislation, it began the resettlement of surplus farm labor from the mountains to hitherto empty or inadequately exploited lowland areas through land reclamation, flood control, and irrigation projects. At the same time it commenced plowing back a large part of its petroleum revenue into the establishment of new industries in old population centers, the creation of new industrial centers, and the planning of new residential districts to relieve urban crowding.

NATURAL FEATURES

Geographical Regions

Geographers customarily divide the country into four continental regions, plus the numerous small islands near the Caribbean coast (see fig. 2). There is no consensus with respect to the extent and boundaries of the regions to which a variety of names have been assigned. According to one representative system of classification, however, they are identified as the Northern Mountains, the Maracaibo Lowlands, the Orinoco Lowlands, and the Guiana Highlands.

Some geographers regard the Maracaibo Lowlands as part of a larger region that also includes the Orinoco Delta and the narrow coastal plain fronting on the Caribbean; to this region they give the name of the Coastal Lowlands. A majority, however, prefer to regard the Orinoco Delta as part of the Orinoco Lowlands and the discontinuous northern coastal strip as part of the Northern Mountains. There is also some question as to the region to which the southern slopes and piedmonts of the Northern Mountains properly belong. Topographically they are part of the mountains, and their economic ties are with mountain urban centers. They are part of the Orinoco drainage basin, however, and administratively they belong to Orinoco Lowlands states. They may, accordingly, be considered a transitional zone between the two geographical regions.

Northern Mountains

Broken by several gaps, the Northern Mountains and their spur ranges extend close to the northern coastline from the Colombian border on the west to the peninsula of Paria on the east. At the border, the Eastern Cordillera of the Colombian Andes divides into the Sierra de Perijá, which juts northward along the border toward the Gulf of Venezuela, and the Cordillera de Mérida (also called the Sierra de Mérida), which extends east of Lake Maracaibo. The Cordillera de Mérida chain broadens northward to form the Segovia Highlands, consisting of heavily dissected plateaus decreasing in altitude from 6,000 feet at the latitude of the city of Barquisimeto at their southern extremity of 600 feet in the north before descending to the coastline.

Before rising as the Cordillera de Mérida, the Colombian Andes fall off abruptly into the Táchira gap in the extreme west of Venezuela. The Andean spine crosses this gap as a relatively low saddle, dividing rivers flowing northward to Lake Maracaibo from those flowing southward across the Orinoco Lowlands. This saddle, across which the Pan American Highway passes between San Cristóbal in Venezuela and Cucúta in Colombia, has served historically as an important communication route between the two countries.

The fertile valley of Táchira, almost self-sufficient agriculturally, is connected with Colombia and with the plains to the south but does not have ready access to the coast or to the cities of the Central Highlands. This geographic isolation has made it traditionally a seat of strong regionalism. The Cordillera de Mérida, which varies in width between eight and forty miles, contains intermont basins and valleys from which mountain slopes rise to extensive areas of high-plateau grassland and, finally, to the only permanently snowcapped peaks in the country. Pico Bolívar, at 16,427 feet the highest peak, is located in Mérida State, which is called "the roof of Venezuela." The piedmont band on the north side of this chain, like those of the other Northern Mountains chains, is narrow and more abrupt but much more accessible than the band flanking the Orinoco Lowlands.

Geographically, the Andes terminate at the Yaracuy gap at the eastern end of the Cordillera de Mérida. Topographically, however, the coastal range of the Central Highlands is a resumption of the Andes so evident that some geographers refer to the entire mountain complex of northern Venezuela as the Venezuelan Andes.

The Central Highlands are composed of two ranges approximately parallel to the coast, separated by an intermediate lateral depression that reaches a maximum width of about thirty miles. This is the core area of the country where the densest population, the most intensive agriculture, and the best developed transportation network are found. The coastal range, where altitudes often exceed 5,000 feet and peaks reach from 7,000 to 9,000 feet, is flanked on the north by narrow coastal plains, except at points where the mountain slopes descend directly to the Caribbean. An interior range has maximum elevations of less than 5,000 feet that become progressively lower toward the east.

There are few easy passages through the two ranges. The principal pass through the coastal mountains has easy gradients and permits a highway to connect the city of Valencia with the Caribbean coast. The highway from Caracas to its port of La Guaira, only ten miles distant, formerly followed a zigzag route through a high and tortuous pass; it was replaced in 1953, however, by a superhighway that was tunneled through the coastal range. To the south, the historic pass of Carabobo through the interior range gives Valencia direct access to the Orinoco Lowlands. A second pass cuts through the same range to the east of Lake Valencia.

The coastal range terminates at Cape Codera on the Caribbean, but remnants of the interior system continue an additional fifty miles eastward to end near the Unare River. Beyond an extensive lowland gap that takes its name from the river, the Eastern Highlands (also called the Cumaná Highlands) rise in a broad block commencing between the old port cities of Barcelona and Cumaná and extending eastward to terminate in coastal marches near the Gulf of Paria. To the north, narrow ridges associated with this system extend laterally along the spines of the twin peninsulas of Araya and Paria. To the south, rounded hills with altitudes of less than 1,000 feet extend into the Orinoco Lowlands; they are sometimes called the Llanos Hills. In the core of the Eastern Highlands,

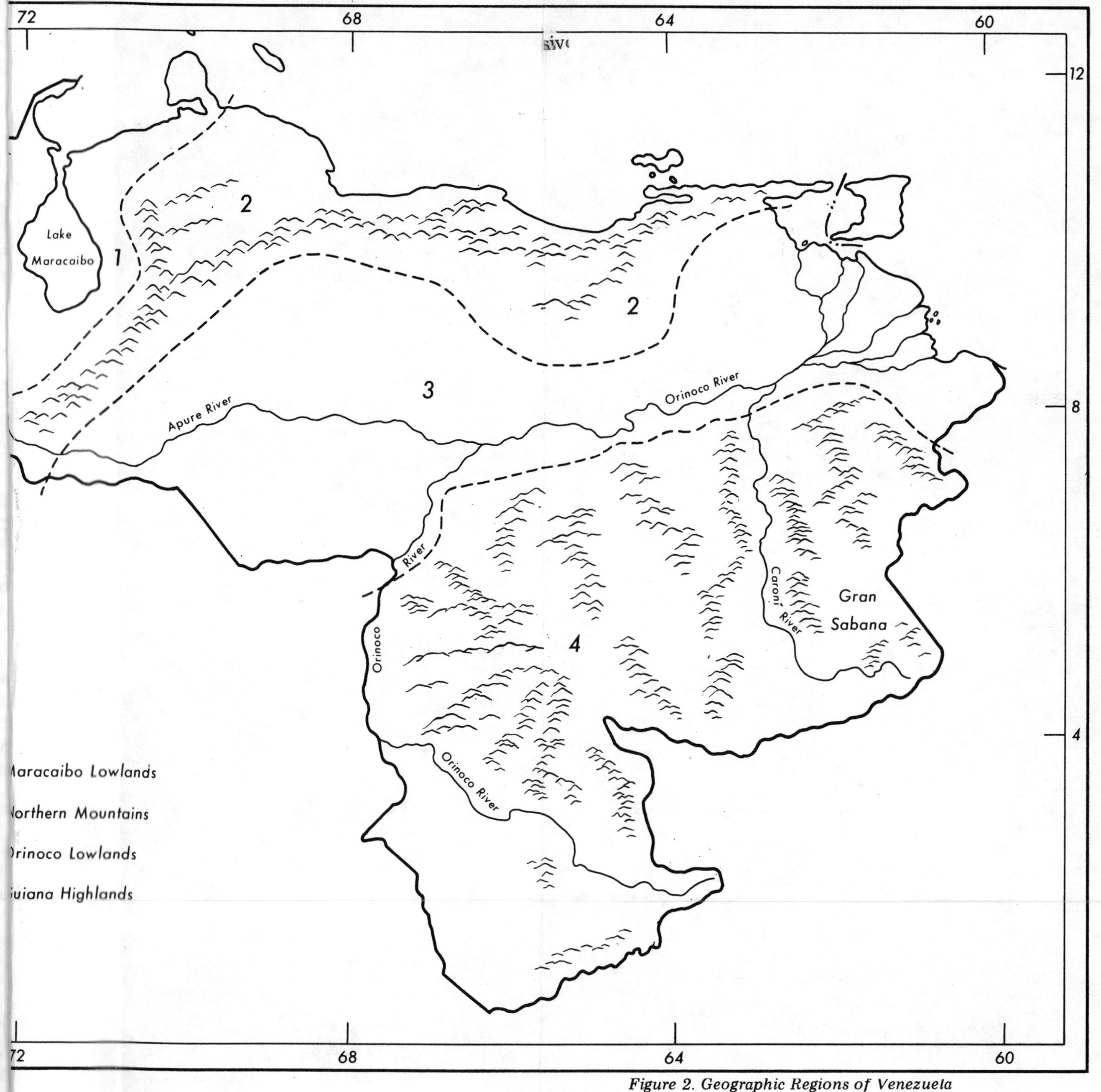

Figure 2. Geographic Regions of Venezuela

peaks reach 8,000 feet, but most of the system is made up of relatively low dissected uplands with a scattering of shallow erosion and rift valleys.

Maracaibo Lowlands

The Maracaibo Lowlands consist of the almost level plains around Lake Maracaibo and the Gulf of Venezuela and extend to the northeast to include the peninsula of Paraguaná. An open oval in shape, the region is delimited on the west by the curve of the Sierra de Perijá and on the south and east by the Cordillera de Mérida and the Segovia Highlands.

Orinoco Lowlands

The Orinoco Lowlands are the plains that extend from the Colombian border to the Atlantic and from the Northern Mountains to the Orinoco River. The region, in places of maximum extension, is nearly 1,000 miles long and 200 miles wide. It is commonly referred to as the *llanos* (plains) although, topographically, the true *llanos* do not include the Orinoco Delta, which extends from the Gulf of Paria to the Guyana border, or the Llanos Hills, which form a bottleneck between the western and eastern *llanos*.

The region tilts gradually southeastward from the Northern Mountains to the Orinoco and northeastward from the Colombian border to the Atlantic, but nowhere are altitudes greater than 600 feet. Gradients are almost imperceptible, and rivers are sluggish and meandering. North of the Apure River, a major tributary of the Orinoco, rivers flowing out of the Northern Mountains have cut out shallow valleys into the western *llanos*, leaving eroded mesa-like ridges that give the land a gently rolling appearance. South of the Apure, the terrain is flatter and altitudes are lower. Open range is unbroken by fences, and great cattle ranches are up to 1 million acres in extent.

Guiana Highlands

The Guiana Highlands (also called the Guayanas) rise almost immediately south of the Orinoco River. Comprising 45 percent of the national territory, they consist principally of plateau areas scored by swiftly running tributaries of the Orinoco. The most conspicuous topographical feature of the region is the Gran Sabana, a deeply eroded high plateau, some 14,000 square miles in extent, that rises deep in the interior from lower highland areas in abrupt cliffs up to 2,500 feet in height. From its rolling surface emerge massive flat-topped bluffs reaching considerable altitudes. The loftiest of these, Mount Roraima at the Brazil-Guyana tripoint, is over 9,000 feet above sea level. Elsewhere the region consists of plateaus varying from 1,000 to 3,000 feet in elevation, with occasional peaks rising to above 7,000 feet, except in the south of Amazonas Territory, where swampy flatlands drain northward into the Orinoco near its headwaters.

The Islands

In addition to the mainland, there are seventy-two islands of varied size and description. The most important is Margarita, the principal island in the small group that constitutes the state of Nueva Esparta. Although Margarita is rocky and mountainous and has little rainfall, it is nevertheless heavily populated, and its valleys are intensively farmed. Two other inhabited islands complete Nueva Esparta; the better known is Cubagua, once famous for its pearl fisheries and the site of the ruins of Nueva Cádiz, the first Spanish settlement of South America. The other islands vary in character from bare rocks to coral reefs to sandbars. The most distant, the minute island of Aves, situated 300 miles north of Margarita, is near the Leeward Islands and was transferred from Spain in 1865.

Climate

Although the country lies wholly within the tropics and its southern extremity is less than one degree north of the equator, its climate varies considerably by locality. These variations are determined primarily by elevation and secondarily by topography and the direction and intensity of prevailing winds. Seasonal variations in temperature are almost nonexistent, but rainfall is subject to variations so pronounced that the rainier months are customarily referred to as winter and the remainder of the year is considered summer.

Temperature is determined almost exclusively by altitude. Caracas, at an altitude of a little over 3,000 feet, has an average temperature of 70° F.; La Guaira, only ten miles distant but at sea level, has an average of 81° F. In all parts of the country, lowland temperatures average 80° F. or more, and averages decline with increasing elevation to freezing or below at 15,000 feet and higher. The seasonal range does not exceed 6° F. at sea level and decreases with elevation. The diurnal range is 15° F., or slightly more, and is not significantly affected by altitude.

There are five temperature zones in the country's loftiest highland complex, the Cordillera de Mérida. Below 3,000 feet is the hot zone (*tierra caliente*), with temperatures averaging 75° F. to 85° F. and with a seasonal range of between 3° F. and 4° F. The temperate zone (*tierra templada*), found between 3,000 and 6,000 feet, has temperatures of 65° F. to 75° F. and a seasonal range of 2° F. to 3° F. In the cold zone (*tierra fría*), between 6,000 and 10,000 feet, the annual range is from 55° F. to 65° F., and the seasonal variation declines to zero. Between 10,000 and 15,000 feet is the zone of the high mountain pastures (*paramos*), with mean temperatures declining to the freezing point. Higher still are the mountain peaks with permanent snows, glaciers, and ice caves. Because elevations do not reach 10,000 feet elsewhere in the country, freezing temperatures occur only in the Cordillera de Mérida.

The country lies south of the customary path of hurricanes, and cyclonic storms occur infrequently. Trade winds, which have an important influence on weather conditions, vary seasonally in intensity in accordance with the position of the permanent center of the permanent high pressure area of the North Atlantic. These winds customarily have deposited their rains over the sea and accordingly exert a drying effect on the coast. Local winds include the *barines* that blow across the interior lowlands into the southeast, the *calderetes* that sweep northward across the country with rain and thunder during the months of June through September, and a Caribbean wind called the Red Wind of Coro that periodically during the dry season blows in from the Caribbean to spread a fine deposit of sand over the Maracaibo Lowlands.

Humidity is generally high, with an average of 81 percent. Coastal lowlands are relatively less humid, with an average of between 65 and 77 percent and an annual variation of about 8 percent. In the interior the average is between 68 and 82 percent, with annual variations of 12 or 13 percent. Values tend to be higher toward the east, with the eastern *llanos* having high humidity conditions like those of the more heavily watered Amazonas Territory and the southern part of the Maracaibo Lowlands. Relatively low humidities are characteristic of the Northern Mountains.

Although there is some rainfall in most of the country during every month of the year, the heaviest precipitation tends to occur from May through November. Near the Colombian border and in the Cordillera de Mérida and in the southern part of the Maracaibo Lowlands, however, there are two rainy seasons; the heavier rainy season reaches its maximum in October, and the lighter, in May. The maximum variations recorded by a meteorological station are at San Fernando in Apure State, where rainfall rises steadily from a low of 0.04 inches in January to a maximum of 11.3 inches in October.

Yearly rainfall averages range from less than twenty inches in the peninsula of Paraguaná and some other areas near the Caribbean to over eighty inches in parts of the Orinoco Delta and in the eastern part of the Cordillera de Mérida. In the southeastern part of the *llanos* yearly averages are from sixty to eighty inches, but in the remainder of that area and in most of the Guiana Highlands the range is from forty to sixty inches. In the southern half of Amazonas Territory, however, the average is from sixty to eighty inches, and in some localities more than eighty inches are reported. In the Northern Mountains rainfall varies from valley to valley, depending on the prevailing winds and the location of the area in relation to mountain features. In the valley of Caracas it is about thirty-two inches annually, with more than half of the total falling from June through August.

Hydrography

Although there are more than 1,000 rivers in the country, its river systems are dominated by the Orinoco. Flowing more than 1,300 miles to the Atlantic from its source in the Guiana Highlands at the Brazilian border, it is the world's sixth largest river and the largest in South America after the Amazon. Its flow varies substantially by season, the high water level in August exceeding by as much as forty feet the low levels of March and April. When the river is low, Atlantic tidal effects can reach Ciudad Bolívar, 260 miles upstream.

Through most of the river's course, the gradient is almost imperceptible and, as it passes through the central part of Amazonas Territory, it divides its waters. Through the Casquiare Channel, it sends one-third of its volume to the Amazon along navigable waterways. Accordingly, an inland waterway from the Amazon to the mouth of the Orinoco is navigable by light craft except where the Atures Falls and Maipures Falls separate the upper and lower reaches of the Orinoco near the town of Puerto Ayacucho.

The Orinoco, together with its innumerable tributaries, provides drainage for about four-fifths of the country. It gathers the interior runoff from the Northern Mountains, most of the water from the Guiana Highlands, and the seasonal waters of the *llanos*. In addition, it provides drainage for the eastern slopes of the Colombian Andes through the Meta and other Colombian rivers.

The runoff from the Northern Mountains is carried to the Orinoco by sluggishly meandering rivers that are subject to extensive seasonal flooding over the alluvial flats of the northern *llanos*. As a result, semiaquatic conditions prevail during the height of the rainy season. After the conclusion of the rains, the waters recede, leaving stagnant pools that evaporate under the hot sun, and the land becomes parched.

Most of the rivers rising in the Northern Mountains flow southeastward to the Apure River, itself a tributary of the Orinoco. From its headwaters in the Cordillera de Mérida, the Apure crosses the *llanos* in a generally eastward direction. Few rivers flow into it from the poorly drained region to its south, and much of the southeastern extremity is swamp forest.

The other major Venezuela river is the Caroní, which originates in the Gran Sabana and flows northward to join the Orinoco at the site of the new city of Ciudad Guayana after gathering the waters of the other major Gran Sabana streams. It is believed to have the largest hydroelectric power potential of any river in Latin America, and Angel Falls, located on one of its tributaries, is the highest in the world.

Most of the rivers flowing from the Northern Mountains into Lake Maracaibo and the Caribbean are short and rapid, with deeply etched valleys. An important exception is the Tuy River, which passes slowly through the intermont depression of the Central Highlands to drain the country's most prosperous agricultural lands. A minor drainage system is provided by the Unare River, which flows into the Caribbean through the gap between the Central and Eastern Highlands. It drains the lowlands of the Unare Gap and a portion of the Central Highlands.

Because of the country's near-equatorial location and the absence of mountains with elevations sufficient to permit much snow accumulation or retention, the rivers are almost wholly dependent on rainfall for their flow. The seasonal character of the rainfall in the Northern Mountains and the consequent irregularity of the flow of rivers southward out of them have discouraged agricultural development of the piedmont and the northern fringes of the *llanos*. The taming of these rivers by construction of dams to permit irrigated farming during the dry season—a program begun during the 1950s—by 1970 had begun to show an important effect on the country's economy (see ch. 17, Agriculture).

Lake Maracaibo, the largest body of inland water in South America, provides convenient transportation of coffee and other agricultural products from the surrounding plains and the Andean mountain slopes. In the north, it is directly connected with the Gulf of Venezuela by an island-dotted narrows some twenty-five miles in length. Although the lake has an average depth of thirty feet and is navigable to its southern end, the exit from the narrows into the Gulf of Venezuela was originally blocked by a sandbar only seven feet beneath the surface at low tide. Because of the importance of Maracaibo petroleum production, the government has dredged a channel to permit passage of tankers through the narrows to the loading port of Maracaibo. The connection of the lake with the sea, however, makes its waters somewhat brackish and unfit either for drinking or for irrigation.

Second in importance among the lakes is Lake Valencia, a body of water eighteen miles in length and ten miles in width located about sixty miles east of Caracas in the heart of the country's best agricultural lands. Originally the lake drained southward toward the Orinoco, but excessive forest clearing on surrounding mountain slopes and overplanting of adjacent level ground during the colonial period caused rainwater to run off in spates rather than gradual underground seepage replenishing the waters of the lake. As a consequence, by 1800 its waters had subsided to a point where it was left without a surface outlet. The wars of independence caused forestry and crop planting to be neglected and permitted second-growth forest to appear. A quarter of a century later the lake had risen and once more had found an outlet. In the twentieth century, however, forest clearing and intensive agriculture have continued, and the drilling of numerous artesian wells in the vicinity once more curtailed the lake's natural water supply. During the late 1960s it was again without a surface outlet.

Third in size among the bodies of inland water is the Guárico Reservoir, the artificial lake formed in 1956 by containment of the waters of the Guárico to open a substantial area in the *llanos* to irrigated farming. In addition, there are numerous small tarns in the Cordillera de Mérida, lagoons scattered among coastal lowlands, and a sizable lake and lagoons in the swampy land east of Lake Maracaibo.

Vegetation

During the 1960s an estimated 21 percent of the country was forested, 20 percent was in pasture, 3 percent was arable, and the remaining 56 percent was in other categories (see ch. 17, Agriculture). Other categories included inland waters and swamps, high mountain zones with alpine vegetation, and arid territory covered by scrub forest and semidesert vegetation. Inclusion of such regions as those covered by mangrove thickets and scrub woodlands in the forested portion would increase the area in forests to over 40 percent. More than 500 types of wood have been identified in forest areas, but the classification is not complete. Slopes in the Northern Mountains have been cleared by timber cutting and shifting agriculture, and valuable woods, such as the accessible mahogany in Barinas and Portuguesa states, have been depleted. Proportions in forest, pasture, and crops may be increased substantially by the reforestation, swamp drainage, flood-control, and irrigation programs that the government initiated during the late 1950s and in the 1960s.

In the Northern Mountains, at altitudes ranging up to 3,000 feet, tropical forests with lichens, mosses, and dense shrubbery prevail where rainfall is persistent and heavy; elsewhere, a type of dry forest is found. Between 3,000 and 6,000 feet the vegetation varies from scrubby woodland to luxuriant forests where tree ferns and orchids grow. Above 6,000 feet a transitional cold zone occurs, with natural vegetation becoming sparser and grasses and herbaceous plants replacing the forests. High pastures and alpine vegetation extend from about 10,000 feet to the snowline at about 15,000 feet.

Because of its higher maximum elevations, the greatest variety of mountain vegetation is found in the Cordillera de Mérida. In the Segovia Highlands, branching off to the north, forest growth in valleys near the southern extremity gives way to scrub forest and brush, thistles, and cacti. The Central Highlands are naturally favored to support a wide variety of tree, plant, and shrub life, but forest clearing and intensive cultivation have inhibited the proliferation of flora. In the Northeastern Highlands poor soils and scanty rainfall have combined to limit most of the vegetation to scattered dry forest and scrub growths.

High humidity, heavy rainfall, and an absence of wind currents in the lower portions of the Maracaibo Lowlands have resulted in luxuriant tropical-forest growth, but closer to the Caribbean there is a transition through semideciduous dry forest to sparse shrub and desert growths like those of the Segovia Highlands.

The light soils and alternating wet and dry seasons of the *llanos* have been conducive to growth of a savanna type of vegetation consisting principally of natural pasture. The most common of these is *yarafuá*, a short grass found in wet areas; high grass called *camelote* is found in drier localities at higher altitudes. There is also some scrub growth and areas of reed and mixed vegetation, but in general the soil and climate are not conducive to the growth of a wider variety of species. Ribbons of broadleaf evergreen forest line the courses of waterways, however, and palms and occasional clumps of mixed forest are scattered about the *llanos*. To the east, the Orinoco Delta is a land of swamp forest and mangrove thickets.

In some places the soils of the Guiana Highlands are so badly eroded that little natural vegetation remains. Most of the region, however, is blanketed by semideciduous tropical forest, tangled with vines and parasitic plant growth, and by the rough natural grass of open savannas scattered among the forests. Among the wide variety of trees that grow mixed in the forested areas are the *balata*, from which a kind of rubber is produced, and the *tonka*, which bears a bean yielding an aromatic essence.

Wildlife

Because there are no effective natural barriers to isolate the country and the physical characteristics of the country are like those found elsewhere in the northern part of the continent, there are many animal species, although the advance of civilization has caused most of the larger animals to retreat to the south of the Northern Mountains. Among members of the cat family are the jaguar, the ocelot, and the puma or mountain lion. There are six kinds of monkey, several of bear, and two of deer. Other varieties include wild pigs and dogs, martens, otters, sloths, anteaters, foxes, opossums, and armadillos. Manatees and dolphins are found along the coastlines.

Alligators have been almost eliminated from the northern parts of the country, but many kinds have survived in profusion in the rivers and streams of the interior. Other reptiles include maritime and freshwater turtles, lizards, striped rattlesnakes, coral snakes, bushmasters, and ànacondas. There are a dozen kinds of rodent. Amphibians include the tree frog and the salamander.

Birds, both migratory and nonmigratory, are plentiful. Various cranes, herons, storks, and the scarlet ibis inhabit the shores of streams and lagoons. More than thirty kinds of eagle are found. Game species include dove, quail, and various ducks, including a Muscovy duck weighing as much as twenty pounds. Some migratory birds come from as far as the Arctic.

The best fishing grounds are located in coastal waters of the Atlantic and the Caribbean, north and west from the Guyana frontier to Cape Unare. In this zone the catch includes red snapper, Spanish mackerel, bluefish, mullet, and sardines. Further offshore, between Blanquilla and Orchila islands, tuna and related species are taken. The western fishing zone, from Punta Chichirivache to the Colombian frontier, is rich in kingfish, drum, shark (used as a food fish), snapper, small mullet, jack, characin, sawfish, and snook. Shrimp are found in Lake Maracaibo; spiny lobsters, in the Las Roques archipelago; and oysters, near Margarita Island and along the eastern beaches. Experiments in the artificial cultivation of mussels were in progress during 1970.

Freshwater fish, most plentiful in the rivers and streams of the Orinoco Lowlands, are so numerous in species that many have not yet been fully studied biologically. Among the most common edible species are various kinds of catfish and the bagre, a native fish weighing up to 200 pounds. There are also rays, electric eels capable of powerful discharges, and the ferocious piranhas, known locally as caribes.

Soils and Minerals

Most of the arable land is found in the alluvial bottoms of valleys and basins of the Northern Mountains, particularly in those of the Central Highlands and the Cordillera de Mérida. In some of these depressions the otherwise fertile land is poorly drained and saline. Adjacent mountain slopes have thinner soils that have been heavily eroded by deforestation and shifting agriculture. On plateaus at higher levels, soils are poorer still in quality but support grains and pasture.

The southern part of the Maracaibo Lowlands is made up of young alluvial soils rich in minerals, but unfavorable climatic conditions have discouraged their development. As the land rises southward into the windward slopes of the Cordillera de Mérida, it becomes suitable for the cultivation of coffee and cacao. Northward, the central portion of the plain deteriorates into an immature tropical bog that is believed unsuitable for reclamation. On the other side of the bog, in the direction of the town of Machiques, the land is suitable for pasture, but fertile alluvial soils are scarce. As the land slopes upward in the west toward the Sierra de Perijá, soils are deep and fertile. Around the Gulf of Venezuela and on the Paraguaná Peninsula they are of poor quality.

The clay and loam topsoil of the western part of the Orinoco Lowlands is thin and suitable mainly for pasture, although accumulations increase in depth near the Orinoco Delta. In the delta itself, deep alluvial deposits are found on the natural levels of the many river branches, but the bogs that lie between are of unproved value. The Llanos Hills are covered by poor, sandy soils. To the northwest, land with a high agricultural potential is found in the states of Barinas and Portuguesa along the fringes of the Cordillera de Mérida. The mountain slopes consist of residual soils that are only moderately fertile but, as the many mountain rivers reach the plains, they lose their velocity and leave thick layers of young alluvial deposits. Rich in minerals and capable of retaining water and plant nutrients, these soils occur in a band, about twenty miles wide, from Arcigua in the state of Portuguesa to the Colombian frontier.

Along the northern fringe of the Guiana Highlands there is a border of alluvial flatland following the course of the Orinoco River, but the plateaus and ridges of the interior are made up of poor, residual soil on ancient parent rock. Most of it is in the form of a thin, sandy, and lateric blanket over compact layers of kaolin and other clay undersoils. Because the open savannas of the region are mixed with thickly forested areas, however, their soils have been less leached and eroded than those of the Orinoco Lowlands, and some authorities believe that only the relative inaccessibility of these savannas prevents them from providing pasturage as suitable as that of the *llanos*.

The country's enormous petroleum wealth is widely distributed, but the most important of its oil-bearing formations—and the most extensive in South America—lies along the eastern shore of Lake Maracaibo and beneath its waters. The lakebed consists of sediment saturated by organic material that has been deposited by rivers flowing rapidly out of the encircling mountain ranges. The increasing weight of the material has caused the older deposits to subside gradually, and increasing pressure and heat have converted the decayed organic content of the deeper sedimentary layers into subterranean reservoirs of petroleum. In places, drillings have reached more than 16,000 feet beneath the lake floor before reaching the granite bedrock.

Oil is also produced from sedimentary deposits located in the Barinas-Apure and Maturín petroleum basins. The first extends from the piedmont of the Cordillera de Mérida southward across the western *llanos*. The second includes the hills to the south of the Eastern Highlands and extends eastward as far as the Orinoco Delta, where a commercially important asphalt lake is located on the San Juan River about twenty-five miles from the Gulf of Paria.

Bituminous coal, the country's other mineral fuel, occurs most extensively in Táchira State and in the Guiana Highlands. Old coal mines in the Northeastern Highlands were reopened during the 1950s in preparation for supplying the new steel mill at Ciudad Guayana on the upper Orinoco.

The most important of the metallic minerals produced is iron, with known reserves amounting to 3 or 4 billion tons or ore. Government geological reports indicate that in the 36,000-square-mile Imataca Belt, extending from the Guyana border across Bolívar State and continuing westward into Apure State, reserves of about 1.5 billion tons of ore range from 55 percent to nearly 70 percent in metallic content. Production comes principally from mines located at El Pau and Cerro Bolívar, both located near the Caroní River above its juncture with the Orinoco. Gold, the country's most important commercial mineral during the nineteenth century, is still mined in diminished quantities at El Callao, also on the Caroní. Diamonds, the country's only precious stone, are found in both gem and industrial grades in connection with alluvial deposits near the same river.

Other than magnesite on Margarita Island, there are no known deposits of metallic minerals in lowland areas. In the Guiana Highlands and Northern Mountains, however, deposits of chrome, tungsten, manganese, nickel, copper, and lead may be of future importance. In addition, it is believed that still unsurveyed portions of the Guiana Highlands may prove to contain extensive deposits of metallic minerals.

In various parts of the country there are commercially important deposits of gypsum, lime, phosphate rock, asbestos, and salt. Among the other known nonmetallic resources are kaolin, sulfur, graphite, quartz, slate, and marble.

BOUNDARIES AND POLITICAL SUBDIVISIONS

After repeated delays, a treaty completing delineation of the 1,274 miles of the Colombian frontier was signed in 1941. In addition, much of this line has been demarcated. Most of the border passes through tropical wilderness where, in some localities, tribal Indians have discouraged survey operations. Southward from the Caribbean, it follows straight lines along the Guajira Peninsula; natural divides in the Sierra de Perijá; and mountain features, rivers, and straight lines to the Meta River. At that point it turns eastward along the Meta to its juncture with the Orinoco. It then follows the Orinoco and other rivers southward to the Brazilian tripoint, except in one short sector where a straight line connects two rivers.

The 1,243-mile boundary with Brazil, based almost entirely on watersheds and small rivers, was determined in protocols dating from 1843 to 1930. In 1970 it had been entirely delineated, and unmonumented river segments were considered demarcated. Some question over the true source of the Orinoco River, however, remained a matter for possible future disagreement. Early in 1970 it was announced that separate Venezuela-Colombia and Venezuela-Brazil commissions would meet later in the year to discuss remaining boundary issues.

The 462-mile border with Guyana (formerly British Guiana) runs eastward from the Brazil tripoint to Mount Roraima along straight lines, rivers, and watersheds to the Atlantic at a point near the lower extremity of the Orinoco Delta. The border, established at approximately its present location by an arbitral tribunal in 1899, was demarcated pursuant to a protocol signed in London in 1930.

Venezuela has maintained that the arbitral award was fraudulent and that its frontier should extend to the Essequibo River. The area in question consists largely of trackless swamp and rain forest, but its 53,000 square miles represent three-fifths of the national territory of Guyana. Dispute over the area became lively in 1965 on the eve of Guyana's independence and continued until June 1970. At that time a twelve-year moratorium was agreed to by the two countries in a protocol signed in Port of Spain (see ch. 13, Foreign Relations).

Although in 1970 no important questions remained unresolved concerning the continental boundary with Colombia, a potentially difficult one had emerged with respect to sovereignty over the waters of the Gulf of Venezuela. The basic issue appeared to be rights to petroleum deposits believed to lie beneath the bed, although this had not been formally stated by either government.

Between 50 and 100 miles wide at its entrance (depending on the points between which the entrance line is drawn), the Gulf of Venezuela has a maximum width of 120 miles. Its shore lies entirely within Venezuelan territory except in the northeast, where there is a short stretch of Colombian shoreline on the upper part of the Paria Peninsula. Venezuela holds the gulf to be an inland body of water under its sole jurisdiction and has asserted that its entrance should be a line drawn from the frontier on the Paria Peninsula to the end of the Paraguaná Peninsula in Venezuelan territory. Colombia, however, claims the waters offshore from its portion of the coastline to the midpoint in the gulf, an arrangement that would give to it a triangular sector also claimed by Venezuela.

Quiet discussions between the two countries had been held intermittently beginning in the mid-1960s. In the early part of 1970 these discussions reached higher levels and were reported extensively in the press. In August, at a sea rights conference held in Lima, fourteen American countries, including Colombia, resolved that all nations had an inherent right to claim as much of the sea and seabed near their coasts as might be necessary in order to protect their present and potential wealth. Venezuela, not wishing to be a party to any resolution that might further open the waters of the gulf to dispute, was among the minority that stood in opposition.

States and territories, the main political subdivisions, coincide generally with geographic regions. The states of Zulia and Falcón coincide approximately with the Maracaibo Lowlands; and Bolívar State and Amazonas Territory, with the Guiana Highlands. The other states are contained primarily within either the Northern Mountains or the Orinoco Lowlands. The political subdivisions also correspond to population distribution in the sense that the smallest states, located in the Northern Mountains, have the densest populations and the largest state, Bolívar, has the lightest population density. This traditional correlation between size and density of habitation has been modified somewhat by urbanization and industrialization of the country during recent years. For example, development of the petroleum industry has changed the large state of Maracaibo from a sparsely populated to a densely populated one.

In general, the structure of the internal subdivisions has exercised a favorable influence on the development of the country, and there is no pressure on the government to change their arrangement. Dense populations in small states and sparse populations in large ones facilitate internal political administration and make possible planning and installation of socially useful facilities, such as schools and hospitals, on a rational basis. Political subdivisions coincide with geographic and economic regions, and their borders generally coincide with natural features; development of internal transportation systems has been facilitated accordingly.

SETTLEMENT PATTERNS

In 1970 the population averaged about 30 persons per square mile, but the density was extremely uneven. The 1961 census showed that political subdivisions making up well over half of the national territory had populations averaging less than 5 persons per square mile, while the states of Carabobo and Nueva Esparta and the Federal District had concentrations of over 200 per square mile (see fig. 3). Because the borders of the political subdivisions for which populations were reported in the 1961 census do not exactly correspond to borders of geographic regions, no exact figures are available with respect to population by region. The census data, however, do indicate that population density in the Northern Mountains was more than five times the national average and in the Maracaibo Lowlands it was nearly twice the average. In the Orinoco Lowlands it was less than half the average, and in the Guiana Highlands it was about one-fifteenth the average for the country as a whole.

From the Spanish conquest to the end of World War I the country remained sparsely populated and predominantly rural. Patterns of settlement during this period were determined almost entirely by climate, soils, and location in relation to other settled areas and to the Caribbean coast.

The valleys and basins of the Central Highlands were advantageous with respect to all of these considerations, and it was in this core area of the country that population—both urban and rural—was to remain concentrated for almost four centuries. Elevations of the intermont depressions were sufficient to modify the near-equatorial temperatures of the lowlands, and rainfall and soil conditions were conducive to development of a strong agricultural base for the economy. The lateral depression between the coastal and interior ranges facilitated good internal communication, and the clusters of population had relatively easy access to Caribbean ports.

The climate and soils of valleys in the Cordillera de Mérida were also suitable for development, and they became secondary centers of population. They were far from the other populated areas and poorly located with respect to access to the sea, however, and they were to develop in relative isolation. The Eastern Highlands were favorably located with respect to access to the coast, and elevations were sufficient to permit escape from equatorial temperatures, but they lacked the fertile intermont valleys of the other two principal mountain systems and, as a consequence, were to remain peripheral population centers.

The Maracaibo Lowlands remained almost entirely neglected. By a quirk of history, the settlement of Coro was established at the foot of the Paraguaná Peninsula in 1527, well before the founding of any permanent ports on the coast north of the Central Highlands. Spaniards entering the interior from Coro, however, found the region inhospitable; semidesert surrounded Lake Venezuela, and the oppressive heat, swarms of malaria-carrying mosquitoes, and wide expanses of swampland around Lake Maracaibo made the thought of settlement near it highly unattractive.

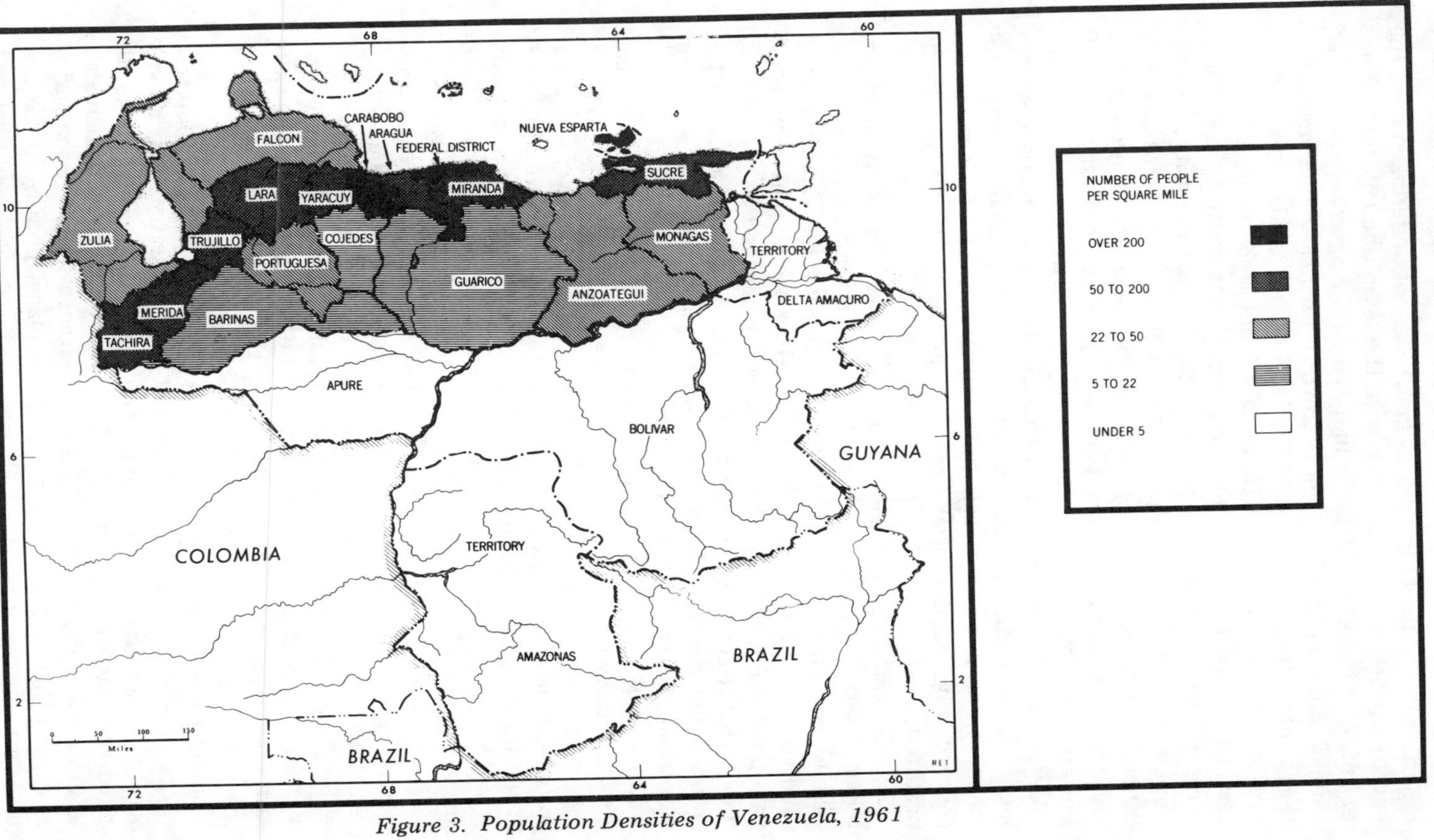

Figure 3. Population Densities of Venezuela, 1961

Settlement of the Orinoco Lowlands was not undertaken until the end of the seventeenth century with the establishment of Calabozo in 1695, followed by Maturín in 1710, and Angostura (now called Ciudad Bolívar) in 1764. These towns served as trading and transport centers and, in the case of Ciudad Bolívar, as a base for mineral prospecting in the Guiana Highlands. Thin soils, heat, alternating seasons of flood and drought, and remoteness from markets, however, dictated that this region be devoted to cattle raising, and the population remained scanty and unevenly scattered across its wide *llanos*. Settlements grew up only in localities not subject to the seasonal floods and droughts, particularly along the rivers that, until the construction of roads during the twentieth century, were the only routes of transport and communication. Agricultural development of the northern fringe of the Orinoco Lowlands did not commence on an important scale until the second half of the twentieth century when agricultural crowding in the Northern Mountains occurred.

The Guiana Highlands remained too distant to be of much interest to settlers, and even in 1970 much of it remained unexplored. Ciudad Bolívar is the capital of the state of Bolívar, a political subdivision of the region, and it served as the shipment point of gold production from the highlands, which reached its peak during the nineteenth century. Topographically, however, it is a part of the Orinoco Lowlands rather than the highlands to the south, as is the new urban center of Ciudad Guayana.

The scanty population of the Guiana Highlands is heaviest near the Orinoco, where there are some cattle ranches and rice paddies, and near the Caroní River, where most of the country's mineral production and hydroelectric power installations are concentrated. In the interior the population in 1970 still was made up principally of Indians, who practiced shifting cultivation in the forests or lived clustered in villages around mission stations on navigable streams.

Although most of the country remained sparsely settled, a prosperous agricultural economy was experiencing slow but steady growth in the Central Highlands and the Cordillera de Mérida. The center, both of population and of intensive agriculture, lay in the intermont depression between Caracas and Valencia and in the eastward extension of the depression along the deep valley of the Tuy River

Valencia was founded in 1555 in the center of what was later to become the leading agricultural district of the country. Caracas was founded in 1567 in a rift valley penetrating the coastal range. It lacked the extensive agricultural hinterland of Valencia, which also was more favorably located with respect to accessibility to the Caribbean and other regions. There was some placer mining during the early years in the vicinity of Caracas, but the city's political and commercial functions rather than its natural advantages enabled it to grow to an estimated 2 million in population by 1970, while Valencia, with a little more than 200,000 people, was the country's fourth city in size.

During the colonial period the valley bottoms were quickly divided into large estates and distributed among the Spanish officers. First Indians and later Negro slaves were settled in clusters of huts around the manor house of the estate owner. Smaller farms were established in poorer lands scattered between estates and, when the lower levels had largely been occupied, agricultural development pushed up the mountainsides, where the prevailing practice of shifting agriculture resulted in the destruction of much of the thick forest that had originally covered the slopes between elevations of 3,000 and 6,000 feet.

In older developed areas population pressures began to be felt, and after World War I the fragmentation of farmholdings had become such that small farmers were forced increasingly to turn to sharecropping arrangements with the proprietors of the remaining larger estates in order to gain access to a sufficient acreage of workable land.

The same kind of pattern had evolved in settlement of the valleys and basins of the Cordillera de Mérida and, to a lesser extent, in the occasional wet depressions of the Eastern Highlands. In 1970 the latest available data estimated that in the country as a whole some 100,000 farms ranging from large to small were producing for the market and that 200,000 families were working small plots at the subsistence level, many of them still engaging in shifting cultivation (see ch. 17, Agriculture).

During the nineteenth century and the early part of the twentieth century, agricultural activity in the Maracaibo Lowlands was confined largely to the sugar, coconut, and cacao estates and to subsistence farming in forest clearings. There were a few fishing villages on the shores of Lake Maracaibo and a few village population clusters on the navigable rivers flowing into the lake. These villages owed their existence to fishing, farming, and service as loading points for coffee brought by muleback from plantations on the slopes of the Cordillera de Mérida.

In the Orinoco Lowlands cattle continued to be the sole important economic endeavor and, in the late nineteenth and early twentieth centuries, political figures exercised an important influence on the growth of settlement through their influence on the industry. President Antonio Guzmán Blanco introduced better breeds of cattle and demanded better care of them. By 1883 the number of animals reached an all-time high of more than 8 million, and there was a demand for additional *llaneros* (cowboys of the region) to herd them. General Juan Vicente Gómez also took a direct interest in pastoral activities, but in his later years he virtually monopolized the cattle business and arrogated the pastures to himself through the simple device of imposing a confiscatory tax on cattle driven across state boundaries. By 1920 the cattle population had dropped to below 3 million head, and the human population in the *llanos* had declined.

Agricultural settlement of the region was confined largely to the high ground of the Andean piedmont where great estates were devoted to the cultivation of tobacco and indigo. After the termination of slavery in 1854 and the removal of indigo from the world market as a consequence of the development of coal-tar dyes, however, agricultural activity came to an end, leaving nothing to attract settlers to this potentially productive area until after the end of World War II.

The first agricultural resettlement legislation was enacted in 1949. In 1956 the creation of an artificial lake, by impoundment of the waters of the Gúarico River, at Calabozo in the *llanos* at the foot of the piedmont made possible the creation of some 500 new farms.

Since 1958 various other resettlement projects have been initiated under the agrarian reform program with the aims of raising agricultural productivity, slowing the flow of the rural population to already crowded cities, reducing agricultural unemployment and underemployment, providing land for landless farmers, opening up hitherto empty lands to settlement, and achieving a more even distribution of the rural population (see ch. 17, Agriculture). A majority of these projects have been in the northern reaches of the *llanos* and in the adjacent piedmont because much of this area is already in the public domain, having been once owned or controlled by General Gómez. It includes good natural pasture, particularly in the states of Barinas and Portuguesa.

During the 1960s the government also initiated a project to open up the sparsely populated public lands of the Orinoco Delta by reclamation of swamps in order to make an anticipated 4 million acres available for year-round agricultural use. In addition, in 1970 the National Agrarian Institute announced plans to establish 12,000 families on virgin lands along the country's frontiers (see ch. 17, Agriculture).

Until after the beginning of the twentieth century the urban population had increased at a rate not conspicuously greater than that of the country as a whole, and the overall rate of growth had been slow. In 1800 the population is estimated to have been about 1 million, and at the end of World War I it was not much more than 2 million. The postwar growth rate, however, has soared in response to development of modern public health and sanitation programs. By 1950 the population had reached 5 million, and by 1970 the population was approaching 11 million. Between 1960 and 1970 the urban population sector increased by about 3 million; the rural, by about 100,000.

This fast rate of urbanization has resulted from an interaction of population pressure on the limited rural employment opportunities, causing young people to leave the crowded farms in increasing numbers, and the increase in urban job opportunities that followed the discovery of oil in the Maracaibo Lowlands in 1917 and, later, in other parts of the country (see ch. 4, Population and Ethnic Groups).

The city of Maracaibo, with a population of less than 50,000 in 1915, by 1970 had become the country's second largest urban center, with a population of more than 600,000. Most of the new jobs that have made this growth possible were not in the capital-intensive petroleum industry itself but in other industries attracted to the new urban area and in the services sector. The village of Cabimas on the eastern shore of Lake Maracaibo had become the seventh largest city, with a population of 140,000. It served as the principal supply center for nearby oilfields. Until 1938 Puerto La Cruz was a small agricultural port in Anzoátegui State. It had no nearby petroleum wealth, but it became the terminus for pipelines to fields in the interior. By 1970 it had become the eighth city in size, with a population of 130,000.

By 1970 the little coastal town of Morón, near the Caribbean port of Puerto Cabello, had been engulfed by a petrochemical complex connected by pipeline with oilfields in Barinas State. Another petrochemical complex, at Tablazo, directly across the Maracaibo narrows from the city of Maracaibo, seemed destined to become an entirely new industrial city. The Ministry of Public Works, in cooperation with the Venezuelan Institute of Petrochemicals, was planning to provide housing and other facilities for 13,000 residents by 1975 and for 330,000 by 1990. The planners hoped that the development of the petrochemical nucleus would attract subsidiary and satellite industries, thus further contributing to growth of the new city (see ch. 18, Industry).

The government has not confined its activities in connection with urban development to those localities where urban growth has been directly related to the petroleum industry. During the 1960s it has engaged in a program aimed at broadening and strengthening the country's industrial base through the establishment of new industries in old population centers and the creation of industrial centers in previously unpopulated localities. The program is commonly referred to as sowing the oil—plowing back petroleum revenues into industries designed to support continued economic growth when the reserves of oil are eventually exhausted.

The most ambitious phase in the program is the construction of Ciudad Guayana, a new industrial city at the confluence of the Orinoco and Caroní rivers in almost empty country between the eastern *llanos* and the Guiana Highlands. Established in 1961 on the site of the little river town of Puerto Ordáz, by 1970 it was already the country's tenth city in size, with a population of well over 100,000. It was expected eventually to replace Maracaibo as the second largest city. The first major heavy-industry establishments to commence production had been a government-owned integrated steel mill and an aluminum plant of mixed ownership (see ch. 18, Industry).

As a means of combating unemployment and urban crowding in other cities, the government during the 1960s sponsored the establishment of new manufacturing plants in such cities as Valencia and Maracay and planned the establishment of more than 200 light-industry installations in Barcelona, an old northeastern port city that had fallen into decay with the growth in prosperity of the nearby oil-loading port of Puerto La Cruz. In 1970 it was engaged in the planning of Ciudad Satelito Tuy Medio, a satellite city to be constructed thirty miles east of Caracas in order to relieve unemployment in the capital city and spread urban development in the Tuy River valley. With its own industrial, commercial, and service establishments and its own schools and hospitals, it was to house 115,000 people by 1975 and more than 400,000 by 1990.

CHAPTER 3

HISTORICAL SETTING

In 1970 Venezuelans continued to take pride in the fact that theirs was one of the first colonies in the New World to revolt against Spain, and the native son who led the revolt—Simón Bolívar—was honored as a national hero. The history of the country was clearly reflected in its national language, its cultural heritage, and its ethnic structure.

The territory, first on the South American mainland to be explored by the Spaniards, was discovered by Christopher Columbus in 1498. Settlers were initially attracted by pearl fisheries, but these were soon exhausted. After the conquests of Mexico in 1519 and Peru in 1532, Spain paid scant attention to Venezuela, which at the time had little more to offer than hides and agricultural produce.

Factors shaping the society were: the mingling of Spanish, Indian, and African bloodstreams; the influence of the Roman Catholic Church; the exploitation of large landholdings with the help of slaves; the rise of political strong men in the nineteenth century; and the discovery of oil in the twentieth century.

During the colonial period descendants of Spanish settlers developed a society not entirely dependent on Spanish connections. Their distance from the great viceregal capitals enabled them to avoid the more onerous Spanish controls, but resentment of neglect by the colonial authorities and ill-feeling generated by their arrogance led to a desire for complete independence. In 1811 Venezuelans declared their independence of Spain and, after years of fighting, achieved freedom in 1821.

Heavy losses of life and a virtual collapse of civil government resulted from the wars of independence, and Spanish colonial rule was replaced by the oppressive administrations of *caudillos* (regional political strong men). The country, together with what are now Panama, Colombia, and Ecuador, was part of a union known as the Republic of Gran Colombia until 1830, when it became a sovereign state.

During the nineteenth century the country's history was characterized by recurrent periods of dictatorship, political instability, and revolutionary violence. Long periods of authoritarianism in the twentieth century included the dictatorships of General Juan Vicente Gómez (1908—35) and General Marcos Pérez Jiménez

(1952—58). Between 1936 and 1938 and after 1958 efforts were made to develop effective representative government, and after the overthrow of Pérez Jiménez in 1958 there were three consecutive elections.

Rómulo Betancourt (1959—64) of the Democratic Action (Acción Democrática—AD) party was the first popularly elected president to complete his term of office. Raúl Leoni (1964—69) became the first president to preside over the peaceful transfer of power to a member of a different political party—Rafael Caldera of the Committee for Independent Political and Electoral Organization (Comité de Organización Política y Electoral Independiente—COPEI), commonly called the Social Christian Party, who took office in March 1969.

DISCOVERY AND EXPLORATION

On his third voyage to the New World in 1498, Columbus reached the mainland of South America and sailed along the northeast corner of what is now Venezuela into the Gulf of Paria, where he discovered four of the many mouths of the Orinoco River. He reported that he found the natives of the coast wearing pearls as ornaments, and it was these that drew the first Spaniards to Venezuela.

In 1499 two Spanish adventurers discovered the source of the treasure in the oyster beds of the islands of Margarita and Cubagua, off the northeast coast. A year later, the first European settlement in Venezuelan territory was established on Cubagua. Here, until the settlement was destroyed by a combination of hurricanes and earthquakes in 1543, the Spaniards exploited the pearl fisheries, using many hundreds of Indian slaves as divers.

Alonso de Ojeda, a member of Columbus' second expedition, was the first European to explore all the Caribbean coast of Venezuela. Accompanied by Amerigo Vespucci and Juan de la Cosa, he set out from Spain in May 1499 with four ships, following the route of Columbus' third voyage. Continuing west along the coast, he sailed into the Gulf of Venezuela and thence into Lake Maracaibo.

The Indians living around the gulf and lake often built their villages on piles over the quiet waters—a feature said to have reminded the explorers of Venice and to have led them to name the area Venezuela (Little Venice). The name soon came to be applied to all the territory of northeastern South America from Lake Maracaibo to a point east of the mouth of the Orinoco River. Definite inland boundaries were not to be established for centuries (see ch. 2, Physical Environment).

The Spanish explorers and conquistadors were accompanied or followed closely by priests. Noteworthy among these was Bartolomé de las Casas, who became famous as the Apostle of the Indians. After two unsuccessful attempts, in 1513 and 1518, by las Casas and other priests to establish monasteries on the coast, Captain Gonzalo de Ocampo laid foundations of a city to be called Nueva Toledo near present-day Cumaná. These projects failed, however, because of Indian attacks brought on by the Spanish slave raids (see ch. 9, Religion).

As Spanish mines and plantations in the Antilles used up the local Indian populations, raids on the relatively docile Indians of the coast became more frequent. To control such traffic and to protect the Indians, Spain sent Jácome Castellón, who, after subduing the Indians of the northeast area, in 1523 founded a fortified city called Nueva Córdoba, known today as Cumaná.

Slave raiding soon shifted to western Venezuela, centering on the Maracaibo area. To reduce the severity of these raids and also to bring the area under royal control, it was decided to establish a center of royal authority and religious influence on the mainland. Juan de Ampúes, sent from Spain in 1527 to select the site, landed on the Paraguaná Peninsula and, after some searching, selected a location at its base and laid out a city to be called Santa Ana de Coro. This was the first European settlement in western Venezuela.

Until 1528 scant attention was paid to the interior except for short forays inland, principally in search of slaves. Rumors of fabulous treasures of gold and jewels and of other wonders to be found behind the coastal ranges began to circulate. There was the legend of El Dorado (the Golden One), the king of a golden city who covered himself with gold dust. As these rumors filtered back to Europe, interest in the exploration and exploitation of the interior increased.

Charles I of Spain—in order to outbid Francis I of France for the vacant title of Holy Roman Emperor—borrowed money from two German banking houses, the Fuggers and the Welsers. These loans were secured by indefinite leases on territory in the New World. Thus, in 1528 Venezuela was leased to the Welsers with the right to found cities, open mines, and take slaves. Not knowing how long their lease might run, the Germans were principally interested in looting the area of its rumored wealth. Successive German governors, using mostly Spanish soldiers of fortune, led expeditions into the interior in search of El Dorado or other elusive sources of booty. Most of the expeditions were financial failures, marked by extreme hardships for the Europeans and by ruthless treatment of the Indians.

One of the German adventurers, Nicholas Federmann, in 1538 pushed southwestward from Coro into what is now the Colombian Andes, but on arrival in the valley of Bogotá he encountered Gonzalo Jiménez de Quesada, who had marched south from Santa Marta, Colombia, and Sebastián de Benalcázar, who had been sent north by Francisco Pizarro from Peru. All three laid claim to the area but, instead of fighting, they agreed to submit their claims to the new Holy Roman Emperor, the Spanish king who had assumed the title of Charles V. In 1546 the emperor revoked the Welser lease and restored the Venezuela area to direct Spanish control.

Exploration and looting continued under the Spanish, but little ready wealth remained to be gathered. The Indians' gold had been largely in the form of personal ornaments (the accumulation of generations), and the mines, when taken over by the Spaniards, were found to be nearly exhausted. Only the land, the Indians, and increasing numbers of Negro slaves remained to be exploited through the slower processes of ranching and agriculture.

CONQUEST AND COLONIZATION

The main period of exploration and plundering ended in the mid-sixteenth century, and an era of conquest and colonization began. To encourage settlement the new governor, Juan Pérez de Tolosa, distributed the available Indians in groups (*encomiendas*—see Glossary) to the conquistadors to work the mines and to cultivate the fertile lands of the mountain valleys. He sought out the best farmlands and sent expeditions to seek sites for future cities. Among those founded were San Cristóbal, Barquisimeto, and Valencia.

With the establishment of towns and cities, civil government appeared in the form of *cabildos* (town councils). Since the *alcaldes* (mayors) and *regidores* (councillors) were usually appointed by the royal representative from among the Spanish settlers or on the recommendation of *criollos* (native-born persons of Spanish descent), the *cabildo* became a form of oligarchy drawn from a colonial aristocracy. The *cabildos* drew up and published municipal ordinances and handled local matters of law enforcement, so that the successors of the conquistadors early became accustomed to local government.

Higher justice was handled by the *audiencias* (royal tribunals), which also exercised the functions of a council of state for the executive. These could refer important cases to the Supreme Council of the Indies in Spain, who members, like the governors, viceroys, and captains general, were also appointed by the crown. Whatever the title of the chief executive of a region, he was also president of the *audiencia* if one was allotted to his seat of government.

All major executives were required to account for their administrations at the termination of their appointments through a public hearing and audit of their conduct in office (*residencia*), both administrative and fiscal, held usually by a senior member of the *audiencia*. The crown might also, at its own initiative, send a *visitador* (inspector) at any time to inspect the affairs of the colony.

These measures of control were often nullified by the ambition and greed of the inspectors, who might accept bribes for a good report on a bad administration or castigate a good one with a view to succeeding to the position.

Early Government

Until 1550 the colony was under the jurisdiction of the Audiencia of Santo Domingo, but in that year Spain established the Audiencia of Santa Fé (de Bogotá) with jurisdiction over what are now Colombia and Venezuela, then collectively called New Granada. The regime became a viceroyalty in 1718, and this arrangement continued until 1777, when Venezuela was made a separate captaincy general directly under the crown. Isolated from both Bogotá and Spain, Venezuela experienced long periods of virtual independence from royal and viceregal supervision during most of its colonial existence.

The towns multipled as the mines and the best farm and ranch lands were seized from the Indians and put into production. Each city was the center of a productive area, dominated by royal officials. Caracas, founded in 1567 after fierce fighting with the Indians, was soon the center of the most prosperous province in the colony.

Some Indian chiefs belatedly sought to unify the tribes against the Spanish but with little success. Fighting was prolonged and bitter; communications were extremely difficult; and the Indians, in their separate tribal groups, had to be conquered piecemeal.

A Portuguese ship, arriving in 1580, brought smallpox to the area. It decimated the Indians; in one year, tens of thousands died, and whole tribes perished without a survivor. By the time the epidemic was spent, a large proportion of the Indian population had disappeared. Negro slaves had already been imported from Africa, and the loss of so many Indians gave added impetus to the slave trade.

Piracy and Trade

Spain's possessions in the Americas were allowed to trade only with the mother country, but the colony produced so little bullion or other exportable commodities that the annual Spanish treasure fleet, carrying loot from Mexico and Peru, did not touch at any Venezuelan port. Only an occasional ship, at intervals sometimes greater than a year, visited the country. Such neglect encouraged a defiance of Spanish authority, which often took the form of buying from and trading with English, French, Dutch, and Portuguese smugglers, who, since they paid no customs duties, offered better bargains.

The weakness of Spanish authority also made its ill-defended ports easy prey for the privateers and buccaneers infesting the

Caribbean from the mid-sixteenth to the mid-eighteenth centuries. France and England granted letters of marque to privateers and encouraged them to harass Spanish possessions and ships.

Many English sea captains learned their trade as privateersmen in the Caribbean. The names of Sir John Hawkins, Sir Francis Drake, Sir Walter Raleigh, and Henry Morgan were well known on the coast of Venezuela, and one English corsair, Amyas Preston, landed at La Guaira in 1595 and marched on Caracas, which he seized and plundered for ten days. Raleigh once seized and burned Cumaná. Later he sent an expedition up the Orinoco River in a vain search for El Dorado. Morgan's raid on Maracaibo and the lake region in 1669 set a new record of massacre and pillage.

Production of agricultural commodities, salt, and hides increased as settlement of the country progressed so that Spain became interested in some of the more valuable exports. By the beginning of the seventeenth century the growing of food products, which had been varied and sufficient to support the local economy, was largely eliminated in favor of cacao and tobacco, the principal cash crops. This served to make the country even more dependent on Spain, as many items of food had to be imported.

Spain's trade with her colonies was constantly interrupted by European wars and the Caribbean pirates. The kingdom found it difficult to furnish the necessary ships. During the War of the Spanish Succession (1701–13), Spain gave a contract for limited trade to a French company. The French were supplanted at the end of the war by a British firm. In 1728 Spain decided to form its own trading company, to which all trade with Venezuela would be allotted. The Guipuzcoana Company was organized, staffed, and financed principally by Basques.

This economic monopoly, in which the colonists had no voice, quickly became unpopular. The company took every opportunity to increase its profits at the expense of the colonists, and the Basques were soon insinuating themselves into positions of administrative, as well as economic power. So widespread was the local opposition that in 1749 the colonists revolted. The revolt was suppressed in 1752, but the extent of its popular support led to a number of reforms.

In 1777 Venezuela, as a captaincy general, was opened to restricted foreign trade, and the crown established a new form of economic control, the intendancy, as an agency for the main purpose of stimulating agricultural and other production. With the increasing loss of its monopoly and power, the Guipuzcoana Company finally failed and was liquidated in 1784. This, plus active support of trade by the intendancy, inaugurated a new economic era. The colony was finally authorized free trade with the other Spanish possessions. It was the last colony to receive this privilege.

Although landowners rejoiced, some merchants protested the increased competition and decreased profits that free trade would bring them. Both groups were made aware more than ever of how completely they were under the domination of Spain.

THE STRUGGLE FOR INDEPENDENCE

Origins of Rebellion

The example of the British colonies of North America with their Declaration of Independence and successful revolution against King George III of England, followed in 1789 by the French Revolution, had powerful attraction for the *criollos* of the Spanish colonies of the Americas. Spanish-American aristocrats, well educated and often well traveled and widely acquainted abroad, resented the exploitation of their country by Spain. On the other hand, the prospect of political change had little or no meaning for the submerged classes. The *mestizos* (see Glossary), the Indians, and the Negroes were serfs or slaves and remained ignorant and illiterate.

Venezuela became the leader in the struggle of Spain's South American colonies for independence, partly because of its situation as one of the least-regarded provinces of Spanish America and its remoteness from the administrative centers, first of Santo Domingo and later of Bogotá. This operated to increase the authority of the local *cabildos* and gave to the *criollos* who sat in them a taste of independence and experience in government, which increased their intolerance of Spanish rule.

After the abortive revolt of 1749 no significant rebellions occurred until 1797, when young *criollos* tried to rouse planters and army officers to revolt. Their plot was exposed, however, and the participants were executed. The leader, José España, who was hanged and quartered, is honored as the country's first martyr in the cause of independence.

Early Efforts

The independence movement got its real start through the activities of Francisco de Miranda, a *criollo* lieutenant colonel who left the Spanish colonial army to represent a revolutionary group in Venezuela. He sought aid for his country's liberation from the new United States in 1784 and later from most of the capitals of Europe. After the French Revolution in 1789, he was made a lieutenant general in the French revolutionary army. By 1805 he was back in the United States recruiting and raising money for an expedition that set sail in 1806. With help from the British at Trinidad, a landing was made at Coro, but there was no popular uprising; the Spanish, with superior numbers, forced Miranda and his little forces to reembark. He went to England, discouraged, but still seeking aid for Venezuela's liberation.

In 1808, when Napoleon usurped the Spanish monarchy and made his brother Joseph king of Spain, the *cabildo* in Caracas deposed the Spanish governor and formed a governing council as a form of trusteeship for the deposed Ferdinand. This junta sent a mission to England to seek British support. The leader of the mission, a young *criollo* colonel of the militia named Simón Bolívar, persuaded Miranda to return to Venezuela in December 1810.

With Miranda's return, the movement for complete independence intensified. The junta resigned and surrendered its power to the first Venezuelan Congress, which, after prolonged debate, voted independence from Spain on July 5, 1811. Venezuelans are proud of being the first Latin Americans to take such definitive action.

Instead of taking prompt military steps to clear the country of all Spanish forces, the Venezuelans gathered in Caracas to debate the constitution of the new state. Meanwhile, the Spanish forces, supported by many Venezuelan royalists, took the offensive. Miranda was made supreme military commander of Venezuela with dictatorial powers. He was mobilizing his forces against the Spanish threat when, on March 26, 1812, most of the patriot cities in the mountains were wrecked by an earthquake, which, however, did not affect the royalist centers on the coast. This was enough for the doubtful among the *criollos* and especially for the superstitious *mestizos*, Indians, and Negroes. Royalist sympathizers among the clergy promptly proclaimed the quake God's judgment against those who would deny their rightful king. Deserters from the patriot camp swelled the ranks of the Spanish forces. By July 30, 1812, it was all over. Miranda surrendered, to die eventually in a Spanish prison, and the First Republic was ended.

The Liberator

One of the patriot leaders who avoided Spanish retaliation after the fall of the First Republic was Bolívar. Born in Caracas on July 24, 1783, of a wealthy *criollo* family long prominent in Venezuelan affairs, he enjoyed all the advantages of his class. His father had corresponded with Miranda in seeking aid for Venezuelan independence. Orphaned early, Bolívar was greatly influenced by his favorite tutor, Simón Rodríguez, a devotee of Jean Jacques Rousseau and an advocate of liberty for Spanish America.

In Colombia, which had declared its independence shortly after Venezuela, patriot factions were still fighting the Spaniards, so Bolívar went to Colombia. Given a small command, he fought his way back into western Venezuela during 1813. Here, apparently for the purpose of forcing the people to take sides, Bolívar issued his famous proclamation of "war to the death" against the Spaniards but clemency for Spanish Americans. This had the effect of detaching from the royalist cause wavering *criollos*, some *mestizos*, and even many of the clergy. Gaining strength as he advanced, Bolívar, in a brilliant campaign, forced his way back into Caracas on August 7, 1813. The joyous capital conferred on Bolívar the title of El Libertador (The Liberator) and, as dictator, he proclaimed the Second Republic. But the remaining Spanish forces on the coast were reinforced from Spain, which was now free of the Bonapartes. Also, they were joined by a horde of *llaneros* (cowboys) from the plains of the Orinoco, who were glad to fight for loot and who had been promised land and revenge on their masters by a Spanish leader named Tomás Boves. By the fall of 1814 the patriots were in full retreat, and the Second Republic ended.

Forced into exile for the second time, Bolívar returned to Cartagena only to find the Colombian patriots divided and the Spanish, heavily reinforced, moving to the siege of Cartagena. Again Bolívar left South America, this time for Jamaica. There he composed the famous "Letter from Jamaica," in which he reaffirmed his faith in independence for Spanish America and visualized for South America a collection of autonomous states, each under a centralized, unitary form of government and headed by a lifetime president.

Later Bolívar went to Haiti, where President Alexandre Pétion offered ships and men for a new attempt. A landing on the Venezuelan coast in 1815 was repulsed. Bolívar then changed his plans. Collecting reinforcements from Haiti, in 1817 he struck into the heart of the plains country to seize Angostura (now Ciudad Bolívar) on the Orinoco River. There, in 1819, Bolívar called a congress to frame a new constitution. This Congress of Angostura, adopting a constitution embodying few of Bolívar's ideas, nevertheless elected him president of Venezuela's Third Republic.

In the plains of the Orinoco River Bolívar won the support of the *llaneros*, who were now under a *mestizo* patriot leader, José Antonio Páez. Here, with a secure base, his forces were strengthened by the arrival of European adventurers recruited from the soldiers—mostly English, Irish, and German—disbanded after the Napoleonic wars in Europe. After some successful skirmishes against Spanish sallies from the mountains, Bolívar made a dramatic march west over the Andes into Colombia and at Boyacá surprised and destroyed a Spanish army. The Spanish asked for a truce, which was signed in 1820, but it proved short lived, and in June 1821 Bolívar, in Venezuela, won the decisive victory at Carabozo, which effectively ended Spanish control of Caribbean South America.

To carry out his plans of combining the states of Colombia, Venezuela, and Ecuador into one state of Gran Colombia, Bolívar called a congress to assemble at Cúcuta in the spring of 1821. After the victory of Carabozo, the new Republic of Gran Colombia was announced, with its capital at Bogotá. Bolívar was elected president; and Francisco de Paula Santander of Colombia, vice president. Venezuela, as a state within a state, was administered by Carlos Soublette with General Páez, the *llanero* leader, in charge of the armed forces.

In the south, until 1826, Bolívar was engaged in the liberation of Ecuador, Peru, and Bolivia. No sooner had Bolívar gone south, however, than regional rivalries in Gran Colombia broke out. Even after Bolívar returned, victorious but broken in health, his prestige was not enough to hold the states together. Venezuela broke away in 1829, and Ecuador, soon after. Bolívar died at Santa Marta, Colombia, in 1830, penniless and almost alone, but he is honored as the principal architect and outstanding hero of Latin American independence.

AUTHORITARIAN GOVERNMENT

The Setting

The new state was divided by natural barriers into regions, and communications were by foot, roads, and horse trails. The traditional subjection of the *mestizo*, the Indian, and the Negro to local leaders encouraged personal, rather than national, loyalties. Long years of struggle had reduced the population and accustomed the remaining people to the rule of the military. The surviving military leaders either assumed, or were rewarded with, control of provinces in which they were strong.

To the submerged classes independence meant only that most Venezuelans had exchanged the Spanish yoke for that of local *caudillos*. From a population of approximately 700,000 in 1800, the country had suffered losses of about 300,000 during the thirteen years of revolutionary struggle. The land was devastated, the country was deeply in debt, and bandits roamed the countryside.

Administration of the country was characterized by a succession of military dictators, each of whom governed as much territory as possible for the benefit of himself and his supporters. Generally, each of these president-dictators remained in power only until some rival *caudillo* gathered sufficient strength to overthrow the incumbent. Centralization or decentralization of government was not a response to political theories but depended on how much territory a given president could control by force of arms. Each victor endeavored to give his accession an aura of legality by controlled indirect elections for the president and congress and constitutional changes to suit his needs. Written constitutions provided for executive, legislative, and judicial branches, but the distribution of power was invariably weighted in favor of the executive (see ch. 11, The Governmental System).

The Caudillos

The first of the military dictators was General José Antonio Páez, whom Bolívar had left in charge of the armed forces and who was soon in full control of the country. He led the separation movement from Gran Colombia in 1829 and in 1830 convoked a constitutional convention to draw up a separate constitution for Venezuela. In 1831 Páez was elected the new Republic's first president.

For the next eighteen years Páez was either president or, because of his control of the army, the power behind Carlos Soublette, with whom he alternated. The Constitution of 1830 provided for a modest property qualification for the voter and a substantial one for the holders of political office. The Roman Catholic Church was shorn of many of its special powers and privileges, including tithing rights, tax immunities, and the monopoly of education. Similarly, the army lost its autonomy and was made subservient to the central government, a situation that brought on unsuccessful revolts in 1831 and 1835. The country made remarkable progress in reconstruction and in building its credit abroad. Schools were built, some slaves were freed, and efforts were made to draft a law granting complete emancipation (see ch. 11, The Governmental System).

Since trusted and proven officials tended to form a small governing clique, political opposition began to develop, mainly among disappointed officeseekers and the losers of the 1831 and 1835 elections. In 1840 the Liberal Party was formed. In 1847 the incumbent president, the former rebel, General José Tadeo Monagas (who had been pardoned by Páez), ousted his conservative ministers and replaced them with Liberals. Though Páez tried to intervene, the president had built up enough military and political support to defeat the old *llanero* and have him exiled.

During the 1848–90 period, known as the era of the Liberals, the succession of military dictators and their ministers conducted governments notable for corruption and treasury-raiding. Páez had upheld the laws and the constitution, at times against his own best interest. The dictators who followed him showed little regard for the laws and the constitution.

From 1847 to 1858 the Monagas brothers, José Tadeo and José Gregorio, alternated in the office of the presidency. Their regime was noteworthy for the emancipation of slaves. First suggested by Bolívar in 1819, this was finally accomplished in 1854.

After the Monagas regime was overthrown in 1858 by a revolt supported by both parties, there was a struggle among local *caudillos* in what came to be known as the Federalist War. The Federalists, who drew their strength from the Liberals, were opposed by the conservative Centralists. The war ended in 1863 with the Treaty of Coche, in effect, a Federalist victory.

The new dictator in 1863, General Juan Falcón, proclaimed a new constitution with many reforms, including universal suffrage, greater autonomy for local governments, freedom of the press, and the outlawing of capital punishment. Since political opposition was suppressed, however, universal suffrage meant only the right to vote for government candidates. Greater local autonomy made each local *caudillo* supreme in his area.

The Falcón government was overthrown by a coalition of Liberals and Conservatives in the Blue Revolution, so called from the color of its flag. The Liberal, General Antonio Guzmán Blanco, who emerged as military dictator in 1870, controlled Venezuela for the next eighteen years. Guzmán Blanco's principal interests were in amassing a fortune and living in Europe, but he demanded honesty and efficiency in his government personnel. He pacified the country, restored its credit, and proclaimed many reforms. He was hostile to the church and virtually destroyed its remaining power in Venezuela, exiling the archbishop, confiscating church properties, and abolishing ecclesiastical privileges. He suppressed all opposition. In the end his own picked candidate turned against him and, in 1888, Guzmán Blanco went into exile.

After two civilian presidents during the next four years, the pattern of military dictatorship was resumed with General Joaquín Crespo. The first Venezuelan Incident occurred during his regime. The border between British Guiana and Venezuela had long been in dispute, but in 1895 Venezuelan authorities jailed some British Guiana police, charging them with violation of the border, and broke off diplomatic relations. United States President Grover Cleveland invoked the Monroe Doctrine, and the contending parties agreed to arbitration. In the process, Venezuela lost most of the territory in dispute, which involved about two-thirds of Guyana, formerly British Guiana (see ch. 13, Foreign Relations).

Crespo's term ended in 1898 and, in the fighting over the election of his successor, he was killed. Cipriano Castro, an Andean from the southwestern state of Táchira, on the Colombian border, saw in the death of Crespo and in the accompanying chaos his opportunity to seize power. He had previously opposed Crespo and, to escape reprisal, had taken refuge in Colombia. Now, rallying a group of fellow exiles, mostly kinsmen and retainers of a shrewd *mestizo*, Juan Vicente Gómez, Castro, with sixty men, crossed into Venezuela on May 23, 1899. Gathering strength as he advanced, he marched along the Andes toward Caracas, often catching the government forces divided and beating or outwitting them. At Tocuyito near Valencia, Castro lured the pursuing forces into a trap and won a decisive victory. The remaining opposition disappeared or joined Castro. On October 26, 1899, Castro and his followers marched into Caracas.

Castro assumed the presidency, but for two years regional *caudillos* contested his rule. Finally Castro's supporter, Gómez, vanquished all opposition. Again the country was governed by a dictatorship. Castro involved the country in squabbles with foreign powers, mostly through his mistreatment of foreign businessmen and diplomats. He sought a new source of revenue by assessing fines against foreign firms and denied the claims of foreign governments and nationals for destruction of their property in the repeated disorders.

Joaquín Crespo had bankrupted the country, and Cipriano Castro undertook to raise funds for the normal operation of the government. He forced bankers to provide him with money but, when England, France, Italy, and especially Germany pressed him for repayment of loans, Castro arrested their ministers. The second Venezuelan Incident occurred when England, Germany, and Italy, the principal creditor nations, sent warships to blockade the Venezuelan ports in 1902. Venezuelan naval vessels were seized, and German cruisers bombarded Puerto Cabello and Maracaibo. Castro was defiant, but the hostilities ended when United States President Theodore Roosevelt prepared to send United States battleships to the scene and persuaded European powers to accept the arbitration of the International Court of Justice at The Hague. Despite the adverse decision of the court, which found for the intervening nations, Castro defaulted on loans (see ch. 13, Foreign Relations).

Castro's health failed, and in November 1908 he went to Europe. He left Gómez, then vice president, in charge of the country; Gómez within a month usurped the presidency, and Castro became an exile for life.

Gómez, a *mestizo* from Táchira, ruled from 1908 until his death in 1935. He punished or eliminated those he could not trust and placed relatives and supporters from his area into most of the key posts. His first concern was the army and, after he had shifted the top commanders, he reorganized, modernized, and expanded the armed forces. He established a military academy at Caracas and employed a military mission from Chile, trained in the Prussian military system (see ch. 23, The Armed Forces).

To facilitate military operations, Gómez began a system of military roads reaching into hitherto inaccessible parts of the country. He also developed an efficient intelligence service that covered all branches of government, including the army and the foreign service. Incipient opposition to his regime was immediately stopped by the arrest and imprisonment of all who exhibited insurrectionist tendencies.

Gómez did much to restore economic prosperity in the country and to present an attractive field for foreign investments. He bolstered credit by paying off the interest on the nation's foreign and domestic debt and even part of the principal. He also honored claims against the government. It was Gómez and the progressive elements of his government who, in the early years of the twentieth century, welcomed the oil prospectors who were to make Venezuela a rich country and Gómez one of its richest men.

Oil seepage had been noticed along the shores of Lake Maracaibo from the times of the early explorers. An asphalt lake in northeastern Venezuela near Guanocó first attracted North American and British investors. In 1913 a successful test well was drilled in that vicinity.

In 1914 a British company (later absorbed by Royal Dutch Shell) began pumping from the first commercial well of the great Maracaibo pool. Maracaibo, a village in a swamp and one of the world's most unhealthful spots, became the second largest city in Venezuela. Though the first oil companies at Maracaibo were British and Dutch, by 1918 North Americans were drilling, and soon all the large companies of the United States were represented. In the same year Gómez's government drafted an oil law that, while protecting national interests, also allowed the oil companies to expand their investment. Gómez took a share of every concession, but he paid off the country's foreign debts (see ch. 16, Character and Structure of the Economy).

Petroleum changed the economy from one that was primarily agricultural and pastoral, producing most of its own food and other basic needs, to an economy which, after 1920, was dominated by the extraction of oil. Prices rose, and agricultural production by small farmers fell off as high wages drew people to the oilfields and the cities. The large *haciendas* (plantations) principally produced export crops, such as cacao or coffee. Venezuela began to import food, including sugar, which it formerly grew itself. Little of the new wealth was expended on internal improvement—education, health, diversified agriculture, or local industries.

The repression of all contrary opinion, involving imprisonment and other penalties, created a determined but ineffectual opposition. There were a number of attempts at uprising or invasion by exiles, all unsuccessful. The dictator, with his intelligence system and his modern army, was more than a match for all such actions, and he never hesitated to use his troops in suppressing them.

The uprising of greatest importance was the student revolution of 1928, which started when a young student, Jóvito Villalba, and two others at the University of Caracas began making antigovernment speeches. When they were jailed by the police, other students challenged the dictator to jail them, too, and over 200 more were promptly arrested. This aroused the people, who demonstrated in the streets. The police dispersed them with firearms, killing and wounding many. By this time a few young Army officers had joined the students and attempted to revolt. The mob stormed the Miraflores Palace and took it but were soon repulsed; this effectively ended the revolt. A student strike was called, but Gómez closed the university, rounded up the students and sent them under guard to work on the roads. Some students died in prison, many were held for years, and others were exiled or voluntarily left the country. Those of the "generation of 1928" who survived became, after the death of Gómez, the leaders of the country. One of them was Rómulo Betancourt (see ch. 7, Education).

Another attempt to overthrow Gómez occurred in 1929 when a number of exiles landed and tried to capture Cumaná. Gómez's army, after heavy fighting, repulsed the invaders, who lost their military leader, General Ramón Delgado Chalbaud, in the battle. Two years later another attempt by General Rafael Simón Urbina was suppressed. The dictator's death on December 17, 1935, brought an end to the regime.

After the death of Gómez, violence erupted, notably in Caracas and Maracaibo. Mobs attacked Gómez supporters, massacred them or forced them to flee, and looted their property. In Maracaibo the oil companies' installations were attacked, and the families of the foreign personnel had to be evacuated on tankers.

The people had no organization or leaders, and the army was still under the control of Gómez appointees. Congress acted quickly to choose as provisional president General Eleazar López Contreras, who had been minister of war under Gómez. He also was a native of Táchira and had joined Castro and Gómez in the 1899 revolt. He promptly sent troops to quell the disorders.

López Contreras subsequently released the political prisoners and invited the exiles to return. He removed members of the old regime and sent them out of the country. In February 1936, when the students called for a general strike and led a mob to the palace to protest against the establishment of a board of censorship, he submitted to their demands. He abolished censorship and removed most of the remaining Gómez men from office. He also promulgated a liberal labor law. In April 1936 the National Congress elected him as the new president. By July 1936 López Contreras began to tighten controls. Again a general strike was called by the opposition, but this time the government arrested the ringleaders (see ch. 19, Labor).

The liberated politicians and returning exiles, especially the Generation of 1928, were busily forming political parties, campaigning for followers, and setting up labor unions; all were in opposition to the government. Communists, outlawed under the Gómez regime, organized openly for the first time in 1937. Conservatives formed a party, and Rómulo Betancourt set up a leftist liberal group, the predecessor to the AD, which openly organized in 1941 (see ch. 12, Political Dynamics).

During the López Contreras regime the franchise was restricted, and there was no direct election of the president or members of the National Congress. The electoral system, under which the president was chosen by the congress and the members of congress by the state legislatures, still prevailed. The labor law was withdrawn. Demonstrators were arrested and fined and, in March 1937, twenty-seven young politicians were branded as Communists and exiled. All opposition political parties were suppressed.

In December 1936, resenting the cancellation of the labor law, the oil workers staged a strike that paralyzed the industry. Within a few weeks the president ordered an end to the strike and sent the strikers back to work with a small pay increase. Labor agitators were arrested and expelled (see ch. 19, Labor).

With the political opposition stifled, López Contreras initiated a plan to build up and diversify agriculture and improve communications, education, and health. New oilfields were opened in eastern Venezuela, and the Maracaibo output increased. It was at this time that the phrase "sow the petroleum" (*sembrar el petróleo*) was used to indicate that oil revenues should be used to develop and modernize the country.

The López Contreras government passed a new oil law more favorable to Venezuela, but the representatives of the oil companies insisted on continuation of the old Gómez agreements. López Contreras picked his minister of war, Colonel Isaías Medina Angarita, as his successor, and, with the established election system, had no difficulty in having Medina chosen as president in 1941. López Contreras went back to his old post as minister of defense to await the end of Medina's term. In the pattern established in 1899, the new president was still another man from Táchira. He announced his intention to carry on the policies of his predecessor and amplified the national development program in a new four-year plan.

Aside from its effect on the oil industry World War II had little impact on the country until the entry of the United States into the war. Venezuela broke diplomatic relations with the Axis Powers on December 31, 1941. German submarines attacked oil tankers in the Caribbean, sinking seven in the first attack. As the campaign continued, a shortage of tankers developed, so serious as virtually to put a halt to the shipment of Venezuelan oil. Revenues fell off by one-third in 1942, and President Medina decided that the time was appropriate to make new agreements with the oil companies more favorable to Venezuela than the original Gómez agreements.

In this, he received assistance from the United States, which was concerned lest Venezuela might otherwise cut off the flow of oil, so essential to the war effort. Agreement was reached with the oil companies, and the law was passed in Venezuela on March 13, 1943, which made a sweeping revision of the old concessions. It provided for the increase of income from royalties and taxes to Venezuela to equal the profits taken out by the companies. All concessions were to be renewed for forty more years—that is, until 1983 (see ch. 18, Industry).

By 1944 the submarine menace had been overcome and, with increased shipping and the increased wartime demand for oil, Venezuela's revenues, at the new rate, rapidly built up United States dollar reserves. In February 1945 Venezuela declared war on the Axis powers and qualified for membership in the United Nations.

President Medina ignored the Táchira clique and chose new appointees for key posts. He released political prisoners, allowed exiles to return, and proclaimed free speech, freedom of association, and freedom of the press. Seeking popularity for his party in the election of a successor in 1945, the government passed more liberal legislation, including provisions for women's suffrage in municipal elections and the direct election of the Chamber of Deputies. This, however, did not affect his safe majority in the chamber then sitting, which had been elected by indirect means in 1944.

The Chamber of Deputies nevertheless contained a highly vocal minority of AD members and sympathizers, the more effective because of Medina's resolve not to reverse himself on his recently adopted course. He was more concerned about the oldtime conservative group supporting López Contreras, composed of the owners of great estates, the senior army officers, professional people, and to a great extent representatives of the church. Moreover, Betancourt and the AD had agreed with Medina on joint support for a liberal candidate, Diógenes Escalante (see ch. 12, Political Dynamics).

The situation changed rapidly in the early fall of 1945. Escalante fell ill just two months before the election; the Medina-controlled convention then nominated Angel Biaggini as substitute. Betancourt and the AD withdrew their support. Medina continued to concentrate on averting a takeover by the conservatives. While threats were being exchanged between Medina's supporters and the conservatives, on October 18, 1945, the government was seized suddenly by an unexpected coalition of junior army officers and the AD.

The young officers had formed a secret organization, the Patriotic Military Union (Unión Patriótica Militar—UPM) and, when the AD separated from Medina, the UPM had covertly offered it army support. After considerable hesitation, the offer was accepted.

Seizing the military academy and the presidential palace and barracks in the early morning and fighting it out with the police and loyal troops, the rebels were in control by nightfall. Medina was forced to resign, and he and López Contreras were ordered into exile. Betancourt became the provisional president, organized a governing junta of seven men (two of whom were army officers), and took over the government.

THE LIBERAL EXPERIMENT

The new head of state hastened to convert what in its outward aspects had been a standard coup into a revolution. Betancourt with his seven-man junta promised a new constitution with free elections as soon as possible and debarred any member of the junta from being a candidate for president. For over two years the AD junta ruled by decree. In March 1946 a new electoral law was promulgated. Suffrage was universal for all citizens over age eighteen (including women) except criminals and members of the military on active duty. All political parties were authorized, and there was proportional representation in the National Congress.

With restrictions on political rights lifted, several political parties emerged to contest the elections. The dominant one was the AD, which, with the young officers, had staged the overthrow. It attracted the more extreme liberals who did not favor communism. More conservative, but with a moderate social-welfare program, was the COPEI, essentially a Christian-socialist (Catholic) party, which drew church support as well as appealing to many moderates in the professions (see ch. 12, Political Dynamics).

In October 1946, in elections held for a constituent assembly, the AD gained a large majority. The constitution produced by the assembly, which went into effect on July 5, 1947, reflected AD principles (see ch. 11, The Governmental System; ch. 12, Political Dynamics).

The elections under the new constitution were held on December 14, 1947, under careful supervision. Again the AD polled the most votes. Its candidate, Rómulo Gallegos, a leading novelist, teacher, and former congressman from Caracas, was elected president, and the AD won comfortable majorities in the Senate and in the Chamber of Deputies. The new government was inaugurated on February 15, 1948.

Rómulo Betancourt and the junta had already decreed a new petroleum law, which brought the equal division of profits up to date and imposed an extraordinary tax of Bs67 million (4.5 bolívars equal US$1) on the industry. No new concessions were granted, and the junta and later the new Gallegos government set out to put Venezuela in the oil business in competition with the foreign companies (see ch. 18, Industry).

Production increased so rapidly that in 1948 petroleum revenues alone were over Bs1.2 million. This was more than twice as much as the total income of the government in the last year of Medina's presidency.

The AD adopted López Contreras' slogan of "sowing the petroleum" and set up a program for reinvesting oil revenues to develop the national economy and improve working and living conditions of the people. Acts to provide extensive reforms in education and agriculture were swiftly legislated, and many projects to promote economic development were planned (see ch. 7, Education; ch. 16, Character and Structure of the Economy; ch. 17, Agriculture).

The reform measures alienated those elements of society that throughout history had been accustomed to controlling the country. The raising of wages and the favoring of labor worried employers in both urban and rural areas, whereas the Agrarian Reform Law appeared to threaten the landed aristocracy (see ch. 19, Labor; ch. 17, Agriculture).

The AD owed its rise to power to the army and, in spite of AD popularity with the masses, the army, still the source of power, was becoming increasingly suspicious. Opposition elements at all levels of society fed the suspicion.

In mid-November 1948 the UPM sent President Gallegos an ultimatum demanding several cabinet posts for the military, a coalition government with COPEI participation, and the exile of Betancourt. Gallegos refused, and on November 24, 1948, the army seized power. Gallegos, Betancourt, and other AD leaders were sent into exile, and a three-man military junta was set up.

RESURGENCE AND REJECTION OF AUTHORITARIAN RULE

The senior officer of the junta was Lieutenant Colonel Carlos Delgado Chalbaud, an organizer of UPM, the secret military society that had conducted the 1945 revolution. He had been selected to serve on the AD junta and was later defense minister under Betancourt and Gallegos. During this period, a group of young officers from Táchira led by Major Marcos Pérez Jiménez, chief of staff, were growing increasingly hostile to the AD government. When in November they decided to oust the AD, Chalbaud joined them to lead the coup.

Pérez Jiménez, though second on the junta, was the foremost in his hostility to the AD and its program. In 1943 he had joined the UPM and soon became one of the leaders. He had been arrested before the 1945 revolution, but its success set him free. As leader of the Táchira faction he had great influence in the army, and when the AD was ousted in 1948, he became minister of defense. The third man on the junta, Lieutenant Colonel Llovera Páez, also a prominent member of the Táchira group, was a close friend and associate of Pérez Jiménez.

The junta ruled Venezuela for two years. After ousting the leaders of the AD opposition, outlawing the party, revoking the 1947 Constitution in favor of that of 1936, and nullifying most of the AD reforms, the members of the junta fell out over the form to be taken by the new government. Chalbaud promised early elections and a return to constitutional government. He seemed reluctant to persecute the AD opposition. Pérez Jiménez and Llovera Páez were opposed to such moderation and preferred military government.

Chalbaud was assassinated on November 19, 1950, and Pérez Jiménez became dictator. He appointed a civilian, Germán Suárez Flamerich, as provisional president and made preparation to have himself elected. In April 1951 an electoral law was issued by the junta that provided for direct election of the president and permitted all parties except the AD to compete. The junta then formed a new party, the Independent Electoral Front (Frente Electoral Independiente—FEI). Opposing were the COPEI and the Republican Democratic Union (Union Republicana Democrática—URD). The COPEI campaigned for a moderate reform government, but the URD outdid the AD in calling for socialistic reforms.

When early returns in the election of November 30, 1952, indicated a victory for URD, Pérez Jiménez clamped a tight censorship on election news and, on December 2, proclaimed an FEI victory. The junta was dissolved, Llovera Páez and Flamerich were sent abroad, and Pérez Jiménez took over as the provisional president.

In January 1953 Pérez Jiménez appointed the Constituent Assembly under FEI control. The COPEI and URD delegates refused to take part. In March, however, the constitution was promulgated, giving the president extensive powers. A congress made up of FEI delegates was chosen in April, and on April 16 it elected Pérez Jiménez constitutional president for five years.

Under the Pérez Jiménez regime leaders of all opposition parties were jailed, exiled, or forced into hiding. Workers' unions were dissolved and leaders prosecuted. Teachers were repressed. Student demonstrations resulted in the closing of the Central University in Caracas. The press was censored and forced to print government handouts. The armed forces was given many special rewards and privileges.

By 1957 opposition to Pérez Jiménez was growing rapidly. In May the church openly denounced him. Instead of holding elections as scheduled, Pérez Jiménez suppressed all campaign activity and announced a plebiscite in which the voters could vote "yes" or "no" for him to continue as president. This plebiscite was held on December 15, 1957, and, within two hours after the polls closed, the government announced that 85 percent of the votes were affirmative.

The leaders of all political parties, the AD, URD, COPEI, and the

Communist party, met in secret and formed the Patriotic Junta, dedicated to the overthrow of the dictatorship. Again the military was the deciding factor. In spite of Pérez Jiménez's favors, many of the military officers were dissatisfied. Few relished having their careers put at the mercy of a clique of officers from Táchira who held all the important posts for themselves. The air force and navy resented army domination; many officers had received training in the United States during World War II and had absorbed democratic ideas and a dislike for dictatorships. Revolutionary groups formed in the three services.

The air force was first to strike. On New Year's Day 1958 planes from the Maracay Air Base flew over Caracas and dropped several bombs. Pérez Jiménez was able to send army forces that he believed were loyal to him against the Maracay force to suppress the rebellion. Though these troops on arrival in Maracay joined the revolution, Pérez Jiménez—by promising compliance with all Maracay demands—was able to persuade the revolutionists to surrender and permit themselves to be disarmed. Thereupon, Pérez Jiménez imprisoned the dissidents. Though temporarily suppressing the revolt, this served to turn more of the military and the civilian population against him.

Meanwhile, the Pérez Jiménez-Táchira clique persuaded the president to take measures to pacify the opposition. The chief of the secret police and several other officials were dismissed. To win over the navy, a popular officer, Admiral Wolfgang Larrazábal, was put at its head, although he was not a Pérez Jiménez sympathizer.

When, on January 21, 1958, the Patriotic Junta called a general strike, street fighting broke out in Caracas and other cities. On January 22 the navy revolted, whereupon a group of army officers forced Pérez Jiménez to resign. He escaped the next day and took refuge in the Dominican Republic. After some maneuvering, a provisional junta of civilian and military leaders, headed by Larrazábal, was organized; it appointed a predominantly civilian cabinet. In December 1958 it was succeeded by an elected AD government with Betancourt as president.

During his five-year term President Betancourt faced the problems of a rapidly growing population, the question of the distribution of wealth and land, illiteracy, and a bankrupt national treasury. The country was importing food staples. Slumdwellers, for the most part unemployed, were easily moved by leftist agitators, as were militants in the Central University, where many students and faculty followed Communist teachings.

President Betancourt's public health program was carried out. Elementary school enrollment increased, and the illiteracy rate dropped. Land reform advanced. Industrialization was stimulated to such an extent that the proportion of the country's domestically manufactured consumer goods increased from about one-third to two-thirds. The country gained political stability that continued into the 1970s (see ch. 6, Living Conditions; ch. 7, Education).

Other difficulties that President Betancourt faced were a recession in the 1960—61 period; criticism of his action in increasing the government's share of petroleum receipts; his denial of new concessions; and his proposal that a national petroleum corporation be formed with a view to taking over all existing concessions when they expired (see ch. 18, Industry).

President Betancourt's political enemies included Communists and supporters of Cipriano Castro, who participated in revolts at two naval bases in 1962 and who, joining with some extreme rightists, organized terrorist groups. In 1963 the government reported discovery of a cache of arms and ammunition on a Caribbean beach evidently delivered by Castro agents for the use of Venezuelan terrorists. Nevertheless, the election of Raúl Leoni as Betancourt's successor in December 1963 was conducted with almost no violence and made possible a peaceful succession (see ch. 12, Political Dynamics; ch. 13, Foreign Relations).

When Raúl Leoni took office in March 1964 he faced the challenge of carrying out the programs initiated by his predecessor while dealing with those who opposed Betancourt—Communists, Castroites, terrorists, and rightists. Nevertheless, an upturn in the economy, which had begun in 1962, continued, and a large public works program was launched. The currency remained stable, and there were moderate increases in the gross national product (GNP).

In the late 1960s the agrarian reform program launched by Betancourt was progressing. Industrial activity and power production had increased greatly, compared with levels in the 1940s and 1950s; the government was investing oil profits in a variety of state enterprises; and large sums were being assigned to the educational system. The country was solvent (see ch. 12, Political Dynamics).

In December 1968, in free and peaceful elections, the people chose Rafael Caldera to succeed President Leoni.

CHAPTER 4

POPULATION AND ETHNIC GROUPS

In 1970 the population was close to 11 million, and the rate of population growth was among the highest in the world. The growth had occurred primarily as a consequence of a rising birth rate and a death rate progressively lowered by improvement in sanitation and health conditions. Heavy immigration from Europe was also an important factor during the years immediately after World War II, but this flow had declined during the 1960s at a time when emigration by natives of the country was on the increase. A substantial addition to the population, however, was being furnished by the undocumented immigration of people from Colombia crossing the border in search of better paying jobs. Internally, a continuing movement of people from country to town during the years since World War I had transformed the country from a rural to an urbanized one and showed no signs of slackening.

With the unbroken rise in the rate of growth, the age of the population had lowered progressively during most of the twentieth century, and in 1970 nearly half was under the age of fifteen. Males continued to outnumber females by a margin that had remained statistically negligible for more than a generation.

The great majority of the population is an amalgam of white, Negro, and Indian ancestry but shares a common culture based on Hispanic traditions, enriched by African and Indian contributions. The bulk of the people belong to the Roman Catholic Church, speak Spanish, and consider themselves primarily *venezolanos* (Venezuelans), members of essentially the same ethnic group.

Since no national census has classified Venezuelans according to ethnic group since 1926, only rough estimates of the national ethnic composition can be made. In 1970 between 10 and 25 percent were white; between 3 and 10 percent, Negro; between 4 and 17 percent, *mulatto*; between 2 and 5 percent, Indian (of whom relatively few were tribal Indians); and between 60 and 90 percent, *mestizo* (persons of mixed ancestry—see Glossary). Ethnic mixing has occurred at all social levels, and ethnicity does not serve to distinguish either separate groups or classes.

The *mestizo* population is dispersed throughout the country, but other groups tend to display some regional concentration. Most of the white population is found in major urban centers, such as Caracas, Maracaibo, and Valencia; Negroes tend to inhabit the coastal lowlands; and Indians are largely restricted to the remote forests of the Guiana Highlands, the Sierra de Perijá, the Maracaibo basin, and the Delta Amacuro. East of Caracas are areas where the lifestyle of the Negro population is little changed from that of their African forebears.

The early Spanish explorers and colonists encountered highly developed Indian societies, in many cases living in towns and practicing intensive agriculture. The more advanced groups were ruled by chiefs and supported priesthoods to serve the local temples. Under Spanish influence, however, the Indian population rapidly declined through enslavement of the native population, famine, disease, and internal wars. The decline in numbers continued in the period after independence: in 1800 tribal Indians were 13 percent of the total population; in 1926, 7 percent; in 1950, less than 2 percent; and in 1970. under 1 percent.

Large numbers of Negroes were imported into the country in the sixteenth, seventeenth, and eighteenth centuries to satisfy the growing demand for labor on the sugar, coffee, and other plantations. Many were former slaves from other Spanish colonies and had already adopted much of the Spanish culture; others were imported directly from the west coast of Africa, but the tribal mixing in transit was so extensive that few were able to retain much of their African heritage. Most Negroes were gradually assimilated into the *mestizo* groups. In 1970 Negroes constituted approximately the same proportion of the population as they did in 1800. Although large numbers of Negroes immigrated from the West Indies in the 1920s to find jobs in the mushrooming oil industry, in the years from 1929 to 1966 no Negroes were permitted to immigrate. By the late 1960s West Indians represented only 1 percent of the total population.

The proportion of whites has been more or less stable or has increased slightly for, although their numbers have been subject to diminution by *mestizaje* (ethnic mixing—see Glossary), there has been a degree of replenishment through the postwar wave of European immigration. About two-thirds of the immigrant stream was of Spanish, Italian, or Portuguese origin and therefore shared many traits common to Latin cultures. Although some immigrants were leaving the country in the late 1960s and in 1970, the foreign born continued to constitute about 8 percent of the total population.

The most significant ethnic minorities in 1970 were tribal Indians, who continued to follow their traditional way of life, and unassimilated immigrants, who formed isolated ethnic communities in the major cities or in agricultural colonies in the countryside. Both groups were slowly becoming incorporated into the mainstream of national life and were adopting Hispanic cultural patterns.

Spanish is spoken by almost all Venezuelans; only among the tribal Indians and immigrant groups are other languages in common use. The indigenous Indians display great linguistic variation; but, as contacts between the *venezolano* culture and the Indians increase, many adopt Spanish as a second language, and it gradually replaces the native tongue.

POPULATION

Structure and Dynamics

The country's population grew from less than 3.9 million in 1941 to 5 million in 1950 and to 7.5 million as counted in the census of 1961. In 1970 it was estimated at about 10.7 million. The rate of growth registered a steady gain from an average of 2.7 percent annually during the years 1936 through 1941 to 3.5 percent for 1963 through 1967. Estimates for the 1970 growth rate ranged from 3.4 to 3.7 percent; a precise count awaited the next demographic census in 1971.

In 1966 an estimated 46 percent of the people were under the age of fifteen, and 70 percent were under the age of thirty. Slightly over 10 percent were fifty or older, and 3 percent were sixty-five years of age or older. The median age for the population as a whole in 1966 was seventeen years. In 1950 it had been between eighteen and nineteen, and in 1941 it had been about nineteen years.

The crude birth rate moved up unevenly, in response to improving living conditions, from 36 live births annually per 1,000 in 1940 to 46 to 48 in the years 1963 through 1965 before dipping to 42.3 in 1966 and 41.3 in 1967. In 1970, however, the government estimated the current rate at slightly more than 43 per 1,000. Recorded deaths declined steadily from 18.9 per 1,000 annually during the years 1926 through 1930 to 7 for the 1963 through 1967 period and 6.6 in 1968. According to a United Nations estimate, however, the actual annual rate during the years 1960 through 1965 was between 9 and 10 per 1,000.

Recorded infant mortalities per 1,000 live births declined from 53 in 1961 to 47 in 1967. Sustained high birth rates coupled with a sharp decline in mortalities lifted life expectancy at birth from sixty-one years in 1960 to sixty-six in 1970, an expectancy among the highest in Latin America.

During the years since World War II, males have continued to outnumber females by small margins. The male margin increased from 35,000 in 1941 to 70,000 in 1950 and to 123,000 in 1961 before declining to an estimated 50,000 in 1967. This pattern reflects a heavy and predominantly male immigration rate during the years between 1945 and the late 1950s and its subsequent decline. In 1961 about 8.9 percent of the male and 5.9 percent of the female population was made up of aliens. Females outnumbered males in the urban sector as a whole by 1.9 percent in 1950 and by 1.8 percent in 1961; males were in the majority in the rural sector by about the same margins.

According to a 1969 estimate, about 6.4 million people were ten years of age or older. Of these, slightly less than 3.5 million were economically inactive. Included in this number were 1,701,000 homemakers, 1,537,000 students, 143,000 incapacitated persons, and 103,000 in other categories.

Migration

Immigration and Emigration

Under the influence of a government policy actively encouraging the immigration of skilled workers under provisions of the 1936 Law on Immigration and Settlement, there was a wave of immigrants during the first years after World War II. Initially, a number of displaced families were settled, but later arrivals were principally unattached young Western Europeans, about two-thirds of them male. During the 1950s arrivals of aliens exceeded departures by about 340,000. After reaching a high for the decade of more than 57,000 in 1955, the gain slackened with the progress of economic recovery in Europe. The government in 1959 suspended the previous administration's policy of encouraging immigration, but the flow had already slowed to a relative trickle of fewer than 16,000 in 1958, and during the early 1960s foreign arrivals and departures were approximately equal in number. Between 1945 and 1962, however, more than 680,000 immigrants had established residence in Venezuela.

Many of these new arrivals had settled in large urban centers, where they contributed extensively to the country's industrial growth. It has been estimated that not fewer than one-third of the enterprises brought into being during the 1950s were established by or on the initiative of immigrants. There was also considerable immigrant participation in small artisan undertakings, such as shoemaking and furniture and mechanical repair shops. In addition, immigrant farm operators made an important contribution to the fund of technical and managerial skills in the countryside, particularly in commercial agriculture.

A new law on immigration and settlement was enacted in 1966. Superseding the previous legislation on the subject, it was directed primarily at skilled agriculturists. Provision was made for the establishment of an office under the Ministry of Agriculture to help unemployed immigrants find work and for various incentives, including relief from some costs connected with arrival in the country and transportation to the place of intended residence. In addition, agricultural settlement in the country was declared to be a matter of public utility, and expropriation of land for settlers was specifically provided for if none could be found available for purchase.

Enactment of the 1966 legislation did not at once lead to an increase in immigration. During 1966 the departures from the country by persons classified as immigrants or resident aliens exceeded their arrivals by 5,866. In 1967 the negative balance rose to 9,975, and in 1968 it remained negative, with departures exceeding arrivals by 4,654. Resident aliens are those who have qualified for resident status after at least one year's domicile in the country.

According to the records of the Aliens Division of the Ministry of Interior Relations, there were some 831,000 foreigners registered at the end of 1968, about 8.7 percent of the total population. Many of these, however, were residents of long standing—since the beginning of the nineteenth century fewer than 97,000 foreigners had become Venezuelan citizens.

Emigration by Venezuelans has been moderate but increased during the 1960s. During the 1950—54 period the number of citizens returning to the country approximately equaled the number departing from it. Subsequently, departures exceeded arrivals, and during the years 1965 through 1968 the excess of departures totaled more than 33,000.

In addition to the officially recognized immigrants entering the country, many Colombians have entered informally. The actual number is a matter for conjecture, but the figure of 250,000 is frequently mentioned, and estimates run as high as 500,000. The migrants, most of them farm or urban laborers, have come principally in response to the lure of salaries several times as high as those prevailing in Colombia. Some are seasonal workers. About 10,000 are reported to enter annually to work as harvest-season hands. Others enter to take jobs on farms or in factories for a limited time, with the intention of returning to their homes after saving a little money. Most, however, are believed to be in the country with the intent of remaining indefinitely or permanently. Many remain as farm laborers or as squatters on subsistence farms in the northwestern states of Táchira and Zulia, where most of the crossings have taken place, but others go on to the cities. The largest urban concentration of undocumented Colombians is probably in Maracaibo, where they have found work in construction, in the petroleum industry, and in factories.

The migration is almost impossible to control. The border is long, and the two peoples are virtually identical in ethnic composition and in culture. Property lines of some estates extend across the frontier, and persons living on one side of the border may work on the other. At several main crossing points in the north, paved roads extend from Colombian towns to towns and cities in Venezuela or to the Pan American Highway, and many of the routes used regularly both by migrants and by smugglers are referred to locally as the "green roads"—footpaths through dense forest.

Both countries have been concerned over the movement, which received extensive press coverage during 1969 and 1970 and has been the subject of discussion at high levels between the two governments. Some show of resentment has been evident on both sides of the frontier. There have been complaints that border crossers have established themselves illegally on farmlands and have resisted efforts to remove them and that undocumented rural and urban workers have deprived Venezuelan workers of jobs by accepting below-standard wages. There have also been countercomplaints from Colombia that undocumented newcomers have been physically mistreated.

In 1970, however, the migration had yet to become a serious threat to the traditionally close relations existing between the two countries. Leading Venezuelans have acknowledged that, on balance, the undocumented labor has made a positive contribution to the development of their country, and it has seriously been suggested that these migrants be encouraged to settle on lands in undeveloped localities.

Internal Migration

The population is highly mobile. In 1950 the census showed that about 19 percent of the native-born Venezuelans lived in a state other than that of their birth, and the 1961 census indicated that this percentage was continuing.

Population movement took place chiefly from the most densely populated states. There was a constant movement by the people of the three Andean states—Táchira, Mérida, and Trujillo—to the Caracas area, to the oilfields of Lake Maracaibo, and to the newly opened farmlands in the foothills of the Andes. There also was a comparable movement from the populous state of Nueva Esparta to the Caracas area and to the eastern oilfields. The iron mines and steel plant of Bolívar State drew men from all states, but particularly from the eastern part of the country.

Urbanization increased rapidly between 1950 and 1961. The population of the urban sector increased from 53.8 percent of the total in 1950 to 67.8 percent in 1961 and to an estimated 75 percent in 1970. Urban here is defined as those places with populations of 1,000 or more, the measure used in United Nations and some Venezuelan publications, although the Venezuelan census lists those localities with 2,500 or more inhabitants as urban, those with between 1,000 and 2,500 as intermediate, and those with fewer than 1,000 as rural. The population of metropolitan Caracas (urban parishes of the department of Libertador in the Federal District and an urban part of the Sucre District in the state of Miranda) increased by nearly 93 percent between 1950 and 1961 and by an estimated additional 50 percent between 1961 and 1968.

Between 1950 and 1961 the most substantial growth occurred in and around Caracas, in the oil-producing states of Zulia and Anzoátegui, in the iron-producing state of Bolívar, and in the states of Barinas and Portuguesa, where new farmlands were being opened up. Proportionally, the smallest gains were registered by the states of the Cordillera de Mérida and in Sucre and Nueva Esparta because of extensive migration to new localities from these areas.

Except for the oil center of Maracaibo, all the six cities with 1961 populations in excess of 100,000 were in the Northern Mountains, and most of the twelve cities with between 50,000 and 100,000 persons were also in the mountain region or in the oil-producing areas. By the end of 1968 the number of cities with populations in excess of 100,000 had grown to nine, and among the new additions to the list were Cabimas on the shore of Lake Maracaibo and Ciudad Guayana on the upper Orinoco River.

Between 1950 and 1970, while the population of the country as a whole was increasing by nearly 6 million, the rural sector's growth was negligible. It increased by a scant 125,000 between 1950 and 1961 and by an estimated 78,000 between 1961 and 1970.

Statistics concerning the distribution of the population by age group are available only for the census year of 1961, but from these alone it is possible to conclude that the failure of the rural sector to increase more substantially during the 1950s had resulted principally from the migration of young adults from rural to urban localities during the period. This movement presumably continued at the same or a higher rate during the 1960s.

In 1961 the rural proportion of each age group under the age of fifteen was well above the proportion for the rural population as a whole (32.4 percent of the total). At subsequent ages the rural proportion dipped progressively lower up to the age group between thirty and thirty-four years. It then increased successively for each group, reaching the highest proportion between the ages of sixty and sixty-four, before decreasing again for those sixty-five and over.

Because the pattern of rural settlement during 1961 was shaped by successive migrations of young people during preceding years, the actual ages at which the movements occurred were substantially younger than the thirty to thirty-four year age group at which the lowest proportion of rural habitation was reached. The pattern for groups under the age of fifteen, however, had yet to be shaped substantially by out-migration. It was made up of children born in, and still living in, rural localities. Many were destined at later dates to move to cities and towns, but in each of the groups under fifteen the concentration was substantially higher than the national average. This indicates a high rural birth rate and a fairly high survival rate through infancy and early childhood which, were out-migration not later to occur, would result in a relative increase rather than a relative decline in the level of rural population.

After experiencing a steady relative increase in age groups over that of thirty to thirty-four, the rural population again declined sharply for those over the age of sixty-five. This resulted from the earlier mortality of males coupled with the relative preponderance of males over females in the rural population. It was also presumably in some part the consequence of the migration of rural widows to cities and towns to join relatives who had migrated at earlier dates.

During the years after the end of World War II reverse migration from urban to rural areas was limited. A few migrants were presumably unable to adjust to urban life and returned to their former homes, but the most substantial return to the countryside has been by workers in the oilfields who have saved their earnings in order to return to the coolness of the mountains and buy farms of their own.

Because of the high degree of concentration of agriculture in the Northern Mountains, most of the migration from one rural locality to another has taken place from mountain valleys and basins to previously unfarmed areas, primarily in the foothills of the mountains and in adjacent lowlands in places where soils are generally superior to those at higher altitudes. Malaria and other diseases have long prevented the use of these lands, but in recent years the government has made great progress toward eliminating disease.

These interregional rural migrants have tended to be older than those moving to the cities and towns. Often married and with children, through practical experience they have learned some farming techniques, and they move for such reasons as the failure of a subsistence farm to support a growing family or the inability to secure land under satisfactory tenure conditions.

Most of the migration to new rural lands during the late 1950s and the 1960s took place as part of the government's rural colonization and resettlement programs (see ch. 2, Physical Environment; ch. 17, Agriculture). There was, however, some spontaneous movement of farmers along newly opened roads leading from the Northern Mountains to piedmont and adjacent lowland areas. The appearance of new farms along the borders of these routes indicated that the accessibility of land to markets provided sufficient incentive to lure farm-bred people away from subsistence plots in the older agricultural areas.

Population Problems

With a 1970 average of fewer than thirty persons per square mile, the country's population problems related to distribution by physical locality and by age group rather than to overpopulation of the country as a whole. It was estimated, however, that under conditions prevailing in 1970 the population would double in twenty-one years, a shorter period than that anticipated for any other South American country with the exception of Ecuador, where a duplication in twenty-one years was also anticipated. Assuming a continuation of 1970 trends, about 30 million people could be expected in the year 2000.

Uneven population distribution is reflected in the excessive concentration of industrial development in a few large cities and of agriculture in crowded farms in the Northern Mountains. Beginning in the late 1950s the government has addressed itself directly to the problems entailed. It has invested heavily in the creation of new industrial centers and the establishment of new industries in old centers. At the same time, it has undertaken the resettlement of subsistence farmers on new land made usable through road construction, land reclamation, and irrigation (see ch. 2, Physical Environment).

The rapid process of urbanization has brought with it increasing pressure to provide adequate services and housing. Schools, medical facilities, and systems of public services have grown at rates faster than the rate of population increase, but urban housing has not kept pace and represents a major problem for the 1970s (see ch. 6, Living Conditions).

The rise in the birth rate coupled with increased longevity has been reflected in a progressive decline in the size of the labor force as a proportion of the total population and faced it with the problem of supporting an increasingly large inactive sector. Moreover, even if the increase in the birth rate and in longevity were to cease at the beginning of the 1970s, the better part of a generation could be expected to pass before the attainment of equilibrium unless there were to be a considerable increase in job opportunities.

Underlying these immediate issues is the ultimate problem of excessive population growth itself. A pilot family planning program had been undertaken by 1970 at the Concepción Palacios Maternity Hospital in Caracas, and the government had established a population center in the Ministry of Health and Social Assistance.

DEVELOPMENT OF THE ETHNIC STRUCTURE

The Indian Background

At the beginning of the sixteenth century the territory that is now Venezuela was a kaleidoscope of numerous Indian groups of widely varying cultural levels and linguistic affiliations. Certain tribes—notably those inhabiting the Andean zone of what are now the states of Táchira, Mérida, and Trujillo and those of the northern coast, the valleys of the Central Highlands, and the coastal mountains near Caracas—had achieved a relatively high level of technology and social organization, living in fairly large permanent villages. Others—for the most part occupying the rain forests of the western Maracaibo shore, the more forested portions of the Guiana Highlands, and certain portions of the *llanos* (plains)—lived as seminomadic farmers who used slash-and-burn agriculture (see Glossary), occupying small villages that were moved at frequent intervals. Finally, in certain portions of the *llanos*, along parts of the Maracaibo shore, and in the Delta Amacuro the population consisted entirely of small bands of wandering hunters and gatherers (see ch. 2, Physical Environment).

These culturally diverse peoples spoke a large number of mutually unintelligible languages. According to the generally accepted classification made by the North American linguist Joseph H. Greenberg, the majority of Indian languages known to have been spoken at the time of the conquest fall into four major sets of related tongues: the Cariban, the Arawakan, the Paezan, and the Chibchan groups.

The more advanced aboriginal societies were organized as chiefdoms, ranging in size and complexity from single villages of perhaps 100 people to multivillage confederacies. Although there was considerable variation in social organization and technology, all chiefdoms shared certain characteristics. All were organized into political units under the recognized authority of a chief or chiefs, whose succession was usually hereditary. The great majority had at least an incipient class system, based upon a combination of hereditary status and distinction in warfare. For all chiefdoms, subsistence was based upon intensive agriculture, supplemented only in minor degree by hunting, fishing, and the gathering of wild plants.

Although there were numerous chiefdoms in the Andes, all of them had disappeared as distinctive societies very shortly after the conquest, and the Spaniards recorded information on only a few groups. The best known of the Andean chiefdoms were those of the Arawak-speaking Timoté, whose villages were located in the higher valleys in the zone near present-day Mérida.

The Timoté and their Andean neighbors lived in orderly, well-planned villages, usually laid out around a central plaza and containing up to 800 inhabitants. As a rule such settlements consisted of a dense collection of houses clustered around a town temple and often a group of large, stone-faced bins intended either for the storage of maize (corn) or for burials. Well-constructed roads and suspension bridges made of lianas connected neighboring villages and made possible what was reported by Spanish observers to be an active trade. Salt and cotton mantles were commonly used as money to facilitate trade between communities.

The agriculture of the Andean chiefdoms was distinguished by a well-developed technology and an impressive list of crops, including potatoes, maize, squash, sweet manioc, tobacco, and many varieties of beans. Archaeological remains of villages of the Timoté and other Andean groups indicate that irrigation was known and extensively practiced. Remains of stone-lined irrigation ditches, water reservoirs, and terraced fields on the steeper hillsides reflect the sophistication of the culture.

Little is known of the social and political life of the Timoté and their neighbors, except that villages and groups of villages were under the recognized authority of chieftains. The roads, irrigation systems, and terraces all attest to the strength of that authority, for they represent the coordinated and supervised effort of large work forces. In addition to Spanish reports of chieftaincies, archaeological evidence, in the form of special stone tombs and richly engraved gods, suggests the existence of social stratification.

Religious life centered in large ornamented temples, which imply the existence of a strong priesthood. The bat, mountain peaks, and the deer, which represented a war god, were particularly venerated; common offerings included thread, deer horns, and grains of cacao. There are indications that human sacrifice may have been practiced on occasion.

Along the entire northern coast, from the western shore of the Gulf of Venezuela to the Orinoco Delta, there were numerous tribes organized as chiefdoms, for the most part settled in the lower valleys and foothills of the Sierra de Perijá, the central valleys, and the coastal ranges. The best known of the northern chiefdoms were those of the Jirajara and the Caquetío in the west, the Caraca in the central portion, and the Palenque, the Cumanagoto, and the Aruacay in the east. Like those of the Andes, the chiefdoms of the north disappeared very shortly after the arrival of the Spaniards.

All of the northern chiefdoms were extremely warlike, a fact attested to by the layout of villages, which were invariably surrounded by tree-trunk palisades and in which special buildings were usually set aside as arsenals. The reasons for incessant warfare among the chiefdoms are not entirely clear, but it seems likely that ritual motives were extremely important. Spanish observers indicate that many groups systematically sought live captives for purposes of sacrifice and, in the case of at least one chiefdom, ritual cannibalism. In addition, the existence of slavery suggests that many wars were essentially forays for the purpose of obtaining bondsmen.

In the denser tropical forests of the lowlands, there was a large number of groups, speaking diverse tongues, whose social and cultural attainments were considerably below those of the peoples of the chiefdoms. For many of these peoples the basic subsistence pattern was almost identical—cultivation of maize, manioc, and other tropical staples—but largely because of the rigors of farming in dense jungles, their efforts failed to support the relatively large populations characteristic of the coastal and mountain groups. In addition, the slash-and-burn techniques, leading to rapid depletion of soils, necessitated the periodic shifting of village sites.

In contrast to the chiefdoms, the more primitive tropical forest peoples lacked clear-cut systems of social stratification and, as a rule, temples and organized priesthoods. Intervillage alliances, confederations, and states were nonexistent, and within individual settlements only a minimal authority was exercised by an informally chosen headman.

The wandering hunters, gatherers, and fishermen who occupied the marginal environments of Venezuelan territory were usually organized into very small kinship-based bands. The groups living on the *llanos*—the best known of whom were the Guahibo and the Chiricoa—depended primarily upon peccaries, deer, and other animals of the savannas and on wild plums and palm fruit. Along the tributaries of the Orinoco were bands of Yaruro, aquatic nomads who depended almost entirely upon fish, turtles, and riparian mammals. They were reluctant to travel on land and limited their exploitation of the *llanos* to gathering wild food in the gallery forests bordering the rivers.

The Conquest

The Spanish conquest of Venezuela resulted in a rapid and widespread extermination of Indians. Enslavement under inhuman conditions, constant warfare, epidemics of hitherto unknown diseases, and famines all took immediate tolls. Since no population statistics are available, it is impossible to estimate the loss of Indian life in the first years of Spanish rule, but it can be stated with certainty that in the first century at least twenty of the most populous tribes had passed into total extinction.

By 1499, one year after the landing of Columbus on the South American mainland, Spaniards were ranging the Venezuelan coast seeking slaves. With the establishment of an active and lucrative pearl fishery on the island of Cubagua, there was a sudden demand for manpower that could be filled expeditiously only through the use of slaves. Under a crown order, which remained in effect well into the sixteenth century, Indians could be legally enslaved if they were in any way hostile to their Spanish conquerors or if they were known to have practiced cannibalism. In the earlier years there were no difficulties in finding apt and legal victims for enslavement, for cannibalism was practiced among the northern chiefdoms, and armed skirmishes between natives and Spaniards occurred frequently (see ch. 3, Historical Setting).

Even after 1513, when the pearling activity of Cubagua underwent a decline, Indian slaves were in demand, for the growth of agricultural enterprise in the more settled Spanish colonies of the Antilles placed a pressing demand upon available manpower. In consequence, the Spanish slavers redoubled their efforts, and the slave trade was extended to virtually all of the Venezuelan territory. A measure of lip service was paid to the legal prescription for enslaving the Indians by automatically branding all captives on the face and arms with the letter *C* (for *caribe*—cannibal).

Enslavement of the native population not only dispersed and directly exterminated many Indian groups but also stimulated warfare. On the one hand, the most accessible chiefdoms (the Caraca and the Jirajara, for example) were mobilized to continuous action against the white invaders and, on the other, such groups as the nomadic Guahibo of the *llanos* were apparently spurred to slave raids on their neighbors. The resulting disruptions of normal activity had further effects in producing food shortages and famines.

In 1580 the decimation resulting from warfare and wanton mistreatment was virtually completed by an epidemic of smallpox. The disease took a severe toll of the Spanish population, but its effects were particularly disastrous to the Indians, who had had no prior exposure and hence had absolutely no resistance. Within one year the epidemic is known to have totally exterminated several large tribes in the valleys of the Central Highlands. The resulting decimation brought to an end the era of effective resistance on the part of the natives.

With the establishment of permanent and stable Spanish colonies based on commercial planting of cacao and tobacco and on cattle ranching, essentially completed by the end of the sixteenth century, another facet of colonial Indian policy came into play. The work of Christianization was effected in three ways: the founding of mission outposts by various religious orders; the forcible resettlement of dispersed Indian groups in accessible towns (*reducciones*) under the supervision of church authorities; and the establishment of the *encomienda*, an institution by which individual colonists (*encomenderos*) were given the right to collect tribute from Indians within a specific territory in return for undertaking the pacification and conversion of their charges (see ch. 3, Historical Setting).

Each of the three techniques of pacification and conversion produced profound cultural effects on the native peoples. The missions, established for the most part in the more remote jungle and *llanos* areas, were islands of peace and order in a territory rent with war and depredation. As such they attracted large numbers of Indians of diverse groups who had fled the excesses of Spanish settlers. Under the guidance of missionaries who ruled their settlements with absolute and final authority, such refugees were rapidly Christianized and at least partly Hispanicized in language and way of life. Old ethnic identities were lost and old languages were forgotten, with the result that Indians of diverse origins tended to become part of a new population of Spanish-speaking peasants, living either as marginal subsistence farmers or as entailed tenant laborers on Spanish-owned plantations and cattle ranches.

Loss of cultural identity was paralleled by *mestizaje* for the earliest invaders and settlers brought with them no Spanish women. The halfbreed offspring of liaisons between Spaniards and native women were usually raised as Indians with their maternal kinsmen. In the turmoil of early colonial days, however, it was common for such *mestizos* to seek shelter and work in Spanish settlements. On the otherhand, it was by no means rare for a white man to legitimize his *mestizo* children and raise them as Spaniards. Indeed, the crown generally favored a policy of miscegenation and facilitated the integration of at least a few chosen *mestizos*, the offspring of legal marriages between Spaniards and the daughters of Christianized native chiefs, by granting them patents of nobility (*hidalguía*). Thus in early colonial days at all levels the ranks of the white conquerors assimilated persons of mixed blood. With the establishment of permanent settlements and the arrival of Spanish women, however, legal marriages between white and Indians became quite rare.

By the end of the sixteenth century, the role of the Indians in the national ethnic structure had been fully set. The most populous tribes—those of the chiefdoms—were virtually extinct, with their surviving members reduced to bondage to the Spaniards. Remnants of such once populous and powerful peoples succeeded in evading the conquerors by withdrawing to more marginal territory, particularly the jungles, but, not having found an environment that would support large sedentary populations, they quickly lost the more complex patterns of their social and political life and came to resemble the primitive forest peoples. For their part, the shifting tropical-forest farmers and the nomadic hunters and gatherers continued as they had before the conquest, merely falling back to more inaccessible territory before the encroachments of white men. Being small, dispersed populations, occupying remote lands that held little attraction for the Spaniards, they were left more or less in peace. Although their numbers continue to diminish, they are the sole surviving groups of Indians in the country living under aboriginal conditions.

The Negro Background

During the latter part of the sixteenth century Venezuela, which had earlier been a neglected backwater in the American colonies, was developing a flourishing agricultural economy. Tobacco and cacao plantations producing exportable surpluses were established in the valleys of the Central Highlands and along the northern coast. As their enterprises grew, the Spanish planters found themselves faced with a need for recruiting labor far in excess of that available from the remnants of local Indian populations. To meet their needs they readily turned to Negro slaves.

Both the scanty historical evidence and identifiable cultural survivals among present-day Venezuelan Negroes indicate that the origins of the slave population were diverse. They were drawn from a variety of ethnolinguistic groups (particularly the Yoruba, the Ibo, and the Fon) from the African west coast, extending from Angola in the south to Senegal in the north.

Uprooted individually from their native groups and held, often for months, in slave ports along with widely differing peoples, the slaves had little opportunity to maintain either their native languages or their tribal customs. Hence, those who survived the rigors of the ocean crossing and a few years as field laborers in Venezuela tended to see themselves much more as Venezuelan slaves than as Ibo, Fon, or Yoruba. Moreover, many of the slaves introduced into Venezuela came not directly from Africa but from other American colonies, particularly the nearby Antilles. This large number of already acculturated Negroes served, in some degree, to impede the extensive reestablishment of African cultural patterns in Venezuela.

Although in many instances the Negro slaves of Venezuela were mistreated and worked under inhuman conditions, they occupied a social and legal status vastly different from that of slaves in the English colonies. In the system that developed in North America, the slave was considered the absolute property of the master, who could not therefore be held responsible before the law for any mistreatment. The Spanish colonial system, however, provided several means of recourse for a slave who felt himself ill-used. Homicide and physical cruelty to a slave were legally punishable, even if committed by the master. In addition, any slave who established that he had been badly treated could demand in court that he be forcibly sold to another master. Similarly, while Anglo-American law held that a slave had no civil rights—and was, in effect, not a legal person—that of Spanish America gave him the right to contract binding marriages and to own, bequeath, and dispose of property. In general, Spanish colonial law also encouraged manumission, whereas that of North America was designed to discourage the freeing of Negro slaves.

The result of this legal and social tradition of slavery was the rapid growth of a population of freedmen working as manual laborers in the cities or living as peasants on marginal lands. Although throughout colonial days Negroes, whether free or slave, occupied a very low social status, they never felt themselves to be part of a foreign and segregated ethnic group but, rather, identified themselves freely with the society and culture of the Spaniards.

Only a relatively few Negro uprisings, never of overwhelming proportions, marred the otherwise peaceful relations between masters and slaves. Those that did take place represented local responses, usually on the part of groups of field hands, against specific abuses, rather than mass attempts on the part of Negroes to throw off the yoke of slavery, like the uprising that was to occur in Haiti. Bands of such slave rebels usually fled to the jungles, where they lived as nomadic farmers and outlaws (*cimarrones*) until, as was usually the case, they lost their identity by interbreeding with Indian neighbors.

During the eighteenth century the importation of Negroes declined, and the slave trade was abolished formally in 1817. Emancipation came in 1854 by decree of President José Gregorio Monagas. Despite the formal persistence of slavery as late as the middle of the nineteenth century, many historians believe that, even among fullblooded Negroes, the slave population had come to be smaller than that of freedmen as early as 1800.

The Colonial Ethnic System

By the early eighteenth century the outlines of the modern ethnic structure had become apparent. The majority of Indians had either disappeared into the burgeoning population of mixed bloods or had withdrawn to be marginal zones. The peak of Negro importation had been passed, and the Negroes were themselves being subjected to the process of *mestizaje*. Finally, the mixed bloods formed a clear-cut social group, distinguished from each of the three ethnic components.

The social structure of colonial Venezuela was rigidly stratified, with a small number of more or less pureblooded whites at the pinnacle. Status distinctions among the Spaniards, such as that between the *peninsulares* (those born in Spain) and the *criollos* (native-born persons of Spanish descent) were for the most part minor in degree. Much of the white population consisted of individuals who had belonged to the lower class in Spain, but the economic opportunities afforded by the abundance of land and cheap labor made it possible for many to improve their status in the New World. Thus strongly motivated, many who had been peasants and manual workers in Spain gravitated toward upper class status as planters and merchants. Those who were less successful, on the other hand, tended to become assimilated, through both association and intermarriage, to the racially mixed lower class. Hence the association of ethnic background and social class was maintained, for the majority of lower status persons came to be automatically identified as *pardo* (dark-skinned persons).

Far below the Spanish elite were the masses of *pardos* and manumitted Negroes who made up the bulk of the free population, living as marginal subsistence farmers or as manual workers and petty merchants. Finally, there were the slaves who, by virtue of their position of bondage, formed a totally separate caste (see ch. 5, Social Structure; ch. 3, Historical Setting).

The tendency of the Spanish population to gravitate toward landholding and mercantile pursuits left open a wide variety of roles for the *pardos* and free Negroes. Virtually all forms of manual labor, both skilled and nonskilled, and much of the minor retail trade were thus monopolies of the nonwhites. Negroes, trained as slaves, did virtually all the metalworking, carpentry, leatherwork, and other skilled work seen by their masters as beneath their station. As freedmen they continued to dominate the crafts. *Pardos*, who flocked to all colonial cities, also entered the handicraft trades and petty commerce. In consequence, although nonwhites occupied a definitely lower stratum of the society, they were thoroughly integrated socially and economically into that society.

By the end of the colonial period all the bases of the present-day ethnic structure had been established. Indian and Negro cultural traditions had been almost completely obliterated—and with them, their separate ethnic identities. Economic integration, extensive intermarriage, and a gradual liberalization of policies and attitudes toward ethnic and racial differences have made it possible for Venezuelans, regardless of racial heritage, to consider themselves as one people, rather than as a mosaic of distinctive ethnic groups.

THE CONTEMPORARY ETHNIC STRUCTURE

Venezolanos

The vast majority of the population participates in the mainstream of national life and culture, speaks Spanish, and shares basically Hispanic traditions and values. Although the term *venezolano* formally designates all nationals of the Republic of Venezuela, it is popularly used to refer to this ethnic group. Thus, the tribal Indians are officially Venezuelans in the sense of nationality, but they are not *venezolanos* in the ethnic sense. Similarly excluded from the ranks of *venezolanos* in the popular view are those naturalized citizens whose way of life continues to show the notable influence of foreign traditions. The term *criollo*, which was originally applied to American-born children of Spanish or other European descent during the colonial period, has come to refer to approximately the same social group and is commonly used to contrast the *venezolano* population with tribal Indians.

In spite of some regional diversity in ethnic composition and cultural patterns, a strong sense of ethnic identity binds all Venezuelans. The isolation experienced by the country throughout much of the colonial period contributed to this sense of distinctiveness, leading many to see themselves as separate even from their Colombian neighbors, with whom they share an almost identical racial background and history (see ch. 3, Historical Setting).

Although the social structure in 1970 was fluid and presented many people with opportunities for social mobility, the ethnic composition of the social classes revealed vestiges of the colonial system of ethnic stratification. The most powerful and wealthy upper class groups, such as the landowners, industrialists, and merchants, and the relatively small middle class tend to be of white ancestry, but lower class urban workers and subsistence farmers are for the most part of a mixed ethnic background.

An individual is not born into a distinct ethnic group but is characterized only by his own appearance. Racial categories are regarded as points along a continuum of variation rather than as discrete entities. Popular terms, such as *blanco* (white), *negro* (black), *mulatto* (mixture of Negro and white), *zambo* (combination of Negro and Indian), and *mestizo* (which has been extended from its original usage, denoting white-Indian crosses, to denote all forms of mixture), serve primarily as a means of describing individuals.

No population census since that of 1926 has included an enumeration by ethnic groups. The only consideration given to such categories in subsequent censuses has been in the form of a separate count of tribal Indians.

Vestigial attitudes of white supremacy from the colonial period have persisted to some extent among the upper levels of society, but they are generally on the decline. A 1936 law that prohibited immigration of nonwhites was superseded in 1966 by a law that dropped this stipulation. Members of the predominantly white upper class retain some sense of exclusiveness. They are, however, aware of the generous mixture of nonwhite in their ranks.

The cultural heritage that underlies the distinctiveness of the Venezuelan people is formed of a basic Hispanic stratum to which the generous influences of many Negro and Indian groups have been assimilated (see ch. 10, Social Values). The national language is Spanish, which is spoken by all *venezolanos* to the exclusion of any aboriginal or African tongue. As spoken in Venezuela, however, the language contains in its vocabulary many words drawn from diverse Indian and Negro languages and used by all people, regardless of racial background. Elements of folklore, superstition, and religious practice derived from Indian and Negro traditions have been thoroughly mingled with those brought from Spain by the conquerors and appear as part of a cultural heritage shared by all.

The Indian contribution to the national culture is most apparent in rural areas and among subsistence farmers, whose style of life is little altered from that of the preconquest period. The techniques of slash-and-burn farming and the digging stick (*coa*) long antedate Spanish influence; furthermore, the staple foodstuffs that provide the subsistence of most Venezuelans, particularly in rural areas, were all domesticated by the indigenous Indian population. Maize and *arepa* (maize bread), manioc, black and broad beans, squashes such as the pumpkin, potatoes, and tobacco are all widely consumed.

Other traits of material culture still in common use include the hammock, the thatched stone-walled house of the Andean zone, and the wattle-and-daub hut of the lowlands. Rural Venezuelan households reflect their Indian heritage in the use of corn-grinding stones and, in the tropical lowlands, of a wickerware tube to squeeze the poisonous sap out of shredded bitter manioc (see ch. 6, Living Conditions).

The Indians have also contributed a number of words that are in daily use by Spanish speakers. Many have passed to other Spanish-speaking countries, and some have even been incorporated into English. From the Arawak of coastal Venezuela and the nearby Antilles, for example, came *hamaca* (hammock), *barbacoa* (barbecue), and *tabaco* (tobacco). From the Cumanagoto came *butaca* (in their language, stool), which came to have wide currency in Spanish America as a word for theater seat.

Of the many elements of religious practice that have persisted from the Indian culture, the numerous dances that became part of Catholic fiestas are the best known. The famous devil dancers of the states of Lara and Falcón, whose costumed performances are a well-known part of the fiesta of Corpus Christi in their region, derived their dance styles and many of their musical instruments, almost unchanged, from the Ayomán Indians, who had used them as part of non-Christian celebrations. Other elements of dance and fiesta practice drawn from the traditions of the Timoté, the Zorca, and many other groups have survived to provide part of Venezuela's varied local color long after the extinction of their Indian originators.

Although vestiges of Indian influence are apparent in the material culture, social organization, and religious beliefs of the rural areas, the trend among the rapidly expanding urban groups is to replace traditional patterns with more modern traits and attitudes. Urban slum dwellers may retain Indian styles of housing, furnishings, and belief, but after prolonged urban residence and improved socioeconomic status, they tend to lose many of these traits.

The Negro contribution to Venezuelan culture embraces virtually every aspect of religious life, folklore, and music. Although there is little evidence that non-Christian cults, such as the Haitian *vodum* or the Cuban *ñañiguismo*, specifically ascribable to African sources, ever took root in Venezuela, the Negro slaves who were among the country's earliest settlers added many African elements to the folk practice of Catholicism.

Old African festivals, celebrated at the time of the solstices, came to be cloaked under the names of Christian saints. Thus, the fiesta of Saint John, June 21, became a particulary important point in the ritual calendar of the coast, where Negroes predominated after the seventeenth century. Within the framework of the fiesta, basically an old Iberian tradition, there are abundant survivals of African music, played on instruments—particularly drums—known in Angola, the Congo, Nigeria, and Senegal. From the predominantly Negro coastal areas, the strong devotion to Saint John and the music, dances, and instruments of his fiesta have diffused to other parts of the country, and what had begun as African transplantings have become the common cultural property of the descendants of Indians and whites in the Andes and on the *llanos*.

Another important Negro contribution to the folk Catholicism of all Venezuelans is the fiesta of Saint Benedict (in late December), who commands the special devotion of Negroes all over Latin America. Originally one of several Negro fiestas observed as part of a cycle of winter solstice celebrations, the cult of Saint Benedict, along with its associated music and dances, has passed to all parts of the country. Indeed, one of the most famous celebrations of Saint Benedict occurs in the *mestizo* town of Betijoque in the Andes of Trujillo (see ch. 9, Religion).

As a result of the fact that for centuries most upper class white children were raised by Negro nursemaids, much identifiably African folklore has crept into the national tradition. A typical West African theme is to be seen in the cycle of tales about Tío Tigre and Tí Conejo (Uncle Tiger and Uncle Rabbit), who are almost identical to Bre'r Fox and Bre'r Rabbit of the southern United States. Such stories of wit pitted against strength are told by Venezuelans of all racial backgrounds, who are only dimly, or not at all, aware of their African derivation.

In addition to the Negro and Indian influences that have so profoundly affected the basic Hispanic stratum, new elements have been added to the language and culture of Venezuela by the flood of North Americans attracted to the country by the petroleum boom. Particularly in the realm of sports and other recreation the *yanqui* influence is perceptible. Baseball has assumed the status of a national sport, and its English vocabulary has been taken over bodily. Thus, the sports announcer speaks of *bol uán*, *bol tu* (ball one, ball two), *estrai tri*, *estrocao* (strike three, struck out), and *jonrón* (home run). Other fields in which North American influence is visible are business, where technical terms are adopted untranslated in many cases, and slang, to which *OK* and *olrai* (all right) have been thoroughly assimilated, at least in the speech of urbanites.

The wholesale importation for foreign words has often offended the sense of cultural nationalism that Venezuelans feel strongly. A law designed to protect the purity of Venezuelan Spanish requires that all brand names and advertising copy used by foreign firms be totally translated into Spanish. For example, the Venezuelan company producing deviled ham under the license of a North American firm is known as Diablitos Venezolanos S.A., and the hot dog is commonly advertised as a *perro caliente*. The popular tolerance of the novel and the foreign is such, however, that there is little attempt to enforce this and other similar laws. Thus, new elements are slowly but continuously assimilated to the distinctive Venezuelan linguistic and cultural compound.

Tribal Indians

The number of tribal Indians is small and continually shrinking. Arriving at exact population figures is very difficult, since many areas inhabited by Indians are remote and inaccessible. Furthermore, the definition of a tribal Indian is inevitably imprecise. The national census classifies a person as indigenous (*indígena*) if he habitually speaks a native language or if his way of life is so obviously aboriginal that he could not be classified with the peasant population. There are many groups, however, in a transitional phase, in which some members speak a little Spanish or have adopted various *criollo* customs and beliefs, such as agricultural practices or folk Catholicism, but retain intact much of the traditional culture.

According to the 1961 census, the country had 31,800 tribal Indians. A 1970 source gives an estimate of 36,000, but a noted anthropologist who studied the Indian population in the Guiana Highlands in the early 1960s found far fewer Indians than reported even in the 1961 census. The Indian population has been declining rapidly throughout the twentieth century, both from decimation by disease and from acculturation into the mainstream of *criollo* culture. The 1926 census recorded 136,147 Indians; by 1941 there were only 100,600; and by 1950 there were 56,706. If this trend continues, the tribal Indian population will be virtually nonexistent by the end of the twentieth century.

Tribal Indians generally live outside the main population centers, in a crescent-shaped band following the national borders. The largest concentration is the the Amazonas Territory, with considerably smaller numbers in the states of Zulia, Bolívar, Apure, and Sucre and a few scattered groups in the rest of the country. The population is divided into at least forty separate tribal groups. A precise tally is difficult, since a single village may be identified as a tribe although it is actually only a segment of a larger tribal grouping, or several distinct tribes erroneously lumped together in the past by untrained observers may continue to be identified as one.

The population is linguistically highly diverse. According to a comprehensive survey made in the mid-1950s, there were as many as 170 distinct languages and dialects spoken in the country, which could be classified into about 50 different language groups. With the decline in the Indian population, many languages are becoming extinct.

A variety of legal and constitutional provisions defines the nation's responsibilities to the Indians. The 1961 Constitution, for example, states the government's intention and obligation to integrate the aboriginal population into national social and economic life and, to that end, establishes the right of Indians to the special protection and tutelage of the nation. In practice, most services provided tribal Indians and most official policy specifically concerning them are the responsibility of the Ministry of Justice, through the work of its Indian Commission. In addition, an act concerning the federal territories, passed in 1948, defines the protection of Indians as a specific duty of the governors, who are empowered to use all territorial police and educational facilities to that end.

In 1951, at the instance of the Indian Commission, an executive decree was issued requiring all persons or agencies proposing to make expeditions into Indian areas to obtain a special license from the Ministry of Justice, to be issued only after an exhaustive examination of the intentions and good character of the petitioners. In addition to providing health, education, and protective services through official agencies, the government also makes financial contributions to Catholic missions that, by prior agreement, engage in the same work in specified parts of the country (see ch. 9, Religion).

Most Venezuelan Indians live a very simple life as slash-and-burn cultivators, herdsmen, or hunters, gatherers, and fishermen. Their staple diet generally consists of maize or manioc, often supplemented by fish, game, bananas, beans, squash, or potatoes. Because of their isolation, most have little regular social or economic contact with *criollo* society. No tribe, however, has been entirely without contact, and the process of acculturation—the adoption of elements of Venezuelan culture—has begun to some extent in almost all tribes.

A few, such as the fierce Motilones, resist the process, but the majority are anxious for the material goods, such as the clothing, radios, different foods, and rum, that civilization has to offer. The Indians must therefore enter the cash economy to earn money to purchase the goods and to trade with the *criollos*, entailing increased cultural contact. In many cases hunting and gathering societies have adopted simple farming from the *criollos*, and in a few areas Indians work for wages in *criollo* factories. Villages of the same tribe may have reached very different levels of acculturation, depending in large part on their proximity to *criollos*.

Missionaries, significant agents of acculturation, are active among many of the more remote tribes. In 1967 Catholic missionaries were working with the Warrau, Guajiro, Piaroa, Makiritare, and the southern, or "wild" Motilones; and Protestant evangelists were active among the Makiritare and the Waica on the upper Orinoco River. Other outside agencies penetrating into the Indian areas are the National Agrarian Institute (Instituto Agrario Nacional), which has attempted to introduce modern agricultural methods, the government malaria service, which has visited remote villages to spray for mosquitoes, and state governments, which are beginning to build schools in isolated Indian communities.

Indians generally view their *criollo* neighbors with hostility and distrust, an attitude often aggravated by *criollos* who take advantage of the Indians. Intermarriage is becoming more frequent, although a temporary liaison ending with desertion by the *criollo* man is also common. In spite of these attitudes, however, a significant number of Indians establish residence in Spanish-speaking towns and are gradually assimilated to the lower class *criollo* group. The long-term trend is toward the absorption of distinct Indian communities into the *criollo* way of life.

One of the best known and largest tribes in Venezuela is the Guajiro, a group of semidesert pastoral nomads who live in the Guajira Peninsula and the western portion of the Maracaibo basin. Their subsistence is based on the pasturage of cattle, sheep, and goats and the cultivation of maize during the short wet season. Owing to their pastoral way of life, most Guajiro live in temporary villages, often sheltered by no more than a lean-to or windbreak. The society is organized into totemic matrilineal clans, headed by chieftains who inherit their office through the maternal line. The social organization is based on the division of society into noble and commoner classes.

The Guajiro have retained a strong ethnic consciousness yet have adopted many traits of *criollo* culture and are to a considerable extent integrated into the money economy. Most are nominally Christians, and many speak Spanish. They have long been traders, exchanging salt, cattle, meat, and dairy products for cloth, firearms, rum, and hardware. More recently they have also become active in various forms of smuggling, both overland from Colombia and by sea from the nearby Netherlands Antilles. Many Guajiro dig salt or gypsum for sale to *criollo* merchants, and it is not uncommon for an Indian to work for a period of time on the roads or the oil derricks near Maracaibo. Intermarriage between the more acculturated Guajiro and non-Indians is not rare; in many cases such marriages take place between Levantine Arab merchants and the daughters of more affluent and successful Guajiro smugglers.

Also inhabiting the northwestern corner of the country is the most feared tribe in Venezuela, the Motilones of the Sierra de Perijá and neighboring areas of Colombia. Long known as implacable foes of the occasional whites who have strayed into their territory (many petroleum-company employees have fallen to their arrows), the Motilones really belong to at least two distinct tribal groups, the Chaké in the north and the Mape in the south. The name *motilon* (those with cut hair) was applied to the fierce tribes of the zone by the early Spaniards, whose haste in retreat never permitted them the time to learn the intricacies of local tribal division.

The northern Motilones are relatively peaceful farmers, only occasionally fighting among themselves. Their villages are customarily surrounded by eight- to ten-foot fortifications, which serve as a protection against pumas as well as marauding Indians. It is the southern branch, the Mape, or Motilones Bravos, that has earned the tribe its reputation. Continually driven back by the expansion of *criollo* farms, this group has been forced to raid surrounding communities in order to survive in times of hardship. Their hostility to any white invader, usually expressed by a well-placed arrow, has resulted in their continued isolation from *criollo* society. In the 1960s the Capuchin order of priests succeeded in making contact with a few villages, but the majority continue to shoot at passing government and oil exploration parties.

The tribes of the Guiana Highlands are among the most primitive and least affected by *criollo* contact. The Piaroa are one of the largest tribes in the Amazonas Territory and are typical of the region. Originally fishers, hunters, and gatherers, they have recently adopted a simple slash-and-burn agriculture, and some of the most acculturated groups practice more complex farming practices in imitation of the *criollos*. The traditional hunting weapons were the bow and arrow and the blowgun, often made more effective by the application of the deadly curare poison to the arrow points. The most common fishing technique was harpooning or shooting the fish with bow and arrow; a milder poison was often used to stun the fish before harpooning. Their large communal houses are conical in shape, rising to a sharp point or a cupola.

Another tribe typical of the Guiana Highlands are the Makiritare, a branch of the river Caribs, notable for their dugout canoes (*curiaras*), which they handle with great skill on the rapid waters of the upper Orinoco, Cauca, and Ventuari rivers. They, too, utilize the blowgun and the poisoned bow and arrow for hunting and, in addition, practice a rudimentary agriculture. Bitter manioc, maize, and bananas are grown with a simple slash-and-burn technique. Many groups are becoming more familiar with *criollo* culture. For example, in 1969, when the forests of the Caroní Valley were being slowly inundated by the rising waters backed up by the Guri Dam, scores of Makiritare Indians helped government workers capture and preserve the fleeing animals.

Northeast, along the crescent of Indian-inhabited territory, live the Warrau, a tribe of simple fishermen who inhabit the swampy lands of the Delta Amacuro. A small percentage engage in desultory farming, but the majority depend on the gathering of wild foods, such as larvae and wild yams, and on hunting with traps and bows and arrows to supplement their primarily fish diet. Their small, semipermanent villages of about 100 persons are typically raised on stilts, and often an entire village will occupy one platform above the swamp. In one respect these Indians are unique, for alone among the hunters and gatherers of tropical South America they have a temple cult, probably derived from neighboring circum-Carribbean culture. Each of the larger villages has a special building housing an idol of a supreme god called Our Grandfather and served by a full-time priest.

The Karinya Indians, inhabiting the eastern part of the *llanos*, are typical of several Venezuelan Indian tribes that are less isolated than those of the Guiana Highlands or the Delta Amacuro. Since the 1930s they have suddenly entered the mainstream of national life with the development of the oil fields in the area. The Karinya villages have generally maintained their sense of ethnic identity and distinctness, while adopting many traits of *criollo* culture. A desire for commercial goods and some participation in the national economy were among the earliest changes in the community. In recent years some villages have also adopted the use of Spanish and the Catholic religion, although retaining the native curer. Wage labor in nearby factories is common among some groups, but relatively few separate themselves entirely from their Indian community (see ch. 5, Social Structure).

Modern Immigrants

Immigrants have contributed substantially to the ethnic composition of the population in the post-World War II period. During the late 1940s and the decade of the 1950s the disruption in Europe, the economic opportunities offered in Venezuela by government public works projects and oil prosperity, and an active campaign on the part of the Pérez Jiménez regime to encourage migrants combined to stimulate a flood of immigration. In 1935 only 1 percent of the population was foreign born, but by the mid-1950s the proportion had risen to 8 percent and in 1968 was estimated at 8.7 percent.

The great majority of immigrants are of either Spanish or Italian origin. At the end of 1968 the foreign population was 30 percent Spanish, 30 percent Italian, 9 percent Portuguese, 8 percent Colombian, 8 percent North American, and smaller numbers, in order of decreasing size of Cubans, British, Germans, Syrians, French, Lebanese, Argentines, Dutch, Ecuadorians, and a sprinkling of natives of Eastern Europe and of other parts of Latin America. Census figures from 1961 indicate a roughly similar ethnic makeup: of the total foreign-born population of 556,875, 54 percent were Spanish or Italian, 8 percent Portuguese, and 19 percent Colombian.

The few migrants who arrived before World War II generally settled in Caracas or in one of the petroleum centers and were, for the most part, readily absorbed into the local population. Inspection of membership lists of upper class social and professional clubs in Caracas shows a liberal sprinkling of foreign surnames—particularly Italian, French, English, and Irish—contributed by the trickle of foreigners who, since the War of Independence, had come to the country had been integrated into local society by marriage. A result of this combination of scanty immigration and ready absorption was an almost total lack, in pre-World War II days, of foreign ethnic enclaves.

Immigrants in the postwar period have continued to settle largely in urban areas, particularly Caracas and Maracaibo, where they became petty merchants, taxicab drivers, or factory workers. Portuguese, Italian, and Spanish immigrants are particularly active as commercial entrepreneurs in the *barrios* such as Caracas and Ciudad Guayana, where they operate drugstores, barbershops, dry good stores, garages, bakeries, and restaurants and provide other services to the native residents. Lebanese are frequently involved in marketing textiles. Over a period of time, immigrants have entered all levels of society and are, in many cases, innovators in the fields of industry, commerce, and agriculture.

As a result of the urban concentration of large numbers of foreigners, self-isolating ethnic enclaves have developed whose residents maintain only minimal social and cultural contact with the *venezolano* majority. Even in the more remote countryside, there are villages of agricultural colonists in which, according to observers, one hears more Italian than Spanish spoken in the streets. A German agricultural colony founded in 1843 in the coastal range near Caracas has recently gained popularity as a tourist center because it has faithfully preserved the architecture and life style of a Bavarian village. The town has maintained its German language and customs, including a local brewery.

Many of the displaced persons—a majority of them East European and German Jews who came to the country shortly after World War II—sought and received naturalization. Nations of other European countries, particularly Italy, Spain, and Portugal, who have arrived in great numbers, often come with the intention of ultimately returning to their homelands. Attracted by the multitude of economic opportunities—many Italians, for example, came to work in the booming Caracas construction industry—they came in the hopes of earning considerably more than would be possible in their home countries. In the 1960s and in 1970, however, significant numbers of Spanish and Italian immigrants were leaving the country.

United States citizens, who in 1968 made up 8 percent of the foreign population, are in most cases employees of oil companies and other foreign concerns. The majority spend only a few years in the country, and most never have more than peripheral contact with local society. Living very often in segregated quarters and working under conditions that make it unnecessary in many cases even to learn Spanish, the North Americans form one of the most visible (and resented) ethnic enclaves in the country.

Since the European immigrants constitute much of the Venezuelan commercial class and are active in the skilled trades, many lower class Venezuelans feel that they have taken away many of the best paying jobs. Nevertheless, although a certain amount of resentment is directed at foreigners who hold top commercial and industrial positions, the professional skills, commercial enterprise, and capital of the foreign populations have added visibly to national prosperity.

In the past the immigrants were not seen as offering destructive competition within fields of endeavor traditionally pursued by Venezuelans but, with the emergence of a Venezuelan class of small businessmen and skilled labor, competitive immigrants are regarded as less desirable. The law on the promotion of immigration enacted in 1966 concentrates on encouraging only agricultural immigrants, in contrast to the previous law of 1936, which emphasized both agriculturists and skilled urban workers.

CHAPTER 5

SOCIAL STRUCTURE

For some forty years the country's society has been undergoing pronounced changes with far-reaching effects. The changes—in class structure, in institutions, and even in basic attitudes—have accompanied the transformation of the national economy from its agrarian base to a primary dependence on the export of mineral resources and, more recently, on a growing manufacturing sector.

A measure of the social change may be seen in a comparison of population characteristics for the years 1936 and 1970. In the earlier year the country was overwhelmingly rural, with almost two-thirds of the population living in the countryside. By 1970 this proportion had been reversed, and approximately 70 percent were living in urban areas. Similarly, the people had become more mobile, with the ratio of persons living outside their native localities increasing from 11 percent in 1936 to over 30 percent in 1970. A further indication of change is evident in the contrast in literacy figures for the same period; in 1936, 21 percent of the people were able to read and write, whereas in 1970 the literacy rate had risen to more than 80 percent of the population over the age of ten.

Other changes have affected the basic structure of the society. As late as the 1920s the fabric of the nation's social system was little different from what it had been in colonial times. Its principal characteristic was the domination of the country by a small upper class whose members owned most of the valuable land and who maintained a monopolistic control over political and economic life. The vast majority of the people belonged to a lower class of peasants and laborers, who had little interest, and less voice, in the formulation of national policy. There was virtually no group that could be described as middle class, and a lack of educational facilities or employment opportunities in characteristically middle class specialties effectively inhibited status-improving mobility.

The prevailing social view divided the population into two classes, the cultured people and the ordinary people. Membership in the former group implied a combination of wealth, education, and power, whereas the ordinary people were those marked by illiteracy, menial occupations, and poverty. For the relatively few persons who fell between these status extremes, there was a nebulous place in the social structure. Such individuals (most often impoverished members of upper class families or persons of lower class origins who had achieved a degree of wealth or education) constituted an ill-defined group largely lacking entity or class consciousness.

The change brought about by the petroleum boom in the twentieth century and its subsequent economic expansion had its greatest impact in the urban areas. It resulted in the rapid creation of an industrial proletariat and the rise of a genuine middle class. Oil-based prosperity was invested in an expanded school system, and ambitious members of the poorer classes found new opportunities to move into higher status and more remunerative occupations. As their numbers grew, the industrial working class became an increasingly powerful bloc in national life, and the middle class developed a marked degree of social cohesion and group consciousness that made it an important cultural and ideological force.

Change came to the rural areas as well, although more slowly than that which characterized urban life. Although by 1970 a majority of the rural population had not advanced much beyond the fringes of national economic, cultural, and political life, improvement in communications, construction of roads, and establishment of schools had begun to have visible effects in changing old attitudes. Rural inhabitants were suddenly thrust into the twentieth century, and rapidly rising aspirations were reflected in large-scale migration to high-wage urban areas as well as in increased political activism in the countryside.

The change in the class structure has resulted in a significant shift in the balance of political power throughout the society. The voice of the rural population seeking economic improvement has grown increasingly audible to the government, and even the most authoritarian regimes have found it impossible to ignore the interests of the lower classes. The result has been a gradual, but steady and comprehensive, program of beneficial social and economic reform.

Keeping pace with the transformations that have taken place in other areas over the past four decades, family and kinship patterns have undergone significant change. The family and the wider kin group, traditionally the focus of social stability within the structure, have lost some of their primacy in the face of pressures resulting from economic change and urbanization. The deeply rooted Hispanic legacy of patriarchal family life is slowly giving way to more modern egalitarian domestic patterns.

DEVELOPMENT OF THE MODERN SOCIAL STRUCTURE

The Colonial Basis

From its beginnings in the sixteenth century, colonial society was stratified into rigid castes along ethnic lines. A relatively small number of Spaniards occupied the pinnacle of the structure; the majority of the population—mixed-bloods, Negroes (whether slave or free), and Indians—were relegated by law and social usage to a position of subservience, poverty, and political impotence (see ch. 4, Population and Ethnic Groups).

The white colonists, who acquired the best lands and slaves in the early years of the colony, came to regard themselves as members of a local aristocracy with an inherent right to absolute control over the land and over their social inferiors. Their supremacy was maintained by laws that effectively blocked nonwhites from social or economic improvement, denying them access to education, service in the Royal Army, or membership in the clergy. It was made visibly obvious by sumptuary laws that forbade to nonwhites the use or wearing of certain symbols of affluence and refinement, such as mantles, capes, silk, lace, or pearls.

The whites in effect formed a single upper caste in colonial society, but in time their own ranks were sharply divided by differences in political, economic, and social status, by divergent loyalties, and by conflicting economic interests. This gave rise to dissension within the white population, ranging from smoldering resentment to occasional armed conflict. Most important was the division between *peninsulares* (whites born in Spain) and *criollos* (those of Spanish descent born in the colony). By the policies of both crown and church, only the former were eligible for high office in the colonial government and the clergy. This officially imposed subordination was strongly resented by the *criollos*, who felt their interests to be impaired by it, and it constantly stood as a sore point in the relationships between the two groups.

The *criollos* came to dominate local colonial government and preserved for themselves a monopoly over offices in the *cabildos* (town councils) as a means of opposing or neutralizing the acts of the crown officials. Most of the important political issues of the period were the subject of conflict between the *criollo*-dominated *cabildos* and the colonial government run by *peninsulares* (see ch. 3, Historical Setting).

In addition to controlling the local councils, the *criollos* held most of the economic power—land, slaves, and commerce. Although as members of a privileged white upper class they enjoyed special legal and social status, not all *criollos* prospered, and many were little, if any, better off than most nonwhites. Conversely, despite formidable obstacles, individual *pardos* (dark-skinned persons) or *mestizos* (persons of mixed ancestry—see Glossary) were occasionally able to raise their status from peasant or laborer and achieve a marked degree of success, usually through commercial enterprise.

Economic success led to ambitions to improve their social lot, and many wealthy *pardos* sought to enter their children in schools or applied for licenses to practice professions considered white monopolies. Their efforts were abetted, to an extent, by the crown government, whose officials did not usually share the white supremacy convictions of the *criollos*. During the latter years of the colonial era any *pardo* could apply, through payment of a substantial fee, for a royal patent declaring him to be the equal in rights and privileges of the whites.

By the end of the colonial period the *pardos* constituted a sizable majority of the population and were as varied in social status, loyalties, and economic interests as the whites. They formed the backbone of the peasant labor force, working as sharecropping tenants on the estates of the whites and as cattle herders on white-owned ranches. There were also large numbers of them in the cities, where they dominated the artisan crafts and much of the petty retail commerce, activities that had been largely abandoned by the whites.

Over the course of colonial history there were indications that the *pardos* nurtured a deep resentment of their subordinated place in the social order. It was not a militant disaffection, however, as the *criollos* firmly held the economic and military power and usually were in full control. There were, nevertheless, occasional slave and peasant uprisings, mostly in the latter eighteenth century, which were usually put down brutally, but effectively, by the authorities.

The other components of the nonwhite lower caste—the Indians and the Negroes—although seldom worse off economically than the *pardos*, had even less opportunity to improve their position in colonial life. What had been a relatively large aboriginal population in the sixteenth century was decimated by the end of the seventeenth century. Dispersed by wars and epidemics, the survivors were subjugated by the colonists by a variety of means, including slavery and tenant bondage. The Negro slaves, although their material and social lot was generally better than that of their fellow bondsmen of the English colonies, were dependent on the will of their masters and usually powerless to seek such economic opportunities as were afforded by the society.

Republican Society

During the War of Independence (1811—21) the disunity and underlying enmities of the colonial social order flared continually. Loyalties reflected lines of ethnic and economic division, and most of the armed combat of the period was motivated as much by preexisting animosities as by adherence to either the royalist or the rebel cause. Bolívar's famous "war to the death" decree, threatening death to *peninsulares* who did not cooperate with the patriot forces, may have been a partially successful attempt to exploit the animosity toward the Spanish-born (see ch. 3, Historical Setting).

In the earliest days of the independence struggle, the movement was spearheaded by the *criollo* landholders and the wealthier merchants and received little support from any other group. The *pardos* and free Negroes inclined in their loyalties toward the royalists, partly through their longstanding animosity toward the *criollos* and partly in response to promises of equality and opportunity made to them by royalist leaders. Only after such *criollo* leaders as Bolívar gave parallel assurances of social and economic reform did the revolution gain any support from the nonwhites.

As a result of the war and ensuing political confusion, the *criollos* suffered considerable erosion of their economic power, and for a time their leadership was successfully challenged by military freebooters who roamed the countryside at the head of hordes of restive Negroes and *pardos*. By 1830, however, order was finally restored by the authorities, and the old social system was substantially reestablished. The Constitution of 1830, written by a coalition of white landowners and merchants, again restored control of political and economic affairs to the hands of the *criollos*.

The promises and assurances made to the nonwhites went largely unheeded, and the social and economic orders established in the 1830s differed little from those of colonial times. Although slavery persisted until 1854, there were some theoretical advances: all legal provisions restricting opportunity and privilege on the basis of race were abolished, and a man could presumably no longer be barred from access to wealth and position solely because of his ancestry. But the continued concentration of land and power in the hands of the predominantly white oligarchy made it virtually impossible for the mass of the citizens to hope for any improvement in their status.

By the mid-nineteenth century the traditional system of ethnic castes had almost completely disappeared, but it had been replaced by a form of social and economic class stratification no less rigid. The society continued to be divided between a small upper class, predominantly white, and a mass of underprivileged, illiterate, and powerless laborers and peasants, overwhelmingly nonwhite. Such few *pardos* as succeeded in rising above their origins were generally assimilated into the ranks of the oligarchy, and their success had little impact on the lower class from which they had emerged.

The latter part of the nineteenth century witnessed some liberal reforms—slavery was abolished and suffrage was extended—but nothing was done about the fundamental economic inequities or about the serious lack of educational opportunities. The masses saw little change in their lot, and this was reflected in the popular support rallied for the numerous violent changes of government that took place in the nineteenth and early twentieth centuries. Despite widespread discontent, the social order underwent virtually no modification until well into the twentieth century, when the economic effects of the petroleum boom ushered in a new era.

URBAN SOCIETY

The burgeoning growth of commercial and manufacturing prosperity that has marked the new economic era has been most apparent in the country's large cities, where most of this activity has been concentrated. In addition to the old established metropolitan centers of Caracas and Maracaibo, by 1970 there were seven other cities with populations of over 100,000. It is, consequently, in the urban centers that social change has been most intense, and its effect on the class structure has been most evident.

The middle class has grown up around the many opportunities offered by the bustling economy, and the demand for industrial labor has resulted in the development of an aware and organized working class, which makes up a large segment of the population. In addition, the influx of people from rural areas has outstripped the demand for labor and created a large slum element of unemployed that has been fertile ground for political agitation and possible subversion.

Changes in the class structure have not been as pronounced in the smaller cities and towns, most of which (except for those lying within the oilfields) still subsist on a predominantly agrarian economic basis. Here life is more tranquil and conservative: the growth of the middle class has been more restricted by the lack of economic opportunity, and a lower rate of urban migration has helped avoid the social problems of widespread unemployment and need.

The Upper Class

The bulk of the upper class is concentrated in Caracas and in the more populous state capitals. Although upper class economic interests were predominantly agrarian until well into the twentieth century, the wealthy plantation owners, who were the basis of the privileged class, generally preferred to spend most of their time in urban residences. The towns laid out by the Spanish settlers were, in fact, designed to serve as places of upper class residence as well as ceremonial, administrative, and marketing centers.

In origins and sources of wealth the upper class is an extremely heterogeneous group, its core formed by the old agrarian elite, who in the past derived their preeminence from landownership and control over the agricultural economy. Descended in many cases from prominent colonial families, this traditional group generally considered itself a local aristocracy. With the recent economic expansion, however, membership in the upper class has expanded to a marked degree, to include those whose wealth derives from commerce or industry or even from the successful practice of a profession. Although some members of this new upper class are drawn from the old landowning families, many are from modest origins, and some are of visibly mixed ethnic backgrounds.

Strong ties of association and kinship have developed between the two upper class segments. Economically successful people of lower class background have always been able to gain social acceptance by the landowning upper class, but this acceptance was most often hard won. Intermarriage has been the primary means of unifying the two groups, and the joining of an old aristocratic name with a recently acquired fortune has gone far in bringing the two components together. Business association, common membership in social clubs, and a developing network of kin connections have further unified this group.

An important part of traditional upper class ideology is the view held regarding work and leisure. Most forms of remunerative effort are looked on as demeaning, and ideally a gentleman lives a life of genteel leisure. Although most upper class men receive a college education, and frequently professional training, the practice of a profession is looked on more as a symbol of elite status than as a means of subsistence. Members of the newer elite derive social status and power more from wealth than from distinguished ancestry, and they tend to be less preoccupied with pedigree. They are generally highly conscious of their success and take pride in their achievements in business or commerce (see ch. 10, Social Values).

In contrast to the ingrained conservatism of the traditional landowners, members of the newer elite tend to be more receptive to social change. They have generally backed government-proposed reform measures and have been the main support of privately administered institutions and foundations active in social work and educational endeavors.

The upper class has always maintained a dual cultural allegiance, and since colonial times elite families have commonly sent their sons abroad for advanced schooling. The somewhat restricted intellectual life in the colony and resentment of Spanish rule led many *criollos* to seek intellectual stimulation in North America and Europe. This tradition of foreign education and cultural influence carried over well into republican times.

In the twentieth century North American influences on clothes, leisure-time activities, and other aspects of daily life have become increasingly evident among the upper class, particularly in such cosmopolitan centers as Caracas and Maracaibo. Although some of these influences have reached most segments of the society, they are most apparent in a group whose members have interests outside the country and who can afford the purchase of imported luxury goods. By reason of their way of life and their business and social association with foreigners, members of the upper class are frequent targets of attack by leftist or extreme nationalist politicians.

The Middle Class

The middle class consists of successful small businessmen; professionals, either independent or employed; managerial and technical personnel; and administrative functionaries. It is an almost entirely urban phenomenon. Its membership is drawn from those who, by economic and social status, are not identifiably upper class but who, because of a comfortable income, education, and nonmanual occupation, are not considered lower class.

The middle class is a new social category in Venezuela that has developed since the 1930s. Although there had always been a few individuals who, by economic and social status, fell into an intermediate group, a defined middle class hardly existed as a recognizable entity. Such persons were often men of lower class origins who had achieved a measure of success but had not been assimilated into elite society. Others were persons of upper class background who through reverses were no longer able to maintain an appropriate style of life, and still others were literate, but poorly paid, white-collar workers, such as teachers and petty functionaries.

The economic boom spurred by oil and the consequent broadening of the base of opportunity has created numerous roles that do not fit traditional patterns. The expansion of commerce and industry, in particular, has created a demand for trained technical and managerial personnel that cannot be filled from the small numbers of the upper class. The increasing concentration of population in cities has resulted in a need, previously unknown, for administrators and such professionals as doctors, dentists, and lawyers as well as in expanded markets for small businesses. At the same time a continuous growth of educational facilities, particularly in the larger cities, has placed the necessary training within reasonably easy reach of many ambitious persons of humble origin (see ch. 7, Education).

The group that has grown up to fill these newly created roles consists predominantly of persons from lower class families who, through education and hard work, have achieved a measure of economic success and social status. Like the members of the new industrial elite, they take pride in their progress, and this pride forms the basis of a strong class consciousness. To an extent the middle class merges with the upper, as its wealthiest members find little difficulty in moving into elite society, at least in the larger cities. These instances are relatively few, however, and in actuality, as its members have grown, the middle class has developed a defined social life of its own. In addition to numerous social clubs, its members belong to a wide variety of associations and professional groups based on occupational interests. In effect, from forming an isolated and unorganized segment on the periphery of upper class society, it is being transformed into a structured social entity in its own right.

Few members of the middle class feel any commitment to the traditional social order. In political and economic orientation, probably a majority tend toward positions ranging from mildly reformist to radically leftist. Staffing the news media, teaching in the schools and universities, and operating the publishing enterprises, they have exerted a powerful influence toward reform.

The Lower Class

The urban lower class includes all those who have traditionally been called the ordinary people—domestic servants, artisans, petty tradesmen, and common laborers—along with the newer industrial proletariat and the swollen population of unemployed or marginally employed squatters of the large cities. In the Venezuelan social view, it is identified with low-status (usually manual) occupations, poverty, and illiteracy. There is, however, considerable variation in the economic status of its members.

A group consciousness embracing all the varied elements of the lower class hardly exists. Because of the wide divergence in economic interests, the union-organized industrial laborers, for example, have little in common with artisans or petty merchants or with the squatters of the large cities. Reflecting the diversity of interests, lower class political participation covers the gamut from patently Communist groups to the more conservative and moderately liberal parties. Organized labor, particularly, has become a powerful pressure group, whereas by contrast small tradesmen and other lower class elements that are not well organized have little impact on the country's politics other than through their individual votes.

Lower class economic expectations have undergone a spectacular rise since the oil boom. The oil-born prosperity has stimulated a tendency toward high wages that has been felt in every sector of the economy and, although no other industry can approximate the pay scales of the petroleum companies, the wage structure of these companies stands as a constant example to the rest. Lower class Venezuelans living in urban areas have been exposed to the allures of the outside world to a greater extent than most of their counterparts in other Latin American nations. An abundance of communications media, particularly motion pictures, radio, and television, which are available to most city dwellers, not only spurs material demands but also heightens public awareness of political and economic issues.

Related to the general rise in economic expectations has been a drive toward social advancement on the part of many lower class families, particularly noticeable in increasing school enrollments. It has become common for parents who themselves lack a primary education to struggle in order to educate their children through secondary school. The traditional route to progress in the society has been through academic and professional instruction; recognition of this fact by members of the lower class has resulted in a marked growth in the demand for such schooling in preference to more narrow vocational and technical training (see ch. 10, Social Values).

RURAL SOCIETY

Rural social life has been molded by an agrarian economy that, until very recently, remained little changed from colonial times. A concentration of the most productive lands in the hands of a very few owners and a generally primitive farming system combined to keep most of the rural population at the margins of the national economy, living in poverty in rudimentary housing with low nutritional standards.

A survey published in June 1970 by the United States Agency for International Development (USAID), titled *Land Reform in Venezuela*, indicated that 79 percent of all cultivated lands were in the hands of fewer than 2 percent of all proprietors. By contrast, two-thirds of all landholders owned less than 3 percent of all cultivated lands. The same survey further indicated that only one-fourth of those listed as farmers or farmworkers owned any land at all (see ch. 17, Agriculture).

The majority of rural inhabitants are wage laborers, sharecroppers, or squatters on private or state-owned lands, and in any of these conditions few command the resources or have the incentive to produce much beyond the demands of simple subsistence. Wages to cash laborers and payments in kind to sharecroppers are low, and such small proprietors or uncontested squatters as can operate independently generally occupy poor land. Their farms are usually marginal in size and productivity and often so inaccessible to markets that modernization and production increases would be both difficult and uneconomical.

Along with the character of the land tenure system and a primitive technology, the geographic and cultural isolation of the majority of the rural population has long stood as a barrier to social change. Longstanding neglect of rural education, the traditional immobility of the countryman, and the dearth of literate, politically conscious people in rural areas had, until around the mid-twentieth century, left agricultural workers almost entirely outside the range of national influences. Events on the national scene, short of all-out civil war or widespread rebellion, had, therefore, little impact on life in the countryside.

Since the late 1930s economic and social change has become slowly, but steadily, apparent. In 1963 the implementation of the 1960 Agrarian Reform Law resulted in the distribution of titles to some 25,000 landless families; by 1969 the total of distributed farms had reached over 160,000. Increased population mobility has sent thousands of peasants to the cities and the oilfields, and contacts with their home villages have provided considerable stimulus to change. There has been increasing interest in farm modernization and commercial production on the part of small landowners and extensive migration from overcrowded and wornout Andean lands to the richer lower slopes.

Community Structure and Character

Regional variations in settlement patterns reflect geographic conditions, land-use practices, and historic traditions. In the Northern Mountains, the heart of Spanish colonial settlement, most *campesinos* (peasants) live in small, fairly dense aggregates. This pattern has roots dating from colonial times, when the Spaniards concentrated Indian and Negro laborers in satellite villages in the vicinity of their own towns. Even after the abolition of slavery, the traditional form of the compact farm hamlet persisted.

In those areas where large plantations are still worked by cash-paid laborers or sharecroppers, the worker population continues to be housed in small, centrally located collections of habitations. Geographic considerations have been influential in determining settlement patterns and are particularly noticeable in mountainous zones, where compactness of settlement reflects the effort to conserve arable lands by the location of houses in small unproductive areas. Similarly, a tendency to concentrate near water supplies and travel routes has resulted in line villages strung out along roads and streams.

By contrast, in the Orinoco Lowlands, or *llanos* (plains), and some other areas remote from early colonial settlement, the pattern is predominantly one of isolated farmsteads and widely dispersed cattle ranches, often at some distance from the nearest settlement or town. Rural communities are similarly varied. In the densely populated northern part of the country, rural settlements, whether plantation hamlet or farm village, are typically closely knit and interdependent, and their residents are usually bound together by bonds of kinship or economic interest. In other areas a dispersed settlement pattern tends to make each household more independent of its neighbors, with a resultant looseness of social bonds.

The typical *campesino* hamlet, particularly in the northern zones, is, for the most part, self-sufficient. Although the residents buy little in the cash economy, they maintain a tradition of labor sharing that often enables them to meet most of their needs locally. Relating to this economic self-sufficiency is a tendency toward strong social integration. In most communities there is an active social life centered on field parties at planting and harvest times and on the periodic celebrations of religious fiestas. In many villages the communal veneration of a patron saint further enhances strong local identity and attachment to the group.

Some contact with national life is nevertheless maintained by even the most tightly knit and self-sufficient settlement. Dispersed throughout the countryside are small towns, usually of fewer than 2,000 inhabitants, that serve as administrative, religious, and marketing centers for the more remote villages. Here the isolated farmer goes periodically to renew old acquaintances, take care of official business, sell his goods, or take advantage of services not available in his home community, such as medical facilities or pharmacies. It is also an opportunity for him to shop for a wider variety of consumer goods, such as clothing or tools, than he can find in his hamlet store, if his community has one at all.

The *campesino* population is, for the most part, poor and within itself is largely classless. Differences in wealth do exist, and ownership of land or even the slightest prosperity lends increased social status. It is between the *campesino* and the townsman, however, that lines of class distinction are clearly marked. Most merchants and minor functionaries who make up the small towns' populations are literate. Although many are relatively poor by urban criteria, their standard of living is considerably higher than that of the peasants. Many have a modicum of political power through holding municipal jobs, and the higher plane of their social position is readily acknowledged by the *campesinos*. The relationship between the two groups is usually friendly and cordial but generally marked by deference and respect on the part of the farmer and a tolerant paternalism on the part of the townsman.

Dynamics

For more than four centuries the *campesinos* have given evidence of dissatisfaction with their lot, whether as slaves, sharecroppers, or independent farmers. They have been readily enlisted over the years in support of rebel leaders in return for promises of reform, but their participation in revolts and other forms of civil disorder has been largely ineffective in bringing about any improvement in their condition. In the past their leaders have seldom fulfilled their promises of change and, added to this, the isolation of most *campesinos* from the centers of political power and their lack of familiarity with more sophisticated national ways have made it impossible for them to act in their own interests. Further, the dispersal of the rural population into small isolated communities has militated against unified action except under the leadership of outsiders.

In response to the basic social and economic changes taking place throughout the society, by 1970 the traditional helplessness and disunity of the rural population were showing signs of disappearing. Increasing communication with the outside world has resulted in a growing political awareness and the beginnings of an articulate leadership. Over the past few decades peasant leagues (*sindicatos campesinos*), similar in organization and aims to labor unions and affiliated with national labor federations, have been formed in many areas. The rural bloc is receiving ever-increasing attention and concessions on the national scene. Most political leaders recognize that the future peace and stability of rural society could depend in large part on the continuation of economic and social reform.

THE FAMILY

The Hispanic heritage upon which Venezuelan society was founded places great emphasis on bonds of family loyalty and accords them moral priority over virtually all other social obligations. In this context families have traditionally seen their best hopes of security and well-being in intimate and extensive blood ties and kin-based mutual aid. The tendency to seek personal security in the kin group and the readiness to lend it assistance have been reinforced by an ingrained distrust of impersonal authority and alien institutions.

Wealth in the old agrarian economy was largely concentrated in the hands of a few families and was handed on along lines of blood ties. The combination of family-controlled wealth, power, and privilege has traditionally been reflected in strong tendencies toward dynastic organization in upper class society. Groups of relatives, aware of their community of interest and collective social status, forged bonds of intimate and unquestioned loyalty that have persisted over generations and include the most distant kinsmen. In addition to affection and trust, collective control over the behavior of the individuals was a prominent feature. For the small elite, class consciousness has, in effect, been kinship consciousness.

Although the ideals of intimate kinship bonds are most evident in the upper class, they are shared at all social levels. The changes in the tempo of daily life since the oil boom, however, have tended to undermine the centrality of the family and the kin group. The focus of economic power has shifted from the hereditary control of lands and from family-organized enterprise to commercial and industrial activities dependent primarily on impersonally organized and often foreign-controlled corporations. Expanding economic opportunity has brought to the ranks of wealth and prominence large numbers of men with no family ties to the old upper class. In the society newly based on commerce and industry, wealth has largely replaced pedigree in determining social status.

In the traditional ideal of family life, the husband and father, in addition to being protector and provider for the household, is also its undisputed head. As such he retains ultimate control over all aspects of family life, although much of his authority is commonly delegated to the mother in routine matters. A man enjoys the freedom to come and go as he pleases and to spend his leisure time without accounting to his wife—a freedom that does not frown on his liberty to engage in extramarital liaisons, provided such affairs are carried on with discretion. By contrast, the ideal for wives, held in various degrees at all social levels, emphasizes dependence and submission. In this view, women are seen as properly limited in their activities and concerns to the household and kinship circle (see ch. 10, Social Values).

For upper and middle class families, kinship solidarity rests upon stable marriage. Formal weddings before church and civil authorities give rise to permanent parental responsibilities that can be neglected only at the risk of profound social disapproval. In addition, the complex of paternal and maternal responsibilities is generally viewed as outweighing the personal relationships between husband and wife. The emphasis of responsibility is on a man's legal wife and legitimate children, and public opinion views casually his obligation in the case of an unsanctified union. In the urban lower class and among the peasants, common-law marriage is almost as prevalent as formal matrimony. Attitudes toward such unions vary widely. In some rural communities a majority of common-law unions are fully as durable as legal marriages and are seen as entailing the same degree of responsibility. In the cities and in most parts of the countryside, however, common-law marriages are typically casual arrangements, and paternal desertion is commonplace.

The patriarchal ideal of family life has been subject to ever-increasing challenge, both by changing social conditions and by the emergence of feminist sentiment among many educated women of the middle and upper classes. Since the 1930s the Constitution and the civil law have provided for complete equality between the sexes in political and economic matters, and employment opportunities traditionally limited to men have been opened to women. As they have played a progressively more active role in national life, many women have come to reject their subordinate and dependent status in marriage. Despite the trend toward change, however, in 1970 probably a majority of all Venezuelans continued to accept the old ideal, and prevailing family patterns still bore the imprint of male supremacy. The civil law continued to recognize paternal dominance within the household and provided that the final right of decision in matters affecting the welfare of his family or minor children resided with the husband.

For most Venezuelans parenthood is a welcome role. Men see fatherhood as a fulfillment and evidence of masculinity, and women are taught from childhood to look on maternity as their most exalted role. The birth of a baby is therefore an occasion for rejoicing and the gathering of kinsmen. The typical domestic unit consists of a father and mother living in permanent, though not necessarily formal, union along with their unmarried and minor children. About 20 percent of all family groups have other kinsmen as regular members. Upper class families tend to be larger, including grandparents and more distant relatives, but few middle or lower class households have the space or resources to support an extended family.

CHAPTER 6

LIVING CONDITIONS

Income per capita during 1970 was the highest in Latin America, and living conditions were correspondingly favorable. The conditions under which people lived have changed remarkably since the beginning of the twentieth century, particularly since World War II. Directly and indirectly, the development of the petroleum industry created the wealth necessary for more people to be able to enjoy more of the amenities of life and for the government to be able to extend more services to them.

The urban sector of the population was the chief beneficiary of the expansion of services, but improvements in transportation and communication made possible improved distribution of goods and services to rural people. At the same time an effective rural environmental health program vastly improved health conditions in the countryside and made possible the opening up of new lands for agricultural exploitation.

New job opportunities in the petroleum industry, in other industries established with petroleum money, and in construction were largely responsible for a massive migration from country to town during the years after World War II, and this resulted in a population shift that profoundly affected living conditions. The population as a whole was growing at an unprecedented rate and, because an ever-increasing proportion of it was clustered in cities and towns, both the demand for, and the feasibility of supplying, medical, sanitary, and other services increased sharply. Educational facilities were closer at hand, and exposure to the complexities of urban life was itself an educational experience. This increase in education, informal as well as formal, was another factor that contributed substantially to the change in the way in which people lived. In addition, the migration from farm to factory spelled an end for the migrants to the traditional welfare arrangement in which the countryman looked to the estate owner for his protection. Although business and private voluntary groups assumed important protective responsibilities, a comprehensive institutional welfare system was increasingly needed, and in 1967 the country's first national retirement and survivor-benefit plan became effective.

The countryman transplanted to the city did not abandon the neat and conservative habits of dress characteristic of all Venezuelans, but his higher income and the greater variety of offerings enabled him to enlarge his wardrobe somewhat and to acquire manufactured cotton clothing instead of the yard goods for home fabrication that he had customarily purchased in the countryside. In the abundantly stocked urban markets he was able to buy a greater variety of imported foodstuffs as well as the unusually varied supply of domestically produced meats, fruits, and vegetables. His diet benefited accordingly.

The urban migration of so many people, coupled with the fast rise in population, had resulted in a critical housing shortage, and the countryman's urban home was more often than not a makeshift shack not much different from the one he had occupied in the countryside. The materials were somewhat better, however, and in a majority of instances there was electric lighting and access to a public supply of piped water. The rate of housing construction increased during the 1960s, but at the end of the decade it had yet to reach a point permitting much replacement of submarginal units.

In the city there was more leisure time than there had been on the farm, a circumstance that afforded the new arrival greater opportunities to enjoy recreational pursuits. In the countryside his recreational outlets had been informal and few in number. In the city he often became a fanatic over baseball, the country's favorite sport, risked a small sum weekly on the lottery, and was able more frequently to indulge his fondness for motion pictures. He could not join one of the many social clubs that were popular among men of more substantial means, but there was a nearby bar where he could meet with other men after work for a few glasses of beer and a game of dominoes.

DIET AND NUTRITION

Venezuelan nutritional habits vary with respect both to quantity and quality of the diet; the Pan American Health Organization reported in 1968 a marginal shortage of less than 5 percent in the average daily caloric intake. Statistics, however, are unreliable. One dietetic count by an international agency listed an increase in the average content of the diet from 2,310 to 2,552 calories daily between 1961 and the 1963–64 period. Another cited the same figures but attributed them to the years 1964 and 1968, respectively.

The 1963–64 dietary analysis listed an average daily consumption of seventy-one grams of protein and sixty grams of fats and oils. It was estimated that, for the population as a whole, about 70 percent of the calories in the diet were derived from carbohydrates, but that in the lowest income brackets the starchy element accounted for 80 percent or more of the intake. Over half of the protein came from vegetable sources, with beef and milk providing 30 percent and fish providing 8 percent of the animal proteins. Animal-derived fats did not contribute materially to the diet, and most of the fatty foods were relatively unsaturated.

Anemia is the principal dietary problem. According to a 1967 report of the National Institute of Nutrition, an estimated 40 percent of the population had some kind of anemia, most of it deriving from dietary deficiency. At all social levels iron deficiency was common in Caracas and in other urban centers. Protein deficiency was most acute in the countryside where a check of rural medical units found 65 percent of the children below the age of seven to be suffering from some kind of malnutrition or to be vulnerable to it. Protein deficiency was attributed to an insufficient intake of meat, eggs, and milk. The shortage resulted as much from lack of knowledge as from lack of money, and a particular point was made of the increasing preference of young children for carbonated beverages over milk, fruit, and fruit juices.

Starches and sugars are consumed in relatively large quantities. The traditionally favored staple of *yuca* (cassava) is being replaced by corn, wheat, rice, potatoes, soybean, and black bean (*caraotas*). A kind of unrefined sugar called *papelón* is the principal sweet.

Meat consumption, relatively low for the population as a whole, is subject to considerable regional variations. In all parts of the country beef is the preferred meat, although there is some lamb and goat consumption. Many farm and low income urban households keep a few pigs, but pigs tend to represent a store of wealth rather than a ready source of nourishment. Ham and turkey are status symbol foods.

Poultry is frequently kept in limited numbers by farmers and by city slumdwellers but primarily for egg production. Although farmers occasionally consume some of the eggs their hens produce, the eggs are more frequently sold because they bring a fairly high price. Egg production is sufficient to meet market demand.

The limited consumption of milk is attributed variously to high cost and lack of education at the consumer level in respect to its advantages. Whatever the cause, the annual consumption per capita declined from approximately 117 quarts to about 85 quarts between 1960 and 1970. About 70 percent is consumed in powdered and 30 percent in fresh form. Some 30 percent of the domestically produced milk is pasteurized, and 10 percent is converted into milk products. The substantial imports consist principally of whole, powdered milk.

Fish is an important part of the average diet, particularly along the coast, and is consumed in such quantity that the national annual per capita consumption is about twice that in the United States. Ocean fish are regarded as superior to freshwater varieties. A substantial production of fishmeal (6,167 tons in 1967) is supplemented by imports from Peru. Bacalau (dried codfish) is also an important element in fish consumption. It is dried locally from fish taken in the North Atlantic by Venezuelan trawlers.

Most tropical fruits grow readily, and temperate climate fruits, such as apples, peaches, and pears, grow fairly well. Consumption is moderately heavy; fruits account for about 14 percent of the calories in the diet. Species of the banana family are most popular, particularly among farm families, and the consumption of fruit juices is remarkably high. Consumption of vegetables is moderate; tomatoes are the most important vegetable crop, and onions are the second. Carrots, broccoli, lettuce, squash, and various legumes are also eaten regularly, but tomatoes and tomato products represent half of the total vegetable consumption.

The availability of foods is highly uneven by locality. Markets and processing facilities are found principally in urban localities, and rural transportation and storage facilities are poor. As a consequence, the farm population is often deprived of what should be a readily available varied food supply while the urban population has an excess. This imbalance is accentuated by socioeconomic conditions, particularly in the case of the subsistence farmer who practices little crop diversification. On the other hand, the climate is such that food crops are relatively easy to produce on a very small scale, and the poorest subsistence farmers enjoy some variety in foods. Better balanced and more varied diets are available in urban areas, even to lower income groups, and an important feature of the Venezuelan diet is the variety in menus made possible by the wide variety of fruits and vegetables produced.

For most people, the well-to-do as well as the working class, the day starts, early, breakfast being finished before 7:00 or 8:00 in the morning. The meal is light but tends to be more substantial than the continental breakfast of coffee and rolls customary in most Latin American countries. Rural workers may content themselves with a cup of coffee at sunup; the more affluent urban people frequently breakfast on eggs (a breakfast dish unusual in Latin America), and hot chocolate is often substituted for coffee. Luncheon is a leisurely meal with several courses; a substantial tea in the late afternoon may include sandwiches, meat cuts, eggs, and a variety of sweets. A heavy dinner, the day's principal meal, is served late in the evening. Mealtimes and menus vary with locality and with socioeconomic status. Families with limited incomes subsist largely on rice and beans, although their diet is varied and has more fruits and vegetables than in most Latin American countries. In rural areas a heavy dinner at sunset may be the only important meal of the day.

The most frequently encountered item on the menu for people of all classes is *arepa*, a flat corncake toasted on an earthen pan.

Stuffed with chicken, pork, eggs, olives, and capers and boiled while wrapped in a plantain leaf, it becomes *hallaca*, the national dish that is served primarily at Christmas. A thick soup of vegetables and beef or chicken called *sancocho* may serve as an entire meal; *mandongo* is a soup of tripe and vegetables; *hervido* is soup with chunks of meat, chicken, or fish boiled with vegetables and roots; and *chipi-chipi* is a clam soup. *Pabellón* is a dish of shredded meat, rice, beans, and friend plantain; *paticas de cochino*, a dish for the accustomed palate only, consists of pig's feet in a pepper sauce; and *cachapa* is a sweetened corncake wrapped around a white domestic cheese. Among the popular sweets is *huevos chimbos*, egg yolks boiled and bottled in sugar syrup.

Coffee is consumed in large quantities after meals, but except at breakfast it is customary to drink only water while eating. The Venezuelan coffee is considerably stronger than the North American beverage. Wine is seldom drunk, but there is a considerable market for beer and carbonated soft drinks. The Venezuelan beer has an alcoholic content as much as twice as high as that produced in North America, and it is cold-stabilized at much lower temperatures than in most other countries. Venezuelans are fond of their excellent and heady beer, and they like it very cold.

HOUSING

The housing deficit, an estimated 785,000 units in 1970, is probably the country's most serious socioeconomic problem. The rate of building construction was generally upward during the 1960s, particularly in public housing, and the total of 52,000 units built in 1969 was greater than that in any of the four preceding years. It was barely sufficient, however, to accommodate the year's growth in population without permitting replacement of substandard and dilapidated structures. The government estimated that 100,000 new units would be needed annually to allow for a reasonable rate of replacement.

In the late 1960s the Ministry of Health and Social Assistance, the Ministry of Public Works, the Labor Bank (Banco Obrero), the National Agrarian Institute (Instituto Agrario Nacional), and the Venezuelan Guyana Corporation (Corporación Venezolana de la Guayana), were all directly engaged in public housing programs. In addition, in 1969 some twenty-one savings and loan associations had 118,000 members and resources amounting to Bs421.7 million (4.5 bolivars equal US$1), managed through the National Savings and Loan Bank (Banco Nacional de Ahorro y Prestamo). During the decade ending in 1967, some 104,000 urban homes and apartments were constructed for the low-income population, and 70,000 units were built in the countryside. The rural units, replacements for substandard or dilapidated dwellings, were constructed with cement floors, concrete block walls, and asbestos roofing. Each had several bedrooms, living and dining areas, and a kitchen and bath. Running water and electricity were provided.

During this period, publicly financed homes constructed outnumbered the private ones by a substantial margin, although per-unit costs for the private construction were twice those in the public sector. The market for homes for high-income families—particularly in Caracas—was almost saturated, and insurance companies and other private interests had yet to participate extensively in ventures for middle and lower income families.

The single largest private program was that of Popular Housing (Vivienda Popular). A nonprofit corporation, it built and sold some 9,000 houses at prices listed in 1968 at between Bs7,000 and Bs40,000. Concerned over the slow pace of private-sector building activity in the face of a growing housing shortage, the government in mid-1969 brought into effect the first in a series of administrative measures taken to provide incentives to the private construction industry. They were taken in order to facilitate the administration's announced goal of 500,000 new homes during its five-year term of office. The initial measures provided exemption from income tax on certain rental incomes, profits from sales, and income from housing loans. In 1970 the Labor Bank was empowered to purchase certain low-cost housing units for 95 percent of the offered price if they had not been sold within two years after an occupancy permit had been issued.

In late 1970 an up-to-date count of the number and kind of dwelling units in the country would not become available until publication of the findings of the next population census, scheduled for 1971, and government agencies were still quoting data extracted from the census of 1961. At that time there were 1,472,000 units, of which 93.3 percent were occupied and 68.5 percent were occupied by their owners. Less than one-third of the unoccupied houses were on the market for sale or rental. Some 491,000 units were in rural localities (on farms and in settlements with fewer than 1,000 inhabitants).

Some 52.4 percent of all dwellings were separate units, 7.1 percent were apartments, and 7.1 percent were rented rooms or suites located in the dwellings of others. The remainder were listed as *ranchos* and similar structures. The *rancho* (also frequently named in the diminutive as the *ranchito*) is defined by the International Bank for Reconstruction and Development (IBRD, commonly called the World Bank) as a shelter below minimum requirements constructed by the occupant with makeshift materials.

A majority of the dwellings were small; 33 percent of the rural and 55.1 percent of the urban units had only one room used for sleeping purposes. The number of occupants averaged 5.5 per unit, occupancy being slightly higher in the country than in town. The rate of occupancy was 5.7 for houses, 5.3 for *ranchos*, 4.5 for apartments, and 3.2 for rented rooms.

Some 60.7 percent of the dwellings occupied in 1961 had electric light. For cooking 48.6 percent used kerosine, 34.7 percent used wood or charcoal, 14.5 percent used gas, and 2.2 percent used other fuels. About 29.9 percent of the units had refrigerators or iceboxes, 13.2 percent had mechanical washers, 6.9 percent had water heaters, and 30 percent had showers or other bathing facilities. About 46.7 percent had piped water, 14.7 percent used a public tap or trough, 14.2 percent drew their water from wells and streams, 9.3 percent used water carried by truck or other means of transportation, and 3 percent used other sources. According to a Pan American Health Organization survey, in 1967 some 88 percent of the urban and 50 percent of the rural, or 74 percent of the total, had access to a piped water system.

Some 27.4 percent of the units had flush toilets, 25 percent had septic tanks or other intermediate means of disposal, and 35 percent had open disposals or no facilities. According to a 1964 estimated, about 42.6 percent of the urban population lived in homes connected with sewer systems.

Earthen and cement materials predominated as building materials. In 1961, 65.2 percent of the floors were made of cement, 33.1 percent of earth, 1.2 percent of brick, and 0.5 percent of wood. In rural areas two-thirds of the floors were of dirt. In rural areas more than three-fourths of the walls were made of adobe or mud, and in the country as a whole earthen materials were used in 49.2 percent of the walls. Cement was used in 38.3 percent (the proportion including a small number made of brick). Wood was used in 4.4 percent, principally in fishing-village huts along the coastline and in alpine chalets high in the mountains; and 9.9 percent were made of scrap materials or palm fronds, cane, or grass. Some 17 percent of the roofs were of clay, oval ceramic tiles predominating. Various cement roofs (*platabondas*) represented 15 percent; 46.4 percent were of metal; 5.5 percent were made of asbestos roofing; and 16.7 percent were of palm fronds, grass, wood, and scrap materials.

During the 1960s the principal trend was toward the use of cement floors and walls and away from the traditional mud and thatch in walls and roofs. The newer homes in *rancho* settlements were fashioned out of concrete blocks with metal roofs. Some 70,000 cement houses were built under the agrarian reform program, and in early 1970 a private company commenced production of reinforced concrete sections for prefabricated houses at the rate of one unit each day and a production goal of 4,200 units annually.

Deficient or dilapidated housing is more frequently encountered in the country than in towns, but it is in urban localities in general and in Caracas in particular that the actual number of housing units is insufficient to meet the demand. The need for more housing has increased in tempo with the city's impetuous growth since the conclusion of World War II, fed by the constantly increasing flow of people from the countryside seeking better living conditions and better employment opportunities in the country's capital (see ch. 2, Physical Environment).

Caracas before World War II was a little city with winding streets and spacious parks. In the working class neighborhoods, solid rows of single-storied houses of adobe with red-tiled roofs faced abruptly on rutted streets, and the colonial houses of the well to do were quadrandular buildings of one or two stories built on spacious shady lots about patios, where there were flowering shrubs and fountains. After World War II much of old Caracas was flattened to make way for the current megalopolis of high-rise structures, superhighways, civic centers, and monuments.

A large part of the area previously devoted to residences was taken over for these purposes and, as the population continued to increase, the limited amount of usable land suitable for housing in the narrow rift valley where the city is located became occupied. By 1970 the supply of this land (defined as unused terrain with a slope of less than 40 percent and otherwise unimpaired) was virtually exhausted. Much of the older urban housing in Caracas and other cities that would ordinarily have become available to lower income groups as middle and upper income people moved to the suburbs had been destroyed. Moreover; municipal ordinances providing for maximum densities of occupancy, minimum sizes of plots, and minimum proportions of free space area practically excluded low-cost housing.

The natural result was a spate of apartment building. By 1961 nearly 72 percent of the country's apartment units were located in the Federal District, and between 1950 and 1966 apartment units increased from 12 to 40 percent of the units of housing in metropolitan Caracas. Apartment construction was at its peak under President Marcos Pérez Jiménez, but it has continued at a fast rate under subsequent administrations. Late in 1970 a government agency was reported engaged in constructing some 7,000 new units in connection with the redevelopment project for the center of the city.

Although land itself is free or almost free in rural areas and, as a consequence, there is little actual housing shortage, it is in these localities that most of the substandard housing is found. In 1961 about 70 percent of the deficient units—virtually all of them *ranchos*—were in the countryside. The manor houses of estate owners and the houses of managers of commercial farms are usually one-story structures built in the colonial pattern with corridors on all four sides to enclose a patio. Kitchen, pantry, and storerooms are in separate buildings, and single workers attached to the estate sleep in a bunkhouse. In rural towns the more affluent townspeople have simple colonial style houses with adobe walls and tiled roofs. Grilled windows and patios are customary, and electricity and running water are common. Families who operate a nearby farm usually live in an adobe *rancho* on the town's outskirts.

The most frequently encountered residential dwelling, both in country and in town, is the *rancho*. In the country it is the makeshift shelter of the subsistence farmer and the farmhand who is not provided housing by the employer. In the town it is the shack constructed by people newly arrived from the country. Second generation urban *rancho* dwellers are few but, although the *rancho* is the poorest of urban dwellings, it is fairly often occupied by skilled and white-collar workers unable to find another kind of home. *Rancho* residential settlements (*barrios*—see Glossary) are customarily found in the outskirts of the cities where land is cheap or where squatters are tolerated. The inner-city slums of North America find in Latin America their closest counterpart in the suburban slum *barrios*. Between 1950 and 1966 the Caracas *rancho* units, installed principally along the steeper slopes of the mountains fringing the city's metropolitan area, were estimated to have increased in number at an annual rate of about 13 percent.

Garbage and waste disposal facilities of any sort and inside piped water facilities are extremely rare, but many of the urban *ranchos* are equipped with electric light, and furnishings are usually of much better quality than the houses themselves. When improvements are made, they tend to take the form of adding another room rather than of painting or otherwise improving the existing property. In general, however, the *ranchos* tend to be somewhat larger than the corresponding slum dwellings in many other Latin American countries, and the considerable use of concrete blocks for walls and coated iron for roofing makes them somewhat more substantial in construction.

DRESS

The urban well to do are well dressed, the styles following a modified North American trend. Women continue to be influenced by European modes, however, and those with limited budgets prefer a few stylish garments to a greater number of less elegant costumes. Black is considered the most fashionable color among women, and subdued colors are usually selected for men's suits. Short-sleeved shirts are customary for office wear in tropical localities, but dark, lightweight suits are worn in the evening. Summer weights are worn during the day throughout the year in localities below 5,000 feet; at elevations above 3,000 feet, heavier clothing is usually worn in the evening.

The generally conservative preferences in wardrobe are reflected in the requirement in the better restaurants and motion picture theaters that coats and ties be worn and, except at sporting events, men seldom appear in public less formally dressed. Shorts are not worn. Hats are seldom worn by members of either sex. Styles in shoes are generally similar to those of North Americans, but lasts are usually somewhat wider.

For the unskilled workers and their families, money considerations severely restrict the choice of wardrobe. The typical costume consists of cheap cotton manufactured apparel, frequently khaki. Men usually wear trousers and open-necked shirts, and women wear print dresses or blouses and skirts. Few can afford more than one or two changes of dress, but women in particular almost always have at least one set of good clothing. The display aspect is important to women, and for the roughest household tasks the housewife prefers wearing her oldest dress to wearing an apron. Clothes of both sexes are neat and seldom patched, and there is considerable aversion to secondhand garments. The smallest children in slum settlements are permitted to run about virtually naked during the week, but on weekends they are carefully dressed in holiday garb. Class distinction in the clothing of older children is minimized by the fact that the wearing of simple uniforms in school is customary.

The costume of the countryman consists of light clothing bought readymade or sewn from manufactured goods. Men usually wear cotton shirts and trousers, the latter often cut off below the knee, and women wear cotton shifts or blouses and skirts. Because a great part of the working day is spent outdoors, men wear broad-brimmed hats usually made of straw. The most popular footwear is the *alpargato*, a cheap fiber sandal. Leather shoes are relatively expensive and for this reason are worn only by the relatively well-to-do. Men wear shoes more often than women, but both sexes frequently go barefoot.

Dress in country towns and villages is only slightly more formal than in the countryside. A majority of the people wear informal cotton clothing, which is usually somewhat more stylish and of better quality than that of the peasant but generally similar to it. Even the leading figure in a small rural town may be seen in the streets without jacket or tie. Shoes are customarily worn by children as well as adults, however, and the average person has one or two more formal costumes for attending church, motion pictures, or important social occasions.

In the countryside and in the small towns, particularly in mountain localities, traditional costumes are still sometimes seen. At high altitudes both men and women wear the *ruana*, a short poncho, and a broad-brimmed sombrero of black felt, which women decorate with flowers and ribbons. In the lowlands the traditional costume for men is the *liquiliqui*, a suit of white cloth consisting of trousers and a large shirt fastened with gold or leather buttons. It may be worn with a wide sash. The traditional female costume is the *joropera*, a full skirt of brightly colored cotton or other material worn with the *cota*, an embroidered white blouse worn very loosely in order to leave the shoulders bare.

PATTERNS OF LIVING AND LEISURE

Holidays and Business Hours

The law requires that urban employers grant nine holidays to their personnel. These are January 1 (New Year), April 19 (Declaration of Independence and Day of the Indian), May 1 (Labor Day), July 5 (Independence Day), July 24 (Birthday of Bolívar), October 12 (Columbus Day), December 25 (Christmas), and the movable dates of Holy Thursday and Good Friday. Other official and traditional holidays sometimes observed include January 6 (Epiphany), March 19 (Saint Joseph's Day), June 24 (Army Day and Anniversary of the Battle of Carabobo), August 15 (Assumption), November 1 (All Saints' Day), December 8 (Immaculate Conception), December 17 (Death of Bolívar), December 31 (one-half day on New Year's Eve), and the movable dates of Ash Wednesday (one-half day), Holy Saturday, Ascension, and Corpus Christi. Local holidays are observed on March 10 in La Guaira and on October 24 and November 18 in Maracaibo. The two days of Carnival in March (Monday and Tuesday before Ash Wednesday) have been declared working days, but guidebooks for businessmen traveling to Venezuela from abroad caution them against visiting during Carnival or Holy Week.

The law requires that employers grant most of the regularly employed personnel vacations of fifteen working days a year. Vacations are most frequently taken during the months of August and September.

Business firms are customarily open from 8:00 A.M. to noon and from 2:00 to 6:00 P.M. Stores remain open until 9:00 P.M., and drugstores maintain a rotating system of taking turns in remaining open all night for emergency purchases. Banking hours are from 8:30 to 11:30 A.M. and from 2:00 to 4:30 P.M. Monday through Friday. Saturday is not an official day of rest, but most firms and offices close at noon or do not open on Saturday.

Recreation

Probably the most popular recreational outlet for the average Venezuelan is watching a baseball game. Baseball is the national sport, and every town of fair size boasts its own stadium. There are numerous amateur and professional leagues; the professional season commences in October—after the close of the season in the United States—and lasts through mid-February. Venezuelan teams participate internationally in the Caribbean Baseball Federation championship series with teams from Puerto Rico, the Dominican Republic, Panama, and—formerly—from Cuba. The series was renewed in 1970 after having been suspended in 1963 for economic reasons. The professional teams often use players from the United States and have contributed many star players to the major leagues.

Soccer, the other national sport, has passionate devotees, and there are professional as well as amateur leagues and teams scattered about the country. Venezuela, however, has developed few players of international caliber, and the top teams draw heavily on Brazil and other Latin American countries to fill their rosters. Professional boxing is very popular, and wrestling matches, basketball and volleyball games, and auto and bicycle races are well attended. Caracas has indoor ice skating facilities, and in 1970 an international bowling tournament was held in Puerto Cabello.

Games of various kinds are favored diversions, particularly among the upper classes. Card playing is popular among women as well as men. Dominoes are played frequently at men's clubs, pool tables are standard equipment in neighborhood bars, and there is a Venezuelan Chess Federation. The devotion of at least a part of the population to chess is attested to by the proposal presented at a recent convention of the federation that the government be urged to make chess a required subject of study in the public schools.

Along the Caribbean coast there is sailing, swimming, water skiing, skindiving, and deep sea fishing. An annual marlin tournament is gaining an international reputation. There is also good river and lake fishing for such species as rainbow and brook trout, striped catfish, and *dorada* (South American salmon). For hunters, numerous species of large and small game are also at hand.

From ten to twelve bullfights are held annually in the Nuevo Circo ring in Caracas, most of the fighters and bulls coming from abroad. The Corrida de Prensa Deportiva (Bullfight of the Sports Press) takes place regularly in January, but there is no regular bullfight season, and most of the events are scheduled in connection with fairs and festivals. Bullfights also take place regularly in Maracay, Valencia, and San Cristóbal and may be scheduled elsewhere. The spectacles are very expensive, even the sun seats in Caracas costing Bs50. For those who like spectator sports violent but are of limited means, cockfights under strict government supervision are legal. Cockfight pits are found in many working class residential neighborhoods.

Horseraces are held in several cities. The Rinconada track in Caracas seats 30,000 and is one of the most beautiful tracks in the world. It is filled regularly, and in 1970 the federal agency that operates the track was planning to build a comparable installation in the industrial city of Valencia. Races are held Saturdays and Sundays throughout the year, and hundreds of thousands who do not visit the track watch regularly on popular television presentations. Wagers are sometimes high, and government-controlled off-track betting is permitted at hundreds of offices scattered about the city. Betting on the ponies is so widespread a practice that the phrase *cinco y seis* (five and six)—a popular type of bet similar to the daily double—has become imbedded in Venezuelan Spanish as meaning any long-odds possibility.

The other major form of gambling is the lottery, which is also under government control. In 1967 lotteries in the Federal District and in seven states held 1,810 drawings, and tickets costing about Bs236 million were sold. Bingo is also played regularly in working class neighborhoods.

Cultural entertainment is centered in Caracas, although touring musical groups and theater companies visit other cities. The Venezuelan Symphony Orchestra, which receives a substantial government subsidy, holds an annual concert series; programs are also offered by several chamber music groups, the Venezuela Concert Association, and choral societies. Opera and ballet are provided by touring foreign companies. There is relatively little legitimate theater, although dramas, comedies, and musical comedies are offered by one repertory theater, the drama section of the Central University, and visiting groups. Plays in English are presented at the Caracas Theater Club.

For the great majority of the people, motion pictures represent the most important form of recreation outside the home. In 1967 about five paid attendances per person were reported. United States and European films with titles in Spanish predominate, and the government classifies all films for acceptability with ratings ranging from "A" for children to "C" for adults only. Radio and television also provide recreational outlets for many. It was estimated in 1970 that nearly 80 percent of the homes in the country had radios and 45 percent had television sets; 80 percent of the population lived within range of at least one television signal (see ch. 14, Public Information).

Casual visiting and entertaining in urban homes are rare and, when practiced, are restricted to relatives and close friends of many years' standing. Visits to houses of relatives and close friends and attendance at their weddings, funerals, baptisms, and birthday parties provide the entire range of joint participation for many families. Heads of families differentiate sharply between the social life and diversions they share with their families and those that are solely their own. The occasional shared diversions are sought most commonly in Sunday outings, in attendance at motion pictures and sporting events, and in religious fetes.

Club membership is widespread among prosperous families, but the club is primarily a male retreat where men can gather to drink, gamble, and converse with friends. On Sundays, however, clubs with such facilities as swimming pools and picnic grounds serve as a locale for family outings. Balls and other periodic functions held in them also furnish occasion for a sharing of recreation by husbands and wives. Club membership is beyond the means of working class men, but for them a bar or cafe provides the corresponding place for recreation outside the home.

Although on a scale usually more limited than that of their husbands, well-to-do wives lead active social lives of their own, largely in connection with women's clubs of various kinds. They also find much of their diversion in informal gatherings with friends, most frequently at afternoon teas and card parties. Working class women have little time or money for explicit social and recreational activity but find diversion in marketing and other tasks that take them out of their homes.

A kind of recreation enjoyed both in urban and in rural localities—but which is of greatest importance in the market towns—is the celebration of festival days or fiestas. In Caracas the principal fiesta is Carnival, a time when business comes to a near halt and there are dances, street celebrations, games, and races. Localities have their particular festive day or days. New Year's, for example, is a national holiday, but it is observed with greatest enthusiasm in the state of Falcón, where fireworks are set off and there are various street celebrations. Local saints' days and other religious holidays are observed in the various towns with religious processions, dances, and games. A typical instance is the Day of San Benito, celebrated on December 29 in several towns of the state of Zulia. Merrymaking begins two days ahead of time when bright decorations are festooned in the streets. Festivities are under the direction of a corps of *chimbángueles* (vassals of the saint) who, after an early mass on the saint's day, place his image on a litter and dance with it through the streets to the beat of drums. Others join in the dance, and from time to time participants refresh the saint—and themselves—with local liquors.

Rural families, who have little or no regular access to commercial entertainment and other organized pastimes, find diversion largely in conjunction with their work and in the informal social life of the neighborhood. In many parts of the country, collective work sessions provide an occasion for social diversion. Some rural communities have the custom of requiring male residents to contribute work on public projects (*convite*), and groups of friends sometimes harvest one another's fields cooperatively (*a mano vuelto*). Gatherings of this kind have a festive atmosphere and are also attended by families of the workmen. The beneficiary is expected to contribute food and drink, which are prepared and served by the wives. The working day frequently ends with a fiesta, which may continue well into the night.

For most rural Venezuelans the year is climaxed on the day of the patronal saint of the neighborhood, when elaborate festivals are sponsored by lay religious societies (*cofradías*), merchants, or other prominent local individuals. All families living within the trading area of a town usually attend, and the visit is the occasion for taking part in the masses and processions, attendance at cockfights and other special events, visits with friends, and a visit by husbands and older sons to a drinking establishment.

In the larger settlements the local general store (*pulpería*) provides a center for male social life. Men from the settlement and nearby parts of the countryside congregate in them, particularly on Sundays, to drink beer and country liquors and sometimes to play *bolas criollas*, a form of lawn bowling. When men are gathered socially, the occasional woman or child who wishes to make a purchase may enter timidly and retire quickly from the scene of festivity.

Expenditure Patterns

Urban markets are abundantly filled with imported products as well as the varied products of agriculture and the fast-diversifying manufacturing industry. As a consequence, both the standard and cost of living are high. It is more expensive to live in Caracas than in any other city on the continent.

Although the diet of lower income groups, including that of the poorer paid elements in the middle class, consists principally of the cheaper commodities, food accounts for a minimum of half of their monthly earnings. At all levels of income, housing and clothing are substantial expenditure items. Most people own their own houses, but rentals are high; even in the urban slum areas some of the newer cement block houses are built specifically for rental, and the cost of renting one of the older *ranchos* for a year may exceed its sale price. Because of the unusual importance of the presentation or display aspect in the attitudes toward dress, the proportion spent on clothing is probably higher than in most Latin American countries.

Consumption patterns in the countryside are different from those in the city. With limited cash and little surplus from crops, the small farmer is not an active consumer. Homegrown food is rarely supplemented by market purchases, and living quarters are built by the owner from cost-free materials. Cash expenditures are largely for such items as salt, kerosine, cookware, clothing or yard goods, and whatever modest diversions the budget may allow. The farm laborer and his family are more dependent on the cash economy, but a garden plot and a few animals are usually kept; housing is often provided by the employer as a part of the wage or for nominal rental. The lowest agricultural daily wage under collective contract during 1969—about Bs7 for men and less for women—was far under the minimum in urban commerce and industry and insufficient for much purchasing of any kind (see ch. 19, Labor). In a good year the immediate consumption needs of farmpeople may be met, but they seldom have money left for savings or improvements; attachment to the land and to the agricultural way of life is frequently not strong enough to overcome the lure of an easier existence in urban areas.

Many migrate to the cities and, once arrived, are quick to change their consumption patterns. Livestock (*cria*) are still often raised for consumption, but the few chickens or pigs are expensive to maintain and are slaughtered for food only occasionally. This marginal livestock raising is an expressive activity undertaken in remembrance of life on the farm rather than a project of major economic importance. Clothes are purchased in the store rather than made at home. The wattle-and-daub or scrap materials employed in building of the rural and the older urban working class homes are giving way to commercial materials. The traditional custom of building one's own house or drawing on the help of neighbors has become regarded as countrified, and even the poorer homeowners employ carpenters and masons with increasing frequency.

At all levels of the country's newly urbanized society, people participate fully in the cash economy. This participation has resulted first from the new jobs and relatively high wages available in the petroleum and petrochemical industries and second from other industrial and commercial jobs created with petroleum wealth. In 1970 even the unemployed and underemployed had learned to copy, to the extent possible, the expenditure habits of those with steadier and more substantial incomes.

HEALTH AND SANITATION

Organization of the Health Program

Primary responsibility for the health of the country rests with the Directorate of Public Health of the Ministry of Health and Social Assistance, which directly administers facilities containing more than half of the country's hospital beds. Hospitals and outpatient facilities are also maintained by the Ministry of Defense, the state governments, the social security system, mutual benefit and charitable organizations, the petroleum and iron-mining companies, and private institutions.

At the national level, the Directorate of Public Health is divided into various divisions with responsibilities for such concerns as adult health, maternal and child health, environmental sanitation, and hospital and outpatient facilities.

Within the states there are varying numbers of health districts in which services are provided in ascending sequence through rural health posts, rural dispensaries, health centers, and hospitals. The health posts are staffed by auxiliary personnel with six months training in first aid, diagnostics, and health education. They carry out immunization programs, conduct sanitary inspections, provide limited advisory and curative services and, when necessary, refer patients to dispensaries. The rural dispensaries, more than 460 in number as reported in 1968, are staffed by one or two visiting doctors and by auxiliary personnel. They provide preventive and ambulatory curative service to a population ideally of about 2,000 and are associated directly with health centers or hospitals. The health center is in effect a small hospital with a director, resident medical officers, graduate and auxiliary nurses, laboratory technicians, and a sanitary inspector.

Health Hazards and Preventive Medicine

The Venezuelan delegation in 1970 to the Eighteenth Panamerican Sanitary Conference reported that the country's principal causes of death—other than those occurring in early infancy—were cancer, heart disease, and accidents. These were causes typical of an urbanized and advanced society. The endemic ailments, such as malaria and tuberculosis, that had taken the heaviest toll one or two generations earlier had been more characteristic of a primarily rural country in an early stage of development.

The shift in focus was accompanied by a substantial overall improvement in health statistics. Between 1941 and 1969 average life expectancy at birth increased from forty-one to sixty-six years (although the 1961 census had shown expectancy for city dwellers to be nearly seven years greater than that for countrypeople), and between the 1951—53 period and 1966 the maternal mortality rate was down by 32.8 percent to 1.2 per 1,000 of the population. Between 1960 and 1969 the general mortality rate decreased from 7.2 to 6.4 per 1,000—one of the lowest in the world—and the rate of infant mortality from 55.2 to 41.5 per 1,000 of the population.

The improvement reflects the success of the national health program in effect since the late 1930s. Its first phase placed emphasis on the eradication or control of widespread tropical diseases, such as malaria. The second, beginning in 1959, but particular emphasis on preventive medicine and environmental health and was directed primarily at those diseases that could be checked readily with direct and specific measures.

Among the 61,281 deaths reported by the World Health Organization for 1964, the largest number (6,386) were caused by birth injuries and diseases of early infancy. The other major causes were cancer (4,621), gastroenteritis and related ailments (4,028), accidents (3,878), heart disease (3,779), and pneumonia (2,251). Significant causes of death reduced by more than 50 percent by rate of incidence between the 1941—45 average and 1970 included gastroenteritis, tuberculosis, syphilis, typhoid and paratyphoid, malaria, all forms of meningitis, tetanus, whooping cough, dysenteries, and bronchitis.

By ages, the highest death rate continues to be among young children, close to half of all deaths occurring among those under the age of five years. Although childhood diseases, such as whooping cough and measles, are prevalent, the principal causes of death in this age group are directly related to environmental and health practices, particularly in rural areas where infant mortality rates are as much as four times as high as those in Caracas. The overall shortage of country doctors, difficult communications, and an often-negative attitude toward modern medicine result in many unattended rural deliveries.

Few precautions relating to diet or cleanliness are taken to ensure good infant health. Customarily, the child is put on solid foods relatively soon after birth. Moreover, unsanitary conditions in the home, an unbalanced diet that does not include much milk after weaning, and the use of contaminated water produce further negative effects. Because of these conditions, diarrhea is the principal pediatric problem, and gastroenteritis is the chief cause of infant mortality. The incidence of malnutrition and respiratory ailments among young children remains high, particularly in rural localities.

At the time of the 1961 census, accidents—primarily those involving automobiles—were the principal cause of death among those in the five to forty-four age group; cancer and heart ailments were primary causes among older people. The faster tempo of life accompanying urbanization and industrialization has probably contributed to a real increase in the incidence of heart ailments, but better medical attention has resulted in a more complete recorded incidence of both coronary ailments and malignancies.

Government campaigns for the prevention, elimination, and control of major epidemic and endemic diseases have met with outstanding success. Venezuela was the first country in South America to have systematically attacked malaria, and a nationwide DDT-spraying campaign, begun in the mid-1940s, has created the largest malaria-free tropical area on the continent. At the end of 1969 the campaign was being continued under the direction of the Malariological and Sanitation Institute of the Ministry of Health and Social Assistance, and the disease was considered eradicated in an area of about 240,000 square miles, or 77 percent of the area in which it had originally been present. It remained only in the sparsely populated southwest of the Guiana Highlands, and no deaths have been reported since 1962.

A similar intensive campaign against smallpox, begun on a national scale in 1952, has brought about complete disappearance of the disease, and no cases have been reported since 1962. More than 40 percent of the population was vaccinated between 1965 and 1967, however, and to prevent introduction from outside sources, vaccination certificates are required at all ports of entry.

Yellow fever of the jungle variety still occurs among the population not yet inoculated, the greatest prevalence occurring in the far east and west and deep in the southwest. During the 1950–65 period some twenty-five of the eighty-nine yellow fever deaths reported were in the state of Bolívar. A campaign aimed at its eradication was commenced in 1948, and by 1968 the disease had been eradicated in 723 of the 825 localities in which it had originally been found prevalent. The campaign, which included vaccination and spraying to eradicate the *aëdis aegpypti* mosquito, was concentrated in the state of Táchira, which had suffered a consistently high rate of incidence, but a nationwide campaign was planned for the 1970s. There were 30 scattered cases from 1960 through 1966, but none were reported in 1967 and 1968. In 1965 and 1966 there was an outbreak of dengue fever, which was first noticed early in the 1960s. At the end of 1969 about 2,000 cases had been reported in the state of Zulia, the core area of its incidence.

Directly identifiable with the rural population is Chagas' disease, carried by a beetle attached to the straw thatch roofing of country houses. An estimated 20 percent of the countrypeople have the disease, which sometimes affects the heart. The control program—which includes efforts to replace the thatch roofs—by 1969 had eliminated Chagas' disease in the high-density population areas of the northern part of the country with a population of about 6 million. Venezuela was the first country in the world to undertake a campaign against the disease on a nationwide basis.

Poliomyelitis is believed to have been brought to the country by foreigners and has been most serious in Caracas and Maracaibo. A massive vaccination program (more than 3.5 million immunizations in 1965) resulted in the reduction of the incidence of this disease from 10 per 1,000 in 1960 to less than 1 per 1,000 by 1967.

Yaws and the plague have been brought under control. By the early 1960s some 80 percent of the population exposed to yaws, which occurs primarily in the north, had been inoculated. With the assistance of the Pan American Health Organization, authorities have been able to eliminate plague, which has not been reported since the occurrence of a lone case in 1962. Hepatitis, once common, has been held in check by gamma globulin injections. A fair degree of control has been maintained over tetanus by means of an immunization program, which eliminated all but 9.9 reported cases and 5.3 deaths per 100,000 of the population during 1965. A majority of the cases reported were among infants, and nearly all of the remainder were among persons over the age of forty-five. Schistosomiasis (liver flukes) is prevalent in the Federal District and in the states of Carabobo, Aragua, and Miranda, where the snail vectors are plentiful. A program for control of the disease has been particularly successful in reducing the number of serious cases. All available means of control are used, with particular emphasis on the systematic application of moluscicides.

A program for leprosy control, begun in 1956, takes the form of inoculations and surveillance of infected persons to prevent spread of the ailment. Formerly endemic in rural areas, particularly in the southwest, it has been spread to cities by the urban migrations of people. In the late 1960s its incidence was about 1 per 1,000 persons, 92 percent of the known cases being under surveillance and 90 percent ambulatory. Some 664 new cases were reported in 1968.

Once a principal cause of mortality, respiratory diseases have been substantially reduced since World War II. Although tuberculosis remains a serious hazard for persons between the ages of fifteen and fifty-five, a vaccination campaign was instrumental in so reducing mortality that the death rate in the 1966—70 periods was estimated at only about 15 percent of that in the 1941—45 period. In 1968, however, it was estimated that 6,000 persons a year were contracting tuberculosis, and 90,000 were suffering from it. Pneumonia, bronchitis, and influenza are most serious in the cold mountain regions.

Endemic diseases associated directly with environment and personal hygiene, principally enteric and parasitic infections, are particularly high in urban slums and in rural localities. Gastroenteritis, one of the three principal causes of mortality, is associated with those areas in which malnutrition and poor sanitation are most prevalent. After the common cold, internal parasites are the most common cause of consultation in rural health centers.

The more than 5 million vaccinations administered in 1969 as protection against eight communicable diseases represented a continuation of an effective immunization program that had been carried out throughout the 1960s. Public health authorities, however, regarded preventive and curative medicine as having played a less significant role than environmental health work in improving overall health conditions. Elimination of insect vectors, the filling of disease-breeding ponds of occasional water, and the provision of clean drinking water had an effect that it is hard to overemphasize. At the end of World War II the endemic mortality rate among children in some tropical parts of the country was as high as forty times that in developed countries, but by 1970 the once-extreme differential had been virtually eliminated. The change was accomplished at considerable cost. During the late 1960s an environmental health program in a district of the state of Monagas was reported costing an estimated Bs670 per capita annually, the equivalent of a fourth or more of the area's per capita annual income.

Medical Facilities

During the 1960s an active hospital construction program was not sufficient to keep pace with the population growth, the number of hospital beds for each 10,000 population having declined slightly from 36 in 1960 to 33 in 1969, when there were 32,683 beds in 333 hospitals. About 87 percent of the beds were in government-operated institutions. Government hospitals with a total of about 2,000 beds were to be completed in 1970, and in 1970 the Venezuelan Institute of Social Security (Instituto Venezolano de Seguridad Social—IVSS) announced a project for construction of hospitals in six large- and medium-sized cities. Scheduled for completion in 1974, the new units were to have 2,200 beds.

More detailed data available for 1966 show that few hospitals had more than 500 beds and that small units predominated. Most of the larger institutions were government-operated general hospitals, and most of the small hospitals were private or operated for special purposes. Some 19,377 of the 28,678 beds were for general use; 4,317 were for mental cases; 2,983 were for tuberculosis; and the remaining 2,001 were devoted—in order of number of beds—to maternity cases, pediatrics, care in rural facilities, care of the aged, chronic diseases, orthopedics, and cancer. The hospital construction program of the Ministry of Public Works for the 1970—71 period reflected a trend away from the specialized facility. All of the thirty-five new facilities under construction or planned were to be general hospitals, and it was reported that some psychiatric and other special hospitals were to be converted to general use. Special cases would be treated in units of the general facilities.

Hospitals are concentrated in the major urban centers, and shortages in beds are most serious in the eastern coastal region. Government plans during the 1960s gave high priority to hospital construction in rural areas, but in 1966 there were 6.2 beds per 10,000 available in metropolitan Caracas and 2.6 per 10,000 in the remainder of the country.

In 1963 there were about 177,000 hospital releases reported, including more than 75,000 maternity cases. Accidents were second in importance with some 14,000 releases.

Supplementing the hospitals are rural dispensaries, health centers, and other public and private outpatient facilities. These, together with outpatient clinics in hospitals, reported 8.5 million consultations with 3.5 million patients in 1964. In addition, in 1964 some ninety-four public health laboratories performed 1.7 million examinations of various kinds. Serological examinations were the most numerous, followed in order by parasitological, hematological, bacteriological, and other examinations.

The IVSS increased the number of beds operated under its direction from 2,280 in 1967 to 4,162 in 1969. About 3,000 of the beds in 1969 were administered directly, and the balance were maintained under contract in private hospitals and clinics. More than 76,000 admissions during the year represented a bed-occupancy rate of close to 100 percent. The IVSS also maintained forty-four outpatient facilities where 5.8 million consultations were reported.

The cost of hospital and outpatient care at social security facilities is met from payments made to the social security fund. Costs of treatment at public health hospitals are charged to the patient whenever possible, but indigents are treated without cost. There are various payment systems at mutual benefit, charity, and commercial private hospitals, the commercial institutions charging the highest fees. Services are free at public health outpatient units, although there is a nominal charge for medicines. Persons who are not beneficiaries may obtain care at social security outpatient facilities by payment of a small charge.

Overcrowding, particularly in the government hospitals, is a widespread problem, and the deficit in beds is estimated at more than 10,000. Newspapers frequently reported instances in which hospital beds are shared, ambulatory patients sleep in shifts, or makeshift beds are brought into use. In some hospitals there is a shortage of surgical equipment, bioanalysis and other laboratory facilities, and X-ray equipment. Doctors are generally agreed to be of first quality, but other hospital personnel are often poorly trained and in short supply. In particular, hospital administration tends to be faulty. In Venezuela, as in many other Latin American countries, administrators are often doctors or other personnel with little specific training in hospital administration. As a consequence, the flow of medicine and medical supplies to the wards is haphazard at best, and the limited funds available for hospital operation are poorly budgeted. Hospitals reportedly often fail to keep a satisfactory tally of operating costs, suddenly find themselves without funds, and turn to the Ministry of Health and Social Assistance for help on an emergency basis.

Medical Personnel

The 9,114 physicians in the country in 1969 represented about 9 for each 10,000 in the population as compared with 5,045, or 7 per

10,000 in 1960. In the mid-1960s the medical schools were producing about 400 new doctors annually. Most of the specialists and a high proportion of all members of the profession practiced in Caracas and other major urban centers. The proportion of doctors to the population as a whole was nearly four times as great in Caracas as in the remainder of the country. The ratio of doctors to the population outside the large cities, however, was more favorable than in any South American country other than Argentina.

Physicians are trained at six of the country's universities in a six-year course leading to the doctor-surgeon degree equivalent to the North American degree of Doctor of Medicine. The graduate degree of Doctor of Medicine is awarded with the acceptance of a thesis, and specialized courses at the graduate level are offered at the School of Public Health of the Central University under sponsorship of the Ministry of Health and Social Assistance. Most of the graduate work, however, is undertaken in Europe or North America.

Together with law and engineering, medicine has traditionally been the most popular of university studies. Proportionately, the medical enrollment has declined somewhat since World War II but remains very high on the list of preferences (see ch. 7, Education). The profession enjoys a high status; the Venezuelan Medical Federation (Federación Médica Venezolana), which represents its interests, is a prestige organization, and doctors have been among the most prosperous of the professional groups. Doctors often work long hours, however, and even in Caracas, with its relatively abundant supply of medical personnel, some carry an extremely heavy workload. In 1967 doctors at five social security medical centers in Caracas were reported able to devote an average of less than two minutes to consultation with each patient.

In 1966 there were 1,779 dentists, or about 2 for each 10,000 in the population, as compared with 1,140, or about 1.6 per 10,000 in 1960. Dentists are trained in five-year courses offered at the Central University, the University of the Andes, and the University of Zulia, which also offers training for dental auxiliaries. Like physicians, dentists are concentrated in Caracas and other large cities. During the late 1960s the universities were graduating about 125 new dentists annually, a number sufficient to improve the ratio between the number of dentists and the size of the population but probably insufficient to meet the country's needs. In 1967 a Caracas newspaper estimated that about 5,000 additional dentists were needed.

In 1966 there were 4,342 graduate nurses, or about 4.9 for each 10,000 in the population, as compared with 3,113, or 4.4 per 10,000 in 1960. In 1966 the small corps of graduate nurses was supplemented by 12,754 auxiliaries, a ratio of about 14.1 per 10,000 persons. Although a few nursing specialties are taught in schools at the university level, the regular professional nurses are trained in four-year courses at the secondary level at the National School of Nursing in Caracas and at centers operated in Maracaibo and seven other localities by the Ministry of Health and Social Assistance, the Venezuelan Red Cross, and other private entities. In the late 1960s about 400 of these nurses were reported graduating annually. Auxiliary nurses are trained in courses of one year or less in schools operated by the ministry.

The inadequate number of nurses is attributed to the fact that, unlike doctors and dentists, they are unorganized and have not attained recognition as professionals. They are frequently called upon to perform tasks unrelated to their profession and, because hospitals frequently have limited operating funds, graduate nurses are reportedly often employed and paid as auxiliaries. In addition, a traditional reliance on midwives has retarded the growth of the profession.

In 1963 there were 1,450 pharmacists, 587 laboratory technicians, 500 X-ray technicians, 50 sanitary engineers, and 327 sanitary inspectors.

Folk Practitioners and Practices

Of considerable significance as recently as the end of World War II, folk medicine had largely fallen into disuse by 1970. The decline was in part attributable to increased availability of modern medical personnel and facilities, environmental health campaigns, improved nutrition, better transport and communication systems, and the spread of education. Folk attitudes and practices, however, had been characteristic primarily of the rural sector, and their decline accompanied the shift in the population balance from country to town.

Traditional attitudes involve the failure to recognize the need for personal hygiene and the avoidance of contaminated water and food and the association of illness with supernatural influences, weather conditions, and excessive bathing and sweating. Folk health measures are most often employed in the home, are limited to the curative phase of treatment, and customarily involve use of herbal preparations sometimes administered with incantations.

Of the folk medical practitioners, the most familiar is the *comadrona*, or midwife, who is usually consulted in areas with limited access to modern medical facilities. To rural women, she is a familiar figure, more readily to be trusted than a male medical doctor. At one time, efforts were made to dispense with the *comadronas*, whose rudimentary practices may have been closely related to high maternal mortality rates in rural areas. Their services supplement those of the few physicians available, however, and their control and education, rather than their elimination, has become the prevailing policy. *Curanderos*, or healers, who make use of herbal remedies and sometimes of patient medicines and who charge small fees for their services, have tended to lose popularity as other facilities have become available. Countrypeople are reluctant to admit using them, but some *curanderos* are believed still to engage in a limited clandestine practice.

With the introduction of modern medical services, rural people have taken advantage of them, but this acceptance has tended to be superficial. Penicillin has readily been accepted as a means of treating an infection much as an herbal remedy or an incantation might have been accepted in the past. The understanding of modern medical and sanitary principles is less promptly being achieved.

WELFARE

The country's public welfare program is directed by the Venezuelan Social Security Institute (Instituto Venezolano de Seguridad Social—IVSS) under a 1966 law that became effective on January 1, 1967. The 1966 legislation for the first time introduced a system of old age and survivors pensions and increased the benefits that previously had been limited to medical care in cases of illness, accident, occupational disease, and maternity.

Coverage was made general and mandatory for wage earners. Previously covered were domestics, temporary employees, those engaged in cottage industries, agricultural workers, relatives of the employer, and government workers not covered by collective contracts. Not covered under the new law were those employed at home whose working conditions were not similar to those of regular workers, temporary workers employed ten or fewer days a month by the same employer, and those performing occasional work unrelated to the business of the employer. Government workers were placed under a system of partial coverage in which they did not receive free medical care or compensation but paid correspondingly lower insurance premiums pending extension of full coverage by decree.

In 1966, under the old social security program, 439,000 persons had coverage for maternity and sickness, and 454,000, for work accidents and occupational diseases. All beneficiaries were enrolled in the new program in 1967, and coverage has since gradually been expanded by executive decision to include workers in additional regions of the country and in additional occupations. Government workers in all parts of the country, however, were at once placed under coverage for the retirement benefits. At the end of 1967 some 641,000 persons were enrolled in the program. The number increased to 693,000 in 1968 and to 772,000 in 1969. In 1969 some 2,201,000 wage earners and their dependents were protected by the program, and 76,400 business enterprises were participating in it.

The IVSS charged contributions of Bs752.6 million from employers and workers and collected Bs607.1 million, about 81 percent of the total. It also received Bs43.5 million in budgeted funds—about half of its appropriation—and Bs26.6 million in income from investments. It reported expenditures of Bs532.1 million, of which about 62 percent was for medical care and compensation.

Premiums are payable at a flat rate of 4 percent of basic wages up to a maximum of Bs3,000 for private sector workers and from 7 to 9 percent for all employers, the amount of the contribution varying with the degree of hazardousness of the occupation. For government workers the charge is 2.75 percent to the employing agency and 2 percent to the worker.

Medical provisions of the IVSS program call for full medical care for insured personnel, pensioners, and dependents. Temporary disability benefits amount to two-thirds of the compensation subject to social security withholding immediately before the disability was incurred and are payable from the fourth day of disability. Benefits in maternity cases are payable from six weeks before to six weeks after delivery. Employers may be liable for disability or death benefits if IVSS coverage is not available.

Permanent disability must involve the loss of at least two-thirds of the person's ability to perform work. A monthly pension for total or partial disability is paid on the basis of a formula that considers the average wage during the past five years, the degree of disability, and the period of time covered by social security, plus a specified flat amount—Bs150 in 1969. The pension must equal at least 40 percent of the average wage used in computing the amount of the pension.

Workers who have made social security contributions covering 750 weeks are entitled to retirement benefits. In most instances these are payable at the ages of sixty for men and fifty-five for women, but the ages may be reduced in certain cases. The amount is calculated on the basis of the same formula as that used for disability pensions.

Persons who had been employed under social security before 1967 were able to continue longevity credit for retirement purposes if they had been employed in covered positions for at least 250 weeks by purchase of credit for the period worked. In addition, when the law is extended to a new region or to a new group of workers, the newly inscribed personnel are entitled to credits of twenty weeks for each year of age over the age of twenty-five with a minimum of 50 weekly credits and a maximum of 500 credits for the purpose of qualifying for a pension. Persons reaching retirement age without having qualified for a pension may continue working or elect to receive a lump-sum payment equal to 10 percent of the pay from which social security contributions were withheld.

Survivorship pensions are generally payable to all unmarried children under fourteen, those under eighteen if they are undergoing regular schooling, and those of any age if incapacitated. They are also payable to widows of any age with dependent children, to childless widows over the age of forty-five, and to disabled husbands over the age of sixty if they were dependent on the spouse. The widow without pension rights is eligible for a lump sum equal to the amount of two yearly pension payments. The amount of the survivor pension is 40 percent of the corresponding old age or disability pension if there is only one survivor and is increased by 20 percent for each other survivor up to a maximum of 100 percent. Pensions cease for children when they exceed the maximum age under which establishment of eligibility for a pension is allowed and for wives when they remarry.

A fixed amount, Bs500 in 1969, is payable to cover the burial expenses of insured workers and pensioners; and insured workers with credits of at least 100 weekly premiums in the previous three years are entitled to a fixed amount of wedding benefit, Bs750 in 1969, at the time of marriage. There is no specific provision for unemployment compensation, but the 1969 legislation calls for future inclusion of provision for this kind of compensation within a reasonable time by executive decree. In addition, labor law under certain circumstances calls for lump sum payments at the time of termination of employment (see ch. 19, Labor).

The Venezuelan Children's Council, an autonomous entity of the Ministry of Health and Social Assistance, exercises broad legal authority in fulfilling its assignment of ensuring the right of minors to live in conditions that permit normal mental, physical, and moral growth. It concerns itself with matters concerning the orphaned, wayward, abandoned, and underprivileged. Programs range from institutionalized care of abandoned children to family assistance plans in which temporary subsidies may accompany temporary counseling by social workers. In 1969 nearly 95,000 children received preventive assistance in their homes, and 21,000 received help in institutions. Over 100,000 of the preventive cases involved supervised care in playgrounds, and nearly 11,000 of the institutional cases involved placement of children in shelters.

Other activities related to child welfare are administered by the National Institute of Nutrition (Instituto Nacional de Nutrición), which in 1969 served free lunches daily to nearly 230,000 children of school age; provided a smaller number of free breakfasts; distributed free milk and vitamins to schoolchildren and expectant mothers; and furnished low-cost meals to adults in public dining rooms in factories and hospitals. It also provided guidance in nutritional practices in more than 600 nutritional clubs and conducts studies in nutrition. The National Association for Care of the Aged and Infirm (Patronato Nacional de Ancianos e Inválidos) supplements the regular public health programs in providing medical and other care for the elderly, particularly in relation to ambulatory medical treatment and occupational therapy.

Private charitable and social welfare institutions operating in the country are not subject to the income tax. In 1968 there were forty-three private foundations in the country. Among the functions performed by many of these were those of a welfare nature, including such activities as the support of orphanages, provisions of assistance to persons of limited means, and funding of scholarships. Of particular significance is the Voluntary Dividend for the Community (Dividendo Voluntario para la Communidad), founded in 1964 and supported by contributions from the business community. It supports various welfare programs, private education, research, and community development projects. Its prestige was increased in 1967 by its prompt and efficient response to a serious earthquake that affected Caracas.

Welfare activities of the Roman Catholic Church are oriented primarily toward education. Outstanding among these is the Fé y Alegría (Faith and Joy) movement, which was started in the early 1950s. By 1966 it operated fifty-five schools for more than 25,000 poor children. In connection with its educational program, it provided medical and dental services and meals. Among its facilities was a farm boarding school in the state of Apure.

CHAPTER 7

EDUCATION

In 1970 (the 1969/70 school year) nearly 22 percent of the population was enrolled in the country's public and private schools. In 1961 not quite 17 percent had been enrolled.

The upward surge in enrollments had begun in 1958, when a new government came to power. The initial thrust was directed at including as many children as possible in the system at the primary level, an effort so successful that in a two-year period the rolls increased by nearly 50 percent. During the 1960s national authorities were hard put to keep the annual rise in primary enrollment sufficient to match proportionally the increase in population at that age level, but the growth at the intermediate level registered a considerable relative as well as absolute rate of increase; at the university level the growth rate was higher still.

During most of the 1960s the principal emphasis at all levels was on getting more students enrolled in the schools rather than on the quality of education. Despite the unprecedented increase in the numbers enrolled in intermediate and higher institutions, in 1970 more than three-fourths of the school population was engaged in studies at the primary level. Moreover, at each level dropouts continued to outnumber graduates and, except at the primary level, only a small proportion in the age group appropriate to that level was actually attending school. By the late 1960s, however, nearly 80 percent of the population over the age of ten was literate, and the emphasis of adult education had shifted from literacy training to basic and vocational schooling. For the adult population, three years represented the average amount of education.

Until the late 1960s primary schools followed a curriculum dating from the 1940s. At the intermediate level academic schooling in preparation for university entrance was conducted completely separately from training in vocational schools, and transfer between these two main intermediate systems was virtually impossible. At the university level most of the students were enrolled in traditionally favored disciplines, such as law, medicine, and engineering, and studies more closely related to the needs of the society remained relatively neglected.

Increasing awareness during the 1960s that the school system as a whole was in need of modernization to meet the needs both of the individual and the nation led to concrete developments by the end of the decade. At that time primary school authorities commenced a revision of the curriculum and the coordination of primary schooling with the lower cycle of intermediate schools in order to give students additional time in school before committing themselves to preparation for a particular academic field of higher study or for a particular vocation. In the universities plans were being made for supplementing the regular courses of study, most of them requiring four to six years, with short courses in fields where professionally trained personnel were in short supply.

National, state, and municipal governments finance and maintain schools. The national government provides the largest part of the support, however, and the Ministry of Education exercises control over curriculum, examinations, and teacher accreditation for the private as well as the public schools. The predominantly Catholic private sector is small at all levels but plays an important role, particularly in academic intermediate schools. During the 1960s it grew as fast as the public sector.

Politics has become increasingly significant in education. Although students and teachers have been politically active throughout republican history, the relatively free atmosphere after 1958 provided a fertile field for radical leftist activity. Intermediate as well as university students and teachers have been involved, and university activity became so intense in 1970 that the National Congress enacted legislation modifying the autonomous status that the public universities had previously enjoyed in order to give the government direct participation in their administration.

Between 1960 and 1970 the educational system had grown and changed substantially. For the 1970s, however, the system's administrators faced a major challenge in simply maintaining its rate of growth. A measure of the challenge was found in the president's first message to the National Congress covering the country's progress during 1969. It was reported that the Ministry of Public Works had completed school buildings to accommodate 41,900 students. During the same year the school population had increased by 117,519.

HISTORICAL BACKGROUND

Colonial education, almost exclusively conducted by the Roman Catholic Church, was aimed at training future ecclesiastics and cultured gentlemen. For others, only some training in practical skills and the occasional rudiments of reading and writing was available. Most of the early schools were established during the seventeenth century, and these became the nucleus of the Royal and Pontifical University of Santiago de León de Caracas, founded in 1721. Education had a religious emphasis and remained politically and academically conservative until after independence.

One of the principles of the new European liberalism that the leaders of independence wished to incorporate in their several constitutions was that of education for all. Simón Bolívar, although an aristocrat by birth, was firmly dedicated to this principle and included it in the Constitution of Angostura (1819), which was a reflection of his personal convictions. His own liberal education by Simón Rodríguez, a follower of Jean Jacques Rousseau, had been profoundly instrumental in shaping his thinking and later led him to his dedication to the principles and cause of independence. Through this association with, and influence on, Bolívar, Rodríguez holds an honored place in national history.

With the establishment of Gran Colombia in 1821—the amalgamation of Venezuela, Colombia, and Ecuador—the first attempt to incorporate the ideas of public education was begun. The real history of the system, however, did not commence until 1870, when a decree was signed establishing the free elementary education teacher-training schools and school supervision that the Constitution of 1864 had envisioned. During this period the most noteworthy events were the creation of the Ministry of Education in 1881 and the adoption in 1897 of the first Code of Education.

Although the twentieth century had been characterized by periods of greater or lesser attention to education, corresponding to the alternating dictatorships and more liberal governments, overall progress has been considerable. Under the Juan Vicente Gómez regime (1908—35) development was limited, although a few positive measures were instituted. During the next fifteen years of less restrictive government, the desire for change brought about an expansion of facilities and some improvement in the quality of the system. Particularly fruitful was the 1945—48 administration of Rómulo Betancourt and Rómulo Gallegos. Under the Marcos Pérez Jiménez regime, no great interest in developing education was manifested, and gains were modest.

EDUCATION AND SOCIETY

Education has always had a high value in Venezuelan society. Historically accepted as the privilege of the upper class minority and one of the attributes that distinguished that minority, it has since become popularly accepted as the right of all society. Although the traditional system has been modified to include not only the formal classical education but also a more practical type of training, greatest esteem is attached to academic preparation. The old Hispanic concept of the cultured individual of numerous talents who prefers abstract intellectual exercise to the practical application of knowledge remains to a considerable extent the ideal. For the upper class, the growing middle class, and those members of the lower class with upward aspirations, an academic education is the only acceptable one. For this reason the *liceos* (secondary schools), which prepare students for the universities and subsequently for white-collar professional or academic careers, are still more popular than other intermediate-level schools. In the universities, training in the time-honored professions of medicine and law and, more recently, economics and engineering is the preference of the majority.

The expansion of education, particularly since 1958, has increased the opportunity for upward mobility. Nevertheless, despite the growth of free public facilities, students in the *liceos* and universities still represent a small portion of the school population. Consequently, for those who successfully complete an academic education, prestige is assured, and a sound economic situation is probable.

Although official schools have better financial support and, as a result, newer equipment and more highly paid teachers, a private education bears the stamp of exclusiveness for many. The select private *liceos*, which, in addition to a sound education, offer class separation, continue to receive the children of socially prominent families. Teachers value the prestige that positions in the better private schools confer. Frequently they divide their time between private and official schools, thus receiving the benefits each has to offer. The educational process and the school itself are seen as the realm of the teacher. Although parent-teacher organizations exist, parental involvement has never been a popular concept.

In private education circles there has been some resentment toward the tight government controls placed on curricula, requirements for teachers, and examinations. Religious school administrators are more conscious of the dictates of the government than of the church. In addition to "free education," many private educators would like some influence in policy and planning decisions, now handled entirely by the Ministry of Education and its staff, as well as some financial aid, since private schools educate students that the state would otherwise have to support.

ADMINISTRATION AND FINANCE

The product of an evolutionary process, the machinery of the educational system tends to be uncoordinated. Public schools are maintained at all levels of government, and until 1970 the national universities were autonomous. The ministries of health and social assistance, agriculture, development, and communications all maintain specialized schools or otherwise participate in the educational development program. During the late 1960s these ministries assumed about 20 percent of the costs of public education.

The Ministry of Education exercises control over choice of textbooks, curricula, and teacher qualifications to an extent that permits little variation at state and local levels to meet needs of the locality. In addition, it has the authority to inspect and supervise the activities of private schools. These private schools must be registered with the ministry, and their teachers, accredited by it. In order that private diplomas receive official recognition, programs of study and examinations must conform to the public school standards. Accordingly, private education is unrestricted only in matters of internal management.

Under the minister of education, a technical directorate is responsible for such matters as maintaining records and statistics, determining norms for examinations, and preparing curricula. Operational functions are carried out by the directorates of general, higher, and special education; primary education and teacher training; and craft, industrial, and commercial training. A permanent office of supervision provides the channel through which each directorate deals with regional offices, which supervise the system at the local levels.

Reorganization of the ministry is perennially cited as a necessary educational reform. In practice, new subdivisions have been added, and functions have been shifted from one to another. Nevertheless, the traditional independence of each supervisory area has been maintained. At the beginning of 1970, however, the government announced that the structure of the ministry would be simplified by a far-reaching reorganization in which three fundamental entities would be established for planning, execution, and control and evaluation.

A school inspection system has been in existence, at least nominally, since 1870. Under the Control and Evaluation Directorate, it has the responsibility for implementing the impending reorganization of the school administration. Like the school system itself, the inspection program is national, regional, and local, most of the administrative functions and actual inspection being conducted by national authorities. During the 1960s the corps of inspectors was expanded, and the number of administrative regions was increased. Because of the corresponding growth in the number of students and schools, however, the principal role of inspectors has continued to be inspection of the physical facilities.

Although the public financial support of education is the collective function of all three levels of government, more than half of the funds come from the central government, most of the balance coming from the states. The proportions vary from year to year, and the central government contributes frequently to the operating costs of state and local schools. Central government education expenditures increased steadily in real values from a base of 100 in 1961 to 177 in 1968 and a provisional 191 in 1969. As a percentage of general budget expenditures, there was an irregular rise from 12.6 percent for 1966 to 16.2 percent for 1970.

The greatest overall expenditure is for primary schools because of the number enrolled; by per capita cost, however, it is for institutions of higher education. Except in a few urban localities, the expenditures per student in schools operated by states and municipalities are significantly lower than those operated by the national government.

THE SCHOOL SYSTEM

Education is free in public schools and is compulsory up to the age of fourteen. Enrollment in the regular school system as a whole increased from 1,244,000 in 1961 to a provisional figure of 2,218,100 in 1970. Regular schools are at the primary, intermediate, and higher levels. Outside the regular system, the Ministry of Education and other ministries maintain special schools and courses devoted to literacy, vocational instruction, and special instruction for children and adults. Enrollment in 1970 exceeded 300,000.

There are private schools at all levels of regular instruction. In 1970 private enrollment totaled 323,800, an estimated 60 percent being in units operated by Catholic orders (see ch. 9, Religion). The proportion in private institutions, about 14.5 percent of the total, was lower than in most Latin American countries.

In 1969 there were 73,519 teachers in schools at all levels. Except in the institutions of higher education, the supply was adequate, the number being limited only by the shortage of schoolrooms. Much of the teaching staff, however, was inadequately prepared except in the primary system.

Despite construction programs, there were not enough schools to handle adequately the increasing number of students. Furthermore, of schools in existence, many were in buildings not originally designed for instructional purposes. School equipment and teaching materials were also frequently poor, and many family budgets were often insufficient to provide their older children with the necessary textbooks and school supplies.

The school year begins in mid-September and ends with final examinations in July, except in a few universities and higher educational institutes that begin the year in January or February and conclude in November or December. Vacation periods include the month of August and the first two weeks of September, about two weeks at Christmas, and a few days at Carnival and at Easter. The school week is 5½ days, and night classes are offered at the intermediate and university levels. The grading system is based on a perfect score of twenty, and any grade below ten is a failure. For those who fail, makeup examinations are given in September. These examinations—which are oral, written, and practical—are also open to students unable to take them at the proper time. For the intermediate and higher levels, grades are officially issued in transcript form by the Ministry of Education.

Primary

During the 1969/70 school year, 1.7 million students, or 76.6 percent of the school population, were enrolled in the primary system. The figure included 35,000 children in the three voluntary kindergarten grades available in some urban localities for children between the ages of five and seven. In 1967 about 85 percent of those enrolled at the primary level were in public schools, and boys and girls were almost exactly equal in number.

Most of the primary enrollment falls in the seven to fourteen age group; during these ages school attendance is compulsory. In 1967 only 3.4 percent were over the age of fifteen, and about 2 percent were under seven.

Only a small portion of the children entering primary school successfully complete the course six years later, but the proportion increased steadily during the 1960s, rising from 29 percent in 1960 to 37 percent in 1967. During the 1960s the rate of growth in the numbers graduating more than doubled that of the enrollment growth.

At the time of the most recent census, in 1961, some 419,000, or more than one-fourth of all children between the ages of seven and fourteen, were not enrolled in school. Over half lived in rural localities where in many instances nonattendance was the consequence of there being no school to attend. Of the total, nearly 19 percent reported that there was no school available, and an additional 0.7 percent lived in localities where the school did not offer the upper primary grades. For 3.6 percent, there were no vacancies (*cupos*) in the local school.

In addition to the number of pupils who drop out from school altogether, a considerable number repeat one or more grades. In 1967 about 12 percent of the pupils were repeaters, nearly half of them in the first grade. The high proportion in each of the first three grades indicates that, through the third grade at least, children who are not promoted make a second attempt in preference to leaving school altogether.

Both the proportion of school-age children enrolled and the retention rate are lower in rural than in urban schools. In 1967 nearly 35 percent of the country's population was in the primary school age group, but only about 20 percent of the primary school population was in the rural sector. The difference was most pronounced in the last three years of primary school where the retention rate for urban children was more than twice that for rural.

The low retention rate of farm children beyond the third grade reflects the large number of *unitarias* (one-teacher, one-room units that offer only three grades). These schools are located almost entirely in rural localities. They increased steadily in number during the 1950s to reach a total of nearly 9,600 in 1960, when they represented about 75 percent of the school units in the system. Thereafter, their number declined progressively to 6,300 units, representing 60 percent of the total in 1967.

Having a curriculum generally corresponding to that for the first three years of the regular schools, most of the *unitarias* are parts of *núcleos rurales* (rural nuclei) systems of three-year schools located in the same general area. For each system there is a boarding unit at which pupils can complete the remaining years of primary school while receiving prevocational training in skills appropriate to the locality. Supervisors of the *núcleos rurales* are also in charge of community development programs in the area and give assistance and instruction to teachers in the individual schools. The number of *núcleos rurales* increased from 27 in 1954 to 76 in 1961, and to 257 during the 1966/67 school year, when they served 4,163 unitary schools with 200,324 pupils.

The number of primary teachers is generally adequate, the pupil-teacher ratio having been about thirty-four to one in 1969. Because of the shortage of classrooms, however, in the late 1960s it was necessary to hold evening classes in some urban localities.

Virtually unchanged since its initiation in 1944, the curriculum during the late 1960s included language, arithmetic, social studies, nature studies, social and moral development, aesthetics, civics, and hygiene. In some schools there was also a prevocational program available in the last three grades. In 1969 an experimental revision of the curriculum, eventually to be extended to all grades, was introduced in the first grade. At the same time, school administrators began to implement a basic changeover in the structure of the system by means of which the six primary grades were to become part of a nine-year course of studies continuing through the first three years of intermediate school. In the new program subjects were to be presented in relationship to one another. Mathematics was to be offered as a series of studies rather than as the separate subjects of arithmetic, algebra, and geometry. Sciences were to be offered as a general and continuing field of study rather than as individual and unrelated scientific subjects.

Although schooling itself is free, pupils were required to furnish their own textbooks and school supplies until 1967, when a decree was issued to remedy this deficiency. By the end of the year nearly 1 million textbooks had been issued on a loan basis, and exercise books and pencils had been supplied. By the end of the first half of 1968 it was reported that the textbook needs of the first three grades had been satisfied.

Intermediate

Intermediate education, designed for students between the ages of fourteen and nineteen who have completed their primary training, is offered in the public and private sector in secondary, vocational, and normal schools. In the 1967/68 school year some 35.2 percent of the population aged fourteen through eighteen was enrolled in institutions of these types. Between 1961 and 1970 enrollment nearly tripled, but the primary school population increased only a little more than one-third. The greater rapidity of growth at the secondary level was a reflection of greater emphasis by the government on intermediate schooling and the sharp rise in the number of primary graduates who were applying for admission to intermediate schools.

In 1967 the male enrollment slightly exceeded the female, and males had a slightly higher retention rate in the upper grades. About 17 percent of the students were nineteen years of age or older, and a slightly smaller proportion were under the age of fourteen. With the exception of agricultural units maintained by the Ministry of Agriculture, virtually all of the intermediate schools were in urban localities.

The lack of integration in the system has been most evident at this level, where each of the three main branches has operated in isolation from the others, although the similarity between curriculum in the first years of the secondary and the normal school courses has permitted some lateral transfer between the two. This isolation was to be substantially modified by introduction of the nine-year basic schooling to cover all of primary and the first three years of intermediate education. Under this new system, the first elements of which were introduced in 1969, the first three years at intermediate schools of all kinds were to consist of a common basic cycle (*ciclo básico común*), and choice of an academic or vocational field of specialization was to be deferred until the beginning of the fourth intermediate year.

Secondary

The term *secondary* applies only to the academic or general intermediate schools called *liceos*, which are designed exclusively for preparing students for schooling at the university level. Upon the successful completion of their five-year program, *liceos* grant *bachilleratos* (diplomas). A *bachillerato* is usually the requirement for university admission.

Between 1961 and 1970 the secondary school enrollment almost tripled, public enrollment representing about 75 percent of the total during most of the years. The proportion of girls increased from 37 percent in 1961 to near 46 percent in 1967. Some 12 percent of the courses of study were in night schools, at which admission was limited to employed students over the age of sixteen.

The 180,000 enrollment in 1967 included about 74,000 in the first grade and progressively fewer in each succeeding grade to 19,100 in the fifth. Boys and girls registered about the same rates of school retention. Both in proportion of population enrolled and in retention rates, schools in the large urban localities had the best record. Containing about 15 percent of the population, the Federal District had nearly 24 percent of the total secondary enrollment and nearly 30 percent of the enrollment in the fifth grade.

Depending on the course content, the *bachillerato* is awarded either in the humanities (*humanidades*) or the sciences (*sciencias*). As in the universities, credits depend on the successful completion of hours per week per subject. During the first three years, all students follow a general program, which includes Spanish and literature, mathematics, social studies, the sciences, art, English, and physical education. At the end of this first cycle, a certificate of general secondary education is awarded. Specialization in a particular field of study begins for the student during the second two-year cycle, subsequent enrollment in a university faculty or school depending on this choice. The teaching method consists of the textbook in conjunction with the classroom lecture. Partly because of the persistence of this traditional pedagogy and partly because classes are often large, student participation in classroom discussion is limited.

A relatively new development in the *liceo* has been the political involvement of the students, principally in Caracas. Although such activity is limited to small, noisy groups, political manifestations have not been without violence. There have been instances of parents withdrawing their children from official schools to place them in the calmer atmosphere of the private school. Politics at this level have probably been the result of increased Communist concentration of attention on students and infiltration into the ranks of the teaching force. The exalted position of the university student following the coup of 1958 and the high level of political activity that existed after that time probably also served as an example to the secondary schools.

Vocational

The vocational or technical (*técnico*) schools are divided into industrial, commercial, agricultural, and other vocation-oriented fields of specialization. Over 90 percent of the vocational school registration in 1970 was in the public sector, but the small private enrollment had increased at a fast rate during the 1960s. Enrollment as a whole had increased somewhat more rapidly than that of the academic secondary schools.

The quantitative growth was not matched by a corresponding improvement in the quality of graduates produced. Dropout rates were much higher than in secondary schools, and the ablest and best prepared students continued to prefer the academic intermediate education leading to university entrance. Few of the teaching staff were trained in pedagogical methods, and many of the vocational students were employed persons attending night schools.

Beginning with the 1969/70 school year the vocational, like the academic intermediate, schools began the process of shifting to the new general studies system, in which the first three years of schooling at the intermediate level would be made up of a continuation of the general studies pursued at the primary level. Several years could be expected to pass, however, before the old program of initiating vocational specialization at the beginning of intermediate school could be superseded.

During the 1966/67 school year there were over 33,000 students in about twenty categories; this included 5,000 girls in industrial schools. In most, the first two-year cycle was devoted to basic technical instruction, and subsequent years were devoted to specialized course of varying duration. Dropout rates were high, particularly after the first year.

For those who had completed the basic industrial cycle, most were enrolled in four-year courses in mechanical, electrical, chemical, petroleum, mining and geology, and electronic technology. At the end of the first specialized cycle students earned the certificate of industrial expert, and at the end of the second, the certificate of industrial technician. Enrollment figures for 1967 indicated a dropout rate of nearly half after the second year. A majority of those completing the third, however, remained for the fourth specialized year.

Two-year specialized cycles for persons who had completed the basic cycles were offered to a small number of technician-students in civil construction, fishing, woodworking, and typography. Single-year courses were held for locksmiths, blacksmiths, auto mechanics, and sanitary installation workers. One- or two-year courses not requiring completion of a basic industrial cycle were offered by night schools in general mechanics, mechanical drawing, soldering, heating and refrigeration maintenance, and radio repair.

As in the industrial program, courses in the commercial program varied in length. The most popular of the programs offered—commercial studies—attracted in 1967 over 51,000 students, including 36,000 females. The complete five-year course was rewarded by the diploma of mercantile technician, carrying with it qualification for enrollment at the higher education level for studies in administration and, under certain circumstances, in economics. Shorter courses of two to four years led to certificates qualifying the holder as officeworker, secretary-accountant, or mercantile expert.

In 1967 about 25,000 students were enrolled in various other vocational schools. Most numerous were the 2,900 (including 500 girls) students in three-year agricultural schools and 2,200 in schools of nursing; courses ranged from two to four years.

Normal

The enrollment in normal schools, which furnished preparation for certification of teachers in the preprimary and primary system, is primarily female. In 1967 nearly 90 percent of the prospective teachers were girls. Schools were located primarily in large urban centers, almost one-third of the enrollment being concentrated in the Federal District. In 1970 more than 61 percent of the registration was in the public sector.

Normal school enrollment suffered an unbroken decline from 32,400 in 1962 to 10,900 in 1968 before recovering to 14,100 in 1970. This decline resulted from the mass closing of schools that had been opened in the late 1950s to provide teachers for the expanded primary school population. Even at the reduced rate of teacher production, more than 200 qualified new graduates of normal schools were unable to find teaching jobs in 1969.

The normal school course of study was formerly four years. In the mid-1960s some of the schools commenced offering a fifth year, and by 1967 about one-fifth of the students were in five-year courses. In general, the rate of failures is much lower than in the other intermediate educational sectors, and most of those who fail do so in the first year.

Higher Education

The 1969/70 enrollment in higher educational institutions—72,600—was nearly three times that in 1961. Female participation increased from about 31 percent of the total in 1961 to 34 percent in 1967. In 1965 less than one-fourth were under the age of twenty, and more than one-fourth were over the age of twenty-four. In 1967 nearly one-half were in the first year of their studies.

Universities

There are seven public and two private universities. The oldest, the Central University of Venezuela, with a 500-acre campus in Caracas, was founded in 1721 and is the only university with valid claim to a colonial origin. The other older universities are the University of the Andes in Mérida, the University of Carabobo in Valencia, and the University of Zulia at Maracaibo. The private Andrés Bello Catholic University and the private nondenominational University of Santa Maria were both established in 1953. The University of the East (Universidad del Oriente) was established in 1958, with administrative headquarters in Cumaná and branch campuses in five eastern states, thus realizing a longstanding aspiration of the eastern coastal region. In 1968 the Experimental Center for University Studies at Barquisimeto qualified for university status as the University of the Central-West (Universidad del Centro-Oeste), and in 1970 the Simón Bolívar University became the country's ninth, with a student body of 508 at the time of opening.

Having more than 25,000 students in 1969, the Central University had about two-fifths of the total university population. As recently as 1965, however, its enrollment had represented more than one-half of the total. The University of Zulia was next in size with about 8,000 students.

Between 1958 and 1970 all of the universities, including the two private institutions, were governed by the 1958 Law of Universities, which reinstated in the university system the cherished Latin American principle of autonomy, which had been violated by the Pérez Jiménez government. Under the 1958 law the National Council of Universities apportioned the distribution of funds among the several institutions and set common standards and requirements for them. It was composed of the minister of education and the rectors, a dean, and a student representative of each university.

At the individual university level, administration was the responsibility of the university officials, who were elected by all professors and a proportion of students and alumni, and the University Council, made up of student and alumnus representatives in addition to the officials, deans of the faculties and schools, and a delegate of the ministry. Supreme authority rested, not with the rector and other high officials, but with the council.

The University Council had the general function of directing and coordinating university life. It prepared and decreed the budget; dictated university regulations; had authority to create, abolish, or modify the structure of faculties, schools, and institutes; and supervised the administration of personnel matters. Because the powerful student associations in the several faculties were behind them, student representatives on the councils were able to play important roles.

In the faculties (*faculdades*)—academic bodies in the Venezuelan universities somewhat similar to, but with greater autonomy than, the academic departments in North American universities—student influence was also substantial. Highest authority rested with a representative assembly, composed of all professors and a student delegation equal in number to 25 percent of the professors. This body selected the dean and made recommendations with respect to faculty matters to the University Council. Under the assembly a Council handled such matters as budget preparation; study programs; and the proposing of professors for contract, their classification, promotion, and pension for approval of the University Council.

The restoration of freedom to student leaders and organizations that followed enactment of the 1958 legislation was accompanied by an increase of political activity and of sporadic demonstrations and violence that led, in December 1967, to issuance of a decree empowering the executive to maintain public order within the universities while leaving the university authorities responsible for internal administration and order. Disorders continued, however, and leftist political groups were increasingly active in student organization, revolutionary elements playing the leading roles. In September 1970 the 1958 legislation was modified by enactment of a law empowering the government to dismiss existing university councils, appoint temporary bodies to administer the universities, and nominate new councils within three months.

Protests by students and professors over this abridgment of autonomy had been violent when the legislation was still in draft stage. After its enactment the rector of the Central University refused to comply with its provisions and boycotted meetings of a provisional council that had been created demanding that he recognize the reforms under threat of possible removal from his post. The rector promptly tendered his resignation, and on October 26 military and police units occupied the university buildings.

Of the country's higher institutions the Central University has the greatest prestige, although intensive political activity has somewhat lowered its reputation within the country. Its greater number of faculties offer wider opportunities to the prospective student. Moreover, its location in the capital—the heart of political, intellectual, and economic life—increases its attraction. The other universities, particularly the newer ones, with much smaller enrollments and fewer faculties, are by contrast provincial. The quality of education received at their universities is esteemed by Venezuelans, for, although some upper class families prefer to send their children to universities outside the country and the scholarships given by government organs and private groups are readily accepted, a foreign diploma bestows no more, and sometimes less, prestige than a Venezuelan one.

Although the universities have traditionally been centers of political activity and training grounds for individuals who have provided intellectual and often political leadership, they have generally maintained an attitude of aloofness toward the mainstream of national life. The wide social and cultural gulf that originally existed between the university community and the bulk of national society and the classically academic nature of the university's pursuits early served to give it an ivory tower aspect. University autonomy, which was instituted throughout Latin America to stem the meddling by national governments in university affairs, resulted in further isolation. Within the university structure itself, there has been a tendency toward the relative independence of each faculty. As a result, students identify more closely with their particular faculty than with the university as a whole.

The widest choice of fields of specialization is offered at the Central University, which has eleven faculties, each made up of several schools or institutes. In the university system as a whole, a majority of the degree courses have durations of four years. Five-year courses are offered, however, in the fields of fine arts, social science, law, architecture, administration and accounting, engineering, agronomy, and dentistry, and there are six-year courses in medicine and economic sciences. There are courses of three years' duration in veterinary surgery and courses of two years' duration in bioanalysis and in nursing.

The licentiate (*licenciado*) is awarded on successful completion of the undergraduate course of study. The doctorate (*doctorado*) requires presentation of a dissertation and may or may not require study after graduation. It is not, however, a graduate degree per se. The five- or six-year term of undergraduate study often required, coupled with the near impossibility of shifting from one faculty to another, have inhibited the establishment of formal graduate study programs leading to advanced degrees.

The beginning of a graduate studies program was initiated in 1968 with establishment of the Institute of Higher Administrative Studies. Its first graduating class of seventeen students received degrees at the master's level in 1970. In addition, in 1970 the establishment of a graduate school of scientific studies was being planned, and the Simón Bolívar University announced its intention of introducing a graduate studies program. In general, however, the university graduate planning further schooling must seek it abroad.

At the beginning of the 1970s the traditionally favored fields of law and medicine and, more recently, economics and engineering continued to be among the most popular. In the 1966/67 school year some 14 percent of the students were enrolled in engineering; 13.3 percent, in economics; 12.6 percent, in law; and 10 percent, in medicine. The various faculties and school of the social sciences accounted for 22.6 percent of the enrollment; 6.2 percent was in disciplines of the humanities; 3.9 percent, in agronomy; and 3.1 percent, in agriculture. Pharmacy had 2.8 percent; dentistry, 2.3 percent; veterinary science, 2.2 percent; and miscellaneous specialties of medical science, 1.9 percent. Some 2.5 percent were in other fields. Imbalance in popularity of fields of concentration has caused the restless student organizations to tend to regard the sought-after faculties as citadels of privilege and to make them targets of demonstrations and strikes.

The lack of correlation between university enrollment by field of specialization and the real needs of the society was under increasing criticism during the late 1960s. In 1969 one highly critical article pointed out that about 3,000 students were enrolled in schools of medicine and 79 were in university schools of nursing.

Steps were already being taken, however, in some of the newer institutions to make studies more responsive to needs. The University of the East offered primarily technical studies; the University of the Central-West concentrated on agronomy and veterinary surgery, and the Simón Bolívar University concerned itself with technical and scientific studies.

Specifically, one step would involve the adoption by universities of a basic cycle during the first three or four university semesters of study to provide a basic education in sciences and humanities as a foundation for further study. The further study could, in many instances, be confined to intermediate technical training, thus accelerating professional training directly oriented toward getting a job.

The other was that short courses be introduced in the universities for the training of auxiliary personnel in such fields as agricultural extension, electronics, administration, industrial plant operation, and auxiliary medical specialties. These might be established in existing universities or in regional institutes for higher study to supply specific needs for regional development.

In 1970 some progress toward the establishment of short career courses was already reported at the Central University, at which a part of the student body was being provided auxiliary training in scientific and technical fields. In addition, the university reported that it was endeavoring to create a type of intermediate education to enable students to obtain a bachelor's degree in three years, particularly in the relatively new field of administrative procedures, in which nearby 3,000 freshmen were already enrolled.

In September 1968 the Central University accepted 12,500 out of some 23,600 applicants, more than three times the number that had applied in 1961. The heavy and increasing pressure on university facilities has been most conspicuous at the Central University but has been acute in the institutions as well. In Venezuela the number of second-choice schools is limited. Therefore, for those of limited means who are not accepted by a high prestige university, the school nearest home is the only possible choice, and failure to secure admission means the wait of a year or the abandonment of hopes for a college education.

The qualifying test for university eligibility is the *bachillerato* from academic secondary school or, in some cases, successful completion of the full five- or six-year commercial or industrial vocational course.

It has been contended that students with a favored socioeconomic background are unduly favored and that acceptance is based less on ability than on opportunity. As an alternative to the present system, it has been proposed that a means be devised for establishing a differential placement program, admission to be based on achievement potential. The level of socioeconomic background would represent the differential factor. The fact that educational thinking in the late 1960s was directed along these lines constituted a measure of the rapid development of this program.

Another of the many problems confronting university admissions authorities derives from the fact that students have selected their proposed university field of concentration at the beginning of the second cycle of intermediate school and apply, not for entrance to a university, but for entrance to a specific university faculty. In practice, the intermediate training in fields of concentration has been imperfect, and students entering universities have been confused in selecting their faculty.

The fact that the Central University in 1968 was able to accept an entering class representing half of the total enrollment made clear the presumption by its administration that most of the matriculants were destined never to graduate. This presumption was substantiated by the congressional committee that prepared the draft of the 1970 bill on university reform. It found that in 1968 the proportion of university graduates amounted to 20 percent of the matriculants. About 25 percent of the law students and 32 percent of the students in agriculture who had matriculated in 1962 had completed their courses of study. In 1967 about half of the enrollment in all universities was registered in the freshman year, and the class in the second year was less than half the size of that in the first.

A considerable number of students do, indeed, find themselves unable to meet the academic standards, but many others find it necessary to abandon their studies because of economic necessity. Latin America, however, does not attach to graduation the importance that is accorded it in North America. At the intermediate and primary as well as at the higher level the prevailing view, however, is that some education is better than none. Dropout rates are extremely high, but many parents of limited means enter their sons and daughters in a university less with the expectation that they will obtain a degree than with the intent of providing them with some education at the university level.

Other Institutions of Higher Education

Teachers for the intermediate schools are supplied by the six university schools of education and by the public pedagogical institutes. Outside the regular university system, the two largest of the institutes had an enrollment that rose from 2,200 in 1961 to 3,800 in 1970. Offering four-year courses of study, they require a *bachillerato* or a normal school diploma for admission. Their standards are high, and graduates enjoy good professional standing. Like the universities, however, there is a high dropout rate and a high concentration of enrollment in the first year of study, where most of the failures occur.

In the 1966/67 school year the Pedagogical Institute of Caracas had an enrollment of nearly 2,400, and the newer and smaller Pedagogical Institute of Barquisimeto had about 800. In both institutions females slightly outnumbered males. The curriculum was oriented toward preparation for teaching in the academic *liceos*, fields of specialization including biology and chemistry, Spanish literature and Latin, social sciences (geography and history), mathematics, English, philosophy and educational science, and physics. In addition, in 1967 the Pedagogical Institute of Barquisimeto established a department for the teaching of technical subjects, and there is a small polytechnic institute in the same city.

TEACHERS

The phenomenal increase in normal school rolls during the late 1950s and the more recent substantial rise in enrollments at the pedagogical institutes and university schools of education have demonstrated that, when the opportunity for training for a teaching career is afforded, applicants for the training appear. For those in the lower socioeconomic groups, teaching represents a road of access to the ranks of the middle class, and for young women of the middle and upper classes, teaching is one of the relatively few careers that are both available and acceptable.

Teachers at the intermediate and superior levels are held in considerable esteem. Many qualified professionals teach for a few hours at a *liceo*, and the university professorship carries with it a great deal of prestige. Because a traditional view is that anyone can teach, however, primary teachers, with a lower level of training, are less highly regarded. The distinction is reflected in the titles given. Those who instruct in the primary system are called *maestros* (masters), and those in the *liceo* and university are designated *profesores* (professors). This hierarchical view is reflected in the profession itself by the existence of a federation for all teachers and two separate associations for secondary and university educators.

Foreign teachers are usually found in the upper levels and are generally esteemed for their good professional backgrounds, although they provoke resentment on becoming involved in national politics, particularly when they come from other Latin American countries. The resentment is based only on nationalist disapproval of intrusion by outsiders, for partisan behavior is expected of teachers as being among the best educated people in a politically conscious society.

In the 1966/67 school year 87 percent of the primary teaching staff was fully qualified academically. The remainder presumably was made up of personnel with long practical experience or located in remote rural areas. In the *liceos* the number of teachers was sufficient, but only about one in three was a graduate of a pedagogical institute or a university school of education. Many were professional people teaching on a part-time basis. Efforts have been made to attract back to teaching those graduate teachers who have entered private industry because of higher pay.

In the late 1960s there was a near-absolute qualitative shortage of teaching personnel in intermediate vocational schools. Teachers were in most instances graduates of technical schools or institutions of higher education or had practical experience in their fields of specialization, but few were qualified as teachers. In 1970 it was hoped that this qualitative shortage would gradually be remedied as increasing number of teachers graduated in technical fields.

Upgrading and refresher training for employed teachers and school administrators at the preprimary, primary, and intermediate levels are the responsibility of the Institute for the Professional Development of Teachers (Instituto de Majoramiento Profesional del Magisterio), organized during the Pérez Jiménez administration. Its enrollment rose from less than 9,000 in 1961 to nearly 60,000 in 1967. Maintaining regional offices throughout the country, the institute provides upgrading programs for nondegree teachers and programs for improvement of technique for those with degrees. Much of its phenomenal expansion has been brought about by the development of holiday and correspondence courses lasting up to five years.

Selection for positions at the university level is generally based on competition. Most begin at the lowest of the five grades—instructor — and move upward gradually toward the full professorship. Despite the numerous attractions offered by university teaching, there is a chronic shortage of personnel, which has resulted in considerable contracting of foreign professors. During the late 1960s the principal means of attempting to relieve the shortage has been the campaign to encourage occasional personnel to devote all or more of their time to teaching.

The economic situation of teachers at all levels is relatively good despite the high cost of living. In addition to their basic salaries and periodic in-grade raises, they receive allowances for housing and dependents. Teachers without degrees receive the same allowances but lower basic salaries. Because of the number of teachers at secondary and higher levels who teach only part time, there are two basic salary systems. A monthly salary is established for full-time teachers, but basic salary is calculated according to numbers of hours taught by part-time personnel. The levels are somewhat lower in private than in public schools, and announcement of an increase in salaries in the public sector was met in 1970 by an announcement from Catholic educational authorities that, unless a subsidy were received from the government to pay matching increases to teachers in parochial schools, closing of many might prove necessary.

Through the Institute of Social Security and Aid, an autonomous body of the Ministry of Education, teachers receive medical and dental care for themselves and their families. They are also assisted in procuring personal and mortgage loans and are eligible for some low-cost housing. Pensions, given after twenty-five years of service in urban and after twenty years in rural schools, amount to 70 percent of the total salary.

In 1968 the basic monthly salary of a full-time professor at the Central University was Bs3,000 (4.5 bolivars equal US$1). Allowance for dependents and years of seniority substantially increased income, however, which made it possible in some instances for primary teachers to earn almost as much as this amount and for secondary professors to earn substantially more than the basic university salary. Because of salaries on this order and with the several fringe benefits, many teachers were able to afford luxuries, such as cars and domestic help.

Job security has increased considerably during the 1960s. Before 1958 unacceptable political affiliation by a teacher often resulted in his dismissal or transfer to an unwanted rural post. Teachers have generally been transferred only at their own request, and dismissals have occurred only on grounds of incompetence, excessive absence from the classroom, or improper conduct. Where there is suspicion of the motives behind dismissal of a teacher, strong defense is provided by the powerful teachers' associations. In late 1970 the government categorically denied charges brought by the Venezuelan

Teachers Association that political affiliations had been responsible for indiscriminate transfers and reductions in salary affecting some 300 teachers.

The three principal groups are the Venezuelan Federation of Teachers, the oldest and most powerful; the College of Professors, for graduates of the pedagogical institutes; and the Association of University Professors. There are also Catholic groups. One of the principal achievements of the Federation of Teachers was the incorporation of a pay scale system in the 1940s. Other activities have included the preparation of studies published in the newspapers and often brought to the attention of the National Congress, the defense of members faced with dismissal for political reasons, and representations before the ministry. The associations officially restrict themselves to educational affairs, but in the past they have assumed a political role.

LITERACY AND ADULT EDUCATION

Although Venezuela has had one of the highest per capita incomes and lowest percentages of rural population, its literacy rate until recent years was much lower than that of other Latin American countries of comparable wealth and demographic structure. After the 1950 census official sources stated the rate to be 53 percent. By 1968 it was estimated to have increased to 81 percent for the population as a whole over the age of ten. This overall figure included 88.6 percent of the urban and 61.4 percent of the rural population and 84.4 percent of the males and 77.7 percent of the females. The highest rate was among young urban males, and the lowest, among elderly rural females. Since female enrollment in primary schools almost matched that of boys and the female retention rate exceeded that of the male, in 1970 the gap between the sexes in literary attainment was expected to close rapidly. The continuing spread of rural education could be expected to narrow somewhat more slowly the literacy gap between the rural and urban population sectors.

The most notable gain in the literacy program occurred between 1958 and 1961, when it was estimated that nearly 500,000 were taught rudimentary reading and writing. Since most of the readily reachable adults who had not attained literacy through regular schooling had been made literate, the pace of the program slowed during the course of the later 1960s. In 1969 literacy courses were completed by some 11,000 persons in more than 300 national centers of cultural extension and an equal number operated by state and local authorities. Private literacy leagues, civic leagues, and diocesan committees brought literacy to an additional 14,000. Furthermore, some 7,000 persons participated in continuing experimental projects carried on with assistance from the United Nations Educational, Scientific and Cultural Organization in the states of Lara, Trujillo, and Portuguesa. In addition to reading and writing, the projects included training in crafts and agricultural skills.

During the same period over 94,000 people were enrolled in public and private adult vocational and academic study programs. Over 88,000 were receiving primary school training, and some 6,000 were studying such specialties as barbering, dressmaking, draftsmanship, publicity skills, and agricultural techniques.

Because of the progressive extension of literacy during the 1960s, the focus of adult training shifted to other fields; in 1969, with all but the hard core of illiteracy substantially eliminated, the president issued an executive decree calling for establishment of facilities for training adults who had not received a basic education during their younger years or who wished to expand their acquired knowledge. The training—to be free at all levels—would be made up of primary, secondary, technical, special, and cultural schooling, as well as special programs in Indian education. Courses were to be offered directly through schools in the public system or through modern communication means, such as radio, television, press, cultural missions, and correspondence schools, or through combinations of these media.

Adult education at the primary level would be based on continuation of the existing literacy programs. It would also acquaint adults with the problems of the area in which they lived; teach them use of the basic instruments of culture; provide instruction in the techniques of a trade; and stimulate their civic, economic, and social self-development. The third phase would consist of familiarization of the student with the realities of national life, and the fourth, completion of academic and vocational training at the primary level. Adult schooling at the intermediate level would be aimed at continuation and broadening of education received at the primary level to prepare the adult student for higher education or for a trade.

The Ministry of Education was charged with determining procedures and programs for training the physically and mentally handicapped. The ministry and the Ministry of Justice were charged jointly with preparation of special programs for the Indian population.

Since its formation in late 1969, the National Institute of Educational Cooperation (Instituto Nacional de Cooperación Educativo—INCE) has had primary responsibility for the formal vocational training program and for apprenticeship training but has also concerned itself with literacy training and other peripheral activities. An autonomous body under supervision of the Ministry of Education, INCE is directed by a board composed of representatives of the government, employee and worker organizations, and the Venezuelan Federation of Teachers. Its operating costs are financed jointly by the participating ministries, trade and labor associations, and private industry.

In 1969 INCE offered nearly 10,000 large and small courses and trained 109,000 persons, as compared with 87,000 in 1967. It offered regular and special programs, with particular emphasis on industrial training. Other major programs were in the fields of commerce (including literacy training) and agriculture.

CHAPTER 8

ARTISTIC AND INTELLECTUAL EXPRESSION

Cultural expression in 1970 reflected an amalgamation of European and Western Hemisphere influences. The aesthetic styles that had been most prominent in arts and letters had originated primarily in Europe and to a lesser extent in the United States, Mexico, and other Western Hemisphere nations, but since independence they had generally been applied to the depiction of local subject matter. Spanish influence has been dominant in the country's folklore, especially in its melodic qualities, but African rhythmic forms have also been incorporated, and the monotonous chants of the indigenous peoples could still be heard in some areas.

In the twentieth century an increasing preoccupation with national characteristics and problems has been apparent in philosophy and science as well as in all of the various art forms. That trend has been accompanied by an expansion of the sector of the population participating as producers and consumers of literature and works of art. Traditionally, a certain proficiency in arts and letters was almost a prerequisite for the cultured gentleman. The ideal was the Renaissance man, a versatile individual capable of accomplishment in a wide variety of fields. Thus, a novelist was likely a poet, essayist, and journalist as well.

Greater educational opportunities, especially since 1958, have brought more people into a sphere that once belonged to only a few and have expanded the audience interested in the results of artistic and intellectual labors. Increased prosperity has resulted in a larger buying public, so that economic self-sufficiency is not always a prerequisite for the creative individual. Thus, professionalism in the arts has become increasingly widespread.

Most aspects of the country's cultural development are of relatively recent origin. During the colonial period development was limited as the colony was small, economically backward, and largely neglected by Spain. Spanish priests wrote most of the early chronicles and scholarly works, and there was little musical or artistic activity other than that sponsored by the Roman Catholic Church.

In the early nineteenth century the emphasis on metaphysics in the colony's philosophical expression gave way to the doctrines of the Enlightenment, which motivated Simón Bolívar and other leaders of the revolutionary movement. Political polemics, patriotic verse, and historical treatment of the revolution and its leaders in the neoclassic and romantic styles were fashionable throughout the nineteenth century, but *costumbrismo*, the depiction of the customs and daily lives of the common people, also gained popularity. Toward the end of the century philosophy became imbued with empiricism and the theories of evolution.

Early in the twentieth century the intellectual stimulation of empiricism focused attention on previously neglected aspects of the national existence. Scholars began to examine the colonial period and to note the influence of Spain on the country's social system. Meanwhile, in poetry and the novel the sentimentality of romanticism gave way to an aesthetic form of Western Hemisphere origins that became known as modernism. *Costumbrismo*, responding to European trends, gave rise to the more vivid descriptive detail of realism and naturalism. Innovators in music and painting broke with the neoclassic tradition and experimented with the forms of the French impressionists.

Since the mid-twentieth century the natural sciences have received increasing attention as international organizations and private foundations have cooperated with the national government in promoting research, and philosophical expression has been greatly influenced by the works of the social scientists. Trends in social and political thought have in turn been influential in creative literature.

Realism, strongly imbued with social consciousness, has been the most prominent contemporary trend in the novel and the short story, and experimental groups, applying avant-garde treatment to social and political themes, have popularized the previously neglected medium of drama. Nationalistic sentiment has been expressed in music through the incorporation of native melodies and rhythms into orchestral and choral compositions.

Contemporary painting and sculpture are dominated by abstract forms, but the stylized realism of the Mexican revolutionary painters is also influential. In architectual design the simple lines and funtionalism of the modern international school have been complemented by the incorporation of murals and sculpture.

THE COLONIAL PERIOD

In contrast to some of the wealthier colonies, Venezuela was a rather small, rustic province. After the initial onslaught of conquerors and adventurers who worked to subdue the region throughout the sixteenth century, society became agricultural and static. Lack of economic importance placed the colony in a position of relative neglect, which permitted a somewhat independent life within the Spanish administrative structure but also retarded cultural development. Without wealth or much official attention, few imposing townhouses, government buildings, or churches were built in colonial cities. A university was established only after 200 years of colonial life had passed. Even the Roman Catholic Church was poor in the number of its representatives and the amount of its material resources (see ch. 3, Historical Setting).

Yet the church was responsible for providing the framework in which culture developed. From its monasteries and sanctuaries came most of the scholars, intellectuals, and writers. Its hierarchy was the best educated and most cultured segment of society. As a patron, it offered instruction in the arts and provided a setting and audience for works produced. From its religious, philosophical, and moral teachings came the themes and orientation that shaped the artistic and intellectual expression of almost three centuries.

Spanish priests, arriving soon after the conquerors, produced the first literature of the colony in their eyewitness accounts of experiences and first records of indigenous oral traditions. A mixture of geography and history, legend, and myth, these chronicles were unpretentious, loosely woven journals that continued the Spanish medieval style.

By the seventeenth century the churchmen had retired to the monasteries to set down the native languages in lexicons and grammars and to study and write on theology and philosophy in the medieval scholastic tradition. From the earlier ingenuous accounts of the often unlettered missionary priests, these men passed to the complex, often obscure intricacies of the baroque style that had developed in Spain. Aristotle and deductive reasoning were still the guides in the resolution of metaphysical problems, but for many the word became more important than what it described.

In the eighteenth century portraits began to appear among the simple religious paintings executed by the untrained hands of artisans and, after 1784, plays could be seen in Caracas's first theater. In this final phase, however, the colony produced its finest artistic expression in the medium of music. The originality, vigor, and sophistication of the musicians and composers who arose in Caracas were unequaled in the colonial empire. The group formed the "School of Chacao," named for the small town outside Caracas where it frequently met to play. Chief promoter behind the musical movement was Padre Sojo, who had traveled to Europe and returned with instruments and compositions. The Philharmonic Society that had been founded in 1750 gave way several decades later to the Academy of Music, where works by Giovanni Pergolesi, Arcangelo Corelli, Dominico Scarlatti, Franz Joseph Haydn, and Wolfgang Amadeus Mozart were played. More than 30 composers and 150 musicians were involved with Padre Sojo and the Chacao school at some time or another during the period preceding independence.

THE QUEST FOR A NATIONAL CULTURE

In the education of young intellectuals of Caracas society during the final quarter of the eighteenth century, the philosophy of Aristotle and his medieval interpreters gave way to the doctrines of the Enlightenment, expressed by the Encyclopedists. The power of reason, the efficacy of empirical methods, the rights of man, a scientific universe, and political liberalism were exciting new concepts. Although the university remained committed to traditional Roman Catholic teachings, there were those who incorporated some of the ideas of the new philosophies in their lectures. Names like René Descartes, John Locke, Isaac Newton, and Etienne Condillac began creeping into theses. Most of the new knowledge, however, was obtained from books, conversations, and travels to Europe. Unique was the experience of Bolívar, whose unorthodox instructor, Simón Rodríguez, modeled his classroom on Jean Jacques Rousseau's principles.

This new body of thought encouraged and reinforced the spirit of rebellion that was arising among the young *criollos* (see Glossary). Perhaps because their colony had never been as closely tied to Spain as some other colonies of Spanish America, they were more receptive to ideas that augured change. Moreover, these ideas were more easily transmitted, as the Inquisition—an institution that had begun as a purely religious measure and developed into an instrument for political suppression—never achieved much strength in Venezuela and consequently did little to check new intellectual currents. Francisco de Miranda and others participated in or witnessed the French and American revolutions and thus saw the translation of these new intellectual positions into reality.

The demands of conspiratorial, later military and, finally, administrative action made this a period of action and ideas, rather than one of concrete literary and artistic production. Some writers expressed feelings of the new patriotism in short dramatic works with titles like *Morir por la patria es gloria* (To Die for the Nation is Glory) or in popular martial airs, but most turned to political polemics in pamphlets and in the embryonic newspapers.

Although known principally as a revolutionary, military leader, and statesman, Bolívar was also a profound thinker. Contained in letters to friends and associates and in several early constitutions, his most memorable ideas dealt with the political structure and future of Latin America. He clearly realized the incompatibilities between the enlightened political thought of the era and the reality of Venezuela and Latin America and foresaw the political chaos and internecine strife that became the fabric of subsequent history. Although he was one of the most outstanding Latin Americans of his age, his words of counsel were little heeded. Nevertheless, Bolívar was soon to become the subject of innumerable works. Only a few years after his death, the first in the long series of historical and quasi-historical writings appeared with the title *Documentos para la vida pública de Bolívar* (Documents for the Public Life of Bolívar), by Francisco Javier Yanes and Cristóbal Mendoza.

In spite of the turbulence of the times, which tended to lead the best minds toward action or polemical writings, one of the leading intellectuals, Andrés Bello, dedicated his creative talents to the production of a body of apolitical work. Less revolutionary than many of his contemporaries, he concerned himself with the conflict between traditional ideas represented in the scholastic tradition and the new philosophy of rationalism and empiricism. Cautious investigation led him to the acceptance of the thought of the school of John Locke and the reconciliation of spiritualism and the empirical method.

Although letters were the main form of expression in this period, painting also began to emerge, replacing music as the most significant artistic idiom. The same desire to reveal the new nation that had led writers to dwell on political and quasi-historical themes moved painters to incorporate historical subjects into the religious and more recent portrait traditions of pictorial art. The inclination was reinforced by the popularity of classical historical themes with the neoclassical European school whose influence had been felt in Venezuela. Although many of his contemporaries adopted this stylistic approach, Juan Lovera employed the unsophisticated realism of a self-taught artist. His most famous paintings were group portrayals of the independence leaders, with stiffly posed detail. Important men of the new Republic were also subjects for numerous individual portraits by Lovera.

With the establishment of the new nation and the destruction of old institutions, the rejection of Spain and the past, expressed politically in the independence movement and intellectually in the sharp shift in ideological orientation, was consolidated. Permanently lost was the cultural hegemony that the church, now eclipsed in power and resources by an unsympathetic state, had formerly exercised as patron, practitioner, and spectator in arts, letters, and thought. For inspiration the people now turned to the glorious moments of the immediate national past; for stylistic direction they continued to look to France. To a limited degree the ruling elite assumed the role of patron, as it shared and encouraged the aspirations of intellectuals for cultural as well as political progress.

In 1830 the Military Academy of Mathematics, the first official institution devoted to such studies, was established under the direction of Juan Manuel Cagigal. In the same year the Italian geographer Agustín Codazzi was commissioned to prepare a national atlas and geography. At the university, modernization of the rudimentary medical courses was effected by José María Vargas, who later became president of the country. Under the influence of these men a whole generation of naturalists and scholars arose. Public education, an innovation with the republican government, was placed under the direction of José Luis Ramos, a self-taught classical scholar and author of Spanish and Greco-Spanish grammars and dictionaries.

Eagerness to establish the national identity attracted many to historical themes, but simultaneously a throng of lesser talents were caught by the appeal of distant times and places. Division also existed along stylistic lines. Artists and many writers continued the neoclassicism of Bello; musicians and an increasing number of writers inclined toward a new tendency-romanticism. The outstanding follower of the older school, Rafael María Baralt, became the classical historian of the independence period with his *Resumen de la historia de Venezuela* (Summary of the History of Venezuela).

Fermín Toro, a contemporary of Baralt, served as a bridge between the two schools. A man of wide interests—natural history, the social sciences, poetry, and philosophy—he dispersed his ideas on the ills of Venezuela, English utilitarianism, and jurisprudence in articles, speeches, and essays. In these he employed the harmony and balance of a neoclassicist. In his fiction and poetry, however, a feeling for history, which was the fascination of the romantics, led him to a more emotional, restless form of expression. With Fermín Toro and many of the lesser creators of his day, the novel made its first appearance in the country. A product of the romantic movement, it was sentimental and often grandiloquent.

Juan Vicente González was the prime exponent of this early romanticism and in many ways the most representative of his age. A restless, exuberant individual, passionate in his loves and hates, González typified the romantic ideal. Inspired by François Chateaubriand, Lord Byron, and Victor Hugo, among others, he exalted the independence period, seeing it as a classical era of Venezuelan history. González had many followers. Chief among them was Felipe Larrazábal, author of the first biography of Bolívar and also a political polemicist for the liberals. Favorites of the era and remembered beyond their time were Abigaíl and Maitín Lozano.

In the shadow of the lofty neoclassic and romantic histories and coexisting with the quickly forgotten sentimental serials, cloak-and-dagger dramas, and journalistic political crossfire was a less pretentious genre, *costumbrismo*, the depiction of the customs and daily lives of the common people. Inspired initially by the inquiring, investigative spirit of the Enlightenment and later by the idyllic pastoral of a romanticism purged of its ecstatic fervor, *costumbrismo* became an increasingly popular form and eventually gave rise to realism in the novel and the short story. Writing for the newspapers of the 1830s and 1840s, Luis Correa presented the Caracas of that period, paying particular attention to the less grand elements. Daniel Mendoza, who appeared somewhat later, incorporated a satirical, critical tone that would become characteristic of the *costumbrista* writers.

Under the firm, though frequently unscrupulous, hand of President Antonio Guzmán Blanco, a mood of relative calm replaced the hectic atmosphere of experimentation and confusion of previous days. During his twenty-year period of influence Guzmán Blanco sought to bring a measure of cosmopolitanism to the capital in the tradition of the enlightened leaders of the European continent he so admired. Many beautification projects were carried out in Caracas; the Municipal Theater was built; public education was stimulated; and the first Academy of Fine Arts was established. A man of some literary pretensions, Guzmán Blanco's pride was the Venezuelan Academy, modeled on, and correspondent of, the Royal Spanish Academy of Language.

In Martín Tovar y Tovar, called at the end of his long lifetime, "the master of Venezuelan painting," Guzmán Blanco had an official artist. Although Tovar y Tovar was not necessarily an adherent of Guzmán Blanco, the nature of the art world of his day kept him in close association with the government. In the absence of wealthy private clients, the artist was dependent for his livelihood on official commissions. In accord with official taste most of Tovar y Tovar's canvasses depicted battle scenes, classical allegory, and important figures in past and present public life. Equally responsible for the choice of subject matter, however, was the prevalence of the influence of the staid French neoclassic school. Under the influence of the instructors at the newly established Academy of Fine Arts and the demands of the only important art market, Tovar y Tovar's disciples, such as Arturo Michelena, Cristóbal Rojas, and Tito Salas, remained with only slight modification within neoclassicism throughout the rest of the nineteenth century.

Less static was the literary world, where along with somewhat modified older traditions, new tendencies were cautiously emerging. The exuberance of early romanticism was still visible in such words as *Venezuela Heróica* (Heroic Venezuela), an extremely popular epic portrayal of the glory of Bolívar and the War of Independence, by Eduardo Blanco. More typical was the spirit of moderation and introspection in the poetry of Pérez Bonalde. In nostalgic verse, inspired by the calmer, mysterious, romantic poets of northern Europe, he reached a level of sentiment unattained since Bello. The mixture of the stylistic elements of realism and naturalism, with romantic plots and descriptive, picturesque passages in the *costumbrista* tradition, was new. The setting of these narratives was no longer some distant, exotic place, but Venezuela.

As more and more novels appeared, the national current became stronger. Romero García's *Peonía* was the most complete expression of the embryonic tendency. For the first time there was a conscious attempt to exalt a native region, the *llanos* (plains). Moreover, a critical reform spirit and the suggestion of the power of geography over the inhabitants of the land represented a new concern for national themes that previously had been reflected only in the historical and *costumbrista* pieces. The theater, in the outbreak of plays of social satire and popular or *costumbrista* inspiration, showed similar inclinations.

In nonfiction this national preoccupation led to the study of natural sciences, folklore, ethnology, linguistics, and economics as well as history by men like Cecilio Acosta and Aristides Rojas. Although romantic touches were apparent in the vivid historical writings of Rojas, he, Acosta, and their associates favored a disciplined humanistic approach. At the Central University of Venezuela, Rafael Villacencio and Adolfo Ernst introduced new concepts that sparked vigorous philosophical discussion. Challenging the traditionalists and theologians, whose influence had not completely disappeared, they introduced the works of Charles Darwin, Auguste Comte, and Herbert Spencer. A new practical science and the theory of evolution shattered the old philosophical idealism of absolutes.

TWENTIETH-CENTURY INNOVATIONS

With the young, university-trained generation, intellectual activity quickened in tempo and broadened in scope. A generally scientific approach, moreover, produced more professional attitudes, which in turn led to the creation of a continuous and solid body of work. Engendered by widespread agreement in ideas and methods, a feeling of unity developed that resulted in the appearance of schools and movements, thus ending the tradition of the isolated scholar or writer. The generation set out to modernize or abolish traditions, first in the areas of scholarship and prose fiction, later in painting, poetry, and music. For most, the thematic point of departure was the national existence in its various manifestations. Some sought merely to depict; others, to explain or criticize. In reaction, there were also those who chose elegantly to evade the reality of the local scene.

The effects of the scientific philosophy were most visible in the expanding social sciences. Historians wanted an objective, comprehensive explanation of the past. The first to bring the modern methods of analysis to historiography was José Gil Fortoul. He methodically reconstructed the past in a series of epochs rather than events. Moreover, in works like *El hombre y la historia* (Man and History), he gave a new importance to the society behind the heroes, bringing in the effects of economics, psychology, geography, and ethics on historical development. Similarly, a contemporary of Gil Fortoul, Lisandro Alvarado, revealed the social content of the mid-nineteenth century Federalist War period in his *Historia de la revolución* (History of the Revolution).

The school that these men generated paid considerable attention to the previously neglected colonial period as well as to the republican era. Beginning with a doctoral thesis submitted in 1909 by Angel César Rivas, the trend toward the reinstatement of Spain in national history culminated in the work of Mario Briceño Iragorry. Exalting Spain, he attributed all of Venezuela's ills to Anglo-Saxon influence and activity.

The developing interest in the social factor in history led to the appearance of sociological studies, the majority of which emphasized the colonial contribution. Ethnic background, social and political evolution, and the origins of national institutions were among the subjects pursued. The application of Social Darwinism to Venezuelan history brought Laureano Vallentilla Lanz and Pedro Manuel Arcaya to a formulation of that pessimistic sociology that was arising throughout Latin America. As a result of the factors of race, climate, and culture, they saw society as unstable and incapable of government by representative democracy; by the process of natural selection, the strongest emerged to become the necessary dictators. Since the writings that put forth this theory appeared during the regime of Juan Vicente Gómez, they were seen as an apology for the authoritarian ruler (see ch. 3, Historical Setting).

Although in the creative arts the nativist tendency, accompanied by important stylistic modifications, crystallized and became dominant, the most striking development represented a temporary departure from this theme. Two literary reviews, *El Cojo Ilustrado* (The Illustrious Cripple) and *Cosmopolis*, which appeared in the 1890s, brought together a group of young writers eager to absorb the new European currents. Throughout Latin America the assimilation of French symbolism and metrical form and Italian decadence brought a refined elegance, a richness of sensual imagery, and a spirit of artistic rebelliousness and disenchantment that resulted in a new aesthetic form, namely modernism. The color, mystery, and exoticism of the romanticists were present but stripped of their sentimental projections. Although in most places modernism found its earliest and best expression in poetry, in Venezuela the novel was its primary vehicle. Adopting the modernist orientation, the young group brought the novel to maturity and developed a new medium, the short story.

Looking for a world that corresponded to their new style of expression, many modernists abandoned Venezuela. Some writers, such as Pedro César Domínici, who developed the theme of exoticism in pre-Christian Alexandria in his *Dynonysos*, accomplished this through the use of distant times and places. In the works of others the attitude was more clearly one of spiritual rejection. Setting his novels, *Idolos Rotos* (Broken Idols) and *Sangre Patricia* (Noble Blood), in Caracas at the turn of the century, Manuel Díaz Rodríguez created an artistic world of the aristocrat in conflict with sordid realities. Unable to accept or change such unpleasantness, his pessimistic protagonists pursued a course of evasion in suicide or exile. Like many a contemporary writer or artist, the characters saw themselves as superior individuals above a society that could never understand nor appreciate them.

In contrast, the critical writers plunged directly into the life around them, enlivening the satirical bent of the *costumbrista* tradition. Often using *costumbrismo*, in fact, as a protective veil, they addressed themselves to the political and social ills of the period. Books like *El cabito*, by Pedro Morantes, painted a bitter picture of Caracas social life, with dictator Cipriano Castro as the main character.

Most prominent, however, in this realistic trend was Rufino Blanco Fombona. Beginning his literary efforts as a poet within the modernist movement of *El Cojo Ilustrado* and *Cosmopolis* groups, Blanco Fombona turned to a more blunt prose for his sharp portrayals of contemporary life. In a dynamic, almost journalistic style, best expressed in short stories, he recreated familiar persons and places. As a critic, Blanco Fombona used satire and caricature in novels, articles, and pamphlets in waging a personal war against Castro's successor, Juan Vicente Gómez.

A contemporary of Blanco Fombona, Luis Urbaneja Archelpohl, combined modernism and realism in a synthesis that set the course of prose narrative. To the *criollo* themes he brought the artistic preoccupations of the modernists. In *En este país* (In This Country) he presented the same conflict between the cultured aristocracy and reality as the modernists but, unlike them, opted in favor of the new, willful, dynamic society of change and progress. Similarly, his stylistic consciousness elevated the *costumbrista* pieces to true short stories.

Younger writers who followed adopted almost without exception the *criollo* theme. Grouped around the magazines *La Alborada* (The Dawn) and *Sagitario* (Sagittarius), they reacted against modernism, with its disdain for sentiment and strong emotional involvement. Within a generally realistic vein, one group tended toward naturalism; the other was more consciously artistic.

Of the naturalistic group was José Rafael Pocaterra, a self-declared antiliterary writer. Between 1913 and 1922 Pocaterra wrote a number of novels and short stories about people and life in the different social strata of his native Valencia. Ironic, sarcastic, and satirical, these works reflected the influence of the Russian realists as well as those of France and Spain. Jailed toward the end of the Gómez regime for political involvement, Pocaterra wrote only two books after his early prolific period. *Memorias de un venezolano en decadencia* (Memoirs of a Venezuelan in Decadence) related the corruption of the ruling class, its adulation of Gómez, and what the author felt was the inherent cruelty of the Venezuelan nature.

Less brutal in his prose, but with an equally strong reform spirit, Rómulo Gallegos gave fullest expression to the *criollo* theme begun earlier by Romero García in his novel *Peonía.* The development of Gallegos as a writer was gradual, beginning with essays, short stories, and dramatic writings that were tentative and incomplete steps toward the central issues of his novels. In his first novel, *El último solar* (The Last Mansion), he brought in the theme of a destructive natural environment and the social concerns that disturbed his generation. *La trepadora* (The Climber) was a less pessimistic novel that reflected the possibilities of a new, constructive society. Most famous, however, is *Doña Bárbara,* which brought Gallegos international recognition and made him the grand man of national letters. Reflecting the unchanneled, disruptive forces of the *llanos*, the character Doña Bárbara is a symbol of the barbarism that must be destroyed before the country could free the sleeping spirit of civilization. Shifting among lyric, psychological, sociological, and *costumbrista* positions, Gallegos achieved a previously unattained universality within the specifically *criollo*. In *Cantaclaro*, considered by many critics a finer novel, the author again chose the *llanos* as a setting but in more poetic language sought a more tranquil mood. Later works retained the themes of nature and social protest but were set in the Guianas Highlands and Barlovento. As the country's best known author, Gallegos became the object of systematic, critical studies and achieved sufficient prestige to merit election to the presidency in 1948 (see ch. 3, Historical Setting).

Teresa de la Parra belonged to neither tendency of the realist school. An aristocrat by birth, she described for the first time the intimate world of the *criollo* woman. *Memorias de Mamá Blanca* (Memories of Mama Blanca) is the pleasant nostalgic recollection of a Venezuela that was disappearing with the advent of petroleum. This introspective, quiet, feminine prose has inspired a number of later works.

With a group of young poets who emerged in 1918, verse began to show the effects of the nativist inspiration. Francisco Lazo Marti had forecast this inclination in 1901 with "Silva Criolla," a nostalgic, symbolic eulogy to the *llanos*, in the tradition of Bello and

Peréz Bonalde. Martí's contemporaries had been lost in the symbolism, Parnassian, and later modernist movements, none of which produced memorable names. Most popular and best known outside Venezuela, Andrés Eloy Blanco brought back the folk couplets and romance of the Spanish tradition. Although not lacking in concept and abstraction, his poetry is rich in popular proverbs and myths in the troubadour style. Others were less lighthearted, interpreting nature, folklore, and legend in an introspective, brooding manner. Under the influence of the Spanish poets of 1898, they discarded the sumptuous imagery of the modernists for a deceptive simplicity, which in great synthesis aspired to capture the essential.

Artists also entered a new era of activity and innovation. To a greater degree than other forms of expression, art had been held fast by tradition. Breaking with the neoclassic painting of the Academy of Fine Arts, a group of artists formed the Círculo de Bellas Artes (Fine Arts Circle) in 1912. In this way they hoped to bypass the academy and bring their work directly to the attention of the public. Led by a Romanian, Samys Mutznez, they painted the landscape surrounding Caracas from nature instead of in the studio. The rigidity of form and the dark palette of neoclassicism disappeared from their work. Further stimulation toward the out-of-doors method was provided by Nicolas Ferdinandov and Emilio Boggio, the latter a Venezuelan who had spent most of his life in France under the influence of the impressionists.

Only one member of the School of Caracas, however, pursued the problems of light, form, and color with the intensity the French artists had exhibited forty years earlier. Armando Reverón left Caracas in 1920 to spend his remaining thirty-four years in rare dedication, painting by the sea in a small primitive hut. At work in the dazzling tropical sun, he sought to capture the brilliant white light on canvas. This permeating light came to dominate Reverón's paintings of the figures, forms, and landscape around his retreat.

Music also awoke from the decline into which it had fallen after the independence period. Spurred by the presence of foreign musicians in Caracas, the appearance of phonograph records, and the introduction of European currents, talented individuals, such as Juan Bautista Plaza, José Antonio Calcaño, and Vicente Emilio Sojo, reactivated, the once—great tradition in the early 1920s. In style they leaned toward the French impressionists and incorporated a stylization of national musical elements on a much more sophisticated plane than had the sentimental romantic or popular composers. Many of the so-called generation of 1920 soon gave up active composing for criticism, historical research, and teaching. Sojo helped found a choral group, Orfeón Lamas, which brought back many of the old colonial compositions and stimulated public interest in music. He also helped promote the establishment of the

Venezuelan Symphony Orchestra and became its director. As director of the National School of Music, founded in 1936, he was influential in the creation of a generation of musicians and composers.

CONTEMPORARY TRENDS

Since the 1930s intellectual and creative tendencies have been less unified. The spirit of dissatisfaction that was manifested politically in the student revolt of 1928 was also felt in the world of arts, letters, and thought and initiated a search, still in progress, for new orientations and methods. The result has been the destruction of the cohesion that the widespread acceptance of inevitable evolutionary progress in thought and nativism in creative activity had brought about. The entrance into an era of greater prosperity and modernization, marked by social as well as material change, acted as a stimulus to the establishment of contact with the new trends in Europe and, more recently, the United States. The resulting eclecticism has led, in varying degrees, to modification and innovation in form and content in the modes of artistic and intellectual expression. Hence, the realistic portrayal of local elements coexists with more cosmopolitan international styles.

Affluence, aspirations toward greater sophistication, and increased educational opportunity, with a resultant rise in public interest, have sustained and augmented cultural activity. The proliferation of names, generations, and schools has been noteworthy. According to one leading writer, intellectuals are more conscious of the demands of an expanded audience, which is now no longer merely an isolated collection of friends and associates. Although facilities for bringing works to public attention and for promoting scholarship and research are still limited, the efforts of government and private entities have prompted a considerable improvement. Government-supported editions of classics and outstanding contemporary works overshadow the limited activity of commercial printers and publishers (see ch. 14, Public Information).

National prizes in literature are given each year, alternating between poetry and prose. Similar awards are given in the plastic arts and in music, supplemented by the private prizes created by individuals and organizations. Museums, with the aid of related associations, and foreign diplomatic missions also contribute significantly to supporting and publicizing cultural activity. Similarly, the universities serve an important function as cultural centers, engaging in publishing, holding expositions of various types, sponsoring public lectures, and generally bringing together leading representatives of various fields. In addition to open involvement in politics and public life, interrupted only during periods of dictatorship, many artists and intellectuals become associated at some time during the course of their careers with institutions of higher learning, preferably the Central University of Venezuela (see ch. 7, Education).

Philosophy and Science

Of the natural sciences, medicine and the physical sciences have been the most vigorously pursued. Scientific investigation has been stimulated by the expansion of the Ministry of Health and Social Assistance and the awards of private organizations, such as the Creole Foundation. The Latin American Institute for Forestry Research was established in 1957 at the University of the Andes (in Mérida) by agreement between the Venezuelan government and the Food and Agriculture Organization of the United Nations. At the institute scholarship students from various countries engage in research aimed at advantageous utilization of the great forest resources of the Western Hemisphere.

History, politics, sociology and, more recently, economics occupy many writers, of whom the outstanding representative is Mariano Picón Salas. His talent for the lucid exposition of ideas has been revealed in his numerous essays on a variety of topics in the Caracas daily *El Nacional* as well as in a number of books. A humanist with a broad cultural background, his works on cultural history—*De la colonia a la independencia* (From the Colony to Independence), *Historia y proceso de la literatura venezolana* (History and Process of Venezuelan Literature), and *Comprensión de Venezuela* (A Comprehension of Venezuela)—are especially noteworthy. The activities of Picón Salas have extended beyond letters to include three professorships, two ambassadorships, and representation on the Venezuelan delegation to the United Nations Educational, Scientific and Cultural Organization (UNESCO).

In philosophy, and particularly in social and political thought, national preoccupation is strong and is probably responsible for the mood of pessimism and anxiety that has been called the common denominator of recent generations. For many, unfulfilled expectations of rapid economic, political, and cultural progress have generated disillusionment and intense national self-analysis. Although the old pessimistic sociology has not been totally abandoned, more adequate explanations are sought. A variety of systems of thought—Marxism, existentialism, and neohumanism—have won adherents. One contemporary thinker, Ernesto Mayz Vallenilla, in dealing with the question of originality has developed a theory of the need for a process of continuous origination, which he contrasts with the two positions that he believes divide his countrymen: attachment to the past and, more widespread, the "mañana complex," or the abiding conviction that everything will come at some future date.

In his approach to historical philosophy, Augusto Mijares combines nineteenth-century scientific rationalism with twentieth-century idealism, the latter being especially apparent in his concepts of reality. Spanish Americanism is the fundamental trait of his thought; in that end and other aspects his works resemble those of the Spanish philosopher Miguel Unamuno.

Like Picón Salas and others, his varied career has included representing his country abroad. He also served as minister of education from 1948 to 1950. In 1956 he was awarded the national prize for literature. His most important book is *La interpretación pesimista de la sociología hispanoamericano* (The Pessimistic Interpretation of Hispanic American Sociology), written in 1938, shortly after the death of Gómez. In this work he rebels against the interpretation of Spanish American history as centering on the phenomenon of dictatorship and finds cause for optimism in the persistence of the ideal of a civil society.

In addition to his more prominent political activism, Rómulo Betancourt has contributed to the literary expression of the ideals and goals of his generation. Democracy, socialism, and nationalism are the most persistent themes of his many works, which include: *Dos meses en las cárceles de Gómez* (Two Months in the Prisons of Gómez), 1928; *Problemas venezolanos* (Venezuelan Problems), 1940; and *Trayectoria democrática de una revolución* (Democratic Trajectory of a Revolution), 1948.

Creative Writing

Developments in letters have been among the less revolutionary. With few exceptions novelists have continued in a fundamentally realistic vein. Yet with foreign influences and stylistic modification, their realism is generally of a subtler, less ferocious quality than that of their antecedents. Strong symbolism and the dominance of nature have been replaced by an emphasis on man, but social consciousness and the reform spirit are still present. Many critics see a shift to realism in the appearance in 1930 of Arturo Uslar Pietri's *Lanzas coloradas* (Scarlet Lances), an excellent novel that dealt with the wars of independence in a vivid and lyrical manner. In rapid, impressionistic strokes, Uslar Pietri painted the masses that composed the rebellious colony.

Other authors followed the same synthetic technique. Antonio Arraiz, in *Puros hombres* (Real Men), was representative of the writers who, in the 1930s and 1940s, explored the repressive atmosphere and rural poverty of the Gómez period. Country life, revealed with social consciousness and introspection, has provided the theme for numerous novelists, among them, Julian Padrón, whose works were usually set in eastern Venezuela.

There are indications that the popularity of the rural setting is beginning to diminish, but few have turned to the new, urban, and cosmopolitan Venezuela for inspiration. One exception is Ramón Díaz Sánchez, who developed the social aspect of life in the oilfields in an early novel *Mene* (1936) and, more recently, in *Casandra* (1957). His latest novel *Borburata*, which came out in 1960, deals with the infrequently treated theme of the rise of the urban middle class and the corresponding decline of the landed aristocracy. The decay of the traditional society also found expression in Miguel Silva Otero's *Casas muertas* (Dead Mansions), as did the social problems of the oilfields in his *Oficina numero 1* (Office Number One). Other novelists with less success, have emulated popular foreign writers in the search for new techniques and themes, but a satisfactory course has not yet been found; there is concern that the national novel is in a period of crisis.

More vigorous and inventive, the short story has achieved great popularity and has been cultivated by most novelists. The stylistic and thematic renovation of this genre has been accomplished to a greater degree of satisfaction than the novel. Conscious of the innovations of writers like Aldous Huxley, James Joyce, D. H. Lawrence, and Erskine Caldwell, the short story writers have attempted to incorporate their work into modern narrative trends. The reality of which they write is tragic, introspective, and poetic. Although the approach is usually subjective and the particulars are taken from the local scene, the themes are universal, with an emphasis on social content and reform.

Among the short story writers, Uslar Pietri is again the innovator. In his several collections, he manifests his concept that the short story should be the creation of an impression rather than the mere narration of an incident. Writing on the genre in general, Uslar Pietri attributes its growing popularity to the nature of the local atmosphere, which offers numerous distractions and impediments to the pursuit of a literary career. This theory is well supported by the writer's own experience for, in addition to being an essayist, biographer, and playwright, as well as short story writer and novelist, he has held the portfolio of three ministries, had three professorships, had been secretary general to the president of the Republic and a national senator and, in the 1963 elections, was an independent candidate for the presidency (see ch. 12, Political Dynamics).

An upsurge in the attraction of poetry has tended to alter somewhat the country's image as a land of prose writers. The modern movement dates from 1928, when young poets liberated poetry from traditional forms. Europe was the source of stylistic innovations, and image and metaphor inspired by contemporary life were modernized. Native themes were retained, but a more universal outlook was injected. "Aspero," written in 1924 by Antonio Arraiz, led the way with its use of free verse and tone of lyric grandeur somewhat reminiscent of Walt Whitman. A political opponent of Gómez, founder and editor of the Caracas daily *El Nacional* and author of numerous works in prose, Arraiz nevertheless continued writing poetry, producing in the "Unfinished Symphony" a poem that many rank among the country's greatest.

Soon afterward, the Viernes group, so called for the magazine it published, which sought to dignify poetry and introduce trends of all directions, went further. Reacting against nativism, Vicente Gervasi and Otto de Sola, among others, adopted an introspective, often highly personal form of expression that explored the many facets of European vanguard movements. The desire was to move as far and as quickly as possible from past traditions. Within the group there was considerable variety, and the atmosphere was one of experimentation. In a short time the magazine disappeared, and the group disintegrated.

Contemporary poetry proceeds in the spirit of innovation begun in 1928 and represents a fusion of the contributions of the Viernes and the groups that arose in reaction to it. With the modern symbolism of the vanguard is combined an intellectual, orderly approach that reexamines human values on a variety of levels. Venezuelan themes, politics, society, geography, and folklore have been reintroduced in a paradox of anguish and affectionate pleasure. Of the great number of poets writing today, critics single out Juan Liscano, writing in the folklore vein, and José Ramón Medina, most promising members of the younger generation. Medina's intimate lyrical verse, which has merited the national prize in literature, deals with idealized love, human fraternity, and a tranquil, pure nature.

The Performing Arts

Drama

During the 1950s and 1960s considerable activity was apparent in the theater, a consistently minor medium in the past. Stimulus was provided by two foreigners—Juana Sujo, an Argentine actress, and Brazilian director Horacio Peterson—who had been hired by a film company to provide technical aid. Both contributed to the training of actors, technicians, and directors through their activities and experimental and student theater groups. The establishment of several small theaters encouraged writers in other fields to produce works for the stage.

In addition, young writers have emerged who have dedicated their efforts exclusively to drama. Isaac Chocrón, influenced by the English theater, has dealt with the general theme of man and Venezuela in a refined, poetic, and psychological manner. Working with the same basic issue, Román Chalbaud employs the existentialist treatment of shock, sharp contrast, and apparent insensitivity. Either directly or indirectly, politics is strongly reflected in the current dramatic output. Among the foreign works staged, those of Tennessee Williams and Eugene Ionesco have had particular success. Preference is for the avant-garde, which incorporates dramatic social problems. Efforts have had a reception sufficient to inspire the creation of the annual Festival of the Theater.

An annual National Drama Prize was established in 1970 by the Institute of Culture and Fine Arts. The prize of Bs5,000 (4.5 bolivars equal US$1) in cash and a medal is intended to encourage and recognize the works of Venezuelan playwrights.

Music

The contemporary trend toward national self-expression in serious music has been characterized by the use of native melodies and rhythms. Notable compositions in this style include the vocal works of Vicente Emilio Sojo and Maria Luisa Escobar's ballet, *Orquideas Azules* (Blue Orchids), based on Venezuelan folklore.

Renewed interest and activity in music since the early 1950s, inspired by nationalistic innovations, has been evidenced by the popularity of the Venezuelan Symphony Orchestra, the organization of new orchestral societies and free Sunday concerts, and the large number of internationally famous artists who have visited the country. Festivals devoted to the music of the Americas were held in Caracas in 1954, 1957, and 1966. A Caribbean Song Festival, involving participants from eight countries, was held in the northern coastal city of Coro in December 1970.

Amateur and professional opera, choruses, and children's musical groups have also been enthusiastically supported. An experimental orchestra, formed under the sponsorship of the Venezuelan Symphony Orchestra as a training medium for young musicians, gave its first concert in May 1970. The orchestra comprises sixty-six students from public and private conservatories in the country and is directed by Evencio Castellanos, the accomplished conductor, composer, and pianist.

The Graphic Arts

Painting and Sculpture

The most significant innovations and broadest acceptance of international styles have taken place within the plastic arts. Around 1930, the painters, while retaining a preference for landscape, began to explore different creative problems. Following the course of the French school of painters, such as Paul Cézanne, Pablo Picasso, and Georges Braque, their work showed a new concern for structure. The first painters instructed at the National School of Applied and

Plastic Arts, established four years earlier, began to emerge by 1940, and there was a return to figurative art. Simultaneously, the influence of the Mexican school of stylized realism, with strong emphasis on social themes, began to be felt. Although a whole group of artists adopted this approach, Héctor Poleo was the most notable. His best work dates from the 1940s and explores the expressive possibilities of strong color, simplified form, and patternistic composition. Inspired by the horror of war, his canvases also had a surrealistic quality of fantasy that has not appeared in the work of others since that time. Other figurative painters adopted the social themes of the Mexican school but not the style. Instead, they carried them to satire and caricature or worked with the human form in the manner of the cubists.

Although these variations of objective painting are being continued, abstract art is overwhelmingly dominant. This movement began in the late 1940s with a group of students who went to Paris to study in rebellion against what they considered the outmoded styles popular at home. Calling themselves the dissidents, they created a magazine to express their views. Until 1958 they refused to submit their work to the national salon, which had been in existence since 1940. When their work did appear, it consistently won the top prizes, although local reception was generally quite restrained. Greater enthusiasm for their work has been shown internationally.

Originally, the abstractionists, led by Alejandro Otero, embraced a cool, precise, geometrical style. By the early 1960s, however, this approach had been largely abandoned for kinetic investigations, exploration of the materials themselves, or the informal expression of texture, surface, and color, as well as the studies of movement in space of Jesús Soto, one of the best known contemporary artists. Noteworthy is the considerable number of foreigners and women who have made important contributions.

Sculpture, never prominent among the arts, is currently becoming more important. Most of its best practitioners, however, are painters, who incorporate the same styles and experimentation found in contemporary painting. Among the country's outstanding contemporary sculptors are Francisco Narvaes and Alejandro Colina.

The center of the creative art movement has been the Museum of Fine Arts in Caracas. Other galleries have also made important contributions to the country's cultural development. In 1970 the Juancho Capriles Gallery presented a unique exhibition of fifty-one paintings by twenty-seven inmates of the Caracas jail. The exhibition—promoted by the wife of the president of the National Congress, Senator Miguel Angel Capriles, owner of the gallery, and the Ministry of Justice—was so well received that plans were initiated to open an art school in the jail.

Architecture

Although modern architechtural activity began late, the country has rapidly become a principal area of achievement. The tremendous expansion in government building programs, which changed the face of Caracas, served as a stimulus, but the aesthetic and technical orientations were largely the result of the efforts of Carlos Raúl Villanueva. Educated at the Beaux Arts School in France, Villanueva returned to Caracas in the 1940s to become the primary force in the creation of the College of Architecture of the Central University of Venezuela, where he taught for sixteen years. Many of his students came to form the ranks of the Venezuelan Society of Architects, of which he was founder and first president. Villanueva also exerted influence through his positions of counselor to the Labor Bank (Banco Obrero), principal constructor of numerous low-cost housing projects, and director of the Commission of Urbanization.

Lacking a long and outstanding tradition in the field, contemporary architects have escaped the excessive formalism that has hampered development elsewhere on the Spanish American continent. Training has been obtained in a wide variety of foreign institutions as well as locally with the result that most buildings fall stylistically within the so-called modern international school. A negative effect noted by some observers has been that full advantage has not generally been taken of local climatic and geographical factors.

The customary building materials are masonry and reinforced concrete, with decorative effects supplied by the materials themselves, window arrangement, large murals, and sculpture-in-the-round. Although the concept of functionalism enjoys great acceptance, aesthetic quality is given equal importance. Typical is the considerable collaboration between architects and artists, who form an intimate community in contrast to the professional separation characteristic in the United States. In spite of the fact that most important commissions come from the government, the architect is allowed great freedom in his work and in the choice of his associates. The prestige that comes to a government from supporting an important architectural accomplishment is a significant factor in this liberal official attitude.

Most imaginative and successful, the Central University of Venezuela, rebuilt under the direction of Villanueva, has been called by art authority Paul Damaz the best example in the world of the "beneficial influences that architecture and other plastic arts can have on each other." The complex of buildings, arranged in an asymmetrical fashion, is complemented by free-standing murals and sculpture created by the country's leading artists, such as Alejandro Otero, and by such well-known international figures as Alexander Calder, Fernand Leger, and Jean Arp.

Folklore

Since the early 1960s there has been a revival of interest, especially among the young, in the country's rich folkloric tradition. Spanish influence on songs and dances is dominant and is reflected in the popularity of the *cuatro*, a four-stringed guitar.

The *joropo*, Venezuela's national dance, is Spanish in origin and is performed in six-eight time to the accompaniment of the *cuatro* and maracas, which are made of dried gourd shells. The rhythmic pattern of the *pasillo* (dance) is also characteristically Spanish. The *tanguito*, a version of the Argentinian tango, and the *merengue*, danced throughout the Caribbean area, are also popular in Venezuela.

African influence is manifest in the rhythmic aspects of folk music in some areas. Syncopated rhythms and a variety of percussion instruments accompany drum dances or are used in combination with melodies of Spanish origin.

Other types of folk music, such as the *tono llanero*, sung by the cowboys of the plains, are associated with certain occupations, chores, or with certain regions of the country. For example, a dance known as *Los Diablos Danzantes de Yare* (The Dancing Devils of Yare) is performed every year on Corpus Christi Day in the state of Miranda.

Although aboriginal musical traditions have had little influence on the common folk music of the country, they remain strong in certain isolated regions, especially south of the Orinoco River. The Indians' songs, generally associated with religious rites, take the form of monotonous chants. Their instruments include flutes and a number of percussion instruments, such as a half coconut covered with parchment and placed in a hole in the ground.

The government has encouraged the study and performance of folk music through the Institute of Folklore Studies in Caracas and the promotion of foreign tours for the folklore dancing ensemble, Venezuelan Dances (Danzas Venezuela), headed by Yolando Moreno. The dance ensemble completed a ten-week tour of the United States in March 1970 and, after Venezuela reestablished diplomatic relations with the Soviet Union in April 1970, made arrangements for a two-month tour of the Soviet Union and other Eastern European countries.

CHAPTER 9

RELIGION

At the close of 1970 the vast majority of the people were Roman Catholics. As a result of missionary efforts, about 1 percent of the population was Protestant, and the number was growing slowly. Several thousand Jews were concentrated in the major cities. A small number of Indians continued to practice their traditional religions, but many were becoming Catholics. Religious freedom was guaranteed by the Constitution of 1961, as it had been since 1836. Although there was no state religion, the Roman Catholic Church had close ties with the government.

During the period of Spanish domination the church played a highly influential role in secular as well as spiritual matters, but this very power, which the church sought to increase, eventually provoked resistance on the part of the state. A series of restrictions on the church's prerogatives enacted by the nineteenth-century republican governments severely reduced its scope of power and influence and undermined its prestige.

During the twentieth century, however, relations between the church and state have been harmonious, based on the acknowledged predominance of the state in temporal affairs. From the nineteenth century until 1964 the state retained the right of ecclesiastical patronage: congressional consent to the papal nominations of bishops was required. An agreement was reached between the Holy See and Venezuela in 1964 that redefined the crucial issue of patronage and granted somewhat more autonomy to the church. According to the 1964 modus vivendi, the president of the Republic has the privilege of knowing the names of the candidates proposed by the Holy See before their official nomination and is permitted at this time to make any objections of a general political nature he wishes. Since the overthrow of the Marcos Pérez Jiménez government, church-state relations have been extremely cordial.

An acute shortage of clergymen has plagued the church throughout much of its history, but there were indications in late 1970 that the situation was improving. The ratio of priests to inhabitants increased after World War II, largely as a result of an influx of foreign clerics. Consequently, in 1970 well over half of the clergy was foreign—largely Spanish. In some cases it was hampered in pastoral duties by a lack of knowledge of Venezuelan problems.

Efforts made by the church in the 1960s and in 1970 to recruit native-born Venezuelans have been only moderately successful.

Attitudes toward the church are changing, in part because of its increased social concern and involvement with temporal problems. The social attitudes that developed in Latin America in the 1960s in response to encyclicals by popes from Leo XIII to John XXIII, and Paul VI, the Second Vatican Council, and the ideas enunciated at the Latin American Bishops' Conference (Consejo Episcopal Latinoamericano—CELAM) in Medellín, Colombia, in 1968 have been accepted by much of the hierarchy, the clergy, and many laymen.

The Archbishop of Caracas, José Humberto Quintero, in effect the leader of the national church, has repeatedly spoken out in favor of social justice, the elimination of ignorance and poverty, and the need for dealing with the country's social problems. Many prelates and clergymen are also concerned with pastoral reforms to increase the level of church participation and knowledge of religious doctrine. Efforts have been made to reduce the size of dioceses, archdioceses, and parishes, to develop a lay apostolate, and to form new pastoral organizations. Minor conflicts have developed between younger clergymen and laymen and the hierarchy over the speed of change and the use of violence. The church gained prestige from the nomination of the archbishop to the College of Cardinals in 1961.

The ability of the progressives in the church to translate their ideas into action has been restricted by limited financial resources. With little property and few contributions, the church is largely dependent on government subsidies for its programs. It has succeeded, however, in establishing a large number of schools with limited or no tuition to serve urban working-class children, in many cases those living in the large *barrios* (settlements of substandard housing on the fringes of major cities).

If the image of the church in the public view has changed, traditional attitudes and reactions toward religion show little modification. Venezuelans continue to practice Catholicism, which is doctrinally nonrigorous but deeply emotional. Adherence to traditional Catholic beliefs is particularly strong in rural areas in which the old agricultural way of life is basically unchanged, as in the Andean states of Mérida, Táchira, and Trujillo. Catholicism in these areas tends to penetrate many aspects of daily life. In some regions, African and Indian elements have been added to a basically Christian pattern, but relatively few syncretistic Afro-Catholic or Indian-Catholic cults exist.

The social changes produced by urbanization and industrialization generally result in a lower level of religious practice as the traditional religious community is disrupted and the urban environment fails to recreate a viable religious life for the migrant. For the long-term resident of an urban area, an attitude of religious indifference is often typical.

HISTORICAL BACKGROUND

Colonial

The Roman Catholic Church was established soon after the country's discovery, but for several reasons it never became deeply rooted. The long years of conquest bred factionalism and individualism throughout the society between church and state and within the church itself. More concerned with the wealthier colonies, Spain did little to establish order. Limited attention from the crown resulted in insufficient money and personnel. Furthermore, the administration of the church, divided between Bogotá and Santo Domingo throughout the colonial period, decentralized ecclesiastical authority in the territory.

Both the local and more distant hierarchies were unable to maintain effective control for the difficult geography and consequent lack of communication made supervision in all but the coastal cities impossible. Another factor was the indigenous population, which in many countries was an important source of support. In the more accessible areas, the Indians were decimated by the white man's diseases and the numerous military campaigns, and those who remained were rapidly integrated into Hispanic society. In the interior, where isolation permitted greater independence and control, the mobility and low cultural level of the Indian groups and arduous physical conditions made success limited. Yet in spite of its lesser relative strength, the church was still the most important civilizing agent and was able to exert considerable influence in social, political, and economic affairs.

Because Spain's Catholic monarchs felt a responsibility for the conversion of the native population to Christianity, missionaries were among the first white men who entered the new colony. Within a few years after Columbus discovered the northern shore in 1498, they were at work in Cumaná. One of these early missions was the work of the famous defender of the Indians, Fray Bartolomé de las Casas. Lack of success in overcoming the hostility of the Indians, which was provoked and intensified by visiting slave traders, resulted in a transfer of activity to the new center at Coro. As early as 1531 a bishopric was established in that city. Although Caracas became the de facto seat of the diocese some fifty years later, Coro remained the legal see until well into the seventeenth century. A third area of missionary activity was the Guianas. Through the colonial period repeated efforts were made to subdue this region, but isolation and economic hardships made success impossible until the end of the era.

The Spanish kings, although concerned about the conversion of the native inhabitants of their new lands, sought royal political control. Since the Vatican represented a potential competitor, the Spanish crown sought to institute a system of civil controls in the colonies similar to that which had evolved during the Middle Ages in Spain.

Through a series of papal bulls promulgated in the last decade of the fifteenth century and in the first decade of the sixteenth century, certain privileges were conceded that enabled the crown to wield even more authority over the church in Latin America than in Spain. The fundamental rights granted were the exclusive privilege of Christianization of the Indians, the tithes of the Latin American church and universal patronage over the church, which meant the right to select candidates for all ecclesiastical positions. As practiced, the privilege was directly exercised by the crown only in the selection of the most important positions; lesser ones were left to the royal representatives in the colonies.

The Spanish kings took advantage of conflicts between the state, the colonial administration, and the church, but royal privileges were never seen merely as political tools to be employed in power struggles. With rights came responsibility. Morally, Spain was obligated to protect and promote the church. Furthermore, it was charged with the complete financial support and administration of the American church, a duty which was generally performed with considerable integrity. In subsequent years, Spain's political heirs in Venezuela expressed equal concern for the necessity of royal patronage (*patronato*) but did not feel as deeply the corresponding responsibilities.

Republican

The church was affected by the War of Independence. Although only a minority of the clergy actively participated, most openly expressed favor for one side or the other. There were bishops originally from Spain who were on the side of independence and *criollo* (see Glossary) parish priests in opposition to it. In some cases, support was motivated by personal ambitions and rivalries within the clergy or between cities.

The increasing subsequent success of the forces for independence won greater support from the church, sometimes in the form of funds and food supplies from the missions. Revolutionary victories also provoked the departure of many of the churchmen most strongly opposed. By 1821 there was no resistance from the church. Although the church's support, both moral and material, was praised by the leaders of independence, increasing attempts were made to restrict its already greatly weakened power. The disorder that had prevailed and the division among the clergy had adversely affected the church's control of its own organization. Many of the important positions had been left vacant during the course of the war and could not be immediately filled upon victory because the issue of patronage had not been settled. In a difficult position, the papacy remained neutral, feeling the need to exercise extreme caution in order neither to offend Spain nor to lose the Latin American continent.

The privilege of patronage was eagerly sought by the liberal leaders of independence as a means of controlling the influence of the church. Anticlericalism, based on a liberal philosophy and political design rather than the church's behavior throughout the war, was strong in the small minority that exercised leadership. In the several constitutions drafted during the war years, measures had been incorporated that restricted the church's influence. A patronage law was drafted during the 1820s when anticlerical attitudes became intensified, but it was ineffective without relations with the Vatican. An eventual tacit recognition came about largely as a result of the groundwork laid by Simón Bolívar, who, despite the anticlericalism of his associates, sought an accommodation with the church. In the troubled times that followed the war, he saw the value of the aid the church could render in promoting stability (see ch. 3, Historical Setting).

After Venezuela's separation from the Gran Colombia federation, anticlericalism resulted in legislation that substantially restricted the church (see ch. 3, Historical Setting). During the rule of the conservative oligarchy (1830—48), the radicalism that characterized its policy toward the church and represented the boldest anticlerical thought in the history of the country fixed the direction of the social and political evolution of the church. In the Constitution of 1830 there were no provisions concerning religion, although the National Congress that drafted the document declared the previous patronage law to be temporarily in effect. During the years that followed, legislation provided for religious freedom and the abolition of the church's tithe. Removal of the tithe was particularly demoralizing because it made the clergy financially dependent upon an unsympathetic government.

In the middle of the nineteenth century policy was less consistent. Through the efforts of the archbishop, who emphasized the spiritual function, a greater harmony with the state developed, and the prestige of the church rose. During this period a concordat with Rome, arrangements for which had been specified in the law of patronage, was finally negotiated. It was accepted by the José Antonio Páez dictatorship in 1862, but his government soon fell, and the subsequent National Congress rejected it on the grounds that various articles undermined the sovereignty of the state.

In the following years tensions grew between church and state and finally erupted during the government of Antonio Guzmán Blanco. A conflict arose between Guzmán Blanco and the archbishop that led to the latter's exile. The refusal of each to deal with members of the clergy who supported the other brought the ecclesiastical organization to a state of paralysis. Guzmán Blanco then sought to lower the reputation of the clergy and destroy what influence the church had managed to retain. Seminaries and convents were closed; primacies were abolished; civil marriage and registry were decreed; the patronage law was incorporated for the first time in a national constitution; inheritance of property by the church was prohibited; government appropriations were lowered; and the establishment of a national church was threatened. During the battle the church lost much of its spirit and integrity.

During the twentieth century governments have adopted a less hostile policy towards the church, but there has been no fundamental change in the legislation affecting freedom of religion and national patronage.

Under the regime of Juan Vicente Gómez, the seminaries were reopened, and foreign priests and religious orders were introduced, which helped alleviate the serious shortages in personnel that the harsh measures of the Guzmán Blanco regime had created. Concessions granted in education and welfare work also increased the church's role in society to a degree. Economically there was little change, for the financial support of the state was used to include a number of new bishoprics and a new archdiocese. Closer ties with the Vatican were established, which resulted in the appointment of the first papal nuncio to the country in 1921. These developments led to an improvement in the prestige of the church, particularly in the years following the Gómez dictatorship.

THE CONTEMPORARY ROMAN CATHOLIC CHURCH

Organization and Hierarchy

In 1970 the country was organized into five archdioceses, sixteen dioceses, one prelature nullius (an ecclesiastical subdivision, not of the rank or organization of a diocese, in the charge of a prelate having quasi-episcopal powers and duties), and four vicariates. The archdioceses, located almost entirely in the north, were Caracas, Barquisimeto, Maracaibo, Mérida, and Ciudad Bolívar. Vicariates are mission territories in remote, sparsely populated regions on the borders of the Republic directly under the Sacred Congregation for the Evangelization of the Nations of the Holy See and administered by regular clergy (members of religious orders). Vicariates are designed primarily for work with the local Indians.

Although the first diocese was founded in 1531, two-thirds of the dioceses and archdioceses and all the vicariates in existence in 1970 were established after 1900. More were created between 1954 and 1970 than in the 423 years since the establishment of the first diocese. The new dioceses formed in the late 1960s and 1970 were San Felipe, Margarita, and La Guaira.

This considerable expansion has come about as the result of general recognition of the need for better organization, made particularly apparent by the large growth in population. As growth has been greatest north of the Orinoco River, the new dioceses have been located in that region, with the exception of the Archdiocese of Ciudad Bolívar, established in 1958, whose jurisdiction extends south into the Guiana Highlands. The less populated areas of the south, the Delta Amacuro region, and the western shore of Lake Maracaibo are in the charge of the vicariates. These regions, which comprise one-third of the national territory, have only 2 percent of the population.

The church is governed by a hierarchy composed of five archbishops, sixteen resident bishops, four vicars, one prelate nullius and, as of 1969, eleven auxiliary and titular bishops. The archbishop of Caracas, José Humberto Quintero, was named to the College of Cardinals in 1961. As emissaries of the pope, the prelate nullius and vicars are directly responsible to him and not to the bishops. In addition, there is the pope's official diplomatic representative, the papal nuncio. With the exception of these papal appointees, the hierarchy is Venezuelan in nationality in compliance with the terms of a 1964 modus vivendi established between Venezuela and the Vatican. The churchmen who hold these elevated positions usually come from the upper class, a practice that has existed since colonial days.

In character, the hierarchy has become increasingly less conservative under the leadership of Archbishop Rafael Arias of Caracas and, later, Cardinal Humberto Quintero. The increased attention given to areas of national interest outside the realm of strictly religious affairs by both these men has encouraged greater social consciousness throughout the hierarchy. In the interests of preserving the now-accepted isolation from partisan conflicts, the approach of ecclesiastical commentary has been from a moral, social, and religious standpoint.

The Clergy

One of the church's greatest concerns has been the shortage of religious personnel, which, in addition to taxing its ability to meet the minimal spiritual needs of the people, serves to weaken its force in daily life. Although this problem has plagued the church since colonial days, the steady and rapid population expansion, which promises to continue, has made it more apparent.

In 1969 the country had 1,970 priests, of whom 884 were diocesan or secular and 1,086 regular or religious, for about 8 million

Catholics. Although the national average was 1 priest for every 4,150 Catholics or for every 4,640 inhabitants, these proportions do not realistically portray the actual situation. Although the bulk of the clergy is in the northern region between the mountains and the coast, the heavy concentration of population, particularly in urban areas, raises the ratio as high as 1 to 30,000 in some city districts.

In the interior, where the number of inhabitants is much lower, dispersion and inadequate communications work against the more favorable conditions that lower ratios would imply. Not infrequently, a small rural town without a permanent priest may receive an ecclesiastical visit only once a year. For those who live some distance from these scattered rural population centers, association is even more limited.

The composition and consequent function of the clergy also modify the situation. In 1969 about 45 percent of the Venezuelan clergy was diocesan or secular, under the authority of the bishops and theoretically charged with the duty of parish work; the rest belonged to the regular clergy responsible to the various religious orders. The great majority of diocesan priests are engaged in parish work, and a significant number of regular priests also perform this function.

In 1962 it was estimated that about 45 percent of all priests were active in parishes, with a ratio of 68 regular clergy to every 100 secular priests. In Caracas, about 11 percent of the regular clergy was engaged in parochial work; the bulk of the regular clergy were working with the many educational institutions located in the capital. This pattern is typical of most dioceses, Valencia, Maracay, and Maracaibo, where the regular priests are more numerous in parish work than the secular, and in the remote regions of the country, where regular priests assume complete responsibility for the administrations of the church.

The number of parishes is small in comparison with the population and size of the country, yet in many cases there is only one priest to a parish. In 1969 the country had 768 parishes, most of which were situated in urbanized areas. The number has been increasing rapidly during the 1960s; the country had 535 in 1956, 640 in 1964, and 768 in 1969. At the same time, there had been a decrease in the average area from 1,441 square kilometers (2.59 square kilometers equal 1 square mile) in 1964 to 1,188 square kilometers in 1969, although the size and population varied considerably in different regions. Some areas in the Andes averaged only 8,000 or 9,000 persons per parish in 1962, whereas large urban centers, such as Caracas and Maracaibo, reported a mean of 18,000 to 21,000. In poor and rapidly growing sections of the cities the ratio was occasionally more extreme. In 1966 one parish in Caracas with a predominately poor, lower class membership contained 55,000 individuals served by a single priest.

Religious orders are also active in providing educational, religious, and social services to the country. There were 1,138 monks and lay brothers and 4,212 nuns and lay sisters active in 1969.

Since World War II the number of clergymen has slowly expanded and the ratio of priests to inhabitants has gradually but steadily improved. The growth in regular clergymen has been most marked, but the major portion of the increase stems from the influx of foreign clergymen in recent years. Toward the end of the nineteenth century foreign religious orders began sending missions to the country as the anticlerical atmosphere created by Guzmán Blanco abated. Interrupted temporarily by the Spanish civil war and World War II, immigration of foreign priests resumed in the late 1940s; by the mid-1960s almost 90 percent of the regular clergy and about 40 percent of the secular clergy were foreign, in great part Spanish, but with representations from the rest of Europe, other Latin American countries, and the United States. The prevalence of regular clergymen engaged in parish work, many of whom were under the direction of headquarters located in foreign countries, led the Venezuelan Bishops Conference of 1965 to request the right of overall supervision over the religious priests assigned to their dioceses.

Of those who enter seminaries few are eventually ordained, for the retention rate is low. The high average age of the clergy, in comparison with the rest of the continent, also indicates that few young people are going into religious vocations.

In spite of efforts to lessen the problem, a severe shortage of vocations exists. In 1966 no priests were ordained for the Archdiocese of Caracas, which had 2 million Catholics, and only one priest was ordained in 1967. In the same year it was estimated that Venezuela had fewer native vocations to the priesthood than any other country in South America. The small number of those young people interested in the priesthood comes largely from the semirural areas and from large families. Well over half come from the three Andean states and Zulia, which have, in many areas, preserved much of the old agricultural existence and the traditional values of religion and family life.

Furthermore, the prospect of becoming a priest is more attractive to the lower middle class and the lower class than to the middle and upper classes. Consequently, most of the clergy is from this level. Enrollment in the seminary offers a free education. If the individual is ordained and given a parish, his family will be able to accompany him to a reasonably comfortable lodging and will receive the benefits of the contributions, often in kind, of the parishioners for the maintenance of the rectory.

A survey of attitudes toward the church made in the late 1960s indicated that 70 percent of upper class parents interviewed would not permit their children to become priests or nuns. Thus, although only the relatively wealthy can afford a secondary Catholic education of good quality, very few vocations come from this group. Often a priest is esteemed for his status as a representative of the church, but he does not always become an integral part of the community, especially in rural areas.

The Church in Society

Relations between the church and the state have been harmonious throughout most of the twentieth century and have continued to be peaceful during the 1960s. Respect is accorded the church through its representatives, who are always guests at important ceremonial functions, such as the opening of a new highway or power plant. The new bridge across the Orinoco River at Ciudad Bolívar, dedicated in 1967, was blessed by Cardinal Humberto Quintero.

The greater harmony of church-state relations in the twentieth century is based partly on the historical evolution of relations and partly on more recent developments. Churchmen are not barred from politics. On its part, the church has gradually defined its role in society in accordance with recognition of the state's preeminence in secular affairs. It has declared itself apolitical and no longer strives to influence choice in this area. The old contest between church and state is seen by all sides as outdated.

This evolution toward more satisfactory relations has been further improved by a greater mutual understanding that events of recent years have brought. Many political figures and members of the hierarchy were against the Pérez Jiménez regime. In May 1957 Archbishop Arias of Caracas published a now-famous pastoral letter that embarrassed the Pérez Jiménez regime by strongly subscribing to labor's right to organize freely and by pointing out many social ills that the government had ignored. The moral support that this ecclesiastical pronouncement lent to a dissatisfied population has not been forgotten.

With the advent of the liberal government of Rómulo Betancourt in 1958, the church declared its support of the government and its program of democratic social reform. Since that time the church has increasingly spoken out for social change, the preservation of moral and civil order, the suppression of atheistic communism, and the support and respect of democratic institutions. The government recognized the value of the church's promotion of issues in accord with its own states principles. Moreover, it found an ally in the church against social and political disorder.

Nevertheless, under Venezuela's Constitution, promulgated in

1961, the church's legal position in relation to the state remains unchanged. As in the past, the only articles dealing with religion are those concerning religious freedom and national patronage. Roman Catholicism is not legally recognized as the state religion, but the privilege of national patronage, abolished by a number of Latin American countries, is stated. Until 1964, according to law, the president presented to the National Congress the candidates submitted by the papal nuncio for approval. Since consideration was given by ecclesiastical authorities to probable official reaction to potential candidates, friction was rare, but the possibility of abuse under an unsympathetic government existed.

A concordat with the Vatican is impossible in view of the existence of the Venezuelan civil divorce law, but the church has long sought to establish a modus vivendi with the Vatican that would terminate or abolish this system. In 1964 an agreement was signed between the Holy See and Venezuela entailing changes in the interpretation and practice of patronage, although not its formal abolition. The church was accorded full authority in religious matters, guaranteed freedom of Catholic teaching, and assured the continuation of state subsidies. The Holy See accepted the Venezuelan stipulation that all bishops and archbishops be Venezuelan by birth. The long-disputed question of the nomination of bishops to vacant dioceses was resolved by allowing the president of the Republic the privilege of knowing the names of the candidates proposed by the Holy See before their official nomination. The president may, at that time, make any objection of a general political nature that he wishes. The consent of the National Congress is no longer necessary.

Thus, although it is not the official state church, the Roman Catholic Church has very close ties to the government and, in fact, functions as a national church. A large part of its operating expenses are contributed by the government through a special division of the Ministry of Justice. Government funds generally provide the salaries of members of the hierarcy, certain lesser functionaries attached to the more important episcopates, a limited number of priests, and the missionaries to the Indians. In addition, government contributions are also available for religious materials, the construction and repair of religious buildings, and projects submitted by bishops and archbishops and approved according to the ministry's estimates of greatest need. As the ministry discharges this duty with the best interests of the church considered, no serious friction exists. The church itself is economically weak, since it possesses little property and receives only limited private contributions. Even government support is moderate; of the 1963 budget of Bs6.2 billion (4.5 bolivars equal US $1), about Bs5 million were allocated to the church.

One of the most significant and traditionally one of the most important areas of church involvement in society is education. During the Pérez Jiménez period, growth in Catholic education was greater than that of the public sector, but in the 1960s growth in public education outstripped the increase in Catholic schooling. It was estimated that 15 percent of total school enrollment in 1963 was in Catholic schools; 10 percent in 1967; and 8 percent in 1969. Statistics for 1969 indicated that 618 schools served 193,000 students, with a substantial portion located in the Archdiocese of Caracas. A pontifical university, Andrés Bello Catholic University, was founded in Caracas in 1953 and by 1967 had an enrollment of about 4,000 students (see ch. 7, Education).

Catholic schools are required by law to observe all regulations concerning public instruction, giving the Ministry of Education jurisdiction over curricula examinations, and teacher accreditation. Public schools are permitted to offer two hours of religious instruction every week but only at the request of the parents. The number of religious teachers in public schools, however, is very small; one source estimated in 1970 that the ratio was 1 teacher of religion for 10,000 students. Consequently, the amount of religious education received by most of the young people in the country—in public and church schools—is minimal. One study in 1970 estimated that 60 percent of the young people in Caracas received no formal religious education at all.

Catholic schools have traditionally educated the children of the middle and upper classes. Since many schools are supported by tuition fees only, the costs are prohibitively high for lower income groups. In recent years there has been some criticism of this situation and, in response, attempts have been made by the hierarchy to establish some control over the schools, to encourage the admission of a greater number of scholarship students, and to increase the number of schools that charge little or no tuition.

Consequently, the situation is changing, and in 1970 a Catholic educator noted that a little more than two-thirds of Catholic schools and colleges, including parish schools, were free or partly free. Many schools have recently been established in urban areas aimed at serving the children of the working class. The fact that the majority of enrollments in 1970 were children of poor families caused considerable financial strain for the church, however, in the same year it faced the prospect of having to close a large number of schools if it did not receive a substantial federal annual subsidy.

Among the schools that cater to the urban poor, the most important and well known are those maintained by Fé y Alegría (Faith and Joy), a movement started in 1955 by a Caracas priest and staffed to a considerable extent by nuns and priests. By 1966 it was running fifty primary schools, five high schools, and two normal schools located in Caracas and twenty other cities, with over

25,000 students enrolled. Although it is designed primarily to provide a basic education and an understanding of Christian morals to urban slum children, Fé y Alegría has established a few farming schools in rural states. The organization receives no direct support from the church; business and individual contributions, an annual raffle, and government subsidies provide the financial backing.

The church plays a minor role in social welfare activities. According to figures for 1962, there were ninety-seven Catholic institutions caring for 12,552 persons. Of these establishments, most of which were located in the major cities, about one-fifth were hospitals or sanatoriums. In 1967 Caracas had thirty church-supported charitable institutions with about 800 persons in residence and fifteen hospitals and clinics. In almost all cases, the staff was drawn from the various female religious orders. Some valuable work is being done in response to the growing problem of orphaned and abandoned children.

A well-received project is Ciudad de los Muchachos (Boys' City), begun in the early 1950s as a school for shoeshine boys and newspaperboys. Its success prompted the establishment of similar institutions in Boconó and La Cruz. Other types of institutions include old people's homes, dormitories for out-of-town students, and nurseries.

In the 1920s, when government interest was aroused in the small remaining indigenous population, the church assumed another of its traditional functions—mission work. Begun through a series of missionary agreements with the government, which assigned the regions of the upper Orinoco and the Caroní, Tucupita and western Zulia to the Capuchins, Dominicans, and Salesians, work in 1970 was being carried out in conjunction with the plans of the Indian Commission of the Ministry of Justice. Although the state is not opposed to evangelization, its principal interest is in the influence the missions exercise through the schools maintained at the various centers in each region. Education is basically of a practical nature, with training in domestic crafts, agriculture, and animal husbandry.

In less traditional areas, ecclesiastical influence, both direct and indirect, is still of only slight importance. Although great interest has been expressed for the working man and his problems, there has been no real campaign to create Catholic-oriented labor unions or leagues as in other countries of the continent. Nonetheless, there is the Confederation of Autonomous Christian Unions (Confederación de Sindicatos Autónomos Christianos), whose greatest strength is in the oilfields (see ch. 19, Labor).

Somewhat more attention has been given to the mass media. In most of the major cities there is a newspaper that represents the Catholic point of view but is not officially linked to the church or its hierarchy. With the exception of Caracas, however, where *La*

Religión, one of the country's oldest dailies, ranks as one of the principal newspapers, this influence is secondary. In orientation these newspapers are the most consistently conservative. In addition, a number of periodicals published by the various dioceses contain articles of general interest and discussions of social issues, such as divorce and birth control, from the Catholic viewpoint. There are four Catholic radio and television stations—in Caracas, Maracaibo, Barquisimeto, and Mérida—that broadcast educational as well as religious programs. The Mérida station transmits part of the adult literacy program as well as information on agriculture and social action (see ch. 14, Public Information).

The church tends to restrict its activities to the nonpolitical spheres. The Committee for Independent Political and Electoral Organization (Comité de Organización Política y Electoral Independiente—COPEI), the ruling party in 1970, drew its ideological inspiration from the social doctrines of the church and other Latin American Christian Democratic parties, but it was not officially connected with the church. COPEI has been sympathetic to the church but not markedly more so than previous ruling parties (see ch. 12, Political Dynamics).

Lay organizations have long been active in promoting social and spiritual welfare. The first secular organization was founded in 1925 as the Society for Catholic Action and has continued to influence manifestations of religious life in the country. The two youth sectors have been innovative and reformist. The Christian Family Movement has expanded slowly but is assuming increasing significance in dealing with the breakup of the traditional family. The lay apostolate has become more widespread in recent years in response to ideological changes in the church. In many cases laymen are taking religion courses and attempting to communicate their knowledge and faith to others. From 1960 to 1965 about 20,000 persons took Christianity Courses (Cursillos de Cristianidad).

Attitudes toward the church vary with education and social class but, according to a survey conducted by the Catholic Press Association Study Committee in the mid-1960s, it was generally viewed as a traditional institution involved more in the externals of ritual and form than in daily life. It is also commonly observed that the church is more concerned with individual salvation than with the social environment. The emerging social consciousness of the church and its recent concern with the problems of ignorance, social injustice, and poverty have considerably increased its prestige in many circles, however, and there is evidence that men, traditionally indifferent, are returning to the church.

Recent Developments in the Church

The awakening social consciousness that developed in the church in Latin America in the 1960s has had considerable impact on the

Venezuelan church. Liberal prelates, clergymen, and laymen are supported by the socially relevant body of Catholic thought that has been developing since 1900 but which gained considerable impetus in the 1960s under the influence of the social encyclicals of John XXIII, *Mater et Magistra* (Mother and Teacher, 1961) and *Pacem In Terris* (Peace on Earth, 1963), and Paul VI's *Populorum Progressio* (The Development of Peoples, 1967).

In addition, the ideas generated at the Second Vatican Council (1962-65) and the 1968 meeting of the Latin American Bishops' Conference (Consejo Episcopal Latinoamericano—CELAM) at Medellín, Colombia, have led to the formation of Latin American principles concerned with social justice for the masses, the dignity of man, institutional reform, the importance of social action to extend Christian influence in the world, and the need for liturgical and pastoral reforms within the church. The principles are generally opposed to violent change, espousing a gradual, evolutionary development. Some groups favor Marxism.

The Venezuelan hierarchy has favored many of these reforms, although generally opposing Marxist principles and violent change. Archbishop Quintero of Caracas, the leading figure in the church by virtue of his position, has repeatedly advocated social awareness and concern on the part of the church. In 1962 he and twenty-two other archbishops and bishops signed a pastoral letter that declared: "To possess extensive capital and keep it unproductive and unused is to fail in social justice and charity . . . two virtues which require recognition of the social function inherent in property as taught by the Church." The letter also dealt with the need for more schools as the population increases, with economic problems, and with the need for agrarian reform.

Archbishop Quintero also donated the Bs380,000 he received for an episcopal residence when he was made a cardinal for the construction of public housing. Other prelates have also spoken out on the problems of hunger, unemployment, violence, low salaries, and the high cost of living typical of Venezuelan society, offering solutions in the social doctrine of the church. The bishop of Maracay has advocated economic reform of the church in which rich parishes would share resources with poorer parishes voluntarily, under the direction of a diocesan commission of pastors from the parishes involved.

In the late 1960s minor conflicts developed within the church concerning the nature and velocity of change. Many young laymen and clergymen are demanding a more rapid implementation of the new social doctrines. A group consisting largely of high school and university students, several of whom were studying at the Andrés Bello Catholic University, occupied a church in Caracas in 1969 to dramatize their demands. They wanted to see a total change in the structures of society and the acceptance of the use of violence if necessary in the struggle for social justice. In his response to the incident, Cardinal Humberto Quintero emphasized the religious nature of the church's mission, as outlined in the Second Vatican Council, and stated his belief that the church should not become involved in temporal struggles.

In the sphere of liturgical reform, the hierarchy has moved slowly. The 1966 meeting of the Venezuelan Bishops' Conference did not accept many of the liturgical changes proposed by the Second Vatican Council. Although guitar masses had been very popular with young people, in 1967 the use of guitars in church was banned except for the Christmas novenas. The hierarchy has favored the lay apostolate, however, and has established pastoral councils and a committee for promoting teamwork in the apostolate.

Much of the church is committed to reform and social action, but practical involvement has been restricted by limited material resources and administrative problems. In recognition of the administrative obstacle, the Archdiocese of Caracas, for example, created a special secretariat to coordinate and support Catholic social work being carried out in its area of jurisdiction. Another function of the secretariat is the distribution of food and goods sent by Caritas, a North American Catholic welfare organization. In addition, special organs have been set up for the study of religious sociology and the supervision of activity of the major lay group, Catholic Action (Acción Católica). Because of the influence that Caracas exercises over the rest of the country, steps are presumably being taken in the other archdioceses.

Religious Life and Practice

The majority of the people would be sincerely offended if their Catholic status were questioned. An emotional attachment to Catholicism, the basis for the individual's self-qualification as a Catholic, does not necessarily influence the actions of everyday life nor the observance of religious obligations. Encouragement of this anomaly is furthered by Catholicism's emphasis of the individual as opposed to the congregation together with the traditional Hispanic concept of individualism (see ch. 10, Social Values).

Of the various elements of religious practice, those with a more solemn aspect are less popular than weddings, baptisms, and the celebration of saints' days, which provide the opportunity for social contact in a festive atmosphere. Frequently the religious significance is secondary to the social for those involved. Moreover, affairs sponsored by individuals of the more affluent elements of society become occasions for a considerable degree of ostentation, as criticisms of the church hierarchy indicate.

In some rural areas these religious events are the principal source of community entertainment and association, but generally community feeling in a religious sense is not highly developed. Historically, the parochial system was not deeply ingrained, as a great part of the country was spiritually served by members of the religious orders rather than by the diocesan clergy. Positive sentiments of group responsibility and activity are not strong. Participation in the lay groups, even Catholic Action, characteristically the largest, is limited; neither is there extensive support of the church and its beneficent projects through the contribution of money or time. In regard to material contribution it is generally believed that the church, because of subsidies from the government, is not in need of great additional private aid.

In rural regions in the Andean states, where traditional values have been least disturbed, persistent conservative attitudes exert a social pressure that results in observance of religious obligations more widespread than in urban areas. A measure of this conservatism comes from the influence of neighboring Colombia, whose national patroness, the Virgin of Chiquinquirá, receives particular veneration in the area.

In the middle class there is less group cohesion in the area of religion. Although this class has produced the leadership in Catholic-oriented political parties and labor groups, it has also been the source of the church's strongest critics. The desire for respectability and status, which is the partial motivation for the enrollment of children in private Catholic schools and active participation in lay groups, is outweighed by the greater tendency toward a spiritually destructive type of materialism. One of these lay groups, which has had the greatest response from the middle class, is the Christian Family Movement, centered principally in Caracas. Its aim is to check what the church considers the disintegration of the family.

In all classes religion is regarded as properly the sphere and function of women. More conscientious in religious practice, within the family they are expected to assume the duty of religious and moral education of children. For girls early training is followed by close supervision in accordance with their socially protected status; however, upon adolescence, boys are discouraged from rigorous religiosity. Moreover, as experience and contacts outside the family circle increase, these attitudes become more firmly fixed. In the university environment, where liberal and, most recently, Communist inclinations are strongest, the negative influence is especially great. Marriage and the establishment of a family may lead to a return to a greater compliance with outward form, but the basic view toward religious practice is likely to remain unchanged. Although devotion may not be openly criticized, it is obviously not a positive element in the Venezuelan ideal of masculinity (see ch. 10, Social Values).

In spite of these variations in belief and practice, the concept of Catholicism held by most Venezuelans is essentially similar. Venezuelan culture is a mixture of Hispanic, Indian, and Negro elements, with comparatively rapid integration of large segments of the population. The cultural homogeneity of Venezuelan Catholicism is symbolized in the national patroness, who is a *mestiza* (person of mixed ancestry—see Glossary) and popular among almost all groups (see ch. 4, Population and Ethnic Groups).

Nevertheless, there are scattered evidences of mixtures derived from the coexistence of the three ethnic types. In the eastern coastal region where Negroes have had the strongest influence, drums of African inspiration are used in a dance in the celebration held to honor Saint John, the patron saint of the area. He is considered to be very powerful, able to solve emotional problems, and assure a good harvest. His celebration occurs at the beginning of the rainy season, when the fields are becoming more fertile from the rains. In some villages Saint John is called San Juan de Guiné, which reflects his African heritage. The religion, however, is essentially Christian in structure with the addition of some African content.

The use of drums and superstitions concerning them were carried from the eastern coast to the Andes, where one of the most important celebrations is in honor of the patron saint of slaves, Saint Benedict, affectionately referred to as "El Santito Negro" (The Little Black Saint). Of the Indian contributions, one of the most colorful is the devil dance, frequently performed, after the celebration of mass in front of the church, on the feast of Corpus Christi in the western state of Lara. This dance is also performed in the east and followed by the bamba, a dance reminiscent of African tribal ceremonials.

The cult of María Lionza is a popular synthesis of African, Indian, and Christian beliefs and practices. María Lionza is worshiped as a goddess of nature and protectress of the virgin forests, the wild animals, and the mineral wealth in the mountains; she is similar to the Arawak Indian water goddess, to West African mythological figures, and to the Virgin Mary. During religious services a priest (*banco*) summons spirits and deities, which are believed to possess mediums who have been initiated into the deity's particular cult. The spirits can then be consulted by the faithful for advice and assistance. The cultic use of tobacco smoke for curing and spiritual cleansing reflects the considerable Indian influence in the religion, and the concept of spirit possession has both African and European antecedents. This sect is particularly popular among the poor urban dweller who has recently migrated from his rural home and feels lost in the city, severed from his traditional Christian community and many of his family ties. At the same time, he is under increased psychological stress in the urban environment. In recent years many middle and upper class individuals have also become adherents of this cult.

Beliefs and practices related to magic and curing that combine expressly Catholic articles with African and Indian elements are widespread, particularly in remote rural areas. In the Andes belief in the supernatural powers of physical objects is witnessed in the use of holy water for curing purposes. Native curers are found in many Indian villages and are often consulted by *criollo* and Indian alike. On occasion a crucifix is an integral part of the ceremony of exorcising an evil spirit or influence (see ch. 4, Population and Ethnic Groups).

PROTESTANTISM

In spite of religious tolerance, Protestantism has made little headway. In fact, the country is considered a difficult mission territory by those in the field. One explanation offered is the widespread comparative indifference toward all religion. Figures available in 1968 indicated that the total Protestant community numbered 52,380, or about 0.5 percent of the total population. Although there has been considerable growth in the number of churches and the size of the Protestant community has approximately doubled since 1961, the total number is still small.

Even though Protestant groups have been active in the country for over 100 years, the churches retain much of their missionary character. The percentage of foreign full-time personnel is declining. In 1957 the percentage of foreign personnel in Protestant groups was 69 percent; in 1961, 62 percent; and in the mid-1960s, 44 percent.

In the liberal atmosphere after the War of Independence, Protestants were able to gain their first foothold in the country. In 1834 an act of the National Congress decreed the freedom of all religious sects, and in the same year the first Protestant church, an Anglican chapel, was founded in Caracas. A Bible society was also established by representatives of the American Bible Society, but a report made by a visiting agent sixty years later indicated that the effort probably died because of lack of activity; within the next few years, however, the work of the society was resumed. During the same period, the first missionaries, associated with a British sect, the Brethren, began to arrive.

As a result of persecution and repression, missionary efforts were of short duration. During this period, some Protestant foreigners were entering the country to find work and, in many cases, settled in Venezuela. After the appearance of American Presbyterians in 1897, and the establishment of missions of other groups, in addition to the colonies of Protestant immigrants established in the country, activity took on a more permanent character. By 1930 there were 111 missionaries representing twelve denominations or sects and 2,310 communicant members. Although at that time Latin America was recognized as a mission field by Protestants, in spite of the existence of a firmly entrenched Catholic church, interest in Venezuela apparently did not increase greatly, for in 1970 only about sixteen denominations maintained missions in the country.

In the mid-1960s almost half the Protestants were members of the Assembly of God Church or the Seventh-Day Adventists. The older denominations—Baptist, Lutheran, and Presbyterian—represented another quarter of the Protestant population. The other church groups were generally much smaller, and many were still tiny missions. The greatest growth in recent years has come in the fundamentalist sects, such as the Pentecostal churches, which are able to win large congregations through militant evangelical activity. The Jehovah's Witnesses, which became active in the 1960s, had about 1,879 preachers in 1962. The eventual aim of the Protestant sects is to convert the missions into national churches administered principally by local personnel, but this had been accomplished only by a few of the churches.

Cooperation among denominations exists to a considerable degree and has resulted in the establishment of regional organizations. As missionary territories do not overlap, there is little cause for conflict. Although there has been a tendency to extend activity farther into the interior, the greatest effort is still in the western coastal area from Caracas to Maracaibo. Most missions maintain elementary schools, but these are relatively unknown outside the congregation. Protestant radio programs are broadcast throughout the country but are not connected with the resident missions.

The appeal of Protestantism has been restricted largely to the lower classes. In the middle and upper classes, association and familiarity with Protestantism is very slight. Departure from Catholicism at these levels would represent a loss of social status.

Protestants have had some of their greatest success in the *barrios*, which often lack Catholic priests. The Protestant sects usually have a higher proportion of ministers to members and tend to establish small, simple chapels, which are convenient to the average *barrio* dwellers. The Protestants frequently congregate on the streets to sing songs and hymns or meet in private to discuss their faith. In many cases they abstain from drinking, smoking, and dancing and are notable for their politeness. One observer found that their Catholic neighbors regarded them as proud and condescending but were tolerant of their presence. Because Protestants are frequently involved in church affairs and not interested in participating in community-wide Catholic celebrations and fiestas, they tend to be somewhat isolated. At the same time, their distinctive behavior further separates them from the mainstream of Venezuelan culture.

In general, attitudes toward Protestantism both on the part of the church and of the people are quite tolerant, and examples of active opposition are few. Friendships between Catholic priests and their Protestant counterparts are not uncommon.

The Jewish population was estimated to number 8,500 in 1966. The large majority lives in Caracas, with smaller groups in Valencia, Maracay, Barcelona, and Maracaibo. They have often become successful importers, businessmen, and professionals. Both Ashkenazic and Sephardic communities have their own synagogues; some 90 percent of the Jewish children in Caracas attended a Hebrew school in 1970.

Relations with the rest of the people are generally good. In 1970 President Raphael Caldera, in response to a Jewish community statement offering prayers for the progress of the country, for peace, and for the success of the government, expressed his gratitude and emphasized the great significance of the harmony existing in Venezuela among men of diverse beliefs and ethnic roots.

CHAPTER 10

SOCIAL VALUES

The values that guide and bolster the country's social life are derived primarily from the Hispanic cultural heritage brought over by the conquistadors more than four centuries ago. Developed in medieval times by the heterogeneous and disunited people of Spain, who forged a national identity in a centuries-long struggle for survival, the value heritage has persisted into modern times with remarkably little change.

Despite political and economic upheaval over the years, as well as strong foreign cultural pressures, in 1970 these same values continued to exert their influence on Venezuelan society. They have left their distinctive imprint on the nation's culture and color the new social and political forms that are resulting from the changes brought about by industrialization and increasing contact with the outside world.

A striking aspect of the Hispanic-derived social view is the primacy accorded individuality. There is a strongly held conviction regarding the uniqueness of the individual and the existence in every person of an inner dignity and personal integrity. These qualities are quite apart from social status and are both inalienable and worthy of respect. These views are reflected in a strong sense of personal honor and sensitivity to praise, insult, and slight.

In the traditional concept of social life and interpersonal relations the emphasis on individuality is reflected in a complex of beliefs and assumptions subsumed under the concept of *personalismo*, which represents a tendency to stress personal qualities and interpersonal trust over abstract ideology and institutionalism. Thus, both national history and national destiny are conceived to be more the product of individual men than of impersonal social forces or the application of abstract ideas. Further, in the view of *personalismo* a man's well-being lies in relations of trust with other men more than it does in the smooth functioning of institutions or in adherence to specific doctrines.

Another key core social value is a deep-rooted tendency to stress the masculine role and to exalt a concept of masculinity as a desirable personality characteristic. The complex of beliefs and attitudes defining this image is called *machismo* (literally, maleness—see Glossary) and includes such qualities as virility, forcefulness, and daring.

Leaders in particular are expected to exemplify the male value and must possess a full share of courage, self-confidence, and personal charm. Although the values associated with *machismo* continue to be upheld by the majority of persons, among more sophisticated and informed men they are less strongly upheld than in the past.

The social tradition includes a strong family consciousness—both a stressing of loyalties among kinsmen above other forms of allegiance and a tendency to ascribe social status to an individual on the basis of his kinship connections. Although concepts of civic morality and responsibility have not been lacking in the abstract, men in positions of public trust have often used their power in serving the private interests of their kinsmen and, in the popularly held view, such behavior has generally been accepted.

In contrast to the sense of personal uniqueness and integrity, but in no way contradicting it, is an equally strong sense of hierarchy and rank. This acceptance is associated with the competitiveness of *machismo*, in which men are seen as being in competition for the validation of personal status. In such competition there are always winners and losers, and their respective positions receive definite social recognition.

The Hispanic value tradition was born in a rigidly stratified society of nobles and peasants, in which privilege and power were largely hereditary. In that society both nobles and peasants recognized and accepted as natural the differences in their status. The inner dignity and uniqueness that are part of the social view of *personalismo* were conceived to endow not only the highborn but also the lowly with a personal honor that made them spiritual, if not temporal, equals and to a degree facilitates the acceptance of stratification.

Implicit in the same concept of hierarchy is a strong conviction that the privileges of leadership and high status involve corresponding responsibilities. Relationships between leaders and followers, employers and workers, and rulers and governed are seen as invested with deference and obedience but also with a well-defined paternalism. In all aspects of social, political, and economic life, the ideal bond between the poor and the rich, and the weak and the powerful, is conceived essentially as a personal contract in which the retainer is rewarded for his respect and compliance by the protection and interest of the leader.

THE INDIVIDUAL

There is a marked stress on respect for individual dignity and personal integrity and a great value placed on free and open self-expression.

North American stress on similarities among men is associated with a strong tendency toward egalitarianism. At least in theory, the ideal society is seen as providing equality of opportunity as a prerequisite to self-expression and fulfillment of individual potential. *Personalismo*, on the other hand, emphasizing uniqueness, conceives personal status to be wholly independent of social status. In this view it is entirely conceivable that an individual can fulfill his personal potential at any social level, no matter how humble. Consequently, there is no inherent contradiction between a strong respect for individuality and an equally strong tradition of social hierarchy and stratification.

There is a clear distinction between the respect accorded social status and that accorded personal dignity. There are elaborate formalities for expressing the respect of followers for leaders and that of the humble for those of superior social status, but the behavior of one person toward another is also prescribed. Cordiality between social equals is emphasized but, in modified form, is also stressed between persons of unequal rank. Although the individual of superior rank is not expected to behave toward his inferior in any way that implies social equality, he is expected to treat him with due recognition of his worth as a person. Hence, relations between employers and employees, leaders and followers, and patrons and retainers ideally reflect the active interest of the former for the latter. One may treat another as a social subordinate but never as a nonentity.

Notwithstanding the respect for individuality and the high value placed on personal uniqueness, the social view also entails a generally accepted range of ideal personal qualities, and an individual derives much of his status from the degree to which he fits these molds. This is particularly the case with the traditions of masculine dominance and the sharply differentiated social roles of men and women, which are reflected in widely contrasting male and female personality ideals.

Masculine Personality Ideals

The ideal prototype of manhood implied in *machismo*, a term and idea of longstanding currency in Hispanic America, is highly stereotyped. It includes such attributes as a zest for action, both physical and vocal, and a will to master both men and nature. It also connotes self-confidence bordering on the daring and demonstrated prowess with regard to the opposite sex. In general, it creates an ideal image of a man of virility, dramatic flourish, and evident heroism.

Besides providing an abstract model of male personality, the values of *machismo* serve as prominent, though not the sole, criteria in forming personal judgments. In politics, and even in intellectual life, forcefulness and daring in expression are major requirements in attracting a following or gaining prestige. It has traditionally been the domineering politician of imposing personality and impassioned oratory, rather than the able but plodding administrator, who has enjoyed the greater success. In intellectual life the brilliant and aggressive polemicist, rather than the quietly intelligent but retiring contributor to substantive knowledge, has most often had the greater appeal to the reading public. Throughout national history the greatest focus of intellectual activity has been in such fields as political and social theory where controversy is most prevalent.

Appreciation of the true *macho* (he-man concept of a male) and his virtues is characteristic of all social classes, but opportunities for gaining the limelight before a large audience, whether in politics, oratorical flourish, or other types of heroic gesture, have been limited largely to members of the small, educated, and influential upper class. Hence, while sharing the general admiration for the virile, the grand, and the heroic, lower class Venezuelans have also tended to express in wit and satire a reaction of sarcasm or ridicule to the same image, presenting the hero as bombastic and pompous. As much a part of folklore tradition as the heroic *macho* is the figure of the antihero, usually a poor, rustic *campesino* (peasant) who bests the great and powerful through a combination of wit and homespun deception.

While the pattern of *machismo* provides a measure of worth for men of all classes, there is also a heritage of values prescribing the ideal characteristics of the upper class man, that of the *caballero* (gentleman). Paralleling the idea of *machismo*, the model of the traditional *caballero* is that of the man of good breeding. This implies refinement, wealth, generosity, leisure, and lack of materialism. His wealth is seen as providing him with the means to lead a gracious and cultured existence and is taken for granted. If he works, his efforts should reflect intellectual and artistic talent rather than the necessity or desire to earn money. He has traditionally been expected to disdain any form of manual work and restrict his efforts to those professions considered socially acceptable, usually such fields as law, journalism, or medicine.

To some degree, the image of the upper status man has been modified by the social and economic changes of the new industrialization. The rise of a defined middle class, and particularly of a powerful industrial and commercial upper class whose members now outnumber the landed gentry, has resulted in an easing of traditional attitudes toward remunerative endeavor. That there remains, nevertheless, a preference for intellectual and professional activities is indicated by continuing high enrollments in the professional courses of the universities. Further, a continued distaste for manual work, even of a skilled nature, is apparent in the preference of socially ambitious secondary school students for academic rather than technical training and the desire of graduates for white-collar rather than skilled manual or technical employment (see ch. 7, Education).

Ideally, the *caballero* embodies elements of both the man of letters and the man of affairs. Appreciation and practice of artistic or intellectual activity, even if desultory, are important aspects of the upper status image. A broad liberal university education is virtually a prerequisite to that status and is ideally reflected throughout adult life by continued endeavors in the intellectual or aesthetic fields. Another acceptable phase, and one which early preoccupies most educated men, is a personal interest or involvement in political activity.

Because of the social changes in the twentieth century and the broadening of educational opportunities, there is clear evidence that the longstanding pattern of the genteel part-time intellectual and artist is undergoing modification. Persons of lower and middle class backgrounds, not reared in the tradition of the cultivated gentleman of leisure, have entered the arts, letters, and professions and have pursued such activities as full time vocations. The same process of change is seen in an increasing number of men studying in the physical sciences and technical professions in response to the needs of the newly industrialized society. Nevertheless, much of the old ideal of the man of letters and affairs persists, and the replacement of part-time gentlemen scholars with full-time professionals is a slow process.

The rejection of materialism characteristic of the traditional *caballero* implies more an interest in concrete ideas than in their spiritual and moral content. Further, the formal teachings of the Roman Catholic Church, in particular a restrictive morality and an emphasis on humility and abnegation, are at direct variance with the salient features of *machismo*. Hence, while subscribing to Catholicism and recognizing it as part of their national and cultural heritage, probably a majority of men look on manifest piety and punctilious observance of church rote as more properly the realm of women and children.

Feminine Personality Ideals

The traditional image of ideal womanhood is in almost every respect the antithesis of that of the ideal man and is no less stereotyped. In contrast to male aggressiveness and zest for competition, the proper female is seen as exhibiting passivity, gentleness, and acceptance of a status derived from that of her husband and family, and she is expected to accept with dignity and resignation the failings and shortcomings of her spouse. If in actuality women exhibit initiative in domestic affairs and, in many cases, work in support of the household, their husbands still expect to maintain a position as the sole and final arbiter of family welfare.

Both motherhood and filial affection are imbued with an aura of devotion and tenderness that is a frequent theme in literature and song. The maternal role also has its reflection in religious observance and prayer through the prominence accorded the Virgin Mary and other female saints. An acceptance of abnegation and self-sacrifice is expected of women in their domestic life. In the social ideal a woman dedicates her whole life to the welfare of her children, assuming almost sole responsibility for their early training and, if necessary, standing ready to provide their sole economic support. She is, in fact, quite often faced with the need to exercise full maternal self-sacrifice, in view of the high incidence of paternal desertion among the lower classes.

One traditional view of femininity, shared by all classes, is that in relations between the sexes the woman is a submissive and passive follower. Premarital chastity and marital fidelity are vital to the ideal image of womanhood, particularly among the middle and upper classes, and this tradition is reflected in the close supervision over unmarried girls in higher status families. Although chaperonage in its strictest form has all but disappeared from the modern scene, there is still a marked lack of freedom in social relations between young men and women and a minimum of unaccompanied dating.

Women have traditionally borne most of the responsibility for the rituals and duties of kinship, and to them have fallen most of the routines for observance of family functions, whether celebrations or mourning. In large part, the cohesiveness of the upper class kin groups is reinforced by constant visiting and socializing on the part of female relatives, and contacts are maintained with even the remotest relatives through calls or correspondence.

Outside of purely domestic affairs and those of the kin group, other activities traditionally seen as a proper realm for women are in religious observance and in charitable affairs. The mother usually has sole charge of ensuring her children's religious education and in general is looked on as the family's representative before the church (see ch. 9, Religion). In the organization and operation of charities, women have always played the prominent role—a role that is an important aspect of the ideal image of upper class women.

As in so many other aspects of daily life, social and economic changes have modified traditional feminine roles. Feminist sentiment has been rather vigorous, particularly among women of the growing middle class, and has resulted in full political rights for women; expanded educational and employment opportunities have also provided many new fields of activity. Nevertheless, no clear-cut value criteria defining these new roles and more aggressive stance of women have as yet emerged. Although the image of womanhood projected in the traditional ideals grows increasingly remote from reality, the old established values continue to persist.

HUMAN RELATIONS AND THE SOCIAL ORDER

Personality and Ideology

The cultural emphasis on personal loyalty and trust over abstract ideology and institutionalism has been a dominant theme throughout national history. To a great extent, the willingness of Venezuelans to sanction and participate in violent overthrows of established governments has resulted from the traditional view that the solution of social and economic problems emerges more from the forceful acts of men than from adherence to ideological principles. Although each of the major insurrections of the nineteenth century was keynoted by a series of high-sounding objectives and slogans, these appear, on close inspection, to have served more as the banners of personalist leaders than as programs of specific actions or reforms.

Social and political life is not, however, lacking in ideological content. Men espouse, defend, and live by widely varying convictions and, to an extent, attract followers on the basis of their ideas. The ideal leader envisioned in the Hispanic tradition is the man of ideas as well as action. Ideological conviction, nevertheless, has a very specialized place in day-to-day political life, and the politician-ideologist develops his public image, at least in part, by brilliant and persuasive writing. His output marks him as an intelligent and forceful man to the literate population and serves to attract the support of other influential men. Conversely, in appealing for a wider base of support, the politician-intellectual must address himself to a population which, until very recently, was predominantly illiterate and which generally mistrusted obviously well-educated and prosperous men. For this reason, he reserves his best intellectual efforts, through literature or lecture, for the limited audience of fellow intellectuals, rather than direct them to the mass group from the candidate's podium.

The wider general appeal for electoral support is, therefore, cast in largely personalistic terms. The politician must present himself as a strong, vigorous, and forthright man and must convince his audience that his personal interest lies in furthering their hopes and aspirations. Finally, and usually of equal importance, he must clearly have the endorsement of someone known personally to his audience.

Friendship and Trust

Reflecting the importance of interpersonal relationships and personal trust, informal social life is much more ritualized than is the norm in North America. People are more conscious of the nuances of personal interchange and of their own stance in such interchange and tend to be more demonstrative of regard and affection. In a cultural tradition emphasizing self-expression, restrained or silent friendship is rare. Overt gestures and words of friendship are common in the most casual encounters. Friends, acquaintances, and even men whose association is largely limited to business often greet each other not only with a handshake but also with an *abrazo*, an embrace that involves a hug accompanied by vigorous backslapping. Even brief meetings of friends include, almost by obligation, a period of mutual and detailed questioning on each other's well-being and that of their families.

The handshake and the *abrazo* are important elements in maintaining a high level of cordiality. Further, the questions regarding one's well-being and that of one's kinsmen are more than mere gestures of politeness but represent the means by which one person expresses his genuine regard for another. Neglect of such rituals can imply a lack of personal interest and, in consequence, evoke a reaction ranging from coolness to downright hostility.

Even in the most casual business relationship the interplay of personality and a climate of cordiality assume a high degree of importance. The personal sensitivities of negotiators are often as crucial to the outcome of a bargaining session as the issue at hand. Because of the tendency to feel greater security in personal trust than in institutions, a man will generally enter into a negotiation with at least as much interest in the person of the man with whom he is dealing as in the firm or institution that he represents. On this basis, negotiations are frequently long and drawn out, with considerable discussion of matters not apparently related to the central issue. Such tangential conversation serves, in effect, as the means by which the negotiators can establish the note of cordiality considered necessary to any exchange of ideas and by which they can judge each other as individuals.

Simpático is a term commonly applied to persons with the social virtue of a pleasing personality and appeal to others. Standard dictionary translations of this adjective, such as "nice," "likable," or "congenial," are not wholly adequate, as there is no precise equivalent in English. The quality of being *simpático* implies a combination of such virtues as a keen sensitivity to the feelings of others, a clear and readily expressed interest in them, a genuine enjoyment of social contact, and a general aura of warmth, good humor, and likability.

On any basis less personal than a well-defined and intimate relationship, whether kinship or longstanding friendship, it is difficult for people to feel secure in trust and loyalty. When it is necessary to evaluate the trustworthiness of a hitherto unknown individual, as, for example, in business or political negotiation, it is common for men to seek out known mutual kinsmen or mutual friends of long standing. When such ties are discovered, the course of the negotiation is usually greatly facilitated, as the participants can recognize each other as men of confidence (*hombres de confianza*).

Kinship and friendship provide the means of cementing loyalties among men of equal social status. There are also well-defined bases upon which those of disparate levels can establish relations of intimacy and trust. In general, a powerful or wealthy man who maintains bonds of personal loyalty with those of more modest status is known as a *patrón* (roughly, sponsor or protector). Men seek aid and protection of *patrones* by attaching themselves to the wealthy and powerful as loyal retainers. Typically, the *patrón* is an employer, a political leader, a landowner or, sometimes in rural areas, a merchant. The relationship sustained with his retainers is a special one, marked by mutual affection, loyalty, trust, willingness to render mutual assistance. Like friendship, *patrón*-retainer ties can develop by long-term association and are often as strong, but unlike friendship the association carries no implication of equality. The *patrón* offers a paternalistic interest, protection, and security, through economic favors or use of his influence on behalf of his retainers, who in turn return not only affection but deference and obedience.

Patrón-retainer ties develop as a natural product of association between the rich and the poor and the powerful and the weak. Employers tend to see the *patrón* role as a normal part of their lives, and workers accept their place as retainers. Local political leaders seek to gain a following by consciously fitting this model. With some frequency the bond is intensified by the establishment of ritual kinship through the traditional *compadrazgo* (literally, cofatherhood—the ties that exist between a child's parents and godparents), in which the *patrón* becomes godfather to the retainer's child. Although this has no implications of equality when the participants are of different social classes, it does mean that the father and the godfather are bound to each other in a mutual obligation that is ideally almost as compelling as that of kinship.

Industrialization and increasing economic complexity, population mobility, and urbanization have all tended to erode the bases on which man-to-man trust can be established, particularly across class lines. In the large cities the quality of everyday life has become largely depersonalized. Similarly, large foreign-based corporations on which many Venezuelans depend for their living provide scant basis for the development of *patrón*-retainer links. The values of the relationship persist, nevertheless, and many are adapted to the new social and economic order. The paternalistic employer or landowner who cared for his retainers and gave them advice and a measure of security is disappearing from the social scene, but many of the attitudes underlying this relationship have been incorporated into the organization of modern industrial firms.

Although personal *patrones* are not easily found in large corporations, aspects of the old bond continue to exist in the form of elaborate housing and welfare programs, schools and recreation facilities, and company hospitals and commissaries. The dependence of the worker on the company considerably exceeds that of a wage contract and encompasses many phases of personal welfare. Furthermore, many employers continue to take an active personal interest in worker welfare and provide their employees with a symbolic *patrón* figure. Hence, even in the complex world of the industrial corporation means are found to personalize the bond between employer and worker (see ch. 6, Living Conditions).

Hierarchy and Leadership

A stress on hierarchy and rank and a preference for strong centralized authority have been major themes throughout the country's social history. The Hispanic social and political traditions emphasized a rigid stratification of power and privilege and a pyramidal structure of command, allowing little leeway for local initiative or collective decisionmaking. Communications barriers made for frequent violations of the laws and practices of the colonial system, but rigid hierarchy and centralization were no less important as ideals. Initiative and rule were seen as properly vested in officials from Spain, and administrators in the colony were considered little more than the executors of imposed policy. Little or no intercommunication was permitted officials at the same level, and most official communication consisted of orders and directives passed down from the home government to colonial administrators.

Although the leaders of the Republic have for the most part expressed adherence to the tenets of democracy and decentralized power and incorporated them into various constitutions, most leaders have in the past conformed to the old Spanish patterns. Thus, numerous presidents in office under constitutions providing for strict division of powers have ignored these precepts; for example, the concept of federalism, an integral part of most constitutions, has had scant application in what has been, in the main, a basically unitary government.

In civic life the sense of hierarchy has its corollary in the acceptance of the wealthiest and most prominent members of the community as the proper spokesmen before outside authority. In small towns and outlying areas local initiative in civic improvement has traditionally taken the form of a petition for aid directed at state or national authorities and circulated almost exclusively among the large landowners and wealthy merchants. That the poorer members of the community see this limitation of initiative as entirely proper is indicated by the fact that in many areas upper class or "cultured people" are also designated the "responsible people" because they fulfill this representative function.

The popular concept of leadership is quite different from that envisioned in democratic doctrine and theory; the leader, whether established by free election or by force, is usually seen less as a moderator and executive for a group of equals than as the spokesman of his group and the unquestioned arbiter of its policies. He can interpret and act in the group's interest with little or no consultation with other members. As long as such a leader remains in command of the situation, largely by the projection of a forceful and persuasive personality, and inspires group confidence in his ability to further the collective interest, there is seldom any strong opposition to his decisions or acts. Such a leader imposes his will by force of personality and by prowess in oratory, inspiring thereby a confidence that he can attain the goals of those associated with him. It is not considered at all unreasonable in the logic of the social tradition that such a man be the best spokesman for group interests. Both out of admiration for his qualities and gratitude for his forceful representation, his followers accord him deference and loyal obedience.

A corollary to this rule of strong man leadership is that any man in power must expect to be constantly challenged, since men are seen as being in incessant status competition. If the followers recognize in a challenger a man better fitted to represent their interests, they will readily shift their allegiance. It is in accordance with this principle that parties and labor groups disintegrate when rivals for leadership carry off their respective groups of followers. The frequent and usually violent changes of presidents during the nineteenth century resulted, at least partly, from adherence to this same rule, as contenders failed or succeeded in their competition for the support of rival groups.

In addition to the assurance that their leader is capable of protecting and furthering their interests, men expect him to be wise and honest in his dealings with them. The traditional image of the *patrón* assumes importance in the quality of leadership, and the *patrón* maintains a bond of trust with his retainers that morally obliges him to act in their interests. He keeps on a footing of intimacy with them and takes pains to communicate his interest in their well-being. In this context the willingness of a leader to be accessible to his followers is vital to their continued acceptance of him. It is both a boast and a technique of popular political figures that they mingle freely and often with their retainers. Personal appearances, particularly at mass functions, assume a significance that surpasses the importance given the contents of an electoral speech, since they symbolize the man-to-man bond between the leader and his faithful followers.

The notable feature about the country's social values is that they have survived for over 400 years with so little change. Bringing to the New World an ethic already long entrenched in Hispanic society, the basic code of guiding principles largely resisted the pressures and vicissitudes of changing conditions in a new and alien environment. For the most part, the values that guided the society in Spain remained valid during the pioneering and settlement of the eighteenth century, the turbulent era of dawning liberalism and violent revolt of the 1800s, and the industrialization and economic upheaval of the twentieth century.

By 1970 the society's social values were confronting what was probably their greatest challenge, as the pace of change in human relations continued to accelerate. Despite significant alteration and adaptation to new conditions, however, these values had demonstrated that their firm roots in the culture would probably ensure their continued acceptance and resistance to rejection for some time to come.

SECTION II. POLITICAL

CHAPTER 11

THE GOVERNMENTAL SYSTEM

In 1970 Venezuela was governed under the provisions of the Constitution of 1961. During more than a century of dictatorships after its declaration of independence from Spain in 1811, the nation's constitutions had preserved in one form or another a federal government comprising semiautonomous states. The executive had enjoyed a dominant position in a government in which the paramount federal power was divided into executive, legislative, and judicial branches.

The twenty-five constitutions that preceded the Constitution of 1961 varied principally in descriptions of executive powers and provisions affecting elections or emergency powers designed to prolong the dominance of incumbent groups or individuals. In the earlier constitutions the franchise was limited to the small number of literate citizens possessing property of at least receiving an income from a trade or profession. Democratic processes were limited, and opposition groups resorted to violence to oust those in power. If the revolt was successful, a new constitution was framed, but it was so similar to the preceding one that new revolts followed. The forcible overthrow of governments and the subsequent revision of constitutions continued into the twentieth century.

The Constitution of 1961, adopted by the National Congress, reflected the reforms regarded necessary by a liberal coalition that took over the reins of government after the overthrow of General Marcos Pérez Jiménez in 1958. The coalition was determined to frame a constitution that would ensure the continuance of popular government and not merely be a convenient instrument of dictatorship. It established a national government but contained provisions that granted the component states narrowly restricted residual powers, confined to those that did not infringe on powers pertaining either to the municipalities or to the national government. Each state had its own legislative assembly, but the qualifications of its members and provisions for their election were prescribed by the central government. The court system was exclusively federal, and governors, appointed by the president, were designated as agents of the national executive and could be removed either by him or by the legislative assemblies.

The independence of the branches of government—executive, legislative and judicial—is established by the Constitution, which also enjoins their collaboration to accomplish the aims of the state. The president and members of the bicameral National Congress are directly elected by the voters; the members of the Supreme Court of Justice, the prosecutor general, and the comptroller general are chosen by the National Congress, whereas the attorney general is appointed by the president. The independence of the Supreme Court of Justice is enhanced by the provision that its members enjoy nine-year terms, longer by four years than any other elected or appointed officers of government. Other judges are assured career status, dependent on good behavior. Individual congressman's immunity for official acts or opinion is preserved.

The Constitution of 1961 may be altered by amendment for minor changes and by revision. Amendments may be initiated by the National Congress or by the legislative assemblies of the states. Constitutional reform follows the same procedure except that the number of members of the National Congress desiring the reform must be at least one-third of the total members, instead of one-fourth—the number required for amendments.

Both restrictive and punitive checks exist. Congressional approval is required for certain acts and for a few important appointments of the president. The president has a delaying, but not an absolute, veto. The Supreme Court of Justice has wide powers of review over both legislative and administrative acts and may nullify those it deems unconstitutional; the prosecutor general is the appointed guardian of the courts of justice and the behavior of officials. Punitive checks include the impeachment of the president by the combined action of the Senate and the Supreme Court of Justice, and ministers may be censured by the National Congress.

The executive is strongly favored in the distribution of powers in spite of measures contributing to the independence of each of the three branches of government and in spite of intragovernmental checks and balances. The president commands the armed forces and has the authority to determine their strength. He is authorized to conclude treaties, to declare a state of emergency and suspend constitutional guarantees, to negotiate loans and administer the national finances, and to issue decrees activating the laws of the National Congress.

The creation of a social security system is fully expounded in the Constitution. The rights of the people to these benefits are set forth in extensive chapters on political, economic, and social rights; the intent of government to create organs to administer the rights is made explicit. The administration of the many agencies necessary to effect such reforms falls within the purview of the executive branch and increases its power by letting it make appointments and allot funds.

In late 1970 there were many general provisions in the Constitution of 1961 that had not been incorporated into law by the National Congress. The separation of power among the executive, legislative, and judicial branches of government, however, had been respected. The civil service act called for in Article 122 was enacted in September 1970. By the end of 1965, 6.7 million acres of land had been distributed under the agrarian reform law to over 114,000 families. The provisions of the electoral law were carried out, and the elections that took place in 1968 were considered to be scrupulously honest. Article 223 of the Constitution of 1961 calls for a system of taxation that would provide a fair distribution of burdens in accordance with the economic capacity of the taxpayer. In 1970 legislation on taxation was still being debated in the National Congress, and the amount of revenue derived from taxation was below that which might generally be expected.

THE COURSE OF CONSTITUTIONAL GOVERNMENT

Early Constitutions

The first constitution, promulgated in 1811, provided for the United States of Venezuela as a federation of the seven original states with a weak central government. Its *criollo* (native-born person of Spanish descent) framers were influenced by the republican forms reflected in United States and French political thought. Suffrage was generally extended only to male citizens who could read and write, and the holding of office was restricted to those who owned property or received an income. Executive powers were vested in an elected triumvirate.

The second constitution, formulated in 1819 at Angostura (later renamed Ciudad Bolívar), created the office of a single president. Simón Bolívar advanced his ideas of unitary government: a life term for the president, a hereditary senate, and a fourth branch of government—a sort of inspectorate. None of these ideas were accepted, although the constitution did proclaim the federal union of states to be indivisible. Powers were divided between executive, legislative, and judiciary branches; the presidential term was set at four years (see ch. 3, Historical Setting).

This pattern persisted when Bolívar united what had been, under the Spanish, the Captaincy General of Venezuela with the Viceroyalty of Nueva Granada (present-day Colombia) and the Presidency of Quito (present-day Ecuador) to form the Republic of Gran Colombia. In 1829, under the leadership of General José

Antonio Páez, Venezuela broke away from Gran Colombia. Its new constitution, adopted in 1830, was again a combination of the federal and unitary systems but included the added concession to federalism that the governors of the Venezuelan states were to be elected by the state legislatures.

Instruments of Personal Rule

After 1850 a succession of dictators changed constitutions at will. These charters differed little in substance and were hardly more than attempts by strong man leaders to legalize their usurpations of power, prolong their regimes, and return to centralized control.

Federalism and centralism were the two opposing ideas during much of the next hundred years, so the constitutions alternated in conferring more or less autonomy on the states. Regardless of slogans, the dictator of the moment generally made certain that he had a strong hold on the national power and seldom gave any rein to local government.

In each of the various nineteenth-century constitutions, guarantees were given for popular government and individual rights, but these were meant, in the context of the times, to apply to the educated minority; voting rights were restricted. Direct election of the president was briefly provided for in 1861. Capital punishment was outlawed by the Constitution of 1864. In 1874 Guzmán Blanco promulgated a constitution that eliminated the secret ballot. It was restored, however, in the Constitution of 1891, which also weakened the powers of the president. Cipriano Castro restored those powers with the Constitution of 1901, which also established the Federal District on a par with the states. Under the long rule of Juan Vicente Gómez, Castro's successor, the constitution was changed to legalize Gómez's continuance in office, but the document was otherwise largely ignored.

The Liberal Trend

After the death of Gómez in 1935 a new constitution, under the pressure of popular reaction, added a number of guarantees of individual rights and privileges. The term of the executive was shortened from seven to five years, and the term of legislators was extended from three to four years. Cabinet ministers were made responsible to the National Congress for their acts. Authorization was made for confiscation of the estates of former officials who had profited at the expense of the nation. Communism was denounced, and Communists were outlawed. Suffrage, however, was still restricted to men possessing property or an income-producing trade. Presidents were again elected indirectly by the National Congress, and the governors of states were appointed by the president.

Simple amendment of a constitution was often accomplished by an act of the National Congress. More usual was complete redrafting by a controlled National Congress or a constituent assembly appointed or chosen by a controlled election. Whereas the early constitutions usually included a more or less formal bill of rights, which was seldom enforced, later constitutions tended to be more specific in stating and enlarging this feature to include increased guarantees and fewer exceptions.

Direct election of the president and of national, state, and municipal legislators, a provision in force since 1947, has given more political power to the people. The power to appoint the governors of states, however, has remained in the hands of the president. A historic feature of all constitutions to date has been some provision granting the executive emergency powers to suspend constitutional guarantees whenever the government appears to be in danger.

THE CONSTITUTION OF 1961

After the overthrow of the Pérez Jiménez regime in 1958, the liberal coalition that took over the reins of government was determined, as announced by President Rómulo Betancourt, to frame a constitution that would be a break with the past. Instead of being an instrument of dictatorship, it would be a document designed to ensure not only the establishment but the continuance of popular government.

The Constitution of 1961 has a preamble and 252 articles, with an appended section of 23 transitory provisions. The preamble cites principles of national independence, unity, security, peace, and stability. It also includes the social aims of welfare and equitable participation by all in the enjoyment of national wealth. It advocates international cooperation, democracy, and self-determination of people and repudiates war, conquest, and economic predominance as instruments of international policy.

The body of the Constitution includes the structure of the government; individual and collective rights and duties; the division of powers between executive, legislative, and judicial branches; certain special economic provisions; and the machinery for amendment and reform.

A feature of the Constitution of 1961 is the length of the appended section entitled Transitory Provisions. The majority of its subsections provide for continuity in government. For instance, all judges in office, whether or not appointed by the previous government, are authorized—unless investigation proves their incompetence—to serve out their terms. Four detailed subsections provide for the recovery by confiscation of national and private property unlawfully used for personal enrichment by members of the Pérez

Jiménez regime and for the punishment of these offenders by court action.

Basic Provisions

The Federal State

The Republic of Venezuela is a federal state within the terms of the Constitution. Its government is declared to be democratic, representative, and responsible and to have periodic elections. Sovereignty is proclaimed to reside in the people, who exercise it by means of their suffrage through elected officials and representatives in the various levels of government; these public officials are to be held responsible for any abuse of their powers and violations of the law.

No official religion is named. Although the Roman Catholic Church comes under the patronage of the government, all faiths "which are not contrary to good order or to good customs" are tolerated. The official language is Spanish.

The Republic is made up of twenty states; two territories, the thinly settled areas of Delta Amacuro and Amazonas; the Federal District, including the national capital, Caracas; and some seventy-two small island dependencies off the coast. National sovereignty is asserted over all of the land and airspace and over the territorial sea extending twelve nautical miles from the coast plus an additional three-mile maritime zone. For purposes of exploitation of resources, claim also is laid to the continental shelf extending from the coast.

Municipalities

The basic unit of local government is the municipality, consisting of an urban center and wide areas of surrounding rural land, governed by an elected municipal council. Such an arrangement is a natural heritage deriving from the cities with their attached lands and their governing councils, or *cabildos* (town councils), as established in colonial times, in turn traceable to the Spain of those times (see ch. 3, Historical Setting).

Although each state has the right to make laws concerning municipalities and to set the limits of the municipal areas within their boundaries, the municipalities themselves are described in the Constitution as autonomous, and they elect their own officials. Municipalities are not permitted to tax agricultural produce, livestock, or fishing, but they may license industry, commercial establishments, and vehicles. They may not dispose of any public lands (*ejidos*) but must retain them for future urban development. Included within the competence of municipal governments are the usual civic responsibilities, such as urban development, utilities, health, culture, social assistance, traffic, and the municipal police.

The States

Reserved to the states is anything that, in conformity with the Constitution, does not involve national or municipal control. In order to promote administrative decentralization, the National Congress may—by a two-thirds vote—grant states or municipalities certain specific matters of national competence. The Constitution describes the states as autonomous and equal as political entities but enjoins them from taxing imports, exports, and livestock.

Each state is required to have a legislative assembly, elected by direct vote with proportional representation of minorities. The assemblies, in addition to legislating on matters of state competence, have two prescribed annual functions: to set the state budget and to approve or disapprove the actions of the governor of the state.

The governors of the states, territories, and the Federal District are appointed by the president of the Republic and may be removed by him. A governor may also be removed by a two-thirds majority vote of the state legislature. There is a provision in the Constitution for changing the system to provide for the election of governors, but this requires passage by a two-thirds majority vote in a joint session of the National Congress and in late 1970 had not been implemented.

States have control of their urban and rural police, and governors have the power to appoint and remove state officials and employees. This feature gives the governor and, through him, the president a strong hand in local politics. The governor is required to enforce the Constitution and laws as well as to carry out the directives of the national executive. Governors also prepare and submit to the state legislative assembly the annual state budget as well as an annual report or justification of their administrations.

Nationality

Venezuelan nationality is accorded to anyone born in the Republic of Venezuelan parents. Others may acquire nationality by a declaration of intention before the age of twenty-five, combined, in some cases, with residence in the country. Naturalization may be lost by sentence of courts or by voluntary acquisition of another nationality. Nationality carries with it certain duties and many individual rights and privileges, as well as social, economic, and political rights and guarantees.

Duties, Rights, and Guarantees

The Constitution of 1961 treats individual and collective duties, rights, and guarantees comprehensively. Six chapters, comprising seventy-four articles, are devoted to these subjects. A major part of the following section, entitled The Public Power, is devoted to limitations on the illegal usurpation of power by the government—its branches and officials. In the preamble to the Constitution, concern is expressed for the protection and guarantee of the dignity and honor of the individual (see ch. 10, Social Values).

The Constitution is specific as to the duties of the people, beginning with the duty of the defense of their country and the protection of its interests. Military service is stated to be compulsory without distinction as to class or social condition. Everyone is obligated through payment of taxes to contribute to the public expenditures. Education also is compulsory, and parents and guardians are responsible for the children's school attendance.

Both Venezuelans and foreigners in the country are required to comply with the Constitution and the laws, decrees, resolutions, and orders issued by the agencies of the government. Foreigners are said to have the same duties and rights as Venezuelans and may even vote in municipal elections. Voting in national elections and election to public office, however, are confined to Venezuelans; election to the higher offices is limited to Venezuelans by birth.

The Constitution states that labor is a duty of everyone fit to perform it and that the state may require services of individuals according to their ability. Many liberal rights and guarantees are modified by conditions and limitations that permit considerable governmental interpretation. For example, "Everyone has the right to express his thoughts by the spoken word or in writing and to make use of any means of dissemination, without prior censorship; but statements which constitute criminal offenses are subject to punishment."

There is no death penalty. All people have the right to the free development of personality, limited only by the rights of others and by the public and social order. Torture is outlawed, and punishments involving confinement are limited to thirty years. No one may be arrested without a proper warrant except when caught in the act of committing a crime. Bail is authorized, and prompt arraignment and trial with full protection of the rights of the accused are required. Self-incrimination is outlawed, as well as the testimony against an accused person by his spouse or close relatives. Discrimination based on race, sex, creed, or social condition is prohibited, and documents of identification must contain no mention of any kind concerning such categories. Also, no one may be tried twice for the same offense, and persons may not be held incommunicado.

The home is inviolable except when a proper court order is issued; correspondence is also protected. Everyone is permitted to travel freely throughout the national territory and to enter or leave the country with only the usual legal limitations. Each person has the right to profess his religious faith and to practice it privately or publicly, provided it is not contrary to the public order and morality.

Religious faiths are subject to regulation by the national executive, but no national religion is established. The right of petition and the right of association for lawful ends are proclaimed. Anonymous communications are prohibited, as are propaganda for war, offenses against public morals, or incitement to civil disobedience.

The state has assumed great responsibilities and powers in connection with social welfare. The family is to be protected, as are marriage and motherhood, without regard to the civil status of the mother. Children are to be aided regardless of legitimacy, the state sharing with the parents in their support if necessary. Indian communities are to be given special attention for their protection and progressive incorporation into the life of the nation. The state is to strive to improve the living conditions of the rural population. The protection of health is also the right of everyone and a responsibility of the government (see ch. 6, Living Conditions).

Education is proclaimed as a right of all, and the state accepts the responsibility for its provision free of cost, though exceptions may be made with respect to higher and special education when persons of means are concerned. The government undertakes to stimulate and protect private schools if they conform to the Constitution and laws. The government assumes the right to organize and guide the educational system and to determine the qualifications of teachers as to morality and competence and to set standards for the practice of all professions requiring academic degrees (see ch. 7, Education).

Having in its preamble stated the aim of "protecting and uplifting" labor and having described labor as a duty, the Constitution proceeds to state that everyone has the right to work and that the state must endeavor to provide all with a decent living. This is followed by the sweeping guarantee that the law shall provide anything necessary to improve the material, moral, and intellectual condition of workers and that no provisions of law in their favor can be denied.

More specifically, the Constitution declares that the law shall provide for an eight-hour day and a forty-eight-hour week, except for night work, which may not exceed seven hours a day and forty-two hours a week, with a paid day of rest each week and paid vacations. The government is committed to a program for the progressive reduction of working hours, to establish a minimum wage, to guarantee equal wages for equal work, to fix the workers' participation in profits, to make wages and social benefits unattachable for debt, and to provide for seniority privilege and unemployment protection. All such guarantees are set forth in terms of promises of future attainment by laws yet to be passed. The Constitution also states that the law shall determine the responsibility of employers toward their employees. The right to strike is granted to workers, but this is to be regulated by law, especially in the case of workers in public services. Women and minor workers are to receive special protection. The Constitution sets as an eventual goal a complete social security system, including not only the employed but also those without any economic means.

The Constitution provides that the law shall favor the development and support of unions, regulate collective negotiations, and foster the peaceful settlement of disputes. Special protection is to be accorded to union organizers and officials against molestation in their organizational activities. These provisions appear in the labor law that was promulgated in July 1966 and was still in effect in late 1970 (see ch. 19, Labor).

The government assumes wide responsibilities in the direction and promotion of the national economy, especially the creation and development of basic heavy industry and the protection and conservation of natural resources. Expropriation of property in the public interest is provided for, and compensation may be immediate or deferred. Oil and mining concessions and the attendant improvements revert to the nation at the termination of concessions, without indemnity. *Latifundism* (system of large estates) is declared contrary to the public interest and subject to elimination by redistribution of the land.

Individuals are protected in their right to engage in private enterprises, provided they conform to the national program of economic development, which includes measures regulating the distribution of wealth. Monopolies are forbidden, though temporary exclusive concessions are permitted, and the state reserves to itself the right to engage in specified fields of industry or services in the national economic interest. Copyrights, trademarks, slogans, and inventions are protected by law. The right to own property is guaranteed, subject to such taxes, restrictions, and obligations as may conform to the public benefit or general interest. Diversification of production is encouraged in order to promote the economic sovereignty of the country, but the Republic is also committed to favor Latin American economic integration.

Voting, in addition to being a stated right and duty, is compulsory for eligible voters. This rule includes all Venezuelans, male and female, who have reached eighteen years of age and who are not otherwise disqualified by law. The freedom and secrecy of the ballot are guaranteed.

The Constitution also states that voters over twenty-one years of age are eligible to hold public office provided they can read and write. For most of the higher offices, however, the age requirement is increased, and candidates must be Venezuelans by birth.

All legal political parties have the right to participate in the supervision of elections, and proportional representation is provided in elected legislative bodies. Resident foreigners may be allowed to vote in municipal elections. Political parties are authorized, but they are to be legalized by the Supreme Electoral Council and regulated by election laws. Peaceful demonstration without arms is authorized so long as it conforms to the law. The right of political asylum is recognized for persons who for political reasons are subject to persecution or danger.

The Division of Power

The National Power

The national power is exercised through the executive, legislative, and judicial branches of the government. Such division of power is made to prevent undue concentration of authority in any one branch and to provide a system of checks and balances between the branches. Although the division of power is real, the executive tends to overshadow the legislative and judicial divisions.

The Constitution of 1961 places within the competence of the national power all the usual functions of government, including foreign relations; defense; public order and the administration of justice; the treasury; taxes and customs; the conservation of natural resources; public works; education; public health; public welfare; agriculture; industry; legislation on all matters of national interest; the postal service; the census; and the system of weights and measures. Of special interest are the provisions for subsidization of the states by annual appropriations from the National Treasury and the nationalization of transportation, communications, and other public services.

Little power is left for the states and municipalities except internal administration. For administrative convenience the National Congress may grant to the states and municipalities specific matters of national concern, but this requires the difficult agreement of two-thirds of the members of each chamber.

The President. The president of the Republic is the chief of state. He exercises power through the executive branch of government. The Constitution of 1961 prescribes that the president of the Republic must be a Venezuelan by birth, over thirty years of age, and not a member of the clergy. He is elected by universal and direct suffrage. The candidate is elected who obtains a plurality of the votes, and the term of his administration is five years. The president is not permitted to succeed himself, nor may he be a candidate within ten years after his term expires.

To complete the term in case of a vacancy, a new president is elected by the National Congress in joint session. Until the election, presidential succession falls on the president of the National Congress or, upon his default, to the president of the Supreme Court of Justice. During temporary absences of the president, he is to designate one of his ministers to fill the office. The president may not leave the national territory without permission of the Senate or of the Delegated Committee of Congress, which acts when the National Congress is not in session. The president as commander in chief of the armed forces is charged with their organization and operation. He determines the size of the military establishment and controls the appointment of officers. He is charged with the defense of the territory and the sovereignty of the Republic in the event of an international emergency. He is also responsible for the enforcement of the Constitution and the laws and therefore ultimately is responsible for internal law and order in a national sense. He is authorized to declare a state of emergency and to restrict or suspend certain constitutional guarantees in the event of internal or external conflict or whenever there is reason to believe that such may occur.

Guarantees that may not be suspended are those forbidding the holding of persons incommunicado, life imprisonment, torture, and the death penalty. The state of emergency, the guarantees suspended, and the reasons for the action must be announced by a decree of the Council of Ministers and be authorized by the National Congress in joint session or, if it is not in session, by the Delegated Committee of Congress.

In the event of well-founded indications of imminent disturbance of the public order, the president, in the Council of Ministers, may adopt measures to prevent such events from occurring. Such measures do not require the approval of the National Congress but are limited to the detention or confinement of the guilty parties and must be submitted for congressional approval within ten days after their adoption. If disapproved the measures must be terminated immediately, but if approved they may be continued for no more than ninety days. Without other limitations the president has also the power to grant pardons.

The president's civil power is exercised through the administrative official whom he may appoint and remove. He appoints the cabinet ministers; ministers of state without portfolio; governors of states, territories, and the Federal District; and national officials and employees whose appointment is not vested in some other authority. Specifically authorized are the appointments of the attorney general of the Republic and the chiefs of the permanent diplomatic missions, but these appointments must have the confirmation of the Senate or of the Delegated Committee of Congress.

Among the most important officials not appointed by the president are the members of the Supreme Court of Justice, the prosecutor general, and the comptroller general, all of whom are chosen by the National Congress. Another general provision of the Constitution empowers the president, with the authorization of the Delegated Committee of Congress, in case of proved emergency during an adjournment of the National Congress, to create and provide the funds for new public services or to modify or abolish those in existence.

The president has full direction of foreign affairs, including the negotiating and concluding of international treaties, conventions, or agreements, whether with foreign countries or between church and state. This facet of presidential power, however, is modified by articles in the Constitution that require the approval of the National Congress for new contracts with foreign states or firms involving the national interest, especially in the exploitation of national resources. All new international agreements are to be reported to the National Congress at the session after their conclusion.

The president may negotiate national loans and is empowered to enact extraordinary measures in economic or financial matters whenever the public interest so requires, and he has been authorized to do so by special law. By congressional authorization he may also expend more funds than the credits allowed in the budget. In addition, he is empowered to issue decrees regulating the application of laws in whole or in part but without altering their spirit, purpose, or reasoning.

The Council of Ministers. The ministers are the direct agents of the president of the Republic and, when meeting together, constitute the Council of Ministers. The Constitution leaves the number and assignment of ministers to an organic law. To be a minister a person must be a Venezuelan by birth, over thirty years of age, and not a member of the clergy. In addition to his functions as adviser to the president and member of the Council of Ministers, each minister is responsible for the operation of the department of government assigned to him.

The ministers have a right to a voice in the chambers and the appropriate committees of the National Congress, and each minister must render an annual report and accounting of funds to the National Congress within the first ten days of a regular session. Ministers as individuals and in council are responsible to the National Congress, which may investigate their acts. Ministers are subject to impeachment, but not removal, by the National Congress.

The Attorney General. The attorney general of the Republic, whose duties are redefined in the 1961 Constitution, must be a Venezuelan by birth, a lawyer, and over thirty years of age. He is appointed by the president of the Republic with the authorization of the Senate.

The attorney general is charged with representing and defending the interests of the Republic, judicially and extrajudicially. He renders opinions in matters that come within his legal purview and gives legal advice to the executive branch and its agencies, all of whose legal advisory services are enjoined to assist him. He has the right to a voice in the Council of Ministers when called upon by the president of the Republic. The office of attorney general formerly combined the duties assigned by the Constitution of 1961 with those of the prosecutor general who, with his subordinates, now acts as public prosecutor at all levels of the court system and performs other duties in connection with the administration of justice. A section among the transitory provisions of the Constitution provides for the interim situation, pending the passage of laws to specify the exact division of duties. In 1970 many of these laws had not yet been passed.

The Legislative Power

The Congress and Its Chambers. The legislative power is exercised by the National Congress, composed of two chambers—the Senate and the Chamber of Deputies. The principal power of the National Congress lies in its capacity to approve, reject, or alter the budget and its right to censor the acts of the executive branch. Senators and deputies must be native Venezuelans; senators must be over thirty years of age, and deputies must be over twenty-one. Senators and deputies are elected by universal and direct suffrage for terms of five years.

Each of the twenty states and the Federal District has a minimum of 2 senators. The two territories have none. A few additional senators are allotted on the basis of a national quotient. Constitutionally elected former presidents are also included in the membership. The number of senators in 1970 was 42. Representatives in the Chamber of Deputies are allotted for each state and the Federal

District on the basis of 1 deputy for each population unit of 50,000. Territories have only 1 deputy regardless of population. Additional deputies may be allotted to minorities on a national quotient basis. In 1970 the number of deputies was 197.

In general, no government official or employee, while holding office, may be elected to the National Congress, but senators and deputies may accept the post of minister, secretary to the president of the Republic, governor, chief of a diplomatic mission, or president of an autonomous institution. Senators and deputies may resume and complete the term of their elected office after terminating the appointed one, but they may not hold both positions simultaneously.

Parliamentary immunity is provided for members of the National Congress in the execution of their functions, although this has not always served to protect those who foment violent opposition to the government. In October 1963 the Supreme Court of Justice confirmed as constitutional a presidential decree issued in May 1962 banning the Venezuelan Communist Party (Partido Comunista Venezolano—PCV) and the Movement of the Revolutionary Left (Movimiento de la Izquierda Revolucionaria—MIR) to include the loss of immunity of the members of the National Congress from those parties. The Constitution provides that each of the two legislative bodies shall have the exclusive right to organize and regulate itself. Each elects its presiding officer, but in joint sessions of the National Congress, the president of the Chamber of Deputies acts as Vice President of the National Congress. Another prerogative of the National Congress is the granting of political amnesty.

Duties assigned to the Senate by the Constitution include: the initiation of bills relating to treaties and international agreements; authorization of public officials to accept posts, honors, or recompense from foreign governments; authorization of Venezuelan military missions abroad or foreign missions within the country; authorization of the promotion of officers of the armed forces above the grade of colonel; and authorization for the president to leave the national territory. The Senate is also charged with authorizing (on the recommendation of the president) the appointment of the attorney general of the Republic and the chiefs of permanent diplomatic missions.

The Constitution assigns to the Chamber of Deputies the initiation of action on the budget and matters of taxation, consideration of whether or not a vote of censure should be made on any cabinet minister, and any other duty indicated in the Constitution and the laws.

The Delegated Committee. While Congress is not in session, a "watchdog" committee, called the Delegated Committee of Congress, is provided. It must include the president and vice president of the National Congress and twenty-one members who, with their alternates, are to be selected to reflect, as far as possible, the political composition of congress. In addition to keeping watch over the government, the committee may authorize the president to make changes in the structure of government and to decree credits not included in the budget. It may, if necessary, convoke the National Congress in extraordinary sessions.

The Judicial Power and the Public Ministry

The judicial power as established by the Constitution is national in scope, but the document prescribes details pertinent to the Supreme Court of Justice only. In addition, the Constitution of 1961 reverted to the system established by the Constitution of 1947 by re-creating the Public Ministry and separating its functions from those of the attorney general. Headed by the prosecutor general, the Public Ministry is staffed by federal attorneys as public prosecutors at all levels of the court system.

The Supreme Court of Justice. At the highest level is the Supreme Court of Justice, composed of members elected by the National Congress, in joint session, for terms of nine years. They are to be renewed by thirds every three years. Alternates are elected in the same way to fill vacancies as required. Magistrates of the Supreme Court of Justice must be Venezuelans by birth, lawyers, and over thirty years of age.

In addition to being the final court of appeal for such cases as are designated by law, the Supreme Court of Justice has wide powers in adjudging the constitutionality—including the full or partial nullification—of laws, decrees, ordinances, and administrative acts of all branches of government. It is also empowered to decide conflicts between laws and between the competence and jurisdiction of the lower courts. When the Republic, a state, or a municipality is party to a case involving one of the others, the Supreme Court of Justice hears the case, except when the issue is between two municipalities of the same state. When charges are brought against one of its own members, a minister, a governor, or certain other high officers—including members of the National Congress (unless protected by constitutional immunity)—the court investigates, tries the case if the offense is political, or refers it to a lower court if it is not. Finally, the court investigates charges of impeachment against a president and, if the Senate concurs, conducts the trial.

The Constitution provides for the creation of the Council of the Judiciary, to have representatives from the three branches of government. Its purpose is to ensure the independence, efficiency, and proper conduct of the judiciary and to guarantee career status for its members.

The Prosecutor General. In addition to heading the entire corps of public prosecutors (*fiscales*), the prosecutor general is given broad powers in seeing that constitutional rights and guarantees are observed and that the course of justice runs speedily and correctly. He is also responsible for overseeing the enforcement of laws, the performance in office of public officials, and the operation of prisons to ensure that the human rights of convicts are respected. He must have the same qualifications as a Supreme Court of Justice magistrate and is elected by the National Congress.

Economic Provisions

The Public Finances

Matters of revenue, budget, and expenditures are grouped in the Constitution under the heading of The Public Finances. The tax system is based on the principle of progressive rates and a fair distribution of burdens in accordance with the economic capacity of the taxpayer. No changes in taxes may be made other than by law except as provided under the emergency powers of the executive. This condition also applies to unauthorized expenditures from the National Treasury or credits that are in addition to those provided for in the authorized budget.

Loans may be obtained only for income-producing activities except in case of evident national necessity or advantage. Public credit operations must be authorized by special laws.

Claims and obligations against the government are limited to those contracted by legitimate agencies in accordance with the laws. The public finances of the states and municipalities are to be governed by the same provisions of the Constitution, insofar as they are applicable, that govern national public finance. A special provision of the Constitution requires that the annual budget include an allotment of money for distribution to the states, the Federal District, and the territories. Thirty percent of this is divided equally among them, and 70 percent is divided in proportion to their populations.

The Comptroller General

Designated as a subsidiary agency of the National Congress, the office of the comptroller general is another special agency of government that has guaranteed autonomy of operations. It is entrusted with the control, supervision, and auditing of the national revenues, expenditures, and assets and of associated operations. The Constitution provides that its functions may be extended to states, municipalities, and autonomous institutions without impairing their guaranteed autonomy.

The office functions under the comptroller general of the Republic, who is elected by the National Congress within the first thirty days of its constitutional term. He must be a Venezuelan by birth, over thirty years of age, and a layman. The comptroller general reports annually to the National Congress on the activities of his office as well as on such accounts of other agencies as the National Congress may require of him. From time to time he makes any other reports that the executive branch or the National Congress may request.

Amendment and Reform

The Constitution of 1961 may be altered by amendment or reform. Amendment is used for minor changes, and reform implies a basic rewriting. The amendment may be initiated by one-fourth of the members of one of the chambers of the National Congress or by one-fourth of the states by majority decisions made in their respective legislative assemblies. The bill of amendment is acted on in the National Congress and, if passed, is then transmitted to the states for consideration in their legislative assemblies. If the amendment is ratified by two-thirds of the states, the National Congress declares it approved, and it is added to the Constitution.

The whole Constitution may be revised by a somewhat similar procedure except that the initiative must come from either one-third of the members of the National Congress or from a majority of the legislative assemblies of the states. If the National Congress accepts the initiative by a two-thirds vote, the bill for reform is then processed like any other law, but if approved it must be submitted to a national referendum to be decided by a majority of all the voters. The president of the Republic may not veto amendments or reforms of the Constitution but must promulgate them within ten days of their passage.

THE FUNCTIONAL ASPECTS OF GOVERNMENT

The structure and powers of the branches and agencies of government as prescribed in the Constitution provide a balanced operation of government, with a considerable measure of independent action allowed to the legislative and judicial branches as well as to the executive. For instance, although the president is above censure, he may be impeached through the concurrence of the Senate and the judiciary; and the ministers, individually and in council, are responsible to the legislature.

On the other hand, the many powers granted in great detail to the executive ensure that virtually all initiative in the operation of government rests with that branch and, in all essentials, with the person of the president. Even in legislation, although the National Congress has specific power to initiate, most important bills, including the budget, are submitted to it by the executive branch. Again, even though the National Congress may override a presidential veto, the executive branch is enabled to retain its initiative by requesting reconsideration of only those parts of a bill that it finds objectionable, thus avoiding a direct conflict with the legislators.

Another feature that greatly strengthens the power of the executive branch is that the Constitution avowedly and explicitly is directed toward the creation of a state that has an economy planned in considerable detail. Such projects ensure the presence, throughout the country and at all levels of government, of representatives responsible to and under the patronage of the executive branch.

The Executive

Under the Constitution the executive branch includes the president, his personal staff, and his secretariat; the ministries; the armed forces; the governors of the states, territories, and the Federal District; and the heads of certain autonomous and specialized institutions and agencies.

The principal functions of the executive power are the enforcement of the Constitution and laws and the administration of the national finances. These together with the patronage and political influence of the presidency, amount to a manifest concentration of power in the exectuve branch. The president may also negotiate foreign loans and, with the authorization of congress or of its delegated committee, may decree credits outside of the budget.

The president is assisted by thirteen ministries: interior relations, foreign relations, finance, defense, development, public works, education, health and social assistance, agriculture, labor, communications, mines and hydrocarbons, and justice. Collectively the ministers form the Council of Ministers, which fulfills the functions of a cabinet. The president's acts and decrees must be countersigned by the appropriate minister or ministers to be valid.

The attorney general assists the president and ministers with legal advice on national and international matters and defends the national interests in any legal action involving the state. He may sit and have a voice in the Council of Ministers when the president desires. Through the minister of interior relations the president controls the political subdivisions of the nation and the National Police. Through the minister of justice he controls the Technical Corps of Judicial Police (see ch. 22, Public Order and Internal Security).

Through the minister of defense he controls the national guard and the regular army, navy, and air force (see ch. 23, The Armed Forces).

By Article 190 the president, in an emergency, is authorized to create and to appropriate funds for new public services. Such a service, called the Central Office of Coordination and Planning (Oficina Central de Coordinación y Planificación), was created in 1959. Although directly responsible to the president, it is a semi-autonomous agency principally concerned with the preparation of successive four-year social and economic plans, for which it may seek the submission of contributory plans from any ministries that may be involved.

For coordination in manners of public administration the president may assemble any or all of the governors of the federal entities. He may also convoke the National Congress into extraordinary session.

The Ministries

The Ministry of Interior Relations has a number of important functions in critical areas of government. It furnishes the channel of communication and direction for all matters concerning the internal territorial administration with the states, territories, Federal District, and dependencies and disburses the allocation of federal budgetary funds that are an important increment of state income. It is responsible for the maintenance of public order and safety and to this end directs some police operations. It is in charge of official information, publicity, and publications and also acts as budget coordinator and paymaster to the National Congress, the Office of the President, and the Supreme Electoral Council (see ch. 22, Public Order and Internal Security).

The Ministry of Foreign Relations has the usual responsibilities for treaties and agreements, diplomatic missions, and protocol. It has the added responsibility for the delimitation of the national frontiers. In late 1970 negotiations to resolve border problems were being carried on with both Colombia and Guyana (see ch. 13, Foreign Relations).

The Ministry of Finance is responsible for the National Treasury and supervision of the banking system, including the relationship between the national government and the Central Bank of Venezuela (Banco Central de Venezuela). It also supervises the operations of the Customs Service (see ch. 21, Finance).

The Ministry of Defense is charged with the organization, operation, and maintenance of the national armed forces, which, besides the army, navy, and air force, also include the Armed Forces of Cooperation, generally known as the national guard. The national guard has the mission of internal security (see ch. 22, Public Order and Internal Security; ch. 23, The Armed Forces).

Important functions of the Ministry of Public Works are the development of the national system of highways and bridges and the construction of dams, drainage systems, seaports, airports, public buildings, and low-cost housing in connection with urbanization programs.

The Ministry of Development has the responsibility for the guidance and coordination of the country's economic development, including the drafting and implementation of the trade policy, the planning and execution of an overall policy of tourism, the obtaining and publication of national census and other statistics, the supervision of the rent control law, and the supervision of the operations of the cooperatives and of the industrial property register.

The Ministry of Education has the responsibility for providing free education for the children of the nation and also for adult education centers for illiterates. In addition, it is responsible for teacher training and provides and maintains museums and libraries (see ch. 7, Education).

The Ministry of Health and Social Assistance operates hospitals and laboratories (some semiautonomous), in addition to dispensaries and centers for maternal care, as part of a general program of sanitation and health.

The Ministry of Agriculture, in addition to the promotion of agriculture and livestock raising, is charged with the protection of the national flora and fauna. It supports the semiautonomous National Agrarian Institute (see ch. 17, Agriculture).

The Ministry of Labor is concerned with the promotion of union organization and the protection of workers' rights and privileges. A law of July 1966 provides that organized labor shall be represented on the boards of directors or equivalent governing bodies of state autonomous institutions, economic development agencies, and enterprises in which the state holds all, a predominant percentage, or a majority of the shares (see ch. 19, Labor).

The Ministry of Communications is responsible for the operation of the postal service and telephone, telegraph, and radio system. This includes control of vehicular, rail, maritime, and air transportation. The ministry is also responsible for the operation of airports (see ch. 20, Trade).

The Ministry of Mines and Hydrocarbons is principally concerned with the enforcement of agreements between the national government and foreign oil and mining firms. Under it are several semiautonomous government corporations that are concerned with the development of government participation in the oil and mining industries.

In addition to administrative support of the whole judicial system and the office of the attorney general, the Ministry of Justice controls the Technical and Judicial Police and operates the national penal system (see ch. 22, Public Order and Internal Security).

The Legislature

The legislative branch has, in practice, two principal functions: to discuss and vote on the national budget and taxation and such other legislation as is properly introduced; and to act as censor of the performance of the executive branch. So long as the government can command a majority in the National Congress, it may encounter little difficulty in promoting its program, but such majority in a multiparty system depends on the stability of coalitions that can seldom be depended on for long-range continuity (see ch. 12, Political Dynamics).

The National Congress is required to meet twice a year, from March 2 to July 6 and from October 1 to November 30. Sessions may be prolonged by a majority vote in joint session, and extraordinary sessions may be convoked by the president of the Republic or at the request of either chamber. A quorum cannot be less than the absolute majority of the members of each chamber.

Legislation may be introduced in either chamber by no less than three senators or deputies. The national executive, the Supreme Court of Justice, and the Delegated Committee of Congress may also introduce bills. Furthermore, a bill may be introduced by direct petition if sponsored by 20,000 registered voters.

Every bill must have two hearings in each chamber. When it is finally passed, with or without modifications, by both houses, it becomes sanctioned as law. The new law is then sent to the president of the Republic for promulgation. The president, if in agreement, must promulgate the law within five days by having it published in the *Official Gazette* of the Republic. If the president objects, he returns the bill to the National Congress with his recommendations. On questions of constitutionality he may call for a ruling of the Supreme Court of Justice, which must be given within ten days. The National Congress in joint session considers the president's recommendations and may repass the law, rewrite it, or withdraw it. If repassed by a simple majority, the president may again return the law for reconsideration, but if passed by a two-thirds majority, he must promulgate it within five days. If he should fail to do so, the president and vice president of the National Congress proceed with the promulgation either in the *Official Gazette* of the Republic or in the *Gazette of Congress.* Laws may be repealed or amended only by other laws.

The Judiciary

Article 204 of the Constitution of 1961 states that the judicial power is exercised by the Supreme Court of Justice and by other courts as prescribed by law. The nine members of the Supreme Court, together with their alternates, are elected for nine-year terms by the National Congress. One-third of the justices are elected every three years. All other judges are selected by the Supreme Court of Justice from lists of names submitted by the minister of justice.

The Supreme Court of Justice generally conducts its business through three divisions (*salas*): a political-administrative division; an appeal division for civil, commercial, or labor cases; and an appeal division for criminal cases. Each division has at least five justices. In order to be eligible for the Supreme Court of Justice, a person must be a lawyer who is a native-born Venezuelan over thirty years of age. The Constitution also permits the setting up of the Federal Division to handle cases of secondary importance. The Federal Division is presided over by the president of the Supreme Court of Justice and has as members at least two representatives from the three divisions of the court.

Below the Supreme Court of Justice are two types of courts: ordinary courts and courts of special jurisdiction. Ordinary courts include superior courts, courts of first instance, municipal or parochial courts, and courts of investigation. Courts of special jurisdiction include military, treasury, labor, traffic, income tax, commerce, and minors' courts.

Justice at the village level is usually handled by the mayor. Courts of investigation may order arrests and make preliminary reports in criminal actions. Municipal or parochial courts handle minor civil and commercial cases and misdemeanors. The courts of first instance are competent in the more serious civil, commercial, and penal cases. Appeals may be made to the superior courts and, finally, to the Supreme Court of Justice.

To ensure that constitutional rights and guarantees are respected and that justice is administered properly, the National Congress elects a prosecutor general, who supervises the functioning of the Public Ministry. The prosecutor general must have the same qualifications as members of the Supreme Court of Justice and is elected within the first thirty days of each ordinary session of the National Congress. The Constitution also authorizes the appointment by the president of an attorney general of the Republic, whose functions are to represent and defend the interests of the country judicially, to render opinions, and to give legal advice to the national administration.

Local Government

The states are declared by the Constitution to be autonomous except for certain restrictions, but the governors are appointed by the president of the Republic, and this gives the national government a strong position in the administration of the states. The state legislative assemblies are elected by direct and universal suffrage, but otherwise the governors are generally free to organize their staffs and conduct the executive functions of state government. State executive organization and operation tend to parallel that of the Republic in miniature, with deletions as to foreign relations, defense, and justice.

The states have the power to merge, alter their boundaries, or cede parts of their territories to other states of the federal government with the consent of the Senate. They also exercise residual powers—anything that, in conformity with the Constitution, does not pertain to national or municipal jurisdiction. Also, the National Congress, by a two-thirds vote, can give a state or a municipality control over national matters in order to promote administrative decentralization. The states are forbidden to tax imports or exports or other revenue items that are under national or municipal jurisdiction.

In 1968 there were 330 representatives to the legislatures of the 20 states and the 2 territories and 1,193 councilmen for the 636 municipal councils. The municipalities were grouped into 172 districts. Each district council had 7 members, with the exception of the Federal District, which had 35. The 2 territories and the dependencies are administered by the Ministry of Interior Relations. The traditional centralization of the national government in Caracas helps to keep local government relatively unimportant, as practically all of the central administration is located in the capital city, and the regional offices with which local governments would deal are limited in their powers.

Municipal governments also retain a measure of autonomy. They uniformally include an elected city council and a mayor, though provision is made for variations so long as they remain democratic and locally acceptable. Small villages may have only a mayor, who handles all government functions, including those of justice of the peace.

ELECTORAL MACHINERY

Universal adult suffrage has existed since the Constitution of 1947 was adopted. All Venezuelan citizens over eighteen years of age are eligible to vote, unless they are subject to a prison sentence or conviction that carries the loss of political rights. There is no literacy, property, or sex requirement, and registration and voting are compulsory for all eligible citizens. Members of the armed forces on active duty may not vote.

Electoral matters are regulated by the Venezuelan Election Law of April 8, 1962, and controlled by the Supreme Electoral Council. The Supreme Electoral Council has thirteen members elected for two-year terms by the National Congress during the first thirty days of its ordinary session. The law does not set any requirements for membership, but no political party may have a dominant representation on the Supreme Electoral Council or on any of the lower electoral councils. If any electoral board has a majority from one party, substitutions must be made.

The Supreme Electoral Council is required to regulate the functioning of the electoral bodies, call elections, appoint the members of the principal electoral boards, determine the registration date, decide appeals from lower boards, count the final vote and proclaim the president, and award legislative seats on the basis of the national quotient. There are 23 principal electoral boards for the 20 states, the Federal District, and the 2 territories. Under them are 172 district electoral boards of five members each and 636 municipal electoral boards of five members each.

Candidates for president of the Republic may be nominated by political parties or organizations represented in at least seven of the twenty-three electoral districts, provided that the number of members is at least 200. Candidates for all other elective offices may be nominated by duly constituted parties or organizations that represent at least 5 out of each 100 registered voters over twenty-one years of age and literate. The twenty-three principal boards receive the nominations for candidates for the National Congress and the state legislatures, and candidates for municipal councils are nominated before the district boards.

To facilitate the voting for those who are illiterate, cards of various colors are used for the presidential candidates and for all the political parties. Except for the president, voters do not vote for individuals, as the method of proportional representation requires a list that is drawn up by each party. In the 1968 election helicopters flew low over cities with loudspeakers exhorting the people to vote. In that election only 91 percent of those registered voted.

At the end of the voting period the ballot boxes are opened in public, and the votes are counted. The totals are forwarded from municipal and district boards to the principal boards, and from them to the Supreme Electoral Council in Caracas. The Supreme Electoral Council announces the winner of the presidential election; the principal boards announce the winners of the national and state legislature election; and the district boards announce the winners of the municipal council seat election.

CIVIL SERVICE

Article 122 of the Constitution of 1961 states that the law shall establish an administrative career service and the standards for entrance, advancement, transfer, suspension, and retirement of employees and shall provide for their incorporation in the social security system. In 1958 an advisory commission on public administration had been established to study and make recommendations on a civil service system. The commission recommended a system based on seniority and qualification through a special school of administration. For twelve years this recommendation was not adopted as a national law, and several ministries instituted their own systems, generally based on entrance examinations and seniority credits for time in office. In September 1970 President Rafael Caldera signed into law a civil service bill approved by all the political parties represented in the National Congress, to be supervised by the Public Administration Commission and other governmental agencies.

Public employees are in the service of the state and have no political partisanship. Every political official or employee is obliged to comply with the requirements established by law for holding his position. Positions in government are eagerly sought, and appointments have customarily depended on political power, patronage, and nepotism. Change of the party or leader has usually meant a widespread turnover in personnel, in which government has suffered through lack of continuity and experience.

CHAPTER 12

POLITICAL DYNAMICS

In 1970, after more than a decade of stable democratic government, the habits of voter participation and peaceful transfer of office had been implanted. Political power had been diffused throughout the population through universal suffrage, direct elections, and large-scale party and interest group organization. All of the major contenders within the multiparty system advocated social reform and sought mass bases of support.

Throughout the first century after independence political power had rested almost exclusively with the landed aristocracy and the military. The military, monopolizing the authorized use of force, protected the interests of the aristocracy. The Roman Catholic Church was also influential, but its power was exercised primarily through education and moral sanctions. In the early 1930s the development of the oil industry began to transfigure the social structure, giving rise to a new upper class of entrepreneurs, a middle class to serve the needs of the growing urban population, and an urban working class.

After the death of the authoritarian ruler Juan Vicente Gómez in 1935 the new groups began to organize politically and, despite the repression of overt political activity by the regime of General Marcos Pérez Jiménez (1950-58), organizational and constitutional mechanisms for popular participation in government were institutionalized after 1958. The major parties, most of which had their origins in student movements and all of which had developed since the 1930s, have looked to workers and peasants as well as to the middle and upper classes for support. Furthermore, popularly elected governments, respecting the institutional prereogatives of the military on the one hand and exploiting interservice and interpersonal rivalries on the other, have been able to command the loyalty of the dominant groups in the armed forces.

Among the important elements in society competing for influence in domestic and foreign policies and, in general, for leverage within the political system have been the landed aristocracy, organized labor and peasant groups, the business community, the armed forces, the Catholic church, and student organizations. As the primary sources of competing political leaders and movements, the armed forces and the university community have carried on a struggle throughout much of the country's history. The universities, as centers of leftist political activism, had provoked military intervention and governmental controls.

The traditional conservatism of the Catholic hierarchy had been largely replaced by advocacy of social reform. The commercial sector continued to have considerable influence on government policies, but its pressures were offset by well-organized urban labor and peasant groups.

The Democratic Action party (Acción Democrática—AD), the first party to develop a meaningful platform, large-scale organization, and broad popular support, elected its leader, Rómulo Betancourt, to the presidency in 1958. In March 1964 one popularly elected president relinquished office to another for the first time in the country's history. The AD, under President Raúl Leoni, retained control of the government but, as in the 1959-64 term, had to rule through coalition. The AD lost much of its following after 1960 to left-wing splinter groups, the largest of which, the People's Electoral Movement (Movimiento Electoral Popular—MEP), broke with the party before the 1968 elections.

The Committee for Independent Political and Electoral Organization (Comité de Organización Política y Electoral Independiente—COPEI), also known as the Social Christian party, has been the second-ranking party in total voting strength since 1963. With a reformist platform similar to that of the AD and with greater cohesion of leadership, it placed its leader, Rafael Caldera, in the presidency in 1969. Having failed after his election to establish a workable coalition with smaller parties, President Caldera in 1970 depended upon the majority AD party for cooperation on major legislation.

SOCIOPOLITICAL DEVELOPMENT

Most constitutions, including that of 1961, have included the statement that "sovereignty resides in the people." Although this implies that political office depends upon the free choice of the people, historically it has seldom been the case. Almost without exception since 1830 a succession of military dictators altered constitutions, restricted suffrage, and manipulated elections to suit their purposes. Political power was based on military force, usually allied with a small aristocracy of wealthy landowners. The people as a whole had no real choice (see ch. 3, Historical Setting).

With the advent of liberal reforms, universal suffrage, and direct elections, greater political power came into the hands of the people. The military retained its capability of seizing the government, but more and more its leaders recognized the importance of popular support. The old landed aristocracy has been giving way politically to a new group, based on industrial wealth and ability, which has also sought the support of the people. Hence, the people—the voters—have become a principal source of political power.

Since 1946 all men and women over eighteen years of age, except criminals and the active military, have had the right and duty to vote. In the 1958 presidential election about 36 percent of the population exercised this right, whereas in 1970 the percentage was nearer 40. About 88 percent of the voters are found in the mountains and the coastal plains in the northern fringe, 10 percent are in the *llanos* (plains) south of the mountains, and 2 percent are in the Guiana Highlands further south. More than half of the voters are concentrated in the larger cities and towns. About one-third are *campesinos* (peasants). Although the least well educated of the *campesinos* and urban workers have tended to be politically inert, their votes have rewarded vigorous campaigns of organization and leadership, such as were instituted in the 1940s by the AD and since 1959 by COPEI. It has been largely the rural vote in support of the major parties that has counteracted the general antipathy to parties in the capital city.

The growing middle class of small traders, office workers, technicians, and professional people, which in 1950 was estimated at 8 percent of the population, probably exceeded 10 percent by 1970. This group has been divided in its allegiance, part tending to identify with the upper class and a smaller part with the lower class. The middle-class voters have, nevertheless, shown themselves likely to be the least predictable at election time; they have also formed the active core of most of the political parties.

The upper class, estimated at about 2 percent of the population, has also been growing, mostly by elevation of individuals and their families from the middle group. By virtue of the traditional dependence of the people on their landlords, the old upper class was usually able to dominate the political field. Even with the political awakening of the lower class, the upper class has retained much influence, but its composition has been changing. The old, conservative landed aristocracy is giving way politically to the new upper class of industrial and professional leaders (see ch. 5, Social Structure). This new group, which includes many who profess liberal principles, has furnished many political leaders. Candidates for president are usually either high military officers or professional men, usually in the field of law, medicine, the arts, or political science. The historic cult of the strong leader often makes the struggle for votes a contest of personalities (see ch. 10, Social Values).

THE EMERGENCE OF PARTIES

For more than a century after independence from Spain in 1821, political parties were of little importance. The traditional labels of Liberal and Conservative were variously employed by a succession of military dictators to mobilize personal followings. New names, Federalists and Centralists, took the place of Liberals and Conservatives, respectively, with no real change in political significance (see ch. 3, Historical Setting).

Political parties based on broad popular support did not develop until after the death of Juan Vicente Gómez in December 1935. The strength of the popular reaction to the long rule of Gómez constrained his successor to grant a number of liberal reforms, including the legalization of political parties and the recall of political exiles. First in importance among the exiles were the former university students, the Generation of 1928, who had rebelled against Gómez. These included such political figures as Rómulo Betancourt, Jóvito Villalba, and Raúl Leoni (see ch. 3, Historical Setting).

In 1936 this group formed a political front, the Venezuelan Revolutionary Electoral Organization (Organización Revolucionaria Venezolana Electoral—ORVE). Soon outlawed by Gómez's successor, Eleazor López Contreras, the leaders of the ORVE regrouped in 1937 as the National Democratic Party (Partido Democrática Nacional—PDN).

The Communist elements were expelled from that party in 1937 and formed the Venezuelan Communist Party (Partido Comunista Venezolano—PCV). Both the PDN and the PCV were outlawed but, just before the elections of 1941, Betancourt and other liberal-minded PDN leaders organized the AD. It too was suppressed under the López Contreras regime but was legalized under the new president, Isaías Medina Angarita.

Although the AD undertook the innovation of organization in depth to ensure a broad base of popular support, neither it nor any other opposition group was able to compete successfully in elections against the government machine because of the old indirect election system whereby the president was elected by the National Congress and the congressmen by state legislatures. This gave the existing government almost complete control of the election machinery.

Under these circumstances the AD accepted an offer of military support by an organization of junior officers, the Patriotic Military Union (Unión Patriótica Militar—UPM). When the UPM led a coup d'etat in October 1945, the AD rode with it into power (see ch. 3, Historical Setting).

The AD has advocated a strong program of civil rights and public welfare measures, but above all it had advocated electoral reforms to include direct election of the president and of members of the National Congress through universal suffrage. Such reforms, along with freedom of speech, the press, and assembly, were put into effect; elections for a constituent assembly were held in October 1946; and a new constitution was adopted the following year.

These measures encouraged the formation of several political parties. Jóvita Villalba broke with the AD and in 1945 formed the Republican Democratic Uníon (Unión Republicana Democrática—URD), with a predominantly middle-class membership and a program almost indistinguishable from that of the AD. A third party, COPEI, was formed in 1946 from a basically conservative Andean student movement by a young lawyer, Rafael Caldera. Often referred to as the Social Christian party, it sought support from the more religious and conservative of the voters while it also advocated a moderate social welfare program. The Communists also competed as a single political party in the election of 1946 though their party, the PCV, through dissension between leaders, had previously been split into two factions.

All four parties (the AD, the URD, COPEI, and the PCV) campaigned for the vote, but the AD was well organized and vigorous in presenting its program throughout the country; its reward was an overwhelming victory at the polls. In 1947 its candidate, Rómulo Gallegos, was easily elected president, and with its representatives in full control of the National Congress, the AD appeared as an authentic example of political power through popular suffrage. It had the mandate to carry out its program of political, economic, and social reforms, but the government's methods alienated not only the entrenched conservative elite but also many of the liberally inclined middle class, who saw their economic position threatened. More serious, however, were an aroused suspicion by the military of AD hostility and antagonism on the part of the church because of AD anticlericalism.

When the military demanded control in November 1948, the AD, despite its majority of voter support, did not take the risk of civil war. The first popular government was superseded by a military junta. AD leaders were exiled, and the party officially was dissolved (see ch. 3, Historical Setting).

During the next ten years persecution by the Pérez Jiménez regime drove underground all political parties except the government's own, the Independent Electoral Front (Frente Electoral Independiente—FEI), and a small Communist splinter group. Student agitation against the government was answered by the closing of the Central University of Venezuela in 1952. The students set up the clandestine National University Front in 1955.

By the summer of 1957 the underground leaders of the AD, the URD, COPEI, and the PCV met and formed a coalition called the

Patriotic Junta (Junta Patriótica) in opposition to the authoritarian government. When that government was overthrown in January 1958, the exiled leaders of the AD, the URD, and COPEI met in New York City, without the PCV, and formed the Venezuelan Civil Front (Frente Civil Venezolano—FCV), pledged to cooperate for a return to constitutional government. Attempts to agree on a single candidate for president were unsuccessful. Each party nominated its own candidate, but all three parties agreed to support the one elected.

Elections were held on December 7, 1958, and again the AD won, though with a smaller majority than in 1946. The AD candidate, Betancourt, won the presidency, and the AD elected a comfortable majority in both houses of the National Congress. President Betancourt formed a coalition government including URD and COPEI members but no Communists.

The AD, the URD, and COPEI were all committed to social reform programs, but by 1960 the more radical elements of the AD rebelled against the slow processes of cooperative government. Upon being expelled from the party, the rebels set up a party of their own, called the Movement of the Revolutionary Left (Movimiento de la Izquierda Revolucionaria—MIR). Their program is Marxist, anti-United States, pro-Castro, and for nationalization of the oil and iron industries.

The AD had another split in 1962, when Raúl Rámos Giménez broke with Betancourt and formed what later adopted the designation AD-*oposición* (AD-op) to contrast with the parent party, or AD-*gobierno* (AD-gob), alternatively called the Old Guard. AD-op accused the government party of interfering with the electoral process and muzzling the press and the universities and proclaimed the government's agrarian reform policy a fraud. The most serious effect of this split was that the four AD senators and twenty-two AD deputies in the National Congress went with AD-op, thus negating the AD's majority in the Chamber of Deputies. In spite of policy differences, the defection of AD-op is generally regarded as resulting principally from a clash of personalities between leaders.

Other parties have experienced splits and the formation of splinter parties. The URD had a faction that early in 1963 broke away from Jóvito Villalba in support of the candidacy of Vice Admiral Wolfgang Larrazábal. It adopted the title the Independent National Electoral Movement (Movimiento Electoral Nacional Independiente—MENI).

Important less for its size than for its militance and its readiness to ally itself with other opposition parties to gain power was the PCV. Communists had been active in the 1930s. They early joined ORVE but were expelled in 1937. Although the PCV split during the 1940s because of nationalist factionalism, it reunited for the election of 1958, where it won two seats in the Senate and seven in the Chamber of Deputies as well as one each in the legislatures of five states.

With elections for president of the Republic and the members of both houses of the National Congress scheduled to be held December 1, 1963, political activity increased as the time grew shorter. Although only four parties had competed in the elections of 1958, seven were registered for the new elections by November 1, 1963, the closing date for political parties to qualify. The three older parties, the AD, the URD, and COPEI, had been active all year. The opposition parties attacked the record of the Betancourt government. Although some parties had platforms that differed little from the present government's program, all opposition parties argued that they could do better.

COPEI, in particular, beginning in January, sought to broaden its popular support. Its leader, Rafael Caldera, conducted a vigorous campaign both in the more populous states and in the slum areas around the capital. As the least radical of the older and larger parties, COPEI counted on support from the more conservative elements of the population, especially from much of the military, the church, and the business community. Hence it made every effort to widen voter support by carrying the Social Christian program to the more numerous, the economically depressed, and the least secure elements of the population.

The URD also presented its leader, Jóvito Villalba, as the "Candidate of the People." Posing as a left-of-center party, it attracted support from restless middle-class elements and from educated younger citizens dissatisfied at the slowness of reform. Withdrawing in 1960 from the coalition government, it favored Fidel Castro's regime in Cuba and accused the AD of bungling the reform program, of subservience to foreign interests, and of repressive action against Venezuelans for political purposes, such as the suppression of the PCV and the MIR and several revolutionary newspapers. The party was subject to considerable internal dissension; some student members branded the leaders as reactionary, whereas older members considered it too sympathetic to Castro and Moscow.

Nevertheless, the URD was second only to the AD in the 1958 elections, and there was a feeling among some older people that Jóvito Villalba, as the orator who sparked the rebellion of the Generation of 1928 against the Gómez dictatorship, deserved his turn at the presidency. The URD opposition was sufficiently radical to expect to profit by the votes of members of the outlawed Marxist parties.

The AD had been the best organized and most broadly based political party since it came to power in 1945. Even when outlawed during the rule of Pérez Jiménez and forced to operate underground, it could command more organized popular support than the government party (FEI). In the free election of 1958, it gained almost twice as many votes as the URD, its nearest competitor. It was the AD that implemented the strong public welfare and civil rights program that did much to improve the position of the *campesino* and the urban worker. Its early fostering of labor unions built for the AD a broad base of support.

Since 1958, as the party in power, it had been the target of criticism not only by the opposition parties but by some of its own following. Impatience with the progress of the AD reform program and the party's anti-Castro stand resulted in the defection of some leaders and alienated some workers but, as long as the AD Old Guard, or government part (AD-gob), retained its image as the principal organizer and protector of rural and urban labor, its political power seemed assured.

At the AD-gob party convention early in July 1963, Raúl Leoni, an old party stalwart and comrade of Betancourt, won enough support to be named candidate for the presidency on the second ballot. Leoni, two years older than President Betancourt, had been president of the Venezuelan Student Federation (Federación Estudiantil de Venezuela) of the Generation of 1928 and in later years head of the party's powerful labor bureau. His image as the workingman's friend was reinforced by a popular belief that he would continue to have the backing of Betancourt, which would promote the continuity of the AD's program. This included the extension of the welfare program, agrarian reform, and an increase of the national share in the development and marketing of natural resources.

Notwithstanding its apparently favored position, AD-gob mounted a vigorous campaign. Its political posters covered the country, and Leoni conducted a strong campaign, making speeches in nearly every state. All resources of the party, including the army of government employees, were mobilized to help elect an AD-gob president as well as a working majority in the National Congress. AD-gob stood on its record as the farmer's and laborer's friend, as the vested champion of economic progress, and as the enemy of colonialism, imperialism, and of all dictatorships, especially that of Cuba.

Among the opposition leaders the best known was Larrazábal, who was popular with leftist elements, especially among students and the unemployed of the capital. He was supported by remnants of his old party of the 1958 election—the MENI—and also had the support of a new party, the Democratic Popular Force (Fuerza Democrática Popular—FDP), which appeared in March 1963. Although of the military, Larrazábal had little popularity with the armed forces other than elements of his own naval branch.

A new candidate, who attracted some defectors from the URD

and AD-op, as well as considerable support among the many small parties and uncommitted voters of the middle class, was Arturo Uslar Pietri, an author, senator, teacher, businessman, and former cabinet member. He ran as the "Independent Candidate of National Understanding" for a coalition of parties called the National Front of Opposition (Frente Nacional de Oposición—FNO).

Both the PCV, the authentic Communist party, and the MIR, the radical faction expelled in 1960 from the AD, were the subjects of a presidential decree of May 1962 denying them permission to enter the elections of 1963. Subsequently, President Betancourt also applied to the Supreme Court of Justice for a decision that the two parties were unconstitutional, and on October 3, 1963, the court handed down a decision outlawing both parties. When the PCV and the MIR were denied the right to present candidates of their own, they threatened in consequence to boycott and sabotage the election. They also tried to conclude an arrangement with one or more of the parties in opposition to the government whereby in return for votes they would receive concessions from any candidates they might help to elect.

Meanwhile, a band of revolutionaries known as the Armed Forces of National Liberation (Fuerzas Armadas de Liberación Nacional—FALN), made up largely of students and supported by the PCV and the MIR, had launched a campaign of urban guerrilla warfare. Their activities led in turn to a mass roundup of Communists in October 1963, including those in the National Congress, carried out by the military, the national guard, and the police.

INSTITUTIONALIZATION OF THE DEMOCRATIC PROCESS

Despite the FALN threat of violent disruption of the electoral process in 1963, almost 90 percent of the qualified voters appeared at the carefully policed polls, and election day passed without incident. Raúl Leoni, the AD-gob candidate, led with 33 percent of the vote, followed by Rafael Caldera, leader of COPEI, with 20 percent. Although the AD margin of victory was considerably smaller than in 1958, the combined vote for the two parties indicated majority satisfaction with the government coalition.

The URD, the leading contender in 1958, ran third with 19 percent, and the independent Uslar Pietri ran fourth, carrying Caracas and gaining 16 percent of the national vote. The FDP, the party of Larrazábal, ran fifth with 9 percent, and trailing far behind in sixth place was Raúl Rámos Giménez, the candidate of the AD-op. The sole avowedly rightist candidate, Germán Borregales of the National Action Movement (Movimiento de Acción Nacional—MAN), received too few votes even to quality for a seat in congress under the proportional representation system. One of the most significant developments indicated by the election returns was that none of the major parties attracted widespread support in Caracas and its environs. Another was that more than half of the electorate was voting for the first time.

On March 11, 1964, for the first time in the history of the Republic, a duly elected president turned over the sash of office to another duly elected president. With only 24 of 48 senators (even including the three ex-presidents who were lifetime members) and 65 deputies in a chamber of 197, AD-gob was once again forced to establish a coalition government. President Leoni refused to accept COPEI's terms for reconstituting the former coalition and moved instead to construct a broad-based government embracing the two major opposition parties, the URD and Uslar Pietri's newly organized Democratic National Front (Frente Nacional Democrático—FND), which was to the right of AD-gob. In addition, he made conciliatory gestures toward the Catholic hierarchy and the business community. COPEI cooperated fitfully with President Leoni's government.

Economic boom and relative political tranquillity characterized the 1964—65 period. The MIR and the PCV adopted more moderate policies and attempted to discourage the radical youth from their guerrilla tactics. The heterogeneous government was unable, however, to undertake significant reform, and by 1966 the coalition had begun to crumble. The FND, representing the urban middle class, was often in sharp disagreement with the labor- and peasant-oriented URD and AD, and in March 1966 it fragmented and withdrew from the coalition.

All opposition parties, the business community, and representatives of the urban middle class objected when in the summer of 1966 President Leoni submitted a proposal for income tax reform. The crisis provoked by the proposal was such that the economy suffered from the flight of capital, and in October 1966 there was a small military uprising, which was quickly put down by loyal forces. In December of that year Leoni yielded to the demands of the military and allowed the army to occupy the Central University of Venezuela in Caracas. With this move and with a substantial modification of the tax proposal Leoni was able to placate the right; meanwhile, however, many of the more liberal members of his own party had become alienated.

In an AD party primary in September 1967, Luis B. Prieto Figueroa, party president and leader of the left wing, was nominated with 70 percent of the vote as the AD presidential candidate for the 1968 elections. The party's executive committee, dominated by the right wing, chose to disregard the primary and push through the nomination of Gonzalo Barrios, secretary general of the party and former minister of interior relations. At that point the AD-gob split down the middle, with about half of the party regulars following Prieto into the new People's Electoral Movement (Movimiento Electoral Popular—MEP). In April 1968 the URD also withdrew from the government coalition in order to gain maneuverability in preparation for the upcoming elections.

There were eighteen active political parties on the eve of the 1968 elections but only six presidential candidates. Rómulo Betancourt had returned after a four-year absence from the country to bolster the candidacy of AD's Gonzalo Barrios. COPEI for the fourth time nominated its leader, Rafael Caldera. The Revolutionary Party of National Integration (Partido Revolucionario de Integración Nacional—PRIN), a collection of left-wing splinter groups from the AD and the URD, joined the MEP in support of Prieto. The URD, the FDP, and the FND, in an unlikely coalition known as the Victory Front (Frente de la Victoria), supported the candidacy of the former diplomat and law professor Miguel Angel Burelli Rivas. The newly founded Democratic Socialist Party (Partido Socialista Democrático—PSD) nominated the nationalistic businessman Alejandro Hernandez, and the small ultraconservative MAN again nominated the columnist Germán Borregales.

Ninety-one percent of the approximately 4 million registered voters turned out on election day, December 1, 1968. The closely contested election resulted in the victory of Rafael Caldera. COPEI had carried out a vigorous and well-financed campaign, and Caldera doubled his 1963 vote in sixteen of the twenty-three states and territories, scoring marked advances in all others. With 29 percent of the vote, however, he gained less than a 1 percent margin over the AD's Barrios, and COPEI won only one-fifth of the seats in the National Congress. Burelli Rivas and Prieto ranked third and fourth, respectively, with 22 percent and 19 percent of the vote. Hernandez and Borregales trailed far behind.

One of the most notable developments of the 1968 elections was the resurgence of Pérez Jiménez as a political force. Extradited from the United States in 1963, Pérez Jiménez was imprisoned on a conviction of embezzlement of public funds until August 1968. After his release from prison he went into self-imposed exile in Madrid, but his followers, who had formed the National Civic Crusade (Cruzada Cívica Nacionalista—CCN), listed him as a senatorial candidate in the Federal District, where he led his congressional slate to a landslide victory. Observers attributed this outcome to the fact that the Pérez Jiménez regime had favored the capital over the outlying regions, to the general lack of enthusiasm in Caracas for the major parties, and to the sense of personal insecurity in the city in the 1960s as a result of leftist terrorism and the police repression it invoked.

The completion without notable violence or irregularities of an election in which the major opposition party gained control was another landmark in Venezuelan political history, but COPEI's position upon assuming the reins of government was tenuous. The AD, with the largest membership in the National Congress, established an opposition coalition embracing the URD, the FDP, and the PRIN; in order to elect its candidate to the important post of president of the senate, COPEI was forced to enter into coalition with the MEP, the FND, and the CCN.

Beyond the congress, however, President Caldera was moderately successful in conciliating real or potential enemies on both the right and the left of the political spectrum. Legal status, revoked in 1962, was restored to the PCV, and amnesty was offered to guerrillas who were willing to lay down their arms. Initial responses to the offer of amnesty were negative, but by 1970 the standing offer had produced divisions within the movement, and representatives of one of its top leaders, Douglas Bravo, had entered into negotiations with the government. Several other leaders had already surrendered.

Concessions to the right had proved more troublesome. Upon assuming office Caldera had consulted at length with the leadership of the Federation of Chambers of Industry and Commerce (Federación de Cámaras de Comercio e Indústria—FEDECAMARAS), assuring them of big incentives for investment and of a permanent dialogue between the government and the commercial sector. The commercial sector was thus able to block full Venezuelan entry into the Andean Common Market in 1969 and 1970. The government's 1970 proposal for broad tax reform was not approved by the National Congress.

The position of the COPEI government was greatly improved in 1970 by the establishment of a modus vivendi with the heretofore obstructionist AD congressional delegation. Although it rejected any measure designed solely to enhance COPEI's position, the AD pledged to give full support to those government measures that were clearly in the national interest.

POLITICAL FORCES AND INTEREST GROUPS

The Armed Forces

The decisive voice in the resolution of major conflicts has often been that of the armed forces. Three governments since the death of Gómez in 1935 have been overthrown by military coups. The armed forces, including the three service branches plus the national guard, with a combined strength of some 42,700 in 1970, although experiencing internal differences, continued to operate as a semiautonomous political force in 1970.

Although the balance of power among contending factions since

1958 had favored those groups committed to upholding the elected government, many officers continued to believe that the ultimate judgment concerning the legitimacy of any government or policy rested with the military.

Elected governments since 1958 have taken advantage of inter-service rivalries to isolate their opponents; several attempted coups against the government of Betancourt and one against that of Leoni were put down by more powerful branches or factions loyal to the government. Governing parties and coalitions have courted the favor of the dominant groups in the military by leaving intact their institutional prerogatives, including the traditionally liberal defense budgets, by emphasizing the importance of their professional role and giving them a relatively free hand in dealing with suspected insurgents, and by convincing them that to depose the elected government would be to play into the hands of leftist extremists.

The Roman Catholic Church

Although the country is overwhelmingly Catholic, the influence of the Roman Catholic Church on political life has never been very strong. Until the middle of the nineteenth century the high clergy were closely associated with the governing conservative oligarchy, and the church played a dominant role in the educational system.

The rise to power of the Liberals in the latter half of the nineteenth century, however, ushered in a period of anticlericalism. It was not until the mid-twentieth century when, under the influence of the Christian social movement, it began to criticize the maldistribution of wealth that the church regained some of its former influence.

Catholic laymen were prominent in the founding of COPEI in 1946, and the announced disapproval of the church contributed to the fall of Pérez Jiménez in 1958. In the 1960s the involvement of the church in educational and welfare activities increased and, although there is no formal tie between the church and the COPEI, it is generally believed that the support of many clergymen and church-affiliated institutions contributed to the electoral success of COPEI in 1968.

Governmental Entities and the Civil Service

The adoption of far-reaching reformist goals since 1958 has generated a proliferation of government agencies and a greatly enlarged bureaucracy. Such entities as the Central Office of Coordination and Planning (Oficina Central de Coordinación y Planificación —CORDIPLAN), the Venezuelan Development Corporation (Corporación Venezolana de Fomento—CVF), the Venezuelan Petroleum Corporation (Corporación Venezolana de Petróleo—CVP), the National Agrarian Institute (Instituto Agrario Nacional—IAN), and the Office of Integrated Educational Planning (Oficina de Planificación Integrada Educacional—EDUPLAN) have acquired institutional objectives that they actively promote in their dealings with legislators and other policymakers. Overlapping authority among such entities, as well as competing demands on limited resources, often leads to discord.

Until 1970 the power of patronage had been an important resource for cementing party loyalty and interparty relationships. The allocation of available posts for political appointees was an important factor for consideration in the formation of coalition governments. Furthermore, government employees had played a significant role in electoral campaigns. Although a number of individual ministries had instituted their own internal administrative systems, thereby limiting political manipulation, the numerous proposals set forth since 1958 for general standardization of government personnel policies were not acted upon until September 1970, when President Caldera signed into law a civil service bill providing standards for entrance, promotions, transfers, suspensions, and retirements.

The Commercial Sector

As commercial and industrial magnates have moved up to replace the once-dominant landowning class in the transposition of economic power into political power, the informal means of exerting pressure, through family relationships and social clubs, have been complemented by the collective efforts of associational interest groups. In 1970 most of the country's private business groups were organized into a single federation, the Federation of Chambers of Commerce and Industry (Federación de Cámaras de Comercio e Indústria—FEDECAMARAS). It represents a great number of interests, including petroleum, agriculture, banking, industry, commerce, and services. Many of its members, such as the Bankers' Association, the Ranchers and Livestock Association, the Chamber of the Petroleum Industry, and the Caracas Chamber of Industry, carry on large-scale lobbying operations on their own. In 1966 FEDECAMARAS succeeded in persuading President Leoni to allow leaders of the business community to participate in the formulation of development policy.

In 1962 a group of financiers and industrialists who wanted to participate more directly in electoral politics organized the Independent Venezuela Association (Asociación Venezolana Independiente—AVI). In 1963 they supported the candidacy of Uslar Pietri, who opposed what he called the rapid pace of socioeconomic reform. A more recently organized group of businessmen known as

Pro-Venezuela announced its opposition to foreign participation in the exploitation of national resources. In 1970 they were lobbying against United States participation in the exploitation of liquid gas.

Labor and Peasant Organizations

Organized labor is the largest and most cohesive of the political pressure groups that have emerged since the mid-twentieth century. Effectively stifled under military rule, it did not begin to affect the political balance until the early 1940s. It backed the October 1945 revolution, and unionization was actively promoted by the short-lived AD government, but as a political counterpoise to the armed forces labor proved ineffective in the November 1948 coup d'etat.

Unionization was again suppressed under Pérez Jiménez, but with the return of constitutionality in 1958 there was a resurgence of the movement. By the late 1960s more than half of the labor force was unionized. The Venezuelan Workers' Confederation (Confederación de Trabajadores de Venezuela—CTV), organized by AD militants, includes in its membership twelve urban labor federations representing some 600,000 workers and the Peasants' Federation of Venezuela (Federación Campesina de Venezuela) with some 800,000 members (see ch. 19, Labor).

A number of leftist unions, opposing the collaboration with the government, split with the CTV to form their own Sole Central Union of Venezuelan Workers (Central Unica de Trabajadores Venezolanos—CUTV). By the late 1960s, however, the numerical strength of the CUTV had declined to less than 40,000. There is also a small Catholic labor organization, the Committee of Autonomous Unions (Comité de Sindicatos Autonomos—CODESA), but its political role has not been significant.

The CTV has enjoyed varying degrees of support from all of the major parties since 1958. Dissension and divisions in the AD in the 1960s were reflected in heated contests for leadership positions in the CTV. When the MEP defected from the AD in 1967, an active member of the MEP, José Gonzalez Navarro, retained the presidency of the CTV. At the Sixth Workers' Congress in 1970, however, the AD slate, with COPEI support, regained control. COPEI gained several directing posts formerly held by Communist leaders.

University Students

The universities have always had a strong catalytic role in the political processes. They have been the principal source of new political ideas as well as of civilian leaders and movements. In the latter half of the nineteenth century university students were in the forefront of the struggle against political repression and for individual liberties and constitutional government. In the twentieth century social reform became a major concern of the politicized students.

Rómulo Betancourt, Raúl Leoni, and other leaders of the AD, as well as Jóvito Villalba and Gustavo Machado, leaders, respectively, of the URD and the PCV, were student leaders of the Generation of 1928 that fought against the authoritarian rule of Gómez. COPEI traces its origins to the National Student Union (Unión Nacional de Estudiantes—UNE), created in 1946 to defend the Roman Catholic Church and to oppose the Marxist-oriented Venezuelan Student Federation.

The uncompromising opposition of student groups, especially after the traditional autonomy of the universities was revoked in 1952, contributed greatly to the downfall of Pérez Jiménez. Their public protests and demonstrations and their work with the underground Patriotic Junta leading to the general strike on January 23, 1958, were particularly effective.

When Betancourt assumed the presidency in 1959 student groups were important collaborators in the establishment of the democratic government but, as the new political elites found it necessary to compromise with the military and with powerful economic interests, most of the student leadership moved into opposition.

The Central University of Venezuela in Caracas has generally been the fulcrum of student activity. Nationwide student political action groups are generally headquartered there. Most of these groups are identified with the national political parties, but the parent parties have little control over them and are sometimes embarrassed by their actions and pronouncements. Students have made up a considerable proportion of the membership of the Movement of the Revolutionary Left (Movimiento de la Izquierda Revolucionario—MIR) that splintered off from the AD in 1960 and of its militant revolutionary band of irregulars, the Armed Forces of National Liberation (Fuerzas Armadas de Liberación Nacional—FALN).

Student elections in June, before the occupation of the Central University by the army in December 1966, indicated that the PCV had the largest following, with COPEI and the AD ranking second and third, respectively. The general alienation of the students from the political system was deepened when the army again occupied the campus of the Central University in 1969 and when in 1970 legislation was passed putting an end to the autonomous status of the universities (see ch. 7, Education).

THE PARTY SYSTEM

The country's multiparty political system is of recent development. The division between liberals and conservatives still has some validity in the social and political life of the people, but it is diluted, principally by the system of proportional representation prescribed in the election laws. This enables small parties to win seats in the National Congress and in the legislatures of the states and, by coalition with other parties, to exercise influence often greater than warranted by their popular support. Organization in depth may ensure for a party the plurality of votes necessary to elect a president but, in order to have a working majority in the National Congress, coalition with one or more of the other parties is necessary.

With the beginnings of liberal government after Gómez, labor unions, which under the dictatorship had had a rudimentary and mostly clandestine origin among the oil workers, emerged into the open. The socialistic leaders who in 1936 laid the foundations of the AD early extended their party system into the union movement, for the most part originally under Communist domination. The AD was successful in organizing new unions and winning members away from older ones that had been either independent or Communist-sponsored. This represents the first effective attempt at popular organization by a Venezuelan political party, and it was this development that was largely responsible for the AD's overwhelming victory at the polls in the free elections for the congress in 1946 and for president in 1947.

Growing liberalism in government, the new constitution, and an electoral law providing for proportional representation of minorities in state and national legislatures encouraged the formation of political parties. Supplanting the old factionalism of the ins and the outs that had supported contending *caudillos* (regional political strong men) under the labels of Federalist and Centralist, a multiparty system has developed in which new parties spring up, often to be absorbed in coalitions with others, and the larger parties suffer splits and the withdrawal of splinter groups.

The two-party system that preceded the multiparty situation began in 1840 with the formation by *criollos* (see Glossary) outside of government of a so-called liberal party to oppose the conservative group that had monopolized the administration of government under José Antonio Páez. By 1860 the struggle for power between local *caudillos* brought about a change in labels from Liberal and Conservative to Federalist and Centralist, respectively. This division survived through the long succession of dictators that followed, but party activity remained confined to the few who constituted the literate electorate. Parties were not divided by conflicting ideologies, and statements of principle or program were sufficiently vague to allow almost complete freedom of action to the leader and party in power; in any case, the voter was influenced by the prestige of the man rather than by the principles of the party.

The tendency to put personality above doctrine still persisted in 1970, but there were indications that it was to a lessening degree. Nevertheless, minor parties generally remained loosely organized groups of followers of persuasive and politically ambitious personalities. Although opposition party platforms might differ little from that of the party in power and might even resemble it, each party chief promised the voters better and more vigorous leadership in carrying out the commonly advocated reforms. Potential candidates sought to enhance their prestige by becoming party leaders and attracting a local following. By this means they might hope to gain the best political price from some stronger party leader in return for the support they could command.

Splintering of parties occurs often as a result of personal ambitions and personality clashes rather than of ideological differences. A further encouragement to the proliferation of parties is the fact that any candidate for the presidency can run at the same time for the National Congress and for a state legislature. This, under the system of proportional representation, multiplies the chances for even a small party to gain one or more legislative seats for its leaders and, conversely, severely limits the chances the winning party has of gaining a working majority in the National Congress without forming a coalition government (see ch. 11, The Governmental System).

The fact that a president cannot, constitutionally, succeed himself tends to reduce his prestige as elections approach and to weaken his party. A very popular government party candidate, a strong organization, or both are needed to hold the party together in order to win the election. The government party must depend largely on organization, for rarely can it expect to produce a candidate of national prestige equaling that of its retiring president. In any case, a vigorous political campaign is in order. The older and better organized and financed parties start their candidates out early in the election year, and even the newest parties present their candidates to as large a public as possible. Candidates campaign by speaking to crowds, especially in the more populous centers. They also make use of radio, television, the press, handbills, and posters to carry their images, slogans, and the colors assigned to their ballots to the people. Political debate through television and radio broadcasts has been used since 1963.

The Major Parties

Democratic Action

Of the eight parties represented in the National Congress in 1970, the Democratic Action (Acción Democrática—AD) party, with nineteen senators and sixty-six deputies, had the largest delegation. In its early years the party was militantly drawing its leadership from young middle-class intellectuals and relying almost entirely on peasants and workers as a power base. After the 1948 coup, however, and a decade of authoritarian rule, the party leadership became convinced of the necessity of accommodating economic interests, the Catholic hierarcy, and the military.

Until the early 1960s the AD was the only party with an effective national pyramidal organization, a clearly identifiable program stressing agrarian reform, education, housing, social welfare measures, and economic nationalism, and sustained popular support distributed nationally. A gradual drift to the center and the refusal of the party's founding generation to share power with younger generations of aspirants to leadership were partially responsible for the three major splits in the AD between 1958 and 1968 that greatly reduced the party's strength. In 1970 Gonzalo Barrios was serving as president of the party, but Rómulo Betancourt continued to the the AD's most popular and most powerful figure.

Social Christian Party

The Committee for Independent Political and Electoral Organization (Comité de Organización Política y Electoral Independiente—COPEI) was organized by leaders of the UNE in 1946 as a conservative church-oriented alternative to the anticlerical Venezuelan Student Federation and the AD. After several years of exile in Europe while Pérez Jiménez was in power, however, the party leadership, especially Rafael Caldera, had become ideologically aligned with the Social Christian movement.

When the leaders returned to Venezuela to compete in the electoral contest of 1958, the party had a regional base of power in the Andean southwest but no nationwide grassroots organization. In the years that followed, however, COPEI began to penetrate labor unions and peasant communities throughout the country and to attract middle-class professionals. Participation in the Betancourt government entitled the party to a share of the patronage and allowed it to claim some credit for the government's accomplishments while disavowing its failures. Thus by 1963 the party had risen in total voting strength from third to second place, where it remained in the 1968 elections.

COPEI maintains close ties with other Latin American Christian Democratic parties but has been more pragmatic than doctrinal in its approach to most issues. Its platforms have differed more in means of implementation than in substance from those of the AD. In 1970 the party's congressional delegation consisted of sixteen senators and fifty deputies. COPEI had managed to avoid the divisions that had weakened the AD, but relations between its left and right wings were sometimes tense, and the parent party had denounced its youth movement.

People's Electoral Movement

The People's Electoral Movement (Movimiento Electoral Popular—MEP) ranked third in the 1968 elections, placing five senators and twenty-six deputies in the National Congress. Since that time it has made important inroads into the leadership of the CTV. It continued to be led in 1970 by Luis B. Prieto Figueroa, who initiated the split with the AD in December 1967. The party entered into a united front with the URD and the FDP in 1970 to oppose the government from a leftist nationalistic position. It opposed, for example, the university reform law enacted in 1970 (see ch. 7, Education.)

National Civic Crusade

The National Civic Crusade (Cruzada Cívica Nationalista—CCN) was the fourth-ranking party in voting strength in 1968, electing to the National Congress one senator and twenty deputies. The creation of Pérez Jiménez, the party called for strict enforcement of law and order and served as a rallying point for the discontented, especially in the Caracas metropolitan area. By 1970, however, the party had virtually disintegrated.

The Supreme Court of Justice in April 1969 invalidated the election of Pérez Jiménez to the Senate on the grounds that he had not been properly registered as a voter, so the party's titular head remained in self-imposed exile in Madrid. By early 1970 the party had split three ways with one group retaining the original name, another calling itself the Popular Justicialist Movement (Movimiento Popular Justicialista—MPJ), and the third defecting to COPEI.

Republican Democratic Union

The Republican Democratic Union (Unión Republicana Democrática—URD) ranked fifth in the 1968 elections, placing one senator and fourteen deputies in the National Congress. The party's strength had declined greatly since 1952, when, with the support of the clandestine AD, its leader, Jóvito Villalba, won the presidential election. The election was promptly annulled, and the URD leaders were exiled.

In 1958 the party formed an electoral alliance around the candidacy of the provisional president, Larrazábal, who ranked second in the presidential elections. After a difficult period in which the party opposed both the violence of the extreme left and the government's repression of leftists, the URD, with Villalba serving again as its standard bearer, dropped to third place in the 1963 elections. The party's continuing decline since that time has resulted in part from ineffective organization and in part from the splintering off of its left wing in 1964 and its right wing in 1966.

The Minor Parties

Smaller parties with representation in the National Congress in 1970 included the FDP, the FND, the PRIN, and the PVC (the Communist party), which participated in the 1968 elections through a front known as the Union for Advancement (Unión para Avanzar—UPA). Since it was legalized in 1969, the PVC, under the leadership of Gustavo and Eduardo Machado, has been gaining adherents. Membership in 1970 was estimated at 8,000 to 10,000. It was weakened by internal dissension, however, as the nationalist Teodoro Petkoff challenged the Moscow-oriented leadership and founded a new party, the Movement Toward Socialism (Movimiento Al Socialismo—MAS) in late 1970.

CHAPTER 13

FOREIGN RELATIONS

The country's most notable foreign policy objectives in 1970 were the expansion of exports and the extension of diplomatic and commercial ties. The government had departed from the precedent of a decade in abandoning the so-called Betancourt Doctrine in favor of a nonideological approach to the maintenance of diplomatic relations.

Under the Betancourt Doctrine the country from 1959 through 1968 had denied recognition to regimes that seized power by extra-constitutional means. In his message to the National Congress in early 1970, President Rafael Caldera explained his policy in this manner:

> Without denying the reasons which underlay the earlier positions, it falls to us to express a real national desire for the opening up of our foreign relations sector, with the gradual reestablishment of links with those Latin American countries from which we had become alienated, to no good purpose, and through the establishment or renewal of relations with other countries in the world which we cannot afford to ignore.

In 1970 relations with the Soviet Union were renewed after an eighteen-year hiatus. The country maintained diplomatic relations with most of the countries of the world, although in many cases, for reasons of economy, a single chancery served more than one country. Only a few countries, such as Haiti, Cuba, the Republic of South Africa, Communist China, North Vietnam, North Korea, and East Germany, were excluded from this open policy.

The government has shown particular interest in expanding relations with Middle Eastern and African countries. To this end, in 1970 it sent a fact-finding mission to visit seven African countries and to attend a preparatory meeting for the Third Conference of Chiefs of State of Nonaligned Countries.

With the exception of newly independent Guyana (formerly British Guiana), Venezuela was, in 1970, the only South American country that had never fought a war with one of its neighbors. The country did, however, become embroiled in boundary controversies immediately after gaining independence as a result of the indefiniteness of the inherited Spanish claims, especially in portions of the virtually unexplored interior. Boundaries were delimited through arbitration and negotiation with Brazil and Colombia by the mid-twentieth century, but the Guyana boundary has continued to be a source of controversy. In the 1960s the prospects of drilling for oil in the Gulf of Venezuela precipitated a dispute between Colombia and Venezuela over underwater rights in the gulf.

European claims for debts and damages affected the country's foreign relations in the latter half of the nineteenth century. When British, German, and Italian warships blockaded Venezuela's Caribbean coast in 1902, the United States, acting upon the principles of the Monroe Doctrine, intervened and directed the claims controversies to the World Court in The Hague.

The threat of intervention by European powers subsided thereafter, but relations with the United States became strained during the first three decades of the twentieth century as a result of United States interventions in Central America and the Caribbean. Relations improved with the inauguration of President Franklin D. Roosevelt's Good Neighbor Policy in the 1930s, and Venezuela contributed to the Allied cause in World War II.

Warm relations between the United States and the government of General Marcos Pérez Jiménez (1950—58) caused resentment among the forces that toppled the authoritarian Pérez Jiménez regime in 1958, but this resentment was largely overcome in the early 1960s by cooperation under the Alliance for Progress and by the friendship between Presidents John F. Kennedy and Rómulo Betancourt. Exploitation of Venezuelan oil by United States-based companies has been a recurring source of disagreement. The United States has been the largest market for the oil, and Venezuela has claimed an increasing share of the revenues from its sale.

Simón Bolívar, the most prominent of the country's founding fathers, was the initiator of the first inter-American conference in 1826. Since World War II Venezuela has become a party to the Inter-American Treaty of Reciprocal Assistance and the Latin American Nuclear Free Zone Treaty and has been an active participant in the Inter-American Development Bank, the Organization of American States, and other hemispheric organizations.

Relations with individual Latin American states have varied in accordance with the nature and predispositions of Venezuela's own government at a given time. Under Pérez Jiménez, for example, the country's closest relations were with other authoritarian governments, whereas during the governments of Betancourt and Raúl Leoni closest relations were with democratic governments. In fact, under the Betancourt Doctrine, generally adhered to from 1959 to 1968, the country withheld recognition from regimes, in Latin America as elsewhere, that seized power in an extraconstitutional manner.

Venezuela participated in the League of Nations and became a charter member of the United Nations, in which forum it has strongly advocated the sovereign equality of nation-states and arms limitations and opposed colonialism and, since 1958, dictatorship. The country is also a member of the International Coffee Agreement and the Organization of Petroleum Exporting Countries.

Before World War II the majority of the domestic population showed little interest in foreign policy, and the president maintained almost complete control over the decisionmaking process. Since the war, however, and particularly since 1958, the country's contacts have extended to all parts of the world, and the vital interests of many citizens have been affected by commercial relations and movements toward economic integration. Thus, in recent years the president has been assisted by a rapidly expanding corps of foreign affairs specialists, and the patterns of foreign policy decisionmaking have incorporated new pressure groups and institutions.

HISTORICAL BACKGROUND

In the late eighteenth century Venezuelan revolutionists sought recognition and material aid from the United States and the principal European powers. First Francisco de Miranda and later Simón Bolívar won sympathy and some unofficial support, but it was not until the end of the Napoleonic wars in Europe that Bolívar was able to attract enough trained foreign soldiers and military supplies to aid him significantly in ending Spanish rule in Colombia and Venezuela.

Bolívar dreamed of a federation, a sort of United States of Spanish America, and his prestige was sufficient to unite Colombia, Venezuela, and Ecuador in the Republic of Gran Colombia. The United States promptly extended recognition in 1822, but in Europe the Holy Alliance—proposed by Russia and joined by Austria, Prussia, and other monarchies—was formed in part to promote the restoration of Spain's rebellious American colonies. The Monroe Doctrine, proclaimed in 1823, was a warning by the United States to the European monarchies to stay out of the Western Hemisphere. President James Monroe knew that Great Britain, with its superior sea power, favored the prohibition as a measure of protection for its growing trade with the young republics of the Americas.

Territorial Demarcation

By 1830 Bolívar's federation of Gran Colombia had fallen apart, and Venezuela, Colombia, and Ecuador became separate states. Independent Venezuela was at once faced with boundary problems. Because of the vagueness of the Spanish delineation of the boundaries of the former captaincy general, as well as the inaccessibility and the lack of accurate maps of the frontier areas, negotiations and surveys extended over the next hundred years (see ch. 3, Historical Setting).

With Brazil, the negotiations were amicable. Limits were defined in agreements signed in 1859 and 1905, and much of the boundary has been surveyed and marked by the members of mixed commissions.

Negotiations with Colombia were more prolonged and involved. Lacking final agreement, Spain and later Switzerland were called upon to arbitrate the boundary. The principal controversy revolved about the source of a small stream, the Río de Oro, emptying into Lake Maracaibo and, when it was found to have two branches, both Colombia and Venezuela claimed the territory between the two branches. This controversy and further disagreement over an area south of the Meta River and west of the Orinoco and its tributaries led to an agreement in 1881 to accept arbitration by the Spanish crown.

A decision was rendered in 1891 but, as further interpretation became necessary, Colombia and Venezuela agreed in 1917 to arbitration, this time by the Swiss government. The award was handed down in 1922, but it was not until 1932 that the boundary was marked. Until 1952 relations with Colombia continued to be complicated by the question of the ownership of a small group of unoccupied islands, the Los Monjes Archipelago, just off the Guajira Peninsula. In November 1952 Colombia finally withdrew its claim in favor of Venezuela, thus ending the matter.

The most serious boundary dispute was that with Great Britain over the frontier with British Guiana. Except for early explorations, Spain had paid little attention to the Guiana area. The Dutch, French, and English attempted settlements and fought each other for control, but the Dutch dominated the area that is now Guyana from 1648 to 1814. Since their plantations were located principally on and east of the Essequibo River, they had little contact with the Spanish, whose eastern outposts were far to the west near the mouths of the Orinoco, although the Spanish claim, based on discovery and exploration, reached to the west bank of the Essequibo.

In 1814 Holland ceded the western part of its Guiana territory to Great Britain, and British kept pushing their settlements westward. By 1840 the British, resting their claims on de facto occupation and control, had surveyed and marked a western boundary, whose northern terminus rested on the eastern mouth of the Orinoco, giving them a position of strategic controls over that river. Venezuelan protests resulted in a succession of alternative proposals but no agreement, and Great Britain refused to submit the matter to arbitration. After the discovery of gold in the disputed area intensified the disagreement, Venezuela severed diplomatic relations with Great Britain in 1887 and made a strong appeal for the good offices of the United States to settle the question.

In April 1895 Venezuelan border guards arrested two minor British officials on the Cuyuni River and charged them with violation of Venezuelan territory. Great Britain threatened to send warships to protect British subjects and interests. Although the two British officials were soon released, the incident aroused public opinion, especially in England and the United States. President Grover Cleveland, in an address to the United States Congress, denounced the British attitude and stated that it was the duty of the United States under the Monroe Doctrine to determine the boundary and resist British advances beyond that line, even at the risk of war.

Great Britain was so involved in competition with France and Germany in Africa and the Middle East that British leaders were disposed to view the Guiana boundary problem as a minor incident. Arbitration was agreed upon, and in 1899 the tribunal handed down a decision establishing the boundary in such a way that Venezuela gained control of the strategic area at the eastern mouth of the Orinoco.

Both sides accepted the decision, but Venezuelans continued to feel that their rights were not well protected, especially since, having invited the chief justice of the United States to present their case, they were not represented on the tribunal by one of their own nationals. In 1962 Venezuela reopened the issue, placing before the United Nations its nineteenth-century claim to two-thirds of the territory of British Guiana. The United Nations voted to suspend debate on the subject, but Great Britain and Venezuela in December 1963 entered into bilateral discussions.

Foreign Creditors and Debt Collection

In addition to the British Guiana boundary dispute, Venezuela became involved with European powers and the United States in a number of other incidents, mostly over matters of protocol and foreign debts. Dictators, faced with empty treasuries, floated foreign loans at ruinous rates of interest. They also demanded contributions from foreign business interests in Venezuela and did not hesitate to confiscate foreign assets on occasion. These practices, and the looting and damages incident to a succession of civil wars and disorders, resulted in a mounting list of foreign claims that successive dictators generally sought to ignore (see ch. 3, Historical Setting).

In 1849 British and, in 1856, Dutch warships were sent to Venezuelan ports to enforce the collection of claims. Matters culminated in 1902, during the regime of President Cipriano Castro. Great Britain and Germany, finding their claims ignored, joined in an ultimatum, which was rejected by Castro. Thereupon, British and German warships seized or sank the few vessels of Venezuela's navy and bombarded Puerto Cabello. Later, joined by Italian warships, they blockaded the whole Caribbean coast of Venezuela.

The Latin American republics, fearful of the precedent of the collection of claims by force and possible annexation of territory, in lieu of specie payment, sided with Venezuela. Their position was expressed in the Drago Doctrine, a protest sent to Washington in December 1902 by Louis María Drago, foreign minister of Argentina, in which it was asserted that no public debt should be collected by armed force from a sovereign American state or through the occupation of American territory by a foreign power.

Opinion in the United States swung to the side of Venezuela, and President Theodore Roosevelt championed the cause of arbitration. His intervention was sufficient to break the blockade and throw the question of the claims against Venezuela into the World Court at The Hague, which decided that the intervening powers should have first priority in claims against Venezuela. Such a decision seemed to Latin Americans to encourage future foreign intervention in similar cases. President Roosevelt then adapted the Drago Doctrine in a statement, announced in 1904 and amplified in 1905, that barred intervention in America by European powers but claimed that right for the United States. This was known as the Roosevelt Corollary to the Monroe Doctrine and, although not invoked in regard to Venezuela, it was designed to protect the Western Hemisphere and especially the Panama Canal, which was just being built.

After investigation by a claims commission meeting in Caracas in 1903, the World Court in the following year awarded to the claimants (England, Germany, Italy, Holland, France, Spain, Belgium, Norway, Sweden, the United States, and Mexico) approximately one-fifth of their original claims. The United States assumed responsibility for collection of the awards.

As an additional consequence a doctrine of nonintervention, originally asserted about the middle of the nineteenth century by Carlos Calvo, an Argentine historian and authority on international law, gave rise to what is known as the Calvo Clause. It required foreign contractors to waive the right to involve their government's diplomatic intervention with regard to disputes about a contract. This principle was applied in the early part of the twentieth century and was reaffirmed in the Venezuelan Constitution of 1961.

The Hague settlement did not end Cipriano Castro's problems with the larger foreign powers. In rapid succession, between 1906 and 1908, he antagonized France, Belgium, and the Netherlands, the latter to the point of naval retaliation. In the face of the Monroe Doctrine, however, none of the European creditors attempted annexation or forcible partition of the country.

Credit and good diplomatic relations with the great powers were finally reestablished by Castro's successor, Juan Vicente Gómez. The new dictator was impressed by foreign military power, especially the growing strength of Germany and the United States. He cultivated good relations with them and with all other principal powers. He acknowledged just foreign claims and, with income from the new oil concessions, restored Venezuela's credit by paying off the nation's foreign debts. In spite of pressures from the Allies and the Central Powers, Gómez kept Venezuela neutral during World War I.

RELATIONS WITH THE UNITED STATES

United States intervention in several Latin American countries in the early twentieth century led many Latin Americans to regard the Monroe Doctrine less as a protection than as a means of coercion. Because of increasing stability in Latin America and the decreasing dangers of foreign threats to the Panama Canal or further foreign intervention in the Western Hemisphere, however, the United States increasingly turned to the Good Neighbor Policy and renounced the right of intervention on any grounds in 1936.

Relations with the United States in the twentieth century have been primarily concerned with oil. Production and development under the Gómez concessions were controlled by British, Dutch, and United States companies, with United States participation increasing rapidly. By 1928 Venezuela had become second only to the United States in oil production. In 1970 it continued to be among the world's leading oil producers and exporters (see ch. 18, Industry).

After Gómez, Venezuelan policy was aimed at changing the original concessions to obtain the maximum possible revenue from the oil companies. The companies resisted this, but the example of expropriation of the oil companies in Mexico in 1938 and the advent of World War II, making Venezuelan oil vital to the Allied war effort, worked to aid the Venezuelan effort. New agreements were concluded in 1943, increasing Venezuela's royalties from 11 percent to 16 2/3 percent and providing a more favorable basis for the calculation of Venezuela's share. This step, along with taxes on the oil companies, was designed to produce revenues for Venezuela equal to the profits of the companies (see ch. 18, Industry; ch. 20, Trade).

In World War II Venezuela's foreign policy was again one of neutrality until the Japanese attack upon Pearl Harbor, which brought about a rupture of diplomatic relations with the Axis powers on the last day of 1941. On January 15, 1942, the United States and Venezuela signed a defense agreement under which United States airplanes patrolling the approaches to the Panama Canal and the Caribbean were allowed to fly over Venezuelan territory. Also, three battalions of United States troops were allowed to land at Barcelona to assist in guarding oil refineries. In February 1945 Venezuela entered the war on the side of the Allied powers; this had little effect other than the impounding of German and Italian vessels in its ports.

The friendly atmosphere engendered by the Good Neighbor Policy and subsequent wartime cooperation deteriorated thereafter. United States recognition of the government of President Pérez Jiménez aroused resentment, which found violent expression after the overthrow of Pérez Jiménez in January 1958 and was reflected in a demonstration against Vice President and Mrs. Richard Nixon during an official visit in March 1958.

The United States decision in 1958 to restrict imports of foreign oil and Venezuela's action the same year in raising taxes on the companies operating oil concessions also strained diplomatic relations, but relations improved with the announcement of a United States policy of coolness toward dictators and of friendship for popularly elected governments. In August 1960 the United States joined Venezuela and other members of the Organization of American States (OAS) in an agreement to break diplomatic relations with, and impose economic sanctions against, President Rafael Trujillo of the Dominican Republic, who had supported the subversive activities of exiled Pérez Jiménez.

President Kennedy's announcement on March 13, 1961, of the plan for the Alliance for Progress, a ten-year economic and social development program of aid to Latin America, was generally well received in Venezuela. In 1961 a United States district court ruled that Pérez Jiménez, who had been arrested in Miami in 1959 at Venezuela's request, should be extradited and turned over to the Venezuelan authorities for trial. Although the attorneys of Pérez Jiménez appealed the case, the ruling improved relations, as did the final denial of the appeal and extradition to Venezuela of the ex-dictator in August 1963.

Further improvement in relations resulted from the cordial reception of President and Mrs. Kennedy on their visit to Venezuela in December 1961. After the United States announcement in October 1962 of the discovery of Soviet missile bases in Cuba and the unanimous OAS approval of quarantine action and the use of armed forces to enforce withdrawal of the missiles, Venezuela was the first, on October 27, 1962, of the Latin American republics to order the mobilization of its armed forces in support of this action.

Venezuelan naval vessels participated in the quarantine patrol of Cuba.

President Betancourt returned President Kennedy's visit in February 1963. He found a most cordial reception and assurance of continued United States cooperation with Venezuela and the OAS.

With the United States, Venezuela has treaties of amity, extradition, and the pacific settlement of disputes. There are agreements on aerial mapping, atomic energy, air transport, customs, maritime matters, passports, technical cooperation, telecommunication, and trade and commerce. Special arrangements provide for United States Army, Navy, and Air Force missions in Venezuela.

RELATIONS WITH LATIN AMERICA

Venezuela has no historic enemies among the other Latin American countries. The Gran Colombia idea, embracing Venezuela, Colombia, and Ecuador, has been reflected from time to time in the twentieth century through economic cooperation and coordination of foreign policies. Consultation among the foreign ministers of the three countries in 1958 resulted in the Declaration of Bogotá, which expressed, among other things, the intent of working toward a common market (see ch. 20, Trade). Pérez Jiménez was accused by Guatemala in 1954 of conspiring with El Salvador, the Dominican Republic, and Nicaragua to overthrow the leftist Guatemalan government, but the charges were denied, and the dispute was soon forgotten. In 1957 Argentina interrupted diplomatic relations, charging Venezuela with giving asylum to its deposed dictator, Juan Perón, and with aiding him in plotting to overthrow the new Argentine government. Later in 1957 Chile briefly severed diplomatic relations with Venezuela after its arrest and expulsion of one of the attachés of the Chilean embassy.

After the overthrow of Pérez Jiménez and the advent of a liberal government in 1958, Venezuela's foreign policy underwent a reversal. Dictatorships were no longer looked on with favor, and President Betancourt proposed that membership in the OAS be limited to freely elected governments.

Venezuela broke diplomatic relations with the Dominican Republic in June 1959 and accused that government of responsibility for terrorist bombings in Caracas in October 1959. In February 1960 Venezuela persuaded the OAS to investigate mass arrests in the Dominican Republic, the first instance of united action against a dictatorship in the Western Hemisphere.

When a terrorist assassination attempt against President Betancourt in June 1960 was attributed to agents from the Dominican Republic, Venezuela called for an emergency meeting of the OAS. Early in January 1961 the OAS voted condemnation of, and sanctions against, the Trujillo government, prohibiting shipments of military equipment, as well as oil, trucks, and truck parts. Late in May 1961 Venezuela again accused the Dominican Republic of complicity in an antigovernment plot, which had been crushed in Caracas. Trujillo's assassination in the same month, followed by an elected government in the Dominican Republic, resulted in restored relations.

In 1962 military coups d'etat in Argentina and Peru met with nonrecognition of the ruling juntas by Venezuela, in accordance with what came to be called the Betancourt Doctrine. Relations were suspended, to be resumed upon the restoration of constitutional governments. On May 29, 1963, relations were broken with Haiti because of President François Duvalier's unconstitutional retention of power. Venezuela refused to attend the 1964 Inter-American Conference in Quito because Ecuador was under a government set up by a military coup d'etat. Likewise, the assumption of power by the military in Brazil in 1964 resulted in the severance of relations, and Venezuela declined to attend the special foreign ministers' conference held in late 1965 in Rio de Janeiro.

Venezuela's relations with Cuba were stormy throughout the first half of the 1960s. The country's liberals were initially sympathetic with the overthrow of Fulgencio Batista but, as Fidel Castro's relations with the Soviet Union were intensified and his encouragement of subversive acts in Venezuela became apparent, diplomatic relations cooled rapidly and were severed by Venezuela on November 11, 1961. Subsequently, relations worsened until in November 1963 Venezuela requested a meeting of the OAS council, before which it laid specific charges of Cuban intervention in Venezuelan affairs.

INTERNATIONAL ORGANIZATIONS AND COMMITMENTS

Regional Cooperation

It was Simón Bolívar, the great Venezuelan patriot and liberator, who furnished the inspiration for the Pan American conferences that led to the formation first of the Pan American Union in 1889 and then of the OAS in 1948. At the first conference, held at Panama City in 1826, Venezuela was represented by Gran Colombia, the federation to which it belonged until 1830.

At the next two conferences, held in 1847 at Lima, Peru, and in 1856 at Santiago, Chile, Venezuela and many other Latin American states were absent. Since the first conference called by the United States, at Washington, D.C., in 1889, however, Venezuela has taken a full part in the development of the policies, acts, and charters by which the OAS promotes inter-American peace and friendship, mutual defense against aggression, and economic, social, and cultural progress in the American region.

In furtherance of these purposes, the country supports and participates in the several subsidiary councils and specialized organizations of the OAS, such as its economic and social, cultural, and peace and juridical councils and its organizations concerned with agricultural, health, women's, children's, and other affairs. Along with the other hemisphere nations, it joined, in 1942, the Inter-American Defense Board, which, like the Pan American Union, was absorbed into the OAS in 1948. It also became a party in 1947 to the Inter-American Treaty of Reciprocal Assistance (better known as the Rio Treaty), which provides for collective defense in the event of aggression from within or beyond the hemisphere against a signatory.

With the change from authoritarian to liberal government, the country has taken a much more prominent part in the OAS, coming out strongly against dictators and advocating the elimination of European colonies in the Western Hemisphere. In 1960 Venezuela, on three occasions, invoked the Rio Treaty and the machinery of the OAS against the aggressive and subversive activities of the government of the dictator Trujillo of the Dominican Republic. This action resulted in the first instance of application of economic sanctions under the OAS, when the OAS Council voted to prohibit members from supplying war materials to the Dominican Republic. At the OAS meeting to consider the problems of a Communist Cuba, held at San José, Costa Rica, in August 1960, Venezuela supported the resolution condemning the intervention of any foreign power in any state of America.

On November 29, 1963, Venezuela, invoking the Rio Treaty, called for a meeting of the OAS Council and charged the government of Cuba with "intervention and aggression." It cited the discovery on the Paraguaná Peninsula of a cache of arms that it claimed were traceable to Cuban sources. The evidence presented by Venezuela, including the fact that the cache contained bazookas and rockets of a type provided by the United States to the Batista government in 1956 and 1957, was sufficient to convince the OAS investigating committee of the validity of Venezuela's claims. As a result, the OAS adopted sanctions against Cuba, including an economic embargo and the severance by member states of diplomatic relations.

Although the government has consistently favored collective measures against Cuba, it has on other occasions refused to sanction the collective use of force by the OAS. When the United States intervened unilaterally in the Dominican Republic in April 1965, Venezuela refused to support the creation of an inter-American peacekeeping force under OAS auspices to provide collective backing for that action.

In May 1970 the country was represented on a special committee that recommended that the issues of terrorism and the kidnapping of diplomats be included in the agenda of the next extraordinary session of the OAS General Assembly.

Venezuela has been a participant in the Inter-American Development Bank since it was created in 1959. In 1966 it joined the other South American states and Mexico in the Latin American Free Trade Association (LAFTA), and in 1967 it became a party to the Latin American Nuclear Free Zone Treaty (see ch. 20, Trade).

Other International Activities

After World War I Venezuela, which had remained neutral, joined the League of Nations when seventeen Latin American states became members. The United States did not join and, when in the 1930s the league proved itself impotent to protect small nations against aggression, several Latin American states withdrew. Venezuela withdrew in 1938 but continued to cooperate with the International Labor Organization, of which it was a member, and with the International Court of Justice.

Since Venezuela had declared war on the Axis powers in February 1945, the country became a member of the United Nations and ratified its formal charter on November 15, 1945. The International Labor Organization and the International Court of Justice were transferred to the United Nations from the League of Nations, and Venezuela continued its interest in them as well as in the United Nations Educational, Scientific and Cultural Organization (UNESCO). In the United Nations General Assembly, Venezuela has spoken against dictatorship and colonialism and has favored elimination of the veto in the Security Council. In the Korean conflict Venezuela offered medical supplies worth US$100,000. A Venezuelan, Carlos Sosa Rodríguez, was elected president of the General Assembly for the eighteenth session (1963—64).

In furtherance of trade relations, Venezuela maintains a delegation to the European Economic Community. The country was a participant in the Latin American Coffee Agreement, which was in force in 1958 and 1959, and in its more widely based successor, the International Coffee Agreement (see ch. 20, Trade).

Venezuela participates with the Middle Eastern oil-rich countries in the Organization of Petroleum Exporting Countries (OPEC). At the second meeting of the OPEC, held in Caracas on January 16, 1961, President Betancourt addressed the delegates in behalf of cooperation, and the members agreed to demand that the oil companies maintain steady prices (see ch. 20, Trade).

Noteworthy in connection with international relations are Venezuela's claims on coastal waters. Territorial waters extend 12 nautical miles from the coast. The Constitution of 1961 also provides an addition of 3 nautical miles to this zone for purposes of maritime supervision and policing. Furthermore, the Republic lays claim to the seabed and subsoil of the continental shelf, adjacent to the coast and beyond the zone of territorial waters. These claims had not been extended in 1970, despite the concerted attempts of several Latin American countries to establish claims of up to 200 nautical miles.

Venezuela signed the Nuclear Non-Proliferation Treaty on July 1, 1968, but had not ratified it when the National Congress adjourned in 1970.

FOREIGN POLICY DECISIONMAKING

The country's commitment to the pacific settlement of disputes was incorporated into the Constitution of 1961. Article 129 states:

> In international treaties, conventions, and agreements concluded by the Republic, there shall be inserted a clause by which the parties bind themselves to decide by peaceful means recognized by international law or previously agreed to by them, if such is the case, all controversies that may arise between the parties by reason of their interpretation or execution, if not inapplicable, and if permitted by the procedure followed in their conclusion.

The powers and duties of the president include the direction of foreign affairs and the making of international treaties, conventions, or agreements. Such commitments, however, must be approved by the National Congress. The stationing of Venezuelan military missions abroad or of foreign missions within the country must be authorized by the Senate.

The president is assisted in the making of foreign policy by the Council of Ministers and in the operation of foreign affairs by the minister of foreign relations. The Ministry of Foreign Relations includes, besides administrative personnel, the Office of International Policy, the Office of Foreign Commerce and Consulates, the Office of Frontiers, the Diplomatic Service, the Consular Service, and the Office of International Cooperation. In 1970 the Office of Cultural Relations was being established.

In the making of critical decisions and the formulation of major policies, the president has been increasingly influenced by groups and institutions that form his constituency. These include the political parties and coalitions, the military, organized labor, the business community and, in some cases, government agencies, such as the Central Office of Coordination and Planning (Oficina Central de Coordinación y Planificación) (see ch. 12, Political Dynamics).

Since 1958 governments have sought consultation with organized labor, represented primarily by the Venezuelan Workers' Confederation (Confederación de Trabajadores de Venezuela—CTV), and the private sector, represented by the Federation of Chambers of Commerce and Industry (Federación de Cámaras de Comercio e Indústria—FEDECAMARAS), on such issues as membership in LAFTA and revision of the commercial treaty with the United States. Both groups have been represented since 1966 on the permanent national commission on LAFTA.

The president consults the military when an issue relates to border controversies, arms purchases, hemispheric security, or friction in relations with neighboring countries. Military interest has been evident, for example, in the decisionmaking process relating to policies toward Cuba.

The persons most immediately and extensively consulted by the president, however, in situations perceived as crises or in the making of policies expected to have widespread domestic repercussions are the leaders of the major parties and the president's personal advisers.

Once foreign policy has been decided upon by the president and his advisers and, when necessary, approved by the National Congress, the Office of International Policy prepares and transmits any necessary diplomatic documents, and the Office of Foreign Commerce and Consulates handles any trade or commerce agreements involved and alerts Venezuelan consulates to policy changes. The diplomatic and consular services have conventional functions of administering the personnel of these offices. The Office of International Cooperation is concerned with all matters relating to the United Nations, the OAS, and the European Economic Community. The Office of Frontiers, when not engaged in the settlement of boundary disputes, is principally concerned with the mapping and marking of the international boundaries of the Republic.

The foreign service has undergone considerable expansion since 1968 as a result of the country's increasing contacts. In 1970 it consisted of some 400 officers on overseas assignment and about the same number on duty in Caracas. As a rule, ambassadors were political appointees, but since 1962 the lower ranks had been filled by competitive examination and constituted a career service.

POLICIES OF THE CALDERA GOVERNMENT

One of the top priorities of the government in 1970 was the expansion of exports and, in regard to this and other matters of trade and economic development, President Caldera had appealed to the developed countries to accept the principle of "international social justice." He maintained that unless the developed countries accepted such a principle the less developed ones would not receive just prices for their exports or support for their development processes.

In accordance with this principle, Venezuela has sought and received loans and technical assistance from various international organizations, private foundations, and individual countries, including the United States, West Germany, France, Great Britain, Italy, Austria, the Netherlands, Switzerland, Poland, Romania, Israel, and Japan. In turn, it has provided technical assistance, primarily in the form of scholarships, to Bolivia, Colombia, Costa Rica, Ecuador, El Salvador, Guatemala, Honduras, Panama, Paraguay, and the Dominican Republic.

In its efforts to promote trade and development in the Andean region, Venezuela entered into the multilateral negotiations with Chile, Bolivia, Peru, Ecuador, and Colombia that led to the signing in May 1969 of the Andean Subregional Integration Pact; however, opposition of the domestic business community precluded Venezuela's participation in that pact. The country joined the Andrés Bello Convention, which provided for educational integration, and the Andean Development Corporation; both were established in 1969 by the same countries. In the meantime, Venezuela has intensified both economic and cultural relations with its Caribbean and Central American neighbors (see ch. 20, Trade).

Venezuela participated in the meeting of the Latin American Economic Coordinating Committee (Comité de Coordinación Economica de América Latina—CECLA) in Santiago in April and May 1969. The position paper drawn up at that meeting and later presented to United States President Nixon called for a more equitable balance of trade between the United States and its trading partners in the hemisphere.

Economic nationalism, expressed particularly in a desire to increase state control over foreign-owned petroleum companies, has been an important determinant of foreign trade policies and problems since 1958. In that year the government announced that no new concessions to foreign companies for the exploitation of Venezuelan oil would be granted and that existing concessions would not be renewed after they expired, beginning in 1983.

New exploitation by foreign companies was to be carried out through service contracts with the Venezuelan Petroleum Corporation (Corporación Venezolana Petróleo—CVP). No such contracts had been negotiated by October 1970, and both the volume of Venezuelan exports to the United States and the terms of trade had deteriorated. In August 1970, however, the Venezuelan National Congress for the first time provided legislative authorization for the service contract arrangements, and the government expressed optimism that satisfactory contracts would be negotiated (see ch. 20, Trade; ch. 18, Industry). Contracts were awarded in November 1970 to three international companies.

On the occasion of his official visit to the United States in June, 1970, President Caldera appealed to President Nixon and to the United States Congress for a growing share for Venezuela of petroleum imports into the United States. President Nixon subsequently responded with measures increasing Venezuela's share in the United States oil market.

The approach of the Caldera government to border controversies and other frictional situations with neighboring countries has generally been conciliatory. The most significant development relates to the historical conflicting claims of Venezuela and Guyana (formerly British Guiana), which gained full independence in 1966.

In 1966, before the establishment of independent Guyana, the United Kingdom, British Guiana, and Venezuela agreed to the formation of the Venezuela-Guyana Mixed Commission to discuss disputes arising out of Venezuelan claims. The commission expired in February 1970 without resolving the disputes, but Guyana and Venezuela subsequently engaged in talks on the island of Trinidad and on June 18 signed the Protocol of Port of Spain. This protocol to the Geneva Agreement of 1966 had the effect of shelving the dispute for at least twelve years. The period was to be automatically extended unless either country chose after twelve years to raise the issue again.

The Guyana issue has been important in domestic politics, as it has served as an escape valve for nationalistic feelings. President Caldera agreed to submit his decision on the moratorium to the National Congress for its approval, where it was still pending in 1970 (see ch. 2, Physical Environment).

A boundary dispute that had delayed the exploitation of oil deposits in the Gulf of Venezuela had been a source of friction between Venezuela and Colombia in the 1960s. High-level discussions, underway since 1965, had produced no agreement by late October 1970. Venezuela, which possesses a greater extension of coast on the Gulf of Venezuela than does Colombia, has held that the delimitation of the gulf should be carried out in accordance with the "extension of the land border" formula, whereas Colombia has proposed to delimit marine and underwater areas along a "median line" between the coasts of the two countries (see ch. 2, Physical Environment).

The illegal immigration of large members of Colombians into Venezuela and illegal cross-boundary trade have also been sources of friction. Discussions concerning both these issues and the boundary controversies have generally been carried out in an atmosphere of cordiality, however, and the two countries have continued to cooperate and coordinate efforts in other important areas, such as joint development of water basins and communication and transportation networks.

CHAPTER 14

PUBLIC INFORMATION

In 1970 the people were served by some 35 daily newspapers, more than 100 radio stations, and 5 television stations, with repeater transmitters in various parts of the country. The combined circulation of 11 leading newspapers was in excess of 0.5 million; the estimated number of radio listeners was almost 8 million; and the estimated number of television viewers was close to 4 million. The extent to which the population as a whole benefited from mass media was affected by differences in the distribution of wealth, population dispersion outside the urban centers, and variations in literacy. Contrasts in cultural level and economic position affecting use of the media were probably most noticeable between city and country, but extremes were also found in large population centers.

Taking the country as a whole, the most effective means of mass communication was radio, which reached every populated area. The size of the national radio audience was increasing rapidly as more and more people acquired transistor sets, and those who did not own receivers could listen in public places or in friends' houses.

During the 1960s the impact of the press had increased as a result of literacy campaigns and a growing political and social consciousness among the people. The fall of the Marcos Pérez Jiménez government in 1958 was followed by a proliferation of newspapers and increased confidence in the written word. Distribution by airplane made metropolitan dailies quickly available in cities and towns throughout the country, but readership was still most widespread in urban areas, where newspapers enjoyed their greatest influence—particularly among the middle and upper classes. Newspapers were privately owned.

In 1970 television was extremely popular and growing in importance. Telecasts by candidates in national elections had their greatest influence in urban areas, where the largest number of receiving sets were located. Among the owners of television sets, radio listening tended to decline. The government owned one radio station and one television station. All others were owned by private enterprises or by individuals.

Under the Constitution of 1961, which prohibits disruption of civil and social order, and under legislation charging the Ministry of Communications with the general supervision of radio and television, government intervention in media operations was legal. In 1970, however, there was no government censorship of the media. The Ministry of Communications issued licenses, set frequencies, and administered regulations affecting the number of stations that might be established.

Most of the periodicals published commercially were of general interest. The combined circulation of four leading weeklies was about 160,000. A number of journals were published by universities. In the publishing industry many books were financed by their authors, and the largest book producer was the government. Annual attendance at almost 700 motion picture theaters was approximately 25 million. A large proportion of feature films shown were of North American origin.

Great Britain, West Germany, France, Italy, the United States, and several Latin American countries maintained binational centers, cultural officers, and educational and cultural exchange programs. Activities of foreign governments in the public information field also included radio broadcasts from Cuba and other Communist countries; circulation of Cuban, Communist Chinese, and Soviet publications; maintenance of a Telegrafnonoe Agentsvo Sovietskovo Soyuza (TASS) news bureau; and motion pictures made in Communist countries shown occasionally in commercial theaters.

Informal channels of information played a significant role, particularly in the more isolated areas, where other means were not readily available. The *botiquín* (small cafe) was a popular place for the exchange of news and views, and the drivers of rural taxicabs operating between towns were often dispensers of news. In urban areas men's clubs were centers for the exchange of information and ideas.

FREEDOM OF EXPRESSION

Venezuelans have long subscribed to the principle of freedom of expression. The principle was adapted from the liberal doctrine of the eighteenth-century Enlightenment and has customarily appeared in national constitutions throughout republican history. In the Constitution promulgated in 1961 Article 66 states that everyone "has the right to express his thoughts by the spoken word or in writing and to make use of any means of dissemination." Free exercise of this right, however, has not always been allowed. National leadership has at times suppressed freedom of expression in varying degrees.

Under Pérez Jiménez (1950—58) any criticism of the regime, verbal or written, was potentially dangerous. Although foreign news services were allowed to operate with minimal official interference, local newspapers and radio and television scripts were subject to prior censorship by the Ministry of Interior Relations. Unfavorable opinions of the government were communicated through techniques of omission, veiled irony, and studied ambiguity. When these methods became too obvious, leading newspapers were fined or suspended, and the commentators on occasion were jailed.

Clandestine newspapers, usually the organs of political parties that were ruled illegal under Pérez Jiménez, circulated throughout the period of dictatorship, especially in the final years. At the same time, opposition within the country became more active, resulting in a newspapermen's strike and the refusal to print a repudiation, demanded by the government early in 1958, of reports of the Maracay uprising. After these events, the organizers were sought by the secret police, and newspapers were published under surveillance until the overthrow of the Pérez Jiménez government some weeks later (see ch. 3, Historical Setting).

Subsequently, complete freedom of expression was restricted only when the preservation of public order was threatened, chiefly by the subversive activities of the Communists and their fellow travelers. On these occasions, the government usually imposed limited censorship in addition to the suspension of constitutional guarantees. During periods of great unrest, information regarding guerrilla and terrorist activities was completely curtailed by means of censorship carried out by representatives of the Ministry of Interior Relations. At no time was inflammatory or inaccurate coverrage of such events permitted. When bounds were overstepped, fines or suspensions were imposed. Government interference did not go uncriticized but, as Article 66 of the Constitution contains a clause that forbids propaganda that "incites disobedience of the laws," such measures were legal and therefore not appealed.

Although in the early 1960s censorship affected all media engaged in news reporting, principal attention was given to the press, partly because the Communists and their sympathizers had been most active and influential in this medium. As important collaborators in the anti-Pérez movement, they were able, immediately after the overthrow of the regime, to obtain positions with some of the large newspapers and to establish their own press without hindrance. They also became the dominant faction in the Venezuelan Association of Newspapermen (Asociación Venezolana de Periodistas—AVP).

After November 1960, however, the Communists did not have a regularly published newspaper. The riots they provoked caused the government of Rómulo Betancourt to suspend constitutional guarantees and to close down the Communist and extreme leftist press for approximately fourteen months. Subsequently, extremist newspapers continued to print articles that often advised violent opposition and were therefore subject to frequent suspension for periods of from one week to several months. During the first half of 1962, for example, *Clarín*, the organ of the extremist faction of the Republican Democratic Union (Unión Republicana Democrática—URD), was suspended on six occasions (see ch. 12, Political Dynamics).

Government action was particularly vigorous from May to August 1962 and from October 1962 to January 1963, periods in which unrest led to the suspension of constitutional guarantees. The decision of the Supreme Court of Justice, handed down in October 1963, on a decree that made illegal the political activities of the Venezuelan Communist Party (Partido Comunista Venezolano—PCV) and the Movement of the Revolutionary Left (Movimiento de la Izquierda Revolucionaria—MIR) resulted in the closing of the press of these two parties on the grounds that their newspapers constituted political propaganda.

In 1962 the editors of both *El Mundo* and *El Universal* were arrested for not complying with government policy. Such incidents reinforced the hesitancy of newspapermen to give extensive coverage to those local events that the government might construe as objectionable. Nevertheless, the minister of interior relations in the spring of 1963 criticized the press for what he considered exaggerated, distorted reports of guerrilla activities.

Engaged principally in the presentation of entertainment, radio and television have been less affected by official intervention. During critical periods, news broadcasts have been subject to limited censorship in accordance with government policies. After 1963, however, the exercise of controls declined until, in 1970, censorship of the media was virtually nonexistent.

NEWSPAPERS

The country's first newspaper, the *Gaceta de Caracas*, appeared in 1808, shortly after the arrival of the first printing press. Published by young intellectuals dedicated to the independence movement, the *Gaceta de Caracas* presented extensive discussions of the new political theories emanating from Europe, in addition to news of local developments in the issue with Spain. Soon thereafter, a number of newspapers sprang up in Caracas, and by 1821 a news organ, the *Correo Nacional*, was also being published in Zulia. The emphasis on ideas and doctrines, typical of these early journals, continued after independence, finding especially vigorous expression during the Conservative-Liberal controversy of the mid-nineteenth century. Intellectuals and writers tended to function simultaneously as journalists. Newspapers were often short lived, sometimes disappearing after the publication of a single issue. An exception was *La Religión*, which was founded in 1890 and still published in 1970.

Table 1. *Major Venezuelan Dailies**

Name	Circulation (estimated, 1970)	Orientation
Ultimas Noticias	100,000	Independent; liberal.
El Nacional	105,000	Do.
El Mundo	85,000	Independent.
El Universal	70,000	Independent; conservative.
Panorama (Maracaibo)	50,000	Do.
La Verdad	15,000	Independent.
La Religión	14,000	Catholic; independent.
Daily Journal	12,000	Independent (in English).
La Tarde	5,000	Opposition.

*Unless otherwise noted, newspapers are published in Caracas.

Source: Adapted from Richard P. Stebbins and Alba Amoia (eds.), *Political Handbook and Atlas of the World, 1970,* New York, 1970; and *Editor and Publisher Year Book, 1970*, New York, 1970.

In the atmosphere of optimism that prevailed after the fall of Pérez Jiménez in 1958 and the removal of previous restrictions, a number of new dailies appeared, and newspaper circulation doubled. Although some of the new dailies, irresponsible and extreme, proved to be ephemeral, those that endured together with the older, established newspapers numbered about thirty-five by late 1970. The publication of newspapers was overwhelmingly concentrated in the major cities, one-third of them being published in Caracas alone. The rest were distributed among some ten to fifteen cities of the interior. There were also weekly newspapers, and a variety of foreign newspapers were available at large hotels and a few newsstands.

In 1970 the preeminence and national influence of the Caracas press was virtually unchallenged (see table 1). Although Maracaibo's principal daily had a circulation equal to, or greater than, that of some of the leading newspapers in Caracas, its distribution was largely confined to the immediate area. By a system of air transportation, Caracas newspapers are immediately available in all towns and cities in the interior. In most cases, however, provincial sales, limited to the relatively small educated groups, account for well under 50 percent of the total circulation of the individual newspapers.

With a large number of newspapers in comparison to the potential readership competition for readers and advertisers is strong. Very few dailies show a profit. Well staffed and well equipped, the seven or eight major newspapers are technically good and editorially well organized, but business organization does not generally reach a comparably high level of development. Although chief financial support comes from advertisers, few of the dailies have advertising departments, and fewer still make use of salesmen. Placement is handled largely by advertising agencies. Circulation is generally left to administrative departments, which rely on newsboys and newsstands for sales. Subscribers are limited in number.

Privately owned, the largest dailies are controlled by several families. Family members generally hold top administrative positions and, not uncommonly, contribute articles. In the increasingly cosmopolitan society of the capital, however, these newspapers are not personal vehicles. Political influence may be exerted by the support of, or opposition to, national figures, but the families themselves seldom engaged actively in politics. One of these families has acquired a chain that includes morning dailies, Caracas's only afternoon daily, and popular weekly magazines.

In the past all the major parties have maintained official party newspapers, most of them weeklies. Some parties, principally those of the extreme Left, have employed additional news organs that followed the party policy in news coverage but did not identify themselves as to party affiliation. Similarly, organized labor has published a number of weekly, twice-monthly, and monthly newspapers directed at union members. In 1970, however, the leading publications were independent, and their policies were not dictated by any particular political party.

Special-interest newspapers include those aimed at foreign groups concentrated in Caracas. In 1970 few had circulations of over 10,000, and most were weeklies or monthlies. The one foreign-language daily was the English-language *Daily Journal*, distributed rather evenly between Caracas and Maracaibo. The Italian, French, German, and Jewish communities have each maintained weekly newspapers.

The provincial press offers a sharp contrast to that of the metropolitan area. Lacking adequate funds, local newspapers tend to employ outmoded equipment and untrained, primarily part-time personnel. Consequently, they are largely limited to coverage of local news. The national news that appears is usually rewritten from the Caracas newspapers. Because of competition from Caracas dailies, provincial newspapers find their limited readership further reduced, and few have a circulation of more than 6,000. Advertisers are not as plentiful in many of these areas, with the result that dependence on government advertising for a substantial part of their income is not uncommon. In policy, the provincial press is generally independent, and in tone it ranges from conservative to moderately liberal.

Reflecting current urban attitudes, the editorial tendency of the principal newspapers has been generally liberal. To some extent, all are influenced by nationalism. Self-declared political independence is the rule. In style and tone, the newspapers range from sensationalism to moderate conservatism. Along these lines, reader preference tends to correspond to socioeconomic levels. Politics, national news, and sports—especially horseracing and baseball, both local and North American—are universally popular and consequently well covered by all newspapers. International events, business developments, and the affairs of society are treated most extensively by the less sensational dailies, whereas crime and personal scandal get most attention from the popular newspapers. Special features include comic strips (many of which are North American), horoscopes, and columnists.

All but one of the major dailies use the standard eight columns. Technical excellence, efficient format, and brisk style and presentation characterize Caracas' morning daily, *El Nacional*, the country's most widely read newspaper. It had a circulation of over 100,000 in 1970. With extensive national coverage, large sports and social sections, a wide range of advertisements and international news, and stories on cultural events and business affairs, *El Nacional* appeals to a general audience. The quality of its columnists, including foreign contributors, is also an important factor in its popularity.

A major reversal of editorial policy in the spring of 1963, through fundamental changes in administrative and editorial personnel, brought *El Nacional* from a leftist to a near-center political position. Motivating this action was the severe economic pressure that had begun a year and a half before. Opposed to the considerable number of Communists in editorial positions and the frequent use of Communist and far-left contributors of the country's leading daily, influential conservative elements brought about a boycott by advertisers that placed the newspaper in an increasingly precarious financial position.

El Nacional's director was replaced by Raúl Valera, who resigned as minister of labor, with President Betancourt's approval, to take over the position. Directives were issued that established the newspaper's political independence. With the lifting of the boycott, *El Nacional* doubled in size and regained its advertisers.

Founded in 1909, the second oldest newspaper, *El Universal*, had a circulation in 1970 of about 70,000. Like other newspaper editors in Venezuela's past, its founder, Andrés Mata, was primarily a literary man and a poet. In style, editorial policy, and coverage, *El Universal* is directed at the upper class and the business community. Its front page usually carries few pictures, many lead articles, and two- or three-column headlines in relatively small type. *El Universal* is frequently cited for its excellent coverage of international news. A considerable portion of its first section is devoted to world events. Similarly, business news and classified advertising are covered. In contrast, political affairs and crime receive less attention than in other newspapers.

The morning tabloid *Ultimas Noticias*, founded in 1951, is popular among the lower class of Caracas. Its estimated circulation in 1970 was 100,000. In policy it has tended to be liberal, and during the Pérez Jiménez dictatorship it was known for its outspoken opposition. Articles critical of the policies of both the United States and Venezuelan governments have not been infrequent. Less sensationalist than *Ultimas Noticias*, *El Mundo* had a circulation in 1970 of about 85,000. *El Mundo* is directed at a general audience.

La Religión, established in 1890, is the country's most prominent Catholic daily. It has been independent and liberal in its policies, and its endurance has been largely owing to the efforts of its longtime director, Monsignor Pellín, who enjoyed great respect both within and outside the field of communications. Unlike most other newspapers, *La Religión* counts on subscribers for about half its total circulation of 14,000.

Panorama is Maracaibo's only large daily and, with a circulation of more than 50,000, has little competition from the other two dailies there. Running about forty pages in two sections, its coverage is comprehensive. In the early 1960s it reflected the conservative attitudes of business-oriented Maracaibo.

Although some of the major dailies maintain special correspondents abroad, most international news is supplied by foreign news agencies. In 1970 the heaviest user was the Caracas press, which typically subscribed to several of the foreign services. The United States Associated Press (AP) and United Press International (UPI), both of which maintained bureaus, and the Agence France Presse (AFP), the Spanish Agencia EFE, the British Reuters, and Italian Agencia Nazionale Stampa Associata (ANSA) were the most active. Other wire services with bureaus in Caracas were the West German agency Deutsche Presse Agentur (DPA) and the Mexican news agency Amex. In late 1970 *El Nacional* started using the newly established Latin American news service (La Agencia Latinoamericana de Información—LATIN).

As a profession, journalism is relatively young. The staffs of many newspapers have a number of part-time employees who actively engage in other professions as well. Contributors seldom have regularly scheduled columns, although they may appear frequently. As they represent a wide range of ideas on the political spectrum, their articles, usually brought together on the editorial page, may run from Left to relative Right in the same edition, despite the general policy of the particular newspaper. Editorial control permits the writer to select material and approach according to individual preference. Opinions and ideas and their presentation are the main concern, and deviation is not seen as contradictory to general policy. With the exception of contributors who usually are well known, bylines are infrequent.

Salaries in 1970, determined by union scales, were relatively high within the national economy. On smaller newspapers, which employed few full-time workers, salaries and payment for articles were considerably lower. Training in journalism and in the techniques of the other mass media is available at the Central University, the University of Zulia, the University of the Andes, and the private Andrés Bello Catholic University. Based on North American models, the four-year programs include practical experience as well as theory. With one of the finest physical plants in Latin America, the School of Journalism at Central University has enjoyed a distinct advantage.

Professional union is accomplished through the AVP. The fact that a number of its members are simultaneously politicians associated with the major parties adds to its importance. It had considerable prestige after the overthrow of Pérez Jiménez, when the organization had been involved in opposition activities and had had democratic leadership, but controlling influence was lost to the Communists from 1960 until 1963. At that time opposing elements worked together to regain the positions of leadership. Also, in reaction to Communist domination, a group of Catholic-oriented newspapermen had broken off from the AVP to form a second association, but its influence was minimal. Similarly, several newspapers banded together to form the Venezuelan Newspaper Publishers' Association (Bloque de Prensa).

In 1970 the Venezuelan Newspaper Publishers' Association inaugurated a series of monthly dinners with personages and organizations of national importance. The first dinner honored the Federation of Chambers of Commerce and Industry (Federación de Cámaras de Comerico e Indústria—FEDECAMARAS). In September 1970 the seventh national conference of the AVP was addressed by President Caldera.

The Venezuelan Advertising Council has as its objectives the promotion, protection, and defense of the interests and prestige of the advertising industry. Its membership includes the Venezuelan Newspaper Publishers' Association, the National Association of Announcers, the Venezuelan Federation of Advertising Agencies, the Venezuelan Chamber of Radio Broadcasting, the Chamber of the Television Industry, and the Chamber of the National Cinematographic Industry.

RADIO

In 1970, with one or more radio stations in each of over fifty towns and cities, there were few people in the country who did not at some time listen to the radio, either at home or in some public place. General supervision of radio operations was exercised by the Ministry of Communications under the Radiocommunications Regulation of 1941. All stations must be licensed and must broadcast on frequencies set by the ministry. Licenses for five-year periods are granted after the issuance of a provisional permit for the installation of equipment and a short trial broadcasting period, monitored by the ministry.

Only Venezuelan citizens or corporations that have boards comprised of Venezuelan citizens and capital that is 80-percent Venezuelan are eligible. Likewise, technical personnel must possess the certificate of qualification issued by the ministry. Expansion of the number of stations is controlled by provisions that permit the establishment of a new station for every increase of 150,000 inhabitants in metropolitan areas and of 50,000 in the interior.

Radio tends to be locally oriented. Most stations program broadcasting according to the interests of the immediate area in which they can be heard. Broader scope is afforded by the four networks in operation in 1970, which, through more powerful transmitters and affiliated stations broadcasting network programs in full or in part, reached a great portion of the country. Three belonged to corporate enterprises, and the other was maintained by the government. Operated by the Central Office of Information of the Ministry of Interior Relations the Venezuelan National Broadcasting Station carried a domestic and international service. Reestablished in June 1961 after several years of inactivity, the international service was beamed at English-speaking audiences in Europe and the United States. Popular and folk music, cultural talks, and news were broadcast on a shortwave frequency. Station call letters were YVKO. The transmitter was used by the domestic service at other times. Similar programs were carried daily in Spanish on the domestic service, YVKA (see table 2).

Of the commercial networks, Radio Rumbos was heard directly throughout the country. This transmitter was used to broadcast on mediumwave at 560 kilohertz (kilocycles) with call letters YVLX. The network also broadcast from Caracas on mediumwave and on shortwave. Broadcasting was continuous for twenty-four hours a day, and news was given every half-hour. The other networks' rebroadcasts on affiliated and other stations reached nationwide audiences. Gran Radio Circuito Nacional RT, "Radio Tropical," broadcast on shortwave and on mediumwave. Radio-Continente Network, "Radio Continente," broadcast on two frequencies, one mediumwave and one shortwave.

In 1970 the number of listeners to foreign international radio broadcasts did not appear to be large. Programs transmitted by the British Broadcasting Corporation (BBC) and the Voice of America (VOA) were relatively popular. Radio Moscow, Radio Havana, and broadcasts from Communist China and European Communist countries could also be heard. Cuba's thrice-weekly broadcasts to hemisphere nations included a program called "Venezuelan Realities".

In 1970 the electronics industry was producing a variety of radio and television sets. More than twenty assembling firms, most of them in Caracas, usually imported components in bulk and purchased some parts locally. There were indications that within approximately three years the industry would be in a position to supply the total domestic demand for receiving sets.

In 1970 there was no FM (frequency modulation) broadcasting. FM was used principally as a carrier for repeater stations—from commercial station to transmitter. It was also used for music piped into shopping centers and apartment and office buildings.

TELEVISION

Television in Venezuela is a well developed and established medium. Telecasts were begun in 1953 on the government-owned Televisora Nacional; a few months later the first commercial station, VeneVisión, was opened. In 1954 a second commercial station, Radio Caracas TV, began operations. After the establishment of these three stations, all in Caracas, stations were set up in Maracaibo and Valencia.

In 1970 each of the five television stations operated its own network and its own independent transmission system. Audience concentration and best reception were in the heavily populated western coastal region stretching from Maracaibo to Caracas. Daily broadcast hours varied from station to station, but all were required by law and union regulations to maintain 50 percent live programming, which according to the local definition included tape recording. All had excellent facilities and were equipped to handle remote telecasts and video tape (see table 3).

The government station, operating without relays, can be seen in a large portion of the country since the installation of a transmitter on one of the mountains near Caracas. Live shows constitute a large percentage of the programming that is broadcast from 4 P.M. to 10 P.M. daily. Shows are predominantly of a cultural or educational nature. In 1970 President Rafael Caldera was holding weekly press conferences that were televised.

Television is popular at all social levels. Although sets are found mostly in middle and upper class homes, it is not uncommon to see television antennas in the shantytowns that dot the urban areas. Key viewing hours are between 4:30 P.M. and 9:30 P.M., the peak occurring between 7:30 and 8:30. The earliest part of this period is dominated by popular children's programs from the United States, but these give way to adult fare in the evening. Local programs telecast at these hours are mainly news programs or variety shows featuring popular local personalities. Daytime television, which caters largely to women and children, consists chiefly of children's

Table 2. Major Venezuelan Radio Stations[1]

City	Station and owner	Call letters	Wavelength (in meters)	Frequency (in kilohertz)[2]
Acarigua	Radio Acarigua Ramon Ramirez H. (affiliated Radio Continente)	YVQV	256.40	1170
Anaco	La Voz de Anaco (L. J. Arreaza Almenar)	YVQZ	247.90	1210
Barcelona	Radio Barcelona Radio Rumbos (Felipe Serrano M.)	YVQJ	277.80	1080
Barinas	Radio Barinas Ricardo Sosa Rios	YVRE	252.10	1190
Barquisimeto	Radio Cristal Radio Cristal	YVSE	491.80	610
	Radio Barquisimeto Hermanos Segura	YVMR	434.80	690
	Radio Universo Hermanos Segura	YVMT	411.00	730
	Radio Juventud Hermanos Segura	YVMY	357.10	840
	Radio Lara Hermanos Segura	YVMP	340.90	880
	Radio Lara Hermanos Segura	YVMO	62.50	4800
	Radio Universo Hermanos Segura	YVMS	61.48	4880
	Radio Juventud Hermanos Segura	YVNK	61.22	4900

	Radio Barquistimeto Hermanos Segura	YVMQ	60.12	4990
	Radio Barquistimeto Hermanos Segura	YVXJ	31.55	9510
Cabimas	Radio Libertad Radio Libertad	YVNO	483.90	620
	Radio Cabimas Compania Anonima Radio Cabimas	YVML	240.00	1250
Cagua	Radio Aragua Prospero Castillo R.	YVPC	297.00	1010
Caracas (Villa de Cura)	Radio Rumbos Radio Rumbos (Felipe Serrano M.)	YVLX	535.70	560
Caracas	Radio Continente Compania Anonima Radio Continente	YVKL	508.50	590
	Radio Nacional de Venezuela Light Program Radio Nacional de Venezuela (government)	YVKA	476.20	630
	Radio Rumbos Radio Rumbos (Felipe Serrano M.)	YVLL	447.80	670
	Radio Caracas Radio Caracas	YVKS	400.00	750
	Radio Tropical Antonio J. Isturiz	YVRT	303.00	990
	Radio Nacional de Venezuela Radio Nacional de Venezuela (government)	YVKZ	285.70	1050
	Radio Cultura Antonio J. Isturiz	YVKE	272.70	1100
	Radio Tiempo Radio Tiempo	YVOZ	250.00	1200

Table 2. *Major Venezuelan Radio Stations*[1] *(Cont.)*

City	Station and owner	Call letters	Wavelength (in meters)	Frequency (in kilohertz)[2]
	Radio Rumbos Radio Rumbos (Felipe Serrano M.)	YVLK	60.36	4970
	Radio Nacional de Venezuela Radio Nacional de Venezuela (government)	YVKO	59.76	5020
	Radio Nacional de Venezuela Radio Nacional de Venezuela (government)	YVKO	48.62	6170
	Radio Rumbos Radio Rumbos (Felipe Serrano M.)	n.a.	31.02	9670
Caripito	Radio Caripito	YVSF	294.10	1020
Carora	Radio Carora Carlos J. Gonzales	YVNI	263.20	1140
Carupano	Radio Nacional de Venezuela Radio Nacional de Venezuela (government)	YVSJ	545.50	550
	Radio Carupano Radio Rumbos (Felipe Serrano M.)	YVQT	270.30	1110
Caucagua	Radio Barlavento Compania Anonima Radio Barlavento	YVNT	243.90	1230
Ciudad Bolívar	Radio Bolívar Antonio J. Isturiz	YVQF	441.20	680
Coro	Ondas de los Medanos Radio Inversionista	YVNA	454.50	660
Cumana	Radio Sucre Radio Rumbos (Felipe Serrano M.)	YVQB	500.00	600
	Radio Cumana Reinaldo Marin Q	YVQR	416.70	720

El Tigre	La Voz del Tigre	YVQM	306.10	980
	Carlos Poleo (affiliated Radio Continente)			
Guanare	Radio Guanare	YVQY	291.30	1030
	C. Delgado Nino Y. J. Delgade Olavarria			
Guarenas	Radio Industrial	YVRR	258.60	1160
	Radio Industrial			
Isla de Margarita	Radio Margarita	n.a.	294.10	1020
Los Teques	Radio Miranda	YVLT	361.40	830
	Radio Miranda			
Machiques	Radio Perija	YVOV	277.80	1080
	Ali Segundo Rachid			
Maiquetía	Radio Aeropuerto	YVRQ	329.70	910
	Marcos Hernandez Solis			
Maracaibo	Radio Nacional de Venezuela	YVSI	556.00	540
	Radio Nacional de Venezuela (government)			
	La Voz de la Fe	YVMJ	517.20	580
	Diocesis de Maracaibo (Catholic church)			
	Radio Popular	YVMH	428.60	700
	Jose a Higuera Miranda			
	Radio Maracaibo	YVNC	405.40	740
	Radio Rumbos (Felipe Serrano M.)			
	Radio Mara	YVMD	333.30	900
	Luis A. Govea			
	Radio Servicio	YVND	306.10	980
	Lius G. Cristalino			
	Radio Calendario	YVMX	294.10	1020
	Maria N. de Rosales (affiliated Radio Continente)			

Table 2. Major Venezuelan Radio Stations[1] (Cont.)

City	Station and owner	Call letters	Wavelength (in meters)	Frequency (in kilohertz)[2]
	Ondas del Lago Nicolas Vale Quintero	YVMF	267.90	1120
	La Voz del Zulia Luis G. Cristalino	YVMB	254.20	1180
	La Voz de la Fe Diocesis de Maracaibo (Catholic church)	YVMI	88.89	3375
Maracay	Radio Girardot Confederacion de Trabajadores Venezolanos	YVLH	461.50	650
	Radio Maracay Radio Maracay	YVLJ	322.60	930
	Radio Central Radio Central (affiliated Radio Continente)	YVLR	309.30	970
Maturín	Radio Monagas Luis J. Arreaza Almenar	YVRB	312.50	960
	Radio Maturín Ruben Sifontes	YVOR	254.20	1180
Mérida	Radio Los Andes Guillermo Lobo L.	YVON	288.50	1040
Morón	Radio Mil Antonio J. Isturiz	YVNM	300.00	1000
Petare	Radio Crono Radar Octavio Suarez	YVKH	230.80	1300
Porlamar	Radio Nueva Esparta Luis J. Arreaza Almenar	YVQX	326.10	920
Puerto La Cruz	Ondas Portenas Rafael Bellorin M.	YVQO	468.80	640

	Radio Puerto La Cruz Hermanos Arreaza a	YVQQ	394.70	760
Puerto Ordáz	Radio Puerto Ordáz Jesus Gonzalez B.	YVQH	240.00	1250
Punta Fijo	Radio Punta Fijo Radio Rumbos (Felipe Serrano M.)	YVNN	319.10	940
	Ondas del Caribe Antonio J. Isturiz	YVMV	260.60	1150
San Cristóbal	Radio Nacional de Venezuela Radio Nacional de Venezuela (government)	YVSL	476.20	630
	Ecos del Torbes Gregorio Gonzales L.	YVOD	384.60	780
	Radio Junin Diocesis de San Cristóbal (Catholic church)	YVOL	348.80	860
	La Voz del Tachira Jesus M. Diaz Gonzalez	YVOB	300.00	1000
	Radio San Cristobal Radio San Cristobal	YVOE	383.00	1060
	Radio San Cristobal Various San Cristobal Broadcasters	YVOM	31.35	9570
	Ecos de Trobes Gregorio Gonzales L.	n.a.	31.12	9640
San Felipe	Radio Yaracuy Hermanos Segura	YVPB	275.20	1090
	Radio Yaracuy Hermanos Segura	YVPA	60.73	4940
San Fernando	La Voz de Apure Rosa Cestari	YVRD	245.90	1220

Table 2. Major Venezuelan Radio Stations[1] *(Cont.)*

City	Station and owner	Call letters	Wavelength (in meters)	Frequency (in kilohertz)[2]
	Radio Nacional de Venezuela Radio Nacional de Venezuela (government)	YVSQ	234.40	1280
Santa Tome de Guayana	Radio Nacional de Venezuela Radio Nacional de Venezuela (government)	YVSI	526.30	570
Tovar	Radio Occidente Diocesis de Mérida (Catholic church)	YVOP	272.70	1100
Upata	Radio Guayana Socrates Hernandez	YVSH	365.90	820
Valencia	Radio Nacional de Venezuela Radio Nacional de Venezuela (government)	YVKK	389.60	770
	Radio Ocho Cientos Diez Radio 810	YVLP	365.90	820
	Radio Valencia Miguel Ache	YVLD	352.90	850
	Radio America Bernado A. Heredia	YVLW	337.10	890
	La Voz de Carabobo La Voz de Carabobo	YVLB	288.50	1040
Valera	Radio Turismo Pedro J. Fajardo	YVSD	258.60	1160
Zaraza	Radio Zaraza	YVPZ	267.90	1120

n.a.—not available.
[1] 10,000 watts and over.
[2] 1 kilohertz equals 1 kilocycle.

Source: Adapted from Foreign Broadcast Information Service, *Broadcasting Stations of the World*, Part I: Amplitude Modulation Broadcasting Stations According to Country and City, Washington, 1969.

Table 3. Venezuelan Television Stations

City	Name and owner of station	Channel	Power video-audio (in watts)	Frequency video-audio (kilohertz per second)*
Agua Linda (Vargas Area)	Corporacion Venezolana de Television	A9	12500	187250
Barquisimeto	Radio Caracas TV	A3	20000	61250
Barquisimeto (Terepaima)	Corporacion Venezolana de Television	A6	76000	83250
Carabobo	Radio Caracas TV	A7	12800	175250
Caracas	Radio Caracas TV	A2	62600	55250
	Corporacion Venezolana de Television	A4	75000	67250
	Televisora Nacional (government)	A5	37200	77250
	Colteve and Proventel	A8	n.a.	181250
	Ricardo Espina	A11	n.a.	199250
	Teleinversiones	A13	50000	211250
Curimagua	Radio Caracas TV	A10	165000	193250
La Guaira	Radio Caracas TV	A7	10000	175250
Maracaibo	Radio Caracas TV	A2	600000	55250
	Corporacion Venezolana de Television	A4	40000	67250
	Teleinversiones	A13	n.a.	211250
Picacho	Corporacion Venezolana de Television	A9	76000	187250
Valencia	Radio Valencia (Miguel Ache)	A3	4000	61250
Valencia-Maracay	Radio Caracas TV	A7	13000	175250
Valencia	Teleinversiones	A13	50000	211250

n.a.—not available.
*1 kilohertz equals 1 kilocycle.

Source: Adapted from Foreign Broadcast Information Service, *Broadcasting Stations of the World*, Part IV, Television Stations, Washington, September 1, 1969.

programs and other shows aimed at homemakers. Television awards, called the Guaicaipuro de Oro, are given annually in a variety of categories. Selection is made by a panel of television critics.

In August 1970 the government-owned station announced plans to build five repeater stations at various locations, the program to start in 1971. There were indications that some basic color equipment would be incorporated. In November 1970 plans were materializing to join the international network of satellite communications, and an earth satellite station was inaugurated.

MOTION PICTURES

In 1970 the local film industry was devoted principally to the production of newsreels, documentaries, and commercials for television and the theaters. Full-length feature films were produced only intermittently. Among the local companies, competition in the newsreel business was especially keen. Commercials generally used live actors in Venezuelan settings, as did the documentaries. Costs were set by the Chamber of the National Cinematographic Industry. With good facilities and well-trained technicians, the local companies produced films of excellent quality. The leading companies were equipped for the entire process of producing pictures, including developing, printing, and editing.

Documentaries were commissioned by government entities, such as the ministries of labor and of education, and by the major oil companies for the purposes of public relations and education. These films were shown free of charge in schools, worker camps, labor centers, rural areas, and occasionally commercial theaters. Films produced for the government sometimes appeared on its television station. In 1970 the Italian Latin American Institute, sponsoring the International Festival of Folklore Films in Rome, awarded a gold medal to a Venezuelan documentary "El Paraiso Amazónico" (The Amazonian Paradise)—a study of the Yanohama Indians produced by the Central Office of Information.

Most of the full-length features shown in commercial motion picture theaters are imported. The single largest exporter of films to the country was the United States. Following closely was Mexico, films from Argentina, Europe (including a few from the Soviet Union and its satellites), and other places making up the remainder. Foreign-language features produced by Puerto Rican or Mexican firms, which have Spanish dubbed in, circulate mainly in the urban areas. Rural sections of the country receive mainly Spanish-language pictures, a great number of which are produced in Mexico. Distribution is handled by companies located in Caracas, of which several represent the major United States film producers.

Censorship boards exist for the purpose of giving audience classifications of A, for general audiences; B, for adults; and C, strictly for adults. Although theoretically all municipalities are entitled to maintain boards, in practice the designations of the Caracas board are used throughout the country, with the exception of Maracaibo, which exercises its privilege. The Roman Catholic Church has a similar classification system, but newspaper listings generally carry only the municipal classifications.

Although television, where available, has reduced theater attendance, films still constitute one of the most popular forms of entertainment among all social classes. Urban tastes are quite cosmopolitan. In the principal cities, there are three shows daily—at 3:00 P.M., 7:00 P.M. (the most popular), and 9:00 P.M. Theater schedules in the smaller towns of the interior are usually limited to weekend performances. Although admissions are low, only the reasonably well off can afford to attend frequently.

PERIODICALS AND BOOKS

In 1970 over 100 periodicals of various types were being published, many of which were issued by organizations or groups to readerships. The market for commercial magazines was precarious, with the result that many disappeared after the first few issues. This has been especially true of the cultural magazines, usually started by a young "generation" of authors, artists, and intellectuals to express its particular theories and to afford outlets for the works of its members (see ch. 8, Artistic and Intellectual Expression).

Most popular and enduring were the large general-interest weeklies that cover current events, both local and international, with a heavy reliance on photographs. Readership was concentrated in the cities among the upper and middle classes. The number of subscriptions was limited, but circulation of four leading weekly magazines was estimated at 160,000.

Venezuela Gráfica and *Momento* were among the largest magazines. All were well equipped and able to use color art. Carrying articles on recent news, the motion picture and television industries, romance and human interest, *Momento* was somewhat less sensational than the others. A popular news weekly was *Semana*.

Other magazines frequently reprinted material from European periodicals, and other articles were divided between staff and freelance writers. Also popular was the magazine *Gaceta Hípica*, dealing mainly with horseracing. Strong competition is offered by such foreign periodicals as the Spanish edition of *Reader's Digest; Bohemia;* and, to a lesser extent, the weekly news magazine *Visión*, printed in Mexico.

Of all the media, books probably had the smallest mass impact in 1970. Excluding schoolchildren under the age of fifteen, there was a potential audience of several million nominal literates, but minimal education, uneven distribution of income, and the high prices of books (the result of the high cost of labor and the use of imported paper) significantly reduced this figure. Book reading was frequent only among a portion of the top socioeconomic group, and readers were primarily students, intellectuals, and the well educated. Popular sales were largely illustrated domestic fiction and imported romantic novels. Books could be bought at about seventy-five shops.

Libraries were not especially numerous. Moreover, the general public had access to only a few libraries, as a great many are privately supported by clubs, foundations, or learned associations. In general, libraries tend to be small. The oldest and largest, the Biblioteca National (National Library), had over 400,000 volumes. University libraries were not especially extensive, the largest by far being that of the Central University in Caracas. Secondary schools, few of which had library facilities, rarely had over 5,000 volumes.

Considering the small market, the book-publishing industry was rather well developed. An important factor was the desire on the part of many educated Venezuelans to publish various kinds of manuscripts for, in the absence of commercial book publishers, it was usually the author himself or his representative who contracted and financed publication with a job printer. Sales and distribution are likewise handled by the author or an agency engaged for that purpose. Promotional activities are limited or nonexistent.

The government also engages in printing and publishing. All ministries and autonomous agencies have printing facilities, and there is, in addition, the Imprenta Nacional (Government Printing Office), which prints government-sponsored works. Books, both privately and officially published, are usually in paperback form, although excellent hard-bound editions can be produced on a limited scale. Press runs are small, the average being about 2,000. Demand may go as high as 5,000, and a bestseller or government-subsidized classic may run to 10,000 copies.

Imported books make up a significant percentage of the market. Chief exporters to the country are Spain, the United States, Italy, France, Argentina, Mexico, Canada, and West Germany. Spain, a large exporter, is most active in the field of scientific, technical, and craft publications, many of which have been translated from English. Textbooks, the second largest import category, are supplied by most of these countries, especially Italy, in accordance with the official lists published by the Ministry of Education. A small market exists for foreign fiction.

The organization representing the book trade in Venezuela is the Cámara Venezolana del Libro (Venezuelan Book Association), with headquarters in Caracas. In 1970 there were at least thirty importer-exporters of books, most of them located in Caracas.

CHAPTER 15

POLITICAL VALUES AND ATTITUDES

In 1970 political activities were characterized by vigorous competition among parties for popular support and general acceptance of the legitimacy and authority of the Constitution and the ballot. In recognition of the diffusion of power among all social groupings and the expectations of advancement on the part of the lower classes, all of the major parties had stressed their commitment to social reform.

Political values and attitudes have been transformed in the past half century. The emergence of new social groups—industrialist, middle class, urban labor—and the acceleration of urbanization that began with the exploitation of oil in the early 1930s created pressures for greatly increased participation in the political processes. Thus, political leadership gradually shifted away from the agrarian elite and came to rest in the new classes.

The process of transmission of values has also undergone significant changes. With the expansion of the educational system and of political and functional organization in the last three decades, particularly since 1958, the inculcation of political values, formerly carried out almost exclusively by the family and the Roman Catholic Church, has been carried out to a greater extent by the public schools, unions, local political organizations, and the communications media.

Relative racial and ethnic homogeneity and the gradual breakdown of regionalistic sentiment in the twentieth century have contributed to national unity. Class antagonisms have sometimes been a divisive force, but education, urbanization, and political organization have given formerly isolated peasants a greater sense of participation in the national community, and social reform and welfare programs instituted since 1958 have given them a stake in the existing political system.

Traditional sources of national identity and nationalistic sentiment include the isolation of Venezuela from other settlements on the continent during the colonial period and the central role played by Venezuelan revolutionaries in the independence movement. Sources of national pride in the 1960s have been the political maturity indicated by the institutionalization of a democratic system and the realization of reformist goals, especially in the areas of land redistribution and educational advancement. Economic nationalism, expressed primarily in the advocacy of national control over petroleum resources, has been increasing since 1958.

The traditional distrust of governmental institutions and cynicism toward the political process have been largely overcome since 1960 as the government has extended services and channels of communication to the formerly neglected or repressed lower classes. The voter turnout of about 90 percent in the elections of 1963 and 1968 indicated that the overwhelming majority of the adult population believed in the ability of the individual to influence the course of government. Vestiges of traditional values and attitudes have nevertheless persisted. Foremost among these is a tendency to value personal loyalty over civic trust and to emphasize personality rather than substantive issues in electoral campaigns. It has not been unusual for bitter rivalries to develop between leaders or parties of similar ideologies.

DETERMINANTS OF POLITICAL VALUES

Social Structure and Urbanization

Until the 1930s political attitudes reflected a social structure that was traditional and relatively simple. A small group of landowning families, many of whom had held title to their estates since the colonial era, controlled the economy and, in alliance with the military, the government. There was general fatalistic acceptance of a dualistic society of cultured people (*gente culta*) and common people (*gente cualquiera*). Those among the peasants who sensed that they were being exploited had no means of channeling discontent and bringing it to bear on the political system. No middle class existed to span the gulf between the elites and the masses (see ch. 3, Historical Setting).

With the development of the petroleum enterprise, the change from an agrarian base to reliance on subsoil deposits, and the concomitant drive toward industrialization, however, the social structure underwent far-reaching changes, and irreversible revolutionary forces were unleashed. Within three decades, from 1936 to 1966, a country that had been 70-percent rural transformed itself into one that was 70-percent urban. Census figures indicate that in the 1930s about 11 percent of the people lived outside their native states; that figure had almost doubled by the 1960s (see ch. 18, Industry).

Physical mobility was accompanied by upward social mobility. By the end of World War II a new upper class comprising industrialists and other entrepreneurs, a commercial and professional middle class, and an urban working class were demanding a significant role in the political processes. As the agrarian oligarchy was unwilling to accommodate the new groups, the middle class aspirants to political leadership looked for support to the urban and rural lower classes (see ch. 5, Social Structure).

Attempts of such middle class groups to organize and mobilize urban workers and peasants as a counterforce to the oligarchy began with the death of the authoritarian ruler Juan Vicente Gómez in 1935 and were greatly accelerated under the leadership of the Democratic Action party (Acción Democrática—AD) from the October revolution of 1945 until the overthrow of President Rómulo Gallegos in 1948 (see ch. 3, Historical Setting). When the AD returned to power in 1958 after a decade of authoritarian rule, it had maintained its peasant and working-class base, but it sought accommodation with the military and with upper class elements as well.

Agents of Political Indoctrination

Among the agents that have influenced the political values and attitudes of the individual have been the family, the Catholic church, the educational system, the parties, the military, labor and peasant unions, and the communications media. The influence of these agents has operated unevenly in urban and rural areas, and a rural-urban cleavage has been reflected in voting patterns.

The orientation of the child to the nation and to political life is derived largely from the family, the church, and the educational system. Of the three the schools are increasingly assuming the political indoctrination role formerly allocated to the others. In well-to-do families traditional relationships and kinship solidarity reinforce political ties, but among lower class families broken homes are more common and family ties weaker, with a correspondingly weaker influence on political views and affiliations.

Likewise, the socializing role of the church is less operative among the lower classes. Although adequate schooling was by no means universal in 1970, overall enrollment figures have risen phenomenally since 1958, and possibilities for advancement were generally seen by the lower class in terms of education. The child's earliest concepts of the nation and its governmental system are often those projected by the schools (see ch. 7, Education).

For the adult, the structuring of political attitudes and recruitment into active political roles are often functions of military service or of membership either in student organizations or in urban or rural labor unions. The unions, for example, have contributed to a recognition of mutual interests that are affected by government policies and of the effectiveness of collective action. The direct linkage, however, of union to party and party to government has discouraged the initiation of independent action by union leaders.

In addition to their organizational and electoral campaigns, the political parties sponsor a variety of activities—social gatherings, soccer (*futbol*) games, discussion groups, and regional and national conventions—to bring the members into contact with one another and with the leaders and to heighten the sense of identity with and commitment to the party.

With increasing literacy the country has seen a proliferation of newspapers and other periodicals, most of which present the views of a particular party or faction. Television has become particularly significant in political campaigns since the 1963 elections. In 1970 there were almost 1 million television receivers in the country, or about 1 for every 10 persons. Although the urban areas are almost saturated with the various media, however, the impact of periodicals and of television drops off sharply in the rural areas. Only the radio provides an almost universal means of communication (see ch. 14, Public Information).

The extent to which urbanization, the emergence of new social groups, and the spread of education, organization, and communication have drawn the heretofore uninvolved masses into the political processes since 1958 is indicated in the fact that in the presidential elections of 1963 and 1968 about 90 percent of the eligible voters turned out to vote. Voting patterns suggest that the relative electoral strength of the major parties is determined more by organizational successes within particular geographical communities than by perceived differences in program or ideology.

None of the major parties has been very successful in Caracas. This has been attributed in part to the fact that political organizations in the metropolitan area were more easily suppressed under the regime of General Marcos Pérez Jiménez in the 1950s than were the decentralized and loosely organized peasant unions and in part to resentment, especially among middle class elements, of what has been considered disproportionate official attention to the rural problems.

ATTITUDES TOWARD THE NATION

Nationalism

Although they share with other Hispanic Americans a common language, cultural heritage, ethnic background, and historical experience and recognize this basic kinship, most Venezuelans are conscious of their distinctiveness as a people. They are quick to point to differences in folk culture, speech, and attitude that underscore that distinctiveness, marking them off even from their Colombian neighbors, with whom they sustain very close ties (see ch. 4, Population and Ethnic Groups).

An important root of national identity lies in the isolated and neglected status of Venezuela in the Spanish colonial system. Exciting little interest on the part of the crown and playing a marginal role in the mercantile economy, the country enjoyed only sporadic communication with other parts of the Hispanic world. Very early in colonial history, therefore, the planters, merchants, and officials who constituted the elite became accustomed to an independence of action considerably greater than that exercised by their counterparts in the more prosperous and important colonies. This de facto independence was easily translated into an attitude compounding a strong local pride with a sense of distinctiveness (see ch. 3, Historical Setting).

Another root of nationalism lies in a keen pride felt in the continent-wide leadership exercised by the country in wars of independence. Venezuelans of all classes and degrees of education are aware that the names of their countrymen Simón Bolívar and Antonio José de Sucre are venerated throughout the continent and that decisive battles fought on Venezuelan soil—Carabobo, for example—are memorialized in street names in scores of distant cities.

Related to this indelible and focal point of national pride is the traditional self-image held by Venezuelans, and largely accepted as a stereotype of them by other South Americans, as a courageous people, quick to oppose by armed force any threat to their independence. Despite the fact that the nation has not been involved in a major international military action since independence, pride in its martial traditions continues to serve as a symbolic rallying point of nationalism. The importance of that tradition is perhaps most succinctly expressed in the national anthem, which offers homage to the *bravo pueblo*, which could be translated with equal accuracy as the "brave" or the "fierce" people.

The economic and social dynamism arising out of the petroleum boom but sustained in such indices as industrialization, strong labor organization, rapidly increasing literacy rates, and urbanization has also been a point of national pride. Several influential writers have expressed concern at the massive social upheavals attending the growth, but a majority of people of all political persuasions are proud of the country's development. Worldwide importance as a major petroleum producer has long been a key aspect of national self-esteem and so, in equal measure, are the visible trappings of material advancement—massive urban construction and superhighways.

Nationalist sentiment has traditionally contrasted with that of some other Spanish American countries in reflecting less of a tendency toward cultural exclusivism and isolationism. Partly as the result of frequent and easy communications with their non-Hispanic neighbors in the British and Dutch Antilles during colonial times, Venezuelans have more readily assimilated cultural and linguistic influences from foreign sources, and the very integration of such traits into the national culture has been taken as a point of distinctiveness.

Although a few writers—notably those influenced by the historian Mario Briceño Iragorry—have seen such receptivity as antinationalist and disloyal to the country's Hispanic heritage, they have not succeeded in mustering wide support for their position. On the contrary, a majority of artists and intellectuals are vocally proud of what they consider a lack of provincialism, and overwhelming numbers, especially in the cities, have continued to display a readiness to incorporate the novel and the foreign into their own way of life (see ch. 4, Population and Ethnic Groups; ch. 8, Artistic and Intellectual Expression).

Notwithstanding the lack of cultural exclusivism, nationalist sentiment implies a strong sense of political sovereignty and an immediate reaction to any act of foreign governments or nationals that could be construed as abridging that sovereignty. In this spirit, anti-United States feeling has occasionally been mobilized around such issues as interventionism. By the same token, much of the widespread opposition to the activities of such Communist groups as the self-styled Armed Forces of National Liberation (Fuerzas Armadas de Liberación Nacional—FALN) can be ascribed to the general conviction that the movement is inspired and supported from foreign bases (see ch. 22, Public Order and Internal Security).

Nationalism has had perhaps its most vocal expression in attitudes, debate, and policy regarding the country's economic resources and development. Although a majority of informed persons concede that United States and European capital and technical capability were indispensable in the development of the vital petroleum and iron industries, continued domination of those fields by foreign companies has given rise to increasing popular resentment. Issues arising out of the preponderance of foreign capital in the petroleum industry have been raised most prominently by politicians of the extreme left, but there is also a much wider segment of public opinion that sees such domination as an affront to national independence.

Thus, for example, many political observers believe that the act of ex-dictator Pérez Jiménez of granting further petroleum concessions during the 1950s contributed materially to his unpopularity and ultimate downfall. Similarly, President Rómulo Betancourt, while seeking to foster confidence among investors by offering explicit guarantees against summary expropriation, nevertheless felt constrained to decree an end to the concession system in petroleum and iron production and in this action incurred no opposition from any political sector.

National Unity

A sense of national unity has increasingly overshadowed the traditional ethnic and regionalist divisions. Since the largest and most advanced Indian groups were either decimated or assimilated early in colonial history, Venezuela has no numerically important enclaves of aboriginal culture and ethnic identity. Similarly, the descendants of the Negro slaves have merged culturally and racially into the national amalgam with somewhat more completeness than in many parts of Brazil. Some members of the upper class are vocally proud of their predominantly European ancestry, but such feelings of racial superiority are, for the most part, submerged in a more general pride in the easy and democratic assimilation of diverse people into national life. Indeed, most educated persons are quick to point to the generous influences of Negro and Indian traditions on the folk culture, and much of the effort of folklorists and ethnologists has been aimed at demonstrating the importance of such influences to national distinctiveness (see ch. 4, Population and Ethnic Groups).

Although there are identifiable differences in cultural tradition among the diverse regions of the country and regionalistic sentiment has not been lacking, such differences have played a relatively minor part in determining political attitudes. The succession of military dictators from the Andean states and the unity in the ranks of their supporters reflected deep-seated regionalist loyalties. Nevertheless, improving communications, population mobility and, not least important, the vigorous suppression of local political leaders by the most powerful of the Andean *caudillos* (see Glossary), Juan Vicente Gómez, have acted to blunt the divisive effects of regionalism. In the mid-twentieth century popular attitudes toward such divisions were largely confined to humor and stereotypes.

If racial and regionalist divisions have offered little impediment to the growth of national unity, class antagonisms have presented a clear and recurrent threat. That the mass of Venezuelans—the majority of whom until recently were illiterate peasants—have nurtured profound resentments toward the elite is evident in virtually all aspects of the country's rich folk culture. Folksongs—especially the traditional *décimas*—express a constant preoccupation with poverty, injustice, and abuse and, in fact, sometimes voice popular resentment against specific governments. Folk tales and folk humor frequently deal with similar themes, often telling the story of the poor and humble man who—through wit and innate superiority—bests his rich and powerful exploiter. In this tradition, Juan Bimba, the popular caricature of the Venezuelan, is seen as a thin, humble, and obviously poor man dressed in peasant garb. As the subject of jokes and cartoons, he views his world sardonically, making biting comments from behind a mask of deceptive humility.

Education, urbanization, and population mobility have all brought the mass of traditionally dispersed and isolated peasants into closer contact with national life. In this process, economic aspirations have risen sharply; mass political appeals to both the farmer and the urban lower class—made possible through improved communications and through labor union organization—have awakened in them a new sense of power. The increasing clamor for land redistribution, beneficent labor legislation, and other types of social and economic reform has consequently become the dominant note in contemporary political life.

The reform programs of the democratic governments since 1958 have apparently gone far toward allaying lower class discontent; politicians of the far left, promising more immediate and radical change, have not succeeded in capturing wide popular support. Nevertheless, isolated incidents during the early 1960s—in particular, the periodic organized invasions of private lands by peasants dissatisfied with the progress of agrarian reform—suggested that there remained a latent resentment.

As the attitudes of the lower class have been transformed from inchoate resentment to political militance, those of the wealthier and more educated classes have also undergone a change since about 1940. Until well after the death of Gómez, the traditional elite of landholders and their generally conservative military allies maintained a stance of implacable opposition to substantial social and economic change and to the establishment of a genuinely popular suffrage. Under the leadership of such men as Eleazar López Contreras, they formed the decisive sector of opinion until the 1945 AD-military coup. The same elitist conservatism was undoubtedly an important factor in the 1948 counterrevolution, which overthrew the elected AD government of Rómulo Gallegos. With the reestablishment of constitutional government in 1958, however, what had been a strong voice in opposition to reform appeared to have been all but silenced.

Most members of the heterogeneous upper class have become convinced that the clamor of a majority of Venezuelans for a greater share of the national wealth can no longer be ignored. A graphic reflection of the recent change in prevailing upper class attitudes is to be seen in the passage of a land reform law in 1960. In part, this rapid change in upper class social attitudes has resulted from the influx of men of lower or middle class origins who had achieved business success in an expanding economy. Such men, either by virtue of their origins or because the basis of their wealth lay in industrial and commercial, as opposed to agrarian, pursuits, have had little reason to defend the vested interest of the old elite; eclipsing the traditional elite in number and wealth, they have come to be the more effective spokesmen of the upper class.

The emergence of the small, but growing and articulate, middle class, itself a product of the massive social change since about 1940, has been an important factor in the national movement toward reform. Its members have provided the most vocal support and much of the leadership of the AD, the Republican Democratic Union (Unión Republicana Democrática—URD), and the Committee for Independent Political and Electoral Organization (Comité de Organización Política y Electoral Independiente—COPEI). In addition, probably the bulk of ideological leadership and support for the radical left comes from the middle class.

ATTITUDES TOWARD THE STATE AND THE POLITICAL SYSTEM

Although the principle of orderly and constitutional succession of governments has gained wide acceptance, the evolution of political interactions in harmony with this ideal was, until the late 1950s, hampered by a heritage of attitudes and values that afforded scant basis for respect and loyalty toward institutional authority. Central in this heritage was the mistrust of government traditionally expressed by the peasants and the urban lower class—a mistrust of institutions that they saw for the most part as responding only to the needs and interests of the small elite.

At another level, the growth of an orderly and constitutional government was impeded by the deep-rooted and persistent value of *personalismo* (a concept that represents a tendency to stress personal qualities and interpersonal trust over abstract ideology and institutionalism). In the context of such values, failure by those in power to reward personal associates and supporters from public resources could be seen as more reprehensible (and politically dangerous) than an occasional lapse in probity. Conversely, only those with personal ties to men in power were able to feel a ready confidence in public authority.

Related to the traditional mistrust of the political process is a widespread cynicism, shared alike by those in power and by the governed. Instances of overt nepotism and self-serving have been so frequent in the country's political history that such practices have been popularly accorded an amused toleration. The traditional use of public employment as a means of cementing political loyalties has been greatly curtailed, however, as a result of the passage in 1970 of a comprehensive law standardizing entry into and promotion within the civil service.

The elected governments since 1958 have had considerable success in overcoming traditional threats to stability and constitutionality. Moreover, it is increasingly apparent that popular attitudes toward government in general are undergoing significant change.

Loyalties directed to the AD and COPEI governments have been demonstrably wider in base and more profound than those accorded any of their predecessors. Further, grounded in this popular support, both the governments and the major parties have arrived at working accommodation with economic interest groups and with the armed forces (see ch. 12, Political Dynamics).

ATTITUDES TOWARD THE CALDERA GOVERNMENT

The attitudes of the majority toward the government of President Rafael Caldera in 1970 ranged from acceptance to enthusiastic support. Even in Caracas, where election returns had generally indicated a negative attitude toward all of the major parties, a majority of the persons interviewed in a newspaper public opinion poll conducted in late 1969 rated President Caldera's management of the nation from "average" to "good."

The popularity of the COPEI government was based on both the personal appeal of President Caldera and the proposals and successes of various governmental projects. Already well known in the country after his fourth campaign for the presidency, Caldera proceeded to visit every state and territory before completing his first year in office. Furthermore, President Caldera, a polished speaker, has made extensive use of television. In 1970, through a weekly televised press conference, he gave a considerable proportion of the population a sense of participation in the affairs of government. Through his many years in public life Caldera has acquired a reputation for perseverance and hard work and, although critics freely assail the COPEI party, the government generally, or specific policies, few have attacked the president personally.

President Caldera's approach to real or potential opponents of his government has generally been conciliatory. One of his first acts in office was to institutionalize periodic consultations with the Federation of Chambers of Commerce and Industry (Federación de Cámaras de Comercio e Indústria—FEDECAMARAS), the powerful organization representing the business community (see ch. 12, Political Dynamics).

He has dealt generously with the military, granting their requests for counterinsurgency weaponry and maintaining for the officer corps a salary level that ranks among the world's highest. As a result of the university reform law passed in 1970 and the occupation of the Central University of Venezuela in Caracas by the armed forces, many of the students who formerly supported COPEI had become alienated from the party and the government (see ch. 7, Education). The president, however, had legalized the Venezuelan Communist Party and had offered amnesty to those guerrillas who would lay down their arms; as a result, terrorist activity had greatly diminished (see ch. 12, Political Dynamics).

Although the government's housing construction program has fallen short of the proposed 100,000 units per year, that program, considerable advances in education, and the beginnings of the construction of a subway in Caracas have generated popular support for the government. The imagination of Venezuelans has also been stirred by the government's plans to develop the country's relatively untapped resources south of the Orinoco River.

SYMBOLS OF THE NATION

The flag is a tricolor of yellow, blue, and red horizontal stripes. In the center of the blue stripe there is an arc of seven white stars representing the seven original states. In the yellow (upper) stripe, next to the hoist, is the national coat of arms (omitted on the merchant flag).

The tricolor, often referred to as the Bolívarian colors from its use as a battle standard of the armies of independence, was actually designed by Francisco de Miranda and first flown by him on the ship *Leander* (see ch. 3, Historical Setting). The intended symbolism in the flag's design expressed the separation of Venezuela (represented in gold) from Spain (represented in red) by the sea. As a plain tricolor, the flag was adopted by the Republic of Gran Colombia, and it is presently used, with variations, by Ecuador and Colombia.

The national coat of arms consists of a shield surmounted by two horns of plenty linked by a laurel branch, flanked on the right by a laurel branch and on the left by a palm branch. The upper half of the shield is divided into two square fields. In the left section, colored red, there is a bundle of wheat stalks, symbolizing both union and agricultural wealth; in the right field, colored yellow, there is a trophy of arms and national flags. The lower half is a blue field on which is represented a white horse running free, symbolizing liberty. Connecting the flanking branches is a ribbon in the national colors bearing, to the left, the inscription 10 de Abril de 1810—Independencia; to the right, 1850—Federación; and in the center, República de Venezuela.

The national tree is the araguaney (*Tecoma chysantha*). The national flower is a species of white orchid called *flor de mayo* (*Cattleya mossiae*).

A campaign song from the wars of independence, "Gloria al Bravo Pueblo" (Glory to the Brave People), is the national anthem, adopted as such by decree of Antonio Guzmán Blanco in 1881. The lyrics were written by Vicente Salías and the music by Juan Landaeta.

Of the official fixed holidays, six commemorate events of historical or patriotic significance. These are: Declaration of Independence and Day of the Indian, April 19 (1810); Labor Day, May 1; Army Day and the Anniversary of the Battle of Carabobo, June 24 (1823); Independence Day, July 5 (1811); Bolívar's Birthday, July 24 (1783); and Columbus Day, October 12.

SECTION III. ECONOMIC

CHAPTER 16

CHARACTER AND STRUCTURE OF THE ECONOMY

In 1970 rapid economic expansion over three decades, largely based on exports of petroleum, had brought the country's estimated gross national product (GNP) to Bs50 billion (4.5 bolivars equal US$1), or to over Bs4,762 per person, despite a rate of population increase that had been an average of 3.5 percent per year during the 1960—69 period (see ch. 4, Population and Ethnic Groups). In 1969 petroleum accounted for 90 percent of the country's export earnings, nearly two-thirds of fiscal revenues, and 17 percent of the GNP.

Production of crude petroleum had increased by over 4 percent per year during the 1958—63 period but by 1.2 percent per year during the 1964—68 period. The reasons for the decline included a policy decision by the government in 1959 to discourage further exploration for petroleum under the concession system and also increased competition in world markets from new low-cost producers elsewhere in the world. Crude oil production decreased slightly in 1969, but unsettled conditions in North Africa and the Middle East led to a recovery in 1970. The government projected an average growth in production of 2.5 percent per year during the 1970—74 period on the assumptions that secondary recovery techniques would increase production from existing fields and that new exploration would again be initiated under service contract arrangements approved late in 1970.

In 1970 continuing ample foreign exchange earnings made possible importation of a wide range of goods (see ch. 20, Trade; ch. 21, Finance). Money wages were relatively high, partly as a result of standards set by the petroleum sector (see ch. 18, Industry; ch. 19, Labor). Tariffs and subsidies had been used by the government both to increase labor productivity per man and to improve the distribution of income. Through 1970 this intervention had been oriented toward promoting the substitution of domestic production for imports (see ch. 20, Trade).

The primary result of the government's intervention had been a rapid rise during the 1950—69 period of the share of manufacturing in the GNP from 10 percent in 1950 to 19.5 percent in 1969 (see ch. 18, Industry). Industrialization had been associated with a rapid process of urbanization (see ch. 4, Population and Ethnic Groups).

Geographic concentration had come with urbanization. The core area of the country can be identified as including the Federal District and the adjoining states of Aragua, Carabobo, and Miranda, which together accounted for 2.4 percent of the national territory (see ch. 2, Physical Environment). By 1970 about 70 percent of the nation's industrial production originated in this area. Three-quarters of industrial employment was found there, and about one-third of the total population was contained in it (see ch. 2, Physical Environment; ch. 4, Population and Ethnic Groups).

In 1970 the government considered the most immediate prospects for expansion of exports to be steel and petrochemicals, both based on natural resources outside the core area. The government estimated that additional export potential also existed in a range of intermediate and finished goods, including processed foods, beverages and tobacco, clothing and footwear, chemical products, and some metallic products. For these, investment and employment were viewed by the government as likely to continue to concentrate in the core area in the light of the early advantages achieved there through the availability of complementary industries and services, overhead facilities, a trained labor force, and ready markets.

A public investment program to cover the 1970—74 period was still in preparation in late 1970. The government had submitted to the National Congress an extraordinary investment program consisting of a list of individual projects for which external borrowing authority was required during the 1971—73 period. The government considered this list as an interim and partial component of the full 1970—74 public investment program (see ch. 21, Finance). The binding constraint on the size of the public investment program was the amount of financing likely to be available. With nearly two-thirds of the current revenues of the national government deriving from the petroleum sector and with petroleum production increasing only slowly, the government estimated that, unless the National Congress enacted the fiscal reforms advocated by the government, revenues could not be expected to increase in step with development needs. The country's unused taxable capacity remained ample in 1970. Current nonpetroleum revenues of the national government in 1969 were lower per person than they had been ten years earlier; they amounted in 1970 to only 7.5 percent of the nonpetroleum GNP.

In 1970 the government anticipated that pressure on the country's balance of payments could be expected to rise with a rate of growth of GNP and of imports in excess of the expected rate of expansion of exports of petroleum. Despite continued restraint on credit, the government expected the cumulative deficit on the balance of payments current account to deteriorate from Bs1.1 billion in the 1965–69 period to Bs7.2 billion in the 1970–74 period (see ch. 20, Trade; ch. 21, Finance). The country's capacity to meet interest and capital payments on additional external debt was considered by international financial organizations to be substantial in 1970. The total external debt outstanding at the end of 1969 was Bs30 million (see ch. 21, Finance). Interest and capital payments on the external debt during the projected 1970–84 period were an average Bs23 million, less than 3 percent of net exports of goods and services in 1969, after deducting investment income payments. The country had an excellent international credit rating, had traditionally adopted a conservative approach to external borrowing, and had met all its foreign obligations since 1906 (see ch. 21, Finance).

PETROLEUM

The government's oil policy in 1970 aimed, as it had for eleven years, at conservation of petroleum, support of oil prices, increased national participation in the benefits of the petroleum industry, and direct national participation in petroleum operations. The government during the 1960s had increased the income tax on petroleum operations (see ch. 21, Finance). It had created the state oil enterprise, the Venezuelan Petroleum Corporation (Corporación Venezolana de Petróleo), which explored for and produced petroleum and refined and marketed it at home and abroad. The government, nevertheless, sought to encourage foreign and local private capital to enter the petroleum sector.

The government that came into office in 1959 had decided against granting any new petroleum concessions because existing areas under concession were far from fully explored. It also developed the concept of service contracts, under which the Venezuelan Petroleum Corporation would contract out certain services, including exploration and production, to expedite the growth of the corporation in competition with existing concessionaires (see ch. 18, Industry).

Subsequent governments had through 1970 continued to prefer to maximize petroleum revenue per barrel rather than total revenue on an absolute or present-worth basis. The government had sought to support oil prices by taking an active part in the Organization of Petroleum Exporting Countries (OPEC), by discouraging until 1967 large discounts off posted prices, and, thereafter, by introducing reference prices for assessment of income tax (see ch. 21, Finance).

The last concessions to foreign companies were granted in 1956 and 1957, bringing the area under concessions to 16.6 million acres.

Subsequent to 1957, 10.6 million acres had reverted to the nation, leaving 6 million acres under concession at the end of 1969. The number of wells drilled during the 1966—68 period was from 300 to 400 per year, mostly production wells in known fields; the number rose to 489 wells in 1969. This level of exploration in the 1960s was about half that of the previous decade.

As a result of the steep decline in exploration, proven reserves had fallen. End-year reserves of proven recoverable crude oil, which had declined from their peak of 17.4 billion barrels at the end of 1960 to 16.8 billion barrels in 1962, were sustained until 1965 by new extensions to reserves. These resulted from a fresh analysis of existing fields, progress in systems of production, and secondary recovery techniques. Subsequent to 1965, however, reserves had fallen to 14.9 billion barrels by the end of 1969. As a result of increasing production, reserves (expressed in years-of-life at then-current production rates) fell steadily from 17.7 years in 1958 to 11.3 years by the end of 1969 (see ch. 18, Industry).

The annual rate of growth of petroleum production declined by 0.3 percent from the 1968 level to 3.6 million barrels per day in 1969. Production was about 3 percent higher in the first half of 1970 than in the same period of 1969 and was expected by the government to average about 2.5 percent higher than 1969 for the whole year. The government had estimated in 1970 that production of crude oil would increase by an average of 2.5 percent per year during the 1970—74 period. This estimate assumed no constraint on the supply of crude oil on the reasoning that the average recovery factor of 18 percent prevailing in 1970 could be economically increased to 30 percent with secondary recovery techniques and that there was scope for new development drilling on existing concession areas.

In September 1967 the Venezuelan Petroleum Corporation announced that it would accept offers for service contracts to explore for and produce oil on five blocks each of 123,500 acres that the government had assigned to the corporation in the southern part of Lake Maracaibo. The chief executive of the Venezuelan Petroleum Corporation informed the press in November 1970 that three private companies had submitted acceptable bids and that he anticipated the service contracts for the five blocks would be awarded by December 31, 1970.

The government estimated the nation's share of total earnings from production of petroleum under service contracts to be not less than 85 percent, compared to the 69 percent (1969) share received under the concession system. The southern area of Lake Maracaibo was in 1970 a test case for the concept of service contracts as a means of preventing reserves from falling below their 1970 level.

The service contracts were also intended by the government to reanimate investments in the oil industry, improve the potential for production and export of oil, strengthen the Venezuelan Petroleum Corporation, and bring the nation into direct participation in producing its oil.

Refining operations in the country began in 1943, and by 1969 there were twelve refineries with a total distillation capacity of 1.3 million barrels per day. They included two of the world's largest refineries, which were the refinery at Cardón and the refinery at Amuay. During 1969 the country's refineries processed an average of 1.2 million barrels per day.

Of the country's output of crude petroleum in 1969, 5 percent was refined domestically for internal consumption in local sales, ship's bunkers, and the petroleum industry itself; 27 percent was refined for export. The remaining 68 percent was exported as crude petroleum; within this balance, 20 percent was shipped to offshore refineries in Aruba and Curaçao for re-export as refined products. These refineries operated essentially on crude petroleum from Venezuela, and international petroleum statistics conventionally treat Venezuela and the Netherlands Antilles as a single exporting unit. Another 5 percent of the country's output of crude petroleum was shipped to a refinery in Trinidad for re-export as finished products. In total the country exported 95 percent of its production in the form of crude petroleum and refined products.

The volume of crude petroleum and refined products exported from the country's ports, which had registered a compound annual growth of 6 percent during the 1954—63 period, grew by 1.2 percent per year during the 1964—68 period and by 1.3 percent from 1968 to 1969, when it averaged 3.4 million barrels per day. This total comprised about 2.5 million barrels per day of crude petroleum, around 700,000 barrels per day of residual fuel oil, and over 200,000 barrels per day of other refined products. Treating Venezuela and the Netherlands Antilles as a single exporting unit, the compound annual growth rate of exports was 4.6 percent during the 1959—63 period, 1.6 percent during the 1964—68 period, and 2.1 percent from 1968 to 1969.

In 1969 the country was still the world's largest single exporter of oil, but the government estimated in 1970 that it was likely to be passed in that year by Iran, Libya, and Saudi Arabia. The country's share of world exports of oil had fallen steadily in the 1960—69 period and was 15.1 percent in 1969. The United States was its most important customer, and Canada, its second. Much of the country's exports to the Caribbean area represented exports to refineries in Puerto Rico and to Trinidad, the latter mainly for re-export to North America.

In 1970 the country had unused potential for the export of manufactured goods in three lines of industrial activity: the processing of natural resources, production of high-quality consumer goods, and the processing of agricultural products. The country's human resources included a relatively literate labor force and a middle class with a rather cosmopolitan outlook and a strong inclination toward being or becoming businessmen (see ch. 5, Social Structure). Substantial immigration had contributed entrepreneurial talent and knowledge learned in more industrialized countries (see ch. 4, Population and Ethnic Groups). The country's natural resources included ample iron ore deposits, considerable supplies of natural gas, cheap hydroelectric power, and a heterogenous agricultural base (see ch. 2, Physical Environment; ch. 17, Agriculture).

Processing of natural resources included the transformation of iron ore into finished steel, the utilization of natural gas to produce ammonia for nitrogenous fertilizers and petrochemical products, and the use of cheap electric power to produce aluminum. By 1970 the country was exporting some steel, mainly in semifinished form; in terms of weight these exports represented almost one-third of the capacity of the principal metallurgical plant. Utilization of natural gas for export had not yet begun in 1970, but plans to build an export-oriented petrochemical complex at El Tablazo in the Maracaibo Lowlands region were well advanced. The country had only started in 1970 to use its cheap electricity as an input into export industries. An aluminum plant had been opened in the Guiana Highlands in the late 1960s; its capacity in 1970 was below optimum at about 25,000 tons, of which 10,000 tons were to be sold in the domestic market and the remaining 15,000 tons were to be exported.

The country had two advantages in the production of high-quality consumer goods. Its domestic market had long been supplied with imports in this field, such as footwear and clothing. Domestic competitors had consequently had to meet world market standards in quality and design. The country has also had considerable foreign exchange at its disposal. As a result, producers possessed very modern equipment in most branches.

The prices of the country's agricultural products were generally above world market prices, but meat, fruits, and fish could be purchased at competitive prices. The country could meet the capital requirements for canning of these products and could maintain the high standards of quality and hygiene necessary for exporting (see ch. 6, Living Conditions; ch. 21, Finance). The country, therefore, had the potential in 1970 of becoming one of the principal exporters of canned food in the Caribbean area.

During the two decades from 1950 to 1970 the share of the manufacturing sector in the GNP had doubled from 10 percent in 1950 to 14.6 percent in 1960 and to 19.5 percent in 1969. The country was very unusual among developing nations in that its industrial output was not outweighed by the product of the agricultural sector but, in fact, exceeded it almost threefold.

Although industrial growth had been much higher than the growth of the GNP, this trend had been decelerating. In the first half of the 1960s the average annual growth rate of industry (excluding petroleum refining) was 11 percent, double the growth rate of the GNP in this period. During the second half of the 1960s the rate of industrial growth slackened; the average annual growth rate was 5 percent, little more than the 3.5 growth rate of GNP. The fall in the rate of growth of the industrial product was the result of the creation of a substantial industrial base, the larger proportions of family budgets absorbed by consumption of industrial goods, the shift of demand to technologically more complex manufactures that are often unavailable in the domestic market, and the larger scale required to produce substitutes for imports.

In 1970 consumer goods contributed almost half of domestic industrial production, with intermediate and capital goods each contributing about one-quarter. The four most marked structural shifts over the 1964—69 period were: a growing share of transport equipment, a rising share of basic metals, a fall in the share of petroleum products, and a drop in the share of food products. Most of these shifts had been induced by government policy. After protection had made profitable the assembly of imported automobile parts, over eighty types of passenger vehicles marketed in the country began to be assembled domestically. Output of basic metals grew with increased utilization of productive capacity in the government steel plant associated with a change in its product mix. The fall in the share of petroleum products reflected the reluctance of foreign companies to continue investing until the future of the oil sector had been clarified. The declining share of food products indicated a decreasing resilience of demand for food relative to income.

In 1970, in addition to export promotion, exploitation of the country's considerable underutilized resources for industrialization depended upon a widening of the domestic market. The country had over 10 million inhabitants and a highly unsymmetrical distribution of income. A study prepared by the Central Bank of Venezuela (Banco Central de Venezuela) showed that in the 1960s as much as 44 percent of all families received only 11 percent of the total income. The same study also indicated that income was disproportionally distributed between rural and urban families. Only 21 percent of families in larger cities, but as many as 67 percent of rural families, earned income of less than Bs6,000 per family per year. Investigations by the Central Bank also revealed that incomes were highly concentrated among cities, with families in Caracas in 1969 enjoying an average income of Bs19,000 per year, compared to about Bs10,000 per family per year in Maracaibo, Barquisimeto, and Barcelona.

A considerable share of the country's industry was foreign-owned in 1970. Excluding petroleum refining, foreign ownership in 1966 accounted for 22 percent of all share capital (see ch. 21, Finance). One-third of foreign capital was concentrated in electrical machinery, largely in small firms run by immigrants who had not acquired nationality (see ch. 4, Population and Ethnic Groups; ch. 5, Social Structure). Foreign capital was also substantial in the chemical industry and in the food industry. The return on capital of foreign investment in manufacturing was lower than the average return for the country's industry as a whole (see ch. 21, Finance).

Public policy had not fostered increased competition in industry. The market was protected as most industrial imports were subject to licensing (see ch. 20, Trade). Investments in new industrial projects and in important extensions of existing industrial capacities were registered with the authorities and, if approved, benefited from important protective measures. Imports of materials and components were duty exempt, registered firms were protected against competing imports, and investors benefited from subsidized interest rates (see ch. 21, Finance).

Direct public investments have been made through transfers from the central government to specialized agencies, such as the Venezuelan Guyana Corporation (Corporación Venezolana de la Guayana) and the Venezuelan Institute of Petrochemicals (Instituto Venezolano de la Petroquímica), which have been responsible for construction of large industrial enterprises. Public investment in industry in 1960 reached a substantial level of Bs2.7 billion channeled into steel and petrochemical plants. It had subsequently declined and stood in 1970 at about Bs85 million annually. During the 1970—74 period, however, the government intended to increase its investment in industry, again mainly in metallurgy and petrochemicals. The share of public sector investment in industry was expected in 1970 to rise from the nearly 25 percent registered in the late 1960s to over 40 percent of total investment in industry (see ch. 21, Finance).

Between 1961 and 1969 the labor force grew at an average rate of 3 percent annually, achieving a total growth of 26 percent by 1969 (see ch. 19, Labor). An estimated 700,000 jobs were generated between 1961 and 1969, an increase of about 87,500 annually. Between 1965 and 1968 new jobs were reportedly created at a rate of 109,000 per year. During the 1960s the tertiary (services) sector created over 490,000 new jobs, whereas agriculture registered a decline of nearly 40,000 jobs.

The share of nonskilled and semiskilled workmen in the labor force was declining in favor of the occupations that required more training, notably professionals and managers. From 1961 to 1969 professional jobs increased by 191 percent. Changes had also occurred in the age structure of the labor force. Whereas persons below twenty years of age made up 19 percent of the labor force in 1950, the figure dropped to 15 percent in 1961 and 14 percent in 1969. In March 1969, 3 percent of the labor force had attained a higher education; 12 percent, some secondary education; and 37 percent, more than four years of primary schooling. The remainder of 51 percent had little or no formal schooling (see ch. 7, Education; ch. 19, Labor).

AGRICULTURE

Agriculture provided in 1970 about 7 percent of the GNP and less than 2 percent of export earnings (see ch. 17, Agriculture; ch. 20, Trade). Because of the large number of people employed in agriculture—over 29 percent of the labor force in 1970—agriculture had a social importance out of proportion to its economic contribution. The country had a total area of 352,000 square miles and an estimated rural population of 2.5 million persons, giving a density of less than 8 rural inhabitants per square mile (see ch. 2, Physical Environment; ch. 4, Population and Ethnic Groups). Much agricultural land, however, suffered from seasonal deficits or surpluses of water, unsuitable terrain, or poor soils. Although the Northern Mountains and Maracaibo Lowlands regions are generally productive and there are possibilities for the extension of rainfed agriculture, elsewhere heavy investment is necessary in irrigation, drainage, or flood control for land development (see ch. 2, Physical Environment). Large areas of the Orinoco Lowlands and the Guiana Highlands are suitable only for extensive exploitation in pasture or forest.

Traditional technology and the limited availability of financial resources to farmers are major constraints to increased agricultural production among both small and large farmers (see ch. 17, Agriculture; ch. 21, Finance). Although the use of machinery, fertilizer, and other agricultural inputs had increased rapidly in the 1960s, this increase had been largely restricted to the production of rice and industrial crops. The public Agricultural and Livestock Bank (Banco Agrícola y Pecuario) had been the principal source of agricultural credit, but its activities had had a heavy social orientation, emphasizing short-term loans at low rates to small producers.

Public sector participation in agriculture is based on the Agricultural and Livestock Bank, the Ministry of Agriculture, and the National Agrarian Institute (Instituto Agrario Nacional), whereas the Ministry of Public Works is responsible for basic investment, including irrigation. The government was attempting in 1970 to improve coordination between the different agencies, the planning and exploitation of irrigation projects, the administration of the price support and credit program, and the extension and research services.

In 1970 the agrarian reform program had been a major component of agricultural policy for twelve years. During this time more than 11 million acres of land had been distributed to over 160,000 families. Whereas this program by its very size had a considerable effect on the rural sector, the benefits to the resettled families appeared in most cases to have been slight. A comprehensive survey by an international organization found that in 1967 the average family income of beneficiaries under the agrarian reform program was Bs3,553, of which nearly one-half was derived from employment away from the farm. The same survey showed that in purely economic terms only one-third of the families were better off than before the reform. An integrated program of agricultural development for 111 agrarian reform settlements, supported by a loan from the Inter-American Development Bank (IDB), was expected by the government in 1970 to play an important role in providing much needed investment in crucial aspects of farm development and in improving the efficiency of the institutions administering the program. Further expansion of agrarian reform settlements was also planned.

The value of agricultural production had maintained a growth rate of over 5 percent annually over the 1960—69 decade. This had been achieved largely by rapid increases in production of sesame, rice, sugarcane, milk, and poultry in response to active government policies and heavy expenditure in this sector. Agricultural exports had grown, but the three principal commodities—coffee, cocoa, and rice—were sold abroad at a loss to the government (see ch. 20, Trade; ch. 21, Finance).

In 1970 past agricultural policy had depended on heavy government subsidies and a protected domestic market in which high production costs were passed on to the consumer. Increased production had led to marketing problems, however, and substitution of domestic products for imports was nearly complete for several commodities. The country's agricultural sector, in its form in 1970, was generally uncompetitive both in the domestic market for capital and in the foreign market for sale of its agricultural products. For certain commodities, however, such as corn, beans, and beef, substitution for imports still offered opportunities for increased production. Advantage could be also taken of the country's well-developed commercial base to supply high-value processed agricultural commodities to a selective world market (see ch. 20, Trade).

CHAPTER 17

AGRICULTURE

In 1970 agriculture generated about 7 percent of the gross national product (GNP) and employed over 29 percent of the labor force. Nearly one-third of the country's total area was agricultural land—used or unused. A national economic policy of agricultural diversification aimed at achieving self-sufficiency in food and fibers and promoting agricultural exports had in four years succeeded in reducing imports of food products from 20 to 8 percent of total imports. The country had become an exporter of some agricultural products that it previously had imported. For seven consecutive years through 1969, except for one year, the output of the agricultural sector had risen at rates greater than the annual increases in GNP as a whole. The annual average rate of increase in production of food in the 1963—69 period had been 7 percent, twice the rate of population growth (see ch. 4, Population and Ethnic Groups).

There still remained a need in 1970, however, for the agricultural sector to improve its productivity in harmony with other sectors of the economy in order to provide its economically feasible portion of the food and fiber needs of the country. The value in 1969 of the product of each economically active person employed in the agricultural sector was calculated at about Bs4,470 (4.5 bolivars equal US$1), about one-fourth of the average product per person for all sectors in 1969.

The latest data available in 1970 indicated that the area devoted to agricultural operations, including livestock raising, was the equivalent of 101,160 square miles, or about 29 percent of the total area of the country. Of this area, 6,500 square miles were under crops, 10,600 square miles were under improved pastures, and 54,000 square miles were under natural or partially improved pastures. The rest was fallow land, land out of use, scrub, and forests, from which a limited amount of timber was removed; an estimated one-fifth of the land covered with forests was potentially tillable (see ch. 2, Physical Environment).

Governmental statistics cited in 1969 showed that two-thirds of all farms were subsistence farms of less than 12 acres, operated by sharecroppers or squatters. The remaining third was owned by larger farmers, who operated the large cattle ranches, the commercial plantations, and the small mixed-crop and specialized farms producing for the market. The large landholdings of from 2,500 acres to 6,125 acres were sugarcane, rice, and cotton plantations. Over 80 percent of agricultural output was produced by the commercial scale farmers.

The Agrarian Reform Law enacted in 1960 established the bases and provided the instruments for a policy aimed at altering the land tenure system and incorporating the rural population into national economic and social development. According to the government's statistics, from the beginning of the program through the end of 1968, there had been allocated for reform purposes 11.2 million acres of private and public lands, private lands being acquired by expropriation or purchase, and 162,137 families had received allotments of land. During 1969, through September 30, the government paid Bs15 million in agrarian debt bonds and Bs13 million in cash to owners of confiscated lands that were part of the over 135,000 acres acquired for agrarian reform in this period and on which 3,395 families were settled.

Subsequent to 1962, the government had given greater attention to the construction needed to consolidate land reform settlements. In 1969 the government had completed a program under which 965 miles of local roads and 337 miles of primary and secondary drainage canals were built; over 116,000 acres were prepared for agricultural production; and irrigation facilities were installed to benefit more than 21,340 acres (see ch. 2, Physical Environment). At the end of 1969 the government prepared an extensive program of agricultural development for four regions, aggregating an area of over 38,000 square miles and a population of nearly 885,000. The program was directed toward benefiting small farmers, mainly those residing in 111 rural settlements containing 12,700 families located in the designated zones. The program included subprograms of settlement consolidation, agricultural research and extension, farm credit and silo construction, irrigation and construction of local roads, and the training of 3,700 professional persons and experts required by the executing government agencies to fulfill their responsibilities under the program.

In 1970 the main crops were corn, rice, potatoes, and sugar. Of the total value of agricultural output in the previous year, 56 percent came from crops; 41 percent, from livestock; 2 percent, from fishing; and 1 percent, from forestry. The predominant portion of agricultural products consumed was produced domestically; only those crops that could not be grown in the country or whose cultivation was not economically sound were imported. The main agricultural imports were wheat and deciduous fruits. As of 1970 the government believed that the country would not be confronted with the severe food crisis that was facing some heavily populated areas of the world. This expectation was based on the facts that very substantial margins existed in the country's natural resource base for raising the output of food and that some progress had been made in increasing the rate of agricultural productivity.

The waters of the country were rich in fishery resources, and the country appeared to have a potentially strong fisheries sector. Inadequate fishing methods and the lack of scientific research, however, had hindered a precise evaluation of the magnitude of these resources. The government had recognized the need for further development efforts in this area and was planning the construction of fishing facilities and the establishment of a fisheries study center.

The production and consumption of forest products was low despite the country's extensive forest resources, but there was an active governmental and private interest in changing this situation. The country's forests in most areas consisted of a mixture of a great many species, of which only a few were of commercial importance, together with thick tropical underbrush (see ch. 2, Physical Environment).

LAND TENURE

The characteristic structure of the country's agriculture has been one in which large concentrations of land are contrasted with small, fragmented holdings; there were a number of large, extensively operated estates and a large number of small farmers trying to make a living on small plots. The nature of production on the large estates was to maximize income while minimizing investments.

Tenure contracts had an important role in the country's agricultural history. Most large landowners who employed tenant farmers were absentee owners whose main source of income was derived from something other than farming. Because tenancy contracts stipulated the type of crops to be raised and the method of cultivation, this provision usually precluded the introduction of new and modern technology. This system retarded development in that neither the landowner nor the peasant was stimulated to invest in the soil. The result was erosion and sterility of the soil (see ch. 2, Physical Environment).

The situation of the squatter was still less conducive to development. The frontier land available for agricultural development was not clearly marked, and there were no clear legal definitions for protection of the peasant squatter. On many occasions a squatter cleared and cultivated land, only to be evicted by the owner who decided to graze his cattle on the cleared land. In such conditions the squatter had no security of tenure and no incentive to invest in the development of his cultivated parcel beyond provision of food for himself and his family.

In 1970 there was still comparatively little pressure of population on the land, considering the country as a whole; there were 5 acres of agricultural land per person. Vast areas of municipal lands and state-owned lands were underdeveloped or not altered by human activity. Although adequate cadastral surveys had not been undertaken to determine precisely the amount of land that could be cultivated more intensively or put into production for the first time, it was estimated in 1970 that without major reconditioning or reclamation at least 15 percent of the total land of the country, or about 33.9 million acres, could be placed in productive use.

In the older, developed agricultural areas, there was some congestion on the land. This had resulted in fragmentation of holdings to the extent that farmers had to rely on tenancy or on sharecropping arrangements with the larger estates to acquire additional workable land. In the agrarian reform settlements, however, the reverse situation had occurred. One case study made in 1966 indicated that, although the size of the plots originally distributed had been small, the average size of a plot had increased because of sharecropping-in-reverse, a process by which a more enterprising farmer hires a less successful farmer who owns a plot of land to work that land, the employer receiving part of the resulting crop at the end of the season.

According to the latest data available in 1970, 67.7 percentof the country's farms were less than 25 acres and were classified as sub-family farms, that is, they employed less than two persons; this type of farm accounted for 2.9 percent of the total area in farms. Farms employing from two to twelve persons, classified as family or medium multifamily and varying in size from 25 to 1,250 acres, made up 30.1 percent of the total number of farms and represented 18.2 percent of the total area in farms. Large multifamily farms, employing more than twelve persons and with a size more than 1,250 acres, accounted for 2.2 percent of the total number of farms and constituted 78.9 percent of the total area in farms.

The land problem in 1970 consisted more of finding people willing to develop and cultivate the vast areas of unused land that were available than of satisfying the strong desire of the landless peasant for acreage. The country was facing the problem of relocating the farm population and developing new lands rather than the redistribution of the limited farmlands in the congested agricultural areas.

There were in 1970 three categories of tenancy that governed the occupancy and farming of land by tenants. One was a form of fixed-rent tenancy, whereby the tenant was granted the full usufruct of a specified area of land, either private or public, and agreed in exchange to pay a predetermined amount in cash or in kind. Generally the tenant was completely free to choose what he wanted to grow or raise on the land and carried on farming operations on his own initiative and bore all the risks of production. A 1967 study indicated that over 9 percent of the total number of farms were operated under this form of tenancy status, known as cash rent, and that such farms accounted for slightly over 2 percent of the total land in farms.

Sharecropping is the occupancy of land through payment of rent in kind by the renter to the owner. Payment on some annual crops occasionally was as high as 50 percent of production. This relationship varied from region to region depending on who supplied the seeds, tools, and facilities as well as on the location of the land and the type of crop grown. The latest data available in 1970 indicated that 8 percent of the total number of farms were operated under this form of tenancy and that these farms represented 1 percent of the total land in farms.

The squatter system of farming had brought devastation to a significant portion of the country's farmland. Using the slash-and-burn method, itinerant squatters settled either on a patch of public land or on private land with the owner's permission. The size, usually from 2-1/2 to 5 acres, depended on the number of members of the family able to work. With handtools, they built a shack, planted corn, potatoes, plantains, manioc, and a few vegetables, and managed to get a few chickens, just enough to feed themselves; some produce had to be sold to buy other necessities. They stayed as long as they were allowed or as long as the soil produced something to eat and then moved on to repeat the process somewhere else. The squatter system encouraged no investments of a permanent nature, such as improved housing, planting of fruit trees, or soil conservation. The system caused the annual migration of these farmers in search of new lands and resulted in a lack of educational, health, and social benefits, which did not reach the migrating people for whom they were intended (see ch. 2, Physical Environment; ch. 5, Social Structure; ch. 6, Living Conditions). The squatter form of tenancy was in operation on 41 percent of the total number of farms, occupying 13 percent of the total area in farms, according to the data available in 1970.

The fundamental characteristic common to almost all types of farms was their extremely low productivity, regardless of size and ownership. The correction of inequality in land distribution and landownership could not provide the efficient use of farm resources nor produce a less inequitable distribution of farm income, for prevalence of low farm income was to a great extent the result of inefficiency in the use of available land and labor. This shortcoming existed because of primitive methods and the poverty of the individual farmers. Improvement of the economic situation of the subsistence farmer required not only widespread ownership of family plots, but increased technical efficiency in agricultural production. In 1970 agricultural output on the agrarian reform settlements was low, mainly because of the lack of sufficient drainage, credit, and assurance that increased productivity would find a market. Agricultural production on farm settlements established by the National Agrarian Institute had increased during the 1961–65 period by over 290 percent, but most of this rise could be attributed to increased extensions of land placed under production. The average value of production per farm family in the agrarian reform settlements in 1965 was nearly Bs3,800, about one-half of the country average of Bs8,000 for the value of agricultural production in that year.

AGRICULTURAL PRODUCTION

Crops

According to the data available in 1970, of the nearly 62 million acres devoted to agricultural pursuits, 1.62 million acres were under permanent crops, and 4.5 million acres were under annual and semipermanent cultivation. Most farmers were engaged in subsistence agriculture, growing corn, beans, yuca, yams, potatoes, plantains, and some other fruits and vegetables, primarily for their own consumption, on small plots in marginally productive lands with very little, if any, surplus to sell to the market. The remaining farmers operated the large cattle ranches, the large commercial farms, the small-sized mixed farms, and the small specialized farms producing for the market. The farmers who were responsible for the substantial increase in agricultural production in the 1960s were those who had cultivated the country's export crops—rice, sugar, coffee, and cacao—and other important commercial crops, such as bananas, copra, sesame, tobacco, cotton, and sisal, for the domestic market.

The expansion of food and industrial crops for domestic consumption and for new exports has meant a shift away from crops grown on irregular terrain by manual labor to the cultivation of the lower, hotter flatlands more suited to mechanized cultivation.

Corn

In 1970 corn remained the principal crop and the traditional basic cereal in the national diet (see ch. 6, Living Conditions). The cultivation of corn was the basis of the structure of rural economic life in almost all parts of the country (see ch. 5, Social Structure). More than half the farmers produced corn. About three-quarters of the crop was grown on small plots, together with beans, yuca, and other starchy subsistence crops, or on land having considerable slope.

Because these lands were frequently badly eroded and the farming techniques were primitive, yields were very low. Some corn was also produced by the larger farms on flat land or rolling land with some modern equipment.

A decrease in direct human consumption of corn per person in the 1960s had been generally offset by the increasing demand for corn in livestock and poultry feeds. Imports of corn had been relatively small in the mid-1960s, amounting to about 10 percent of domestic production, shortages of corn for feed being met by imports of wheat.

In 1969 about 1.5 million acres were planted to corn, harvested production from 1968 plantings reaching 720,000 tons. The government announced late in 1969 a significant reduction in harvested acreage in 1969 because of planted acreage that had been adversely affected by unseasonal rains and floods. The government also made public plans to import in 1970 about 150,000 tons of corn because of adverse weather conditions in 1969.

In March 1970 the government announced its intention to induce the planting to corn in 1970 of an additional 275,000 acres to attain an increase in production of 220,000 tons in the 1971 harvest. In 1971 further acreage was to be planted to corn, and the government would work to increase yields materially with the aim of eliminating all imports of corn by 1972. The plan to increase production of corn was essentially one of maintaining all production areas under control of, and in close contact with, the government's agricultural extension services, recommending and helping producers in all aspects of crop management that contributed to increased yields and better handling practices. The plan also included supervised credit activities plus arrangements for supplying improved seed and fertilizers and other chemical needs of growers.

Rice

Rice, like corn, is a staple of the national diet. The bulk of the crop is of the upland variety, and production for the market is concentrated on the large mechanized farms. Minimum rice prices are guaranteed to producers, crop financing is available, and imports are limited, thus stimulating the production of rice. In response to these inducements, output rose from about 166,000 tons in 1964 to an estimated 380,000 tons in 1969.

Despite the problem of a surplus production of rice in 1968 and 1969, the expansion of acreage planted to rice and of production of rice was continuing in 1970. The government was also encouraging a shift to higher yielding Philippine varieties. The efforts of the government to find export markets for the country's rice surplus had through mid-1970 been successful to some extent but not to the desired volume. Fairly regular shipments had been made to African destinations amounting to about 35,000 tons annually; at the end of 1969 surplus rice in storage amounted to about 225,000 tons. In mid-1970 most of this surplus was removed by the sale of 200,000 tons to United States wholesalers.

Coffee

The country was at one time one of the world's major producers of coffee, but in 1970 it had a relatively insignificant position as producer and exporter. Major causes that contributed to this situation were the failure to replace old trees and rising production costs. Coffee is grown at varying altitudes above 1,500 feet (see ch. 2, Physical Environment). Most of the trees are cultivated in high valleys or on the moderately moist slopes of the Andes and the northern ranges from 1,500 to 6,000 feet above sea level with suitable permanent shade. The country's mild coffee is well known for its high quality. Coffee production for the 1970/71 coffee marketing year (October 1—September 30) was estimated at 48,000 tons.

Sugarcane

Sugarcane is grown in most sections of the country in a wide variety of soils and at various altitudes. Large acreages are concentrated in the alluvial valleys of the northern coastal states. Production of raw sugar for 1969 amounted to 384,000 tons. The sugarcane from the large estates usually goes to the government sugar mills to be refined, but much of the cane from smaller farms is used for making brown sugar loaf, rum, or alcohol or is cut into joints for sale or for household consumption (see ch. 6, Living Conditions).

Cacao

Cacao production, like that of coffee, has been stagnant because of the neglect of groves and the failure to replace deteriorating trees with new, higher yielding varieties. Output in 1969 was 27,000 tons. In addition to aging trees, other factors causing a stagnant level of production have been disease, labor shortages, and drought. Many of the large cacao producers have been deterred from planting by the long-term investment required for cacao production because young trees do not bear until they are five or six years old.

Other Crops

Tobacco was the first plant grown in the country on a commercial basis. Of the two varieties grown in the country, black and light

Virginia, the latter is used for the most part to make certain popular brands of United States cigarettes under license. In 1970 about 7,200 plots grew tobacco on slightly over 31,000 acres. Production in 1969 was around 10,000 tons.

Production of cotton has been continually increasing to meet the demand of the textile industry; in 1969 about 15,000 tons were produced. Yields per acre have been low. Large plantations, of which there were some 7,000 in 1970, use modern cultivation methods. A substantial portion of the crop, however, comes from small farms where such facilities are not used.

The country's cottonseed output has been very small, and future increases will largely depend upon the expansion and improvement of cotton production. Sesame production is on a relatively large scale on fully mechanized farms and in 1969 set a record of 83,000 tons.

Plantains and bananas are an important supplementary food in the local diet. The total area under plantains and bananas is second in importance only to corn. In 1969 some 1.3 million tons of bananas and 660,000 tons of plantains were produced.

Root crops, such as yuca, yams, and sweet potatoes, are widely grown as subsistence crops both on large estates and in small clearings. Because potatoes are particularly well suited to higher altitudes, native varieties are grown in the highland areas. Potatoes were in the late 1960s displacing yuca as the most consumed tuber. Production of potatoes increased yearly in the late 1960s and reached 165,000 tons in 1969. Potatoes are a staple food of the peoples of the highlands and also find an urban market.

The local legumes are mostly black beans, kidney beans, lima beans, and peas. Beans constitute one of the basic foodstuffs in the local diet and provide an important source of inexpensive protein.

Practically every tropical fruit grows well in the country. Oranges are the most important citrus fruit. About 2.2 million plants in eighteen states of the country produce 400 million oranges annually. Other fruits are mango, guava, pineapple, melon, pawpaw, avocado, and numerous small fruits.

Livestock

There were, at the end of 1969, approximately 7.2 million cattle, raised primarily for meat and hides, dairy herds making up a small minority. The production of beef in 1969 reached 195,000 tons. Several factors contributed to the disproportionately low figures for meat production. The great herds of the plains are the descendants of the lightweight Spanish cattle of the colonial period. The heat- and pest-resistant zebu cattle and the Santa Gertrudis cattle of Texas have been imported for crossbreeding; in 1967 over 2,300 zebu cattle were imported, which was double the total number imported two years earlier. Because importation of cattle found particularly adaptable to the country's climatic conditions began on an important scale in the 1960s, the effects of crossbreeding on the quality of domestic cattle were only beginning to be apparent by 1970. The hard and fibrous grass of the plains is not particularly nutritious, and the plains are alternately two wet or too dry (see ch. 2, Physical Environment).

The bulk of the beef from the plains is flown daily to the largest cities in the north-central part of the country. Although plane freight is costly, this means of transport has been found more profitable to the cattleman than taking cattle over long distance by truck, which causes the steers to lose considerable weight in transit.

Cattle range at will over most of the 119,000 square miles forming the five states of Apure, Barinas, Cojedes, Guárico, and Portuguesa. Few properties are fenced. Ranches are so large, some over 1 million acres, that construction of fences or other divisional indicators would be extremely expensive. Cattle belonging to different owners mingle, and the only way to ascertain ownership is through each owner's particular brand. The large herds of beef cattle on the open ranges of the plains account for approximately 70 percent of the cattle population and over 80 percent of the total stock-farming area. The slow and gradual natural increase in the size of the country's cattle stock has been raised by continual illicit movement of herds from Colombia to Venezuela, where prices are higher.

The government's cattle development program, in addition to crossbreeding, includes: construction of artificial lagoons to provide drinking water for cattle in the dry season; erection of silos to store fodder and feed the cattle in the rainy season; construction of new slaughterhouses with ample refrigeration facilities; provision of credits to cattlemen; and the opening in February 1969 on the Paraguaná Peninsula of a quarantine station claimed to be the first of its kind in Latin America. The quarantine station was expected to facilitate the importation of zebu cattle from Brazil. Other measures aimed at increasing the productivity of the country's cattle include the training of technicians in artificial insemination and the improvement of pasturelands.

Milk production had risen to 767,000 tons by 1969, supplying 70 percent of total demand for milk and milk products. The principal dairy region is the state of Zulia, a fertile area with year-round pastures. Zulia is believed to produce from 80 to 85 percent of the total supply of raw milk, and four of the country's five powdered milk plants are located in Zulia. The country's dairy herds were estimated to number about 300,000 in 1970, most being situated in Zulia. Herds are generally rather small, 80 percent of the farms having less than 100 head of cattle each.

A powdered milk plant was opened in March 1969 in the state of Mérida. In the same year construction of a pasteurizing and bottling plant in Puerto Ordáz, part of the growing Ciudad Guayana industrial complex in the southeastern part of the country, was begun; the area was in 1970 continuing to receive its milk by airplane or truck from milksheds as distant as 400 miles (see ch. 18, Industry).

The number of hogs was estimated in 1968 to be about 2 million; about 33,000 tons of pork was produced in 1969. The government has attempted to promote the development of pork production by requiring importers of pork to provide evidence of having purchased 8 pounds of domestic pork for every pound of pork to be imported. In 1969 hogs provided about 15 percent of the country's meat supply.

Goats, estimated in 1968 to number about 1.3 million, are found chiefly in the semiarid coastal regions and in the Andes. They are raised for milk, meat, and hides and subsist on very poor pasturage. The number of sheep was calculated in 1968 to be about 100,000; some wool is produced, spun, and woven in the Northern Mountains. Horses and mules are raised for cattle herding. Burros are widely used as pack animals, but the use of work animals is relatively limited. Oxen are used as draft animals on the medium-sized farms.

The commercial poultry and egg business has expanded with the growth of urban markets and through the protective measures accorded by the government. Egg production was estimated for 1968 at 611 million; self-sufficiency was attained in 1968, and small quantities of eggs were exported to Caribbean destinations.

Fishing

The country's extensive coastline provides some excellent fishing grounds. The coastal waters of the eastern half of the country are sources of tuna, sardines, snappers, Spanish mackerel, bluefish, and mullet. In the western zone from eastern Falcón to the Colombian border, shrimp, shark, croaker, and sea trout are taken. The commercial catch in 1969 totaled 132,000 tons.

The fishing sector was in 1970 registering the important movements initiated in 1967. Several government and nongovernmental projects had been started for the purpose of assessing the country's fishing resources; as a consequence, several government-sponsored programs had been organized to add impetus to the growth of the sector. The value of fish production rose by over 17 percent in 1969, and the government's hopes for continued favorable growth of the sector were high. In 1968, 33,558 persons were directly employed in the fishing sector; there were over 200,000 coastal part-time fishermen; and about 7,000 persons were employed in the fish-processing plants in Cumaná, Punto Fijo, and Maracaibo (see ch. 18, Industry; ch. 19, Labor). The contribution of fishing to the national food supply had increased by nearly 90 percent during the fourteen years ending in 1969 (see ch. 6, Living Conditions).

The government's studies found that the fishing sector had been hampered in its growth by inadequate marketing, high fixed costs for processed fish products, lack of advertising to create a larger domestic market for fish products, little exploration of the possibilities of expanding sales in foreign markets except in the case of shrimp, and failure to meet the needs of the sector for modern fishing vessels and equipment. The government's plans in 1970 included greater investment and more participation in the activities of the fishing sector. The government believed that the national consumption of animal proteins could be significantly increased through the encouragement of increased consumption of fish products. With the planned completion of the major international fishing port at Güiria in the Gulf of Paria in 1971, prospects of expanding the domestic market and creating new export markets for fish products appeared promising in 1970.

In 1966 the government announced that it would finance the establishment of a national fishing fleet of modern vessels equipped with refrigeration and the latest fishing aids and gear. The project provided for 111 trawlers, 21 tuna vessels, and 14 boats for general fishing. The government would finance 85 percent of the sale value of each vessel; repayment was to be made over a five-year period, and interest was set at 8 percent. The government has also provided financial support to five privately owned boatyards. In 1969 there were over 9,290 fishing boats of all kinds; the number of trawlers had increased from 116 in 1968 to 163 in 1969.

Forestry

The country has extensive forest reserves. Surveys indicate that approximately 40 percent of the total land area is covered by forests, which contain many species of trees (see ch. 2, Physical Environment). The development of the lumbering industry, however, has been hampered by inaccessibility of some of the forest regions, restrictive government measures originally designed to correct previous wasteful practices, the shortage of available capital for improvement of equipment, inefficient cutting methods and worker training, and the lack of technical assistance for the requisite intensive investigations and research.

In 1968 an estimated 1.2 percent of the country's total forest area was being used economically; the methods of exploitation were generally very selective and destructive. A limited number of species were utilized because of the lack of integrated enterprises for the exploitation of the forests and the absence of technological information about the numerous species in the country's tropical forests. Fire control services were estimated to be effective for about 10 percent of the country's forested areas. Large forest reserves cover about 13.3 million acres.

A law governing forests, soils, and waters was enacted on December 30, 1965. The law governs the conservation, development, and utilization of the forests and their products, public and privately owned waters, soils, and activities related to these resources. The law asserts that the nation is obligated to promote and conduct the scientific research necessary for a rational development of forests, soils, and waters, for which appropriate research centers are to be established. Protective forest zones and forest reserves are declared to be of public benefit. The following activities were declared to be of public interest: the introduction and propagation of new forest species; prevention, control, and extinction of forest fires; reforestation; and the preparation of a national forest inventory.

ROLE OF THE GOVERNMENT

Planning and Development

Action in planning, coordination, and development in agriculture has been assumed almost exclusively by the government. In addition to setting goals of growth and carrying out the agrarian reform program, it has taken an active part in capitalization, technical study and, in some cases, operations in order to raise and improve the standard of living of the rural population and incorporate it in the nation's economy. The Central Office of Coordination and Planning (Oficina Central de Coordinación y Planificación), the general government planning agency, includes agricultural planning in its scope. Its National Plan (Plan de la Nación) for the 1970—74 period included a part outlining agricultural development policy. Aims of the policy were: to increase the incomes of agriculturists in a manner designed gradually to decrease the discrepancy between agricultural and industrial incomes; to improve the distribution of rural incomes; to obtain a more efficient use of the factors of agricultural production; to decrease progressively the levels of underemployment in rural areas; to increase significantly production of new agricultural exports; to guarantee the availability of raw materials in the quality and condition required by industry at prices and grades satisfactory to the producer and reasonable for the consumer; to execute integrated projects of regional development; and to promote the adequate conservation of renewable natural resources.

The three governmental agencies that in 1970 bore most of the responsibility for planning and executing agricultural development programs were the Ministry of Agriculture, the Agricultural and

Livestock Bank (Banco Agrícola y Pecuario), and the National Agrarian Institute (Instituto Agrario Nacional). The Agricultural and Livestock Development Bank (Banco de Desarrollo Agropecuario) began functioning at the start of 1970; as of late 1970, the ultimate role this agency would play in the agricultural development process was undefined other than its statutory directive of advancing credits to the commercial farming area of the agricultural sector.

The Ministry of Agriculture was concerned primarily with production factors, such as output projections, productivity of resources, rural mechanization, cooperatives and extension services, and research. It also acted as the coordinating body for other governmental and private agencies. In 1969 the ministry established a new section for the promotion of agricultural exports; the section was inaugurated with the aim of coordinating activities that previously had been undertaken by a number of organizations independently and with multiple duplication of effort. Work of the new section was planned to include selection of agricultural products, different from traditional exports, for which the economics of marketing and production were to be studied and trials made with competitive suppliers and experimental shipments. The new section was also designed to deal with specific problems of exportation, such as technical assistance for production, control of quality and sanitary conditions, establishment of grades and standards, development of market information, and financing of exports (see ch. 20, Trade).

The Agricultural and Livestock Bank concerned itself with loans and credits to farmers. It was active in carrying out agrarian reform by providing credit for seeds, tools, and living expenses to the members of agrarian reform settlements. It made loans or gave credit to individuals and cooperatives. The members of the agrarian reform settlements usually pledged a portion of their crop at a supported price as collateral, and the Agricultural and Livestock Bank subsequently marketed the crop or stored it for the next year's seed. The bank also administered a graduated price support program for staple products and operated storage facilities, such as grain elevators, dryers, and warehouses. In addition, the Agricultural and Livestock Bank had sole authority to import agricultural products; it exercised this right only when the domestic crop fell short of internal demand. Corn, beans, and cotton were the products most often supported in this fashion (see ch. 20, Trade).

The funds of the Agricultural and Livestock Bank were controlled by the Ministry of Finance. The bank's controlling board included representatives from the National Agrarian Institute and the Peasants' Federation of Venezuela (Federación Campesina de Venezuela). The bank's representatives, in turn, served on the ministry committees, thus forming interlocking directorates that determined agricultural marketing and price policies.

The National Agrarian Institute is charged with the administration of the agrarian reform program according to the Agrarian Reform Law of March 1960. The institute acquires and purchases land and decides the amount to be paid for the land, the size of the land parcels, and the identity of the beneficiaries. The law provides that the institute be operated by a directorate consisting of a president and four directors, two of whom represent peasant organizations and another who is a professional agronomist; all the members are appointed by the president of the country. There are also bimonthly meetings of a coordinating committee, consisting of representatives from the ministry, the National Agrarian Institute, the Agricultural and Livestock Bank, and the Peasants' Federation of Venezuela. The minister of agriculture is the president of the coordinating committee and has the responsibility of giving direction to agrarian reform and ensuring efficient joint effort.

The National Agrarian Institute is aided in its agricultural colonization program by numerous other agencies. The Ministry of Public Works is responsible for construction of penetration roads on newly opened land and for the irrigation and drainage programs. When the National Agrarian Institute distributes land to the peasants or charters a cooperative, the institute plans for basic utilities and either provides the power, water, schools, and houses itself or calls in other agencies.

The role of private organizations in long-range agricultural development has been small and generally confined to service activities. The Rural Welfare Council (Consejo de Bienestar Rural) has been active in area and development studies and in technical services on a contract basis. The Foundation for Training and Research on Agrarian Reform (Fundación para la Capacitación e Investigación Aplicades a la Reforma Agraria) was in 1970 assigned the task of training 3,700 professional persons and experts required by the executing agencies to fulfill their responsibilities under the agrarian reform program.

Agrarian Reform

The Agrarian Reform Law of March 5, 1960, deals not only with problems of land tenure but also with other aspects of a comprehensive agricultural policy. The stated objective of the law is to transform the agrarian structure of the country and to incorporate the rural population into the economic, social, and political development of the nation by replacing the system of large, landed estates with one of just ownership, tenure, and exploitation of land.

Three kinds of land are subject to expropriation: uncultivated land; farms worked indirectly through renters, sharecroppers, and other intermediaries; and lands suitable for cultivation but devoted to natural pasture for extensive livestock raising. Private lands can be expropriated only if no publicly owned properties are available in the same area. The law also fixes the absolute size limits below which private land cannot be expropriated. Landholdings usually exempt from expropriation are those not exceeding 371 acres of first-class or 741 acres of second-class agricultural land and those with 4,940 acres of first-class or 12,350 acres of second-class grazing land. In certain cases of serious land pressure, however, land can be expropriated without regard to the criteria of size and land use. At the time of the passage of the Agrarian Reform Law in March 1960, approximately 2,500 holdings exceeded the legal limits and could technically be expropriated; these estates included nearly 60,000 square miles.

Under the law present occupants, tenants, and agricultural laborers are given first preference for land parcels. The lands taken over are to be paid for in cash up to Bs100,000. Above this amount, part of the payment is to be in cash and part in bonds; payment is to be made at current market value. The sales price to new owners includes the cost of purchase plus improvements; payment can be extended over a period of twenty to thirty years, and annual amounts are not to exceed 5 percent of gross income from sales of produce. In some cases land can be distributed free of charge. Once the application for land has been accepted by the National Agrarian Institute, applicants are required to form an administrative committee to handle local affairs and act as liaison with the institute. Provisional titles are extended after one year. Permanent title is issued after a farmer has paid for his land in full. In addition to these directives controlling land tenure, the Agrarian Reform Law contains provisions dealing with farm credit, marketing, extension services, cooperatives, land development, and other supplementary measures.

Decree 192 of November 1964 gave unsettled public lands to the National Agrarian Institute for redistribution. Land affected by this decree consisted of 18.7 million acres, mostly in the states of Zulia, Portuguesa, Táchira, Cojedes, and Barinas, where agricultural development had been the greatest in the early 1960s and was believed to have the best future possibilities. Limited land surveys, however, did not allow a definition of the difference between private and public lands. Decree 277 was passed in February 1965 to remedy this situation; the decree established a committee to determine the location and principal characteristics of unsettled public lands.

Decree 746 of February 8, 1967, contained the regulations in effect in 1970 for implementing the Agrarian Reform Law of 1960, giving detailed rules for carrying out the provisions of that law in respect to the allotment of lands and all other aspects. A registry of available lands was to be undertaken progressively by the National Land Office (Oficina Nacional de Catastro de Tierras y Aguas) in each municipality of the country. The registry of lands has three aspects—physical, legal, and evaluative—and involves two steps—a preparatory, or advance, appraisal, including the physical study and preliminary soil classification and legal data, and a definitive assessment in which the lands are evaluated and the legal situation is investigated in full. A registry was to be kept, including maps or charts of all parcels of land, and air photographs covering each municipality were to be studied. In registering each parcel, a title search was to be made as far back in time as records could be found. Each parcel was to be given a code number. All property owners were expected to meet for determination of location and, on the basis of the owner's documents, records of registers, and any other information obtained, a certificate was to be issued in duplicate, one copy for the National Land Office and one for the local office.

The decree prescribed a point system for the classification of lands, which may be used as a basis in considering the allotment and use thereof under various provisions of the Agrarian Reform Law and its regulations, including the size of the parcel reserved to a landowner whose holding is otherwise expropriated. Classification was to be based on soil analysis, topography, climate and water supply, and accessibility to markets.

Production Credits

Agricultural credit is extended by the Agricultural and Livestock Bank, the Venezuelan Development Corporation, and the National Agrarian Institute. In May 1970 the Inter-American Development Bank approved three loans equivalent to US$75 million to assist in financing a program of integrated agricultural development. A law of August 1, 1967, created the Agricultural and Livestock Development Bank to take over the function of lending to commercial farmers, which through 1969 remained one of the two agricultural credit functions of the Agricultural and Livestock Bank.

In the 1964—69 period annual totals of loans extended by the Agricultural and Livestock Bank had ranged from Bs263 million in 1964 to Bs312.1 million in 1969. In these years the Agricultural and Livestock Bank had two separate credit departments: one was for small and medium farmers and included a supervised credit program in which technical advice and assistance were provided, together with financing; the other was designed to meet the needs of the larger commercial farmers and livestock ranchers. The Agricultural and Livestock Bank had increasingly concentrated in the latter 1960s on the credit requirements of small and medium farmers who were participating in the agrarian reform program. Effective January 1970 the responsibilities of the Agricultural and

Livestock Bank in regard to the commercial farming sector were transferred to the new Agricultural and Livestock Development Bank, except for previous loans by the Agricultural and Livestock Bank to commercial farmers amounting to Bs400 million.

The National Agrarian Institute extended directed credit to the agrarian reform settlements in 1969 for the cultivation of corn, rice, cotton, peanuts, sorghum, cassava, and beans. At the beginning of 1969 a directed credit program for the cultivation of coffee was inaugurated; credits amounting to Bs468 million were extended for this purpose in 1969. The institute also made loans of Bs236 million in 1969 under the livestock development program.

One aspect of the integrated agricultural development project for which the Inter-American Development Bank approved assistance, amounting to the equivalent of US$75 million in May 1970, was provision of short-, medium-, and long-term credits to be provided through the Agricultural and Livestock Bank for financing of the cultivation of 12,700 plots and construction of silos with a capacity of 74,000 tons.

Because many of the agricultural credit loans are related to special credit programs for specific commodities, a farmer is able to apply for a number of loans for different commodities. Each loan is processed separately by different officials. The commodity-by-commodity approach has led to emphasis on short-term seasonal credit for crops, which has hampered the investment of public funds in medium- and long-term projects (see ch. 21, Finance).

Marketing and Storage

The development of main roads and air transportation has brought farm producers into closer contact with central markets. The intercity network of highways is generally excellent, making transportation between large centers relatively easy (see ch. 20, Trade). Feeder roads, on the other hand, are insufficient, and the majority of farmers do not have access to good central markets. Prices therefore vary widely between different markets, and the gap between producers' receipts and consumer costs is large; in the case of rice, for example, in 1965 the retail price per pound was three times the price paid to the farmer.

Marketing methods tend to be deficient for such nonstandardized and perishable items as livestock, meat, eggs, fruits, and vegetables; fairly regular marketing channels exist for dairy products, tobacco, sugarcane, oilseed, and cotton. Marketing of processed agricultural commodities is relatively efficient. The majority of agricultural commodities are nonstandardized, ungraded, and traded in small lots on the basis of physical inspection. Farmers either bring their produce to small municipal markets or sell to truckers, who deliver to the public market. The truckers sell to small retailers and to consumers from their trucks.

Most of the retail shops are family enterprises, depending on low volume, slow turnover, and high markups. Storage of agricultural products has been hampered by inadequate sanitary standards, inexpert processing, and nonstandard grading. Facilities for small-scale commercial shortage are few, resulting in seasonal gluts and shortages, particularly for perishable commodities, that are reflected in sharp seasonal price variations.

In response to the almost total lack of an organized marketing system for agricultural products, six members of the Chamber of Deputies cooperated with the Ministry of Agriculture in developing a draft bill to regulate the marketing of agricultural products in their raw or natural state. The first draft of the bill was made public in October 1969. The legislation would cover all agricultural products that have not been processed in any way and all stages from the producing zones to the processing plants and marketing centers. Major objectives of the proposed law would be to guarantee to the farmer a profitable minimum price for his crop and to eliminate the possibility of controlled or monopolized distribution of agricultural produce. A corporation with a separate legal personality and principal offices in Caracas would be formed for marketing agricultural products; all of its personnel would be government employees. The corporation would purchase and sell agricultural products, purchase national crops at the minimum prices fixed by the Ministry of Agriculture, import agricultural products and raw materials necessary to meet deficits in national production, establish distribution channels, fix subsidies and other types of incentives for agricultural production, contract for the construction of storage facilities, and sponsor the formation of farmers' cooperatives.

CHAPTER 18

INDUSTRY

In 1970 the country was becoming increasingly dependent upon an expanding industrial economy. The most dynamic industrial sector in 1970 was manufacturing, which in 1967 contributed for the first time a larger proportion of the gross national product (GNP) than petroleum. Petroleum continued to play a major role; the country's 1969 petroleum production of 3.6 million barrels per day and shipment abroad of over 1.2 billion barrels in that year made it one of the world's leading oil producers and exporters. With the successive implementation of the country's development efforts, however, the relative shares of the GNP generated by other industrial sectors had risen substantially. In 1969 the principal industrial branches generated 44.9 percent of the GNP and employed 24.2 percent of the labor force. The GNP contributions were distributed as follows: manufacturing, 19.5 percent; petroleum, 17.1 percent; construction, 5.8 percent; power production (electricity, gas, and water), 1.5 percent; and minerals, 1 percent.

The government viewed its managerial position in the industrial development field as limited to industries of a basic character that provided essential primary materials and were, consequently, of central importance to the economy. In addition, the government was prepared to participate in the formation of specific industries required in the public interest, particularly those not attractive to private investment because of low initial yield. The government had stated its intention to remove itself from such areas when private capital did become available for them.

The government accorded high priority to the development of the manufacturing sector of the economy. The major objective of this policy was to diversify the industrial base, create employment, lower imports, and reduce the dependence of the economy upon the petroleum sector. The government offered a variety of incentives to private investors in order to encourage industrialization. Included among these incentives were tariff or other import restrictions for the protection of local industries, provision for the duty-free importation of requisite capital equipment and raw materials, and exemption from certain taxes. In addition, the Venezuelan Development Corporation (Corporación Venezolana de Fomento) offered technical assistance, feasibility studies, and loans to industries in which further development was desired.

Partly as a result of these efforts, the average annual increase in the value of manufacturing production during the 1963–69 period had been 6 percent, reaching an estimated Bs10.4 billion (4.5 bolivars equal US$1) in 1969. The growth of the manufacturing sector had promoted import substitution, diversification of potential exports, and the provision of additional jobs for the rapidly growing population (see ch. 4, Population and Ethnic Groups; ch. 20, Trade). In 1969 the manufacturing sector employed 430,900 persons, an increase of 18.6 percent over the 1964 level of 363,200. Chief manufacturing divisions were food and beverages, textiles and wearing apparel, chemicals, metal products, and automobile vehicles.

The petroleum industry continued in 1970 to be of major significance for the national economy; the industry accounted for about 90 percent of the country's foreign exchange earnings and about 65 percent of total government revenues (see ch. 20, Trade; ch. 21, Finance). Since 1960 the government had consistently pursued a policy of not granting further concessions to private companies, encouraging the companies instead to increase activities at existing concessions. In addition, the government had been preparing to enter into service contracts by which private companies would carry out exploration and exploitation activities for the government-owned Venezuelan Petroleum Corporation (Corporación Venezolana de Petróleo). The National Congress had in August 1970 approved minimum acceptable terms for the service contracts.

In a press conference in mid-October 1970, the president announced that the eleven United States and European companies that had originally bid on service contracts for exploration and drilling rights on new potential oilfields in southern Lake Maracaibo had been reduced to four. Although a deadline for announcing the award of the service contracts had not been set, the chief executive of the Venezuelan Petroleum Corporation stated publicly in late October 1970 that he expected the first service contracts to be signed by the end of 1970.

Three basic arrangements, all involving the participation of the Venezuelan Petroleum Corporation, were contemplated under the proposed contracts that could extend for a period of from fifteen to twenty years from the initiation of commercial exploitation. The three basic forms were: mixed enterprises (the Venezuelan Petroleum Corporation and specific private companies) for extraction only; mixed, integrated enterprises to both produce and market; and direct-service contracts to produce and (or) sell petroleum for the Venezuelan Petroleum Corporation. The award of new petroleum exploitation areas was contemplated under the government's plan, with the Venezuelan Petroleum Corporation gradually assuming complete control of all domestic production and marketing.

Proved reserves of petroleum in 1969 were estimated at approximately 14.9 billion barrels. At current rates of consumption, this was equivalent to slightly over an eleven-year supply. The government's petroleum policy emphasized that petroleum was a nonreplenishable asset and that current revenues must be utilized to create new sources of wealth, thus reducing the country's dependence on the petroleum industry. In addition, the government sought to protect prices in international petroleum and petroleum product markets through the country's membership in the Organization of Petroleum Exporting Countries (see ch. 13, Foreign Relations). The government also aimed to increase national participation in the production and distribution of petroleum through the further expansion of the Venezuelan Petroleum Corporation.

Approximately two-thirds of the country's crude petroleum was refined outside the country, mainly in Curaçao, Aruba, Trinidad and Tobago, and the United States. Refinery facilities had expanded rapidly, however, with 32 percent of total 1969 production, or an average of about 1.2 million barrels per day, being refined locally. In 1969 there were fifteen refineries in operation. Except for the government-owned Venezuelan Petroleum Corporation refinery at Morón, all the refineries were owned by private international petroleum companies.

Natural gas was being produced in large quantities as a byproduct of petroleum exploitation, with net production of 107 million cubic feet being realized in 1969. Almost 45 percent of total natural gas production was utilized in the injection method for increasing petroleum-well recovery operations, whereas 18.8 percent was used for household and industrial purposes, and 36.2 percent was flared. The Venezuelan government by the end of 1970 had two proposed gas projects under consideration, but a national policy was slow in evolving.

Construction had been one of the most rapidly expanding sectors in the economy during the 1960s. The growth of the sector had been based upon an increase in private construction, especially in the housing area (see ch. 6, Living Conditions). Private financial intermediaries, such as mortgage banks and savings and loan associations, had increased their role in the 1960s (see ch. 21, Finance). Public outlays, nevertheless, still played a major role in construction activity in 1970 because they gave vital direct and indirect assistance to private construction, as well as permitting an ambitious public works program (see ch. 6, Living Conditions; ch. 20, Trade; ch. 21, Finance).

Electric power capacity and generation had grown rapidly in the 1960s, whereas consumption demand had risen at an even faster rate. During the 1960—69 period installed electric power capacity rose at a yearly average of nearly 20 percent; in the same period total consumption demand grew at an average of over 17 percent per year. The generation of electric power was carried out by national, state, and municipal entities in the public sector and also by privately owned utility companies and specific industrial enterprises. The privately owned utility companies generally provided power to the major urban centers. A number of industrial enterprises in the manufacturing, petroleum, and mining sectors had their own generating facilities that often provided power to both the production enterprises and the surrounding housing and other ancillary areas. These self-supplying enterprises generally utilized gas turbines and diesel plants. The oil companies used a large number of gas turbines for their gas and water reinjection plants on Lake Maracaibo. Thermal power plants were used by some paper mills that required both steam and electric power.

The four main minerals produced were iron ore, gold, diamonds, and coal. The government planned considerable development in the mining sector during the 1970s. Two main goals of these efforts were a considerable increase in the exploitation of known reserves of minerals, such as iron ore, nickel, and phosphates, and the completion of a systematic and intensive inventory of total mineral reserves upon which further exploitation plans might be based.

MANUFACTURING

In 1969 manufacturing account for almost 20 percent of the GNP, with an aggregate output of nearly Bs10.4 billion, calculated at 1968 prices. Manufacturing enterprises employed about 16 percent of the labor force in 1969. Principal manufacturing branches in the early 1970s included foodstuffs and beverages, chemicals, textiles and clothing, primary metals, and transport equipment. In 1969, 230 new industrial enterprises began operating and employed more than 3,000 workers (see ch. 19, Labor).

Manufacturing was in 1970 one of the most dynamic sectors of the economy. Its expansion could be attributed partly to the deliberate national policy of encouraging industrial development to reduce the nation's dependence upon petroleum. The population growth of 3.5 percent annually required many additional employment opportunities that a developing manufacturing sector helped to provide (see ch. 4, Population and Ethnic Groups; ch. 19, Labor).

The government had pursued this objective by direct public investment in a number of basic manufactures and by encouraging private investment. Although public investment played an important role, private investment was expected to be the primary developer of the manufacturing sector.

Manufacturing was encouraged by import policies that protected domestic production by restricting the imports of competing products but permitted the almost unlimited entry, at nominal or exonerated duties, of capital goods or primary materials destined for manufacturing operations. In 1969 exemptions from duties on imports of primary materials, machinery, and equipment destined for manufacturing firms amounted to Bs995 million; the goods benefiting from this procedure were 1 million tons in volume with a free-on-board (f.o.b.) value of Bs1.5 billion. The nation stimulated investment in manufacturing through additional means, such as favorable tax and corporate structure laws (see ch. 20, Trade; ch. 21, Finance).

Nondurable Goods

Foodstuffs and Beverages

A steady increase in the production of foodstuffs is traceable to the increase in demand and to the policy of import reduction that has led to the expansion of existing enterprises as well as the establishment of new ones. The country was, nevertheless, not self-sufficient in foods; in 1969 imports amounted to Bs299 million (see ch. 17, Agriculture).

In the case of meatpacking and storage, a number of modern slaughterhouses have been built with the government assisting breeders' associations by granting long-term credits and, in some cases, by building modern abattoirs and packing plants. There were also many modern poultry slaughtering and packing plants. With the availability of ample supplies of fresh meat, the meatpacking and meat-processing industry had developed rapidly. To protect this industry, the government had imposed import restrictions on most meat products, including soups having a meat base (see ch. 20, Trade).

The meat-processing industry in 1968 consisted of thirty-four plants with over 1,500 employees and an investment of over Bs25 million; this total did not include the eight modern slaughterhouses and rendering plants constructed in the mid-1960s. Output of the industry had increased to over 19,000 tons in 1967. Most of the firms used modern equipment, usually from the United States, West Germany (the Federal Republic of Germany), or Italy, and their products were considered to meet adequate quality and sanitary standards (see ch. 6, Living Conditions; ch. 20, Trade). Utilization of byproducts resulting from slaughtering began in the late 1960s; most of the new slaughterhouses built in the mid-1960s had rendering and byproduct plants. They and a few small commercial plants produced glandular extracts, stearic oils, refined greases, tallow, soapstock, and sulfonated oils and fats.

Steady increases in production of raw milk had permitted a considerable expansion in the country's manufacture of dairy products in the late 1960s (see ch. 17, Agriculture). Imports of powdered milk, still permitted under a gradually reducing quota system, had consequently decreased (see ch. 20, Trade). The entire supply of locally produced raw milk was utilized domestically in the production of pasteurized fluid milk, powdered milk, milk for babies, butter, ice cream, and cheese or in farm use.

Pasteurized and homogenized fluid milk, packed in waxed or plastic-coated containers made by one manufacturer under license from a United States firm, was available in 1970 in all urban centers of the country. The areas were served by a number of modern pasteurization and packing plants, and the distribution system was effective. The containers were dated. There were a total of fourteen pasteurization companies, some of them having several plants in various towns of the country.

In 1970 there were six powdered milk plants in the country; milk was produced carrying domestic, United States, and Danish brand names. Several pharmaceutical companies produced powdered milk for babies. There were numerous small producers of cheese. The quality of domestic cheeses had improved considerably during the 1960s, and the quantity was sufficient to meet domestic requirements of close to 7,000 tons annually. Only specialty cheeses were permitted to be imported, and their retail price was extremely high (see ch. 20, Trade).

Production of butter fluctuated at around 4,000 tons a year. There were over 100 manufacturers of ice cream; most of the firms were very small. Production was stable at somewhat over 20,000 tons annually. Several of the milk pasteurizing firms produced chocolate milk sold in waxed containers. Yogurt, acidified milks, whipping cream, sour cream, and buttermilk were produced by a number of small manufacturers, mostly in the Caracas area.

In 1970 most prepared foods were being produced in the country; imports had been reduced to a small volume, consisting mostly of specialties. The country had sufficient capacity to supply the internal market in tomato products, vegetable juices, peas, fruit, and fruit juices. Government assistance to fruitgrowers also had made available sufficient quantities of tropical fruit, citrus, and such species as tamarind, guava, and guanabana; the juices of these fruits were canned or packed in waxed containers.

Sardines, tuna, mollusks, and shrimp were canned by plants in the eastern half of the country. Approximately 8 percent of the output of frozen shrimp was consumed in the country, with the rest being designated for the export market. Thirteen freezing plants for shrimp existed in 1970 in Punto Fijo and Maracaibo; the output of shrimp virtually represented the country's exports of fishery products. Frozen shrimp accounted for over 85 percent of the country's export of fish; in 1968 exports of frozen shrimp were 3,022 tons in volume and Bs17,658 in value (see ch. 17, Agriculture; ch. 20, Trade). The frozen shrimp were packed in waxed cardboard boxes and airlifted to the United States and Spain; shipments to Japan are moved by Japanese ships (see ch. 20, Trade).

In 1970 there were in operation twelve flour mills and twenty-one animal feed mills, including mixing plants. Consumption of wheat flour had shown yearly increases, and fresh bread was replacing the traditional flat toasted corn cake to some extent (see ch. 17, Agriculture; ch. 5, Social Structure). Two modern corn flour mills were, however, producing precooked corn flour specifically for the preparation of these corn cakes, and these and other corn-flour based products were recovering some of their former popularity (see ch. 6, Living Conditions).

Rice processing and polishing plants were located mainly in the states of Portuguesa and Guárico, the principal ricegrowing areas (see ch. 2, Physical Environment; ch. 17, Agriculture). Rice processing was done by thirty-five plants that produced 60,578 tons of polished rice for sale in bulk and retail pack in 1967. Most of the rice-processing plants were owned and operated by the government.

Domestic animal feed was produced by twenty-one manufacturers. Production had steadily increased during the 1960s, and in 1970 the manufacturing firms were able to meet almost the entire domestic demand for prepared cattle, hog, poultry, horse, and pet feeds. The expansion of production had been accompanied by an increase in the importation of additives not locally available and required for the mixing of balanced feeds, such as mineral mixtures, antibiotics, and hormones. A considerable amount of alfalfa, poultry grains, and soybean meal was also imported to mix with domestically produced raw materials, such as fish and bone meal, oil cakes, and corn (see ch. 17, Agriculture; ch. 20, Trade).

Bread, rolls, and pastries were produced mainly by numerous small bakeries; industrial bakeries were, however, obtaining an increasing share of the market. The largest proportion of bread produced was United States-style white bread packed in glassine or cellophane; some European breads were being produced by small bakeries, of which a great number were operated by immigrant Italian bakers (see ch. 4, Population and Ethnic Groups; ch. 6, Living Conditions).

Through the effectiveness of a national plan for sugar production, there was in 1970 a small surplus of sugar. Large-scale refineries were concentrated in the principal sugarcane-growing areas of Lara, Carabobo, Aragua, and Yaracuy states and in the district of Sucre (see ch. 17, Agriculture). Annual refinery capacity was estimated for 1970 at about 464,000 tons. Sugar production in 1967 amounted to 346,764 tons. There were five privately owned sugar mills; the government operated seven mills and produced close to one-half of the total national output.

The soft drink industry was in 1970 continuing to grow at a rapid rate. Production had reached 147 million gallons in 1967. The number of plants had decreased slightly to seventy-three in 1968 because of the construction of larger and more efficient plants by the large manufacturers. The industry, including its distribution organizations, was reported in 1970 to employ close to 80,000 persons. Distribution was very efficient; bottles, crown caps, and cans, in addition to wooden, cardboard and plastic cases, were manufactured in the country.

The brewery industry was dominated by two companies that owned almost all breweries in the country, and their own brands were distributed nationally. Their production reached 88 million gallons in 1967. The industry imported malt and hops and purchased bottles, caps, and cans locally. Rum produced from domestic molasses and an unrefined sugarcane brandy were the lowest priced distilled liquors; distillation of alcohol of proof grades for rum and gin amounted to 5.7 million gallons in 1967.

Domestic production of edible vegetable oils and fats was an important industry. Its output included vegetable shortening, margarine, sesame oil, cottonseed oil, and coconut oil. There were ten plants with about 1,500 employees. Production of peanut oil was expected to commence in 1970 from a government-assisted peanut-processing plant that was to process 4,000 tons annually of peanut oil to replace yearly imports of about that volume (see ch. 20, Trade).

Chemicals

In 1970 the output of the industry consisted principally of acids, industrial gases, alcohols, synthetic resins, glycerine, soap, toilet preparations, pharmaceuticals, paint, matches, and insecticides. There was also some production of tanning and dyeing material and of explosives.

The Venezuelan Institute of Petrochemicals (Instituto Venezolano de la Petroquímica), an autonomous government agency, operated a large, government-owned complex using natural gas as the major raw material to produce acids and fertilizers. The complex was at Morón, situated on the coast near Puerto Cabello, some 106 miles from Caracas. Output of the group of plants included caustic soda, chlorine, ammonia, and sulfuric, nitric, and phosphoric acids. An ammonia plant at the Morón complex was nearing completion of construction in 1970 and was expected to be in operation before the end of the year; it had been designed for a daily production capacity of 600 tons. Basic engineering studies for a urea plant, with a daily capacity of 750 tons, had been completed, and a soil study of the site was also ready. The primary engineering phase of a project for the production of phosphate fertilizers was almost concluded. The urea and phosphate fertilizer plants were expected to be in production by the end of 1971.

In 1970 the installed annual capacity of the Morón complex included 33,000 tons of ammonia, 66,000 tons of sulfuric acid, 33,000 tons of phosphoric acid, and 61,000 tons of nitric acid. The expansion program being carried out by the Venezuelan Institute of Petrochemicals included a series of additions to the existing Morón fertilizer complex that would result in a fivefold increase in production. The intermediate units of the new complex would produce 198,000 tons of anhydrous ammonia, 660,000 tons of ground phosphate rock, and 82,500 tons of phosphoric acid. The end-products plants would have yearly capacities of 247,500 tons of urea, 99,000 tons of triple superphosphate, 150,000 tons of diammonium phosphate, and 115,500 tons of mixed fertilizers or 65,000 tons of granulated superphosphate. The country was lent the equivalent of US$16.2 million by the Inter-American Development Bank (IDB) in September 1968 to finance 30 percent of the total cost of the projected additions; Japanese suppliers' credits were providing 17.3 percent of the cost, and the government was contributing the remaining 52.7 percent (see ch. 20, Trade; ch. 21, Finance). The projected additions would utilize domestic raw materials, including natural gas piped from the Anaco fields in the eastern part of the country, phosphate rock from the mine (owned by the Venezuelan Institute of Petrochemicals) at Riecito, sixty-two miles west of Morón, and sulfur from an oil desulfurization plant.

In addition to government projects, there was some private production of sulfuric, hydrochloric, phosphoric, and nitric acids. Eight plants produced industrial gases, including oxygen, acetylene, nitrogen, and carbon dioxide. There was also some production of ethyl alcohol, synthetic resins, glycerine, and inorganic chemicals.

Paint constituted one of the principal consumer items in the chemical field. There were in 1970 thirteen plants engaged in the manufacture of paints and allied products. the industry had a work force of about 2,000 employees. The country was self-sufficient in the manufacture of soaps, dentifrices, and cosmetics; the industry was estimated to consist of close to fifty firms, with 2,500 employees. Domestic raw materials used in the manufacture of soap and toilet preparations included coconut oil, tallow, palm oil, and mineral oil; nearly all other materials were imported.

In 1970 there were eighty pharmaceutical and medical products enterprises, with total employment of over 4,000 persons. Almost all the raw material was imported in semifinished or in bulk form.

Standards of hygiene were high, and packaging and presentation were equal to world standards. The industry used modern mixing and packaging methods.

The number of firms in the plastics industry was estimated in 1970 to be over 200, with total employment close to 2,000. The value of production was calculated by various sources to have reached 80 percent of total domestic consumption of molded plastic products. The industry produced consumer goods, including household articles, toys, and novelties, and industrial goods, including containers, laminates, artificial leather, and many other items.

Textiles and Clothing

The textile and clothing industries were in 1970 two of the oldest and most important manufacturing industries of the country. Production figures for 1969 were: cotton yarn, 18,388 tons; cotton fabrics, 16,085 tons; cotton cloth, 458.5 million yards; knitted fabric, 2,945 tons; woolen cloth, 1,411 tons; and synthetic fabrics, 45.4 million yards.

Domestic production of rayon and mixed rayon and cotton fabrics included crepes, taffetas, serges, and twills. Finished products included bedspreads, blankets, towels, underclothing, hosiery, twine, and cord. The industry in 1970 consisted of seventy-six primary textile mills plus another seventy converters, texturizers, and knitting mills, employing over 17,000 workers. In addition, the estimated 500 manufacturers of clothing, most of them quite small, employed another 30,000 persons. The total number of spindles in operation was estimated at slightly over 315,000, and that of looms, at around 6,500.

Estimates of the number of knitting machines installed in knitting mills ranged around 800. Venezuelans considered this equipment the most modern in Latin America.

The auxiliary industries had also expanded to meet the steadily increasing requirements of the textile industry. The supporting industries were able in 1970 to supply the primary textile mills with plastic and paperboard bobbins, certain spare parts, and practically all starches, dressings, bleaches, and detergents. The chemical industry produced chemicals used in finishing and dyeing and for wash-and-wear and wrinkle-proof processing.

The general trend in the industry toward reducing costs had resulted in some mergers and in the construction of spacious, modern plants with efficient quality-control laboratories, climate control, and high-speed materials-handling equipment. The industry viewed reduction of costs and increased efficiency in production as means to improve its competitive position relative to other member countries of the Latin American Free Trade Association (LAFTA) (see ch. 13, Foreign Relations; ch. 20, Trade).

The country's synthetic textile fiber industry produced a considerable amount of synthetic fibers and yarns; total production in 1969 was estimated at 19.4 million pounds. The industry was working close to installed capacity with the exception of the polyester plants, which were utilizing about one-third of their total capacity of 8 million pounds annually. There were seven texturization plants producing texturized and stretch nylon.

Production of woolen fabrics containing less than 30-percent wool in 1969 reached 193 tons, and that of fabrics with over 30-percent wool content amounted to 1,218 tons. Worsted fabrics produced were reportedly of excellent quality, with emphasis on tropical lightweights. The country had four carpet mills; their capacity was estimated at 50,000 square yards annually per work shift. Initiation of production of automobile carpeting for the domestic automotive assemblers had given the industry an impetus. Output of the mills included nylon, cotton, and woolen rugs, carpets, mats, and automobile carpeting; sisal rugs were also popular.

Two companies wove linen. Five lace and embroidery mills jointly satisfied domestic requirements. A number of weavers of small, narrow fabrics, labels, and elastics also had sufficient installed capacity. There was one weaver of curtains and upholstery fabrics.

The country was estimated to have more than 500 manufacturers of clothing; most of these firms were very small, with less than fifty employees. Many of the companies operated under licenses from United States manufacturers. Men's and ladies' wear and underwear, and men's shirts, neckties, handkerchiefs, bathing suits, and sportswear were produced. The industry was protected by extremely high tariffs and import license requirements and was able to satisfy most of the country's requirements for outer garments and underwear. The high protection afforded the industry had encouraged modernization, and only a small amount of production involved piecework.

The country was self-sufficient in production of hard fiber products, with sisal as the primary raw material. The industry was concentrated in the principal sisal-growing area around Barquisimeto. Rope up to 3 1/2 inches in diameter was produced at an average rate of 300 tons per month; nylon rope and nylon and sisal fishing nets were also produced. The principal use of sisal was for sacking, used in the shipping of vegetable products and salt; about 9 million sisal sacks were produced during 1969.

Durable Goods

Primary Metals and Metal Products

In 1970 the country had two primary steel mills, the Orinoco Iron and Steel Company (Siderúrgica del Orinoco) and the Venezuelan Iron and Steel Company (Siderúrgica del Venezolana). The Orinoco Iron and Steel Company was a large, government-owned, integrated steel mill producing pig iron, ingots, blooms, billets, slabs, seamless pipe, and rod and wire. The mill processed locally mined iron ore but imported coal and coke; in 1969 it produced 711,110 tons of finished steel. The Venezuelan Iron and Steel Company, a privately owned mill, produced 110,000 tons of steel in the same year; this firm used scrap metal as raw material.

The Orinoco Iron and Steel Company's mill had been constructed to provide a capacity of 750,000 tons of ingots per year as the basis of annual production of 600,000 tons of finished iron and steel products. The plant was constructed by an Italian firm at an ultimate total cost of the equivalent of US$402 million and was formally inaugurated on July 9, 1962. On December 27, 1966, the government made its last payment to the Italian firm, resulting in liquidation of all debts connected with the original construction. The mill was originally designed to produce 300,000 tons per year of seamless steel tubing, primarily for the petroleum industry. When exploratory drilling for crude oil began to decline in the 1960s, demand for seamless tubing dropped to 100,000 tons per year. On April 14, 1967, the president of the Orinoco Iron and Steel Company informed the Chamber of Deputies that the national steel enterprise had lost Bs322 million during the 1962—66 period, its first five years of operation.

The plant was temporarily closed in 1966 to allow a reduction in inventories, and in 1967 the number of personnel was reduced from 7,000 to 5,876. Labor productivity, as measured by man-hours per ingot ton, improved from fifty-three in 1966 to twenty-four in 1969, when the company employed over 6,000 persons (see ch. 19, Labor).

During the late 1960s the one-half of the mill's output of steel ingots originally planned to be used in production of seamless steel tubing was shifted to use for production of semifinished slabs, blooms, and billets. Partly as a consequence of changed proportions in the product mix, the enterprise moved from a loss in 1966 of Bs59 million to a profit in 1968 of Bs21 million. In 1969 the organization earned a profit of more than Bs30 million on total sales in that year of Bs504 million.

In 1970 bidding was continued on a flat-products mill to be constructed as an addition to the original plant. This mill was estimated to cost Bs783 million and would take approximately four years to build. The new mill was to have a capacity of 385,000 tons annually, about equal to the country's annual consumption. Flat products include plates, sheets, hoops for welded pipe, and tin plate.

In 1970 the country was self-sufficient in the production of aluminum. Caroní Aluminum (Aluminio del Caroní, S.A.), a joint venture of the government and Reynolds Aluminum Inter-American, Inc., produced 10,000 tons of aluminum ingots in that year; the plant began operations in October 1967. The plant used alumina from Jamaica and the United States, shipped to its own dock on the Orinoco River in seagoing ore vessels. Construction was proceeding in 1970 on installation of additional reduction cells to bring the plant's annual capacity to 22,500 tons of aluminum ingots.

Transport Equipment

The country's automobile assembly and manufacturing industry was one of the largest in Latin America. In 1970 there were eleven plants assembling automobiles and two plants assembling only trucks. The industry produced eighty-four passenger car models, fifteen bus chassis models, sixty-seven truck models, and twenty-seven models of general-purpose motor vehicles. In 1968 the industry produced 14,047 commercial vehicles and 48,570 passenger cars; during the first quarter of 1969 the totals were 8,781 commercial vehicles and 22,518 passenger cars. For 1969 as a whole, the industry completed nearly 73,000 automobiles. The industry represented a total investment of Bs380 million, generated Bs280 million in annual consumer spending, employed 14,000 persons, and paid over Bs200 million in annual wages.

Effective February 1, 1963, the government had prohibited further importation of assembled automobiles. Beginning in December 1965, the government had required the incorporation in locally assembled automobiles of a minimum percentage, by weight, of locally produced parts. In addition, the government had prohibited the importation of certain parts as soon as local production was presumed sufficient to meet the demand for assembly and replacement parts. The percentage of local content had been set each September for the following calendar year, divided into semesters; for the second half of 1969 the percentages ranged from 38.5 percent for passenger automobiles and station wagons to 22.0 percent for chassis for buses. The percentages were in relation to the overall dryweight of the vehicle out of the factory and included both mandatory and optional equipment.

On September 2, 1970, the government issued a decree establishing a five-year automotive policy for the 1971—75 period. The decree required that by 1975 local content for passenger vehicles must be increased 150 percent over the base period of July 1969 to June 1970. The formula calculating local content was a computation of locally added weight and value as a percentage of total weight and value in the country of origin. Assemblers were also required to submit to the Ministry of Development by June 1971 a complete list of locally produced parts, including cost and weight, that they planned to incorporate into their production through 1975. The Ministry of Development indicated that it would announce the base local content percentage by the end of 1970; parts manufacturers were required to submit to the ministry statistics concerning their operations that would assist the ministry in determining value added locally in parts manufacture. The ministry announced that the large number of small-scale producers of some parts would be reduced, that different percentages of local manufacture for a single part would not be permitted, and that parts' prices must be progressively reduced.

The decree stated that parts imported from other Latin American countries might be considered as locally produced to the extent that the assembler exported Venezuelan parts; assemblers would be permitted to participate in new projects for the manufacture of parts. Penalties for failure to meet the scheduled requirements, in the form of reductions in imports of knocked-down parts, were imposed; a shortfall of 1 percent below the required percentage would result in import restrictions that would reduce production by 50 percent. The decree also contained a provision requiring discontinuation of models that did not attain 1 percent of total passenger-vehicle production.

Three of the biggest companies assembling principal United States automobiles were General Motors, Chrysler, and Ford. Other firms with assembly plants were Toyota, Mercedes-Benz, Renault, American Motors, Fiat, International Harvester, Nissan, Rootes Motors, and Volkswagen.

Before the decree of September 2, 1970, assemblers had been forbidden by the government to establish parts and components factories. This requirement had caused a large number of new component plants to be built and existing metalworking shops to enter into production of automotive parts. The automotive parts industry was reported in 1969 to consist of 235 companies, with a total employment of close to 10,000 persons.

In 1970 the country was self-sufficient in the construction of bodies and superstructures for trucks and buses. The builders of truck bodies, using locally assembled chassis, produced refrigerated bodies, flatbed trailers, vans, and other body types. Two firms fabricated tanks for petroleum products and other stainless steel tanks for transportation of beer or milk.

PETROLEUM

The petroleum industry continued in 1970 as a sustaining force of the national economy. In 1969 it had accounted for slightly over 17 percent of the GNP and for about 90 percent, by value, of all exports. Industry-wide, total capital investment at the end of 1968 amounted to Bs7.3 billion, and net fixed assets, to Bs6.8 billion. Net profit of the industry in 1968 was Bs2.5 billion; dividends paid amounted to Bs1.9 billion. The industry earned an average net return on capital investment of 35.9 percent in 1968; the highest previous average net return had been the 32.3 percent earned in 1957. In 1969 daily average production in barrels was 3.6 million, and total production reached 1.3 billion barrels; average net return on capital investment was estimated by the government at 31.9 percent.

Despite the fact that annual petroleum production in 1969 was at the second highest level on record, less than one-half of 1 percent below the historical high level reached in 1968, the industry continued to be faced with serious problems that might profoundly affect its future development. During the 1960s competition on the world petroleum market had become more intense. On the one hand, traditional exporting countries had been increasing their output and, on the other, many new potentially large oil-bearing regions had been discovered. An additional competitive disadvantage lay in the fact that production costs were significantly higher in Venezuela than in some of the other new oil-producing countries. For example, productivity per well in Libya in 1968 was 3,000 barrels daily, compared to 300 barrels daily in Venezuela; consequently, average Libyan production costs were significantly below those in Venezuela.

Tangible results of a progressively tighter government control over the industry were continuing to be evident in 1970. The Venezuelan Petroleum Corporation, a government-owned entity established by decree on April 21, 1960, to engage in all aspects of production, refining, and distribution in competition with existing companies, was steadily becoming more important. The same decree had provided that no further petroleum concessions might be granted under the Law on Hydrocarbons of August 10, 1955. The Law on Hydrocarbons, of which Article 3 and Article 107 were amended by a law dated August 7, 1967, was reenacted and published in the Official Gazette (*Gaceta Oficial*) of the Republic, on August 8, 1967, pursuant to the final article of the amending law. Amending Article 107 stated that the Law on Hydrocarbons of August 10, 1955, was repealed. The new Article 3 stated that the right to exclusive exploration and to exploitation, manufacture, refinement, or transport by special means any of the substances covered by the law might be exercised in the following three ways: directly and exclusively by the executive power; by autonomous institutes and enterprises owned exclusively by the state, in which by law the state controls decisions made by those to whom rights may be transferred; and by means of concessions, in accordance with the provisions of Article 126 of the Constitution (see ch. 11, The Governmental System).

Decree 1050 of February 6, 1968, provided that holders of rights obtained in conformity with the second point of Article 3 of the Law on Hydrocarbons were equated with concessionaires of hydrocarbons insofar as the concessionaires' obligations and supplementary rights, which are established in Articles 52 to 62 of that law, were concerned. The president had previously ordered that, in replacement of the concession system, one of service contracts be initiated, whereby the foreign companies would engage in exploration, drilling, and processing for the Venezuelan Petroleum Corporation on a flat fee basis.

The government had been placing increased emphasis upon improved recovery methods, especially by the gas-injection recovery technique. Over fifty gas-injection plants were in operation in 1970, among them the world's largest. A program for the secondary recovery of oil by injecting water into old wells had begun in 1962, and by 1969 the largest oil operator in the country had fifteen such installations in operation on Lake Maracaibo. In 1969 this firm initiated an additional program for secondary recovery by this method; the company began construction of seven new injection plants. The new plants would inject water into three or four wells instead of just one. They would have a daily injection capacity of 5,000 gallons of water and would cost Bs5 million each.

Resources

There were in 1970 three major petroliferous basins that had been discovered to date—the Maracaibo, the Orinoco, and the Apure-Barinas (see ch. 2, Physical Environment). The first found, and most productive to date, is the Maracaibo basin. There are two main producing areas in the basin—the Bolívar coastal field along and under the northeast part of the lake and the various fields in the Maracaibo and Mara districts on the northwest. The second major basin is that of the Orinoco River in the northeastern part of the country. It is second in production and reserves to Maracaibo. The third major basin is that of Apure-Barinas in the Orinoco Lowlands (see ch. 2, Physical Environment). This basin came into production in October 1957.

In 1966, the latest year for which production data by area were available by production basins, the Maracaibo basin accounted for 76.5 percent of total production; the Orinoco basin for 21.1 percent; and the Apure-Barinas basin, for 2.4 percent. Proved reserves of petroleum in 1969 were estimated at approximately 14.9 billion barrels, down from 15.7 billion barrels in 1968. At current rates of consumption, this was equivalent to slightly more than an eleven-year supply. Additional reserves in the three major basins, however, had been estimated to be at least equal to this amount. Deposits of heavy crude oil, moreover, were known to exist north of the Orinoco River in the Gulf of Venezuela, and south of Lake Maracaibo.

Structure of the Industry

The petroleum industry is composed of some fifty companies, of which sixteen operate producing concessions. The remainder either have nonproducing concessions or may be joint owners, though not operators, of producing areas but nevertheless export and sell crude oil on the world market and are thus considered a part of the industry.

The three largest petroleum companies—the Creole Petroleum Corporation (a subsidiary of Standard Oil of New Jersey), Royal Dutch Shell, and Gulf Oil Company—account for 80 percent of domestic production. The Creole Petroleum Corporation, the largest company, alone produces 39 percent of total output. Although all petroleum companies operate under national corporate charters, most are subsidiaries of foreign companies. The sixteen companies with producing concessions had been granted concessions covering an area of 6.7 million acres in 1969; some of them would expire in 1983 and others in 1996 and 1997.

The Venezuelan Petroleum Corporation fulfilled a longstanding national aspiration. The principles underlying its organization were incorporated in part in the 1961 Constitution, which in Article 97 reads, "The State may reserve to itself specified industries, exploitations or services of public interest, for reasons of national advantage" (see ch. 11, The Governmental System).

In 1969 the Venezuelan Petroleum Corporation held a producing concession of 919,134 acres. Its average daily production in 1969 was 30,700 barrels, making a total of 11.2 million barrels in that year; this signified an increase of 81 percent over its production in 1968. The corporation exported 5.9 million barrels of crude oil in 1969.

Concessions

Until the decree of April 21, 1960, prohibiting any further concessions to private companies, exploitation of new oil resources had been governed by the Law on Hydrocarbons of December 21, 1938, and the Law on Hydrocarbons of August 10, 1955. Basically, the laws provided that any legal entity, person or corporate (but excluding states and holders of political office), could through proper application establish a claim to exclusive rights of exploitation over specific lands and processing and transportation of oil taken from them. Four classes of concessions were defined: both exploration and exploitation, exploitation, refining, and transportation. The exploration and exploitation concession provided for a period of exclusive rights lasting for three years, during which the holder was expected to do all necessary exploratory work and during which he could begin exploitation. The exploitation concession was granted upon application and presentation of a plan of operations to the Ministry of Mines and Hydrocarbons for a period of forty years, with a possible extension of another forty years. Concessions for refining and transportation could be granted either to holders of exploitation rights or to entities specifically established for those purposes, provided that the exploiting entity explicitly relinquished rights to engage in those operations.

Most of the exploitation concessions in operation in 1970 had been granted in 1943 and therefore would expire in 1983. In 1956, however, the government had granted 768,000 acres in Lake Maracaibo and along the Colombian border in new concessions and, in 1957, an additional 1.3 million acres in the central and eastern parts of the country were opened. The latter concessions will expire in the 1996—97 period.

Service Contracts

The Venezuelan Petroleum Corporation announced in early 1968 the basis for accepting offers for service contracts from oil companies interested in further development of the country's oil reserves. The corporation stated that service contracts were a substitute for the old concessions policy. Negotiations would cover an area of 617,761 acres south of Lake Maracaibo; the area was divided into five blocks of 123,552 acres and these, in turn, into ten lots of 12,355 acres each. Contracts would be direct-service contracts, under which the contractor was to explore at his own risk the area contracted for, extract the oil, and deliver it to the corporation, which would then turn over to the contractor the amount of oil called for in the contract for sale in foreign markets. This amount would in no case exceed 90 percent of total production.

The contractor would charge to the corporation the cost of production in the area. The contractor's profit would be the value of sales of oil received from the corporation, less the cost of production and other related expenses. He would pay income tax to Venezuela on this profit (see ch. 21, Finance). The duration of a service contract would be twenty years, not counting three years allowed as an exploratory period. Exploration would be financed by the contractor at his own risk. If oil were found in commercial quantities, the corporation would be admitted as a partner for the development of the deposit. The corporation would not be held responsible for any investment loss in case oil were not found. Current standards would be followed in setting the sale price of any oil extracted, with joint participation of the corporation and the contractor in any decision.

Other features of the proposed service contracts included joint approval by the contractor and the corporation of investment plans and projects, training of local executive and technical personnel, free delivery to the corporation at the wellhead of natural gas not used in petroleum production and related industries, and delivery to the corporation of at least 10 percent of the crude oil output. This last feature in particular would lead to greater government participation in the income generated by the petroleum sector. In his annual message to the National Congress, the minister of mines and hydrocarbons estimated that this participation would increase from a maximum of 68 percent of profits before taxes, under existing concessions, to a minimum of 85 percent, under the proposed service contracts.

Production

Crude oil output had increased almost continuously over the forty-five years of active exploitation. Necessarily responsive to conditions affecting world markets, production, though quantitatively higher than ever, had undergone minor fluctuations since 1962, when the 3 million barrels per day figure was attained, as both internal and external conditions change (see ch. 13, Foreign Relations; ch. 20, Trade). During the 1960s, the average annual rate of increase had been 2.3 percent.

Refining

At the beginning of 1970 the country had a total installed annual capacity of refining over 421 million barrels, or one-third of crude oil production. The outlook for expansion of the country's refining industry was affected by the increasing tendency of consuming countries to install their own refineries and to limit their importation to crude oil. About two-thirds of the country's total production was destined for export as crude oil (see ch. 20, Trade).

Two of the largest refineries in the world were located in the country. They were the Amuay refinery, owned by the Creole Petroleum Corporation, with a rated capacity of 345,000 barrels a day, and Shell's Punta Cardón refinery, with 285,000 barrels per day. In 1969 about 90 percent of capacity was utilized.

Concern about the market for the country's fuel oil on the eastern seaboard of the United States, in view of increasingly stringent restrictions on sulfur content, had been allayed by the signing, on January 5, 1968, of an agreement between the government and the Creole Petroleum Corporation for construction of a desulfurization unit at the Amuay refinery. In return for certain fiscal advantages, the Creole Petroleum Corporation agreed to invest the equivalent of US$120 million in a unit to reduce the sulfur content of 155,000 barrels of fuel oil daily to below 1 per cent. The hydrogen required for the process would be derived from natural gas piped 150 miles from Lake Maracaibo, with the pipes being supplied by the Orinoco Iron and Steel Company. It was expected that 300 tons per day of liquid sulfur would be extracted from the oil; the Venezuelan Institute of Petrochemicals would have an option on this production. This plant was expected to be in operation by mid-1971.

Royal Dutch Shell reached agreement with the government during 1968 on the terms for the country's second desulfurization unit. The plant, to be installed at the company's Punta Cardón refinery, would cost an estimated equivalent of US$35.7 million and was expected to produce 50,000 tons of fuel oil for export with a maximum sulfur content of 1 percent. This plant was expected to commence production sometime in 1970.

Among refined products in 1969 fuel oil accounted for 60.8 percent. In descending order, other refined products were: kerosine and distillates, 18.0 percent; gasoline and naptha, 11.8 percent; and others, including asphalts, lubricants, liquefied gases, and refinery gains and losses, 9.4 percent. Domestic consumption of refined products was very small. In 1969 total domestic consumption absorbed 16.8 percent of the output of refined products. In terms of both quantity and value, gasoline was the important product on the local market because the country relied on trucks and airplanes for almost all domestic transportation (see ch. 20, Trade). Gasoline sales amounted to 23.4 million barrels in 1969. Domestic lubricating oils had a growing market for use in motor vehicles and in machinery being installed in new factories; 781,000 barrels had been consumed in 1969, and the average annual growth rate during the 1960s had been 10 percent.

Transportation

At the beginning of 1970 the aggregate length of the pipeline system was 3,720 miles, of which 2,085 miles were trunklines and 1,635 miles were secondary lines. The longest single pipeline in operation extended 210 miles from Campo Silvestre, in the Barinas area, to El Palito, near Puerto Cabello. For the transportation of derivative products to centers of distribution and to the shipping terminals, there were 214 miles of pipelines.

Most of the internal distribution of refined products was in the hands of the petroleum companies, which operated some thirty-three bulk stations and distributing centers. By Decree 187 of 1964 the government required that the Venezuelan Petroleum Corporation acquire 33 percent of the domestic market for refined products by the end of 1968. At the beginning of 1968, out of a total of 1,776 service stations in the country, 190 were operated by the Venezuelan Petroleum Corporation, compared with 650 owned by the Creole Petroleum Corporation, 640 owned by Royal Dutch Shell, and 153 owned by Mobil Oil. The balance of 143 service stations were operated by three small distributors (see ch. 20, Trade). In September 1968 the government issued a new decree, establishing November 30, 1968, as the deadline for fulfillment of the 1964 decree and stating that the six marketing companies involved would, by that date, transfer to the Venezuelan Petroleum Corporation facilities equal to 5 percent of their 1967 sales volume. By the end of 1969 the corporation was supplying over 32 percent of the domestic market for refined products and was operating 613 service stations. Serving the distributing centers was a tank-truck transportation system, partly operated by the companies themselves and partly by independent handlers.

NATURAL GAS

Of all natural gas produced in the country, 98 percent is a by-product of petroleum extraction. Through 1970 the Ministry of Mines and Hydrocarbons had encouraged measures for the conservation and rational use of this valuable resource. Nonetheless, as late as 1969, 36.2 percent of all natural gas produced was wasted; this proportion emanating from oil wells was burned off.

Total natural gas production in 1969 was over 167 million cubic feet. Of this volume, 45 percent was reinjected into the ground to increase petroleum pressure and for storage and 18.8 percent was used in sales to consumers as fuel in various processing operations or transformed into products (in particular, liquid gas).

In 1969 there were 1,575 miles of pipelines for transmission of natural gas to centers of utilization. The petroleum companies owned and administered 609 miles of this system, and the Venezuelan Petroleum Corporation owned and administered 966 miles. The corporation in 1969 controlled 65.4 percent of the distribution of natural gas in the country. Through 1970 the corporation had been engaged in the construction of natural gas pipelines and planned to invest more than Bs200 million in such projects in 1970.

CONSTRUCTION

In 1970 construction accounted for about 6 percent of the GNP and employed about 160,000 persons, or around 6 percent of the labor force. The value of the sector's output had risen by 16 percent in 1964, by 11 percent in 1965, by 7 percent in 1966, by slightly over 3 percent in 1967, and by 10 percent in 1968. The value of the goods and services originating in the sector remained stable in 1969. Except in 1967 and 1969, the annual increases in the product of the sector had exceeded the yearly rates of growth in the GNP during the 1964—69 period.

The variable element in the construction total had been the volume of private construction. Data on private construction are recorded for the Caracas metropolitan area, for the state capitals, and for other urban areas. Private construction in the state capitals had remained relatively stable from year to year, with the annual volume of private construction in the Caracas metropolitan area and in urban areas other than the state capitals flunctuating sharply. The Caracas metropolitan area had accounted for from 40 to 60 percent of the value of all private construction counted in the government's records. Public construction was concentrated mainly in locations outside the Caracas metropolitan area and consisted chiefly of low-cost housing projects financed by the Workers' Bank (Banco Obrero), the Ministry of Health and Social Assistance, and the president's Foundation for Community Development and Municipal Action (Fundación para el Desarrollo de la Comunidad y Fomento Municipal) (see ch. 6, Living Conditions; ch. 21, Finance).

POWER RESOURCES

In 1970 electric power was available almost everywhere in the country, and the integration of regional networks was progressing rapidly. The development of the hydroelectric resources of the Caroní River in the Guiana Highlands had made feasible a completely integrated national power network. The major problem was the supply of fifty-cycle current to Caracas, whereas the rest of the country was operating with sixty-cycle current. The conversion of the Caracas system from fifty- to sixty-cycle current was underway in 1970 at an estimated total cost of Bs160 million. Completion of the conversion in the early 1970s would make possible the integration of the highest consumption area, in which the most important private utility was operating, with the rest of the country.

Power generation and distribution were handled by private utilities, by national and municipal agencies, and by the consuming industries themselves. The Chamber of Electrical Industry (Cámara de la Indústria Eléctrica) estimated installed electrical capacity in 1969 at 2.5 million kilowatts, generation at 9.6 million kilowatt-hours, and subscribers at 1.2 million; these figures did not include energy produced and used within the petroleum and other private industries.

The government enterprise, Electric Administration and Development Company (Compañía Anónima de Administración y Fomento Eléctrico), was in 1970 the major agent in the development of the country's power resources. In addition to operating plants, it was also responsible for the planning, execution, and administration of electrification programs. The agency's main goals were the interconnection of the various regional networks and the installation of generation and distribution facilities in rural areas and in areas where the small number of subscribers and high cost of distribution did not make the installation of private utilities economically attractive.

In 1970 national planning of electrification was focused on centralization of generating capacities in large plants to reduce generation and maintenance costs, interconnection of utility systems, replacement of uneconomical systems, and organization of all private and public systems along a uniform pattern into one national integrated system. A government agency, the Caroní Electrification Company (Electrificacíon del Caroní), was responsible for construction and operation of the huge Guri Dam and hydroelectric project on the Caroní River; this facility was planned to be one of the largest hydroelectric projects in the world.

The Guri Dam was the key factor in a large-scale plan of integrating the northern coastal area of the Central Highlands with the Guiana Highlands (see ch. 2, Physical Environment). The first stage of this plan provided for the interconnection of the systems of the two major national government agencies in the power production field, the Electric Administration and Development Company and the Caroní Electrification Company, with the country's most important private producer of electric power, Caracas Electricity (C.A. La Electricidad de Caracas). The total investment for this interconnection was estimated at Bs1.4 billion. Simultaneously, in 1970, the interconnection of the various networks of the Electric Administration and Development Company with each other and with the private utilities was proceeding vigorously, and integration inside the various regional systems had almost reached completion.

In 1969 the Electric Administration and Development Company operated fifty-six power plants, with an installed generating capacity of 582,000 kilowatts; it had 500,000 subscribers and was estimated to serve 2.6 million persons, to whom it supplied nearly 1.9 million kilowatt hours. It maintained sixty-nine substations with voltage varying from 13,800 to 230,000 volts. During the 1959–68 period it had installed 1,800 miles of transmission and distribution lines, with an investment of Bs111 million.

The president of the enterprise stated in a press interview in May 1970 that his agency would have to invest Bs12 billion during the next ten years for the development of the country's electric-power generation and distribution system. In 1970 the agency was working on the country's electrification plan, originally prepared in the early 1950s and amended several times subsequently, to change it from a general overall plan to a detailed working schedule. The agency intended to finance the plan from profits, bond issues, and internal loans, with foreign financing being requested for major projects, such as power plants and dams.

The most important single project in 1970 of the Electric Administration and Development Company was the Santo Domingo project in western Venezuela. The project, begun in early 1969, included the construction of a dam and a hydroelectric generating plant. The hydroelectric dam would be built on a mountain spur at the confluence of the Santo Domingo and Aracay rivers in the Cordillera de Mérida subregion (see ch. 2, Physical Environment). The power plant was planned to have an eventual capacity of 240,000 kilowatts, produced by four 60,000-kilowatt generators. The project was estimated to involve an investment of Bs200 million.

The major project of the Caroní Electrification Company in 1970 was the Guri Dam on the Caroní River at a point twenty-five miles south of Ciudad Guayana. Initial work on the dam began in 1963; on November 8, 1968, the president of the country officially inaugurated the project. At that time, the first turbine of 175,000-kilowatt capacity was put into use; a second turbine was brought into operation in April 1969, and a third turbine began generating power in July 1969. By mid-1969, therefore, the Guri Dam had an installed capacity of 525,000 kilowatts. As demand for power increased, the powerhouse was to be expanded, and seven additional generating units were to be installed for a total first-stage capacity of 1.8 million kilowatts. As of 1970 the first stage was expected to be completed in 1980.

In its first stage, the Guri Dam was built to a height of 361 feet. The second stage of the planned expansion will constitute raising the dam an additional 82 feet and constructing another powerhouse with six more turbines, for a total capacity of 3 million kilowatts. The third stage would include a further 82-foot rise in the dam and eight more generating units, for a final capacity of 6 million kilowatts.

The Caroní Electrification Company also controlled the Macagua No. 1 plant, which had an installed capacity of 370,000 kilowatts. This plant was located at the confluence of the Orinoco and Caroní rivers and had been inaugurated in 1961. This installation plus the first stage of the Guri Dam provided the Caroní Electrification Company with an installed capacity of 895,000 kilowatts in 1969. In that year the enterprise produced 3.9 million kilowatt hours furnished to twenty-eight industrial factories and sold to other electric power companies.

Installed capacity for power generation and distribution by the consuming industries was estimated in 1970 to be about 523,000 kilowatts. Most of these plants were installations of the oil companies and of sugar mills. Some of the power plants belonging to the oil companies also supplied some residential areas. The number of industrial generation facilities had decreased as more industries could be supplied by the Electric Administration and Development Company; the industrial power plants were in such cases kept as standby units.

There were also numerous very small power generation facilities, practically all of them diesel units, supplying power for a few hours in the evening in small villages, farms, or cooperatives (see ch. 17, Agriculture). Most of these installations had a capacity of less than 100 kilowatts. The Electric Administration and Development Company normally took these installations out of operation or took them over when its distribution network reached the area.

MINING

Mining contributed 1 percent to the 1969 GNP, and exports of 19 million tons of iron ore earned the equivalent of Bs608 million, about 5 percent of the country's total exports in that year. In 1969 foreign capital investment in mining, concentrated in iron, was 4 percent of cumulative gross foreign investment and ranked second to foreign investment in petroleum. The government was engaged in 1970 in a program of evaluation of the country's mineral resources to determine their quantity and quality. The geological investigations were focused on areas in the Northern Mountains and in the Guiana Highlands (see ch. 2, Physical Environment). Particular attention was being given to the possibilities of exploitation of known deposits of nickel, magnesite, mercury, copper, asbestos, and bauxite. The country's mineral wealth was still largely unsurveyed in 1970, however, and production in 1969 could not, therefore, be taken to indicate potential production.

Production of diamonds in 1969 reached 188,000 carats, with a value of nearly Bs17 million. These figures represented increases of 59 percent in volume of output and of 77 percent in value, compared to the 1968 results. The rise in output was primarily due to the discovery and exploitation of new deposits.

Aside from iron and diamonds, commercial mining of any significance was confined to gold and coal. Other minerals mined on a smaller scale included clay, limestone, salt, asbestos, tin, manganese, nickel, phosphates, and bauxite. The country also had varied and largely unutilized quantities of mica, feldspar, silver, sulfur, gypsum, marble, copper, mercury, lead, magnesite, barite, antimony, beryllium, chromium, and uranium.

Despite an apparent abundance of mineral resources, little commercial attention had been paid to mining, except in the case of iron, diamonds, gold, and coal. Exploitation of minerals was governed by the Mining Law of December 28, 1944, and by the Law of Hydrocarbons of March 13, 1943, as amended. All minerals other than those specifically exempt by law or decree were exploited under concessions granted by the national government. Building stone, any other stone not regarded as precious, and several other minor products might be exploited freely by the owner of the lands on which they occurred.

The country's total estimated reserves of iron ore were calculated in 1968 to be about 3 billion to 4 billion tons, with at least 58 percent pure iron content (see ch. 2, Physical Environment). Production in 1969 reached over 19 million tons; almost all of this total was exported. The major producers continued to be the Orinoco Iron and Steel Company, a subsidiary of the United States Steel Corporation, and the Iron Mines Company of Venezuela, a subsidiary of the Bethlehem Steel Corporation. All of the output of the Iron Mines Company is sent to the United States; about two-thirds of the production of the Orinoco Iron and Steel Company is shipped to the United States, with the balance being shipped to Great Britain, West Germany, and Italy.

ROLE OF THE GOVERNMENT

Responsibility for planning, coordination, and development of the country's industrial base has been assumed primarily by the government. In addition to setting overall goals of growth and diversification and providing a favorable climate, it has also taken a direct hand in capitalization, technical study and, in some cases, actual operations.

Three governmental agencies bear most of the responsibility for the planning and execution of industrial development programs. The Ministry of Development is constitutionally charged with executing presidential decrees in all matters affecting economic growth and with the creation of a general climate favorable to continued development. The Venezuelan Development Corporation is a semiautonomous agency, largely independent in administration from the Ministry of Development but required to report annually to the minister; it engages in a broad front of planning and development activities in all sections of the economy. It does feasibility studies in the establishment of new industries, provides technical assistance to established enterprises, provides capital, both by direct loans and through investment in various banks, and operates several governmental industrial enterprises through subsidiary corporations. The Central Office of Coordination and Planning (Oficina Central de Coordinación y Planificación), responsible directly to the president, undertakes broad and long-range planning, as well as specialized planning services for other government agencies involved in economic and social development. Central to its activities is the formulation of multiyear economic plans within which industrial growth occupies a prominent place (see ch. 16, Character and Structure of the Economy; ch. 21, Finance).

In addition to the nationwide development agencies, there is another semiautonomous entity, the Venezuelan Guyana Corporation (Corporación Venezolana de la Guayana), which is specifically charged with the overall development of the mineral-rich Guiana Highlands region. It has engaged in a wide variety of basic construction activities, including roads, ports, and hydroelectric dams, and operates the steel mill in the Orinoco Lowlands. Its most ambitious undertaking is the construction of a new industrial city, Ciudad Guayana, at the confluence of the Orinoco and Caroní rivers. The city will initially provide housing and services for workers in the nearby steel and aluminum plants. It is intended that many new industries will be established around this nucleus, and projections contemplate a probable population of from 200,000 to 250,000 and a labor force of about 50,000 by the 1980s.

CHAPTER 19

LABOR

The 3 million men and women who made up the labor force in 1970 constituted about 30 percent of the population. The proportion actively engaged in or seeking work was lower than it had been in earlier years. An unprecedentedly high birth rate during the immediately preceding years, coupled with a much higher rate of retention in school enrollment, left a progressively smaller proportion of the population available for the labor force.

With its relative decline in size, the working population underwent a change in composition. As people moved from country to town, industrial and commercial employment rose, and agricultural employment registered a relative decline. The economy was experiencing a rapid expansion, and there were many new jobs available in factories producing goods and in the stores selling those goods. Employment in the large personal services sector, however, grew only at about the rate of increase for the labor force as a whole.

The pattern of development was a generally healthy one. With increasing agricultural productivity more people were leaving low-paying farm employment in order to seek work in the cities. At the same time the factories and stores were able to absorb more than their share of the influx.

This pattern of development was for the most part explainable in terms of money. Venezuela during the 1960s had the wealth gained from petroleum sales to plow back into the development of new industries, and it was these new industries that provided the new employment.

Other changes were taking place. In 1970 only about one member of the labor force in five was female, but this proportion was far higher than it had been a decade earlier. Although enrollment in the small vocational training programs was increasing more rapidly than in the academic programs, skilled workers remained relatively few, and most of the training was acquired on the job. Real income of workers was rising, and the pay levels were the highest in Latin America. There was, however, an extreme disparity between the rural and urban averages. A farm laborer's earnings might be less than 10 percent of those of the factory worker.

In 1970 nearly half of the labor force was in some manner

associated with a labor union, but organized labor had been very slow in establishing itself as a social and an economic power. Authoritarian governments had made collective labor action impossible before the middle 1930s, and another administration had suppressed it between the late 1940s and the late 1950s. It was natural, therefore, that when labor finally emerged as a powerful element in the society in 1958 it should be with a high degree of political orientation.

Since 1958 the role of organized labor has been less one in which unions as representatives of workers have negotiated with employers than one in which unions as associates of national political parties have sought to advance the positions of their memberships through political channels.

STRUCTURE AND DYNAMICS OF THE LABOR FORCE

The roughly 3 million persons considered economically active (employed or seeking employment) at the end of 1968 constituted approximately 30 percent of the total population at the time. The proportion had been more than 32 percent in 1961 and 34 percent in 1950. This sustained decline was the result, not of an ebb in the rate of economic activity, but primarily of a sustained high rate of population growth that each year was reflected in a higher proportion of the total population made up of children too young to be employed (see ch. 4, Population and Ethnic Groups). To a less significant extent, it resulted from a spread in the educational system. This resulted in a progressively greater number of adolescents kept out of the labor force by prolonged school attendance (see ch. 7, Education).

The distinction between manual and nonmanual occupations has considerable legal and social significance. The *obrero* (laborer) is defined under the law as a person engaged in an occupation in which he works for another at a trade or performs a service in which manual or physical efforts predominate. An *empleado* (employee) is defined as a person who works for another at work where the intellectual effort predominates over the physical. The *obrero* is paid in daily or weekly wages whereas the *empleado* receives a salary, usually paid on a monthly basis. The white-collar *empleado* usually receives considerably more pay than the blue-collar *obrero*.

In the late 1960s about 200,000 people worked for the government. Administrative personnel predominated, but there were more than 50,000 teachers, and the various professions and trades were represented in the personnel working for government-owned businesses.

Composition by Occupational Sector

Between 1961 and 1968 employment in all other sectors of the economy increased at the expense of agriculture and related activities, which registered absolute as well as relative declines. A decrease of almost 40,000 in the number of farmworkers constituted a decrease in the proportion of the total labor force employed in agriculture of more than 10 percent. The most substantial gains in employment were the 4.8 percent registered in the manufacturing industry and the 4.5 percent in commerce (see table 4).

Growth was most substantial in those enterprises employing the more sophisticated manufacturing processes. On the basis that 1960 equals 100, the index in manufacturing employment as a whole stood at 143 in 1969, but employment in artisanry was at only 128. The traditional manufacturing processes, such as food, beverages, clothing, and furniture, increased to a 1969 index of 135; intermediate industries, such as cement, chemical products, and basic metals, were up to an index of 177; and machinery and mechanical manufactures were up to an index of 254. The highest individual rate of growth was registered in the production of basic metals, which in 1969 was at an index of 660 as a consequence of the

Table 4. Employment in Venezuela, 1961 and 1968

Sector	1961		1968[1]	
	Persons Employed[2]	Labor Employed[3]	Persons Employed[2]	Labor Employed[3]
Agriculture	730	35.1	691	24.7
Mining and petroleum	39	1.9	50	1.8
Manufacturing	250	12.0	473	16.8
Construction	81	3.9	174	6.2
Electricity and gas	22	1.1	37	1.3
Commerce	271	13.0	489	17.5
Transport and communications	86	4.2	158	5.7
Services	524	25.2	724	25.9
Unspecified	75	3.6	2	0.1
Total employed	2,078	100.0	2,798	100.0
Unemployed	329		157	
Total labor force	2,407		2,955	

[1] November 1968.
[2] In thousands.
[3] Percent of total employed.

Source: Adapted from U.S. Department of Commerce, Bureau of International Commerce, "Establishing a Business in Venezuela," *Overseas Business Reports* (OBR 69—64), Washington, 1969, p. 8.

growth of steel production and the establishment of an aluminum plant (see ch. 18, Industry). Machinery manufacturing was at an index of 560. Pulp and paper, chemical products, and electrical and transport equipment were all at indices above 200.

Despite the decline in farm employment, farming and other rural activities in 1968 involved more than 700,000 persons, more than any other occupational group. Factory artisans or workers were next in number, sales personnel were third, and persons engaged in service or entertainment activities were fourth (see table 5).

Age and Sex Distribution

In 1970 females made up an estimated 21.2 percent of the labor force, the ratio being the culmination of a steady increase from 12.2 percent in 1950 and 18.0 percent in 1961. The 1961 census showed female employment to have been highest in the services sector, presumably because of relatively high employment ratios in domestic and other personal services. In the services sector as a whole, females constituted nearly half of the total employed. In manufacturing they constituted nearly one-third, the heaviest concentration occurring in the textiles and clothing industries. Employment in other sectors was substantially lower. Females made up 12.2 percent of the employers and self-employed, 22.0 percent of the salary and wage earners, and 4.9 percent of the unpaid family workers.

The 1961 census showed employment of males and of females under the age of fourteen to constitute 4.3 percent and 0.9 percent

Table 5. Economically Active Population of Venezuela by Occupational Group, November 1968

Occupational group	Number economically active
Professionals and technicians	234,912
Managers and administrators	57,872
Clerical employees	256,546
Salesmen	408,676
Farmers, fishermen, and lumbermen	704,202
Miners and stonecutters	14,291
Operators of transportation or communications equipment	189,941
Factory artisans or workers	510,273
Other artisans or workers	160,151
Service or entertainment employees	377,041
Unidentified or not specified	11,369
Seeking work for first time	30,098
Total	2,955,372

Source: Adapted from U.S. Department of Commerce, Bureau of International Commerce, "Establishing a Business in Venezuela," *Overseas Business Reports* (OBR 69—64), Washington, 1969, p. 8.

of the total. Between the ages of fifteen and nineteen, however, these proportions increased to 62.1 percent and 17.9 percent, respectively. The highest rate of male participation was between the ages of thirty and forty-four, with 98 percent employed. For females the peak was reached between the ages of twenty and twenty-four, with a participation rate of 25.8 percent. For both males and females participation dropped at older ages, but 70.1 percent of the males over sixty-four remained employed. For the heads of households, accordingly, retirement remained a luxury enjoyed by few.

There is a perceptible correlation between age and geographical and occupational sector of employment, particularly with respect to the rural labor force. In a country where over half of the labor force was under the age of thirty, it was estimated in 1970 that 60 percent of the farmers were over forty, an indication that the young farm people were migrating to towns and cities to seek employment rather than remaining in rural localities (see ch. 2, Physical Environment). In addition, however, most of the work performed by young adolescents was on farms. Nearly all of these were presumably helping their fathers in the fields.

Alien Workers

With certain exceptions, foreigners have the same rights and duties as Venezuelan citizens. At least 75 percent of all workers (salaried employees as well as wage-earning laborers) in each enterprise, however, must be Venezuelans. Overseers and employees immediately superior to unskilled workers must be Venezuelans, except in the case of technical specialists. It has been ruled that this includes only positions immediately superior to unskilled laborers. Accordingly, it applies to overseers and foremen but not to managerial and supervisory office positions.

In 1961 about 68 percent of all aliens and 20 percent of all alien women were employed. They constituted about 12 percent of the labor force. Their concentration was highest among the managers and administrators, where they made up nearly 40 percent of the total. About half were in the Federal District and the state of Zulia. The heaviest employment was in industries, followed by sales occupations, services, and agriculture in that order.

Occupational Skills

The shortage of trained manpower is a major problem, even though the ratio of technicians and skilled workers to the overall population is above that of most other Latin American countries. There is a serious shortage of carpenters, electricians, solderers, and metalworkers. The labor force as a whole in 1970, however, remained poorly trained.

The petroleum, construction, and iron-mining industries and some of the larger manufacturing firms have a high level of productivity and are staffed by well-trained personnel. These are, however, for the most part modern capital-intensive operations, requiring relatively few hands. In 1967 the highly productive petroleum and mining sectors employed only about 1.5 percent of the working population. Productivity of labor in the petroleum sector is about thirty times that in the economy as a whole. In general, the incidence of skills is lowest in the services and in the agricultural sector, where most of the workers are employed.

Early post-World War II immigration contributed appreciably to the economic expansion that marked that period and supplied many of the much-needed technical and managerial skills. Many of the immigrants settled in Caracas and in other large urban areas, where they gave impetus to cabinetmaking, shoe manufacturing, and mechanical repair of a number of types. They also contributed substantially to the growth of commercial agriculture. The flow of skilled immigrants virtually ceased in 1959 when the government, concerned over growing unemployment terminated the previous policy of active encouragement to skilled immigrants (see ch. 4, Population and Ethnic Groups).

Legislation was enacted in 1959 to enlarge the pool of skilled manpower through apprenticeship programs and training for the unemployed. The law, administered by the National Institute of Educational Cooperation (Instituto Nacional de Cooperación Educativo—INCE), requires employers to provide training for one worker between the ages of fourteen and eighteen for every twenty workers employed. Programs range from on-the-job training to those combining classroom study with work experience. There are also management training programs and classes for personnel supervisors, plant foremen, and industrial relations experts. In addition, there are programs for the commercial and agricultural sectors. During the 1960s enrollment almost tripled in vocational high schools, but in 1970 the economy still relied heavily on on-the-job training for the production of skilled personnel (see ch. 7, Education).

There is also a considerable shortage of personnel at the managerial level and of skilled engineers, technicians, and agronomists. University enrollment rose precipitously during the 1960s, but so many of the students were in law, medicine, and other traditional prestige fields that in 1970 considerable criticism was being voiced about the lack of correlation between university enrollments and the real needs of the economy (see ch. 7, Education). In general, the output of the upper levels of the educational system in the past has been quantitatively insufficient to staff the higher positions in industry and commerce. According to the 1961 census about 11 percent of the working population with some education earned in excess of Bs1,000 (4.5 bolivars equal US$1), or the equivalent of US$220 monthly. Nearly 44 percent of those in this highest paid bracket had no more than a grammar school education, and only 23 percent had attended school at the university level. The more than 75 percent of the working population that had attended a university, however, were in the highest paid category.

Unemployment

The unemployment rate was 6.5 percent in 1969, having declined steadily from 6.9 percent in 1968, 7.3 percent in 1967, 9.4 percent in 1965, and 13.1 percent as reflected in the 1961 census. Unemployment figures customarily included both persons who had previously been employed and those seeking work for the first time—about 10 percent of the total in 1961 and probably more than that proportion during the late 1960s.

Unemployment remained fairly low during most of the 1950s but moved sharply upward with the overthrow of the Pérez Jiménez administration in 1958. The upturn was the result of the curtailment of an extensive public construction program that had been carried on previously, the dislocation of the economy resulting from the changeover in government, and the arrival in urban centers of a flood of jobseekers from rural localities that had previously been forcibly restrained. The continuing downward trend in unemployment after 1961 accompanied the inauguration of a system of protective tariffs and a plan of credits made available through the Venezuelan Development Corporation to strengthen industries supplying products previously imported.

The 1961 census showed the rate of rural unemployment to have been less than one-third of that in urban localities. The low productivity of agriculture, however, reflects a high rate of underemployment on farms. Urban unemployment is highest in major population centers, primarily because the heaviest incidence falls on unskilled rural migrants newly arrived in towns as part of a flow that, except during the Pérez Jiménez administration, has been sustained since the end of World War II (see ch. 2, Physical Environment). In 1961 unemployment was at 28 percent of the working force in Caracas and 17.5 percent in Maracaibo.

Among the major urban occupational sectors, unemployment has tended to be above the average in construction and manufacturing and below the average in commerce and services. In 1961 nearly half the persons engaged in construction and 17 percent of those in manufacturing were unemployed. For commerce and industry the rates were about 11 and 8 percent respectively. In general, the incidence has been heaviest among unskilled workers in types of employment, such as construction and manufacturing, where a considerable number of skills is needed. There is little unemployment of skilled personnel in any employment sector. Outright unemployment is low in services, where the demand for skills is limited, but the rate of underemployment is high. In general, unemployed persons in urban centers have shown a reluctance to move to another locality in order to find work. There has been little reverse migration from town to country and, when unemployment in Caracas was unusually high in the early 1960s, recruiters encountered difficulty in finding workers willing to journey to the rim of the Guiana Highlands for employment in connection with the building of the Ciudad Guayana industrial complex.

Between the economically active and the economically inactive sectors of the population lie the unemployables, persons who lack the stamina or degree of skill necessary to be productive. Their number was estimated by President Raúl Leoni in 1965 to be 200,000 or less. Other estimates have reached as high as 500,000.

THE LABOR MOVEMENT

Organized labor had a late start after having been firmly suppressed during the regime of General Juan Vicente Gómez (1908—35) and earlier governments, although a few mutual benefit societies had maintained a precarious existence in Caracas and other cities.

General Gómez died in 1935, and the transformation of labor's status commenced promptly. The Labor Office responsible to the Ministry of Interior Relations was established and set about preparing a legislative charter for labor influenced by advanced legislation already in existence in Mexico and Chile. The result was the Labor Code of 1936. It was greeted with some alarm by employers, who regarded it as leftist-inspired, but its substance, modified substantially by 1945, 1947, and 1966 laws, was still in effect in 1970.

During the presidencies of General Eleazar López Contreras (1935—41) and General Isaías Medina Angarita (1941—45) the forces of labor made steady progress, and the ground for further progress was laid. In 1937 the Ministry of Labor and Communications was formed, and labor courts were established; in 1945 the first comprehensive labor legislation with respect to agriculture and animal husbandry was enacted.

In the freer atmosphere that prevailed following the death of General Gómez, the first unions promptly were organized among the oilfield workers and the skilled craftsmen in Caracas and in a few other cities. By mid-1937 there were enough unions to hold the First Workers' Congress. No permanent central labor organization, however, emerged from this meeting.

The López Contreras administration, moreover, became concerned at the growing signs of labor's aspirations and shortly adopted a less liberal policy, which was reflected in the imprisonment or exile of labor leaders and the banning of a second workers' congress planned for 1938. A national committee of workers was established in secret, however, and with the establishment of the government of General Medina in 1941 organized labor once more began to operate openly. During the 1930s and early 1940s the labor movement had been dominated by Communist elements. A significant shift, however, occurred in 1944 at the time of the holding of the Second Workers' Congress, where unions supporting the Democratic Action (Acción Democrática—AD) party emerged as the dominant element. This was accomplished by the Ministry of Labor's removal of recognition from many of the Communist-controlled unions. On reorganization, a majority were controlled by AD supporters. The move came as a distinct surprise, since the AD had been the administration's loudest critic and the Communists had cooperated with it.

As President Medina's term approached its end, the AD, in association with a group of young military officers, engaged in a coup that brought that party into power. During the next thirty-seven months the AD controlled the government, and the number of unions more than quadrupled. More than half of this increase came from the establishment of agricultural union organizations under provisions of 1945 legislation extending rights to farm and ranch workers. Gradually during the mid-1940s the AD built up the regional and occupational labor federations that supported it, and at the Third Workers' Congress, held in 1947, the first central labor organization, the Venezuelan Workers' Confederation (Confederación de Trabajadores de Venezuela—CTV), was established with the support of the great majority of the unions represented in that congress. After an up-and-down history, the CTV at the beginning of the 1970s was an organization of such significance that it completely dominated organized labor and politically played a role of great importance.

In 1948, however, labor lost its position of favor. The new military government was openly hostile to it, and for nearly ten years of military administration its aspirations were suppressed. Labor leaders were imprisoned or exiled and, when a strike developed in the oilfields early in 1949, the CTV was dissolved. In 1952 the government began a conspicuously unsuccessful effort to develop its own system of organized labor. Government-sponsored unions, expensive union headquarters buildings, and vacation resort centers made few friends, and the clandestine remnants of organized labor joined in a popular uprising in 1958 that had its culmination in the collapse of the Pérez Jiménez regime.

Labor, like the government, commenced a rebuilding program. Some 600 local unions that had existed ten years earlier were reconstituted, and another 700 new labor groups were at once brought into existence. Exiled labor leaders returned to Venezuela, and hastily appointed labor inspectors soon found themselves unable to cope with the flood of newly written labor contracts presented to the new government under terms of still existent but half-forgotten terms of labor law. Under the existing law, work contracts were between the individual company and the individual local union. The inspectors were supposed to pass upon these contracts, but the work load proved to be impossible, and labor and management joined in complaining over proposed contracts that could be brought before the labor inspectors only after weeks or months of scheduled delays.

The result was the enactment in 1958 of the Law of Collective Contracts, which led to negotiation of work contracts on regional or industry-wide basis rather than on the basis of the local union presenting its position to the individual company. The new system was effective from the beginning, with management and labor cooperating through central organizations that they brought into existence at that time.

The employer group—the Federation of Chambers of Commerce and Industry (Federación de Cámaras de Comercio e Indústria—FEDECAMARAS)—was to remain in existence as the principal representative of the country's business. The labor group was created on an interim basis to meet immediate needs, and all major political parties were represented in it. Its policy was to encourage the formation of national federations to represent specific industries as well as the reestablishment of the regional federations that had existed before the Pérez Jiménez administration. The new type of union organization proved successful, with nationwide groups, such as construction workers and textile workers, making up some of the largest federated organizations.

Employer and worker representatives were able to reach general agreement to avoid political infighting in connection with the numerous labor elections then occurring. Common lists of union candidates were agreed upon in advance of the elections and, when the CTV was reestablished in 1959, AD elements were elected to less than one-half of the executive posts despite the party's general rank-and-file support in the member unions.

For a time the facade of labor unity remained sufficiently intact for the organized movement to play an important role in maintaining the civilian administration in power. General strikes in 1959 and in 1960 were directed not at collective bargaining goals but at the frustration of attempts at military coups.

Labor unity, however, was collapsing. In 1960 the Communists,

workers employed were hired by direct application at the plant gate and more than 40 percent through friends and relatives. Some 5.5 percent were placed through the official exchanges, 4.4 percent through private agencies and unions, and 2 percent through advertisements.

Working Hours, Days of Rest, and Vacations

The regular schedule for the manual worker of either sex may not exceed eight hours per day or forty-eight hours per week for daytime employment; for night work it may not exceed seven hours per day or forty-six hours per week. Daytime work is that performed between 5:00 A.M. and 7:00 P.M. Positions of supervision or trust and those that by their working characteristics are not subject to working hours do not fall under these limitations. There is, however, an overall limitation of twelve hours in any single work period, and this must include an interim period of at least one hour.

Sundays and the nine regular national holidays are mandatory days of rest (see ch. 6, Living Conditions). Work may be performed regularly on these days only in certain specified categories where exceptions are necessary in the public interest or for technical reasons. For example, public services are generally excepted, and the retail sale of foodstuffs is permitted until noon on holidays.

In addition to the regular national holidays, special holidays (*días festivos*) are frequently declared by national, state, or local governments. The declaration of a special holiday does not, however, carry with it the right to pay without work. Various days, most of them religious days of observation, are often given special notice. These may include Twelfth Night, Corpus Christi, or All Saints. Business custom or collective contract may give workers a half day's or a full day's pay on these occasions, which include local days of observation. In addition, the traditional element in employer-employee relations is recalled in those occasional labor contracts that give the worker a holiday with pay on his birthday. In all, the worker may have as many as eighteen holidays during the year with pay. The average is estimated at from twelve to fourteen.

Paid annual vacations are set at fifteen working days for all employed personnel. The annual vacation must be taken during the year except that, if a worker is dismissed or loses his employment for reasons beyond his control, he is entitled to one day's pay for each full month worked. In addition, if a vacation to which a worker is entitled has not been taken before the termination of his contract, the employer must pay remuneration for the corresponding time involved. If, however, there is an absence without justifiable cause totaling seven or more days in a year, the time absent is counted as part of the annual leave to which the worker is entitled.

Different rules apply to farm laborers, whose regular workday is eight hours during a forty-eight-hour week. The number of hours may, however, be increased to a maximum of sixty. Days of rest are Sundays and seven legal holidays, and the regular paid vacation is four days for those who have rendered uninterrupted service on at least two-thirds of the working days of the year.

Work of Women and Minors

No minors of either sex under the age of fourteen are permitted to work in any industrial, commercial, or mining enterprise. Between the ages of fourteen and eighteen minors may work only with the authorization of their parents or legal representatives. For those between the ages of sixteen and eighteen the working day may not exceed six hours except in agriculture; work may not take place in mines, foundries, enterprises involving risks to life, or those that would impede normal physical development.

Women and minors under eighteen may not work in enterprises that might be injurious to morals or well-being or in retail liquor establishments. In general, work may take place only between 6:00 A.M. and 7:00 P.M. except in nursing or domestic service or in certain other designated occupations. Women over eighteen, however, may under certain circumstances engage in night work when necessity or the type of work so requires.

Apprentices are those minors between the ages of fourteen and eighteen who are given systematic vocational training while working and who have not completed training courses before commencing their employment. Industrial and commercial firms must provide such training for a minimum of 5 percent of their workers, but this ruling may be modified. Special wage scales apply to apprentice personnel.

A pregnant woman may not be employed in a task involving undue physical effort or one that might endanger her health. She must refrain from work from six weeks before childbirth until six weeks thereafter. During that period she receives compensation to provide for maintenance of the child in those localities where the social security system is operative.

Wages

Legislation requires that equal wages be paid for equal work regardless of the sex or nationality of the worker. Where manual work is involved, however, women sometimes receive a lower basic wage than men, presumably because they are believed less able to perform arduous work. In agriculture, for example, the lowest basic contract wage for women in 1969 was about one-third less than that for men. The equal-pay provision, moreover, does not preclude the payment of allowances or performance bonuses if these are made applicable to all workers in similar positions. The labor courts have ruled, however, that wage provisions need not apply to a worker succeeding another in the same work. Wages must be paid not less than once a week to *obreros*, but *empleados* may be paid once a month. Payments must be in legal currency, except that farm laborers may be paid one-third of their wages in kind.

Although minimum pay rates have been fixed in the past under emergency conditions, they are not currently established, and the legal machinery for their determination has never been used. In practice, minimum basic pay is determined by the collective contract in an industrial sector. Noncontract pay, however, tends to lag behind that awarded under contract. The wages of *obreros* employed by the government are fixed by collective bargaining. The government itself, however, fixes the pay of *empleados*.

Overtime and night work are rewarded with 25 percent and 20 percent premiums, respectively. Personnel required to perform work on the weekly day of rest or on a regular holiday receive an additional day's compensation.

Longevity pay increases are not required under the law, and during recent years increases based on contract negotiation have been moderate. Representative increases for contract *obreros* amounted to Bs3.23 (US$0.72) per day in 1968 and Bs1.86 (US$0.41) in 1969. In the fall of 1969 nearly 200,000 government workers ranging from professional to manual received increases averaging 10 percent. Some 30,000 petroleum workers received corresponding increases. In the private sector as a whole, about one-fourth of all personnel covered by collective bargaining benefited from increases ranging between 6 and 15 percent. Though moderate, the gains considerably exceeded the upward movement in the cost of living, which rose from a base of 100 in October of 1967 to 102.41 in November of 1969.

Among the supplementary elements in the wage structure, the most important is profit sharing. The law requires that each business enterprise distribute to workers 10 percent of the year's profits. Determination is made upon the basis of book profits, and a loss during one year may not be used to offset profits in another. When books show no profit, the government is authorized to order payment as a special bonus of seven days of pay to those with seven months' service and one day for each complete month for those with less than seven. The wording of the profit-sharing legislation is not specific, and judgments on individual cases are often necessary.

The amounts apportioned to the various workers in a firm are determined by a formula based on their regular wages plus special payments accrued during the year and may not exceed two months' of regular pay. It is customary practice to pay a portion of this bonus shortly before Christmas and the balance when it legally falls due.

A 1969 survey indicated that 73.4 percent of the wages paid in industry were required by law and that 26.6 percent were general or voluntary. The statutory wage components were made up of: basic pay at 53.5 of the total; profit sharing at 8.8 percent; severance pay at 6.3 percent; government contribution to social security funds at 3.3 percent; night pay at 1.1 percent; and overtime at 0.4 percent. The general pay components included such elements as payment for housing; attendance, cost of living, and family bonuses; food allowances; transportation costs; and medical, schooling, and other occasional cost items.

Among the highest daily industrial wages for contract workers during 1969 were those of electric shovel operators in iron mines at Bs52.65 (US$11.70), foundrymen in steel works at Bs51.50 (US$11.44), and petroleum drillers at Bs50.04 (US$11.12). The highest daily base wage for agricultural laborers was Bs14.00 (US$3.11) for men and Bs10.00 (US$2.22) for women. The lowest basic agricultural wage under collective contracts was Bs7.00 (US$1.56) for men and Bs4.50 (US$1.00) for women. Among office personnel, representative monthly wages included Bs1,425 (US$316.67) for bilingual secretaries and Bs712 (US$158.22) for typists. The salaries of managerial personnel ranged from an average of Bs1,453 (US$322.89) in some food processing industries to Bs4,280 (US$951.11) in metal processing establishments.

LABOR RELATIONS

Employment Contracts

A labor contract is made between an employer or group of employers and an individual worker or group of workers. Where personal services are performed, a contract is presumed to exist. A contract may be for completion of a specific piece of work, for an indefinite period of time, or for work over a specified period of time that may not exceed one year for *obreros* and five years for *empleados*.

The collective contract becomes part of individual contracts made while it is in effect, except that the collective agreement may not impose terms less favorable than those in the individual ones. Employers are required to negotiate a collective contract with a union if so requested by 75 percent of the workers in the same trade or in several trades within the same union.

Petitions for industry-wide contract negotiation may be initiated by either management or labor. Under terms of 1958 legislation, the Ministry of Labor may be asked to call a convention to negotiate such a contract with local, regional, or national applicability in a sector of the industry. The contract must be for a period of not less than two years.

The terms of a contract of this type are binding on employers and workers or their representatives who were called to but did not attend the convention, although parties in attendance have the right to oppose extension of the contract to them. If no agreement is reached after fifty days, the majority of the representatives of the parties may ask that the problem be submitted to a board of arbitration. The award of the board becomes compulsory on publication.

The contract may be declared by the executive to be applicable to other employers and workers in the same branch of industry if it covers a majority representation of both. A decree extending this coverage must be approved by the Council of Ministers, but refusal to extend does not bar the other employers and unions from voluntarily observing the agreement.

Termination of Employment

An indefinite contract may be terminated by either party after one month's uninterrupted work with one week's advance notice, after six months with two weeks' notice, and after one year with one month's notice. The advance notice may be waived by either party through payment of an amount equal to the wages for the period. The law states specific grounds under which either employer or worker is justified in terminating the contract without giving notice.

A worker discharged without just cause or for other reason beyond his control is entitled to one-half the wages earned during the last month of service for each year of uninterrupted work or fraction over eight months. The payment is known as the seniority indemnization (*indemnización por antigüedad*). In addition, when a worker under contract for an indefinite period loses his position because of unjust dismissal or leaves for a justifiable reason, he is entitled to supplementary severance pay (*auxilio de cesentía*) based on the length of employment. The compensation, which may not exceed the wages for eight months, is payable even if the worker is immediately hired by another employer, is entitled to retirement pay or old-age pension, or is protected by unemployment insurance. If a contract terminates because of forces beyond the employer's control, the employer is not required to pay the two forms of severance compensation.

Labor Disputes

Strikes and lockouts are permitted only after exhaustion of conciliation procedures in any enterprise employing ten or more persons. Workers or their representatives must present a summary of the complaints involved to the Labor Inspection Service for the purpose of seeking their settlement. A board of conciliation must be assembled under the chairmanship of an inspector within 72 hours, and work may not be suspended collectively until 120 hours after notification of the dispute. Similarly, employers must notify the inspector of the dispute and may not declare a lockout until 120 hours after the inspector was informed.

The board may recommend specific terms of agreement or referral to arbitration. If the parties do not agree to arbitration, which is not mandatory, the board issues a report stating the reasons for the dispute and the obligations of each party as well as an extract of the conciliatory discussions. The report also establishes that arbitration either has been rejected by both parties or has been accepted or suggested by one but rejected by the other. If arbitration is accepted, a board consisting of two members and an alternate from each side is selected from lists submitted by employers and workers. In 1969 some 600 collective labor contracts were signed, and 105 labor claims were settled amicably through conciliation or arbitration procedures.

After issuance of the report by the conciliation committee, a legal strike or lockout may be declared when there is no arbitration. If the work stoppage involves enterprises that would endanger the health or economic well-being of the public by their closure, the government may decree a resumption of work only to the extent necessary in the public interest.

The strike has seldom been utilized extensively in the country's labor history, and in those instances when it has occurred the motivation has tended to be political; many of the more serious work stoppages have been illegal. These illegal stoppages have often been met with dismissal or suspension of the officers of the unions involved.

The strike was not countenanced under the Pérez Jiménez regime. In the year of 1959 that followed its collapse, the reemerging labor movement called strikes resulting in the loss of over 100,000 man-days. During the 1960—68 period, however, organized labor operated in harmony with the government, and in no single year did the number of days lost reach as many as 50,000. The incidence was sharply higher in 1969—most of the increase a consequence of three major illegal strikes that alone accounted for the loss of nearly 200,000 man-days. This upturn, however, was politically oriented and apparently temporary. The tendency appeared to be downward again in 1970.

LABOR ORGANIZATIONS

Government Organizations

The Ministry of Labor is the principal agency concerned with labor matters. Two autonomous agencies operate under its general direction. The Venezuelan Institute of Social Security (Instituto Venezolano de Seguridad Social—IVSS) is charged with the country's retirement and welfare programs (see ch. 6, Living Conditions). The Institute for Training and Recreation of Workers (Instituto para Capacitación y Recreación de Trabajadores—INCRET) is concerned with worker training and administration or worker vacation resorts and trade union headquarters facilities.

The largest of the ministry's functional directorates, the directorate of labor, employs about two-thirds of the 1,400 persons on the ministry's payroll. It is responsible for the settlement of labor disputes through a conciliation and arbitration procedure under a labor inspection service. The service is based in Caracas but has regional offices in capitals of states and territories. Because labor matters are prerogatives of the national government, state and local governments do not participate in programs of the ministry. The other functional entities are the directorate of administration, the directorate of employment, and the directorate of social welfare, which maintains liaison with the IVSS and conducts the ministry's accident-prevention program.

Unions

Under the law, the rights of people to act collectively in the furtherance of their interests are generally recognized. Employers as well as employees may form unions, and worker unions may be formed either on a trade (the type of work performed) or an industrial or a regional basis. Union membership may not be made a condition of employment, and persons may not be denied employment simply because of union membership, although collective union contracts may be declared applicable to workers who are not union members.

Federations are supported by dues from members of constituent unions. It is probable that slightly less than half of the total federated union membership is in the trade or industrial groupings, but these functional federations are the more active and effective. In 1970 about 95 percent of the local unions had federal affiliations. The state or regional groups serve less as bargaining entities than as organizational links in the structure of the union system.

Labor union membership is open to persons of either sex, including aliens, over the age of eighteen and persons between fourteen and eighteen who have parental or other legal authorization. White-collar government employees and members of the armed forces are not allowed to form unions in order to bargain collectively. Associations of government employees may be formed, however, and these sometimes are politically important as voting blocs.

Union funds come from membership dues and from government subsidies. Government participation in financing is of particular importance at the national union level. In addition, many of the union headquarters are maintained with little cost at the government-owned Union House (Casa Sindical) in Caracas and in publicly owned centers in other cities.

Dues are often collected from the members through the checkoff system, in which the employer withholds union fees from the worker's paycheck. The checkoff is not compulsory but has often been included in collective agreements. Usually, the percentages withheld for the local union and for the federation are specified, with the larger amount going to the former. Unions without checkoff provisions tend to find themselves in relatively poor financial positions.

In union organizations, influence to a considerable extent derives from the chain of personal allegiances that carry up from the lower levels to the higher. As a result, debate and consensus in union affairs tend to be limited. Local leaders assume direct responsibility for the solution of individual problems. When factionalism occurs, it is usually based on differences of opinion between leaders. At higher levels, greater sophistication produces a relatively strong awareness of and attachment to institutions and ideologies.

Because unions are prohibited by law from affiliating with political parties, the close union relationship with parties is maintained on an informal and personal basis primarily through the parties' important labor bureaus. The leading labor union figures in each party are customarily members of this bureau. Government's part in this informal relationship is of particular importance in dealings with management. Without official backing, labor's bargaining position would be greatly weakened, particularly in instances where there was substantial unemployment. Apart from this important de facto working relationship between labor and government, unions are left relatively free from formal government pressures. Where Latin American government systems in many instances make it possible for a strike to be broken by declaring a striking industry to be performing an essential public service, Venezuelan law requires only a resumption of work to the extent necessary in the public interest. The law does permit the president of the country to dissolve a labor union, but this authority has not recently been invoked, and in 1970 both the president and the minister of labor were on record as regarding this authority as arbitrary and supporting its abrogation.

In the late 1960s organized labor had a collective membership of some 1.3 million persons in about 6,500 local unions. About the same membership had been claimed at the beginning of the decade. At any given time, however, the effective membership is debatable. Many workers sign as union members but pay dues seldom, if ever, and the dues-paying membership tends to ebb sharply after a collective contract has been successfully negotiated.

Immediately following the overthrow of the Pérez Jiménez regime in 1958, organized labor enjoyed a gain in strength unparalleled in its history. The 600 recognized unions that had existed previously were at once reconstituted, and legal status was promptly given to another 700 unions. By 1964 nearly 2,000 local union entities were in existence. Between 1964 and 1969 an average of more than 300 new local entities was created each year, but the actual net gain in numbers was limited. Government figures showed 342 unions to have been added in 1969, but the number of new union members was only about 17,000. At that time, it was estimated that between 100,000 and 125,000 were being added annually to the labor force.

The CTV in 1969 claimed a membership of well over 1 million in twenty-three regional and twenty-four industrial or trade federations, half of its claimed membership occurring in rural unions. The claim was undoubtedly inflated, but the inflation was not necessarily a reflection of unjustified claims by the organization itself. Criteria for effective membership were uncertain, and the CTV did represent the bulk of the country's organized labor. Its actual strength may have been 1 million, or three-fourths of organized labor's membership.

As the only real central labor organization in the country, the CTV was of great significance as a focal point of political influence and coordination of labor but was not itself a collective bargaining entity. In the late 1960s there were two other organizations claiming status as labor centrals. Catholic unions were represented by CODESA, with 30,000 nominal members in 1968—about one-third of them dues paying. Its federated entities included three regional groups and industrial groups for the textile industry, gasoline distributors, public health, and education. The CUTV was a Marxist group that separated from the CTV in the early 1960s. It had concerned itself with propaganda rather than collective bargaining activities.

In the late 1960s the largest of the national labor federations organized on an industrial basis was the rural Peasants' Federation of Venezuela (Federación Campesina de Venezuela) made up of unions and landworkers' leagues with a claimed membership of 600,000 in 3,500 local units. Its effective membership was estimated at 45 percent of the CTV total.

The aristocracy of organized labor was represented by the Federation of Petroleum Workers (Federación de Trabajadores Petroleros—FEDEPETROL) with a claimed membership of 20,000. Industrial federations claiming memberships of 60,000 or more were the port workers and transportation, construction, textile, and communication groups.

Employer Associations

Three or more employers engaged in commerce or in the same sector of industry may form an employer's union in order to act collectively in bargaining with organized labor. These associations in general have the same rights and are bound by the same legal restrictions as those applicable to unions. Under the law, management organizations are envisioned as almost exact opposite numbers to labor organizations, and both are referred to generically as unions. In practice, however, only about forty management entities in existence in 1970 performed collective bargaining functions. The primary orientation of the employer association, like that of the labor union, was political.

Employers drew together in associations first in Caracas and later in other parts of the country. The first major grouping was the Caracas Chamber of Commerce, formed in 1893, and the first association of manufacturers was the Caracas Chamber of Industry, formed in 1938. Major management as a whole is represented by FEDECAMARAS. Originally formed in 1944 and suppressed during the Pérez Jiménez regime, it was reconstituted in 1958 and in 1970 counted nearly 150 employer groups in its membership.

Although not itself a collective bargaining unit, FEDECAMARAS serves as a forum for its broad membership. It is outspoken in its presentation of views to the government and in its general opposition to legislation that would increase public control over the economy. For management, it serves a position nearly identical with that performed for workers by the CTV, with which it maintains regular and usually amicable discourse. For example, in 1970 a communiqué with respect to the need for reform of the national social security program was jointly ratified and issued by the two entities.

Among the major functional associations, most of them FEDECAMARAS participants, are the National Cattlemen's Federation, the Industrial Chamber of Caracas, the Chamber of the Petroleum Industry, the Venezuelan Construction Chamber, and the chambers of commerce in Caracas, Maracaibo, and the other large cities. The larger of these, like FEDECAMARAS, are central forums that leave the actual collective bargaining to their member groups. Other employer groups include the Pro-Venezuela Association—an association of investors and industrialists interested in the promotion of new industries—and voluntary business groups. It is not unusual to find a Lions' Club flourishing in a small population center in the interior.

International Affiliations

The CTV is affiliated internationally with the anti-Communist Inter-American Regional Organization of Workers (Organización Regional Interamericano de Trabajadores—ORIT) and its parent organization, the International Confederation of Free Trade Unions (ICFTU). The leftist central labor organization, the CUTV, reflects its political leanings in its affiliation with the Moscow-oriented World Federation of Trade Unions (WFTU). The third labor central, the Catholic CODESA, participates in the Latin American Confederation of Christian Trade Unions (Confederación Latino Americano de Sindicatos Cristianos—CLASC), which in 1970 sponsored in Caracas the Second Latin American Union Conference.

Several union federations have ties with international trade secretariat counterparts. These include the International Federation of Commercial, Clerical, and Technical Employees; the International Metalworkers' Federation; the International Federation of Petroleum and Petrochemical Workers; the Postal, Telegraph, and Telephone International; and the International Transport Workers' Federation. In addition, the American Instutute of Free Labor Development—an organization sponsored jointly by United States labor unions, government, and private enterprise—maintains small programs for worker education and low-cost housing.

Although representatives of largely fictitious Venezuelan labor groups participated in the founding conference of the Pan American Federation of Labor in 1918, the Venezuelan labor movement played very little part in hemispheric labor matters until recent years. Neither the left wing labor movement of the Latin American Confederation of Workers (Confederación de Trabajadores de América Latina—CTAL) active in the late 1930s and the 1940s nor the effort of the Perónist unions in Argentina to form an international group in the 1950s attracted serious Venezuelan support.

The CTV, shortly before its suppression by the Pérez Jiménez government, had been represented at the founding congress of a hemispheric group that was to become the direct ancestor of the moderate ORIT. After the CTV was reestablished in 1959, however, it remained aloof from hemispheric affiliation until it finally joined the ORIT in 1962.

FEDECAMARAS is a member of the Inter-American Council for Commerce and Production, a hemispheric employer group with headquarters in Montevideo. Venezuela was a founding member of the International Labor Organization (ILO) in 1919 and by 1970 had ratified twenty-four of that organization's conventions. Relations between Venezuela and the ILO were strained during the Pérez Jiménez regime, and the country withdrew from the ILO in 1957 as an effort was made to bring the unsatisfactory labor conditions in the country to the attention of the United Nations Educational, Scientific and Cultural Organization (UNESCO). After the collapse of the regime, however, the country returned to the ILO in 1958.

CHAPTER 20

TRADE

In 1970 the country continued its reliance upon petroleum and iron ore for export earnings. Petroleum generated about 90 percent of the country's foreign exchange receipts from exports; and iron ore, another 5 percent. The principal imports were industrial raw materials and machinery, transport equipment, construction material, and food. The United States, Great Britain, Canada, the European Economic Community (EEC) countries, and member nations of the European Free Trade Association (EFTA) were the country's largest buyers and suppliers. Trade with the country's fellow members of the Latin American Free Trade Association (LAFTA) was relatively small.

The country's foreign trade policy was shaped by the goals of promoting industrialization and substitution of imports, encouraging export-oriented industries, and maintaining a balance of payments equilibrium. Tariffs and nontariff controls were used to protect domestic manufacturers by levying high duties or by restricting imports and to spur investment and expansion by permitting relatively unrestricted entry of capital goods and primary materials required for production. The country's foreign trade policy was also directed toward fostering greater economic integration of the Latin American nations. The country had granted to other LAFTA members tariff concessions on an extensive list of items.

In 1970 domestic trade provided about 19 percent of the gross national product (GNP) and employed about 40 percent of the labor force. The principal marketing area was in and around Caracas, the capital and the largest urban center. The country's population had a relatively high purchasing power. A good transportation network allowed easy shipment of agricultural products from the countryside to the capital and other cities and facilitated the reverse movement of manufactured goods. The government continued to place great emphasis on the expansion of the highway system, modernization of major existing airports and creation of new airports, dredging operations in Lake Maracaibo and the Orinoco River, and construction of bridges to replace obsolete ferries at important river crossings.

FOREIGN TRADE

In 1970 the country had recorded a favorable balance of trade for over fifty years. The absolute amount of the favorable balance had fallen in the late 1960s, however, because foreign exchange earnings from exports had remained almost unchanged during the 1965–69 period, whereas payments for imports had risen by one-sixth in the same period. The country's position in foreign trade had been possible because of the sustained production and exports of petroleum, the high rate of investment, the rising incomes, and the development of industry, which had made possible the substitution of domestic products for imports (see ch. 18, Industry). During the 1960–69 decade the proportion of imports of consumer goods in total consumption had declined steadily. The proportion of imports of intermediate goods to GNP had steadily increased, however, so that between the two categories they had virtually kept pace with the growth of output (see ch. 16, Character and Structure of the Economy). Less than a quarter of total imports had been in consumer goods in the late 1960s; just short of a third, in intermediate goods; and nearly half, in capital goods.

Composition of Trade

Exports

In 1970 exports continued to be dominated by petroleum. It had accounted for more than 80 percent of the value of total exports for thirty-five years. In 1969 petroleum and its derivatives represented about 90 percent of total exports by value.

During 1969 direct exports of crude petroleum and derivatives reached 1.2 billion barrels, composed of 73 percent crude and 27 percent refined products. Exports of derivatives were 2 percent higher than in 1968, principally because of an 8 percent increase in the exports of combustible residual derivatives. The exports of these products had grown during the 1960s at an average annual rate of almost 4 percent, whereas total exports of crude petroleum and derivatives had grown during the same period at an average annual rate of slightly over 2 percent.

Increased world petroleum production and the emergence of competitive sources of petroleum have created a surplus of crude petroleum on the world market, resulting in consequent downward pressure on prices. The country was a founding member of the Organization of Petroleum Exporting Countries (OPEC); the signatory countries provide more than 90 percent of the world's total petroleum needs. OPEC is dedicated to the unification of petroleum policies of the member countries and to the assertion of their sovereignty over the petroleum industry. It is attempting particularly to end slumps in world petroleum prices by controlling production and exports. At the eighteenth and nineteenth OPEC conferences, held in June and December 1969, the country affirmed the need for the construction of a program of joint production among the member countries to stabilize the world prices of petroleum.

In 1970 the government believed that, although petroleum would continue as the country's major source of foreign exchange for years to come, its relative position in the country's total export trade would probably decline because of increased industrial diversification and the promotion of nontraditional exports in order to lessen the country's dependence on one commodity. This conviction was borne out by the growth of exports of steel from Bs1 million (4.5 bolivars equal US$1) in 1962 to Bs79 million in 1969 and by the commencement of exports of aluminum in 1969 at a value of Bs26 million.

The two traditional agricultural export commodities, coffee and cocoa, have diminished radically in importance. In 1969 they made up little over 1 percent of the total value of exports.

In 1969 the first steps were taken toward a reorientation of the country's foreign trade and the preparation of an integrated program for the promotion of exports. The government created the Foreign Trade Council (Consejo de Comercio Exterior) and organized a commission to study the formation of the Foreign Trade Bank (Banco de Comercio Exterior). The government asked the United Nations Industrial Development Organization (UNIDO) for technical assistance in determining the possibilities. The private sector was invited to play a major role in the composition and organization of the Foreign Trade Council; the council was expected to examine and express opinions on bilateral and multilateral trade agreements, export promotion, economic integration, and the institutional organization of foreign trade.

Imports

The significant rise in imports of capital goods in the 1960s had taken place outside of the petroleum sector, whereas the proportion of consumer goods to total imports had decreased during the same period. In 1969 imports of raw materials, machinery, transport equipment, and building materials represented 77 percent by value of total imports, an increase of 10 percent in value in relation to 1960.

Efforts had been made to supply some of these needs from domestic sources despite the high costs and the low level of tariff protection. The country doubled its production of intermediate products during the 1960s. The trend toward increased self-sufficiency had met with considerable success in import substitution of consumer goods, especially nondurables (see ch. 18, Industry).

One of the great problems that had characterized the economy for most of the country's history was the necessity of importing a large part of its food for a rapidly growing population that the long-neglected agricultural sector had not been able to supply (see ch. 4, Population and Ethnic Groups; ch. 17, Agriculture). Imports of foodstuffs in 1969 accounted for 5 percent of total imports by value, about 6 percent less than in 1960.

In 1969 consumer goods, excluding foodstuffs, constituted 18 percent of total imports by value, of which 12 percent was nondurable and 6 percent was durable consumer goods. The increase in domestic prices of imported goods caused by government-imposed foreign exchange measures in 1964 had reduced only moderately the volume of imports (see ch. 21, Finance).

Despite increased domestic production, the total cost of imported consumer goods had increased over the years. In 1960 such goods amounted to Bs760 million, and by 1969 they had increased to Bs1,187 million; the rise was in part the result of the increasing size and prosperity of the urban middle classes (see ch. 5, Social Structure).

Direction of Trade

In the 1960s there had been a trend of decreased exports to and a small decline in imports from the Western Hemisphere. Exports to that area in 1961 amounted to 79 percent of the country's total, and in 1969 they had fallen to 49 percent; on the other hand, imports from the Western Hemisphere declined from 60 percent of the total in 1961 to 58 percent in 1969. The decline in exports was the result of increasing competition from petroleum exporters in Africa and the Middle East (see ch. 18, Industry). For the same period, imports from Europe fell slightly from 34 percent to 33 percent of the total, and imports from Asia showed a modest increase of from 5 to 8 percent.

United States

In spite of increasing competition from other countries, the United States has continued to be the most prominent trading partner, accounting for 50 percent of the country's total imports and 34 percent of its total exports in 1969.

The United States in 1969 purchased about 50 percent of the country's total petroleum exports, 86 percent of its coffee, 54 percent of its cocoa, and almost all of its iron ore. The United States in turn supplied machinery and transport equipment, which made up 50 percent of imports from the United States.

Although such imports from the United States as machinery, chemicals, unassembled passenger cars, trucks, buses, and iron and steel products enjoyed an increasing demand, such agricultural imports as tobacco and dairy products continued to decline (see ch. 17, Agriculture). Nevertheless, the country ranked third in the Western Hemisphere in agricultural imports from the United States in 1969. During that year it imported Bs405 million worth of United States farm products. There was also a decline in imports of textile products, pulp paper, paperboard, and many medical and pharmaceutical products. The decrease was partially the result of strong third-country competition and government measures to diversify the national economy and to increase domestic production of crops and livestock products (see ch. 17, Agriculture; ch. 18, Industry). Still another factor was that national subsidiaries of United States companies were producing identical products locally at lower cost than their parent establishments.

The protectionist measures had led to several revisions of the Reciprocal Trade Agreement between Venezuela and the United States, which was originally negotiated in 1939 for the purpose of expanding foreign markets for the products of both countries through tariff reductions (see ch. 13, Foreign Relations). The last revision was in 1952, when certain provisions were modified by either raising import duties or subjecting some products to licensing, or both, in order further to protect local industry. In 1970 preliminary work for the renegotiation of the trade agreement was underway.

Europe

The trade pattern with Europe has appeared to be one of decreases in both exports and imports but with the sharper drop in exports. Whereas exports to Europe declined from 21 percent of total exports in 1961 to 16 percent in 1969, imports fell slightly from 35 percent of total imports in 1961 to 33 percent in 1969.

In 1969 the EEC countries were the leading importers (21 percent), followed by the EFTA member countries (11 percent). For exports the relationship was reversed with the EFTA countries taking 7 percent and the EEC countries receiving 6 percent.

Exports to Europe consist almost entirely of petroleum and its products. During the 1960s a weakening petroleum market had been encountered because of increased competition of low-cost crude oil from other producing areas, despite the special characteristics of the country's crude oil, which seems to be more suitable for European consumption than any other type when mixed with the lighter North African crude oil.

Still in force in 1970 were treaties of friendship, commerce, and navigation, some of which dated back to the late nineteenth century, with Belgium, Spain, Great Britain, and Italy. These countries, plus France and the Netherlands, were given most-favored-nation treatment by Venezuela.

Latin America

Latin America as a whole plays a relatively small part in the country's total trade. Commercial dealings with Central America and the West Indies are relatively negligible, but the tendency has been toward increasing trade with South America. In 1969 exports to Latin America were 15 percent of total exports, and imports from Latin America were 4 percent of total imports. The country enjoyed a favorable balance of trade with Latin America as a whole, although there were some variations with individual countries. The main trading partners were Argentina and Brazil.

The basis of the export trade is petroleum. Argentina, Brazil, and Uruguay are the major Latin American consumers. In the 1960s petroleum exports to Central American countries increased, but to South America they decreased, because Argentina and Brazil were increasingly supplied from domestic sources. The imports from Latin America are characterized by their frequently varying composition and consist basically of agricultural products, with some raw and semiprocessed materials.

Venezuela has bilateral commercial treaties under which it extends most-favored-nation treatment to Bolivia and El Salvador. It has a modus vivendi with Brazil and another with Canada. In 1966 the country became a member of LAFTA (see ch. 13, Foreign Relations).

TOURISM

In 1970 the government was making a concerted effort to attract an increasing number of tourists to the country. The uncertain outlook for the country's petroleum sector had drawn the government's attention to tourism as a significant possibility for diversifying the country's economy and as a source of income, new jobs, and foreign currency earnings. Because of the relatively high propensity of the country's residents to travel abroad, the foreign exchange balance on tourism was largely unfavorable, expenditures of the equivalent of US$134 million in 1969 being about three times receipts of US$46 million in that year (see ch. 21, Finance). Governmental agencies responsible for the development of tourism were the Venezuelan Development Corporation (Corporación Venezolana de Fomento—CVF), the National Hotel and Tourism Corporation (Corporación Nacional de Hotels y Turismo), and the

Tourism Directorate (Dirección de Turismo), a department of the Ministry of Development. The functions of the Tourism Directorate consisted of making policies and plans. The National Hotel and Tourism Corporation, a state enterprise, was mainly concerned with the development of hotels. The role of the Venezuelan Development Corporation in tourism was the provision of credit (see ch. 21, Finance).

In 1970 there were 1,390 hotels and guesthouses throughout the country. Of these, 613 were classified as hotels and provided a total of 16,323 rooms; 777 guesthouses provided a total of 11,550 rooms. There were 40 hotels each with more than 50 rooms; of this total, there were 13 hotels with more than 100 rooms apiece. The government estimated in 1970 that the country had 112 hotels that could be relied on for the development of domestic tourism; of these, about a dozen met the standards required by the international tourism market (see ch. 6, Living Conditions; ch. 21, Finance).

A government survey made in 1970 concluded that the country's tourist accommodations were planned for business-motivated travelers rather than for vacationers. The survey found that the distribution of tourist accommodations throughout the country closely reflected the distribution of the country's population and its economic activities (see ch. 4, Population and Ethnic Groups; ch. 16, Character and Structure of the Economy). The survey also noted that the few resort hotels that did exist were for the most part owned by the National Hotel and Tourism Corporation, managed by foreign hotel groups, and located in the Northern Mountains (see ch. 2, Physical Environment).

Of the 108,203 foreign tourists who visited the country in 1969, 53 percent came from North America; 21 percent, from Europe; 14 percent, from Latin America; and 12 percent, from other areas. On the whole, foreign tourism increased at an average annual growth rate of 22.5 percent in the 1961—69 period. Although a number of pleasure-motivated tourists had been attracted to the country since the mid-1960s, when a number of accommodations of international standard were completed and promotion initiated abroad, business and family-motivated visitors in 1969 accounted for the majority of foreign tourists. The average length of stay and daily expenditure of foreign visitors in the country in 1969 were estimated by the government to be thirteen days and the equivalent of US$30, respectively. Foreign exchange receipts from tourism in 1969 were calculated by the Central Bank of Venezuela (Banco Central de Venezuela) to total the equivalent of US$46 million.

Late in 1969 several first-class hotels, three tour operators, and the country's international airline launched a winter program of package tours, based on group-inclusive tour rates in the United

States. This particular program, offering combined stays in Caracas and on the coast for a total of seven days, proved very successful. On the basis of actual figures of passengers transported to the country in December 1969 and January and February 1970 and of reservations made for March and April 1970, the government anticipated that 12,000 United States vacationers would have visited the country by the end of the season, in addition to the number of United States residents who would have visited the country if the package tours had not been offered.

The great majority of foreign visitors usually arrived by air, the primary access to the country being Maiquetía International Airport. A number of tourists from neighboring Colombia, however, drove to Venezuela, crossing the border at San Antonio in the state of Táchira. Foreign excursionists and transit visitors were also of some importance. Foreign excursionists, primarily cruise passengers landing at La Guaira for an eight-hour visit to Caracas, increased from 30,000 in 1963 to 74,000 in 1969, whereas the number of transit visitors rose from 26,000 to 29,000 over the same period.

The main domestic tourist-generating area in the country was the Federal District, where as much as 20 percent of the population and a higher percentage of the total income produced by the country were concentrated (see ch. 4, Population and Ethnic Groups; ch. 16, Character and Structure of the Economy). The flow of visitors originating in this area made heavy demands on tourist facilities in the nearby littoral, particularly on weekends and holidays. Other tourist destinations popular among domestic vacationers were the Northern Mountains region and the island of Margarita (see ch. 2, Physical Environment). For the most part, residents of the country took pleasure trips during four specific periods of the year that totaled ninety days: the school vacation period from July to September, the Christmas holidays, Carnival, and Holy Week (see ch. 6, Living Conditions; ch. 7, Education).

DOMESTIC TRADE

In 1970, for the distribution of most products, the country was regarded as a single integrated market; the products were imported by firms in Caracas and distributed to branches in other parts of the country. When more than one marketing area was desired, it had been customary to divide the country into three zones. The western zone was served from Maracaibo; the central zone, from Caracas; and the eastern zone, from Puerto La Cruz (see ch. 2, Physical Environment). In the late 1960s, however, the growing importance of Puerto Cabello near the petrochemical complex at Morón and of the industrial center at Cuidad Guayana appeared to be resulting in the creation of new marketing subzones (see ch. 18, Industry).

Wholesale and retail trade was in 1970 characterized by a large number of small firms. Wholesalers generally carried many lines and imported to some extent. They often covered large geographic areas with a relatively small sales staff. Retailers usually specialized in a few products and operated with only one or two salespersons, often family members (see ch. 5, Social Structure). In the 1960s chains of modern department stores and supermarkets had appeared, particularly in Caracas and Maracaibo. The low-volume, high-price basis on which retail trading firms had traditionally operated had begun by 1970 to be reversed by some of the chains, but the country was still a high-cost market (see ch. 6, Living Conditions). Some prices, however, such as those of certain drugs and basic foods, were controlled (see ch. 17, Agriculture).

In 1970 shopping habits varied with the social class (see ch. 5, Social Structure). Supermarkets and department stores catered to the upper middle class and wealthy sector, whereas open-air markets or small variety stores attracted customers from both levels. Indications of the increasing sophistication of the consumer market were the sales of such items as automobiles, refrigerators, radios, and television sets (see ch. 14, Public Information; ch. 18, Industry).

Installment buying was widespread in 1970 and formed a substantial portion of all retail sales. The range of goods sold on installment credit was similar to that in the United States. Under the Law on Conditional Sales of December 26, 1958, the ownership of property sold on installment credit remained with the seller until the final payment had been made. Because consumer credit was scarce, manufacturers generally had to establish their own finance companies (see ch. 21, Finance).

Regulation and Organization

Trade in 1970 was regulated by the extensive Commercial Code (Código de Comercio). Article 96 of the 1961 Constitution guaranteed the right to free practice of trade within the limitations set by law (see ch. 11, The Governmental System). Basically, in addition to legislating in all matters concerning business organization and practice, the government intervened in trade through the maintenance of public monopolies over certain commodities and through price controls.

Public monopolies existed on the importation, production, and distribution of matches, cigarette paper, salt, explosives, and firearms. Such monopolies were exercised either directly, by government agencies, or indirectly, through the granting of concessions to private firms. The manufacture or import of firearms and explosives was regulated through licensing by the Ministry of Defense, and all private trade in such items was forbidden (see ch. 23, The Armed Forces).

Article 96 of the 1961 Constitution authorized the government to control prices. In 1970 such controls were in effect on most foodstuffs, medicine, low-octane gasoline, kerosine, and rents (see ch. 6, Living Conditions; ch. 17, Agriculture; ch. 18, Industry). Price protection to farmers was afforded through government buying and stockpiling of such commodities as corn and black beans (see ch. 17, Agriculture).

Business enterprises were organized by law into five basic categories: individually owned firms; general partnerships or companies; limited or silent partnerships; corporations; and limited liability companies. The various multiple-owned firms were defined as juridical persons independent of their members, whereas the individual enterprises were not deemed to have juridical personality. Individually owned firms were required to be identified by the surnames of their owners. The general partnership was organized and operated by a group of participants who shared joint and unlimited liability for their company's obligations. Limited partnerships were owned by one or more active partners, who bore joint and unlimited liability, and one or more silent partners, whose liability was limited to the extent of capital participation. Corporations were firms in which obligations were guaranteed by a specified capital and whose members were personally liable only to the extent of their holdings. Limited liability companies are obligated to the extent of specified capital, and their members are liable to the extent of their holdings.

Chambers of commerce functioned in the major cities, largely as the spokesmen for business interests before national and local government and before public opinion. The oldest and largest chamber, that of Caracas, had in 1970 more than 400 members, including industrial and commercial firms and such professionals as lawyers and accountants. Its ranks included not only firms and individuals with headquarters in the Federal District but also those based in many other cities throughout the country. Despite the inclusion of many manufacturing firms in the chambers of commerce, analogous trade associations had been formed in other sectors of industrial and commercial activity. The electric light and power industry, for example, had its own chamber of commerce.

All these trade organizations were members of the national Federation of Chambers of Commerce and Industry (Federación de Cámaras de Comercio e Indústria—FEDECAMARAS), which represented the business and industrial community at the highest level. The federation and its affiliates had on several occasions been invited to collaborate in the various government programs of economic development, but such cooperation had generally been limited to purely consultative functions, including membership on the boards of directors of state banks (see ch. 21, Finance). The bulk of its activities had been confined to economic studies and periodic issues of recommendations in its bulletins or in formal resolutions.

Structure and Practices

Wholesale

There were in 1970 wide disparities in volume, organization, and price mechanisms between channels for the wholesaling of industrial and imported goods, on the one hand, and those for the wholesaling of domestic unprocessed foodstuffs, on the other. In general, the distribution of manufactured and imported goods was effected by a relatively small number of specialized, large-volume wholesale agencies centered in Caracas and, to a lesser extent, in Maracaibo and a few other large cities. As a rule such firms possessed or had access to adequate warehousing and handling facilities and were, therefore, able to maintain suitable inventories and a smooth flow of goods to retailers and consumers. Most of them undertook all phases of procurement, storage, processing, and shipping, moreover, with the result that the number of middlemen was minimized.

By contrast, wholesaling of domestic agricultural commodities—excluding only those that required industrial processing and were sold directly to manufacturers, such as sugar, cotton, tobacco, and dairy products—was handled principally by low-volume dealers in widely dispersed locations. The majority of wholesalers dealing in domestic farm produce undertook only one or two phases of collection, transfer, and sale, and such produce often passed through a number of intermediate hands between producer and retail outlet (see ch. 17, Agriculture).

Until the late 1960s large-scale wholesaling was concentrated in the hands of import-export houses handling goods in a variety of lines and representing many different manufacturers. Some of the largest and oldest firms in Caracas still maintained this tradition of broad-based activity in 1970 but, as a result of rapid domestic industrialization and an expanding consumer market, there had been an increasing trend toward specialization. In addition to channels afforded by wholesale houses, manufactured goods reached retail outlets through sales offices maintained by the producers themselves. Several foreign manufacturers had distribution subsidiaries in the country, and many domestic manufacturers sold directly to retailers and large-volume industrial consumers.

Unprocessed domestic foodstuffs were traded through a variety of channels. In agricultural zones with easy access to cities and large towns, many farmers, especially those who operated on a commercial scale, undertook the transportation and direct sale of their produce to wholesalers, to retailers and, on occasion, to consumers in public markets. One important collection point for unprocessed foodstuffs was the village general store, whose owner, in addition to retailing a rudimentary stock of basic necessities, also bought small quantities of produce from his rural customers for periodic resale in large lots to wholesalers in the cities (see ch. 6, Living Conditions). Such village merchants often extended retail credit to their clients against repayment in cash or kind at harvesttime. Truckers were also important in the wholesale distribution of farm produce. In the states of Trujillo, Mérida, and Táchira, truckdrivers often engaged in two-way trade, buying industrially produced goods in Maracaibo for sale to retailers in mountain villages and returning with a load of farm produce.

In several cities and larger towns the Ministry of Agriculture operated produce markets at which farmers might sell directly to consumers and retailers without payment of stallholders' fees. These facilities, called free markets, were usually provided with low-cost restaurants and often with dormitories for sellers from distant areas. Prices in the free markets were set by the Ministry of Agriculture at 20 percent below prices currently prevailing in the municipal retail markets (see ch. 6, Living Conditions).

The Agricultural and Livestock Bank (Banco Agrícola y Pecuario) operated in 1970 the country's only modern foodstuffs market at Coche, in the Federal District. The Coche market had 130 stores and 32,292 square feet of undivided selling space, parking space for 400 trucks, and storage bins and refrigerators for 235,800 cubic yards of produce. For the development and coordination of a nationwide network of storage facilities, the CVF and the Agricultural and Livestock Bank had formed a semipublic corporation called Agricultural and Livestock Warehouses (Almacenes de Depósito Agropecuarios). All public storage facilities, including six cold storage depots and a system of silos for 80,000 tons formerly operated by the Agricultural and Livestock Bank, were turned over to Agricultural and Livestock Warehouses, along with the responsibility for future construction (see ch. 17, Agriculture).

Retail

In 1970 consumers in Caracas and Maracaibo and, to some extent, in other cities had access to a full range of merchandise outlets, including modern specialty shops, department stores, and supermarkets offering wide selections of goods. The bulk of retail trade in the country, however, was concentrated in small, family-owned general stores offering a limited range of merchandise. In rural neighborhoods and smaller towns, the only retail establishment was most often a general store selling a few foodstuffs—largely domestic canned goods and local produce—along with salt, kerosine, alcoholic beverages, soft drinks, a few articles of clothing, and a minuscule stock of small manufactured items, such as flashlights and tools.

In the cities and larger towns another retail outlet was afforded by open marketplaces at which vendors sold small stocks of foodstuffs, clothing, and manufactured items to consumers and bought wholesale lots of produce from farmers (see ch. 6, Living Conditions; ch. 17, Agriculture). Except for the free markets established by the Ministry of Agriculture, the majority of such markets were operated by the municipalities. Prices, both retail and wholesale, were generally set by bargaining within limits imposed by official controls on certain items.

Retail trade in the largest cities had attracted considerable foreign investment. Low turnovers and high markups had traditionally characterized retail trade. Department store and supermarket merchandising practices in Caracas had in 1970 gone far toward modifying this pattern, both by example and by their strong influence on retail price structures. Retail credit was until the mid-1960s restricted to monthly courtesy accounts extended to the prosperous clients of urban stores and to credit extended to farmers against harvested crops by the owners of rural general stores. A combination of relatively high levels of prosperity in the cities, rising material aspirations, and the influence of modern merchandising techniques had resulted in the widespread practice of installment selling.

High-volume, sophisticated consumer markets in the cities and the nationwide availability of radios had made possible an active advertising industry employing up-to-date methods. Advertising was polished and focused on the young person. Television and the press were the most effective media in the mass market (see ch. 14, Public Information). Annual advertising expenses were estimated in 1967 to be divided as follows: television, 51 percent; press, 26 percent; radio, 16 percent; and movies, outdoor signs, and other, 7 percent. Newspapers accounted for about two-thirds of the press share of advertising expenditures. In 1970 neon signs and bus placards were much in evidence in the larger cities.

TRANSPORTATION

In 1970 the country's transportation system was among the best in Latin America. A modern road network connected all the principal cities and towns. Trucking services were available at reasonable rates. Two national airlines provided both domestic and international service. There were ten major coastal and river ports that provided access for coastal and international shipping. Railroads did not play an important part in the transportation system, as there were only about 110 miles of track in 1970. Owing to the concentration of population and economic activity in the north where topography would make rail transportation difficult and expensive, highways had provided the principal means of internal movement in the country, accounting for 70 percent of freight and 90 percent of passengers.

The country's most pressing transportation problem in 1970 was in the metropolitan area of Caracas, where the combination of the heavy congestion of commercial, government, and industrial activity, the elongated configuration of the city, and the limitation of space had led to badly congested traffic conditions. The problem was being attacked through the planned construction of an expressway system that started early in the 1960s. A rapid transit system, which would complement the expressways, was also being planned.

Road Transport

In 1970 the country's highway network consisted of over 23,250 miles. Of these, 10,850 miles were paved; 8,700 miles, graveled; and 3,700 miles, earth. Whereas the overall length of the network had increased by 40 percent in the 1960—69 period, the length of paved highways had more than doubled. The system was densest in the heavily populated areas in the north and had a predominance of east-west roads in conformity with the country's topographical features (see ch. 2, Physical Environment; ch. 4, Population and Ethnic Groups).

Construction of a fifteen-mile four-lane highway on the eastern shore of Lake Maracaibo from Palmajero to Cabimas and of a thirteen-mile expressway along the northern limits of Caracas had been authorized in 1970. In the previous year completion of a series of overpasses and underpasses had made it possible for motorists to drive from the seaport of La Guaira or the nearby Maiquetía International Airport to all parts of the country by skirting Caracas and taking any of the highways going east, south, or west.

The trunk road system was, except in a few areas, basically adequate for the needs of trade in the early 1970s. Most of the system was concentrated in areas of dense population and intensive economic activity. Highway projects completed in the late 1960s or proposed for the early 1970s centered predominantly on improvement of the existing network through the replacement of ferry crossings with bridges, through the construction of new superhighways in areas of high traffic density, and through the construction of roads between points previously connected only indirectly.

In 1967 the cumulative vehicle registration was 642,276, of which 452,449 were passenger automobiles, 14,327 were buses and 175,500 were trucks. About 200,000 vehicles, or around 30 percent of the total, were concentrated in metropolitan Caracas. During the 1960–69 period the vehicle fleet had grown by 9 percent a year; passenger automobiles, by 10 percent; and trucks, by 7 percent. The ratio of population to motor vehicles in 1967 was 14 to 1.

The highway transport industry was in 1970 free of all governmental regulation, except for the requirement to pay license fees. There was no regulation of routes or prices. About 70 percent of the trucks were operated by organized enterprises that faced stiff competition from the owner-drivers who operated the remainder. Interurban bus services were mostly provided by cooperatives, each owning a few buses.

Air Transport

In 1970 there were two international airports and five other major airports that together annually handled about 1 million passengers and around 35,000 tons of cargo, mainly beef from the southern part of the country. Domestic traffic was shared by two airlines, one privately owned and the other government owned. External services were provided by a number of international airlines, including Venezuelan Aviation (Venezolana de Aviación), a mixed public-private company and the only Venezuelan international airline.

The new Maracaibo International Airport was dedicated on November 15, 1969, by the president. It had been built to handle 413,000 passengers annually by 1980; this capacity was about four times the number of passengers using the airport in 1970. On August 21, 1970, the president signed legislation authorizing the Ministry of Public Works to obtain credits for the expansion and modernization of Maiquetía International Airport serving Caracas. Construction of a provisional passenger terminal and a new freight terminal was underway in 1970 and was nearing completion by the end of that year. Immediately thereafter, construction of a new runway and a new terminal building was to begin; this phase was to be completed by 1973 and would be sufficient for expected traffic loads until 1980.

In the late 1970s the second phase, consisting of another runway, an enlargement of the terminal building, and a second new freight terminal was scheduled to be started, with completion projected for 1984. It was intended that the final project would be sufficient for traffic loads up to the year 2000 or later.

Because of a concentration of people and productive activity in a relatively small portion of the country, most passenger and freight transport by air in 1970 was over short hauls that were also served by reasonably good roads. The much higher rates charged by airlines were therefore only to a limited extent compensated for by speed differentials. One area in which air transport had developed and held a considerable advantage was that of shipment of meat. Several companies specialized in airlifting freshly killed steer carcasses to urban markets from points in the interior not served by roads. Large-scale ranchers selling in Caracas and Maracaibo found the relatively high freight charges well compensated for by savings in losses that would have been occasioned by driving their animals on the hoof to markets (see ch. 17, Agriculture).

In 1968 an air taxi service had been established between thirty-two cities, many of which were in the states of Apure and Bolívar and in Amazonas Territory; this was primarily an airmail service designed to improve communications in these areas. Another air taxi operator in the state of Bolívar had ten aircraft and transported 200 passengers daily.

Water Transport

The long coastline, the Orinoco-Apure river system, and Lake Maracaibo formed a system of waterways affording easy transit between many widely dispersed regions of the country (see ch. 2, Physical Environment). Water transport had maintained a position of some importance in foreign trade because of the large-scale iron ore traffic on the Orinoco (see ch. 18, Industry).

In 1970 the country's merchant fleet consisted of thirty-five oceangoing vessels with an aggregate gross tonnage of 315,000 deadweight tons. Of these vessels, fifteen were tankers, with an aggregate gross tonnage of 251,000 deadweight tons. The country's dry cargo fleet was operated by the government-owned Venezuelan Navigation Corporation (Companía Anónima Venezolana de Navegación). In 1969 the corporation carried 580,000 tons, a decrease of 6,000 tons from the tonnage carried in 1968. Coastal shipping was reserved to Venezuelan flag vessels, and the corporation dominated this trade.

Total cargo discharged in the country's ports in 1969 was 3.2 million tons, about 3 percent higher than the 1968 total. In 1967 there were 10,807 international shipping arrivals of many nations at the country's ports, and total cargo discharged amounted to 3 million tons; in the same year there were 9,952 overseas shipping departures and a total volume of 193.5 million tons of cargo.

La Guaira served as the port of Caracas and was the main port of entry for imports. Puerto Cabello served the important agricultural and industrial region surrounding Barquisimeto, Maracay, and Valencia. The administration of the country's ports was the responsibility of the government, which controlled entry, pilotage, docking, unloading, warehousing, and the collection of customs duties and port charges. It also provided bonded warehouses in which goods might be stored without payment of customs duties.

Deep-draft shipping channels were maintained in Lake Maracaibo for oil tankers and in the lower Orinoco River for iron ore and other bulk carriers engaged in international trade (see ch. 18, Industry). Only a small volume of domestic traffic was carried by coastal and inland shipping.

Rail Transport

In 1970 there was one railroad line in operation in the country. This was the 109-mile Puerto Cabello-Barquisimeto line, which was to have been the beginning of a national railroad network; the idea had been abandoned, and there were no plans in 1970 to extend the system. The line carried about 80,000 tons of bulk traffic, most of which was for the Venezuelan Institute of Petrochemicals (Instituto Venezolano de la Petroquímica), which had plants near Puerto Cabello. The line was managed by the Autonomous Railways Institute (Instituto Autónomo de Ferrocarriles) under the Ministry of Communications. Subsequent to 1965, three other older lines totaling about 200 miles, all separate lines unconnected with each other, had been abandoned because of lack of traffic.

On April 1, 1970, the Council of Ministers formally approved the project for the construction of a subway in Caracas. Construction of the first stage, running from the city's western outskirts to near the major governmental offices, was expected to begin in 1971 and to last through 1973. The government was drafting legislation in 1970 to submit to the National Congress for the formation of two companies. One company was to be responsible for acquiring the right-of-way, excavating, and building the permanent physical structures of the line; it was to be a joint venture of the national government and of the municipalities affected. The other company would be an autonomous agency of the national government; it would procure and supply the operating equipment and would later operate the subway when it was completed.

COMMUNICATIONS

In 1970 the National Telephone Company of Venezuela (Nacional Teléfonos de Venezuela) was working toward fulfillment of its 1970–74 investment program. The National Telephone Company of Venezuela was a government-owned autonomous institution; it operated the telephone system throughout the country and was also responsible for the operation of the submarine cables linking the country with overseas destinations, international radio communications, and advanced communications systems such as international Telex. The company was also charged with construction and operation of a satellite earth station.

Progress in telecommunications had been noteworthy. During the 1965–69 period the number of telephones had grown from 283,000 to 372,000, or an increase in telephone density from 3.2

to 3.8 per 100 population (see ch. 4, Population and Ethnic Groups). The company had formulated a program to increase the number of telephones in operation to 770,000 in 1974 and raise the number of Telex subscribers from 1,600 in 1969 to 2,700 in 1974. Achievement of this expansion would raise the telephone density from 3.8 to about 6.4 per 100 population. This density would contribute much to meeting a substantial unsatisfied demand. It would also meet most requirements in Caracas and would incorporate towns of at least 2,000 inhabitants into a national direct-dialing system.

Expansion of postal and telegraph services was also part of the 1970—74 investment program. Domestic telegraph service was the responsibility of the Ministry of Communications (see ch. 11, The Governmental System). International telegraph service was until 1969 provided by two private companies, but on expiry of their contracts in that year the service was provisionally taken over by the government's domestic airline. Discussions were underway within the government in 1970 to establish a new autonomous institution along the lines of the National Telephone Company of Venezuela to manage both the international and the domestic telegraph services.

In 1970 the company was continuing to experience technical difficulties in maintenance, operation, and staff arising from the existence of five different switching systems in Caracas and seven throughout the country. Some standardization was provided in the company's 1970—74 investment program.

On December 15, 1967, the president inaugurated the first long-distance direct-dialing service established in the country. The system consisted of Caracas-Valencia, Caracas-Maracay, and Caracas-Federal District coastal area, which included Maiquetía International Airport and the port of La Guaira. In 1968 a second group of cities was added: Barquisimeto, Maracaibo, Valera, San Juan de los Morros, and Valle de La Pascua. The company's 1970—74 investment program provided for a national long distance network connecting twenty-eight of the principal cities of the country with the capital.

A submarine cable inaugurated on August 4, 1966, gave the country direct voice contact with the United States and replaced a radio system. The submarine cable, with its eighty-channel capacity, was expected to meet the country's needs through 1970. On December 18, 1968, direct dialing from the United States to the Caracas exchange of the National Telephone Company of Venezuela went into operation over thirteen channels of the cable, and on January 15, 1969, an equal number was used to establish direct dialing from the company's long-distance operator in Caracas to the United States telephone system. About 85 percent of the country's international telephone traffic is with the United States.

CHAPTER 21

FINANCE

In 1970 the most important fiscal requirement, in the view of the president of the Republic, was the need to maintain a balanced budget. Before 1958 the national budget had almost always been in balance. After 1958 there had been several years when fiscal deficits occurred and supplemental appropriations were made to the regular budget.

Government fiscal operations affect all sectors of the economy. Government expenditures in 1969 were equivalent to 31 percent of the gross national product (GNP). In addition to the central government's revenues, funds are collected and spent by the state and municipal governments and by the autonomous institutions. In 1968 the central government had a budget of almost Bs8.9 billion (4.5 bolivars equal US$1), but an additional Bs5.1 billion were raised by the autonomous organizations and about Bs1 billion by the states and municipalities.

Although the central government collects the bulk of total public revenues, it spends less than half of total public expenditures. The central government makes annual transfers of funds from its budget to the autonomous institutions, the states, and the local governments to augment their own income. By 1970 it had become obvious to the central government that inadequate control of spending by these other levels of government was a contributory factor to the unbalanced budgets.

The petroleum industry provides the bulk of public revenues. Taxes, royalty payments, and special levies to which the petroleum companies are subject usually raise two-thirds of public income. Because of this dependence upon the petroleum industry the Venezuelan taxpayer has had a relatively low tax burden and has not been accustomed to paying high taxes. The petroleum industry, however, was leveling off during the 1960s because of a stagnation in petroleum exports, and by 1970 the government took the position that the domestic tax burden would have to be increased if planned economic development expenditures were to be maintained.

Public debt has been growing and was over Bs5.4 billion in mid-1970. Over half was external debt and almost 60 percent of the total had been contracted by the autonomous agencies to finance development projects. The relationship of total debt to national income was low, however, and manageable. Only between 3 to 4 percent of the national budget was required to meet amortization and interest payments. The country's credit rating is excellent and loans are easy to obtain.

Since 1962 there has been some difficulty in maintaining a balance of payments equilibrium. Imports have grown continuously, and trade surpluses have been declining (see ch. 20, Trade). Invisibles, such as tourism, freight and insurance, and profit remittances of foreign companies, are almost always negative. New capital inflow usually offsets any deficits in the current account, but in some years it has not done so.

Foreign investment in the country is high. In 1970 it amounted to more than Bs25 billion—most of it in the petroleum industry. Private United States and British firms accounted for 93 percent of total foreign investment. Generally, the government has a policy of encouraging foreign investment. Participation in some fields of economic activity however, is restricted. In addition, certain temporary financial restrictions were imposed on foreign companies in mid-1969 that were still in effect at the end of 1970.

The banking system comprised both state and private banks, savings and loan associations, and mortgage banks. The state banks are used to promote specific economic sectors, such as agriculture and industry, or to satisfy a social need, such as low cost housing. Private commercial banking is fairly well developed. In 1969 there were thirty-one banks with a total of 450 branches throughout the country. Other financial institutions serving to mobilize savings are insurance companies, financing and investment companies, and two stock exchanges.

The bolivar (Bs) was backed so adequately by international reserves that it was designated an international convertible currency by the International Monetary Fund (IMF) in 1966. The official exchange rate is considered Bs4.5 equals US$1 but, in fact, varies from this rate, depending upon the use or source of the exchange.

NATIONAL BUDGET

The central government's budget dominates the revenue element but not the expenditure part of total public finance. It usually accounts for up to three-fourths of all public sector revenues; in 1969 the central government collected over 70 percent of total revenues. It, however, spent only 43 percent of total public expenditures. The autonomous institutions, the states, and the local governments receive transfers from the central government to augment their own sources of revenue. The autonomous institutions collect about 25 percent of total public receipts but account for 45 percent of expenditures; state governments collect about 2 percent of revenues but spend 10 percent of expenditures; local governments collect and spend about 2 percent of each. Mainly because of inadequate control of spending by the autonomous institutions, the budget had not been an effective instrument of economic policy. Each agency has its own working budget, and until 1966 their accounts were not audited. In April 1970 an executive decree was issued to require these institutions to follow uniform rules and to exercise stricter control of expenditures.

In addition to the regular budget, supplemental appropriations are made in some years. When a surplus occurs, it is used either to increase the reserves of the Central Bank of Venezuela (Banco Central de Venezuela) or to retire some of the foreign debt. Starting in 1969, however, there was a growing debate within the government as to whether or not budgetary, borrowing, and tax policies should be amended in view of the frequent need for supplemental appropriations. In November 1970 it became apparent that the government would have to modify its 1971 budget or the National Congress would not approve it.

The annual budget is formulated in accordance with provisions of the Constitution and with the Law of Public Finance of March 17, 1961. In 1962 the fiscal year, which had run July 1 to June 30, was changed to correspond with the calendar year. Since mid-1970 the preparation of the budget has been the responsibility of the National Budget Directorate (Dirección de Presupuesto) of the Ministry of Finance, subject to policy guidelines set by the president.

Preliminary budget proposals prepared by the various entities of the government are submitted to the Ministry of Finance by June 12 for incorporation in the budget law that is submitted to the National Congress by the president. The ministry makes any changes that are necessary to conform with the overall program of the Central Office of Coordination and Planning (Oficina Central de Coordinación y Planificación—CORDIPLAN), and the Council of Ministers makes final approval by July 4. During August and September a detailed estimate of potential tax revenue is made by the offices responsible for tax collections. The president forwards the budget proposal to the National Congress on October 2, except during the last year of a presidential term when it is submitted earlier. The Chamber of Deputies must approve the budget at two separate sessions during which it may make modifications. The budget is then sent to the Senate. Differences between the Chamber of Deputies and the Senate are resolved at a joint session. If the National Congress fails to pass the budget by January 1, that of the previous year remains in force until the issue is resolved.

The 1968 budget was approved for Bs8.9 billion, but a deficit occurred when revenues were less than anticipated. The treasury for the first time had to resort to short-term borrowing to finance the deficit. The 1969 budget was Bs9.3 billion, but a deficit again occurred when expenditures exceeded revenues by Bs1.2 billion. The 1970 budget as originally submitted to the National Congress was less than that for 1969, but it was amended to almost Bs9.9 billion. Although another deficit was anticipated, by the end of August 1970 the budget was still in balance as revenues were slightly ahead of expenditures.

For 1971 a two-level budget was submitted to the National Congress. The lower level was Bs9.7 billion. The upper level was Bs10.56 billion. The difference was to be made up by proposed new taxes. If the new taxes were not approved, then the lower level would prevail. The proposed new taxes included a wholesale sales tax on certain items, a luxury tax, and increased personal income taxes. In addition, a special four-year development budget amounting to Bs2.9 billion was submitted for the National Congress's consideration. The special budget was to be financed entirely from loans, both external and internal.

Expenditures

Government expenditures have increased along with revenue growth. From the 1963—68 period they rose at an average annual rate of 9 percent. In 1969 they rose less than 4 percent. In the 1960s the need to maintain employment levels has resulted in a continued commitment to a high level of public works expenditures.

Despite increases in ordinary income of the government the percentage thereof used for investment has decreased sharply because of increases in current expenses. The proportion of ordinary receipts earmarked for investment was about 30 percent in 1971. Consequently, the public sector has had to obtain foreign financing in order to maintain desired investment levels. About 65 percent of the 1971 budget was for ordinary expenditures, and 5 percent was for amortization and interest on the public debt.

By function, or type of activity, public works projects receive the largest percentage of the budget. In the 1970 budget it was about 21 percent. Education is usually next with between 12 and 15 percent, followed by defense with about 10 percent, and health and social welfare with almost 9 percent. Other activities receive smaller percentages. General administration of the government costs less than 4 percent of the budget.

Among the ministries, the Ministry of Interior Relations and the Ministry of Public Works received the largest percentages of the annual budget in the late 1960s, about 20 percent each. The appropriations for the Ministry of Interior Relations included the funds that were transferred to the states, territories, and the Federal District. These funds must be 15 percent of the annual budget according to the Constitution. The Ministry of Education was next with about 14 to 16 percent of the budget, followed by the Ministry of Defense with 9 to 10 percent. The Ministry of Health and Social Assistance was allotted between 8 and 9 percent; the Ministry of Finance, over 7 percent; the Ministry of Agriculture, under 7 percent. All the other ministries, the judiciary, and the legislature received the balance.

Every ministry receives an allotment that is to be transferred to one or more autonomous decentralized institutions under its general jurisdiction. In 1970 there were over eighty such public institutions, and about 20 percent of the national budget was transferred to about forty of them, through the various ministries, to augment income from their own operations. In 1968, for example, total income of all the autonomous agencies amounted to Bs7.6 billion, of which Bs2.5 billion were transfers from the central government budget. These institutions are of three types: service institutions, such as the Venezuelan Institute of Social Security; financial, such as the government banks; and commercial and industrial enterprises, such as the telephone company, the steel company, or Venezuelan Aviation. Some of the organizations are joint public-private enterprises but also receive funds from the government.

Revenue

Direct taxes—principally those levied on corporate and personal income—assumed a growing prominence in the 1960s. Direct taxes constituted more than 50 percent of ordinary revenues by 1970. The indirect taxes declined to less than 14 percent of the total.

After direct taxes, the two most important sources of ordinary government receipts are: territorial revenues (rentals and royalties on the use of natural resources), 31 percent; and commercial revenues (profits and fees derived from foreign exchange operations, licensing, and consular services), 2 percent. The bulk of territorial revenues are provided by royalties on oil and iron production and rentals on publicly owned lands. Including taxes and royalties, the petroleum industry provides two-thirds of total government revenue. The largest portion of the commercial revenues is derived from exchange operations. Other sources of ordinary revenue include profits from the sale of salt (a government monopoly), interest on loans granted through government banks, and a variety of miscellaneous fees and rentals. Taken together, these remaining sources account for a very insignificant portion of the receipts, about 2 percent in 1968.

Extraordinary revenues, including such items as loans, sale of short-term treasury notes, and sale of government assets, have accounted in different years for a widely varying proportion of total government income—largely in reflection of the amount of new long- and short-term credit contracted. During the 1960s extraordinary revenues accounted for no more than 2 percent.

Although tax receipts are substantial by international standards, amounting to about 27 percent of GNP, most of the burden is on foreign companies, particularly the petroleum companies. Domestic taxpayers have a relatively low tax burden. The minister of finance claimed in 1970 that only 3 percent of the population pays income taxes, which are the most productive of the various domestic taxes.

Because of its great dependence on taxes relating to foreign trade, government income is sensitive to variations in foreign trade, especially the world price of oil. In 1970 the government was aware of the need to increase the share provided by domestic taxpayers. One measure was the new tax proposals submitted to the National Congress in November of that year. Another was a measure under which all tax delinquents and evaders could pay back taxes without penalties by June 30. Afterwards, a double tax penalty would be applied. Tax administration was modernized, including the use of computers. As a condition for engaging in certain activities or obtaining some government service, taxpayers must submit a tax clearance certificate, proving that they have paid their taxes.

Taxation

Income Taxes

The power to tax personal and corporate incomes is reserved to the national government. A new tax law was enacted in 1966 and became effective January 1, 1967. Responsibility for collection and enforcement is assigned by law to the Income Tax Administration of the Ministry of Finance.

Only income derived in Venezuela is taxable. All residents with net income over a stipulated amount, all companies (juridic entities), and all foreigners regardless of amount of net income must file a tax return. Nonresidents whose entire tax burden has been withheld do not have to file. Over 320,000 tax declarations were filed in 1969, and over 346,000 were filed as of June 30, 1970. The government estimated that about 400,000 declarations would be filed during 1970. Certain persons (such as foreign diplomats), entities (autonomous government institutions), and types of income (interest on the first Bs50,000 in savings accounts) are totally exempt from taxation. Other types of income may be partially or totally exempt for a period of time, by order of the president of the Republic, if it is earned from socially or economically useful activities.

At the time of filing for the past year, an estimate of the current year's income must be made by persons not subject to withholding and by all juridic entities. Tax payments are made by them every two months. The income tax law is similar to that of the United States, but rates are much lower, and provisions for dependent allowances and deductions are more liberal. A variety of exemptions for dependents and deductions for charitable and cultural contributions and medical bills are applicable in its computation. The generous allowances result in a virtual exemption from taxes for much of the population. For example, only 110,000 individuals actually paid taxes in 1969 out of the more than 300,000 who filed a declaration.

Since 1967 there have been three classes of taxpayers. Each class pays a different progressive rate. Schedule A applies to nonpetroleum and nonmining corporations, all partnerships, and commercial income of individuals. The tax rates range from 15 to 20 percent of taxable income. Schedule B applies only to oil and mining activities, and rates range from 20 to 52 percent. Schedule C applies to the income of most individuals, and rates range from 4.5 to 45 percent of taxable income.

Fiscal Obligations of the Petroleum Industry

In addition to normal corporate taxes, the petroleum companies are subject to several special levies so that total contributions of the petroleum industry are about 63 percent of total revenues. A production tax (royalties) is payable monthly in cash or kind on crude oil, natural gas, and asphalt extracted. The rate is generally 16.66 percent of a specified reference (market) price, but some concession holders pay a higher rate. The average rate in 1969 on petroleum was 17.34 percent. An initial exploitation tax of at least Bs8 on each hectare (1 hectare equals 2.47 acres) is paid upon acquiring a concession. In effect, however, winning bidders on concessions have been paying more than Bs8. A surface tax is levied on each hectare of land being exploited. The tax is assessed annually but payable quarterly, and the previous quarter's production tax already paid is deducted from the current quarter's surface tax owed. The surface tax rate is Bs5 per hectare for the first ten years of exploitation and then increases by Bs5 every five additional years to a maximum of Bs30 per hectare.

A consumption tax is paid by manufacturers or refiners on petroleum products sold domestically. The tax rate is 50 percent of the import duty applicable to that product. A transportation tax is paid by companies transporting petroleum (pipeline companies) for third parties. The rate varies up to 2.5 percent of the amount received. The special exchange rate at which petroleum companies are required to buy bolivars from the government-controlled Central Bank of Venezuela forms an indirect but important levy.

Under provisions of a law enacted in 1948 the government is entitled to a minimum of 50 percent of all profits derived from domestic oil production. This principle is implemented in what is termed the additional tax, which is set at 50 percent of any excess of profits over tax payments. The additional tax is calculated by subtracting the total of all other taxes already incurred from net after-tax income. Any excess of income is then taxed at 50 percent. In practice, the share accruing to the government has consistently been greater than 50 percent because the level of the other taxes is so high. In 1969 the government's share of net profits was 69 percent. In late 1970 the National Congress amended the income tax law, thereby increasing by 16½ percent (from 52 to 60 percent) the tax rate on the petroleum companies. The amendment also enables the president to unilaterally set reference prices in the future—without consultation with the petroleum companies if he so desires.

Other Taxes

Primarily because of the revenues collected from the petroleum industry, the proportion of income derived from indirect taxes in Venezuela is among the lowest in Latin America. Indirect taxes are divided between those levied on importation in the form of customs duties and consular fees and those levied on domestic production and consumption.

Customs duties bring in about only 7 percent of revenue. With some exceptions, duties are based on the weight rather than on the value of the goods imported. The rate schedule has ten classes with rates ranging from Bs0.05 for one kilogram (1 kilogram equals 2.2 pounds) in the first class to Bs50 per kilogram in the tenth class. These duties are subject to specific surcharges and ad valorem rates or to specific decreases, according to the commodity. In the national interest the president is given wide powers to increase and decrease duties by 100 percent and to grant rebates up to 25 percent. Duties are raised to protect domestic industries. Special rates apply to certain items originating in member countries of the Latin American Free Trade Association (LAFTA), in the United States (under the Reciprocal Trade Agreement), and in countries signing most-favored-nation agreements. Effective in late 1970 was an additional import duty of 2 percent on goods arriving by air.

Various production, sales, and excise taxes bring in about 8 percent of revenue. One of the more important is an alcoholic beverage tax, which was increased in late 1970. An inheritance and gift tax ranges from 1 to 55 percent, depending on the amount of the bequest and the relationship between donor and beneficiary. Other minor taxes are as follows: fiscal stamp taxes, required for most judicial and commercial acts; a telecommunications tax of 1 percent, levied on gross revenue of radio and television stations; public registry fees; a capital-stock tax, levied on new stock issued by companies; and an exit tax of Bs80.

STATE AND MUNICIPAL FINANCES

The Constitution provides that state and municipal finances are subject insofar as possible, to the same regulations that apply to those of the national government. The constitutional allotment of money provided by the national government to the states is their main source of income and is distributed from federal funds through the Ministry of Interior Relations, in rough proportion to population. In turn, the states allocate part of the funds to the municipalities to supplement the municipal taxes and other local charges that constitute their primary financial base. It is estimated that the national government has provided 98 percent of state and territorial revenues in the form of constitutional and supporting grants since 1964. The small balance comes from state lotteries, real estate tax, and sale of state property.

Total revenue of the states grew by better than 10 percent annually between 1964 and 1967 but only 7 percent in 1968. No figures were available for 1969. Total state revenue in 1968 was Bs1.1 billion. By 1970 state budget procedures varied so greatly from state to state that the federal government was encouraging the states to improve and unify them.

State expenditures run slightly ahead of revenues. Education, public health, and social assistance account for two-thirds of total expenditures. Costs of administering state governments run around 18 percent, and other activities account for the balance. From 22 to 24 percent of the total are capital costs, such as schools and other buildings.

Total revenues of all municipalities increased at an average annual rate of 9 percent from 1964 through 1967 but by less than 2 percent in 1968, to Bs790 million. About half of each year's total is received by the Federal District. In contrast to state government revenues, most of local revenue is raised by the municipalities themselves with lesser amounts coming from transfers from the state and federal governments. The largest source of municipal revenue is a license tax on businesses called a *patente*. It varies considerably and usually is administered by a mixed board of businessmen and municipal officials. The rate for the *patente* is based upon the previous year's profits. Municipalities also levy taxes on urban real estate (sometimes exempted to attract new industries), public amusements (usually 10 percent of admission price), commercial advertising, vehicles, and rental receipts. The vehicle tax rate varies so greatly that many owners register vehicles in lower rate jurisdictions. The country is one of the few where local governments may levy a tax on gross rental receipts. If the building is owner occupied, then the tax is based upon the cost of acquisition. Among other sources of municipal revenue are proceeds from the rent or exploitation of communal lands, fines, and state or national subsidies and donations.

Municipal expenditures run slightly ahead of revenues. In 1968 total expenditures of all municipalities were Bs805 million. Disbursements are predominantly earmarked for current expenditures, about 80 percent of the total, mostly for salaries of municipal employees. The balance is for capital expenditures. Over half of total expenditures are made by the Federal District. Most of the municipal expenditures go for sanitation, education, water supply, sewerage, and street maintenance.

State and municipal finances, besides being thoroughly controlled by the national government, are further characterized by the lack of a clear separation between the three levels of government responsibility for such functions as education, sanitation and health, construction of roads, and other public works. Although there seems to be a tendency for the federal, state, and municipal governments to concentrate on selected functions in these areas, there is inevitably some duplication of services.

PUBLIC DEBT

The public debt is divided into two categories—external and internal—each having subdivisions for direct and indirect obligations. The direct public debt consists of government securities and short- and medium-term obligations, whereas the indirect public debt consists of long-term obligations. The total public debt on June 30, 1970, excluding the floating debt, amounted to Bs5.4 billion, of which 53 percent was external and 47 percent was internal. About 60 percent of the total was contracted by the autonomous agencies. The floating debt consists of obligations incurred by government ministries and entities during the year but not yet paid for. In some years it is a considerable sum of money. Total debt is low compared to national income and government revenues. In 1969 it was about 7 percent of GNP and took only 3 percent of the budget for amortization and interest payments.

One of the problems that faced the government between 1959 and 1964 was the matter of the obligations, mostly in short-term loans, incurred by the previous regime. Although no exact figures are available, it is estimated that the dictatorship of General Marcos

Pérez Jiménez left the equivalent of over US$200 million in short-term debts.

The period of troubled public finances that followed the overthrow of the government of Pérez Jiménez did more than highlight the ambitious public works program and the huge floating debt. It pointed out the obvious shortcomings of the law of public credit, first enacted in 1941 and then amended in 1944, which governed the credit operations of the government.

As the law stood before it was again amended in 1959, it was considered to be both restrictive and loose. It required congressional approval for all money loans and the submission of detailed plans for public works projects to be so financed—procedures that were both time consuming and troublesome. On the other hand, the law did not regulate the incurrence of debt on contracts, and it was possible for the various government departments, agencies, and autonomous institutes during the Pérez Jiménez dictatorship to issue, by contract, short-term promissory notes without the approval of the National Congress or any central office in the government. It was the payment of such notes amounting to about Bs2.5 billion that created a difficulty for the government of Rómulo Betancourt.

The public credit law in effect in 1970 provided that, with certain exceptions, the national executive and government departments need prior authorization of the National Congress in contracting public debt. Money loans and other credit operations of the autonomous institutes were made subject to authorization of the national executive upon consultation with the Central Bank of Venezuela and required the consent of the National Congress. States and municipalities, not mentioned in the old public credit law, were required to obtain approval from the national government for any incurrence of debt. They were also prohibited from engaging in external loan operations.

The major exception under the public credit law provides that short-term credit obligations, payable during the current fiscal year and incurred to meet current expenses, do not require congressional approval. Treasury notes issued by the national executive, for example, require no such approval if they are not in excess of 10 percent of estimated ordinary income. Similarly, short-term operations of states and municipalities not in excess of 10 percent of budgeted income are excluded.

The country has a good international credit rating. All foreign obligations have been met since 1906. If any surpluses exist in the annual budget, they are used to retire older debt, both foreign and domestic. The country's good credit permits it to contract for foreign loans for development projects without much difficulty, thereby conserving its foreign exchange reserves.

BALANCE OF PAYMENTS

During the 1960s the balance of payments moved back and forth from favorable to unfavorable. In 1968 there was a balance of payments deficit of the equivalent of US$116 million.

During the 1960s the current account weakened steadily with declining surpluses stemming primarily from a leveling off of petroleum exports and continual growth of imports. Freight and insurance together constituted a large negative annual item because most of the country's foreign trade is carried out by foreign shipping. In 1967, for example, the equivalent of almost US$180 million was spent on freight and insurance. Investment income is also almost always negative, reflecting profits of the petroleum and mining companies remitted abroad. Other invisibles such as tourist travel and private transfers abroad also show annual deficits.

New capital inflow, from private investments and foreign loans, usually offsets any deficit in the current account. In years when this inflow is not large, such as in 1968, the balance of payments is negative. An estimate has also been made that the equivalent of US$100 million annually is sent abroad by private Venezuelans investing in foreign securities, particularly mutual funds. All foreign investment abroad by Venezuelans in securities, real estate, and bank accounts was estimated at the equivalent of US$4 billion.

Foreign Investment

Foreign private capital in 1970 continued to play a significant part in modernization and industrial development. Foreign investment has been characterized by increasing direct investment in capital goods and installations, whereas portfolio investment (in stocks and bonds) has fluctuated. Direct investment remains the dominant form of foreign capital in the different sectors of the economy. At the end of 1967 gross accumulated foreign investment was the equivalent of over US$5.57 billion, the largest amount of any developing country in the world, with over US$5.3 billion in direct investment and almost US$220 million in portfolio investment.

Eighty-six percent of foreign investment was in the petroleum industry; about 5 percent was in industry; another 5 percent was in mining; and the remaining 4 percent was distributed between the different sectors of the economy. The amount of foreign investment in commerce, however, represents about half of all investments in commercial activity. Foreign investment in some fields is restricted. For example, foreign capital cannot own more than 49 percent of insurance companies, is limited in coastal shipping and newspaper publishing, and cannot invest in domestic aviation. The principle of restriction may be extended by the government to other economic areas.

Foreign investment originates almost exclusively (93 percent) in two countries: the United States, which accounts for 71 percent of the total, and Great Britain, accounting for 22 percent.

United States private capital in Venezuela was estimated at US$3 billion in 1969, making it the fourth largest recipient of United States investment in the world. Although the bulk of United States investment is concentrated in petroleum, investment is going into all other sectors of the economy, particularly iron, manufacturing, and commerce.

The most significant role of foreign capital, excluding the extractive industries, has been played in the development and diversification of manufacturing industries. Most of these enterprises were established after World War II by internationally known companies, mostly from the United States, acting as parent companies. Manufacturing is confined to established product lines that were previously imported, such as car assembling, tires, food, and chemical products.

United States firms are represented in a variety of forms. There is also increasing European and Japanese competition. The official policy of the government is one of encouragement to and equality for foreign capital, as long as it does not compete with existing domestic interests. There is no law that regulates foreign investment, although there is legislation that differentiates between national and foreign companies as to form, place of incorporation, and major purpose of the business.

In mid-1969, however, temporary restrictions were placed on companies having a majority of nonresident shareholders and owing money to Venezuelan banks. These affected firms must maintain in the country the proceeds of all foreign loans they contract, all paid-up capital, capital reserves, and earnings. They cannot make investments abroad unless such investments contribute to the expansion of Venezuelan exports and cannot make loans to companies outside the country or maintain interest-earning deposits abroad. They must report on a monthly basis their local bank debit position and foreign credits. The failure to abide by the regulations could cause the cancellation of loans by domestic banks. The purpose of these regulations was to discourage the practice by some foreign companies of borrowing money in Venezuela at relatively lower rates and using the proceeds through their subsidiaries elsewhere in the world. Some aspects of the regulations were later modified, but they were still in effect as of December 1970.

To attract foreign capital the government offers such inducements as high protective tariffs for new industries and exemption from import duties for capital equipment and raw materials. There is also relatively low taxation. Because of government interest in diversifying the economy, many corporations are granted tax benefits when starting a new industry. The comparatively high profits made possible through these measures have constituted the principal inducement for United States firms to establish new industries.

As a further stimulus for new investment, Venezuela and the United States concluded in late 1962 the Investment Guarantee Agreement, which ensures United States investment in Venezuela against expropriation, inconvertibility, and war risks.

Foreign Aid

Despite its relatively high per capita income, the country still qualifies for some forms of foreign economic aid. Several international organizations, the United States government, foundations, and religious and welfare agencies are engaged in a variety of economic aid programs. From January 1, 1961, through September 30, 1969, the country received the equivalent of almost US$735 million in foreign loans. The largest percentage, 26 percent, went into transportation and communications development. Twenty-two percent was used to improve the electric power system; almost 22 percent, for industrial and mining development; 11 percent, for sanitation and public health; over 10 percent, for housing; and the balance, for miscellaneous purposes.

The International Bank for Reconstruction and Development (IBRD, commonly known as the World Bank) made its first loan to the country in December 1961 and by mid-1970 was the major single provider of foreign aid, having extended credits for over US$300 million. The Inter-American Development Bank had made over twenty-five loans to Venezuelan institutions by mid-1970, totaling over US$180 million. The Agency for International Development (AID) gave US$11 million worth of grants for technical assistance during the 1961—69 period. The Export-Import Bank has made available, since 1960, some US$230 million for miscellaneous projects. In 1970 a consortium of private New York banks lent US$100 million for public works projects. There are also members of the United States Peace Corps in Venezuela working on various projects, including teaching, playground direction, and agricultural and home economics counseling. The Peace Corps program cost about US$15 million through 1969. Since 1966 a currency exchange agreement has been in effect under which the United States and Venezuela can each draw up to US$50 million of the other's currency.

Various United Nations organizations have provided advice and technical assistance in numerous fields. Some private foundations and voluntary agencies have also given aid. A DM100 million bond (in October 1963, 3.66 Deutschmarks equaled US$1) was raised and passed in the Federal Republic of Germany (West Germany) in 1968.

BANKING AND CURRENCY

In addition to the Central Bank of Venezuela, the banking system includes several government-owned development banks that provide loans to agricultural and industrial enterprises, thirty-one commercial banks, a system of savings and loan associations (in part publicly financed), and mortgage banks. Services offered by domestically owned institutions are supplemented by those of foreign banking houses. A variety of other institutions also serve to mobilize savings and offer credit. Most important among such institutions are insurance companies, both domestic and foreign, financing and investment companies, and two stock exchanges.

The operations of banks and credit institutions are governed by the General Law on Banks and Other Credit Institutions, promulgated in March 1961. In addition, banks and credit institutions that have been established for specific purposes, such as industry, mining, and agriculture, are subject to special laws. (A law passed in 1970 restricted foreign equity participation in borrowing operations.)

The banking system is supervised and controlled through the Office of the Superintendent of Banks, a special technical service created in 1940 and attached to the Ministry of Finance. Charged with the inspection, auditing, and control of all banks and credit institutions, in accordance with the general law, the superintendent is appointed by the president for a period of three years and may be reappointed. Penalties imposed by the Office of the Superintendent of Banks for violations of the banking laws may be appealed to the minister of finance.

The banks and credit institutions are represented in a National Banking Council, which has its seat in Caracas. The council is composed of one representative from each domestic bank and credit institution, subject to regulation under the general law on banks. In the deliberations of the council, foreign banks operating in the country have a voice but no vote.

Banks

The government banks play an important role in the banking system. They were formed to develop specific economic sectors and to satisfy social needs. They provide about one-third of total credit in the banking system and usually charge from 1.5 to 5 percent less interest than commercial banks. Besides the Central Bank of Venezuela, other official banks include the Venezuelan Development Corporation (Corporación Venezolana de Fomento), Industrial Bank (Banco Industrial), Agricultural and Livestock Bank (Banco Agrícola y Pecuario), Labor Bank (Banco Obrero), Workers Bank (Banco de los Trabajadores), Agricultural and Livestock Development Bank (Banco de Desarrollo Agropecuario), and National Savings and Loan Bank (Banco Nacional de Ahorro y Prestamo).

The Central Bank of Venezuela, established in 1940, is the sole source of banknote issue and, in effect, the head of the banking system. It is a stock company with a capital of Bs10 million to which the national government must by law always subscribe at least half. In 1970 the government held 50.04 percent of the shares, and the remaining 49.96 percent were in the hands of 6,333 private stockholders. The authorized capital is divided into shares of Bs100, transferable only with the approval of the Board of Directors. No individual, natural or juridical, other than the national government may hold more than 100 shares. The bank is governed by special legislation, codified in the Central Bank Law of January 18, 1961. The bank pays dividends on any profits it earns. The bank is run by six directors, three of whom are appointed by the president of the Republic; one, by the private stockholders; one, by the commercial banks jointly; and one, by the business community. In 1970 the bank opened a branch office, its first, in Maracaibo.

In addition to issuing banknotes and regulating the volume of currency in circulation, the Central Bank serves as the government's sole financial agent in both domestic and foreign credit transactions, and represents the country in the International Monetary Fund. It is also the depository of national treasury funds and is permitted, within certain limits of the law, to grant credit to the government to cover temporary cash shortages.

Provisions pertaining to government loans are rather restrictive, however, and allow the Central Bank a limited role in financing long-term credit needs. It is not permitted to hold government credit instruments in value higher than 10 percent of the average ordinary annual revenues over the past five years. In practice, therefore, the Central Bank is confined to the acquisition of short-term government notes due within the next fiscal year. It is possible for the Central Bank to buy long-term government paper on the open market but not directly from the government.

One of the most important functions of the Central Bank is the purchase and resale of foreign exchange to the government and to the commercial banks and the maintenance of international reserves. Other functions of the Central Bank include the establishment of rediscount rates—which usually vary between 4 and 5 percent—and service to the banking community as a source of credit, a depository, and a check clearinghouse. Although it can rediscount to commercial banks, few bankers actually utilize rediscounting because of a belief that such action implies that the bank is not strong. One other weakness is that the Central Bank cannot alter the reserve requirements for commercial banks, which is a congressional responsibility.

Among the various credit institutions established by the government for national economic development, the largest is the Venezuelan Development Corporation (Corporación Venezolana de Fomento—CVF). It was founded in 1946 with an initial capitalization of about Bs90 million. An autonomous institution subordinate to the Ministry of Development, the corporation undertakes the establishment and promotion of new enterprises and extends long-term loans through several banks under its control. It purchases private industrial bonds, issues its own bonds, and makes and guarantees loans. In its early years the corporation centered its credit activities on the development of agriculture. After 1957, however, loans to the industrial sectors exceeded those to agriculture.

One of the major credit outlets of the corporation is the Industrial Bank, in which it holds a majority of shares (approximately 95 percent in 1970). The Industrial Bank grants development loans to domestic manufacturing, processing, and mining enterprises and administers various regional development banks for the CVF.

In 1949 the CVF established regional development banks in areas in the interior where commercial banks were reluctant to operate. In 1970 it held the majority stock of the four regional development banks of Los Andes, Coro, the Guayanas, and Zulia. Three others had been sold to private interests. The regional banks serve as an important policy arm, granting initial capital and improvement loans to enterprises in new and developing industries. The largest of the regional development banks is the one for the Guayanas, called the Venezuelan Guyana Corporation (Corporación Venezolana de Guayana). Its assets in 1970 were almost Bs3 billion.

The Agricultural and Livestock Bank, the first state bank, was created in 1928 to finance the needs of farming, stockraising, and commercial fishing. It was reorganized under a new law of July 3, 1968, and part of its activities were transferred to another state bank. The bank was run by a three-member administrative board. It had sixty-four branches and close to 1,800 employees in 1969 and had total assets of over Bs2 billion. It makes short-, medium-, and long-term loans. Its funds come from the national budget, its own operations, and foreign and domestic borrowing.

The bank also receives deposits from the public, grants home mortgages, sells foreign exchange, and performs some nonbanking activities. It maintains warehouses and storage facilities, develops cooperatives for farmers and fishermen, provides machinery and equipment at reasonable prices, and guarantees price levels of certain commodities to producers. In 1968, for example, price supports were maintained on carrots, potatoes, corn, rice, sisal, and cotton.

The largest percentage of the bank's loans go for livestock and corn and rice production. Since its inception the bank has had difficulty in fulfilling its franchise. It receives more applications for credit than it can grant annually, and it has many unrecovered loans. As a result, in 1970 it decided to limit loans to any one person to Bs15,000 in order to accommodate more borrowers and to cut down the amount of loss it incurs annually.

In 1968 the Agricultural and Livestock Development Bank was founded to take over agricultural credit operations relating to large enterprises. The Ministry of Agriculture, the Agricultural and Livestock Bank, and the CVF were to transfer to it all their agricultural loans granted at 4 percent interest or higher. By June 1970 about half of their combined estimated portfolio of over Bs700 million of affected loans had been transferred. Initial capital of the bank was Bs100 million, of which the government provided half. The other half was to be sold to private stockholders. All public entities were authorized to keep up to 5 percent of their total bank balances in the Agricultural and Livestock Development Bank in order to give it additional funds.

The Labor Bank (Banco Obrero—formerly called the Workers Bank) was established by the government in the same year as the Agricultural and Livestock Bank, for the chief purpose of financing and operating medium-cost and low-cost housing. By 1970 it had become the largest financial institution in the country in terms of assets, with over Bs4 billion. In addition to home mortgages it also makes consumer loans.

A new Workers Bank (Banco de los Trabajadores) was established in 1966. It maintains savings accounts for workers and makes loans for home ownership and to artisans, small industries, and cooperatives. It raises its capital by selling shares of stock to the government and to workers, labor unions, and cooperatives.

In the private sector the importance of commercial banks has grown rapidly. Until 1882 there were no banks in the country, and banking transactions were made through mercantile companies. Three commercial banks were formed between 1882 and the early 1900s. By 1948 there were thirteen banks in operation. Between 1948 and 1958 a major expansion occurred as the number of commercial banks grew to thirty-seven. By 1970 this number had been reduced to thirty-one because of mergers. The thirty-one banks had a total of about 450 branches in 1969. Banking services are very well developed in the economically active areas of the country but not elsewhere. In the Federal District and in Miranda State, for example, there is one bank office for every 12,600 persons, whereas in the states of Cojedes and Táchira, there is one office per 40,000 persons.

The General Law on Banks and Other Credit Institutions of 1961 contained the basic bank legislation and was still in effect in late 1970. A new banking law, however, containing some controversial features, was before the National Congress in November of that year, but there was no indication when it might be acted upon. Reserve requirements were considered conservative in 1970. If total deposits are no larger than six times the banks own resources, then the bank must maintain a legal reserve of 15 percent for demand deposits, 10 percent for savings deposits, and 8 percent for time deposits. Two-thirds of the reserve must be kept in the vaults of the Central Bank. If total deposits do exceed the six to one ratio, then 40 percent of the excess is also required as a legal reserve.

In addition to credit operations, commercial banks may buy and sell foreign exchange, sell letters of credit and travelers' checks, maintain safe deposit boxes, engage in trust activities, lease equipment to businesses, and make collections of past due accounts for their customers. Rates of interest are subject to regulation by the Central Bank. On the whole, in 1970 interest rates charged by commercial banks were quite stable, ranging between 10 and 11 percent, having been set by the government in mid-1969. The rates paid by banks on savings accounts and other deposits varied between 4 and 7.5 percent. They were increased in June 1969 to satisfy middle-income savers.

The largest commercial bank in terms of capital and reserves is the Bank of Venezuela (Banco de Venezuela), formed in 1890 and having fifty-six branches by 1970. It is followed by the National Discount Bank (Banco Nacional de Descuento), formed in 1954 and with twenty-five branches in 1970, and then by the Mercantile and Agricultural Bank (Banco Mercantil y Agrícola), founded in 1946. The latter bank is affiliated with the Chase Manhattan Bank of New York. Another important foreign bank is the First National City Bank of New York, which has operated in the country since 1917.

In 1970 there were six mortgage banks in operation, reportedly operated on their own subscribed capital, making little attempt to attract savings deposits. Their total assets were over Bs1 billion, and they could make mortgage loans up to twenty years.

A savings and loan association system was started in 1962 to encourage savings by lower income groups and to help finance new homes or repair existing ones. The system, although private, received assistance in getting established from both government and from the Alliance for Progress. By 1970 there were twenty-one savings and loan associations in existence, with over Bs500 million in assets and over 118,000 savings accounts. Almost 11,000 loans for new homes had been authorized through 1969. The entire savings and loan system is supervised by a government institution called the National Savings and Loan Bank. This was established in 1967 to help stabilize the mortgage market by rediscounting the mortgages granted by the private associations. It also guarantees loans and deposits.

Other Financial Institutions

A number of investment companies engage in medium- and long-term financing. They may raise funds by the use of time deposits, loans, or bond issuance. The bonds of investment companies cannot have a maturity of more than ten years, and interest must be paid quarterly. The largest and most successful of such companies is the Venezuelan Development Finance Corporation (C.A. Venezolana de Desarrollo, Sociedad Financiera—CAVENDES). It was founded in 1963 and is owned jointly by the CVF, the International Finance Corporation, and about 100 private individuals and companies. It is typical of other investment companies, in that it lends to private manufacturers or to agricultural companies producing raw materials for industry. It may make direct loans or take an equity position in the borrowing firm. It may underwrite securities of private firms and help to market them, and it may provide technical assistance. Another private investment company is the Creole Investment Corporation, a subsidiary of the Creole Petroleum Company, which finances industrial development on either a loan or an equity basis. A third such company is the Shell Investment Corporation which, unlike the others, restricts its investments to companies in the petroleum industry.

Insurance companies, as a depository for personal savings and as a source of investment, have enjoyed a growing prominence. In 1970 there were almost fifty companies with total assets of about Bs1.5 billion. All companies must have a stipulated reserve either in cash or government bonds. Premium rates are approved by the government, and all insurance agents are licensed. For the most part, insurance funds have been invested in real estate, long-term government bonds, and industrial and commercial securities. By 1970, however, they were starting to make loans to industry in response to an acknowledged need.

About eighty private credit unions with almost Bs700 million in assets were in existence in 1969. Five consumer finance companies with total assets of about Bs600 million were also in existence in that year. One unusual financial institution is the Municipal Institute of Popular Credit (Instituto Municipal de Credito Popular), a government-sponsored entity that lends only to municipalities. Most of its loans are for municipal low-income housing and public works projects.

There are two major organized stock exchanges in the country. The Caracas Stock Exchange, controlled by the Caracas Chamber of Commerce, is the older, having been established in 1947. The other is the Miranda Stock Exchange, founded in 1958 and also located in Caracas. A third, smaller exchange opened in the city of Valencia in 1964, but there was no information regarding it in 1970. Trading volume has increased steadily but is still not very large. From a combined total of about Bs100 million in 1960, transactions grew to around Bs500 million in 1969, and a typical trading day might see Bs2 million traded.

In 1970 the government was studying the possibility of creating a more sophisticated securities market in order to increase transactions, make stocks more attractive, raise capital domestically for development needs, and stop the flow of capital flight and investments abroad by Venezuelans. For example, foreign mutual funds were illegal but were being purchased despite the illegality. A new securities and exchange law was submitted to the National Congress in November 1970 in an effort to widen the appeal of securities. The draft law was modeled after those of the United States, Mexico, and Brazil. Among the features contained in the proposed law were: a tax relief for new stock issued by companies; a provision that 10 percent of dividends paid and 10 percent of capital gains would be tax free; and, in order to give wider ownership, the placing of a limitation on the number of shares any one person could hold in any one company.

Currency, Credit, and Money Supply

The monetary system is based on the gold standard, with a basic currency unit called the bolivar (Bs). Historically, the country has had a very stable and sound monetary system. The bolivar has been continuously backed by sufficient international reserves and ranks among the hardest currencies in the world. It was designated an international convertible currency by the IMF in September 1966. Official gold and foreign exchange reserves were estimated at US$937 million in September 1970, with US$404 million of this in gold. Venezuela has the largest gold holdings of any country in Latin America. On a per capita basis, it is one of the highest in the world.

The bolivar is made up of 100 centimos and ranges in value from approximately US$0.22 to US$0.30 under the multiple exchange rate system that went into effect in January 1964 and was still in force in 1970. Generally, the buying rate is Bs4.45 to US$1.00, and the selling rate is Bs4.5 to US$1.00. The export earnings of the petroleum and iron ore mining companies must be sold to the Central Bank at Bs4.40 per US$1.00. The Central Bank sells to commercial banks at Bs4.485. Certain commodities traded in foreign commerce receive a subsidy of Bs1.15. Before this sytem was in effect, a much more complicated multiple exchange rate system existed.

Fractional units of the bolivar are called colloquially the puya (5 centimos), the locha (12.5 centimos), the media-real (25 centimos), and the real (50 centimos). Gold bolivar coins, which were once in circulation, have been replaced by notes in denominations of 500, 100, 50, 20, 10, and 5 bolivars. There are also silver coins of 1, 2, and 5 bolivars.

The law provides that banknotes in circulation must be backed by a minimum of 33 percent gold and foreign exchange. The ratio has, however, been consistently higher in practice. Most increases in the money supply are based upon increases in foreign exchange holdings.

The money supply (cash, coins, and checking accounts) circulating in the hands of the public in June 1970 amounted to Bs6.7 billion. Of this total, bank deposits accounted for Bs4.6 billion and banknotes and coins for the remaining amount. Time and foreign currency deposits amounted to an additional Bs4.6 billion.

The government, through the Central Bank, has generally followed a cautious monetary policy. The credit operations of the Central Bank are considerably smaller than its lending capacity. The banking system, almost wholly dependent on the leadership of the Central Bank, has followed the same conservative line with regard to credit expansion. The resulting inflexibility, although containing inflationary pressures, has limited the flow of funds into productive enterprise and has resulted in a tendency toward capital shortage. Most banks in mid-1970 had high liquidity—more funds than loan applications—with sufficient credit available for most purposes except residential home construction.

Outstanding credit in the entire banking system in April 1970 was equivalent to US$1.6 billion. Over 50 percent of all loans are made by the government banks, about 30 percent by the commercial banks, and the remainder by the savings and loan associations and other financial institutions.

Commercial banks cannot legally make loans for more than two years' maturity. Longer term loans have to be obtained from a government bank. The two-year maximum regulation comes from a belief that long-term loans involve too much risk for the bank's depositors. Most loans made by the commercial banks are from a three- to six-month duration, with three months being the norm. Many of the loans are renewable for additional periods of time. No borrower may be lent more than 10 percent of the bank's own resources. Most banks request excessive guaranties and collateral because they cannot evaluate adequately the financial situation of the borrower and few banks exchange credit information.

The economy appears to be relatively free of inflationary pressures even though the money supply had been expanding slightly faster than the output of goods and services in the late 1960s. Prices have increased less rapidly than salaries. The wholesale price index increased by 29 percent in the decade between 1958 and 1968, one of the lowest increases in Latin America. The consumer retail price index increased by an average of only 0.5 percent annually between 1961 and 1968. The prices in Caracas however, increased at a higher rate during 1968 and 1969, almost 2 percent per year.

SECTION IV. NATIONAL SECURITY

CHAPTER 22

PUBLIC ORDER AND INTERNAL SECURITY

In 1970 the responsibility for both public order and internal security was divided between national and state police forces controlled by four cabinet ministers and the governors of the states and the Federal District. The Armed Forces of Cooperation (Fuerzas Armadas de Cooperación), generally known as the national guard, had the responsibility for internal security throughout the country. Its competence and efficiency had won wide popular support.

Codes of criminal law and procedure are derived largely from European sources rather than from Anglo-Saxon traditions. Comparatively little is left to the discretion of judges and court officials. Trials are held before a single judge or panel of judges without a jury. There is no provision for bail.

The court system was only slightly affected by the change in government in 1958. Judges appointed during the former regime were continued in office so as to maintain juridical stability and lay the foundations for a career judiciary. The continuing prevalence of crime, amounting to emergency conditions at times, has clogged the system, however, and slowed the process of justice.

The penal code in effect in 1970 was that of 1915 and revised in 1946. Its articles define felonies and misdemeanors and provide punishments for each. There is no capital punishment, and the maximum prison sentence is thirty years. The director of prisons, under the minister of justice, operates the national prison system, but the national guard has the function of guarding prisoners working outside prison walls and is also responsible for the exterior security of the prisons. There are twenty-seven penitentiaries, national jails, and municipal jails.

The concern of the government for the treatment of prisoners is reflected in the Constitution of 1961, which instituted the position of prosecutor general and included among his duties that of "enforcing the guarantee of human rights in jails and other prison establishments." In spite of these guarantees, in 1970 many of the national and municipal jails were overcrowded, primarily because of the time that elapsed between arrest and the conviction or release of the accused.

The incidence of crime, particularly in urban areas, showed a steady rise between 1962 and 1970. One reason for this was the constant migration of people from the rural areas to the larger cities, particularly Caracas. Of the 230,000 persons apprehended for various offenses in 1967, more than 66,000 resided in Caracas. Addiction to and sale of drugs was becoming a serious problem. The country's lengthy border with Colombia provided many opportunities for smuggling operations. Offenses included violations of laws or regulations about the international transfer of currency and manufactured products.

By a variety of means, ranging from legal to subversive and including open violence and guerrilla warfare, the Venezuelan Communist Party has been seeking the overthrow of the government. The party has successfully penetrated student and faculty organizations. During 1970 the student manifestations were the principal source of the disruption of public order in the urban areas. Guerrilla operations in the countryside were ineffectual, but in 1970 remnants of these bands remained at large.

THE POLICE SYSTEM

In 1970 the total strength of security forces was about 30,000, giving an approximate ratio of 4 police to every 1,000 citizens. Six organizations were responsible for the maintenance of public order and, except for emergencies, were not under a central command. The municipal police of Caracas were under the juridsiction of the governor of the Federal District. The Directorate of Intelligence and Prevention Services was subordinate to the Ministry of Interior Relations; the Technical and Judicial Police, to the Ministry of Justice; the Directorate of Land Transit (traffic police), to the Ministry of Communications; and the national guard, to the Ministry of Defense. In addition, the state and local police were under the supervision of state and municipal governments. In order to handle emergencies in the greater metropolitan area of Caracas, the Unified Command was established with a central communications center to provide radio and telephone communications in order to facilitate and combine the operations of all police forces.

Each state, and the Federal District, is responsible for preserving order within its own borders. Each controls its own police and has the authority to determine which units are to be placed under the jurisdiction of the various municipal governments. The national guard functions in areas not served by state or municipal police and provides guards for the exterior security of the penitentiaries and jails. The national guard is also dispatched to any area for the maintenance of internal order if requested.

Federal District Municipal Police

The municipal police force of the Federal District was created in 1926. Its jurisdiction is limited to the Federal District, an area seventy miles long and ten miles wide. This force operates under a single command that has operational centers in Caracas and La Guaira, a city on the coast near Maiquetía International Airport. A training center is located at El Junquito, about fifteen miles west of Caracas. The force has a strength of about 7,000, including 800 administrative and clerical personnel and drivers. Force members are recruited on a voluntary basis but must agree to serve for at least one year. All recruits, except those entering the service from the armed forces, must complete a basic training course at the school located in El Junquito. It has dormitory and dining facilities for about 500 persons and operates directly under the governor of the Federal District. The length of the several courses taught varies from one month to one year, but the basic course is six months.

Directorate of Intelligence and Prevention Services

The Directorate of Intelligence and Prevention Services, formerly called the National Security Police, operates under the Ministry of Interior Relations and has jurisdiction over the entire national area. The minister of interior relations serves as the nominal head of the organization but delegates actual administration to a directorate general, appointed upon his recommendation by the president of the Republic.

The basic mission of the directorate is to execute and coordinate police activities designed to preserve public order, and its legal functions include the investigation of specific crimes listed in the penal code and the apprehension of suspects. The specified crimes include crimes against national security and those classified as crimes against the state and national powers, crimes against international law, crimes against political freedom and individual freedom, and crimes against the home.

Additional responsibilities include investigation and control of traffic in narcotics, supervision of the activities of foreigners in the national territory, control of arms and explosives in cooperation with the Ministry of Interior Relations, and those functions not specifically assigned to other police agencies. In practice, the duties of the directorate have been expanded to include the supplying of agents to guard important officials and facilities of the Ministry of Interior Relations and certain industrial concerns that are considered vulnerable to attack by terrorists.

The directorate has over 1,000 agents located in Caracas and eight other zonal areas. These are in Maracaibo, San Cristóbal, Barquisimeto, Valencia, Barinas, San Juan de los Morros, Barcelona, and Maturín. Each zone has jurisdiction over a geographical area that may include one or more states. The directorate is composed of a number of major units concerned with instruction on criminal cases, crime prevention, public order, laboratory work, narcotics control, fingerprint analysis and filing, and radio communications.

Technical and Judicial Police

The Corps of Technical and Judicial Police was established by Decree No. 48 of February 1958. It has nationwide jurisdiction and was created as a direct auxiliary of the judicial power under the Ministry of Justice. Its responsibilities include the investigation of crimes, the apprehension of criminals, the gathering of proof, and the preparation of cases for the courts. Cases handled by the corps include crimes against persons and property, homicides, holdups, woundings, stolen vehicles, and frauds. Also included in an additional list of specific crimes are abuse of authority, adulteration of food supply, gang assault, bigamy, perjury, contraband, corruption of public officials, offenses against public health, extortion, bribery, forgery, arson, resisting arrest, and vagrancy.

In 1960 a laboratory was established, with the responsibility of providing scientific assistance in police investigations. The operations of the laboratory are divided into five sections: biochemistry and toxicology, criminalistics, ballistics and graphotechnics, crime-scene investigations, and planimetry.

The headquarters of the Corps of Technical and Judicial Police is in Caracas, and its operations in the interior of the country are carried out through delegations and, under them, subdelegations. The delegations are at Maracaibo, San Cristóbal, Barquisimeto, Valencia, Maracay, and Mérida. The chiefs of delegations are under the supervision of the central headquarters but have a high degree of local autonomy with regard to their operational activities.

Overall operations consist chiefly of receiving complaints regarding crimes and investigating crimes. Very little preventive work is carried out, and all personnel operate in plainclothes.

Directorate of Land Transit

The country's first traffic law, enacted in 1928, decreed that traffic surveillance was the joint responsibility of the governments of the Federal District, the states, and the federal territories. In 1948 the National Traffic Inspectorate was created under the Ministry of Interior Relations and given nationwide jurisdiction. In 1956 this organization was transferred to the Ministry of Communications, and in 1958 the name was changed to the Directorate of Land Transit.

The major responsibilities of the organization are the enforcement of traffic laws, traffic engineering activities, issuance and control of vehicle titles and license plates, examination of drivers, issuance and control of drivers' licenses, and determination of routes and services for public transportation vehicles. These duties are executed by a Corps of Vigilantes numbering about 1,700; they are assigned to the seven zones into which the country is divided, and the zones are further divided into a total of eighty inspectorates. Over 900 vigilantes are assigned to the First Zone, which includes the state of Miranda and the Federal District, and they are responsible for the traffic services for over 2 million people. The vigilantes are responsible for the enforcement of traffic laws throughout the entire country, with the exception of federal toll roads that are the responsibility of the national guard. They have full police authority but generally limit their activities to traffic control.

State and Municipal Police

The governors of the twenty states and the two federal territories are appointed by the president of the Republic, and they have considerable influence over the operations of police in their respective areas. In two of the states the police are organized on a statewide basis and paid from state funds. In the other states and in the territories they are organized on a district and municipal basis, each with its own command. The overall operations of district and municipal police agencies vary in type and degree in accordance with different needs, conditions, and areas. Police functions in the state capital cities include the use of patrol cars, the guarding of jails and public buildings, and dismounted patrolling.

The National Guard

The Armed Forces of Cooperation (Fuerzas Armadas de Cooperación), generally known as the national guard, was established in 1937. It is a military force of about 12,000 officers and men that also has a civil police responsibility with jurisdiction in all parts of the national territory.

The mission of the national guard is to cooperate with other branches of the armed forces in the event of war, or under such circumstances as it may be required, and to protect the internal security of the country in time of peace. Additional peacetime assignments include vigilance over national offices to protect public funds, protection against the removal of natural resources from forests and waters, security of natural extractive resources, guarding of borders to prevent illegal entrance or exit, outside security of the country's penal institutions, and the maintenance of traffic security on toll roads and railroads.

In 1954, when the Ministry of Defense was established, the national guard was placed under its control as one of the four branches of the armed forces. The organization is headed by a brigadier general, assisted by an inspector general and a chief of staff who supervises the functioning of the five-section general staff. The first four sections are concerned with personnel, intelligence, operations and training, and logistics. The fifth section has five bureaus concerned with the enforcement of forestry, fishing and hunting laws, customs, liquor laws, traffic activities, and special guard service at prisons and penitentiaries.

The national guard maintains three schools for its personnel. The Officers' Academy, established in 1946, provides a four-year course in military and academic subjects for applicants who have finished three years of high school. Graduates are commissioned second lieutenants. The Officers' School of Application was established in 1955 and is attended by those seeking the qualifications for promotion. The nine-month course is usually attended by about sixty first lieutenants and captains, and the goal is to train officers for high command duties and special assignments. The National Guard School was established in 1937 and is the basic training school for enlisted men. The course lasts one year and serves both as a training and probationary period for the guards.

The national guard is the largest police agency in the country and, in addition to foot and motorized patrols, it has aircraft for aerial surveillance and more than 100 boats for lake, river, and harbor patrolling. In June 1970 a presidential decree required the national guard to begin the selection of officers for assignments in command of state and municipal police forces. In July its officers commanded the police forces in fifteen cities of eleven states, and twenty-one officers had been assigned to the traffic police.

THE ADMINISTRATION OF JUSTICE

The Court System

The entire court system is under the national government; no courts are controlled by the individual states. Prosecution is the responsibility of the Public Ministry, headed by the prosecutor general, who is assisted by a staff of subordinate prosecutors (see ch. 11, The Governmental System). The prosecutor general is elected by the National Congress during the first thirty days of its constitutional term and, if there is a vacancy, a new election must be held for the remainder of the term. The principal duties of the prosecutor general are: to see that constitutional rights and guarantees are respected; to ensure that there is speed and proper conduct in the administration of justice and that the courts of the Republic apply the laws correctly; to take criminal action in those cases in which action by an individual is not necessary to initiate and prosecute them; to see to the correct enforcement of the laws in jails and other prison establishments; and to initiate actions on which there are grounds for enforcing civil, criminal, administrative, or disciplinary liability incurred by public officials.

The highest court is the Supreme Court of Justice, organized in three divisions to hear different types of cases—political, civil, and criminal. The Division of Penal Cassation has the sole task of hearing final appeal in criminal cases. The Supreme Court of Justice acts in first instance only in impeachment of the president or other major officials for political offenses. It appoints the judges of all the lower courts, selecting them from a list submitted by the minister of justice, and exercises supervision over their organization and conduct.

Below the Supreme Court of Justice are the superior courts, and below these are courts of first instance. Superior courts may be composed of one or more judges, whereas the lower courts have only one judge. Municipal and parochial courts are competent only in criminal actions for misdemeanors or minor criminal offenses. A special category of court, presided over by an investigating judge (*juz de instrucción*), conducts a full preliminary hearing in criminal cases to determine whether or not a crime has been committed and to order the arrest of suspects where probable guilt is evident, or, if not, to put an end to the case. Complete summation of the case and of all evidence, reduced to writing by the judge, form the basis of the indictment and of the proceedings before the trial court. In very minor cases the judge is empowered to pass sentence himself.

After a crime has been committed, summary proceedings may commence by order of a judge, by the denunciation of an official or private person if the offense is against the public order or, otherwise, accusation by an interested party. When the judge finds that there are reasonable grounds to suspect guilt, he will issue a warrant for arrest or for detention if arrest has been made. Even a person taken in the act of committing an offense must be released unless detention is approved by a judge.

A person arrested must be interrogated within forty-eight hours in the presence of at least a provisional counsel for defense. When the summary proceedings have been completed, or in case more than thirty days have elapsed since arrest, the record must be turned over to the judge having jurisdiction, who will notify the prosecutor. Civil action for damages may be taken along with criminal action, or it may be taken in a separate civil suit.

If the defendant is not represented at the trial by a defense counsel of his own choice, the court will appoint one. Charges must be presented on the third day after the acceptance of a defense counsel by the accused. If the prosecutor and his deputy should decide that charges should not be presented, the presiding judge must decide whether or not to proceed. If he decides not to do so, he must consult the judge of the court immediately superior to his own before ordering dismissal and closing the case. After the charges have been referred, a trial must be commenced at one of the next three sittings of the designated court.

At the opening of the trial the arraignment is read, and the defendant, advised by his defense counsel, makes an unsworn statement of the facts. Evidence is submitted by the prosecutor and by the defense counsel in turn, and rebuttal is allowed in both cases. Judgment is pronounced on the basis of findings on the acts imputed to the defendant in the charges, although the court may give an interpretation of such acts differing from that of the prosecutor.

In criminal cases the findings of the court are automatically sent for review to the next higher court that has the right to order the case retried should its review so indicate. This procedure is considered to be part of the original trial and therefore not to violate the constitutional prohibition of double jeopardy, even though the retrial may reverse the findings or result in a more severe sentence. In the Venezuelan legal system, there is no trial by jury.

The Penal Code

The penal code consists of three books containing 548 articles. The books describe felonies and misdemeanors and allot punishments for each. Felonies are defined as crimes against the independence and security of the nation, freedom of work, the administration of justice, and persons and property. Misdemeanors are defined as offenses against public order, public property, public security, and public morals.

Article 1 states that no one may be punished for an act not expressly described as punishable by law. Punishments are corporal and noncorporal. Corporal punishment may consist of a penitentiary sentence with forced labor, a prison sentence, arrest, detention at a prison work colony, confinement, or expulsion from the country. Noncorporal punishments include fines, loss of political rights, inability to engage in certain professions, suspension from employment, and subjection to vigilance by public authorities.

Punishments for various crimes range from three to eighteen months in prison for insult or defamation of character to twelve to thirty years in prison for murder.

The Prison System

In 1970 there were twenty-seven institutions for the detainment of civil and military offenders. There was one in the Federal District and at least one in each state except Cojedes and Nueva Esparta

(Margarita Island). These consisted of the General Penitentiary at San Juan de los Morros; penitentiaries at Maturín and Valencia; a work colony at El Dorado; an institution for women at Los Teques; six national jails; and sixteen public jails. National jails are operated by the federal government, and public jails are controlled by the municipalities under state supervision.

Penal institutions are supervised by the Directorate of Prisons under the Ministry of Justice, but the governor of the Federal District operates the large jail in Caracas that is under the Ministry of Defense. The creation and direction of industrial and agricultural programs for the prisons is under an autonomous prison industries organization, as are the operations of the institutions' canteens.

Institutions for the detention of persons accused of criminal acts have often been overcrowded. A 1970 report indicated that buildings with a total capacity of 6,500 inmates sometimes housed as many as 15,000. The large public jail in Caracas, with a normal capacity of 500, sometimes houses as many as 1,500 inmates. During the six years from 1958 through 1964 at least 50 percent of the individuals detained were under indictment and had not been convicted at the time the census was taken. Unsentenced personnel, sentenced personnel, and military, political, and juvenile offenders are sometimes confined in the same institution. Military prisoners are in segregated areas within the prison areas and are supervised and guarded by military personnel.

Most institutions have facilities for teaching skills to inmates. These include: carpentry; the manufacture of shoes and slippers; printing and binding; handicraft; manufacture of brooms, mattresses, garments, and metal products; and agriculture. Livestock, eggs, and honey are produced at the penitentiary at San Juan de los Morros where 50,000 acres are available for cultivation.

The General Penitentiary near the town of San Juan de los Morros is about fifty miles southwest of Caracas. The dormitories, workshops, dining hall, hospital, and recreation grounds are in a fenced-off enclosure occupying about twenty acres. Families of many inmates who work on the outside live in small homes at the edge of the prison reservation.

Inmates are paid by the institution for carpentry, kitchen work, maintenance and cleaning, laundry work, and teaching. They also manufacture and sell various articles of clothing and handicraft. Visits take place Thursdays, Sundays, and holidays. Conjugal visits take place in rooms at the penitentiary entrance.

The work colony near the town of El Dorado, about 750 miles southeast of Caracas and 30 miles from the border with Guyana (formerly British Guiana), has a maximum capacity of between 500 and 600 inmates. The work program includes agriculture as well as carpentry and the manufacture of shoes and garments. Agricultural pursuits include the raising of corn, rice, fruits, and hogs. The principal disadvantage is the location of the institution, resulting in a high cost of transportation of prisoners.

The Institution for Women, completed and occupied in 1962, is located near Los Teques about thirteen miles south of Caracas. It is situated on a hilltop outside of Los Teques and built on different levels. The living quarters for the Sisters of the Good Shepherd, who operate the institution, are in the center of the enclosure. At one end are facilities for housing the babies and children of the inmates. There is a capacity for from 250 to 300 women. Other jails for women are located in the cities of Barcelona, Maracaibo, and Valencia.

The governor of the Federal District is responsible for the operation of the La Planta jail in the capital city. This jail is not under the jurisdiction of the Ministry of Justice and is administered by the Department of Police of the Federal District.

INCIDENCE OF CRIME

During 1969 the monthly number of crimes against persons varied from 140 in January to 220 during October. Crimes against property varied from 150 in November to 300 during each of the months of March and May. Of the 232,000 persons apprehended for various offenses in 1967, 214,000 were men and 18,000 were women. Of the total, 66,000 resided in the Federal District. The largest number, 44 percent, were in the nineteen-year to twenty-nine-year age group; 31 percent were in the 18-year age group; 15 percent were in the thirty-year to thirty-nine-year age group; and 10 percent were aged forty or over. Other than misdemeanors, the criminal acts of those arrested included theft, burglary, assault, bombing, attacks on military convoys, kidnapping, and murder.

In the period from 1962 through 1967 there was a continuous rise in the number of persons under arrest for criminal acts. This number varied from 171,000 in 1962 to 232,000 in 1967. About 26 percent were married persons, and about the same number were illiterate. During this period over 5,000 were indicted each year by courts of first instance. Each year there were over 2,000 cases of assault, over 1,000 cases of theft, and more than 700 homicides. The prison population increased steadily, the total number of inmates rising from 7,800 in 1962 to 13,000 at the end of 1968.

Drug addiction was becoming a serious problem in 1970. A police official reported that between 80 and 100 arrests on narcotic charges had been made each month between June and November 1970. The average number of suicides during the period from 1962 through 1967 was about 300, varying from a low of 202 in 1964 to a high of 437 in 1963. Most frequent methods of suicide were strangulation and poison.

THREATS TO PUBLIC ORDER

During 1970 public order was affected by student demonstrations and by the activities of guerrilla bands operating in the mountainous areas in the eastern and western parts of the country. Student demonstrations were frequently based on opposition to the government's university reform law, proposed in 1969 and signed into law in 1970. Students and some faculty members contended that the law destroyed the autonomy formerly enjoyed by the universities by opening the grounds and buildings of the universities to inspection by civil authorities. Public order was also disrupted sporadically by the activities of armed bands operating in the rural areas.

Student Disturbances

The 1958 Law of Universities reinstated the principle of university autonomy that had been ignored by the government of General Marcos Pérez Jiménez and reaffirmed the sanctity of university buildings and grounds. In 1969 and in 1970 the government undertook to dislodge leftist leaders controlling student councils and proposed a university reform bill. When the provisions of this bill became public, student reaction took the form of serious disorders.

Article 7 of the new bill stated that, although the buildings and grounds of the universities were inviolable, civil officials might enter in order to prevent a crime or at the request of the tribunals of justice. In 1969 individuals concealed within the buildings and the wooded area in the Botanical Gardens of the Central University of Venezuela (by far the largest university in the country) fired on law enforcement personnel maintaining order outside the university grounds. Several police were killed and wounded. Police and army units entered the grounds to search for weapons. Students at several other universities, in sympathy with those of the Central University, created disturbances involving property damage and requiring police intervention. These disturbances occurred at the University of the Andes in Mérida and also at the universities at Maracay, Maracaibo, and Valencia.

Rural Terrorism

In 1962 the Venezuelan Communist Party initiated a campaign of rural terrorism. The goal was not to achieve an immediate Communist takeover of the national government but to cause so much unrest that the armed forces would finally initiate a military coup. Outside observers suggested that the Communists believed such a coup would be distasteful to all segments of the population and could be more easily overthrown than the government existing at that time, and this would be their chance to install a government of their own.

In order to stimulate more interest in armed operations in the countryside, university students were urged to participate, and at first many did as "weekend guerrillas." Occasionally students became casualties and, in one case when a student was killed by the security forces, students at a university rioted, claiming he was tortured by the police. Gradually student participation declined, and the Communists were not able to recruit sufficient reinforcements from the rural population.

Many Venezuelans have been trained in Cuban guerrilla schools that teach Communist theory, intelligence collection, guerrilla operations, and demolition. Reports from rural areas have been received, stating that armed men (usually in small bands of ten or less) have entered homes in villages demanding food and money. In 1970 their numbers were dwindling and their threat to the internal security of the country was negligible.

GOVERNMENTAL MEASURES

Article 190 of the Constitution of 1961 authorizes the president to declare a state of emergency and in such cases to restrict or suspend constitutional guarantees. Since 1958 two democratically elected presidents—Rómulo Betancourt and Raúl Leoni—have invoked the emergency measures provided by the Constitution several times. Under such measures censorship was imposed, newpaper publication was suspended, schools were closed, demonstrators were arrested, the writ of habeas corpus was suspended, and congressional immunity was lifted.

Although he may wish to, there are certain constitutional guarantees that a president may not revoke. He may not revoke the guarantee against capital punishment, against being held incommunicado, or against torture, and he cannot increase the maximum allowable court sentence to more than thirty years' imprisonment. He does have the power, without declaring a state of emergency, to adopt measures to prevent disturbances believed to be imminent. A state of emergency was declared to exist in 1960 after extensive pro-Castro student riots, and this was not lifted until 1962. Another declaration of emergency, made in October 1962 at the time of the Cuban missile crisis, was lifted in January 1963.

In 1970 army detachments were sent to assist national guard units in suppressing the operations of terrorist bands in the mountainous areas. The government was being urged to take more drastic steps to eliminate crime and at the same time was being accused by leftist groups of police brutality.

CHAPTER 23

THE ARMED FORCES

In 1970 the total strength of the army, navy, and air force was about 30,000, and the various national and state police forces, including the Armed Forces of Cooperation (Fuerzas Armadas de Cooperación, generally known as the national guard), that could be placed under military command in the event of an emergency equaled the strength of the armed forces.

From Spanish times to independence, under the various dictators and *caudillos* (regional political strong men), the army had been an instrument of rule. Since independence the country has never faced a serious threat of invasion by a foreign power, nor has it resorted to arms in any international dispute. Accordingly, the military forces have been more accustomed to meeting threats to internal security than to thinking in terms of foreign war, although border disputes in the 1960s heightened awareness of the external role. The influence of the military over political affairs has been important and almost continuous.

The country's concern with internal affairs, resulting from factional and regional disputes from independence until the early twentieth century, precluded the development of the armed forces as a truly national defense force. Nevertheless, the attention given them—particularly the army—during the long rule of Juan Vicente Gómez (1908–35) formed the basis of the armed forces as they existed in 1970.

The position of the armed forces in government was clearly defined in the Constitution of 1961, which stated that their principal duties were the defense of the Republic and observance of the Constitution. The president is the commander in chief. The minister of defense controls the armed forces, normally through the chief of the joint staff. Military service is, under the law, obligatory for males for a period of two years.

There is no centralized logistical system, and major items of materiel must be procured from foreign sources—in 1970 primarily from the United States, which maintained missions to assist the equipping and training of the armed forces. The relatively small number of the armed forces and their annual budget have placed slight burden on the country's labor force and its economy.

All branches of the armed forces maintain schools and other facilities for the training of officers, noncommissioned officers, and conscripts. If conscripts are illiterate, they are taught to read and write. All four branches of the armed forces—particularly the army and the national guard—are active in civic action projects. These have consisted of road and bridge construction, building of schools and dispensaries, medical assistance, earthquake and flood refugee work, emergency air transportation, and maritime search and rescue missions.

Under the governments of Rómulo Betancourt, Raúl Leoni, and Rafael Caldera, the armed forces have supported constitutional government and acted effectively in upholding the government against any rural terrorism and urban disruption of public order.

THE PLACE OF THE MILITARY IN NATIONAL LIFE

History

The conquistadors, who began arriving in the country shortly after its discovery by Columbus in 1498, conducted slave raids against the Indians, who retaliated with numerous attacks. Within a century, however, most Indians—except in the tropical forests of the far south—had been subjugated, and tens of thousands had succumbed to the white man's diseases and been forced into slave labor. Before 1600 wars with the Indians had virtually ceased. Order was kept principally by small forces of guards maintained by the town councils.

The governor of the colony and provincial governors each maintained a regular force under arms, mainly for ceremonial purposes but available for emergencies. Although Spanish regular troops were few, there was a modest garrison at Caracas as well as units to man the coastal forts protecting the main ports against buccaneers. All Spaniards, nevertheless, were subject to a call to arms in emergencies. Not until 1760 were forces regularly recruited in the colonies, both as a standing force and as militia. Even then the volunteers were all *criollos* (see Glossary) because the Indians and persons of mixed blood were excluded from military service by Spanish law.

In the wars of independence Simón Bolívar used every means to build up the fighting qualities of his troops. He made full use of great personal dynamism to inspire his men, paid great attention to their material needs, and also used drastic means to discipline the waverers. In 1813 he made his famous declaration, "Death to all Spaniards, even if guiltless, and life for all Americans, even if guilty." Carrying out this policy in 1814, he ordered the execution of 800 prisoners in La Guaira. By the combination of inspiration, solicitude, and fear, Bolívar was able to build and equip a force capable of winning independence (see ch. 3, Historical Setting).

Bolívar was superseded by General José Antonio Páez, who had been his chief aid at the Battle of Carabobo. He became the first of the *caudillos* who ruled the country by personal magnetism and strong-arm tactics. He was a brave, generous leader, often stern but seldom cruel by the standards of the time. He was followed by many other *caudillos*, usually bearing the title of general, who in turn took over the government with strong support from forces from their own section of the country. Under each of these *caudillos*, the army was an instrument of personal rule. Each one successively dismissed the ranking military officers and replaced them with his own appointees while retaining the rank and file (see ch. 3, Historical Setting).

Juan Vicente Gómez perfected this procedure and ruled from 1908 to 1935. He came from the western mountainous state of Táchira and placed his kinsmen and henchmen in command everywhere, with such effect that Táchira men continued to occupy high army posts for more than twenty years after the death of Gomez, and Táchira has provided a large percentage of the officers in the army.

Gómez's first concern was to build up a strong army, so constituted that any successful armed uprising against the government was impossible. He concentrated on training a disciplined force and, after World War I, brought in French officers to train the ground forces and French and Belgian aviators to pilot his planes and to form a school of aviation, which was founded in Maracay in 1920. The expanded military complex in Maracay soon became the seat of an integrated school and training system. In this way Gómez thoroughly reorganized and modernized the army; he paid it well and gave the officers special social and legal privileges.

In 1937 the successor to Gómez, General Eleazar López Contreras, established the national guard as a special force for preserving internal security. Under his successor, General Isaías Medina, more civilian participation in running the government was encouraged, and special consideration was given to the national guard. During the rule of these two generals, the political machine built up by Gómez gradually weakened. One result was a split that developed within the army itself, between the older officers appointed through political preferment and the younger, professionally trained officers who resented their dominance.

This younger group had formed the Patriotic Military Union (Unión Patriótica Militar—UPM), a secret society dedicated to modernizing the army. Displeased with Medina's lack of deference to the army, they allied themselves with members of the Democratic Action (Acción Democrática—AD) party who were anxious to have a more liberal government. On October 18, 1945, they staged a successful coup d'etat by seizing the presidential palace and the military academy. Included in this group were Major Marcos Pérez

Jiménez and Lieutenant Colonel Carlos Delgado Chalbaud (who became minister of defense) as the two military members of the seven-man ruling junta headed by Rómulo Betancourt (see ch. 3, Historical Setting).

The junta adopted a drastic program of reform that worried many vested interests, including the military. Even though the minister of defense reported in 1946 that all professional members of the armed forces faithfully supported the constitution, the chief of staff of the army, Major Pérez Jiménez, was growing impatient with the government's actions. When Rómulo Gallegos was elected president in 1947, the effort to reduce the influence of the armed forces became apparent, and it was evident that he was trying to increase the other internal security forces as a counterbalance to the army. After the government denied a demand from the armed forces for more cabinet representation, the army—under a three-man junta—seized control and exiled Gallegos and Betancourt. A provisional government, completely under military control, was established.

The head of the junta, Delgado Chalbaud, was murdered in 1950, and Lieutenant Colonel Pérez Jiménez assumed power and imposed a strict military dictatorship. He built the police into a repressive force and elevated his own army friends to high positions in government and the army. A group of officers, disillusioned by such abuses, organized a plan for the overthrow of the dictatorship.

After almost ten years the repression, graft, and other excesses of the regime were obvious. Many officers had become disenchanted with Pérez Jiménez. In addition, all the opposition political parties in the country had formed a coalition seeking to reestablish constitutional government.

The revolt against Pérez Jiménez was initiated by the air force when, on January 1, 1958, its planes strafed Caracas from airfields in Maracay that had been seized by the rebel forces. After agreeing to negotiate and after the rebel troops had been disarmed as a result of these negotiations, the president refused to honor the agreements and ordered retaliatory measures.

While the armed forces were leading the revolt, the leaders of political parties were organizing civilian groups to aid in the overthrow of the dictator. Student riots broke out and a general strike occurred. Rioters in Caracas were attacked by police units that were in turn attacked by army units. On January 22 Pérez Jiménez resigned and was exiled by the junta that took over the government. He went to the United States but was extradited in 1963 and was tried and imprisoned for illegal appropriation of government funds. He was released in 1968 and went to Madrid, where he resided in 1970. In 1968 some of his still-loyal followers submitted his name as a senatorial candidate. His electoral list won six seats, but by a court decision his name was withdrawn because he had not resided in the country at the time the nominating and balloting had taken place.

When the country returned to constitutional government in 1958, the armed forces assumed a more apolitical role. The armed forces supported the free elections of presidents Rómulo Betancourt, Raúl Leoni, and Rafael Caldera, who succeeded to the office in 1969. The Constitution of 1961 authorizes the president to appoint and remove all cabinet ministers. President Caldera appointed as minister of defense General Martin Garcia Villasmil. At that time the senior army officer was General Pablo Antonio Flores Alvarez, who occupied the position of inspector general of the armed forces, the second highest military assignment in the country. General Flores made public statements detrimental to both President Caldera and the minister of defense that, according to charges leveled against him by the government, bordered on insubordination.

General Flores was tried and accepted the punishment of the court martial. In January 1969 President-elect Caldera in a public address stated that the armed forces had set a perfect example in their loyal and determined conduct in support of the Constitution and urged an exchange of sentiments and an indestructible solidarity between the civil power and the national armed forces.

Attitudes Toward the Military

Bolívar, the Liberator, is the symbol of the warrior in the eyes of the people. This symbol has given the armed forces an aura that it retains. By their action in the overthrow of Pérez Jiménez, however, and by their adherence to the constitutional governments of Presidents Betancourt, Leoni, and Caldera, the armed forces have overcome the animosity generated toward them during the Pérez Jiménez regime.

The armed services are made up of career officers graduated from the service academies, senior career noncommissioned officers, and conscripts. The conscripts are mostly from the lower levels of society. Officer rank is being increasingly attained by the sons of farmers and laborers who are qualified to enter and who graduate from the service academies. Military officers habitually have been held in high esteem, and the fact that a great majority of the personnel in the armed forces, including some officers, are from the common people created in them a paternal interest in the forces.

Shortly after the Pérez Jiménez regime, the military was criticized for being too aloof from the people, and greater daily contact between the military and civilians was urged. Efforts such as civic action have led to a mutual sympathy between the services and the people, particularly those in the rural areas.

POSITION IN THE GOVERNMENT

According to Article 132 of the Constitution of 1961:

> The National Armed Forces form a nonpolitical, obedient and deliberative institution, organized by the state to insure the national defense, the stability of democratic institutions, and respect for the Constitution and the laws, the observance of which shall always be above any other obligation. The National Armed Forces shall be in the service of the Republic, and in no case in that of any person or political party.

Article 190 prescribes that the president is the commander in chief of the armed forces and is specifically empowered to fix their size, to declare a state of emergency, and "to adopt measures necessary for the defense of the Republic, the integrity of its territories or its sovereignty in case of international emergency." He is the only public official entitled to exercise simultaneously military and civilian authority.

Constitutionally, the National Congress can influence the armed forces in several different ways. Above all, the Chamber of Deputies must initiate discussions of the budget. The Senate must approve all promotions in the armed forces to general or flag rank. At the president's request, the Senate authorizes the entry of foreign military missions and the sending of Venezuelan military missions to other countries.

The framers of the Constitution of 1961 felt a need for stating therein that the role of the armed forces was apolitical. This reflected the fact that in the past there had been many examples of direct military intervention in the political life of the country. During the first 100 years of the Republic the army existed as the personal instrument of the *caudillo* in power, but it became a national force during the time of Gómez. The military have continued to hold a powerful political potential. In the overthrow of the governments of Isaías Medina, Rómulo Gallegos, and Pérez Jiménez, parts of the military forces took direct action to oust the government in power.

The feeling of the military toward the government has been strongly influenced by international political events. In August 1960 a meeting of the Organization of American States at San José, Costa Rica, condemned both the Dominican Republic and Castro-led Cuba as disturbers of the peace. Even the fact that Venezuela joined in the mild denunciation of Cuba set off violent leftist attacks on the government. The measures taken to put down these attacks had the support of the armed forces and, when called upon, they effectively contained the rioters. In January 1962, when the foreign ministers were meeting at Punta del Este, Uruguay, and pro-Castro elements were staging widespread riots in Caracas, the armed forces supported the government efforts to restore tranquillity. The government has deployed armed forces units to international border areas in cases of potential disorder.

THE MILITARY ESTABLISHMENT AND THE NATIONAL ECONOMY

The armed forces consist of four co-equal services and, in 1970, had an estimated strength of about 42,500 officers and men, or about 0.3 percent of the total population. The individual services were: army, 15,000; navy, 6,500 (including 2,500 marines); air force, 9,000; and national guard, 12,000.

There are no organized reserves, but ex-servicemen are available throughout the country in considerable numbers and can be called upon in a crisis. An estimated 80,000 men reach conscription age each year.

During the nine-year period from 1961 through 1969, government defense expenditures averaged 9.4 percent of total expenditures, with a high of 11.3 percent in 1963 and a low of 7.9 percent in 1969. During the same nine-year period defense expenditures averaged 2.19 percent of the gross national product (GNP). The defense budgets varied from a low of the equivalent of US$133.8 million in 1961 to a high of the equivalent of US$201.8 million in 1967. There was a steady annual rise in defense expenditures, but about one-third of this increase resulted from inflation.

FOREIGN INFLUENCE

German military doctrine predominated during the last half of the nineteenth century. Results of German training may still be seen in the exaggerated goosestep performed on parade by the service academies and dismounted military units. A mission from Chile, which had been host to German military missions for many years, trained army units in 1910. After World War I French and Italian missions trained different services, and the French founded the army's air arm. In 1970 some French doctrines were still accepted.

After World War II United States military influence predominated. Major items of equipment for the army, navy, and air force have come from the United States; large numbers of officers of all services have attended school in the United States; and many officers and noncommissioned officers have received specialized military training in the Canal Zone.

MISSION AND TOP CONTROL

Mission

The mission of the armed forces is to defend the national territory from external attack and to help preserve internal security. The army was in 1970 composed of battalion-sized infantry, armored and artillery units, a cavalry regiment, and supporting antiaircraft and engineering units. The national guard, armed as light infantry, combines with the army in preserving internal security. The navy has a functioning destroyer force as well as escort and coast guard vessels that would be useful against a small-scale invasion attempt. The air force, equipped with modern fighters and bombers, as well as transport aircraft and helicopters, can support the army and navy.

Top Control

In 1970 the president, as commander in chief of the armed forces, was advised at the highest level by the Supreme Council of National Defense, which consisted of the cabinet members, the inspector general of the armed forces, the chief of the joint staff, and the commanders of the four military services.

The president exercises his command over the four services through the minister of defense, who normally acts through the chief of the joint staff. Senior in rank to the chief of the joint staff and junior only to the minister of defense is the inspector general of the armed forces, a position that may be occupied by a general or flag officer of the army, navy, or air force.

The chain of command runs directly from the minister of defense to the commanders of the army, navy, air force, and national guard. The chief of the joint staff has no command authority but reports directly to the minister, as do the commanders of the various special staffs that control services common to all four branches of the armed forces. These include recruiting, quartermaster, intelligence, communications, military engineering, medical services, military justice, comptroller, merchant marine, and civil aeronautics.

The commanders of the four services command all units in their respective branches. Each has an inspector general who reports directly to him, and each has a chief of staff who supervises the general staff. The army has a special schools command that oversees all of the army's several schools. The staff organizations are similar in their functions to those in the corresponding United States services.

THE ARMY, NAVY, AND AIR FORCE

In 1970 the army consisted of two armored battalions, three artillery groups, a cavalry regiment, and eleven infantry battalions. In addition, there were engineer, antiaircraft, and support units. The tanks were of the United States Sherman and French AMX—13 varieties.

The navy strength included 2,500 naval infantry men or marines. Principal vessels included one submarine, the *Carite*, acquired from the United States; three destroyers built in Great Britain; six frigates built in Italy; ten patrol vessels; eight coast guard vessels; and about ten transports, survey ships, and tugs.

The air force had about 250 aircraft and was organized into fighter, bomber, training, and transportation squadrons. Materiel included Canberra and Mitchell light bombers; Venom and Vampire fighter-bombers; Sabre jet fighters; Provider transport aircraft; and Texan, Mentor, and Vampire training aircraft.

MANPOWER

The personnel of the military forces comprise a well-paid, professional officer corps; a small, well-paid nucleus of career noncommissioned officers; and two-year conscripts who make up the bulk of the noncommissioned officers and all of the privates and seamen. Except for the career noncommissioned officers, all enlisted men in the army, 80 percent in the air force, and from 60 to 80 percent in the navy are conscripts. The national guard is an exception; it is made up completely of volunteers, 90 percent of whom have already completed their obligatory service in one of the other military forces.

According to the law for obligatory military service, the ages during which this service is obligatory are from nineteen to forty-five. Every male must register by the March 31 following his eighteenth birthday. Selection for the draft is on a lottery basis with quotas to each state, but the law grants exceptions for a number of reasons. It exempts married men, teachers, high school and university students, government employees, railroad employees, members of the clergy, only sons, those with a brother in the service, prisoners, and those with obvious physical impediments.

In the all-volunteer national guard, a considerable number of men follow their father's vocation. The volunteers must be single and not over twenty-five and must have had the equivalent of a sixth-grade education. Once in service, the men usually make the guard a career, and the annual turnover is small. Although most of the officers come from the middle class, some are from the upper class, and an increasing number are from families of farmers or laborers.

The great majority receive their commissions on graduation from one of the four service academies, but some professional persons receive commissions upon entering service direct from civilian life.

One of the problems confronting the armed forces is the relatively low level of education attained by its enlisted men. Although the national illiteracy rate of about 20 percent is low in comparison with most other countries in Latin America and a compulsory education law is in effect, many children leave school after the three-year compulsory period with only a rudimentary education. As a result, the armed forces must teach at least 50 percent of the conscripts to read and write before they can be taught to be effective soldiers, sailors, or airmen, and few of them can aspire to obtain the knowledge required in order to remain in the service as professional noncommissioned officers.

TRAINING

The armed forces maintains an extensive training establishment for officer candidates, recruits, officers, noncommissioned officers, and specialists. Each of the four services has its own academy for training career officers. The military and national guard academies are in Caracas; the naval academy is at Mamon on the coast west of La Guaira; and the air force academy is at Maracay, southwest of Caracas. The four-year course at the military academy is designed to ensure that each graduate has a solid foundation in scientific and cultural studies and an orientation in tactics and techniques of the arms and services of the army, without specializing in one. To be commissioned, a graduate must be at least twenty-one.

Venezuela has a five-year high school cycle, and the naval academy accepts students from the third, fourth, and last years of high school. It has a five-year course oriented toward the sciences, and graduates earn the equivalent of two years of university training in engineering. In 1967 the academy initiated a postgraduate course in mechanical engineering in which the student can present a thesis at the Central University of Venezuela and be awarded a degree in that subject.

The air force academy accepts as cadets only high school graduates. It has developed its curriculum in coordination with the faculty of civilian universities, and its graduating pilots have the equivalent of one year of university-level engineering. The national guard academy accepts only high school graduates.

The applicant for the four service academies must be between sixteen and twenty, be a Venezuelan by birth, have his parents' consent, and be single. He must be in good health and also have a good moral character, with no criminal record or service discharge less than honorable in character. He must renounce all political affiliations upon entry.

Each of the four branches of the armed forces has a senior school for its officers, the students usually being lieutenant colonels, majors, or senior captains (or the naval equivalents). They also have specialist schools for officers. Those of the army include infantry, artillery, armored, engineer, signal, and transportation. In December 1970 the cabinet approved the creation of the National Defense Institute to train high-ranking military and civilian personnel in the modern concepts of national defense and internal security.

A program of vocational training was instituted to offer all conscripts instruction in farming, in livestock raising, or in some agriculturally oriented trade. Because a large number of men from rural areas, when released from their term of service, remained in urban areas where job opportunities were wider, this program was set up in order to encourage more enlisted men to return to the farms with an increased agricultural knowledge. Most conscripts returning to civilian life appreciate the role of the armed forces in preparing them for life in the civilian community, and thus a favorable image of the armed forces is being fostered.

Training is also given in the military schools. In 1951 the Menseñor Jáuregui Military School was opened in La Grita in the state of Táchira. In 1955 the Grand Marshal de Ayacucho Military School was established in Caracas. The minister of defense assigns 320 scholarships to the military schools, which have a combined annual student population of 500. The objective of the military schools is to create a cadre of educated individuals who will have fulfilled their obligatory military service and thus can constitute a pool of reserve officers.

LOGISTICS

The Ministry of Defense coordinates the acquisition and distribution of weapons and equipment for the armed forces. Principal items of military equipment, such as aircraft, naval vessels, and tanks, are procured from foreign sources.

Ninety percent of the navy's ships were built in England and Italy and were provided with equipment adapted for modern naval warfare. The maintenance of this materiel, as well as its subsequent improvement, must be accomplished by the shipyard of origin. The rest of the ships were built for the United States Navy and acquired by Venezuela. The shipyard at Puerto Cabello can provide maintenance for small vessels. It has a 600-foot wharf with a 36-foot water level and can repair hulls, anchors, and decks and also propulsion, steering, and electrical systems.

Air force aircraft were constructed in the United States and Great Britain, most of them being post-World War II aircraft. Other than minor repair, maintenance must be provided by the countries of origin. The equipment for the army and national guard is all of foreign manufacture, obtained from France, Belgium, Italy, and the United States. This results in a diversity of materiel difficult to maintain.

MILITARY JUSTICE

The jurisdiction and composition of military courts are defined in the Code of Military Justice, which is separate from the criminal code of the country, except that under certain circumstances the decision of a military tribunal is subject to appeal before the Supreme Court of Justice. The code provides that military jurisdiction will apply for all military crimes, all common crimes committed by military personnel on military bases, and all common crimes committed by civilians under military jurisdiction. The Military Justice Service, which functions under the minister of defense through the chief of the joint staff, serves all the branches of the armed forces.

The highest military court is the Court Martial, composed of five members and ten alternates. One of the most senior assignments in the armed forces is that of the president of the Court Martial, always a general or flag officer. This is the court of sole instance for general and flag officers and a court of appeal for decisions from the councils of war. These courts have original jurisdiction over all matters not included in the jurisdiction of courts of first instance and hear appeals from those courts. Councils of war have three members.

In times of declared emergency military tribunals can try civilians for offenses against the state if the government so directs. Military tribunals act promptly. In 1962, after the Carupano and Puerto Cabello uprisings, military personnel complained that the military persons involved had been promptly tried and convicted but that the civil courts had not begun trial proceedings against the civilians involved.

UNIFORMS AND INSIGNIA

All four branches of the armed forces have a series of uniforms, including full dress and dress for officers and parade, garrison, work, and field uniforms for all ranks. Both white and beige cotton uniforms are authorized for summer wear. The army winter garrison uniform is dark green; the navy, midnight blue; and the air force, light blue. Cap covers for all navy uniforms are white. Army rank insignia are indicated by shoulder boards—one, two, or three five-pointed, gold-colored stars for second lieutenant, first lieutenant, and captain; one, two, or three similar but larger stars for major, lieutenant colonel, and colonel; and one, two, or three gold sunbursts for brigadier, major, and lieutenant general. In 1970 the highest ranking army officer was the minister of defense, Brigadier General Martin Garcia Villasmil.

Rank insignia for naval officers follow that of the British navy and are worn either on the lower sleeve or indicated by shoulder boards. The top gold stripe in each case has a loop similar to that of British naval officers. Air force insignia are indicated by shoulder boards supporting the series of one, two, or three stars. The parade uniform of the service academies consists of white trousers and a single-breasted, high-collared blouse. These are light gray for the military academy and dark blue for the others. Service caps are worn by the cadets at the military, naval, and air force academies, and the headgear of the national guard academy is a shape similar to that of the United States Military Academy.

AWARDS AND DECORATIONS

The government has authorized the award of nine military decorations and medals. Some of these are also awarded to civilian and foreign military personnel and eminent statesmen. The Order of the Liberator, in five grades, is the country's senior decoration. It is awarded to military personnel and civilians for distinguished service to Venezuela or to humanity. The Legion of National Defense, in three grades, is awarded to both military and civilian personnel for "defense of laws and rights of Venezuela." The Marshal Sucre Medal is awarded to military personnel, both national and foreign, for heroic acts and distinguished service.

The Order of Francisco de Miranda is awarded to military and civilian personnel for outstanding service in the field of science; it is also in three grades. The General Rafael Urdaneta Military Order is awarded to officers of the armed forces for years of honorable service. It is in three grades: ten years, bronze; twenty years, silver; and thirty years, gold. The Order of Naval Merit, in three grades, is awarded to both military and civilian personnel for distinguished service to the Venezuelan navy. The Cross of the Venezuelan Ground Forces, in three grades, is awarded to military and civilian personnel for distinguished service to the Venezuelan ground forces. It has been awarded to individuals who have held the position of minister of defense or commanding general of the army. The Cross of the Venezuelan Air Force, in three grades, is awarded to military and civilian personnel for distinguished service to the Venezuelan air force. The Cross of the Armed Forces of Cooperation is awarded to military and civilian personnel for heroic acts of members of the national guard and also for the authorship of professional works of benefit to the national guard.

Four medals for noncommissioned officers and enlisted personnel are awarded for esprit de corps, diligence, conduct, and marksmanship.

CIVIC ACTION

The armed forces have been active in the civic action field. In 1969 about 3 percent of the defense budget was used for this purpose. Officers have been assigned to remote areas where they have instructed the local inhabitants in collective farming in order to improve the production and distribution of agricultural products. The armed forces have carried out soil and water conservation projects, have assisted in road repair and construction, and have erected dispensaries, schools, and churches in areas where these were badly needed by the local communities.

The army has also assisted in earthquake and flood relief by providing tent housing for the homeless and by dispatching food, clothing, and medical supplies to the inhabitants of the stricken areas. Military medical teams give lectures in health and sanitation, provide emergency medical and dental treatment, give physical examinations, inoculate the communities against typhus and poliomyelitis, and vaccinate them against smallpox.

In 1962 the army engineers initiated Operación Amazonas (Operation Amazonas), designed to increase the socioeconomic development of the southern part of the country. It was the first time the military had played a direct role in civic action. The principal objective was the construction of a hard-surfaced road in the state of Bolívar to connect several towns with the capital city, including the construction of thirteen bridges of various sizes. In 1970 army engineers were also constructing airports in the remote southwestern parts of the country.

CONDITIONS OF SERVICE

Since the beginning of the twentieth century all of the governments, whether dictatorships or freely elected, have recognized the necessity for maintaining the morale of the career professionals of the armed forces at a high level. Morale, in 1970, was good. The annual pay of officers and career noncommissioned officers was the highest of any Latin American country. There were many additional benefits for those who made military service a career. Officers could retire after thirty years with a pension equal to their active duty pay at highest rank attained; noncommissioned officers, at twenty years.

The officers made a monthly contribution of 8 percent of their pay to the Venezuelan Institute of Social Security. These funds were used to defray medical expenses for dependents and for insurance in case of the death of an officer. All active duty personnel, regardless of rank, received free medical and dental treatment and hospitalization. In July 1970 the Chamber of Deputies passed a bill authorizing retired armed forces officers who are available for work to hold public offices and be paid for their services.

Since 1960 efforts have been made to improve the living conditions of the enlisted men. Although the pay of the conscripts is small in comparison with that of career personnel, they receive free board and lodging, which in many cases is better than what they were accustomed to at home. They also receive educational benefits. If illiterate, they are taught to read and write, and many of the specialized branches of the armed forces provide training that can assist in obtaining a position in industry after the completion of military service.

A number of decorations and medals are awarded for competence in the various aspects of military life, and the parade uniforms of the cadets and the branches of the armed forces tend to instill pride in the organization.

BIBLIOGRAPHY FOR FEBRUARY 1964 EDITION

Section I. Social

RECOMMENDED SOURCES

Briceño Iragorry, Mario. *Tradición, Nacionalidad y Americanidad.* Santiago de Chile: Editorial Universal, 1955.

Briceño, Olga. *Cocks and Bulls in Caracas: How We Live in Venezuela.* Boston: Houghton Mifflin, 1945.

Buitrón Aníbal. *Exodo rural en Venezuela.* Washington: Pan American Union, 1955.

Butland, Gilbert J. *Latin America, a Regional Geography.* London: Longmans, Green, 1961.

Consejo de Bienestar Rural. *Problemas económicos y sociales de los Andes venezolanos.* Caracas: 1955.

Dupouy, Walter. "La Clase Media en Venezuela." Vol. V in Crevenna, Theo (ed.), *Materiales para el estudio de la clase media en Venezuela.* Washington: Pan American Union, 1951.

Frank, Waldo David. *Birth of a World.* Boston: Houghton Mifflin, 1951.

Gillen, John P. "Some Signposts for Policy." In Adams, Richard N., *et al., Social Change in Latin America Today.* New York: Harper, 1960.

Grisanti, Angel. *Resumen histórico de la instrucción pública en Venezuela.* Bogotá: Editorial Iqueima, 1950.

Herring, Hubert. *A History of Latin America from the Beginning to the Present.* New York: Knopf, 1960.

Hill, George W. *El estado sucre: sus recursos humanos.* Caracas: Universidad Central de Venezuela, 1961.

Hill, George W., Beltrán, Gregorio, and Marino, C. "Social Welfare and Land Tenure in the Agrarian Reform Program of Venezuela," *Land Economics,* XXCIII, February 1952, 17-29.

International Bank for Reconstruction and Development. *The Economic Development of Venezuela.* (Ed., H. David Davis.) Baltimore: Johns Hopkins University Press, 1961.

International Labor Organization. International Labor Office. *Indigenous Peoples.* Geneva: La Tribune de Genéve, 1953.

James, Preston E. *Latin America.* New York: Odyssey Press, 1959.

Lieuwen, Edwin. *Petroleum in Venezuela.* Berkeley: University of California Press, 1954.

_____. *Venezuela.* London: Oxford University Press, 1961.

Lipsky, George, *et al. Area Handbook for Colombia.* Washington: Foreign Areas Studies Division, Special Operations Research Office, 1961.

Marsland, William D., and Amy, L. *Venezuela Through Its History.* New York: Crowell, 1954.

Masur, Gerhard. *Simón Bolívar.* Albuquerque: University of New Mexico Press, 1948.

Mecham, J. L. *Church and State in Latin America.* Chapel Hill: University of North Carolina Press, 1934.

Munro, Dana Gardner. *The Latin American Republics, A History.* New York: Appleton-Century-Crofts, 1950.

Pan American Union. *Constitution of the Republic of Venezuela, 1961.* Washington: PAU, 1961.

Picón Salas, Mariano, *et al. Venezuela independiente, 1810–1960.* Caracas: Fundación Eugenio Mendoza, 1962.

Rourke, Thomas. *Gómez: Tyrant of the Andes.* New York: Morrow, 1936.

Siso, Carlos. *La formación del pueblo venezolano: estudios sociológicos.* New York: Horizon House, 1941.

Smith, T. Lynn. *Latin American Population Studies.* Gainesville: University of Florida Press, 1961.

Steward, Julian H. (ed.). *Handbook of South American Indians.* IV. (Smithsonian Institution Bureau of American Ethnology Bulletin 143.) Washington: GPO, 1948.

Steward, Julian H., and Faron, L. *Native Peoples of South America.* New York: McGraw-Hill, 1959.

Tannenbaum, Frank. *Slave and Citizen: The Negro in the Americas.* New York: Knopf, 1947.

U.S. Department of Agriculture. *Agricultural Geography of Latin America.* Washington: GPO, 1958.

Vallenilla Lanz, Laureano. *Cesarismo democrático.* (3d ed.) Caracas: Tipografía Garrido, 1952.

Vila, Marco-Aurelio. *Geografía de Venezuela.* Caracas: Fundación Eugenio Mendoza, 1961.

Watters, Mary. *A History of the Church in Venezuela 1810–1930.* Chapel Hill: University of North Carolina Press, 1933.

Whitaker, Arthur P. *The United States and South America: The Northern Republics.* Cambridge: Harvard University Press, 1948.

Wilgus, A. Curtis. *The Development of Hispanic America.* New York: Farrar and Rinehart, 1941.

_____. *South American Dictators During the First Century of Independence.* Washington: George Washington University Press, 1937.

Wise, George S. *Caudillo: A Portrait of Antonio Guzmán Blanco*. New York: Columbia University Press, 1951.

OTHER SOURCES USED

Abercrombie, Thomas J. "Venezuela Builds on Oil." *National Geographic Magazine*, CXXIII, March 1963, 344–387.

Acosta Saignes, Miguel. *Elementos indígenas y africanos en la formación de la cultura venezolana*. Caracas: Universidad Central de Venezuela, 1955.

———. "Gentilicios Africanos en Venezuela," *Archivos Venezolanos de Folklore* (Caracas), 1955–1956.

———. "Orígen de Algunas Creencias Venezolanas," *Boletín Indigenista Venezolana*, VI, 1958, 171–195.

———. "San Benito en Betijoque," *Archivos Venezolanos de Folklore* (Caracas), IV–V, 1957–58, 101–111.

"Adsum"; organo oficial del arzobispado de Caracas. Caracas: 1959–60.

Albornoz, Orlando. "Valores Sociales en la Educación Venezolana (Una Investigación Sociológica)," *Boletín Bibliográfico*, III, July-August 1962.

Alexander, Robert J. *Communism in Latin America*. New Brunswick: Rutgers University Press, 1957.

Almond, Gabriel, and Coleman, James S. (eds.). *The Politics of Developing Areas*. Princeton: Princeton University Press, 1960.

Alonso, Isidoro, *et al.*, *La Iglesia en Venezuela y Ecuador*. Freiburg, Switzerland: Federación Internacional de los Institutos Católicos de Investigaciones Sociales y Socio-religiosos, 1961.

Alvarado, Lisandro. *Obras completas de Lisandro Alvarado,* IV. Caracas: Ministerio de Educación, 1956.

Anderson-Imbert, Enrique. *Historia de la literatura hispano americana*, I and II. (3d ed.) Mexico: Fondo de Cultura Economica, 1961.

Aracaya, Pedro M. *Estudios de sociología venezolana*. Caracas: Editorial Cecilio Acosta, 1941.

Arcila Farías, Eduardo. *Economía colonial de Venezuela*. Mexico: Fondo de Cultura Económica, 1956.

Arciniegas, Germán. *The States of Latin America*. New York: Knopf, 1952.

Arellano Moreno, A. *Orígenes de la economía venezolana*. (2d ed.) Caracas: Ediciones Edime, 1960.

Armas Alfonzo, Alfredo. "A las Puertas del Salón." *El Farol*, XX, No. 179, November–December 1958.

Armas Chitty, José Antonio de. *Tucupido: formación de un pueblo del llano*. Caracas: Universidad Central, 1961.

Banco Obrero and Sección de Investigaciones Social, Económica y Technológica. *El problema de los cerros en el area metropolitana.* Caracas: 1954.

Barrenechea, Manro. "Unionism in Venezuela," *America*, CVII, August 13, 1962, 626.

Betancourt, Rómulo. *Mensaje del Presidente ante el Congreso Nacional, 11 marzo, 1961.* Caracas: n.d.

_____. *V Mensaje Presidencial, 12 de marzo de 1963.* Miraflores: Imprenta Multimpresión, n.d.

Bolívar Coronado, R. *El Llanero.* Buenos Aires: Editorial Venezuela, 1947.

Brito Figueroa, Federico. *La estructura social y demográfica de Venezuela colonial.* Caracas: Ediciones Historia, 1961.

Calcano, José Antonio. "Sintesis Historica de la Música en Venezuela," *El Farol*, XV, No. 150, February 1954.

Caldera Rodríguez, Rafael. *Idea de una sociología venezolana.* Caracas: Librería y Editorial Alma Mater, 1954.

Chang-Rodríguez, Eugenio, and Kantor, Harry. *La América Latina de hoy.* New York: Ronald Press, 1961.

Clark, J. P., and Powell, John D. "To Struggle Is My Destiny." Report for School for Advanced International Studies of Johns Hopkins University, November 1, 1961 (unpublished manuscript).

Clemente Travieso, Carmen. *Mujeres venezolanas y otros reportajes.* Caracas: Avila Gráfica, 1951.

Consejo Venezolano del Niño. *El consejo venezolano del niño y la obra pro-menor en Venezuela.* Caracas: Editorial Sucre, 1955.

Coxill, H. Wakelin, and Grubb, Kenneth. *World Christian Handbook.* (1962 ed.) London: World Dominion Press, 1962.

Damaz, Paul F. *Art in Latin American Architecture.* New York: Reinhold, 1963.

Davies, Howell. *The South American Handbook.* London: Trade and Travel Publications, 1963.

Debuyst, Federico. *La Población en América Latina.* Brussels: Centro de Investigaciones Socio-Religiosas, 1961.

"De la Tradición, el Presente Originalidad : Tema Arquitectonico de América Latina." *Vision*, XXV, September 6, 1963.

"Demos"; Revista de Ilustración y Orientación. Ciudad Bolívar: 1960–62.

Diament de Sujo, Clara. *Art in Latin America Today: Venezuela.* Washington: PAU, 1962.

Díaz Seijas, Pedro. "La Novela Venezolana en los Ultimos Años," *Contrapunto*, No. 2, April/May 1948.

Dorselaer, Jaime, and Gregory, Alfonso. *La urbanización en América Latina.* Brussels: Centro de Investigaciones Socio-Religiosas, 1962.

Ellenbogen, Bertram Leighton. "A Study of the Social Organization of a Plantation Community in the Coffee Producing Region of Southwestern Venezuela." Unpublished doctoral dissertation, University of Wisconsin, 1959 (microfilm).

Fabbiani Ruiz, José. "Algunos Apuntes sobre Literatura Nacional," *Revista Shell*, IV, June 1955.

Fergusson, Emma. *Venezuela*. London: Knopf, 1942.

Fernández y Fernández, Ramón. *Reforma agraria en Venezuela*. Caracas: Tipografía Vargas, 1948.

Ferrer Faria, Ivan. *Ensayo sociológico de un medio rural concentrado venezolano*. Maracaibo: Tipografía Cervantes, 1957.

Fonseca, Jaime. "Reforma Agraria Integral." (National Catholic Welfare Conference News Service.) N.pl.: January 25, 1963 (mimeo.).

Foy, Felician A. (ed.). *National Catholic Almanac*. Paterson: St. Anthony's Guild, 1963.

Goetz, Delia. *Education in Venezuela*. Washington: GPO, 1948.

González Baquero, R. *Análisis del proceso histórico de la educación urbana (1870–1932) y de la educación rural (1932–1957)*. Caracas: Facultad de Filosofía y Letras, Universidad Central de Venezuela, 1962.

Griffin, Charles C. *Los temas sociales y económicos en la epoca de la independencia*. Caracas: Editorial Arte, 1962.

Grubb, Kenneth, G. *The Northern Republics*. New York: World Dominion Press, 1931.

Harburg, Ernest. "Los Medio Superiores: A Description of the Background and Features of an Upper Status Group in a Rural Market Town in the Venezuelan Andes in 1953." Unpublished master's thesis, University of Wisconsin, 1956 (microfilm and typescript).

Hernández Carvajal, Alvaro. *Veritas: estudio socio-económico*. Maracay: Ministerio de Salud y Asistencia Social, 1961.

Hill, George W. *La vida rural en Venezuela*. Caracas: Editorial Vargas, 1958.

Hill, George W., Silva, José M., and Hill, Ruth. *La vida rural en Venezuela*. Caracas: Tipografía Vargas, 1960.

Hill, Howard C. *Roosevelt and the Caribbean*. Chicago: University of Chicago Press, 1927.

Hitchcock, Henry Russell. *Latin American Architecture Since 1945*. New York: Museum of Modern Art, 1955.

Inter-American Indian Institute. "Indians in the Hemisphere Today," *Indianist Yearbook* (Mexico), XXII, 1962.

International Bank for Reconstruction and Development. *The Economic Development of Venezuela*. Baltimore: The Johns Hopkins Press, 1961.

Jankus, Alfred P., and Malloy, N. M. *Venezuela: Land of Opportunity.* New York: Pageant Press, 1956.
Liscano, Juan. *Folklore y cultura: ensayos.* Caracas: Editorial Avila Grafica, 1950.
Medina, José Ramón. *Examén de la poseía venezolana contemporánea.* Caracas: Colección "Letras Venezolanas," 1956.
Mendoza, José R. *Sociología, Ideología y Moral.* Caracas: Editorial Elite, 1938.
Mijares, Augusto. *La interpretación pesimista de la sociología hispanoamericana.* Madrid: Afrodisio Aguado, 1952.
Montesino Samperio, José V. *Demografía venezolana: la población del area. Factores de crecimiento y tendencias futuras.* Caracas: Corporación Venezolana de Fomento, 1956.
Moreno C., José. "Significación Económica de la Ley de Abril de 1834," *Revista Shell,* VIII, March 1960, 36–41.
El Nacional (Caracas), February 19, 1963.
"News of the Christian World," *Christian Century.* September 27, 1961.
Pan American Union. *América en cifras 1960: estadísticas sociales y del trabajo.* Washington: 1961.
_____. *Consumers Price (Cost-of-Living) Indexes of the American Nations, January 1955–June 1961.* Washington: 1961.
_____. *La estructura demográfica de las naciones americanas.* Washington: 1959.
_____. *Exodo rural en Venezuela.* Washington: 1954.
_____. "Situación de la Vivienda 1961," *El Censo de América de 1960,* June 28, 1963 (mimeo.).
_____. *Social Security and Economic Development.* (11th Inter-American Conference, Quito, Ecuador, 1960.) Washington: PAU, 1960.
_____. Department of Social Affairs. *Síntesis de la seguridad social americana.* Washington: PAU, 1960.
_____. División de Educación. Departamento de Asuntos Culturales. "Centro interamericana de educación rural: becas de especialización en educación rural, curso de 1963." Washington: 1962 (mimeo.).
_____. "Centro interamericana de educación rural: boletín informativo." Washington: July 1962 (mimeo.).
_____. Sección de Intercambio Educativo. *Boletín,* Nos. 2 and 6, 1959 and 1960.
Pattee, Richard. *El catolicismo contemporáneo en Hispano América.* Buenos Aires: Editorial Fides, 1948.
Picón Salas, Mariano. *Formación y proceso de la literatura venezolana.* Caracas: Impresores Unidos, 1940.
_____. "Hora de la Literatura Venezolana." *El Farol,* XV, February 1954.

Picón Salas, Mariano, *et al. Venezuela independiente 1810-1960.* Caracas: Fundación Eugenio Mendoza, 1962.

Pineda, Rafael. "Pasado y Presente del Teatro en Venezuela," *El Farol,* XV, February 1954.

Planchart, Enrique. "La Pintura Venezolana," *Revista Shell,* I, February 1952.

Prieto Figueroa, Luis Beltrán. *De una educación de castas a una educación de masas.* Havana: Editorial LEX, 1951.

Pulido Villafane, A., and Loreto, Luis. *Compilación legislativa de Venezuela.* Caracas: Editorial Andrés Bello, n.d.

Ramón y Rivera I. and L. F. "Resumen de un Estudio Sobre las Expresiones Negras en el Folklore Musical y Coreográfico de Venezuela," *Archivos Venezolanos de Folklore,* III, 1955-56, 65-73.

Ramos, Arthur. *Las culturas negras en el nuevo mundo.* Mexico: Fondo de Cultura Económica, 1943.

Reid, John. "Notes and Meditations on Contemporary Venezuelan Literature," *Hispania,* XXXIV, August 31, 1951.

Rohl, Juan. "Ligero Esbozo de la Pintura Venezolana," *El Farol,* XV, February 1954.

Rosenblat, Angel. "El Castellano de Venezuela: la Influencia Indígena," *Boletín Indigenista Venezolano,* III-V, March 1958, 87-107.

Rourke, Thomas. *Man of Glory, Simón Bolívar.* New York: Morrow, 1942.

Rumazo González, Alfonso. "Speaking of Gran Colombia," *Americas,* XIII, November 1961.

Sangróniz y Castro, José A. *Familias coloniales de Venezuela.* Caracas: Editorial Bolívar, 1943.

Schaedel, Richard, and Wisdom, Robert. "Community Development in Venezuela." A Report for the Agency for International Development, February 1962 (mimeo.).

Siso Martínez, J. M. *Historia de Venezuela.* Mexico: Editorial "Yocoima," 1957.

______. *Historia de Venezuela.* Caracas: n. pub., 1962.

Sojo, Juan Pablo. *Temas y apuntes afro-venezolanos.* Caracas: Tipografía La Nación, 1943.

Stuart, Graham H. *Latin America and the United States.* New York: Appleton-Century-Crofts, 1955.

Taylor, Paul S. "Venezuela: A Case Study of Relationships between Community Development and Agrarian Reform." (For Bureau of Social Affairs of the United Nations.) Caracas: August-September, 1960 (mimeo.).

Tejera, Victorino. "Venezuelan Literature: An Interpretation," *United Nations World,* V, July 1951.

de Undurraga, Antonio. "Venezuela en la Nueva Poseía," *Cultura Universitaria*, No. 57, September-October 1956.

United Nations Educational, Scientific and Cultural Organization. *The Demographic, Economic, Social and Educational Situation in Latin America.* (Conference on Education and Economic and Social Development in Latin America. Santiago de Chile, 5–19 March, 1962.) (mimeo.).

_____. *La situación educativa en América Latina: la ensananza primaria: estado, problemas y perspectiva.* Paris: UNESCO, 1960.

U.S. Army Medical Service. Medical Information and Intelligence Agency. *Health and Sanitary Data for Venezuela.* Washington: n. pub., 1961.

U.S. Department of Labor. *Labor Law and Practice in Venezuela.* (Business Information Service Report No. 212.) Washington: GPO, 1961.

U.S. Department of State. *Health and Sanitation Program. Agreement Between the United States of America and Venezuela, Caracas, February 18, 1943.* (Publication 2048. Executive Agreement Series 300–399, No. 348.) Washington: GPO, n.d.

University of California. Center of Latin American Studies. *Statistical Abstract of Latin America, 1960.* Los Angeles: 1960.

_____. *Statistical Abstract of Latin America, 1962.* Los Angeles: 1962.

Uslar Pietri, Arturo. *Letras y hombres de Venezuela.* Mexico: Fondo de Cultura Económica, 1948.

_____. *Materiales Para la estructura de Venezuela.* Caracas: Ediciones Orinoco, 1959.

Van Loon, Hendrik Willem. *Fighters for Freedom, Jefferson and Bolívar.* New York: Dodd Mead, 1962.

Venezuela. Banco Central de Venezuela. *Memoria: correspondiente al ejercicio anual 1959.* Caracas: Artegrafia, n.d.

_____. *Memoria: correspondiente al ejercicio anual 1960.* Caracas: Artegrafia, n.d.

_____. *Memoria: correspondiente al ejercicio anual 1961.* Caracas: Artegrafia, n.d.

Venezuela. Dirección General de Estadística. *Censo nacional de 1950: empadronamiento especial de la población indígena.* Caracas: El Cojo, n.d.

Venezuela. Embassy of Venezuela (Washington). Information Service. "Community Development in Venezuelan National Program," n.d. (mimeo.).

_____. "Teachers Being Trained Here for Venezuelan Universities," *Venezuela Up-to-Date,* Fall 1962.

_____. "Venezuela, A Resume of its Educational System Based on a Study by J. Homer Herriott," n.d. (mimeo.).

Venezuela. Laws, Statutes, etc.
Código civil venezolano. Caracas: Colección Arandina, 1961.
"Ley de Universidades 1958." *Gaceta Oficial* (Caracas). 1958.
"Proyecto de Ley de Presupuesto para el Ejercicio Fiscal 1963," *Gaceta Oficial* (Caracas), 1963.
Congreso Nacional. *La ley de reforma agraria en las cámaras legislativas.* 2 vols. Caracas: 1960.
Venezuela. Ministerio de Educación. *Boletín de la Oficina de Planeamiento Integral de la Educación.* Caracas: March 1962.
_____ . Dirección de Educación Secundaria, Superior y Especial. *Oportunidades de estudio en Venezuela.* Caracas: n.d.
Venezuela. Minister of Education. General Directorate. "General Statement of Educational Achievement in the Last Six Years." Caracas: n.d. (mimeo.).
Venezuela. Ministerio de Fomento. *IX Censo nacional de población, resultados preliminares del crecimiento de los centros poblados y su distribución por tamaño.* Caracas: 1962.
_____ .*IX Censo nacional de población, resultadós preliminares por centros poblados.* Caracas: 1962.
_____ . *IX Censo nacional de población, resultados preliminares por distritos y municipios.* Caracas: 1962.
_____ . *Octavo censo general de población, población urbana y rural y lugar de nacimiento.* Caracas: 1955.
_____ . Dirección General de Estadística. *Boletín Mensual de Estadística* (Caracas), XXII, No. 12, July–September 1962.
Venezuela. Ministerio de Salud y Asistencia Social. Annual Memorias presented to the National Congress for the years 1961 and 1962.
_____ . Dirección de Malariología y Sameamiento Ambiental. División de Vivienda Rural. "El Programa de Vivienda," 1961 (mimeo.).
Venezuela. Oficina Central del Censo Nacional. *Octavo censo general de población (26 de noviembre de 1950): edad y estado civil por entidades y distritos y resúmen nacional.* Caracas: n.pub., 1954.
Venezuela. Secretaria General de la Presidencia de la República. *Plan de la nación 1963-1966.* Caracas: Imprenta Multimpresión, November 1962.
Williamson, René de Visme. *Culture and Policy: The United States and the Hispanic World.* Knoxville: University of Tennessee Press, 1949.
Wood, Bryce. *The Making of the Good Neighbor Policy.* New York: Columbia University Press, 1961.
World Health Organization. "XVI Pan American Sanitary Conference. XIV Regional Meeting of the World Health Organization" (Complete Set of Documents). Minneapolis: August 21–September 3, 1962.

Zuloaga, Guillermo. *Geografía petrolera de Venezuela.* Caracas: Cromotip, 1960.

(In addition, much useful material was found in numerous issues of the *Revista Venezolana de Salud y Asistencia Social* [Caracas], for the years 1960–62, and in *Noticias Católicas* [Washington, by the National Catholic Welfare Conference], for the years 1957–63.)

Section II. Political

RECOMMENDED SOURCES

Bartlett, Ruhl J. *The Record of American Diplomacy.* (3d ed.) York: Knopf, 1954.

Betancourt, Rómulo. *Pósición y doctrina.* Caracas: Editorial Cordillera, 1959.

Cárdenas, Rodolfo José. *La insurrección popular en Venezuela.* Caracas: Ediciones Catatumbo, 1961.

Davis, Harold Eugene. *Government and Politics in Latin America.* New York: Ronald Press, 1958.

Drier, John C. *The Organization of American States and the Hemisphere Crisis.* New York: Harper and Row, published for the Council on Foreign Relations, 1962.

Dubois, Jules. *Operation America: The Communist Conspiracy in Latin America.* New York: Walker, 1963.

Hill, Howard C. *Roosevelt and the Caribbean.* Chicago: University of Chicago Press, 1927.

Ireland, Gordon. *Boundaries, Possessions and Conflicts in South America.* Cambridge: Harvard University Press, 1938.

Masur, Gerhard. *Simón Bolívar.* Albuquerque: University of New Mexico Press, 1948.

Mecham, J. L. *The United States and Inter-American Security, 1899–1960.* Austin: University of Texas Press, 1961.

Munro, Dana Gardner. *The Latin American Republics, A History.* New York: Appleton-Century-Crofts, 1950.

Needler, Martin C. *Latin American Politics in Perspective.* Princeton: Van Nostrand, 1963.

Operations and Policy Research, Inc. *Venezuela Election Factbook, Elections: December 1963.* Washington: OPR, 1963.

Pan American Union. *Constitution of the Republic of Venezuela, 1961.* Washington: PAU, 1961.

———. *A Statement of the Laws of Venezuela in Matters Affecting Business.* (3d ed.) Washington: PAU, 1962.

Peaslee, Amos J. *Constitutions of Nations,* III. (2d ed.) The Hague: Martinus Nijhof, 1956.

Pike, Frederick B. (ed.). *Freedom and Reform in Latin America.* Notre Dame: University of Notre Dame Press, 1959.

Schmitt, K. M., and Burks, D. D. *Evolution or Chaos: Dynamics of Latin American Government and Politics.* New York: Praeger, 1963.

Stokes, William S. *Latin American Politics.* New York: Crowell, 1959.

Stuart, Graham H. *Latin America and the United States.* New York: Appleton-Century-Crofts, 1955.

Whitaker, Arthur P. *The United States and South America: The Northern Republics.* Cambridge: Harvard University Press, 1948.
Wilgus, A. Curtis. *The Development of Hispanic America.* New York: Farrar and Rinehart, 1941.
Wood, Bryce. *The Making of the Good Neighbor Policy.* New York: Columbia University Press, 1961.

OTHER SOURCES USED

Aaronson, Charles S. (ed.). *International Motion Picture Almanac, 1961.* New York: Quigley Publications, 1961.
Abercrombie, Thomas J. "Venezuela Builds on Oil," *National Geographic Magazine*, CXXIII, March 1963, 344–387.
Alexander, Robert J. *Communism in Latin America.* New Brunswick: Rutgers University Press, 1957.
_____ . *Today's Latin America.* (Anchor Books.) New York: Doubleday, 1963.
Almond, Gabriel, and Coleman, James S. (eds.). *The Politics of Developing Areas.* Princeton: Princeton University Press, 1960.
Arciniegas, Germán. "Lógica y Absurdo en lo de Venezuela," *Cuadernos* (Paris), No. 30, May/June 1958.
_____ . *The States of Latin America.* New York: Knopf, 1952.
Arias, Aníbal. "Venezuela: un Regímen Puesto a Prueba," *Cuadernos* (Paris), No. 68, June 1963, 68–70.
Balink, Albert. *My Paradise Is Hell: The story of the Caribbean.* New York: Vista Publishing Corporation, 1948.
Brierly, J. L. *The Law of Nations: An Introduction to the International Law of Peace.* Oxford: Clarendon Press, 1955.
Cereceda, Raúl. *Las Instituciones Politicas en América Latina.* Bogotá: Feres Friburgo, 1961.
Chang-Rodríguez, Eugenio, and Kantor, Harry. *La América Latina de hoy.* New York: Ronald Press, 1961.
Davies, Howell. *The South American Handbook.* London: Trade and Travel Publications, 1963.
Eisenhower, Milton S. *The Wine Is Bitter: The United States and Latin America.* New York: Doubleday, 1963.
Fergusson, Emma. *Venezuela.* London: Knopf, 1942.
Film Daily Year Book of Motion Pictures, 1963. New York: The Film Daily, 1963.
Frank, Waldo David. *Birth of a World.* Boston: Houghton Mifflin, 1951.
Gallegos, Rómulo, *et al. Rómulo Betancourt: interpretación de su doctrina popular y democrática.* Caracas: SUMA, 1958.
Herring, Hubert. *A History of Latin America from the Beginning to the Present.* New York: Knopf, 1960.

Jennison, Peter S., and Kurth, William H. *Books in the Americas.* Washington: Pan American Union, 1960.

Johnson, John J. *Political Change in Latin America: The Emergence of the Middle Sectors.* Stanford: Stanford University Press, 1958.

Legters, Lyman H., *et al. Area Handbook for Panama.* Washington: Foreign Areas Studies Division, Special Operations Research Office, 1962.

Lieuwen, Edwin. *Venezuela.* London: Oxford University Press, 1961.

Lipsky, George, *et al. Area Handbook for Colombia.* Washington: Foreign Areas Studies Division, Special Operations Research Office, 1961.

Los manifiestos de la liberación: recopilación de los manifiestos que circularon clandestinamente desde el 1° hasta el 23 de enero de 1958, día de la liberación venezolana. Caracas: Editorial Pensamiento Vivo, 1958.

Luzardo, Rodolfo. *Notas histórico-económicas, 1928–1963.* Caracas: Editorial Sucre, 1963.

Marsland, William D., and Amy L. *Venezuela Through Its History.* New York: Crowell, 1954.

Merrill, John C. *A Handbook of the Foreign Press.* Baton Rouge: Louisiana State University Press, 1959.

Morner, Magnus. "Caudillos y Militares en la Evolución Hispano-Americana," *Journal of Interamerican Studies,* II, July 1960, 295–310.

Organization of American States. Alliance for Progress. *Public and School Libraries in Latin America,* by Marietta Daniels. Washington: 1963 (mimeo.).

Palmer, Mona. *World Petroleum Report.* New York: n.pub., 1963.

Pan American Union. Columbus Memorial Library. *Directorio de librarias y casas editoriales en América Latina.* (6th ed.) (Bibliographic Series 2, Pt. 3.) Washington: PAU, 1958.

______. *Guía de bibliotecas de la América Latina.* (Edición Provisional. Bibliographic Series No. 51.) Washington: PAU, 1963.

Picón Rivas, Ulises. *Indice constitucional de Venezuela.* Caracas: Editorial Elite, 1944.

Picón Salas, Mariano, *et al. Venezuela independiente 1810–1960.* Caracas: Fundación Eugenio Mendoza, 1962.

Rourke, Thomas. *Man of Glory, Simón Bolívar.* New York: Morrow, 1942.

Sánchez, L. A. "El Vicepresidente Nixon en América Latina," *Cuadernos* (Paris), No. 32, September–October 1958, 75–81.

Siso Martinez, J. M. *Historia de Venezuela.* Caracas: n.pub., 1962.

Testimonio de la República en Venezuela 1° de enero-23 de julio, 1958. Caracas: Tipo Vargas, S. A., 1958.

U.S. Congress. 86th, 2d Session. Senate. Committee on Foreign Relations. *Latin America: Venezuela, Brazil, Peru, Bolivia and Panama*. Washington: GPO, 1960.

U.S. Congress. 87th, 2d Session. House. Committee on Foreign Affairs. *Regional and Other Documents Concerning United States Relations with Latin America*. Washington: GPO, 1962.

U.S. Department of Commerce. Business and Defense Services Administration. Scientific, Motion Picture and Photographic Products Division. *World Survey of Motion Picture Facilities*. Washington: October 1960.

Uslar Pietri, Arturo. "La Venezuela de Lieuwen no es, exactamente, Venezuela," *La Nueva Democracia* (New York), April 1962. 42–44.

Venezuela. *Proposed Budget for Fiscal Year 1963*. Caracas: n.pub., 1963.

______. Laws, Statutes, etc. "Reglamento de Radiocommunicaciones." *Gaceta Oficial de los Estados Unidos de Venezuela,* LXIX, March 5, 1941.

Venezuela. Secretaría General de la Presidencia de la República. *Constitución 1961*. Caracas: Imprenta Nacional, 1961.

Voice of America. *Program Schedule—November 1963–January 1964, Latin America* (pamphlet).

Wilgus, A. Curtis. *Colonial Hispanic America*. New York: Russell and Russell, 1963.

______ . (ed.). *South American Dictators During the First Century of Independence*. Washington: George Washington University Press, 1937.

Zuniga Cisneros, M. "Reflecciones sobre lo Venezolano," *Boletín de la Academia de Ciencias Políticas y Sociales*, No. 21, July-September 1961.

(The following were also used in the preparation of this section: *Copely News Service,* 1963; *Deadline Data on World Affairs,* 1963; *La Esfera, El Universal, El Nacional and La República,* from January through December 1963; and various issues of *Gaceta Oficial* [published by the Venezuelan Ministry of Interior Relations], from January 1962 to October 1963.)

Section III. Economic

RECOMMENDED SOURCES

Coutsoumaris, George. "Policy Objectives in Latin American Land Reform, With Special Reference to Venezuela," *Inter-American Economic Affairs,* XVI, Autumn 1962, 25-40.

International Bank for Reconstruction and Development. *The Economic Development of Venezuela.* (Ed., H. David Davis.) Baltimore: Johns Hopkins University Press, 1961.

Lieuwen, Edwin. *Petroleum in Venezuela.* Berkeley: University of California Press, 1954.

Penn, Raymond T., and George Schuster. "La Reforma Agraria de Venezuela," *Revista Interamericana de Ciencias Sociales,* II, No. 1, 1963, 29-39.

Pogue, Joseph E. *Oil in Venezuela: An Economic Study.* New York: Chase National Bank, 1949.

U.S. Department of Commerce. *Investment in Venezuela: Conditions and Outlook for United States Investors.* Washington: GPO, 1956.

———. Bureau of Foreign Commerce. *Principal Manufacturing Industries—Venezuela.* (World Trade Information Service: "Economic Reports," Pt. 1, No. 8-70.) Washington: September 1958.

U.S. Department of Labor. *Labor Law and Practice in Venezuela.* (Business Information Service Report No. 212.) Washington: GPO, 1961.

OTHER SOURCES USED

Abercromie, Thomas J. "Venezuela Builds on Oil," *National Geographic Magazine,* CXXIII, March 1963, 344-387.

Adler, John H. "Fiscal Policy in a Developing Country." N.pl.: International Bank for Reconstruction and Development, July 8, 1960 (mimeo.).

Alexander, Robert J. *Communism in Latin America.* (2d ed.). New Brunswick: Rutgers University Press, 1960.

Alfonso Pérez, Pablo Juan. "El Petroleo Ruso no es una Amenaza para Venezuela," *Mundo Económico,* No. 8, September 1961, 7-10.

Alliance for Progress. "Address by the Honorable Teodoro Moscoso, U.S. Coordinator of the Alliance for Progress before the Thirteenth Annual Caribbean Conference," University of Florida: December 8, 1962 (mimeographed press release).

Angulo, Manuel R. "Comments on the Status of Foreign Business Corporations Under the Commercial Codes of Argentina and Venezuela," *Inter-American Law Review*, IV, July-December 1962, 159-185.

Arellano Moreno, A. *Orígenes de la economía venezolana*. Caracas: Ediciones Edime, 1960.

Banco Interamericano de Desarrollo. *Reformas institucionales y desarrollo social en América Latina*. Washington: BID, March 1963.

Barrenechea, Mauro. "Unionism in Venezuela," *America*, CVII, August 18, 1962.

Butland, Gilbert T. *Latin America: A Regional Geography*. London: Spottiswodde Ballantyne, 1961.

"Cámara de Comercio Venezolana—Antillana," *Comercio Exterior de Venezuela*, XI, July 1963, 4.

Canalejas, F. I. *Patent and Trademark Law in Venezuela 1955*. Caracas: Cromotip, n.d.

Carroll, Thomas F. "The Land Reform Issue in Latin America," Pages 184-188 and 190-191 in Hirschmar, Herbert O. (ed.), *Latin American Issues: Essays and Comments*. New York: The Twentieth Century Fund, 1961.

Chamber of the Petroleum Industry. "Report on the Venezuelan Petroleum Industry." N. pl.: February 1960 (mimeo.).

Chaves, Fernando Luis. *Geografía agraria de Venezuela*. Caracas: Ediciones de la Biblioteca, Universidad Central de Venezuela, 1963.

Clark, John P., and Powell, John D. "To Struggle is My Destiny: Agrarian Reform, Venezuela." Unpublished study at School of Advanced International Studies of Johns Hopkins University. Washington: November 1961.

"Cloth, Cattle, Candy and Corn," *The Lamp*, XLV, Summer 1963, 3-6.

Confederación de Trabajadores de Venezuela. *Lista completa de los integrantes de las federaciones de trabajadores regionales y nacionales de Venezuela, afiliadas a la C.T.V.* Caracas: 1960.

Consejo de Bienestar Rural. *Problemas económicos y sociales de los Andes Venezolanos*. Caracas: 1955.

Cook, Hugh L. "The New Agrarian Reform Law and Economic Development in Venezuela," *Land Economics*, XXXVII, February 1961, 5-17.

CORDIPLAN. "Public Finance," *News of Venezuela*, I, No. 4, April 1962, 3, 6, 7.

Corporación Venezolana de Fomento. *Memoria y cuenta 1960-1961*. N.pl.: n.d.

_____. *Memoria y cuenta 1962*. Caracas: Cromotip, April 1963.

Corporación Venezolana del Petróleo, *CVP*. N.pl.: n.d.

Creole Petroleum Corporation. *Companía de inversiones creole*. Venezuela: Cromotip, September 1962.

———. *Datos básicos sobre la industria petrolera y la economia venezolana.* Caracas: July 1962.

———. "FEDEPETROL Collective Contract," May 18, 1963 (mimeo.).

Crest, Raymond E. *Venezuela.* Garden City: Doubleday, 1959.

Day, George H., and Quinones, Edward. "Venezuela—Land Reform in Action," *Foreign Agriculture*, XXVI, December 1962, 5-7.

Economist Intelligence Unit, Ltd. *The Economic Resource: Venezuela,* Nos. 13 and 14, May and August 1963.

———. *Economic Review of Venezuela* (London), No. 16, January 1957; No. 23, October 1958; and No. 13, May 1963.

———. *Three-Monthly Economic Review: Venezuela,* No. 13, May 1963. No. 14, August 1963; and Annual Supplement 1963.

Espinosa, Alfonso. "Some Aspects of the Venezuelan Economic Development," *The Statist* (London), March 1960, 174, 175.

Fonseca, Jamie. "Christian Democrats Spearheading Venezuela's Land Reform Program Based on Church's Social Teachings." (National Catholic Welfare Conference News Service.) Washington: January 1963 (mimeo.).

Food and Agriculture Organization. *Report of the FAO Oilseed Mission for Venezuela.* Washington: 1949.

———. *The State of Food and Agriculture.* Rome: FAO 1961.

Forrest, Alan. "Venezuela's Democratic Revolution," *Free Labor World* (Brussels), November 1962.

Francis, David R. "La Guayana Complex: Venezuela Industry Buds," *The Christian Science Monitor*, February 16, 1963, 14.

Golomb, Berl, *et al.* (ed.). *Statistical Abstract of Latin America, 1962.* Los Angeles: University of California Press, 1963.

Hallström, Anders. *Olja och Indianer.* Stockholm: Bonniers, 1960.

Hanborg, C. A. "Venezuela under Betancourt," *Current History*, XL, April 1961, 232-240.

Hanson, Simon G. "The International Coffee Agreement," *Inter-American Economic Affairs*, XVII, Autumn 1963, 75-94.

Hassan, Mostafa, F. "Capital Flight: Venezuela 1958-1960," *Inter-American Economic Affairs*, XVII, Autumn 1963, 53-73.

Hill, George W., *et al.* "Social Welfare and Tenure Problems in Agrarian Reform Program of Venezuela." Pages 293-304 in Parson, Kenneth H., *et al.* (eds.), *Land Tenure.* Madison: University of Wisconsin Press, 1956.

Hinkle, William R., Jr. "Private Investment Possibilities in Venezuela" (Speech delivered at Chicago World Marketing and Economic Development Conference, July 1961). Pages 1-12 in *Panorama of Venezuela.* Miraflores: Imprenta Multimpresión, n.d.

Hollandsche Bank-Unie, N.V. "Economic Review: Venezuela." N.pl.: November 1961–February 1963 (mimeo.).
_____ . "Venezuela: Economic Report for July 1963." N.pl.: September 1963 (mimeo.).
Hunt, James C. "Venezuela Before the Elections: Oil and Expectations," *Statist*, June 14, 1963, 787-789.
Hynes, K. V. "Venezuela: Plan for Readjustment," *Foreign Commerce Weekly*, No. 19, 1959.
"Impulso a la Exportación de Tabaco," *Comercio Exterior de Venezuela,* XI, August 1963, 12.
Inter-American Development Bank. *Reformas institucionales y desarrollo social en América Latina*. Washington: IDB, 1963.
International Bank for Reconstruction and Development. *The Economic Development of Venezuela.* Baltimore: Johns Hopkins Press, 1961.
International Bank for Reconstruction and Development and International Development Association. *The World Bank and IDA in the Americas: A Summary of Activities.* Washington: January 1962.
International Confederation of Free Trade Unions-Organización Regional Interamericana de Trabajadores. *The Permanent Struggle of the Free Trade Union Movement Against Latin American Dictatorships.* (ICFTU-ORIT Special Publications.) Mexico City: June 1960.
International Labour Organisation. International Labour Office. *Freedom of Association and Conditions of Work in Venezuela.* Geneva: ILO, 1950.
_____ . *The Landless Farmer in Latin America.* Geneva: La Tribune de Genève, 1957.
International Monetary Fund. *The Balance of Payments Yearbook*, XIV, 1957-61; and XV, September 1963.
_____ . *Fourteenth Annual Report: Exchange Restrictions 1963.* Washington: IMF, 1963.
"Iron Ore and the Guiana Project," *Latin American Report,* IV, February 1962, 21-23.
James, Preston E. *Latin America.* New York: Odyssey Press, 1959.
Jankus, Alfred P., and Malloy, Neil M. *Venezuela: Land of Opportunity.* New York: Pageant Press, 1956.
Johnson, Betram B. "Venezuelan Oil Crisis Builds." *Christian Science Monitor,* October 8, 1959.
Lieuwen, Edwin. *Venezuela.* London: Oxford University Press, 1961.
Luzardo, Rodolfo. *Venezuela: Business and Finance.* Englewood Cliffs: Prentice Hall, 1957.
Maby, A. C. *Venezuela: Economic and Commercial Conditions.* London: His Majesty's Stationary Office, 1951.

MacLeish, H. William. *Land and Liberty: Agrarian Reform in the Americas.* New York: Visión, January 1962.

Mayorbe, José A. "Economic Trends in Venezuela," *The Statist,* March 1960, 171-173.

Mehren, George L. *El mercado de los productos agrícolas en Venezuela.* Caracas: Consejo de Bienestar Rural, 1954.

Mendoza, Eduardo G. "Agricultura: Factor Clave de Desarollo," *El Faról,* November-December 1953, 57-64.

"Monetary Aspects of the Venezuelan Economy," *Modern Venezuela Moves Ahead* (Special section of *New York Times*), Sec. 12, May 26, 1963, 25.

"Nueva Política de Exportación," *Mundo Económico,* No. 16, May 1963, 10.

Olcoz, Ignacio F. "Déficit Spending: Inflación y Reservas Internacionales," *Mundo Económico,* No. 8, September 1961, 42, 43.

Pan American Coffee Bureau. *Annual Coffee Statistics 1961,* No. 25, USA: AM-AHI-LITHO'D, 1962.

Pan American Union. *A Statement of the Laws of Venezuela in Matters Affecting Business.* (3d ed.) Washington: PAU, 1962.

Parra, Alirio A. "La Industria de Minas y sus Obligaciones Fiscales en Venezuela." (Presented by the Ministry of Mines and Hydrocarbons at the First Venezuelan Petroleum Congress.) Caracas: March 1962.

_____ . "Oil and Stability." (Paper presented by Venezuelan Delegation at Third Arab Petroleum Congress.) Alexandria: October 16-22, 1961 (mimeo.).

Parra, Alirio, A., and Pocaterra, Emma. "The Petroleum Industry in Venezuela." (Paper presented by Venezuelan Delegation at Third Arab Petroleum Congress.) Alexandria, October 16-22, 1961 (mimeo.).

Pérez, Guerrero Manuel. (Speech delivered at Chicago World Marketing and Economic Development Conference, July 1961.) Pages 1-11 in *Panorama of Venezuela.* Miraflores: Imp. Multimpresión, n.d.

Pernaut, Manuel, "Los Dineros del Fisco," *Mundo Económico.* No. 15, January 1963, 55-58.

Poblete Troncoso, Moises, and Burnett, Ben G. *The Rise of the Latin American Labor Movement.* New Haven: College and University Press, 1960.

Pueblo-organo de los sindicatos autónomos cristianos de Venezuela (Caracas), November 1962.

Rayburn, J. C. "Development of Venezuela's Iron Ore Deposits," *Latin American Economic Affairs,* VI. No. 1, 1952, 52-60.

Rojas, Wilson J. *Razón y objectivos para la vigencia de la re-*

forma agraria en Venezuela. Caracas: Instituto Agrario Nacional, 1962.

Roncayolo, Luis Alberto. "Development of the Iron and Steel Industry," *The Statist* (London), March 1960, 177.

Royal Institute of International Affairs. Information Department. *Venezuela: A Brief Political and Economic Survey.* London: Oxford University Press, 1958.

Salera, V. "Broadening the Industrial Front in Venezuela," *Inter-American Economic Affairs,* VIII, Spring 1955, 69–80.

Sarda, J. "Industrial Development in Venezuela," *Inter-American Economic Affairs,* VII, Spring 1954, 38–48.

Shoup, Carl, *et al. The Fiscal System of Venezuela.* Baltimore: Johns Hopkins University Press, 1959.

Silva Guillen, Rafael. *La reforma agraria en Venezuela.* Caracas: Instituto Agrario Nacional, 1962.

Snyder, David E. "Ciudad Guayana: A Planned Metropolis on the Orinoco," *Journal of Inter-American Studies,* July 1963, 405–412.

Sutton, Horace. "Who's Gonna Take De Money and Run Venezuela?" *Saturday Review,* May 11, 1963, 34–36, 39.

Tamayo, Armando. "The National Agrarian Institute and Land Tenure Relations Venezuela." Pages 304–308 in Parson, Kenneth H., *et al.* (eds.), *Land Tenure.* Madison: University of Wisconsin Press, 1956.

Taylor, Wayne C., and John Lindeman. *United States Business Performance Abroad: The Case Study of the Creole Petroleum Corporation in Venezuela.* Washington: National Planning Association, 1955.

"Trojan Horse in Venezuelan Labor," *AFL-CIO Free Trade Union News* (New York), January 1960.

United Nations. Department of Economic and Social Affairs. *World Economic Survey 1962: The Developing Countries in World Trade.* (No. 63, II C. 1.) New York: UN, 1963.

_____ . *Yearbook of International Trade Statistics 1961.* New York: UN, 1963.

United Nations. Economic Commission for Latin America. *Economic Bulletin for Latin America,* VII, October 1962.

United Nations. Economic Commission for Latin America and Food and Agriculture Organization. "Stock Farming in Venezuela: Its Status and Progress." (E/CN/558.) N.pl.: March 1961 (mimeo.).

United Nations. Office of Public Information. *Yearbook of the United Nations 1961.* New York: UN, 1963.

U.S. Agency for International Development. *Alliance for Progress in American Partnership.* Washington: 1963.

_____ . *Report to the Congress on the Foreign Assistance Program in Fiscal Year 1962.* Washington: GPO, 1963.

———. Statistics and Reports Division. *Fiscal 1962 Projects by Country and Field of Activity.* Washington: GPO, 1963.

———. *Voluntary Foreign Aid Programs: Reports of American Voluntary Agencies Registered with the Advisory Committee on Voluntary Foreign Aid.* N.pl.: 1962.

U.S. Committee for Economic Development. *Cooperation for Progress in Latin America.* N.pl.: CED, 1961.

U.S. Congress. 83d, 2d Session. House. *Fuel Investigation: Venezuela Petroleum.* (Report No. 1487.) Washington: 1954.

U.S. Congress. 87th, 2d Session. Senate. *Special Report on Latin America (November and December 1961).* No. 80.) Washington: GPO, 1962.

U.S. Congress. 88th, 1st Session. Senate. *A Report on the Alliance for Progress 1963,* by Hubert H. Humphrey. (Doc. No. 13.) Washington: GPO, 1963.

U.S. Department of Agriculture. *Agriculture Geography: Latin America.* Washington: GPO, 1958.

———. *The World Food Budget 1962 and 1963: The Western Hemisphere (excluding U.S.).* (Supplement No. 1.) N.pl.: 1961.

———. *The 1963 World Agricultural Situation Western Hemisphere.* (Supplement No. 1.) N.pl.: 1963.

———. Economic Research Service. *Notes on the Agricultural Economies of the 20 Latin American Republics.* Washington: GPO, 1961.

———. *U.S. Farm Products Find Market and Competition in Venezuela.* Washington: GPO, 1961.

———. Western Hemisphere Branch (RAD). "Venezuela—Value of Trade by Principal Commodities and Countries, 1951 to 1960." N.pl.: September 1962 (mimeo.).

U.S. Department of Agriculture. Foreign Agriculture Service. *U.S. Agricultural Trade with Latin America.* (FASM-57.) Washington: GPO, 1959.

U.S. Department of Commerce. Bureau of Foreign Commerce. *Basic Data on the Economy of Venezuela.* (World Trade Information Service: "Economic Reports," Pt. 1, No. 59-69.) Washington: GPO, 1959.

———. *Economic Developments in Venezuela, 1958.* (World Trade Information Service: "Economic Reports," Pt. 1, No. 59-49.) Washington: GPO, 1959.

———. *Economic Developments in Venezuela, 1962.* (World Trade Information Service: "Overseas Business Reports," No. 63-73.) N.pl.: March 1963.

———. *Foreign Trade of Venezuela, 1956-1957.* (World Trade Information Service: "Statistical Reports," Pt. 3, No. 58-41.) Washington: GPO, 1958.

———. *Import Tariff System of Venezuela.* (World Trade Information Service: "Statistical Reports," Pt. 2, No. 61-18.) Washington: GPO, 1961.

______. *Patent and Trademark Regulations of Venezuela.* (World Trade Information Service: "Operations Reports," Pt. 2, No. 59-6.) Washington: GPO, 1959.

______. *Utilities Abroad: Electric Power in Venezuela.* (World Trade Information Service: "Economic Reports," Pt. 4, No. 56-16.) Washington: 1956.

U.S. Department of Commerce. Bureau of International Commerce. *Basic Data on the Economy of Venezuela.* (Overseas Business Reports, OBR-63-132.) Washington: GPO, 1963.

______. *Economic Developments in Venezuela, 1962.* (Overseas Business Reports, OBR-63-73.) Washington: GPO, 1963.

U.S. Department of Commerce. *Licensing and Exchange Control of Venezuela.* (Overseas Business Reports, OBR-63-80.) Washington: GPO, 1963.

______. *United States Foreign Trade, December 1962 and Calendar Years 1956-1962.* (Overseas Business Reports, OBR-63-101.) Washington: GPO, 1963.

U.S. Department of Commerce. Bureau of International Programs. *Foreign Trade of Venezuela, 1959-1960.* (World Trade Information Service: "Statistical Reports," Pt. 3, No. 61-40.) Washington: GPO, 1961.

U.S. Department of Commerce. Business Information Service. *Venezuela Economic Review—1953.* (World Trade Series, No. 539.) Washington: GPO, 1954.

U.S. Department of Commerce. Office of Business Economics. *Foreign Grants and Credits by the United States Government, Calendar Year 1962,* (No. 72.) Washington: 1963.

U.S. Department of Commerce. Office of International Trade. International Reference Service. *Economic Review of Venezuela 1949.* VI. (No. 83.) Washington: GPO, n.d.

U.S. Department of Labor. Bureau of International Affairs. *Directory of Labor Organizations—Western Hemisphere, II,* Washington: GPO, 1960.

Venezuela. *Convenios comerciales vigentes: tomo I, convenios bilaterales.* (Estudios sobre Comercio Exterior, No. 10.) Caracas: November 1962.

______. *Disposiciones legales venezolanas que regulan las importaciones y exportaciones.* (Estudios sobre Comercio Exterior, No. 13.) Caracas: February 1963.

______. *Exportaciones venezolanas 1955-1961.* (Estudios sobre Comercio Exterior No. 12.) Caracas: January 1963.

______. *V Presidential Message, 12th March 1963.* Caracas: Imprenta Nacional, 1963.

______. *Inversiones de capitales extranjeros en Venezuela.*

(2d ed.) (Estudios sobre Comercio Exterior, No. 15.) Caracas: April 1963.

———. *Memoria que presenta el Ministro del Trabajo al Congreso Nacional.* Caracas: 1960-63.

———. Banco Central de Venezuela. *Boletín Mensual,* No. 231, April 1963.

———. *Informe económico correspondiente al año 1962.* Caracas: Artegrafia, n.d.

———. *Memoria: Correspondiente al ejercicio anual 1961.* Caracas: Artegrafia, n.d.

———. *Memoria: Correspondiente al ejercicio anual 1962.* Caracas: Artegrafia, n.d.

Venezuela. Consulate General, New York. "President Betancourt Spells Out Fundamental Economic Policy of Venezuela." (Bulletin No. 25.) New York: June 12, 1962 (mimeo.).

Venezuela. *A Resume of the Venezuelan Income Tax Law, Including Labor and Reserves.* N.pl.: n.d. (mimeo.).

———. "Venezuela's Bright Economic Future Highlighted." (Bulletin No. 36.) Washington: May 15, 1963 (mimeo.).

Venezuela. Contraloria General de la República. *Control Fiscal y Tecnificación Administrativa.* No. 26, January-March 1963.

Venezuela. Corporacion Venezolana de Guayana. *The Guayana Region: A Portfolio of Investment Opportunities.* Caracas: Editorial Grafos, July 1963.

———. *Planta siderurgica del Orinoco.* Venezuela: Tipografía Haliana, 1962.

Venezuela. Embassy of Venezuela, Washington. "Resumen del problema de las importaciones de petróleo." Washington: March 1963 (mimeo.).

Venezuela. Instituto Agrario Nacional. *Dos años de reforma agraria.* Caracas: June 1961.

———. *Plan (modificado) de investiones a realizar durante los anos 1962 y 1963 para la consolidación de asentamientos campesinos y la ejecusión de los proyectos de las Majaguas y Guaraunos.* N.pl.: January 1962.

Venezuela. Laws, Statutes, etc.

Congreso Nacional. "Ley de presupuesto general de ingresos y gastos públicos para el año fiscal 1959-1960," *Gaceta Oficial,* No. 595, June 30, 1959.

———. "Ley de presupuesto para el ejercicio fiscal julio-deciembre de 1961," *Gaceta Oficial,* No. 696, June 30, 1961.

———. "Ley de presupuesto para el ejercicio fiscal 1963," *Gaceta Oficial,* No. 819, December 14, 1962.

———. "Ley de presupuesto para el ejercicio fiscal 1964," *Gaceta Oficial,* No. 870, August 23, 1963.

———. "Ley de reforma parcial de la ley orgánica de la ha-

cienda nacional: ley orgánica de la hacienda pública nacional," *Gaceta Oficial,* No. 678, March 17, 1961.
_____ . "Ley general de bancos y otros institutos de credito," *Gaceta Oficial,* No. 676, March 11, 1961.
_____ . "Proyecto de ley de presupuesto para el ejercicio fiscal 1963," *Gaceta Oficial, 1963.*
Embassy of Venezuela. Washington. Information Service. "Law of Hydrocarbons and Its Regulations 1943," *Official Gazette,* n.d.
Junta de Gobierno de la República. "Presupuesto general de ingresos y gastos públicos para 1958–1959," *Gaceta Oficial,* No. 566, June 30, 1958.
Ministerio de Trabajo. *Ley del trabajo: reglamento del trabajo en la agricultura y en la cría.* Caracas: Impresora Ideal, 1959.
Venezuela. Ministerio de Agricultura y Cría. *Exposición de motivos al proyecto de ley de reforma agraria: ley de reforma agraria.* (Colección de Estudios agrarios, No. 1.) Caracas: MAC, 1961.
_____ . *Reforma agraria y desarrollo agropecuario en Venezuela.* Caracas: Editorial Arte, April 1963.
_____ . División Estadística. *Boletín de precios de produción agropecuarios, Septiembre 1962.* (Monografia de Precios, No. 39, Serie III, EEA-63-006.) Caracas: 1963.
_____ . *Informe sobre superficie, producción, rendimiento, importación y exportación de productos agropecuarios.* (EEA-62-101) Caracas: 1962.
Venezuela. Ministerio de Fomento. *III censo agropecuario 1961, resultados preliminares.* Caracas: Servicio Gráfico de la oficina Central del Censo, 1962.
Venezuela. Ministerio de Minas e Hidrocarburos. *La industria petrolera y sus obligaciones fiscales en Venezuela.* Caracas: March 1962.
Venezuela. Ministerio de Obras Públicas. *Cuando los ríos llegan cansados al mar: plan nacional de obras hidraulicos para el mejoramiento de tierras agrícolas.* Caracas: Tipografia Haling, n.d.
_____ . *El plan de obras hidraulicas para el desarrollo de tierras agrícolas: primeras jornadas venezolanas de riego.* Caracas: n.d.
Venezuela. Ministerio de Relaciones Exteriores. Direccion de Comercio Exterior Consulados. *Analisis de los mercados de exportación de petróleo venezolano.* Caracas: 1962.
_____ . *Convenios comerciales vigentes: tomo II, convenios multilaterales.* (Estudios sobre Comercio Exterior No. 10.) Caracas: 1962.

———. *Intercambio comercial entre Venezuela y los países suramericanos.* (Estudios sobre Comercio Exterior No. 14.) Caracas: 1962.

Venezuela. Ministerio de Relaciones Exteriores. Dirección de Política Económica. Oficina de Comercio Exterior. *Importaciones venezolanas de productos aumenticios comestibles y bebidos 1948-1953.* Caracas: Editorial Ragon, 1954.

———. *Importaciones venezolanas de textiles 1948-1954 y un apundice sobre producción nacional.* Caracas: Tipografía la Nacion, 1955.

———. *Principales aspectos del comercio exterior de Venezuela con los Estados Unidos de América 1946-1952.* Caracas: Tipografía la Nacion, 1954.

Venezuela. Oficina Central de Coordinación y Planificación. *Manual de presupuesto programa 1961.* Caracas: Tipo-Lit. Cartografia Nacional, August 1961.

———. "El Plan 1963-1966," *Informaciones de Venezuela,* January 1963, 1-5, 9-14.

———. *Plan de la Nación 1963-1966.* Caracas: Imp. Multimpresión, November 1962.

———. *Plan de la Nación 1963-1966.* Caracas: Sección de Reproduccion de la Secretaría General de la Presidencia, May 1963 (mimeo.).

Venezuela. Secretaría de la Comisión Nacional de Financiamiento a la Pequeña y Mediana Industria. *Programa de financiamiento a la pequeña y mediana industria.* N.pl.: Tipografía Vargas, n.d.

Venezuela. Secretaría General de la Presidencia de la Republica. *Corporación venezolana del petróleo.* Caracas: Imprenta Nacional, 1961.

———. *V Presidential Message.* Caracas: Imprenta Nacional, 1963.

———. *Venezuela and OPEC (Organization of Petroleum Exporting Countries)* Caracas: Imprenta Nacional, 1961.

Venezuela. Sociedad Financiera para el Fomento de Turismo y del Recreo Público. *Panorama de Venezuela, 1963.* Caracas: Grafos, 1963.

"Venezuela Hails Oil Industry Pact," *New York Times,* February 16, 1960.

"Venezuela Passes Austerity Bill, Double Taxes on Company Income," *Foreign Commerce Weekly,* LXVI, September 11, 1961, 9-12.

Vila, Marco-Aurelio. *Geografía de Venezuela.* (7th ed.) Caracas: Fundación Eugenio Mendoza, 1961.

Wallace, W. D. "Trade Prospects: Venezuela," *Foreign Trade,* June 1, 1963, 26, 27.

Wenzel, Peter H. *The Business and Economic Climate in Venezuela.* (A presentation before the Conference for Corporation Executives, Sponsored by SAIS of the Johns Hopkins University.) Washington: February 14, 1961.

The West Indies and Caribbean Yearbook, 1961. London: Thomas Skinner, 1961.

Zuloaga, Guillermo. *Geografía petrolera de Venezuela.* Caracas: Cromotip, 1960.

_____ . "Una Ojeada Geografíca," *El Faról.* November-December 1962.

(Various issues of the following publications were also used in the preparation of this section: *International Commerce.* [U.S. Department of Commerce], from 1961 through 1963: *World Petroleum Report.* [New York], for 1957 and from 1960 through 1963: *Venezuela Up-to-Date.* [Embassy of Venezuela, Washington], from 1960 through 1963; *Foreign Agriculture* [U.S. Department of Agriculture], for 1963: *Hispanic American Report.* [Stanford University], for 1963; *Inter-American Labor Bulletin* [U.S. Department of Labor], from 1957 through 1963; and Boletín de la Cámara de Comercio de Caracas [Caracas], from 1962 through 1963.)

Section IV. National Security

RECOMMENDED SOURCES

Alexander, Robert J. *Communism in Latin America.* New Brunswick: Rutgers University Press, 1957.

"The Atlantic Report on Venezuela," *Atlantic Monthly,* CCXI, May 1963, 31, 32.

Harrison, John P. "The Confrontation with the Political University," *The Annals*, CCCXXXIV, March 1961.

Johnson, John J. (ed). *The Role of the Military in Under-Developed Countries.* Princeton: Princeton University Press, 1962.

Lieuwen, Edwin. *Venezuela.* London: Oxford University Press, 1961.

Masur, Gerhard. *Simón Bolivár.* Albuquerque: University of New Mexico Press, 1948.

Pan American Union. *Constitution of the Republic of Venezuela, 1961.* Washington: PAU, 1961.

——— . *A Statement of the Laws of Venezuela in Matters Affecting Business.* (3d ed.) Washington: PAU, 1962.

Pike, Frederick B. (ed.). *Freedom and Reform in Latin America.* Notre Dame: University of Notre Dame Press, 1959.

Washington, S. Walter. "Student Politics in Latin America: The Venezuelan Example," *Foreign Affairs*, XXXVII, April 1959, 463.

OTHER SOURCES USED

Cárdenas, Rodolfo José. *La insurrección popular en Venezuela.* Caracas: Ediciones Catatumbo, 1961.

Clark, Gerald. *The Coming Explosion in Latin America.* New York: McKay, 1963.

Consejo de Bienestar Rural. *Problemas económicos y sociales de los Andes venezolanos.* Caracas: 1955.

Culhane, Eugene K. "Youth and Politics in Venezuela," *America,* CVII, June 2, 1962, 352, 353.

David, L. "Venezuela Today," *International Socialist Review,* XXIII, Fall 1962.

Donovan, John. *Red Machete.* New York: Bobbs-Merrill, 1962.

Economist (London), "Between Americas," April 13, 1963.

——— . "On the Volcano," February 23, 1963.

Frank, Waldo David. *Birth of a World.* Boston: Houghton Mifflin, 1951.

Gillen, John P. "Some Signposts for Policy." In Adams, Richard N., *et al. Social Change in Latin America Today.* New York: Harper, 1960.

Haar, Charles M. "Latin America's Troubled Cities," *Foreign Affairs,* XLI, April 1963, 536–549.

James, Preston E. *Latin America.* New York: Odyssey Press, 1959.

Lieuwen, Edwin. "Militarism in Latin America: A threat to the Alliance for Progress," *The World Today,* XIX, May 1963, 193-199.

——. "Neo-Militarism in Latin America. The Kennedy Administration: Inadequate Response," *Inter-American Economic fairs* (Washington), XVI, Spring 1963, 11-19.

Madariaga, Salvador de. *Latin America Between the Eagle and the Bear.* New York: Praeger, 1962.

MacDonald, Austin F. *Latin American Politics and Government.* New York: Crowell, 1954.

Operations and Policy Research, Inc. *Venezuela Election Factbook. Elections: December 1963.* Washington: OPR, 1963.

Rivero, Nicolas. "Venezuela's Oil—Its Vital Red Target," *The Washington World,* March 8, 1963.

Rourke, Thomas. *Gómez: Tyrant of the Andes.* New York: Morrow, 1936.

Royal Institute of International Affairs. Information Department. *Venezuela: A Brief Political and Economic Survey.* London: Oxford University Press, 1958.

Stokes, William S. *Latin American Politics.* New York: Crowell, 1959.

Stuart, Graham H. *Latin America and the United States.* New York: Appleton-Century-Crofts, 1955.

United Nations Statistical Yearbook 1962. New York: UN, 1963.

U.S. Congress. 86th, 2d Session. Senate. Committee on Foreign Relations. *Latin America: Venezuela, Brazil, Peru, Bolivia and Panama.* Washington: GPO, 1960.

——. *Study Mission in the Caribbean and Northern South America, November 1959.* Washington: GPO, 1960.

U.S. Department of State. *World Strength of Communist Party Organization.* (Intelligence Report No. 4489R-14) Washington: Department of State, January 1962.

U.S. Information Service. *Communist Propaganda Activities in Latin America in 1961.* Washington: USIS, 1961.

Venezuela. *Venezuela y Cuba.* Caracas: Imprenta Nacional, 1961.

——. Laws, Statutes, etc.

"Proyecto de ley de Presupuesto para el Ejercicio Fiscal 1963," *Gaceta Oficial* (Caracas), 1963.

Venezuela. Ministerio de Fomento. *Anuario estadístico, 1955-1956.* Caracas: 1961.

Venezuela. Ministerio de Guerra y Marina. *Memoria 1944.* Caracas: 1945.

Venezuela. Ministerio de Justica. *Memoria y cuenta 1961*. Caracas: 1962.

Venezuela. Ministerio de la Defensa Nacional. *Memoria 1946*. Caracas: 1947.

Venezuela. Ministerio de Relaciones Interiores. *Memoria y cuenta*. Caracas: 1962.

Venezuela. Secretaría General de la Presidencia de la República. *Constitución 1961*. Caracas: Imprenta Nacional, 1961.

Whitaker, Arthur P. *The United States and South America: The Northern Republics*. Cambridge: Harvard University Press 1948.

Wilgus, A. Curtis. *South American Dictators During the First Century of Independence*. Washington: George Washington University Press, 1937.

The Worldmark Encyclopedia of the Nations—Americas. New York: Worldmark Press, Harper, 1963.

(The following were also used in the preparation of this section: *Hispanic American Report* [Stanford University], from March 1962 through November 1963; *New York Times, Washington Star* and *Washington Post*, from January 1962 through December 1963; *Christian Science Monitor*, from January 1963 through December 1963; *La Esfera* [Caracas,] from January through December 1963; *Futuro* [Caracas], and *Guardia Nacional* [Caracas], of various dates; and *Vision Letter* [New York], from February through December 1963.)

BIBLIOGRAPHY FOR REVISED EDITION

Section I. Social

RECOMMENDED SOURCES

Arratia, Alejandro, and Hamilton, Carlos D. (eds.) *Diez Cuentos Hispanoamericanos*. New York: Oxford University Press, 1958.

Beals, R. "Social Stratification in Latin America." Pages 342–361 in Dwight B. Heath and Richard Adams (eds.), *Contemporary Cultures and Societies of Latin America*. New York: Random House, 1965.

Blanco Martínez, Oscar. "Notas Sociológicas sobre los valores sociales," *Educación: Revista para el Magisterio*, XXV, No. 108, February 1964, 38–41.

Bonilla, Frank, and Silva Michelena, José A. (eds.), *The Politics of Change in Venezuela*, I: A Strategy for Research on Social Policy. Cambridge: Massachusetts Institute of Technology Press, 1967.

Bullrich, Francisco. *New Directions in Latin American Architecture*. New York: George Braziller, 1969.

Butland, Gilbert J. *Latin America: A Regional Geography*. (2d ed.) New York: John Wiley and Sons, 1966.

Cabaldón, Arnaldo. "Salud," *Daily Journal*, October 23, 1970, A9–A17.

"The Church and the Apostolate in Venezuela." Part II of *Pro Mundi Vita: Centrum Informationis*, XIV, 1966, 19–39.

Cohen, J. M. (ed.) *Latin American Writing Today*. Baltimore: Penguin Books, 1967.

Davis, Harold E. *History of Latin America*. New York: Ronald Press, 1968.

———. *Latin American Social Thought*. Washington: University Press of Washington, D.C., 1961.

Gunther, John. *Inside South America*. New York: Harper and Row, 1967.

Herring, Hubert. *A History of Latin America*. (3d ed., rev.) New York: Knopf, 1968.

James, Preston E. *Latin America*. (4th ed.) New York: Odyssey Press, 1969.

Machado de Acedo, M. *Actitudes Ante el Cambio Social*. Caracas: Comisión Nacional del Cuatricentenario de la Fundación de Caracas, 1966.

Mecham, J. Lloyd. *The Church and State in Latin America*. Chapel Hill: University of North Carolina Press, 1966.

Milne, Jean. *Fiesta Time in Latin America.* Los Angeles: Ward Ritchie Press, 1965.
Pan American Health Organization-World Health Organization. *Annual Report of the Director—1968.* (Official Document No. 95.) Washington: 1969.
Peattie, Lisa Redfield. *The View from the Barrio.* Ann Arbor: University of Michigan Press, 1968.
Pollak-Eltz, Angelina. "Probleme der Volkerkunde Venezuelas einst und jetzt," *Mitteilungen der Anthropologischen Gesellschaft in Wien,* XCVI/SCVII, 1967, 125–137.
Price Waterhouse and Company. *Information Guide for Doing Business in Venezuela.* Chicago: 1968.
Republic of Venezuela. Oficina Central de Coordinación y Planificación. *Los Gastos Familiares.* Caracas: 1968.
Robertson, William Spence. *History of the Latin American Nations.* (Rev. ed.) New York: Appleton, 1925.
Schwerin, Karl H. *Oil and Steel: Processes of Karinya Culture Change in Response to Industrial Development,* IV. (Latin American Studies Series.) Los Angeles: University of California Press, 1966.
Sormani, Guiseppe, et al. *The World and Its Peoples: Venezuela, Colombia, Ecuador, Guiana, Uruguay.* New York: Greystone Press, 1966.
Torres-Rioseco, Arturo. *Antología de la Literatura Hispanoamericana.* (2d ed.) New York: Appleton-Century-Crofts, 1941.
U.S. Department of Defense. Office of the Assistant Secretary of Defense. *Venezuela: Nutritional Survey, May-June 1963.* Washington: 1964.
U.S. Department of Labor. Bureau of Labor Statistics. *Labor Law and Practice in Venezuela.* (BLS Report No. 212.) Washington: GPO, 1961. (Revision being prepared.)
Wilbert, Johannes. "Indians of Orinoco-Ventuari Region Studied" (*Indios de la Región Orinoco-Ventuari*). Caracas: 1963. [Translated by U.S. Department of Commerce, Office of Technical Services, Joint Publications Research Service (Washington). JPRS: L3088, 1969.]

OTHER SOURCES USED

Aguilera Ballesteros, Bernardo. "Porqué Educación católica?" *SIC, Centro Gumilla,* XXXIII, No. 322, February 1970, 78–79.
Alexander, Robert J. *The Communist Party of Venezuela.* (Hoover Institution Studies No. 24.) Stanford: Hoover Institution Press, 1969.
______ . *The Venezuelan Democratic Revolution.* New Brunswick: Rutgers University Press, 1964.

Angulo Arvelo, L. A., et al. "Composición de la Población Venezolana," *Revista Venezolana de Sanidad y Asistencia Social*, XXXI, No. 3, September 1966, 479–493.

Annuario Pontifico per L'Anno 1968. Vatican City: Tipografia Poliglotta Vaticana, 1968.

Bayard, Franck. "The Black Latin American Impact on Western Culture." Pages 287-336 in Joseph S. Roucek and Thomas Kiernan (eds.), *The Negro Impact on Western Civilization*. New York: Philosophical Library, 1970.

Beller, Jacob. *Jews in Latin America*. New York: Jonathan David, 1969.

Beyer, Glenn H. (ed.) *The Urban Explosion in Latin America*. Ithaca: Cornell University Press, 1967.

Cámel Vargas, Fayad. "Natalidad y Fecundidad en Venezuela," *Revista Venezolana de Sanidad y Asistencia Social*, XXXI, No. 3, September 1966, 405–430.

Castedo, Leopoldo. "Latin American Painting and Sculpture." Pages 795-801 in Claudio Véliz (ed.), *Latin America and the Caribbean: A Handbook*. New York: Praeger, 1968.

Centro Latinoamericano de Demográfica. *Boletín Demográfico*, I, No. 1, January 1968.

Cohen, J. M. "Spanish American Poetry." Pages 772–778 in Claudio Véliz (ed.), *Latin America and the Caribbean: A Handbook*. New York: Praeger, 1968.

Comisión Nacional del Cuatrocentenario de la Fundación de Caracas. *Como Utilizan Los Caraqueños el Tiempo Libre*. Caracas: Universidad Central de Venezuela, 1966.

Copley International Corporation. *Gallatin Business Intelligence: Venezuela*. New York: Copley International, 1967.

Correa de Azevedo, Luis Hector. "Latin American Music." Pages 814-819 in Claudio Véliz (ed.), *Latin America and the Caribbean: A Handbook*. New York: Praeger, 1968.

Crawford, William R. *A Century of Latin American Thought*. Cambridge: Harvard University Press, 1961.

Demographic Yearbook, 1953. New York: United Nations, 1954.

Demographic Yearbook, 1960. New York: United Nations, 1961.

Demographic Yearbook, 1963. New York: United Nations, 1964.

Demographic Yearbook, 1967. New York: United Nations, 1968.

"La Educación en América," *La Educación: Los Recursos Humanos y la Educación*, LI and LII, Año XIII, July-December 1968, 1969, 161–196.

Erasmus, C. J. "Upper Limits of Peasantry and Agrarian Reform: Bolivia, Venezuela and Mexico Compared," *Ethnology*, VI, October 1967, 349–380.

Europa Yearbook, 1969, II: Africa, The Americas, Asia and Australasia. London: Europa Publications, 1969.

Foy, Felician A. (ed.) *1970 Catholic Almanac*. Paterson: St. Anthony's Guild, 1970.
Franco, Jean. "The Spanish American Novel." Pages 761–764 in Claudio Véliz (ed.), *Latin America and the Caribbean: A Handbook*. New York: Praeger, 1968.
Harris, Marvin. *Patterns of Race in the Americas*. New York: Walker, 1964.
Houtart, François, and Pin, Emile. *The Church and the Latin American Revolution*. (Trans., Gilbert Barth.) New York: Sheed and Ward, 1965.
Institute for the Comparative Study of Political Systems. *Venezuela Election Factbook*. Washington: 1968.
The International Atlas. New York: Rand McNally, 1969.
International Yearbook of Education, 1966. Geneva: International Bureau of Education and United Nations Educational, Scientific and Cultural Organization, 1967.
International Yearbook of Education, 1967. Geneva: International Bureau of Education and United Nations Educational, Scientific and Cultural Organization, 1968.
International Yearbook of Education, 1968. Geneva: International Bureau of Education and United Nations Educational, Scientific and Cultural Organization, 1969.
Inter-American Committee for Agricultural Development. *Inventory of Information Basic to the Planning of Agricultural Development in Latin America: Venezuela*. Washington: Pan American Union, December 1964.
Inter-American Development Bank. *Venezuela 1950–1967*. (2d ed.) Washington: 1968.
Inter-American Development Bank. Social Progress Trust Fund. *Socio-Economic. Progress in Latin America*. (Ninth Annual Report, 1969.) Washington: 1970.
Kantor, Harry. *Patterns of Politics and Political Systems in Latin America*. Chicago: Rand McNally, 1969.
Lambert, Jacques. *Latin America: Social Structures and Political Institutions*. (Trans., Helen Katel.) Berkeley: University of California Press, 1967.
Lieuwen, Edwin. *Venezuela*. London: Oxford University Press, 1961.
Lipset, Seymour M., and Solari, Aldo (eds.). *Elites in Latin America*. London: Oxford University Press, 1967.
López, Victor. "Migraciones en Venezuela," *Revista Venezolana de Sandidad y Asistencia Social*, XXXI, No. 3, September 1966, 471–478.
McQuown, Norman A. "Indigenous Languages of Native America," *American Anthropologist*, LVII, No. 3, Part 1, June 1955, 501–570.

Martz, John D. "Venezuela." Pages 199–230 in Ben G. Burnett and Kenneth F. Johnson (eds.), *Political Forces in Latin America: Dimensions of the Quest for Stability*. Belmont: Wadsworth, 1968.

Mercier Vega, Luis. *Roads to Power in Latin America*. (Trans., Robert Rowland.) New York: Praeger, 1969.

Minerals Yearbook, IV. (Area Reports 1967.) Washington: GPO, 1969.

Moreira, João Roberto. *La Articulación de la Enseñanza Media con La Primaria y Superior*. Washington: Pan American Union, 1965.

Moser, Brian, and Taylor, Donald. *The Cocaine Eaters*. New York: Taplinger, 1967.

Organization of American States. *Datos Básicos de Población en América Latina*. Washington: 1970.

Orono, Angelo Raymond. "The Social Organization of the Margariteno Fishermen, Venezuela." (Unpublished doctoral dissertation, Department of Anthropology, University of California at Los Angeles, 1968.)

Pan American Health Organization. *Facts on Health Progress*. (Scientific Publication No. 166.) Washington: 1968.

———. *Reported Cases of Notifiable Diseases in the Americas, 1965*. (Scientific Publications No. 149.) Washington: 1967.

Pan American Health Organization-World Health Organization. *Health Conditions in the Americas 1960–1964*. Washington: 1966.

Pan American Union. *América en Cifras 1967; Situación Cultural: Educación y Otros Aspectos Culturales*. Washington: 1969.

———. *América en Cifras, 1967; Situación Demográfica: Estado y Movimiento de la Población*. Washington: 1968.

———. *América en Cifras, 1967. Situación Física: Territorio y Clima*. Washington: 1967.

———. *América en Cifras 1967; Situación Social: Hogar, Habitación, Mejoramiento Urbano, Previsión, Social, Asistancia Médica y de Salud, y Trabajo*. Washington: 1969.

———. *A Statement of the Laws of Venezuela in Matters Affecting Business, 1962*. Washington: 1962.

Pan American Union. *A Statement of the Laws of Venezuela in Matters Affecting Business: Supplement 1968*. Washington: 1968.

———. *Venezuela*. (American Republics Series No. 21.) Washington: 1960.

Picón-Salas, Mariano. *A Cultural History of Spanish America: From Conquest to Independence*. (Trans., Irving A. Leonard.) Berkeley: University of California Press, 1962.

Poblete Barth, Renato. "The Roman Catholic Church." Pages 730–735 in Claudio Véliz (ed.), *Latin America and the Caribbean: A Handbook*. New York: Praeger, 1968.

Population Reference Bureau. *Programas Internacionales de Población*. Washington: 1968.

Population Reference Bureau. Oficina en América Latina. *Cifras de Población Mundial*. Bogotá: 1970.

Puffer, Ruth Rice, and Griffith, G. Wynne. *Patterns of Urban Mortality*. Washington: Pan American Health Organization, 1967.

Quijada, Hernán. "Aspectos de la Psicología social en Venezuela," *Revista Venezolana de Sanidad y Asistencia Social*, XXXI, No. 3, September 1966, 593–607.

Ray, Talton F. *The Politics of the Barrios of Venezuela*. Berkeley: University of California Press, 1969.

Republic of Venezuela. *Anuario Estadístico de Venezuela, 1965*. Caracas: Dirección General de Estadístico y Censos, 1967.

_____. *Anuario Estadístico de Venezuela, 1967*. Caracas: Dirección General de Estadístico y Censos, 1969.

_____. *Venezuela en 1969: Primer Mensaje del Presidente de la República, Dr. Rafael Caldera, al Congreso Nacional*. Caracas: Oficina Central de Información, 1970.

Republic of Venezuela. Embassy in Washington. *Here is a Resumé of the Geography of Venezuela*. Washington: n.d.

Republic of Venezuela. Ministerio de Fomento. *Boletin Trimestral de Estadísticas Demográficas y Sociales,* XXIX, No. 31, October–December 1967.

_____. *Boletin Trimestral de Estadísticas Demográficas y Sociales,* XXX, No. 35, October–December 1968.

Republic of Venezuela. Oficina Central de Información. *Introduction to Venezuela*. Caracas: 1970.

Republic of Venezuela. Oficina Central del Censo. *Noveno Censo General de Población, Resumen General de la República, Partes B y C*. Caracas: 1967.

Rippy, J. Fred. *Latin America*. (Rev. ed.) Ann Arbor: University of Michigan Press, 1968.

Roberts, C. Paul (ed.). *Statistical Abstract of Latin America 1969*. (12th ed.) Los Angeles: University of California Press, December 1969.

Rouse, Irving, and Cruxent, J. M. *Venezuelan Archaeology*. New Haven: Yale University Press, 1963.

Sanders, Thomas G. "The Church in Latin America," *Foreign Affairs,* XLVIII, No. 2, January 1970, 285–300.

Schwerin, Karl H. *Oil and Steel: Processes of Karinya Culture Change in Response to Industrial Development,* IX: Latin American Studies. Los Angeles: University of California Press, 1966.

The South American Handbook, 1970. Ed., Andrew Marshall. Chicago: Rand McNally, 1970.

Statistical Abstract of Latin America, 1968. (12th ed.) Los Angeles: University of California Press, 1969.

Terry, Edward Davis (ed.). *Artists and Writers in the Evolution of Latin America*. University: University of Alabama Press, 1969.

Tovar, Ramón A. *La Población de Venezuela*. Caracas: Escuela de Sciencias Económicas y Sociales, Universidad Central de Venezuela, 1968.

United Nations. "Population and Vital Statistics Report—Data Available as of 1 July 1970," *Statistical Papers,* XXII, Series A, No. 3, 1970, 1-27.

United Nations Educational, Scientific and Cultural Organization. *World Survey of Education*, III: Secondary Education. New York: 1961.

U.S. Agency for International Development. *Summary Economic and Social Indicators: 18 Latin American Countries—1960–1969*. Washington: 1970 (mimeo.).

U.S. Department of Commerce. Bureau of International Commerce. "Basic Data on the Economy of Venezuela," *Overseas Business Reports* (OBR–62), Washington: GPO, 1967.

———. *Country Market Survey, Venezuela*. Washington: GPO, 1969.

———. "Establishing a Business in Venezuela," *Overseas Business Reports* (OBR 69–64), Washington: GPO, 1969.

———. "Selling in Venezuela," *Overseas Business Reports* (OBR 69–23), Washington: GPO, 1969.

U.S. Department of State. Foreign Area Research Documentation Center. External Research Staff. *Afro-American-Type Cults and Religious Practices in Venezuela*, by Angelina Pollak-Eltz. (Foreign Affairs Research Series No. 11780.) Madison: University of Wisconsin, October 1969.

Vallier, Ivan. "Challenge to Catholicism in Latin America," *Trans-Action,* IV, No. 7, June 1967, 17–26.

——— "Religious Elites: Differentiations and Developments in Roman Catholicism." Pages 190–232 in Seymour M. Lipset and Aldo Solari (eds.), *Elites in Latin America*. London: Oxford University Press, 1967.

Wilgus, A. Curtis. *Historical Atlas of Latin America*. New York: Cooper Square, 1967.

World Christian Handbook: 1968. Eds., H. Wakelin Coxill and Kenneth G. Grubb. Nashville: Abingdon Press, 1967.

World Health Organization. *Third Report in the World Health Situation 1961-64*. Geneva, 1967.

The World of Learning, 1969–1970. (20th ed.) London: Europa Publications, 1970.

Worldmark Encyclopedia of the Nations, III: Americas. (3d ed.) New York: Harper and Row, 1967.

(Various issues of the following periodicals were also used in the preparation of this section: *Bank of London and South America Review* [London], September 1970; *Daily Journal* [Caracas], October-December 1968 and August-October 1970; *El Nacional* [Caracas], August 15-29, 1969, and March-December 1970; *Gazette* [Washington], October-December 1968 and October-December 1970; *Labor Developments Abroad* [Washington], December 1968-November 1970; *Latin American Airmail* [London], 1968-1970; *Times of the Americas* [Miami], 1969-1970; and *Venezuela Up-to-Date* [Washington], Spring 1966-Fall 1970.)

Section II. Political

RECOMMENDED SOURCES

Alexander, Robert J. *The Communist Party of Venezuela.* (Hoover Institution Studies, No. 24.) Stanford: Hoover Institution Press, 1969.

———. *The Venezuelan Democratic Revolution: A Profile of the Regime of Rómulo Betancourt.* New Brunswick: Rutgers University Press, 1964.

Bailey, Norma A. *Latin America in World Politics.* New York: Walker, 1967.

Bonilla, Frank, and Silva Michelena, José A. (eds.). *The Politics of Change in Venezuela,* I: A Strategy for Research on Social Policy. Cambridge: Massachusetts Institute of Technology Press, 1967.

Burnett, Ben G., and Johnson, Kenneth F. *Political Forces in Latin America.* Belmont: Wadsworth, 1968.

Cooke, Thomas M. "The Dynamics of Foreign Policy Decision-Making in Venezuela." (Doctoral dissertation, American University.) (In University of Michigan microfilm library.)

Editor and Publisher Year Book, 1970. New York: Editor and Publisher Co., Inc., 1970.

Fagan, Richard R., and Cornelius, Wayne A. (eds.), *Political Power in Latin America: Seven Confrontations.* Englewood Cliffs: Prentice-Hall, 1970.

Foreign Broadcast Information Service. *Broadcasting Stations of the World,* Part I: Amplitude Modulation Broadcasting Stations According to Country and City. Washington: GPO, 1969.

———. *Broadcasting Stations of the World.* Part IV: Television Stations. Washington: GPO, September 1, 1969.

Gunther, John. *Inside South America.* New York: Pocket Books, 1968.

Herring, Hubert. *A History of Latin America From the Beginnings to the Present.* (3d ed., rev.) New York: Knopf, 1968.

Institute for the Comparative Study of Political Systems. *Venezuela Election Factbook.* Washington: October 1968.

Lieuwen, Edwin. *Venezuela.* London: Oxford University Press, 1961.

Martz, John D. *Acción Democrática; Evolution of a Modern Political Party in Venezuela.* Princeton: Princeton University Press, 1961.

———. "Venezuela." Chapter 8 in Ben G. Burnett and Kenneth F. Johnson (eds.), *Political Forces in Latin America: Dimensions of the Quest for Stability.* Belmont: Wadsworth, 1968.

Mecham, J. Lloyd. *A Survey of United States-Latin American Relations.* Boston: Houghton Mifflin, 1965.

Pan American Union. *América en Cifras 1967: Situación Cultural: Educación y Otros Aspectos Culturales.* Washington: 1967.

Publishers' World 69/70. New York: R. R. Bowker, 1969.

Ray, Talton F. *The Politics of the Barrios of Venezuela.* Berkeley: University of California Press, 1969.

Republic of Venezuela. Oficina Central de Información. *Primer Mensaje del Presidente de la República al Congreso Nacional.* Caracas: 1970.

Sigmund, Paul E. *Models of Political Change in Latin America.* New York: Praeger, 1970.

Stebbins, Richard P., and Amoia, Alba (eds.). *Political Handbook and Atlas of the World, 1970.* New York: Simon and Schuster, 1970.

U.S. Department of Commerce. Bureau of International Commerce. "Basic Data on the Economy of Venezuela," *Overseas Business Reports* (OBR-62), Washington: GPO, 1967.

U.S. Department of State. Foreign Area Research Documentation Center. External Research Staff. *The Peasantry as an Emerging Political Factor in Mexico, Bolivia, and Venezuela,* by Peter P. Lord. (Foreign Affairs Research Series No. 4984.) Madison: University of Wisconsin, May 1965 (mimeo.).

———. *Student Political Activism in Venezuela,* by Orlando Albórnoz. (Foreign Affairs Research Series No. 7470.) Madison: University of Wisconsin, March 1967 (mimeo.).

———. *Urbanization and Voting Behavior in Venezuela and Chile, 1958-1964,* by George Fleming Jones. (Foreign Affairs Research Series No. 8640.) Madison: University of Wisconsin, March 28, 1967 (mimeo.).

Wainhouse, David W., et al. *International Peace Observation.* Baltimore: Johns Hopkins University Press, 1966.

Whitaker, Arthur P. "Cuba's Intervention in Venezuela: A Test of the OAS," *Orbis,* III, No. 3, Fall 1964, 511-514.

Worldmark Encyclopedia of the Nations, III: Americas. (3d ed.) New York: Harper and Row, 1967.

Zimmerman, Irene. *A Guide to Current Latin American Periodicals—Humanitarian and Social Sciences.* Gainesville: Kallman, 1961.

OTHER SOURCES USED

Agle, Charles. "Urban Sources of Instability in Latin America," *SAIS Review,* XI, No. 4, Summer 1967, 3-9.

Bamberger, Michael. "A Problem of Political Integration in

Latin America: The Barrios of Venezuela," *International Affairs,* XLIV, No. 4, October 1968, 709-719.

Connell-Smith, Gordon. "The Political Problems of Latin American Integration." Pages 395-402 in Claudio Véliz (ed.), *Latin America and the Caribbean: A Handbook.* New York: Praeger, 1968.

Davis, Harold E. *History of Latin America.* New York: Ronald Press, 1968.

Dreier, John C. *The Organization of American States and the Hemisphere Crisis.* New York: Harper and Row, 1962.

Gibson, Carlos. "American Regionalism and the United Nations," *The Annals of the American Academy of Political and Social Science,* CCCLX, July 1965, 120-127.

Horowitz, Irving L. *Masses in Latin America.* New York: Oxford University Press, 1970.

José, James R. "An Inter-American Peace Force Within the Framework of the Organization of American States: Advantages, Impediments, and Implications." (Doctoral dissertation, School of International Service, American University, 1968.)

Kantor, Harry. *Patterns of Politics and Political Systems in Latin America.* Chicago: Rand McNally, 1969.

Lieuwen, Edwin. *General vs. Presidents: Neomilitarism in Latin America.* New York: Praeger, 1964.

Lipset, Seymour M., and Solari, Aldo. *Elites in Latin America.* New York: Oxford University Press, 1967.

Lott, Leo B. "Venezuela." Chapter 12 in Martin C. Needler (ed.), *Political Systems of Latin America.* Princeton: Van Nostrand, 1964.

Mecham, J. Lloyd. *The United States and Inter-American Security: 1889-1960.* Austin: University of Texas Press, 1961.

Mercier Vega, Luis. *Guerrillas in Latin America: The Technique of the Counter-State.* (Trans., Daniel Weissbort.) New York: Praeger, 1969.

_____. *Roads to Power in Latin America.* (Trans., Robert Rowland.) New York: Praeger, 1969.

Nelson, Joan M. *Migrants, Urban Poverty, and Instability in Developing Nations*, XXII. (Occasional Papers in International Affairs.) Cambridge: Harvard University Press, 1969.

Organization of American States. Consejo Permanente. *Informe de la Comisión de Asuntos Jurídicos—Políticos sobre una Resolución Condenatoria de los Actos de Terrorismo, el Secuestro de Personas y la Extorsión Conexa con este Delito.* (OEA Documentos Oficiales, Ser G. CP/Doc. 19/70.) Washington: 1970.

Pan American Union. *Constitution of the Republic of Venezuela, 1961.* Washington: 1968.

Parkinson, Fred. "Latin American Foreign Policies." Pages

414-424 in Claudio Véliz (ed.), *Latin America and the Caribbean: A Handbook.* New York: Praeger, 1968.

Petras, James. "Revolution and Guerrilla Movements in Latin America: Venezuela, Guatemala, Colombia, and Peru." Pages 329-369 in James Petras and Maurice Zeitlin (eds.), *Latin America: Reform or Revolution.* (Political Perspectives Series.) Greenwich: Fawcett, 1968.

"President Nixon Meets with President Caldera of Venezuela," *Department of State Bulletin,* LXII, No. 1618, June 1970, 793-799.

"President of Venezuela Visits OAS," *Inter-American Briefs,* XI, No. 7, July 1970, 2.

Republic of Venezuela. Oficina Central de Información. *Introduction to Venezuela.* Caracas: 1970.

Sormani, Guiseppe (ed.). *The World and Its Peoples: Venezuela, Colombia, Ecuador, Guiana, Uruguay.* New York: Greystone Press, 1966.

Taylor, Philip B., Jr. "Progress in Venezuela," *Current History,* LIII, No. 315, November 1967, 270-274.

U.S. Department of State. *Venezuela Facts Book.* Washington: GPO, 1970.

U.S. Department of State. Foreign Area Research Documentation Center. External Research Staff. *Moscow, Havana, and the Venezuelan Communist Movement, 1964-67,* by D. Bruce Jackson. (Foreign Affairs Research Series No. 5333.) Madison: University of Wisconsin, June 1967.

World Peace Through Law Center. *Law and the Judicial System of Nations.* Washington: 1965.

(Various issues of the following periodicals were also used in the preparation of this section: *Christian Science Monitor* [Boston], June-September 1970; *Daily Journal* [Caracas], August-November 1970; *El Nacional* [Caracas], August-November 1970; *Latin America Airmail* [London], December 1968-November 1970; *New York Times,* April 1969-October 1970; *Times of the Americas* [Miami], January 1969-October 1970; *Venezuela Up-to-Date* [Washington], Spring 1968-Fall 1970; *Wall Street Journal,* December 1968-June 1970; and *Washington Post,* March 1970-October 1970.)

Section III. Economic

RECOMMENDED SOURCES

Alexander, Robert. *Organized Labor in Latin America.* New York: Free Press, 1965.

Banco Central de Venezuela. *Informe Económico—1968.* Caracas: Las Prensas Venezolanas de Editorial Arte, 1969.

——— . *Síntesis de la Economía Venezolana, 1961-67.* Caracas: 1968.

Consejo de Bienestar Rural. *Present Status and Possibilities of Agricultural Development in Venezuela.* Caracas: March 1967.

Constitution of the Republic of Venezuela. Washington: Pan American Union, 1968.

Gallatin International Business Service. *Venezuela.* New York: Copley International, 1967.

Heaton, Louis E. *The Agricultural Development of Venezuela.* New York: Praeger, 1969.

Inter-American Development Bank. *Report on Group of Loans to Venezuela.* Washington: July 1970.

——— . *Venezuela 1950-1967: Variables, Parameters, and Methodology of the National Accounts.* (2d ed.) Washington: 1968.

Inter-American Development Bank. Social Progress Trust Fund. *Socio-Economic Progress in Latin America.* (Ninth Annual Report, 1969.) Washington: 1970.

Levy, Fred D. *Economic Planning in Venezuela.* New York: Praeger, 1968.

Machado Gómez, Alfredo. "The Capital Market and Financial Institutions," *Daily Journal,* XXV, No. 359, October 23, 1970, B-15.

Maroni, Yves. *Petroleum, Politics and the Quest for Prosperity: the Venezuelan Case.* Washington: Board of Governors of Federal Reserve System, March 1967.

Pan American Union. *Mining and Petroleum Legislation in Latin America.* (2d ed.) Washington: 1969.

——— . *A Statement of the Laws of Venezuela Affecting Business, 1962.* (3d ed., rev.) Washington, 1962.

——— . *A Statement of the Laws of Venezuela Affecting Business: Supplement 1968.* Washington: 1968.

Prebish, Raúl. *Change and Development: Latin America's Great Task.* Washington: Inter-American Development bank, 1970.

Price Waterhouse and Company. *Information Guide for Doing Business in Venezuela.* Chicago: 1968.

Puga, William B. (ed.) *Electric World: Directory of Electrical Utilities in Latin America, Bermuda and the Caribbean Islands, 1969-70*. New York: McGraw-Hill, 1969.

Republic of Venezuela. Oficina Central de Información. *Introduction to Venezuela*. Caracas: 1970.

_____ . *Venezuela en 1969: Primer Mensaje del Presidente de la República, Dr. Rafael Caldera, al Congreso Nacional*. Carracas: March 1970.

Republic of Venezuela. Ministerio de Fomento. Dirección General de Estadística y Censos Nacionales. *Boletín de Comercio Exterior*. Caracas: October 1970.

Roberts, C. Paul (ed.). *Statistical Abstract of Latin America 1969*. (12th ed.) Los Angeles: University of California at Los Angeles, December 1969.

U.S. Congress. 90th, 1st Session. House of Representatives. Committee on Banking and Currency. *Food for Progress in Latin America*. Washington: GPO, 1967.

U.S. Department of Commerce. *Venezuela*. (International Marketing Information Service.) Washington: GPO, November, 1969.

U.S. Department of Commerce. Bureau of International Commerce. "Basic Data on the Economy of Venezuela," *Overseas Business Reports* (OBR 67-2), Washington: GPO, January 1967.

_____ . "Foreign Trade Regulations of Venezuela," *Overseas Business Reports* (OBR 69-52), Washington: GPO, October 1969.

_____ . "Selling in Venezuela," *Overseas Business Reports* (OBR 69-23), Washington: GPO, June 1969.

U.S. Department of State. *Venezuela Facts Book*. Washington: GPO, 1970.

Valera, Raúl. "The Developing Labor Force," *Daily Journal*, XXV, No. 359, October 23, 1970, B4-B11.

Wing, Harry E., Jr. *Land Reform in Venezuela*. Washington: U.S. Agency for International Development, June 1970.

OTHER SOURCES USED

Banco Agrícola y Pecuario. *Crédito Campesino*. Caracas: 1966.

Banco Central de Venezuela. *Boletín de la Deuda Pública Venezolana*, X, No. 6, June 1970.

_____ . *La Economía Venezolana en los Ultimos 25 Años*. Caracas: 1966.

_____ . *Memoria—1969*. Caracas: Las Prensas Venezolanas de Editorial Arte, 1970.

"Budget for 1970 Passed," *Venezuela Up-to-Date,* XIII, No. 3, Spring 1970, 5.

Business International. *LAFTA—Key to Latin America's 200 Million Consumers.* New York: 1966.

Cabinet Task Force on Oil Import Control. *The Oil Import Question.* Washington: GPO, February 1970.

Carroll, Thomas F. *Land Tenure and Land Reform in Latin America: A Selective Annotated Bibliography.* Washington: Inter-American Development Bank, December 1965.

Chemical Bank. *International Economic Survey: Venezuela.* New York: April 1969.

Consejo de Bienestar Rural. *Long Term Forecasts of the Supply and Demand of Agricultural and Livestock Products in Venezuela.* Caracas: December 1965.

Day, G. H. *Agrarian Reform in Venezuela.* Caracas: 1962.

Deltec Panamérica, S. A. *El Mercado de Capitales en Venezuela.* Mexico: Centro de Estudios Monetarios Latino Americanos, 1968.

Economist Intelligence Unit. *The Crisis in Latin American Integration.* (QER Special No. 1.) London: 1968.

"Evasión de Capitales en América Latina," *The Economist para América Latina,* III, No. 21, October 15, 1969, 32–33.

First National City Bank. *Venezuela: An Economic Study.* New York: June 1966.

"High Petroleum and Mineral Output Leads Venezuela in Upward Swing," *Commerce Today,* I, No. 9, October 19, 1970, 52–53.

Hutchinson, John E. *Summary and Evaluation of Long Term Forecasts of the Supply and Demand for Agricultural and Livestock Products in Venezuela.* (ERS-Foreign 191.) Washington: U.S. Department of Agriculture, June 1967.

Inter-American Committee for Agricultural Development. *Inventory of Information Basic to the Planning of Agricultural Development in Latin America: Venezuela.* Washington: Organization of American States, December 1964.

Inter-American Development Bank. Group of Controllers of the Review and Evaluation System. *Report on Loans to Venezuela.* Washington: 1970.

"Invests in Venezuela," *Venezuela Up-to-Date,* XII, No. 4, Summer 1970, 10.

James, Preston E. *Latin America.* (4th ed.) New York: Odyssey Press, 1969.

McGinn, Noel, and Davis, Russell G. *Build a Mill, Build a City, Build a School: Industrialization, Urbanization, and Education in Ciudad Guayana.* Cambridge: Massachusetts Institute of Technology Press, 1969.

Maidenberg, H. J. "Venezuela Planning Tougher Stock Law," *New York Times,* CXX, No. 41, 191, November 3, 1970, 49-51.
Organization of American States. Inter-American Development Bank. Economic Commission for Latin America. Joint Tax Program. *Problems of Tax Administration in Latin America.* Baltimore: Johns Hopkins University Press, 1965.
Picks's Currency Yearbook 1969. New York: Pick Publishing, 1969.
Republic of Venezuela. Oficina Central del Censo. *Novena Censo General de Población, Resumen General de la República,* Parte A. Caracas: 1966.
——— . *Noveno Censo General de Población, Resumen General de la República,* Partes B y C. Caracas: 1967.
Republic of Venezuela. Superintendencia de Bancos. *Informe Anual—1968.* Caracas: Artegrafia, n.d.
Rodríguez, Gumersindo. "Los Bancos Venezolanos y el desarrollo económico," *Cuadernos de la C.V.F.,* II, No. 5, March 1966, 15-22.
Roper, Penelope. *Investment in Latin America.* (QER Special No. 6) London: Economist Intelligence Unit, April 1970.
"Savings and Loan System Expanding," *Venezuela Up-to-Date,* XII, No. 11, Spring 1969, 13.
Saxl, Victor. *The Textile Industry in Venezuela.* Atlanta: Smith, 1967.
"Slight Increase in 1969 Budget," *Venezuela Up-to-Date,* XII, No. 10, Winter 1968-69, 13.
Sormani, Guiseppe (ed.). *The World and Its Peoples: Venezuela, Colombia, Ecuador, Guiana, Uruguay.* New York: Greystone Press, 1966.
U.S. Agency for International Development. *Summary Economic and Social Indicators: 18 Latin America Republics—1960-1969.* Washington: 1970.
U.S. Department of Commerce. *The Market for Electronic Data Processing Equipment in Venezuela.* (International Marketing Information Series, IMIS 70-217.) Washington: GPO, 1970.
——— . *Venezuela.* (Foreign Economic Trends Report No. ET 68-10.) Washington: GPO, August 1, 1968.
——— . *Venezuela.* (Foreign Economic Trends Report No. ET 69-44.) Washington: GPO, February 19, 1969.
——— . *Venezuela.* (Foreign Economic Trends Report No. ET 70-17.) Washington: GPO, February 1970.
——— . *Venezuela.* (Foreign Economic Trends Report No. ET 70-91.) Washington: GPO, August 17, 1970.
U.S. Department of Commerce. Bureau of International Com-

merce. "Establishing a Business in Venezuela." *Overseas Business Reports* (OBR 69-64), Washington: GPO, 1969.

______. "Latin American Economic Integration." *Overseas Business Reports* (OBR 69-7), Washington: GPO, April 1969.

______ . "Market Profile for Latin America and the Caribbean." *Overseas Business Reports* (OBR 69-32), Washington: GPO, June 1969.

U.S. Department of Labor. Bureau of Labor Statistics. "Labor Conditions in Venezuela." *Labor Digest* (Bulletin No. 59.) Washington: 1964.

______ . "On-the-Job Training and Wage-Hour Standards in Foreign Countries." *Labor Digest* (Bulletin No. 1610.) Washington: 1968.

U.S. Department of State. *Republic of Venezuela: Background Notes.* Washington: GPO, May 1970.

______ . *Venezuela—Post Report.* Washington: September 1969.

"Venezuela," *International Financial Statistics,* XXIII, No. 9, September 1970, 336-338.

"Venezuela," *International Notes,* No. 165, November 1969, 1-8.

"Venezuelan Tax Increase Proposals Run Into Considerable Opposition," *Business Latin America,* October 15, 1970, 333-335.

Wendt, Herbert. *The Red, White and Black Continent.* New York: Doubleday, 1966.

Worldmark Encyclopedia of the Nations, III: Americas. New York: Harper and Row, 1967.

Year Book 1969-1970. Caracas: American Chamber of Commerce of Venezuela, September 1970.

Yearbook of Labor Statistics, 1969. Geneva: International Labor Office.

(Various issues of the following periodicals were also used in the preparation of this section: *Bolsa Review* [London], August 1969-June 1970; *Daily Journal* [Caracas], July-November 1970; *El Nacional* [Caracas], July-November 1970; *Latin America Airmail* [London], December 1968-October 1970; *New York Times,* February-October 1970; *Noticias* [New York], February 1969; *Times of the Americas* [Miami], January 1969-October 1970; *Venezuela Up-to-Date* [Washington], Spring 1968-Fall 1970; *Wall Street Journal,* December 1968-October 1970.)

Section IV. National Security

RECOMMENDED SOURCES

Alexander, Robert J. *The Communist Party of Venezuela.* (Hoover Institution Studies No. 24.) Stanford: Hoover Institution Press, 1969.

Arcaya, Mariano. *Código Penal.* Caracas: Empresa el Cojo, 1968.

Blackman, Raymond V. B. (ed.) *Jane's Fighting Ships, 1969-70.* New York: McGraw-Hill, 1970.

Constitution of the Republic of Venezuela. Washington: Pan American Union, 1968.

Herring, Hubert. *A History of Latin America from the Beginnings to the Present.* New York: Knopf, 1968.

International Who's Who 1970-1971. London: Europa Publications, 1970.

Johnson, John J. *The Military and Society in Latin America.* Stanford: Stanford University Press, 1965.

Lieuwen, Edwin. *Arms and Politics in Latin America.* New York: Praeger, 1960.

Lingo, Joseph L. *Police Organization and Operations in Venezuela.* Washington: U.S. Agency for International Development, 1963.

SIC-Centro Gumilla. *La Delincuencia en Acción.* XXXIII, No. 332. Caracas: Apartado, February 1970.

U.S. Congress. 90th, 2d Session. Senate. Committee on Foreign Relations. *Survey of the Alliance for Progress.* Washington: GPO, 1968.

US. Department of State. Bureau of Intelligence and Research. *World Strength of Communist Parties.* (22d Annual Report.) Washington: GPO, 1970.

Wood, David. *Armed Forces in Central and South America.* London: Institute for Strategic Studies, 1967.

World Peace Through Law Center. *Law and the Judicial System of Nations.* Washington: 1965.

OTHER SOURCES USED

Alexander, Robert J. *Communism in Latin America.* New Brunswick: Rutgers University Press, 1957.

"Central Committee Submits Draft of PCV Statutes," *Tribuna Popular,* April 22-29, 1970, S2-S4.

Loveland, Frank. *Report on the Prison System of Venezuela.* Washington: U.S. Agency for International Development, 1963.

Pan American Union. *América en Cifras, 1967. Situación Política y Administrativa: Representación Política, Administración Pública y Justicia.* Washington: 1969.

Repúblic of Venezuela. Ministerio de Fomento. Dirección General de Estadística y Censos Nacionales. *Anuario Estadístico de Venezuela 1967.* Caracas: 1969.

———. *Boletín Trimestral de Estadísticas Demográficas y Sociales.* Caracas: 1968.

Republic of Venezuela. Ministerio de la Defensa. Dirección de Gabinete. Departamento de Relaciones Públicas y Protocolo Militar. *Revista de las Fuerzas Armadas de Venezuela,* No. 250. Caracas: 1970.

Republic of Venezuela. Ministerio de la Defensa. Fuerzas Armadas de Cooperacion. *Recopilación.* Caracas: 1966.

Republic of Venezuela. Oficina Central de Información. *Venezuela en 1969; Primer Mensaje del Presidente de la Republica, Dr. Rafael Caldera, al Congreso Nacional.* Caracas: 1970.

(Various issues of the following periodicals were also used in the preparation of this section: *Daily Journal* [Caracas], July 1970–December 1970; *El Nacional* [Caracas], July 1970–December 1970; and *New York Times,* July 1970–December 1970.)

GLOSSARY

abrazo—An embrace involving a hug accompanied by vigorous back-slapping.

AD—Acción Democrática (Democratic Action party).

Armed Forces of Cooperation—Fuerzas Armadas de Cooperación, generally known as the national guard.

barrios—Settlements of substandard housing on the fringes of major cities.

bolivar—Currency unit. Rate in 1970 was 4.5 bolivars to US$1 with certain exceptions. Divided into 100 centimos. Before January 18, 1964, the official rate was 3.35 bolivars to US$1, but multiple rates also existed. On January 18, 1964, new rates became effective and were still in effect in January 1971. A free market rate of Bs4.5 equal US$1 was established for most transactions. Petroleum and iron ore earnings were exchanged at Bs4.4. Coffee and cocoa were exported at the rate of Bs4.485 equal US$1. The rate for certain imports, the list of which varied, was Bs3.35 equal US$1. The Central Bank sold to commercial banks at the rate of Bs4.5 and bought exchange from them at Bs4.48 per US$1; these two rates were also applicable for capital transfers and invisible payments.

caballero—Gentleman.

cabildos—Town councils.

caudillos—Regional political strong men.

COPEI—Comité de Organización Política y Electoral Independiente (Committee for Independent Political and Electoral Organization). Commonly called the Social Christian party; after 1963, the second largest political party.

CORDIPLAN—Oficina Central de Coordinación y Planificación (Central Office of Coordination and Planning).

criollo—Native-born person of Spanish descent.

CVF—Corporación Venezolana de Fomento (Venezuelan Development Corporation).

Delegated Committee of Congress—Committee that functions when the National Congress is not in session.

Deutschmark—In October 1969, DM3.66 equaled US$1.

ejidos—Public lands.

empleado—A person who works for another in occupations in which the intellectual effort predominates over the physical.

encomienda—Spanish royal grant of specified numbers of Indians to the tutelage, protection, and religious influence of a designated Spaniard in return for a definite portion of their labor.

FEDECAMARAS—Federación de Cámaras de Comercio e Indústria (Federation of Chambers of Commerce and Industry).

fiscales—Public prosecutors.

GNP—Gross national product.

hectare—1 hectare equals 2.47 acres.

IVSS—Instituto Venezolano de Seguridad Social (Venezuelan Institute of Social Security).

kilogram—A metric unit of weight equal to 2.2 pounds.

latifundism—A system of large estates; ownership and inefficient use of large areas of land.

llaneros—Cowboys.

machismo—Literally, maleness; complex of beliefs and attitudes defining the image of masculinity.

macho—A man who exemplifies the concept of *machismo*.

mestizaje—Intermarriage and genetic mixing involving various combinations of Negro, white, and Indian blood.

mestizo (mestiza)—Persons with mixed European and Indian ancestry; by extension, all persons of mixed ancestry.

OAS—Organization of American States.

obrero—A person engaged in an occupation in which he works for another at a trade or performs a service in which manual or physical efforts predominate.

ORIT—Organización Regional Interamericano de Trabajadores (Inter-American Regional Organization of Workers).

pardos—Generic term for dark-skinned persons, usually of mixed ancestry.

patrón (pl. *patrones*)—Sponsor or protector.

rancho(s)—A shelter below minimum requirements constructed of makeshift materials by the occupant.

simpático—A term applied to persons with the social virtue of a pleasing personality and appeal to others.

slash-and-burn agriculture—A type of agriculture in which land is cleared and farmed for one year or a few years, usually without fertilizer, until the soil is exhausted. The farmer then moves to another site.

INDEX

Academy of Fine Arts: 155, 160
Academy of Music: 151
Acosta, Cecilio: 156
AD. *See* Democratic Action
AD-*gobierno* (AD-gob): 236, 238, 240
administration and management: personnel, 88, 311
administrative divisions: viii
AD-*oposición* (AD-op): 236, 239
adult education: 125, 146
advertising: 399
Africa: 322
Agence France Presse (AFP): 276
Agencia EFE: 276
Agencia Nazionale Stampa Associata (ANSA): 276
agrarian reform (*see also* land: reform; laws: agrarian reform; resettlement projects): 4, 8, 28, 103, 312, 328, 329–331
agreements and treaties, international: ix, 4, 22, 254, 255, 260–268 *passim,* 391, 392, 418
Agricultural and Livestock Bank: 311, 312, 328, 329, 331, 332, 398, 420; functions, 421–422
Agricultural and Livestock Development Bank: 328, 331, 332, 420
Agricultural and Livestock Warehouses: 398
agricultural products (*see also* crops): 308, 392
agriculture (*see also* agrarian reform; agricultural products; crops; farmers; farms and farming; land: reform; land: tenure; livestock): 308; areas, 10, 24, 26–27, 67, 311; armed forces training in, 454; credit, 311, 312, 316, 320, 321, 328, 331; exports, viii, 311, 312, 315, 320, 328; extension services, 321, 328, 329; government role and policy, 4, 312–326 *passim,* 327–333, 328; imports, 316, 321, 328, 391; methods, 62, 71, 74, 75, 76, 77, 319; production and productivity, 312, 315, 316, 319, 320; workers, 4, 56, 57, 91, 311, 315, 365, 376, 377
aid, foreign (*see also specific countries and international organizations*): ix, 267, 418–419
air force: 51, 444, 448, 449, 450, 451, 453
air taxi service: 402
airfields: ix, 401
airlines and service: ix, 399, 401
Alliance for Progress: ix, 254, 260, 423
aluminum: 308, 346, 389
Alvarado, Lisandro: 157
American Bible Society: 189
American Institute of Free Labor Development: 385
American Motors: 348
Amex news agency: 276
Ampués, Juan de: 33
Andean Common Market: 242
Andean Development Corporation: ix, 267
Andean Subregional Integration Pact: 267
Andrés Bello Catholic University: 137, 182, 185, 277
Andrés Bello Convention: 267
Angel Falls: 16
Apure River: 12, 15
Aracay River: 358
Arcaya, Pedro Manuel: 157
archaeological remains: 63
architecture: 168
area of the country: vii, 1, 7
Argentina: 258, 288, 290, 385; relations with, 261, 262; trade, 392
Arias, Rafael: 177, 180
armed forces: 41, 43; attitudes toward, 445–446; civic action, 454; constitutional role, 446–447; coups and revolts, 47, 49, 51, 242, 245, 443, 444; equipment and weapons, x, 448, 451–452; foreign influences, 447; and politics, 3, 49, 232, 242–243, 249, 293, 443, 446; strength,

x, 441; training, 450-451; uniforms and insignia, 452-453
Armed Forces of Cooperation (national guard): 429, 430, 433-434, 443, 448, 451, 453
Armed Forces of National Liberation (FALN): 239, 246, 296
Arp, Jean: 168
Arraiz, Antonio: 163, 164, 165
Aruba: 337
Asia: 390
asphalt: 21, 44
Assembly of God Church (Seventh-Day Adventists): 190
Associated Press (AP): 276
Association of University Professors: 145
Austria: 267
automobiles: 309, 347-348, 391, 400, 401, 417
Autonomous Railways Institute: 403

balance of payments: 304-305, 387, 406, 416
Bank of Venezuela: 423
Bankers' Association: 244
banks and banking: 406; government role, 419-424; restriction on foreign ownership, v
Baralt, Rafael María: 154
Barrios, Gonzalo: 240, 241, 249
barrios: 105, 172, 190
Batista, Fulgencio: 262, 263
Bautista Plaza, Juan: 160
Belgium: 258, 392, 452
Bello, Andrés: 153, 154, 159
Benalcázar, Sebastián de: 33
Betancourt Doctrine: 253, 254, 262
Betancourt, Rómulo: 3, 32, 45, 47, 48, 49, 51, 163, 180, 232-246 *passim,* 249, 254, 261, 264, 271, 275, 296, 373, 415, 440, 442, 444, 445
Bethlehem Steel Corporation: 360
beverages: 342
Biaggini, Angel: 47
birth rate: 2, 53, 55, 60, 61
Blanco, Andrés Eloy: 160
Blanco, Eduardo: 155
Blanco Fombona, Rufino: 158
Bohemia: 289
Bolívar, Simón: 2, 4, 31, 38-40, 41, 84, 127, 149, 152, 153, 175, 207, 254, 255, 262, 295, 442, 445
Bolivia: 267, 392
Bonaparte, Joseph: 38
Bonaparte, Napoleon: 38
books: 270, 289-290
Borregales, Germán: 239, 241
boundaries, national: 7, 21-22; disputes, 42, 253-254, 255-257, 268, 441
Boves, Tomas: 39
Bravo, Douglas: 242
Brazil: boundary, 22, 254, 256; relations with, 262; trade, 392
Briceño Iragorry, Mario: 157, 296
British Broadcasting Corporation (BBC): 278
British Guiana. *See* Guyana
budget, national (*see also* expenditures, revenue): 221, 405, 406-413; deficit, viii
building materials. *See* construction: materials
Burelli Rivas, Miguel Angel: 241

caballero: 196, 197
Cacao: 63, 67, 312, 322
Cagigal, Juan Manuel: 154
Calcaño, José Antonio: 160
Calder, Alexander: 168
Caldera, Rafael: 32, 52, 191, 230-244 *passim,* 253, 266, 268, 277, 279, 373, 442, 445
Calvo, Carlos: 258
campesinos. See farmers
Canada: 290, 307, 387
Canal Zone: 447
capital (city). *See* Caracas
capital (*see also* investment): flight of, 416, 425
capital goods: 309, 388, 389
Capriles, Miguel Angel: 167
Caracas: 26-27, 35, 36, 39, 78, 86, 87, 99, 108, 109, 111, 115, 117, 119, 134, 173, 184, 240, 241, 273, 274, 276, 278, 279, 294, 300, 301, 310, 356, 368, 369, 370, 374, 394, 395, 397, 398, 399, 401, 427, 430, 444; communications, 404; crime, 430; housing, 104; police, 430, 431; population, 58-59; roads, 10, subway, 403; temperature, 13; traffic conditions, 400
Caracas Chamber of Commerce: 384, 396, 425
Caracas Chamber of Industry: 244, 384
Caracas Electricity: 357
Cardón: refinery, 307
Caritas: 186

Caroní Aluminum: 347
Caroní Electrification Company: 357, 358
Caroni River: 15-16, 21, 26, 356, 357, 358
Castellanos, Evencio: 166
Castellón, Jácome: 33
Castro, Cipriano: 42, 43, 52, 158, 208, 258
Castro, Fidel: 236, 237, 262
Catholic Action: 184, 186, 187
Catholic Press Association: Study Committee, 184
cattle: 26, 27-28, 323; ranches, 8, 12, 91, 315, 320, 324
caudillos: 40, 41-48
censorship: 50, 271, 272
census: 53, 58, 70, 73, 78, 114, 131, 145, 292, 366, 368, 369
Central America: 392
Central Bank of Venezuela: v, 224, 309, 393, 407, 412, 415, 419, 423, 425, 426; functions, 420-421
Central Highlands: 9, 10, 16, 18, 19, 24, 26, 357
Central Office of Coordination and Planning (CORDIPLAN): 224, 243, 265, 327, 360, 407
Central University: 50, 51, 109, 119, 137-141 *passim*, 144, 156, 162, 235, 240, 246, 277, 290, 300, 439, 450; College of Architecture, 168
Centralists: 42, 247
Chalbaud, Lt. Col. Carlos Delgado: 49, 50, 444
Chalbaud, Román: 165
Chamber of Deputies: 47, 218, 219, 333, 346, 407, 446, 455
Chamber of Electrical Industry: 356
Chamber of the National Cinematographic Industry: 277, 288
Chamber of the Petroleum Industry: 244, 384
Chamber of the Television Industry: 277
Charles I of Spain: 33
Charles V of Spain: 34
Chase Manhattan Bank: 423
chemicals: 342-343, 390
children: 95, 99, 114, 117, 123, 124, 198, 213, 279, 393, 376
Chile: 267, 447
Chocrón, Isaac: 165
Christian Family Movement: 184, 187
Christians and Christianization: 65-66, 75
Chrysler Corporation: 348
Círculo de Bellas Artes: 160
Ciudad Bolívar: ix, 15, 26, 39
Ciudad Guayana: 2, 16, 21, 30, 59, 78, 325, 361, 370, 394
Ciudad de los Muchachos: 183
Ciudad Satelito Tuy Medio: 30
civil service: 229-230, 244, 364, 377
clergy: 177-180, 243
Cleveland, Grover: 42, 257
climate: viii, 1, 13-15
clothing: 97-98, 105-107, 111, 112, 338, 345
coal: 21, 338, 359
coat of arms, national: 301
cocoa: exports, viii, 312, 389, 390
Codazzi, Agustín: 154
coffee: 322; exports, viii, 312, 389, 390; plantations, 8
Colina, Alejandro: 167
College of Professors: 145
Colombia: 38, 75, 76, 187, 394; border, 21-22, 23, 224, 254, 256, 268; immigrants from, 53, 57-58; relations with, 267
Columbus, Christopher: 2, 31, 32, 442
commerce: 369, 384, 416; chambers of, 384, 396
Committee of Autonomous Unions (CODESA): 245, 374, 383, 385
Committee for Independent Political and Electoral Organization (COPEI): 32, 48, 49, 50, 184, 232-246 *passim*, 249-250, 299, 300, 373, 374
communications (*see also specific medium*): ix, 1, 403-404; nationalization, 215
communism: 180, 187, 208
Communist countries: public information activities, 270, 278, 288
Communists (*see also* Marxism, Venezuelan Communist Party): 45, 46, 52, 134, 234, 235, 239, 245, 247, 271, 275, 277, 296, 371, 372, 373, 439, 440
Concepción Palacios Maternity Hospital: 61
Confederation of Autonomous Christian Unions: 183
Congress of Angostura: 39
Conservatives: 42, 45
Constitution (1961): vii, 3, 5, 74, 171, 180, 205, 206, 207, 226, 258, 265, 269, 270, 271, 350, 351, 374, 395, 396, 429, 440, 441, 445, 446; amend-

ment and reform, 206, 222; provisions, 210-222, 229
constitutions (*see also* Constitution 1961): 39-42 *passim*, 50, 202, 205, 207-209, 232; of Angostura (1819), 39, 127, 207; (1830), 41, 85, 175, 208; (1864), 127, 209; (1947), 48, 228; (1953), 50
construction: 104, 117, 337, 355-356, 369; materials, 103, 112, 389
consumer goods: 308, 309, 388, 389, 390
cooperatives: 328, 329, 330, 333, 401, 421
Cordillera de Mérida: 9, 10, 13, 14, 17, 18, 19, 20, 24, 26, 27
corn: 320-321
Corps of Technical and Judicial Police: 430, 432
Corps of Vigilantes: 433
Corpus Christi fiesta: 71, 375
Correa, Luis: 155
Costa Rica: 267, 446
Council of the Judiciary: viii
Council of Ministers: 216, 217-218, 223, 265, 379, 403, 407
courts: labor, 370, 377; military, 452; Supreme Court of Justice, viii, 206, 216-220 *passim*, 226, 227, 239, 250, 272, 435; system, 205-206, 220-221, 226-227, 429, 434-436
credit unions: 424
Creole Foundation: 162
Creole Investment Corporation: 424
Creole Petroleum Corporation: 351, 353, 354, 355, 424
Crespo, Gen. Joaquín: 42, 43
crime and punishment: viii, 42, 208, 212, 429-440 *passim*
criollos: 37, 39, 68, 69, 75, 76, 83-87 *passim*, 152, 247, 442
crops (*see also* cocoa, coffee, corn, rice, sugarcane): 316, 320-323, 328
Cuba: 270, 446; missile crisis, 260, 440; relations with, 263, 266
Cubagua island: 13, 32
cultural exchange programs: 270
culture (*see also under* Indians, Negroes, Spain): 2, 53, 70-73, 149, 169, 296
Cumaná: ix, 33, 36, 45, 173, 325
Curacao: 337
currency: basic unit, 425; exchange agreement, 418; exchange rate, 406, 411, 425, 426
Daldera, Rafael: 300-301
Damaz, Paul: 168
dance: 71, 169, 188
death rate: vii, 55, 113, 114, 116
debt, public: 405, 414-416; foreign, 254, 257-259, 305
Declaration of Bogotá: 261
Delgado Chalbaud, Gen. Ramon: 45
democracy: institutions and processes: v, 1, 3, 4, 180, 202, 205, 231, 239-242, 291
Democratic Action (AD): 3, 32, 46-50 *passim*, 232-247 *passim*, 248-249, 250, 293, 298, 299, 300, 371-374 *passim*, 443
Democratic National Front (FND): 240, 241, 242, 251
Democratic Popular Force (FDP): 238, 241, 242, 250, 251
Democratic Socialist Party (PSD): 241
dentists: 119
Deutsche Presse Agentur (DPA): 276
development plans and programs (*see also* Central Office of Coordination and Planning, Venezuelan Development Corporation): 316, 324-329 *passim*, 331-332, 335, 338, 357, 358, 360-361, 408; (1941), 46; (1948), 49; (1970-74), 327, 404
diamonds: 21, 338, 359
Díaz Rodríguez, Manuel: 158
Díaz Sánchez, Ramon: 164
dictatorship (*see also* Gómez, Juan Vicente *and* Perez Jiménez, Marcos): 31, 40, 41, 42, 43, 50, 51, 208, 232, 264, 271, 444
diet: 74, 77, 98-101, 111, 123, 124, 320
Directorate of: Intelligence and Prevention Services, 430, 431-432; Land Transit, 430, 432-433; Public Health, 112-113
diseases: viii, 60, 65, 113-115
doctors: 118-119
Dominican Republic: 260-263 *passim*, 267, 446
Dominici, Pedro César: 158
Drago, Louis María: 258
drainage. *See* irrigation and drainage
Drake, Sir Francis: 36
drama: 165-166
dress. *See* clothing
drugs: sale and addiction, 430, 438
Duvalier, François: 262

economy (*see also* development plans and programs; investment: public; petroleum, *and specific economic sector*): v, 303-313; government role, 4, 214; growth rate, viii; reform, 298; structural changes, 4
Ecuador: 267
education (*see also* adult education; literacy: campaign; schools; teachers; universities; vocational and technical training): vii, 1, 41, 97, 213, 298, 301, 385, 408, 413; administration, 128-129; attainment levels, 369; colonial, 126-127; curriculum, 132; expenditures, 130; and politics, 126, 293
El Mundo: 272, 276
El Nacional: 275, 276
El Salvador: 267, 392
El Universal: 272, 275
elections: 2, 41, 47, 209, 210, 215, 229, 233, 247; (1946, 1947), 48; (1952), 50; (1958), 233, 236, 237; (1963), 2, 237, 239, 251, 292, 294; (1968), 2, 52, 207, 229, 241, 250, 251, 292, 294
Electric Administration and Development Company: 356, 357, 358, 359
electricity. *See* power
employer associations: 384-385
employment: 8, 29, 97, 310-311, 315, 325, 338, 342, 355, 363, 364, 365-367, 379; conditions, 374-378
Ernst, Adolfo: 156
Escalante, Diógenes: 47
Escobar, Maria Luisa: 166
España, José: 37
ethnic groups (*see also criollos,* Indians, *mestizos*, Negroes, *venezolanos*): vii, 2, 53-54, 61-79
Europe: 288, 296, 336, 390, 417; trade, 390, 391
Europe, Eastern: 169
European Economic Community (EEC): 264, 266, 387, 391
European Free Trade Association (EFTA): 387, 391
expenditures, personal: 111-112
expenditures, public: defense, 447; education, 130; local, 413; national, 405, 408-409
exports (*see also under* agriculture, cocoa, iron ore, petroleum, rice, sugar): 266, 308, 336, 340, 388-389, 390; earnings, 311, 387, 425; potential, 304; total, viii
Falcón, Gen. Juan: 42
family (*see also* children, family planning, marriage): 82, 93-95, 194, 213, 291, 293
family planning: 61
farmers: 76, 90. 91-92, 311, 316, 317, 332, 333, 367, 397-398, 399
farms and farming (*see also* sharecropping, squatters): 315-321 *passim,* 329, 451
Fé y Alegría movement: 124, 182-183
Federalists: 41-42, 247
Federation of Chambers of Industry and Commerce (FEDECAMARAS): 242, 244, 266, 277, 300, 372, 384, 385, 386, 396
Federation of Petroleum Workers (FEDEPETROL): 384
Federmann, Nicholas: 33
Ferdinandov, Nicolas: 160
fertilizers: 308, 311, 321, 342, 343
Fiat company: 348
fibers: 322, 345
fiestas: 71, 72, 92, 110
films: 288-289
finance, public (*see also* banks and banking, budget, currency, debt, expenditures, revenue, taxes): viii, 221, 304; local, 413-414, national, 405-427; national credit rating, 305, 415
First National City Bank of New York: 423
fish and fishing: 19, 77, 99, 316, 317, 325-326, 340-341
flag: 301
Flamerich, Germán Suárez: 50
Flores Alvarez, Gen. Pablo Antonio: 445
folklore: 169, 196, 297
food and food products (*see also* diet): 71, 309, 320, 326, 339, 397, 398; exports, 308; imports, 4, 315, 321, 390
Ford Motor Company: 348
foreign exchange: 4, 308, 389, 416, 420, 421, 425, 426; earnings, 303, 336, 387, 388, 393, 409
foreign policy: 253, 265-266; objectives, 4
Foreign Trade Bank: 389
Foreign Trade Council: 389
forests and forestry: 316, 317, 326-327

Foundation for Community Development and Municipal Action: 356
Foundation for Training and Research on Agrarian Reform: 329
France: 270, 290, 447, 452; aid, 267; relations with, 258; trade, 392
Francis I of France: 33
freedom: of association, 47; of expression, 5, 47, 212, 270-272; of the press, 42, 47; of religion, vii, 3, 181
fruits: 100; exports, viii
Fuggers (German banking house): 33

Gallegos, Rómulo: 48, 49, 159, 235, 293, 298, 444, 446
gambling: 109
García, Romero: 156, 159
Garcia Villasmil, Gen. Martin: 445, 453
gas, natural: 308, 337, 355; government control, vi
General Motors: 348
Generation of 1928: 237, 238, 246
Germany: 258, 447
Germany, West: 270, 290, 339, 360; aid, 267, 419
Gervasi, Vicente: 165
Gil Fortoul, José: 156, 157
gold: 21, 26, 33, 34, 257, 338, 359; holdings, 425
Gómez, Gen. Juan Vicente: 27, 28, 31, 42-45 *passim*, 127, 157, 159, 176, 208, 231, 234, 237, 246, 259, 293, 297, 370, 441, 443, 446
González, Juan Vicente: 154
Gonzalez Navarro, José: 245
Good Neighbor Policy: 254, 259, 260
government (*see also* Chamber of Deputies, civil service, Ministry, National Congress, president, Senate): attitude toward, 299-301; autonomous agencies, 409; branches, 223-227; colonial, 35; form of, vii, 1, 210; national, 205-227; state and local, 210-211, 227-228
Government Printing Office: 290
Gran Colombia, Republic of: 31, 40, 127, 207, 255, 301
Gran Sabana: 12
Great Britain: 37, 38, 44, 270, 360, 406, 417, 451; aid, 267; relations with, 256-257, 258, trade, 387, 392
Greenberg, Joseph H.: 62
gross national product (GNP): vii, 4, 52, 303, 304, 309, 311, 315, 335, 338, 349, 355, 356, 359, 387, 388, 405, 410, 414, 447
Guajiro tribe: 75-76
Guárico Reservoir: 17
Guatemala: 261, 267
guerrillas: 239, 300, 430, 439, 440
Guiana Highlands: 1, 2, 12-13, 14, 18, 20, 21, 24, 26, 308, 311, 356, 357, 359, 361
Guipuzcoana Company: 36
Gulf Oil Company: 351
Gulf of Venezuela: 22, 32, 268, 351
Guri Dam: 357, 358
Guyana: boundary, 22, 42, 224, 254, 256-257
Guzmán Blanco, Gen. Antonio: 27, 42, 155, 175, 176, 179, 301

Haiti: 39, 262
Hawkins, Sir John: 36
health (*see also* dentists, diseases, doctors, hospitals and clinics, immunization, nurses): vii-viii, 408, 413; facilities and services, viii; folk practitioners and practices, 120-121; personnel, viii; program, 112-117
Hernandez, Alejandro: 241
holidays: 107, 302, 375
Honduras: 267
hospitals and clinics: 112, 113, 117
hotels: 393
housing: 1, 98, 101-105, 111, 112, 301, 337, 385, 422; public, 101-102, 185, 356
hydroelectric power: 1, 26, 308, 356, 357, 358; potential, 16

illiteracy: 3, 51, 438, 442, 450, 455
immigrants and immigration: 77-79, 368
immunization: 113-116 *passim*, 454
imports (*see also* tariffs *and under* agriculture *and* food): viii, 4, 304, 308, 310, 340, 346, 348, 387, 388, 389-390, 392; policies, 338-339; substitution, 312, 313, 336, 387, 388, 390
income: distribution, 303, 309, 319; per capita, 97
independence: 2, 31; struggle, 37-38, 85
Independent Electoral Front (FEI): 50, 235
Independent National Electoral Movement (MENI): 236, 238

Independent Venezuela Association (AVI): 244
Indians: 2, 26, 27, 32-37 *passim*, 40, 53, 54, 55, 61-66, 73-77, 83, 84, 146, 171, 172, 174, 213, 442; cultural influence, 70-71, 169, 188, 297; languages, 62, 66, 74; population, 73
individualism: 194-199
Industrial Bank: 421
Industrial Chamber of Caracas: 384
industrialization: 51, 52, 61, 172, 201, 292, 295, 304, 335, 387, 416
industry (*see also specific sector*): viii, 8, 29-30, 369, 416; foreign-owned, 310; government policy and role, 335, 336, 338, 360-361; growth rate, 309
infant mortality: 55, 60, 113
information, public (*see also specific medium*): 269-290
Institute of Culture and Fine Arts: 166
Institute of Folklore Studies: 169
Institute of Higher Administrative Studies: 139
Institute for Professional Development of Teachers: 143
Institute of Social Security and Aid: 144
Institute for Training and Recreation of Workers (INCRET): 381
insurance companies: 424
intellectual activity: 149-165, 196, 199
Inter-American Council for Commerce and Production: 386
Inter-American Defense Board: 262
Inter-American Development Bank: ix, 4, 264, 312, 331, 332, 343, 418
Inter-American Regional Organization of Workers (ORIT): 385
Inter-American Treaty of Reciprocal Assistance: ix, 254, 263
intermediate and finished goods: 304, 388, 389
International Bank for Reconstruction and Development (IBRD, World Bank): ix, 102, 418
International Coffee Agreement: ix, 255, 264
International Confederation of Free Trade Unions (ICFTU): 385
International Court of Justice: 43, 264
International Federation of Commercial, Clerical, and Technical Employees: 385
International Federation of Petroleum and Petrochemical Workers: 385
International Finance Corporation: 424
International Harvester company: 348
International Labor Organization (ILO): x, 264, 386
International Metalworkers' Federation: 385
International Monetary Fund (IMF): ix, 406, 420, 425
International Telecommunications Union: x
International Transport Workers' Federation: 385
investment: foreign, 44, 296, 310, 359, 399, 406, 416-418; private, 338, 416, 417; public, 304, 338, 404
Investment Guarantee Agreement: 418
iron industry: 296, 360
Iron Mines Company of Venezuela: 360
iron ore: 8, 308, 338, 402; exports, viii, 359, 360, 390; reserves, 21, 360
irrigation and drainage: 16, 17, 63, 311, 312, 316, 329
islands: 13
Israel: 267
Italian Latin American Institute: 288
Italy: 270, 290, 339, 360, 392, 447, 451, 452; aid, 267

Japan: 343, 417; aid, 267; trade, 341
Jehovah's Witnesses: 190
Jews: 3, 171, 191
Jimenez de Quesada, Gonzalo: 33
John XXIII, Pope: 172, 185
judiciary. *See* courts

Karinya Indians: 77
Kennedy, John F.: 254, 260, 261

La Agencia Latino-americana de Información (LATIN): 276
la Cosa, Juan de: 32
La Guaira: ix, 10, 13, 36, 402, 404, 431
la Parra, Teresa de: 159
La Religion: 184, 272, 276
labor (*see also* employment, labor force, labor unions, unemployment, wages): contracts, 378-379; disputes, 379-380; government organizations, 381; legislation, 370-374

passim; productivity, 303, 346, 368; relations, viii, 201-202; rights, 213, 214; shortages, 368; skilled, 56, 363, 367-369, 370
Labor Bank: 101, 102, 168, 420, 422
labor force: viii, 4, 61, 308, 310-311, 338, 361; structure, 364-369
Labor Inspection Service: 380, 381
labor unions (*see also* strikes): viii, 45, 183, 214, 298, 364, 370-374, 381-384; international, 385; membership, 383; news organs, 274; and politics, 4, 245, 247, 293, 372-374; relationship to government, 382
Lake Maracaibo: vii, ix, 8, 16, 19, 20, 24, 27, 32, 44, 306, 336, 338, 350, 352, 354, 387, 400, 402
Lake Valencia: 16-17
land: reform, 51, 91, 298, 312, 316, 329; tenure, 90, 316, 317-320, 329; use, 315, 320
Landaeta, Juan: 301
languages (*see also* Spanish *and under* Indians): vii, 71, 72-73, 78
Larrazábal, Felipe: 154
Larrazábel, Adm. Wolfgang: 51, 236, 238, 239, 250
las Casas, Bartolomé de (Apostle of the Indians): 32, 33, 173
Latin America: 348; economic integration, 214, 387; trade, 392
Latin American Bishops' Conference (CELAM): 172
Latin American Coffee Agreement: 264
Latin American Confederation of Christian Trade Unions (CLASC): 385
Latin American Confederation of Workers (CTAL): 385
Latin American Economic Coordinating Committee (CECLA): 267
Latin American Free Trade Association (LAFTA): ix, 4, 264, 265, 344, 387, 392, 412
Latin American Institute for Forestry Research: 162
Latin American Nuclear Free Zone Treaty: ix, 4, 254, 264
Latin American Union Conference: 385
laws: agrarian reform, 49, 91, 207, 316, 329, 330, 331; banks and other credit institutions, 419, 423; Central Bank (1961), 420; collective contracts, 372; conditional sales, 395; election, 228; hydrocarbons, 349, 350, 351, 360; immigration and settlement, 56, 79; labor code, 370; public credit, 415; public finance, 407; mining, 360; penal code, 436; petroleum, 47, 48; securities and exchange, 425; universities (1958, 1970), 137, 250
leadership: 203-204
League of Nations: 4, 254, 264
Leger, Fernand: 168
legislature: 226
Leo XIII, Pope: 172
Leoni, Raúl: 32, 52, 232, 234, 238, 239, 240, 243, 244, 246, 254, 370, 373, 440, 442, 445
Liberal Party: 41, 42, 243
libraries: 290
Lions' Club: 385
Liscano, Juan: 165
literacy: campaign, 3, 145-146, 184, 269; rate, vii, 81, 145, 294, 295
literature: 149-165 *passim*
livestock (*see also* cattle): 112, 316, 323-325
llaneros: 39
longevity: viii, 55, 113
López Contreras, Gen. Eleazar: 45, 46, 47, 48, 234, 298, 370, 371, 443
Lovera, Juan: 153
lower class: 68, 70, 75, 79, 81, 82, 89-90, 94, 95, 128, 179, 190, 196, 197, 198, 233, 275, 292, 293, 298
Lozano, Abigaíl: 154
Lozano, Maitín: 154

Machado, Eduardo: 251
Machado, Gustavo: 246, 251
machinery and mechanization: 311, 321, 328, 389, 390, 391, 421
machismo: 193-197 *passim*
Maiquetía International Airport: ix, 394, 400, 404, 431
Makiritare tribe: 76-77
man: ideal, 94, 187, 195-197
manufacturing (*see also specific sector*): 4, 303, 308, 309, 310, 335, 336, 338-348, 365-366, 369, 417
Maracaibo: ix, 16, 36, 44, 78, 87, 115, 184, 273, 274, 276, 279, 310, 325, 340, 369, 374, 394, 395, 397, 398, 420, 431, 432, 438; population, 29
Maracaibo International Airport: 401
Maracaibo Lowlands: 1, 9, 12, 18, 20, 24, 27, 29, 308

Maracay Air Base: 51
Margarita Island: 13, 19, 21, 32, 394
markets and marketing: 92, 332-333, 387, 394, 398-399
Marti, Francisco Lazo: 159, 160
marriage: 94, 123, 213
Marxism: 162, 185, 236
Mata, Andrés: 275
Mayz Vallenilla, Ernesto: 162
meat: 99, 323, 324, 325, 339, 402
Medina, José Ramón: 165
Medina Angarita, Col. Isaías: 46, 47, 234, 370, 371, 443
Mendoza, Cristóbal: 153
Mendoza, Daniel: 155
Mercantile and Agricultural Bank: 423
Mercedes-Benz company: 348
Merchant Marine: ix, 402
Mérida State ("roof of Venezuela"): 10
mestizos: 37, 39, 40, 53, 66, 83
metals and metal products: 345-347
Mexico: 288, 289, 290
Michelena, Arturo: 155
middle class: 2, 70, 81, 82, 86, 88-89, 94, 95, 128, 179, 187, 189, 196, 197, 198, 233, 235, 240, 249, 275, 279, 292, 293, 294, 298, 299, 308, 395, 449
midwives: 120
migration (*see also* urbanization): 53, 54, 56-57, 91, 97
Mijares, Augusto: 163
military academies: 43, 47, 153
milk and milk products: 324-325, 340, 391
minerals and mining: 8, 20-21, 338, 359-360, 416
Ministry of: Agriculture, 56, 128, 133, 225, 312, 327, 328, 333, 398, 399, 408, 422; Communications, 128, 225, 269, 270, 277, 403, 404, 430, 432; Defense, 112, 224, 395, 430, 434, 437, 451; Development, 128, 225, 348, 360, 393, 421; Education, 126-131 *passim*, 144, 146, 182, 225, 290, 409; Finance, 224, 328, 407, 408, 410, 420; Foreign Relations, 224, 265; Health and Social Assistance, 61, 101, 112, 114, 118, 119, 120, 123, 128, 162, 225, 356, 408; Interior Relations, 57, 224, 228, 271, 278, 370, 408, 413, 430, 431; Justice, 74, 146, 167, 181, 183, 225, 430, 432, 437; Labor, 225, 370, 371, 378, 381; Mines and Hydrocarbons, 225, 352, 355; Public Works, 29, 101, 117, 126, 225, 312, 329, 401, 408
Miranda, Francisco de: 37, 38, 152, 255, 301
Miranda Stock Exchange: 425
missions and missionaries: 65-66, 74, 75, 76, 173, 183, 189
Momento: 289
Monagas, José Gregorio: 41, 68
Monagas, Gen. José Tadeo: 41
monetary unit. *See* currency: basic unit
money supply: 426, 427
Monroe, James: 255
Monroe Doctrine: 42, 254-259 *passim*
Morantes, Pedro: 158
Moreno, Yolando: 169
Morgan, Henry: 36
Morón: chemicals, 342, 343, 394
Motilones: 74, 76
Mount Roraima: 12
Movement of the Revolutionary Left (MIR): 219, 236-240 *passim*, 246, 272
Movement Toward Socialism (MAS): 251
mulattoes: 53
Municipal Institute of Popular Credit: 424
Museum of Fine Arts (Caracas): 167
music: 150, 160, 166
Mutznez, Samys: 160

Narvaes, Francisco: 167
National Action Movement (MAN): 239, 241
National Agrarian Institute: 28, 75, 101, 225, 244, 312, 320, 328-332 *passim*
National Association of Announcers: 277
National Association for Care of the Aged and Infirm: 124
National Banking Council: 419
National Cattlemen's Federation: 384
National Civic Crusade (CCN): 241, 242, 250
National Congress (*see also* Chamber of Deputies, Senate): v, viii, 45, 46, 48, 126, 145, 175, 181, 189, 205-211 *passim*, 215, 216, 217, 222-229 *passim*, 239, 246, 247, 250, 251, 265, 266, 267, 268, 304, 336, 353, 403, 407, 408, 409, 412, 415, 423, 425, 434, 446; constitutional power, 218-

220; Delegated Committee, 216, 217, 219-220, 226
National Council of Universities: 137
National Defense Institute: 451
National Democratic Party (PDN): 234
National Discount Bank: 423
National Front of Opposition (FNO): 239
national guard. *See* Armed Forces of Cooperation
National Hotel and Tourism Corporation: 392, 393
National Institute of Educational Cooperation (INCE): 146, 147, 368
National Institute of Nutrition: 99, 123
National Land Office: 330, 331
National Library: 290
National Savings and Loan Bank: 101, 420, 424
National School of Applied and Plastic Arts: 167
National School of Music: 161
National School of Nursing: 120
National Student Union (UNE): 246, 249
National Telephone Company of Venezuela: ix, 403
National University Front: 235
nationalism: 294-299
nationalization: 215, 236
navy: 448, 449, 453
Negroes: 34, 35, 37, 40, 53, 54, 66-68, 69, 83, 84, 85; cultural influence, 71-72, 188, 297
Netherlands: aid, 267; relations with, 257, 258; trade, 392
Netherlands Antilles: 307
news agencies: 276
newspapers: 4, 183-184, 269, 271, 272-277, 294, 399
Nissan company: 348
Nixon, Richard M.: 260, 267, 268
North America: 72-73, 87
North Americans: attitude toward, 79
Northern Mountains region: 1, 9-11, 16, 17-18, 19, 21, 24, 59, 60, 61, 91, 325, 359, 393, 394
Nuclear Non-proliferation Treaty: 265
Nueva Cadiz: 13
nurses (*see also* midwives): 119-120
nutrition. *See* diet

Ocampo, Gonzalo de: 33
Office of Integrated Educational Planning (EDUPLAN): 244
oil. *See* petroleum
oils and fats, edible: 342
Ojeda, Alonso de: 32
Organization of American States (OAS): ix, 4, 254, 260-266 *passim*, 446
Organization of Petroleum Exporting Countries: ix, 225, 264, 305, 337, 388-389
organizations, international (*see also specific organization*): 262-265, 385-386; membership, ix-x, 254, 255
Orinoco Delta: 9, 14, 18, 20, 28
Orinoco Iron and Steel Company: 345, 346, 354, 360
Orinoco Lowlands: 1, 9, 12, 19, 20, 24, 26, 27, 91, 311, 350, 361
Orinoco River: vii, ix, 1, 7, 15, 32, 36, 350, 358, 387, 402, 403
Orinoco-Apure river system: ix, 402
Otero, Alejandro: 167, 168

Padrón, Julian: 163
pardos: 68, 69, 83, 85
Páez, Gen. José Antonio: 39, 40, 41, 175, 208, 247, 443
Páez, Lt. Col. Llovera: 49, 50
painting: 153, 160, 166-167
Pan American Conference: 4
Pan American Federation of Labor: 385
Pan American Health Organization: 98, 103, 115, 262
Pan American Highway: 9, 58
Panama: 267
Panama Canal: 258, 259, 260
Paraguay: 267
Patriotic Junta: 236, 246
Patriotic Military Union (UPM): 47, 49, 234, 443
Paul VI, Pope: 172, 184
PCV. *See* Venezuelan Communist Party
Peasants' Federation of Venezuela: 245, 328, 329, 383
Pedagogical Institute of Barquisimeto: 142
Pedagogical Institute of Caracas: 142
penal code: 436
peninsulares: 68, 83, 84
pensions: 144
People's Electoral Movement (MEP): 232, 241, 242, 250, 373, 374
Pérez Bonalde: 155, 160
Pérez Jiménez, Gen. Marcos: 31, 32,

49, 50, 51, 77, 104, 137, 171, 180, 182, 205, 231, 235, 237, 241, 243, 245, 246, 249, 250, 254, 260, 261, 269, 270, 271, 275, 294, 296, 369, 371, 380, 384, 385, 386, 415, 439, 443-446 *passim*
Pérez de Tolosa, Juan: 34
periodicals: 184, 289, 294
Perón, Juan: 261
personalismo: 193, 195, 299
Peru: 262, 267
Peterson, Horacio: 165
Pétion, Alexandre: 39
Petkoff, Teodoro: 251
petrochemicals: 304, 308, 310, 343
petroleum (*see also* petroleum industry, petroleum products): 4; concessions, 305, 306, 350, 351; deposits, 20-21, 22, 44; and the economy, 44, 49, 112, 336, 348-349; exports, viii, 1, 2, 267, 303, 307, 335, 349, 354, 387, 388, 390, 391, 392; government policy and role, 267, 305, 337; prices, vi, 305, 337, 389, 410; production, 1, 259, 303, 306, 335, 349, 353; public revenue from, v-vi, 4, 46-49 *passim*, 259, 305, 306, 336, 409, 411-412; reserves, 306, 337, 350; service contracts, 305, 306, 307, 336, 350, 352-353
petroleum industry: 2, 8, 29, 296; agreements with, 46-47, 259; foreign investment, 416, 417; social impact, 82, 97, 231, 292; structure, 351; taxes, v, vi, 47, 48, 259, 260, 411
petroleum products: 309, 354, 355, 388, 411
Pico Bolívar: 10
Picón Salas, Mariano: 162, 163
pipelines: 354, 355
Pizarro, Francisco: 34
Pocaterra, José Rafael: 158, 159
Poland: 267
Poleo, Héctor: 167
police forces: x, 430-434
political parties (*see also specific party*): viii, 45, 46, 48, 215, 234-239, 246-251, 274, 294
political subdivisions: 23
politics (*see also* political parties; students: political activity *and under* armed forces, education, labor unions, Roman Catholic Church): 231-242; attitudes, 3; education, political, 3, 293-294; and the farmer, 92-93; source of power, 3, 82, 231, 232-233; and social classes, 88, 89, 233, 235, 240, 249, 292-293
popes. *See* John, Leo, Paul
Popular Housing: 102
Popular Justicialist Movement (MPJ): 250
population: density, 10, 23-24, 25; growth, 8, 28, 53, 55, 59, 61; total, vii, 1, 28-29, 53
ports and port facilities: ix, 399, 402, 451
Postal, Telegraph, and Telephone International: 385
poultry: 99, 312, 325
power (*see also* hydroelectric power): electric, 308, 335, 337-338, 356; electrification plan, 358
Presbyterians: 189, 190
president: office of, 216-218
Preston, Amyas: 36
prices: controls, 395, 396; indexes, 427
Prieto Figueroa, Luis B.: 240, 241, 250
prisons: 429, 436-438
professionals: 87, 88, 119, 311
profit sharing: 377
Protestantism: vii, 3, 75, 171, 189-191
Pro-Venezuela Association: 385
public health: 1, 51
Public Ministry: 434
public order: 429-440
public works program: 52, 408
Puerto Cabello: ix, 258, 342, 394, 402, 451
Puerto La Cruz: 29, 394
Puerto Rico: 307

Quesada, Gonzalo Jiménez de: 33
Quintero, José Humberto: 172, 177, 180, 185, 186

race: attitudes and policies, 69, 212; categories, 70
radio: ix, 4, 109, 146, 184, 190, 248, 269, 272, 277-279, 280-286, 399
Radio Caracas TV: 279
Radio Havana: 278
Radio Moscow: 278
railroads: ix, 399-400, 403
rainfall: viii, 7, 14-15
Raleigh, Sir Walter: 36
Rámos Giménez, Raul: 236, 239
Rámos, José Luis: 154
Ranchers and Livestock Association: 244
raw materials: 389

Reader's Digest: 289
recreation: 107-111
refining and refineries (petroleum): 307, 337, 353-354
regionalism: 297
regions, geographical: 1, 8-13
religion (*see also* clergy; freedom: of religion; Jews; Protestantism; Roman Catholicism): vii, 171-191, 213; attitudes toward, 172, 191, 197; traditional, vii, 71, 72, 171
religious orders: 179, 438
Renault company: 348
Republic (First, Second, Third): 38, 39
Republican Democratic Union (URD): 50, 235-242, 250-251, 272, 299
resettlement projects: 28, 60, 61, 312, 320
retirement: 121, 122
Reuters: 276
revenue, public (*see also* petroleum: public revenue from): 304, 409-410, 413
Reverón, Armando: 160
Revolutionary Party of National Integration (PRIN): 241, 242, 251
Reynolds Aluminum Inter-American, Inc.: 347
rice: 321-322, 332, 341; exports, viii, 312
Río Treaty: 4
Rivas, Angel César: 157
river transportation: ix
rivers: 1, 15-16
roads: ix, 10, 316, 329, 332, 399, 400-401
Rodríguez, Simón: 38, 127, 152
Rojas, Aristides: 156
Rojas, Cristóbal: 155
Roman Catholic Church (*see also* clergy, missions and missionaries, Roman Catholicism, Vatican): 41, 42, 53, 74, 149, 151, 173, 176-189, 197, 289, 291; attitudes toward, 180, 184; church-state relations, 3, 171, 180-181, 210; and politics, 231, 240, 243, 249, 293; schools, 126, 130, 172, 182-183; social role, 176, 180-186; welfare activities, 124
Roman Catholicism: vii, 3, 72, 73, 77
Romania: 267
Roosevelt, Franklin D.: 254
Roosevelt, Theodore: 43, 258
Rootes Motors: 348
Rousseau, Jean Jacques: 38, 127, 152
Royal Dutch Shell: 44, 351, 353, 354, 355
Royal and Pontifical University of Santiago de León de Caracas: 126
rural areas: 294; consumption patterns, 111-112; cultural influences, 71; education, 131, 132; health, 97, 113, 115, 116, 120-121; incomes, 309-310; population, 59-60, 311; power, 357; recreation, 110-111; religion, 172, 187, 189; social structure, 82, 90-93; terrorism, 439-440
Rural Welfare Council: 329

Salas, Tito: 155
Salías, Vicente: 301
sanitation: 112
Santander, Francisco de Paula: 40
Santo Domingo River: 358
savings and loan association system: 423-424
scholarships: 124, 138, 267, 451
schools (*see also under* Roman Catholic Church): construction, 75, 130; enrollment, vii, 51, 90, 125, 130-143 *passim*, 182, 183, 368; medical, 119; military, 441, 448, 450, 451; private, 126-130 *passim*, 190, 213
sculpture: 167
security, internal: 429-433 *passim*, 448
Semana: 289
Senate: 216, 218, 219, 407
services: 369, 370
settlement patterns: vii, 1, 2, 8, 23-30, 91
sharecroppers and sharecropping: 27, 90, 91, 92, 315, 317, 319
Shell Investment Corporation: 424
shipping: ix, 402-403, 416
Silva Otero, Miguel: 164
Simón Bolívar University: 137, 139, 140
Simón Urbina, Gen. Rafael: 45
slavery: 27, 28, 32-37 *passim*, 41, 54, 63-69 *passim*, 83, 92; abolished, 85
smuggling: 58, 75, 430
Social Christian Party. *See* Committee for Independent Political and Electoral Organization
social reform: 3, 4, 291, 298
social security: viii, 112, 121-123, 206, 214, 230, 376, 384
society (*see also* family, lower class, middle class, upper class *and* social structure *under* rural areas, urban

areas): character of, 1-5; human relations, 199-204; ideal, 195; mobility, 82, 128, 292, 298; structure, 2-3, 68-70, 81-93, 292-293
soil: 18, 19-20
Sole Central Union of Venezuelan Workers (CUTV): 245, 373, 374, 383, 385
Sojo, Padre: 151
Sojo, Vicente Emilio: 160, 166
Sola, Otto de: 165
Sosa Rodríguez, Carlos: 264
Soto, Jesús: 167
Soublette, Carlos: 40, 41
Soviet Union: 169, 253, 288
Spain: 290; as colony of, 35-37; conquest, 34-35, 64-66; cultural influence, 5, 149, 150, 169, 193, 204; trade, 341, 392
Spanish (language): 2, 55, 69, 70, 210
sports: 72, 107-108
squatters: 315, 317, 319
standard of living: 92, 111, 327
Standard Oil of New Jersey: 351
states: government, 211; subsidization, 215, 221
steel: 304, 308, 310, 346, 389; mills, 21, 30, 345
stock exchanges: 406, 425
storage facilities: 398
strikes: viii, 45, 46, 51, 214, 246, 371, 372, 373, 379, 380, 382, 444
students: 137; political activity, 50, 126, 134, 138, 235, 245-246, 439, 444; revolt of 1928, 44-45, 161; "weekend guerrillas", 440
Sucre, Antonio José de: 295
suffrage: 42, 48, 85, 208, 228, 233, 298
sugar: estates, 8; exports, viii
sugarcane: 322, 341
Sujo, Juana: 165
Supreme Council of National Defense: 448
Supreme Electoral Council: 215, 228, 229
Switzerland: 267
symbols, national: 301-302

tariffs: 303, 310, 335, 387, 391, 412, 417
taxes (*see also under* petroleum industry): 207, 221, 335, 352, 405, 408, 409, 413-414, 418, 425; foreign-owned companies, v, vi; income, 124, 240, 410; reform, 240, 242
teachers: 128, 129, 130, 135, 213, 364; political activity, 126, 143; pupil-teacher ratio, 132; training, 136, 142, 143
technicians: 88, 367, 368
Telegrafnonoe Agentsvo Sovietskovo Soyuza (TASS): 270
telephones: ix
television: ix, 4, 109, 146, 184, 248, 269, 272, 279, 287-288, 294, 300, 399
Televisora Nacional: 279
Telex: 403, 404
territorial waters: 264-265
textiles: 344-345
Timoté: 62-63, 71
tobacco: 322, 391
Tobago: 337
Topography: vii, 7, 8-13
Toro, Fermín: 154
tourism: 392-394
Tovar y Tovar, Martin: 155
Toyota company: 348
trade: colonial, 35-37; domestic, 387, 394-399; foreign, 267, 387, 388-392, 410
transport equipment: 309, 338, 347-348, 389, 390
transportation (*see also* airlines, pipelines, railroads, roads, shipping): 10, 332, 354-355, 387, 399-403, 411; nationalization, 215
Trinidad: 307, 337
Trujillo, Rafael: 260, 262, 263

Ultimas Noticias: 275, 276
unemployment and underemployment: 28, 30, 86, 123, 327, 368, 369
Union for Advancement (UPA): 251
United Nations: ix, 55, 58, 257, 266, 418; Conference on Trade and Development, x; Development Program, ix, x; Economic Commission for Latin America, x; Economic and Social Council, x; Educational, Scientific and Cultural Organization, 146, 162, 264, 386; Food and Agriculture Organization, ix, 162; General Assembly, 264; Industrial Development Organization, 389; International Atomic Energy Agency, x; membership in, 4, 47, 255, 264; World Health Organization, x, 114; World Meteorological Organization, x
United Press International (UPI): 276

United States: 37, 42, 43, 46, 79, 108, 109, 161, 236, 245, 263, 276, 279, 288, 290, 296, 323, 339, 340, 345, 360, 385, 394, 404, 406, 412, 417, 418, 444, 451, 452; Agency for International Development, 90, 418; aid, 267, 418; attitude toward, 296; Export-Import Bank: ix, 418; military influence, 447; Peace Corps, 418; petroleum, 267, 307, 336, 337, 390; relations with, 254-258 *passim*, 259-261, 266; trade, 322, 341, 387, 390-391; and the Venezuelan armed forces, 441; Voice of America, 278
United States Steel Corporation: 360
Universal Postal Union: x
universities (*see also* students): 126, 128, 137-142, 161, 290; political activism, 3, 126, 232, 245-246, 250; reform law (1970), 300, 439
University of the Andes: 119, 137, 162, 277, 439
University of Carabobo: 137
University of Caracas: 44
University of the Central-West: 137, 140
University of the East: 137, 140
University of Santa Maria: 137
University of Zulia: 119, 137, 277
upper class: 2, 68, 70, 72, 78, 81, 82, 86-88, 93, 94, 95, 110, 127, 128, 138, 179, 180, 189, 196, 198, 203, 233, 275, 279, 292, 293, 298, 449
urban areas: incomes, 309-310; population, vii, 58-59; social structure, 82, 86-90
Urbaneja Archelpohl, Luis: 158
urbanization: 2, 4, 8, 28-29, 58-59, 61, 98, 172, 201, 291, 292, 294, 295, 298, 304
Urbina, Gen. Rafael Simón: 45
Uruguay: 392
Uslar Pietri, Arturo: 163, 164, 239, 240, 244

Valencia: 26, 27, 30, 34, 108, 109
Valera, Raúl: 275
Vallentilla Lanz, Laureano: 157
values: social, 93, 127, 193-204; political, 291-299
Vargas, José María: 154
Vatican (*see also* John, Leo, Paul): 176, 181, 186
vegetation: 17-18
vehicles (*see also* automobiles): ix, 309, 347, 391, 400, 414
VeneVisión: 279
venezolanos: 53, 69-73
Venezuela Grafica: 289
Venezuelan Advertising Council: 277
Venezuelan Association of Newspapermen (AVP): 271, 277
Venezuelan Aviation: 401, 409
Venezuelan Book Association: 290
Venezuelan Chamber of Radio Broadcasting: 277
Venezuelan Children's Council: 123
Venezuelan Civil Front (FCV): 236
Venezuelan Communist Party (PCV): 51, 219, 234-242 *passim*, 246, 251, 272, 300, 430, 439
Venezuelan Construction Chamber: 384
Venezuelan Development Corporation (CVF): 243, 331, 335, 336, 360, 369, 392, 420, 421, 422, 424
Venezuelan Development Finance Corporation (CAVENDES): 424
Venezuelan Federation of Advertising Agencies: 277
Venezuelan Federation of Teachers: 145, 147
Venezuelan Guyana Corporation: 101, 310, 361, 421
Venezuelan Incidents: 42, 43
Venezuelan Institute of Petrochemicals: 29, 310, 342, 343, 354, 403
Venezuelan Institute of Social Security (IVSS): 117, 118, 121, 122, 381, 408, 454
Venezuelan Iron and Steel Company: 346
Venezuelan Medical Federation: 119
Venezuelan National Broadcasting Station: 278
Venezuelan Navigation Corporation: 402
Venezuelan Newspaper Publishers' Association: 277
Venezuelan Petroleum Corporation (CVP): 243-244, 267, 305, 306, 307, 336, 337, 349-352 *passim*, 355
Venezuelan Red Cross: 120
Venezuelan Revolutionary Electoral Organization (ORVE): 234, 236
Venezuelan Society of Architects: 168
Venezuelan Student Federation: 238, 249
Venezuelan Symphony Orchestra: 161, 166
Venezuelan Teachers Association: 144-145

Venezuelan Workers' Confederation (CTV): 245, 250, 265, 371, 372, 373, 374, 383, 384, 385
Vespucci, Amerigo: 32
Victory Front: 241
Villacencio, Rafael: 156
Villalba, Jóvito: 44, 234-237 *passim*, 246, 250, 251
Villaneuva, Raúl: 168
vocational and technical training: 3, 90, 125, 135-136, 147, 277, 363, 368, 376, 451
Volkswagen: 348
Voluntary Dividend for the Community: 124
voting: 212, 215, 292, 293, 294

wages and salaries: 89, 90, 144, 276-277, 347, 363, 364, 369, 376-378
War of Independence: 3, 84, 174
Warrau tribe: 77
welfare (*see also* retirement,· social security): 97, 121-124, 183, 213, 408, 413; programs, 291
Welser (German banking house): 33, 34
West Indies: 392
wildlife: 18-19
women (*see also* marriage): 110, 111, 187, 279; education, 131-136 *passim*, 142, 145; ideal, 94, 197-199; in labor force, viii, 214, 366, 367; population, 55, 56; status and role, 94, 198-199; suffrage, 47, 48; welfare benefits, 123; working conditions, 376
Workers' Bank: 356, 420, 422
World Court: 254, 258
World Federation of Trade Unions (WFTU): 385
World War (I and II): 259-260

Yanes, Francisco Javier: 153

PUBLISHED AREA HANDBOOKS

550—65	Afghanistan
550—98	Albania
550—44	Algeria
550—59	Angola
550—73	Argentina
550—20	Brazil
550—61	Burma
550—83	Burundi
550—50	Cambodia
550—96	Ceylon
550—26	Colombia
550—60	Communist China
550—91	Congo (Brazzaville)
550—67	Congo (Kinshasa)
550—90	Costa Rica
550—152	Cuba
550—22	Cyprus
550—54	Dominican Republic
550—52	Ecuador
550—150	San Salvador
550—28	Ethiopia
550—29	Germany
550—78	Guatemala
550—82	Guyana
550—151	Honduras
550—21	India
550—39	Indonesia
550—68	Iran
550—31	Iraq
550—25	Israel
550—30	Japan
550—34	Jordan
550—56	Kenya
550—41	Republic of Korea
550—58	Laos
550—24	Lebanon
550—38	Liberia
550—85	Libya
550—45	Malaysia
550—76	Mongolia
550—49	Morocco
550—64	Mozambique
550—88	Nicaragua
550—81	North Korea
550—57	North Vietnam
550—94	Oceania
550—48	Pakistan
550—92	Peripheral States of The Arabian Peninsula
550—72	Philippines
550—84	Rwanda
550—51	Saudi Arabia
550—70	Senegal
550—86	Somalia
550—93	Republic of South Africa
550—55	South Vietnam
550—95	Soviet Union
550—27	Sudan
550—47	Syria
550—62	Tanzania
550—53	Thailand
550—89	Tunisia
550—80	Turkey
550—74	Uganda
550—43	United Arab Republic
550—97	Uruguay

☆U.S. GOVERNMENT PRINTING OFFICE: 1971—O436-800 (PO 26)